THEOLOGY IN THE PUBLIC SQUARE

Challenges in Contemporary Theology

Series Editors: Gareth Jones and Lewis Ayres
Canterbury Christ Church University College, UK and Emory University, US

Challenges in Contemporary Theology is a series aimed at producing clear orientations in, and research on, areas of 'challenge' in contemporary theology. These carefully co-ordinated books engage traditional theological concerns with mainstreams in modern thought and culture that challenge those concerns. The 'challenges' implied are to be understood in two senses: those presented by society to contemporary theology, and those posed by theology to society.

THEOLOGY IN THE PUBLIC SQUARE

Church, Academy, and Nation

Gavin D'Costa

© 2005 by Gavin D'Costa

BLACKWELL PUBLISHING
350 Main Street, Malden, MA 02148-5020, USA
9600 Garsington Road, Oxford OX4 2DQ, UK
550 Swanston Street, Carlton, Victoria 3053, Australia

The right of Gavin D'Costa to be identified as the Author of this Work has been asserted in accordance with the UK Copyright, Designs, and Patents Act 1988.

First published 2005 by Blackwell Publishing Ltd

1 2005

Library of Congress Cataloging-in-Publication Data

D'Costa, Gavin, 1958–
    Theology in the public square : church, academy, & nation / Gavin D'Costa
      p.   cm.—(Challenges in contemporary theology)
    Includes bibliographical references and index
    ISBN-13: 978-1-4051-3509-2 (hardcover: alk. paper)
    ISBN-10: 1-4051-3509-3 (hardcover: alk. paper)
    ISBN-13: 978-1-4051-3510-8 (pbk.: alk. paper)
    ISBN-10: 1-4051-3510-7 (pbk.: alk. paper)
    1. Universities and colleges—Religion. 2. Church and education.
    3. Religious pluralism.
    I. Title. II. Series
    BV1610.D36 2006
    230'.01—dc22   2005003250

A catalogue record for this title is available from the British Library.

Set in 10.5 pt Bembo
by The Running Head Limited, Cambridge
Printed and bound in India
by Replika Press Pvt. Ltd., Kundli

The publisher's policy is to use permanent paper from mills that operate a sustainable forestry policy, and which has been manufactured from pulp processed using acid-free and elementary chlorine-free practices. Furthermore, the publisher ensures that the text paper and cover board used have met acceptable environmental accreditation standards.

For further information on
Blackwell Publishing, visit our website:
www.blackwellpublishing.com

For Sachin and Roshan

Contents

Preface

I have been teaching theology of religions for some 22 years and inevitably one reflects on the institutional context of one's intellectual work, for me, the university. This book is the result of such reflection. I hope it will interest those concerned with the future of the university in Anglo-American culture and those who believe that the university might be other than the intellectual production line in the industrial halls of late postmodern capitalist society. This book is also addressed to those who teach and study the disciplines called "theology" or "religious studies" (or "comparative religion" or "history of religion"). To the former, it is yet another voice in a growing symphony that imagines a vital public role for theology so that it may serve both the Church and the wider secular and inter-religious culture in which we live. To the latter, it is a challenge to consider a theologizing of their discipline. In the final chapter of the book I indicate how this theologizing of *all* disciplines is what might characterize a theologized university—a Christian university. Thus, this book might also be of interest to Christian intellectuals who may sometimes wonder what their Christian identity has to do with their university work. Hence, I address a triangular and often overlapping audience: the Church, the university, and the "public square" made up, as it is, of the former two, but also other religions, secularism, and various ideologies.

In chapter one, "Theology's Babylonian Captivity in the Modern University," I reflect on the sense in which both theology and the major site of its production, the modern university, have been secularized. I speak of England and the United States in what follows. This has profound consequences, two of which I explore. The first, more related to my own intellectual interests, is the birth and development of religious studies. I argue that religious studies is locked into an Oedipal relation with theology, as it is in fact a child of secularized forms of theology, and its logic leads to the demise of theology.

Concerned as I have been with theology of religions, I suggest that the reverse would be more productive. I argue for a theological religious studies, for the theologizing of a discipline (religious studies) that should properly serve theology. An example of this is found in chapter five. The second consequence of the secularization of the university and theology within it has been the fragmentation of the disciplines. The rationale for the modern university is increasingly consumerist, reflecting our Anglo-American context. And often it is the Arts subjects, including theology, that are seen as most difficult to justify in financial and educational terms: a theology degree does not obviously help one to become a good economist, nurse, or bus driver. On the contrary, I suggest that theology's pivotal place in the origins of the university in Europe rightly implies that it, with philosophy, has the ability to unify the disciplines. I return to this unifying possibility in chapter six. The consequence of this analysis is my argument for a Christian university, rather than for internal plurality within the modern liberal university. I want to argue that theology can best serve secular society by being properly theological, capable of articulating a vision that both challenges and embraces the best of modernity. This is one virtue of theology.

I am Roman Catholic so I try to work this out in terms of a Catholic vision, drawing heavily on certain Catholic sources, even though many of the most inspiring theologians I have read have been non-Catholics. (I use "Catholic" to mean "Roman Catholic" for brevity's sake, fully realizing that the word can be properly applied more widely.) I started this book envisaging arguments for a Christian university, but soon realized that too many denomination-specific issues had to be faced. Hence, my strategy has been to present arguments for a Catholic university, not in an unecumenical spirit, but rather the opposite. It is important first to envisage what a Catholic university might look like, and other denominations might do the same, before we Christians might work together toward a "Christian university." Certainly, in England, this is more plausible than a denominational institution, even though historically all the major universities that were Christian were first Congregationalist, Episcopalian, Roman Catholic, Baptist, Lutheran, or of other denominations, and then "Christian." I very much hope that non-Catholic readers can enter into the project, realizing that glorifying Christ in the academy has to be worked from the bottom up, through our respective ecclesial communities.

In the second chapter, "Babylon in the Church: The United States and England," I selectively test my comments about the state of the modern university in relation to the United States and England. Reading chapter one, a response might be: "what you say may be true of secular universities, but there are many church-based universities in the United States. Surely the plurality of education you seek can be found in such contexts?" In the United States I focus on Catholic institutions primarily. Although there are glimmers of hope and flashes of brightness, I chart a slow "dying of the light," the growing secularization of the very institutions that might challenge modernity and postmodernity's habits of thought and practice. In England there is a very different situation. There are no great Christian universities left, even in name, as in the United States. However, the history of English universities follows some similar patterns: from church-based institutions of higher learning to secularized universities. Chapter two serves to act as an empirical fleshing out and testing of the thesis of chapter one. It leaves me with a number of further questions regarding the plausibility of the type of Christian university I am proposing, in terms of its social divisiveness, its academic freedom and accountability, and funding.

These issues are the topic of chapter three: "Cyrus Returns: Rebuilding the Temple in Babylon." I argue that liberal modernity is in fact committed to religious plurality and diversity in society and that these goals are best served, in some circumstances, by helping religious communities to learn and practice their traditions faithfully. In the intellectual realm, this means the funding of "sectarian" universities only in so far as they are committed to the "common good" and engagement with other traditions. These two requirements are actually generated from my own theological position, but overlap with elements of modernity. Hence, my metaphor of Cyrus, King of the Medes and Persians, who helped the Jews rebuild the temple, allowing a return to Jerusalem and suggesting that those who remained in Babylon help finance the project in Jerusalem (2 Chron. 36: 22). I inspect the arguments about sectarianism, in part, to explode some of the rhetorical stances taken by critics of the type of position I'm advancing, and in part to respond to some very genuine concerns. After trying to address such concerns, I examine the complex issues of the accountability, freedoms, and funding of a Catholic university in the United States. Can the university serve the Church and society at the same time? If it is Catholic, will it not skew things to the advantage of a minority interest group in our pluralist society? And should society pay for institutions that are accountable primarily to minority communities that can often launch truculent criticism of that wider society? Part of my answer is that the accountability of theologians and others in a Church university, while a complex matter, is no different, formally speaking, from accountability in all professions and all disciplines. And most importantly, there is no clear case that academic freedom is called into question. Rather, the opposite may occur: genuine creativity and interdisciplinary research may occur in universities accountable to a unified vision of life, grace, and love.

Having cleared the ground a little, and I realize that many objections still remain, I turn to a distinctive aspect of a Christian university in chapter four, "Why Theologians Must Pray for Release from Exile," that of prayer. At this point I abandon the rational argumentative mode of the first three chapters and will proceed *as if* the reader is in agreement with the basic project I'm advancing. Up until now, I have been trying to persuade those who might not share my view. This now changes and the following chapters (four–six) speak from within a model of a Catholic university to show how things might be otherwise. They are snapshots of a place that is yet to be built by ecclesial communities (together or alone) in democratic societies. They are also snapshots based on various fragmentary practices within existing Christian—and secular—universities. So in chapter four I chose prayer for two reasons. Prayer is hardly ever imagined as part of the methodology of a rigorous academic discipline. I argue that it is precisely this, both in the history of theology until the modern period, and as a necessary epistemological presupposition. Second, I trace the way in which this necessary requirement for the doing of theology actually forces a reconsideration of the traditional disciplinary lines internal to the discipline called "theology." Theology's own house needs a spring clean. As the argument proceeds I illustrate instances of the fruitfulness of dissolving traditional boundaries, thereby returning theology to a profounder integration with itself and with other disciplines in a manner not unknown prior to modern university "specialization." It is this rich dynamic tradition that offers both the Church and the secular world a considered alternative to the dead ends of modernity and postmodernity, while nevertheless recognizing their great strengths.

In chapter five, "The Engagement of Virtue: A Theological Religious Studies," I return to the discipline of "religious studies" to show what it might look like when theologized. It also allows me to draw together a number of themes. In the early chapters I argued for the practice of virtue for undertaking theology. I return to virtue in a case study of a Christian "saint," Edith Stein, and a Hindu "goddess," a *sati*, Roop Kanwar. I had argued in chapter four that the saint embodies theology, and thus the embodiment of both Stein and Kanwar is my focus here. Their theologically narrated lives generate a painful but challenging conversation regarding virtue and its cross-religious and gendered aspects. Edith Stein's canonization caused much controversy, leading to a high-level Jewish delegation's visit to the Pope in an attempt to block the process. A number of important Catholic theologians supported this Jewish plea. Roop Kanwar's death as a young *sati* caused horror and revulsion in India and abroad. What might these two women have in common, other than their controversial lives? Virtue? This chapter also exemplifies the sense in which I believe a Christian university and its theologians can reach outwards, engaging creatively and positively, but not uncritically, with all creation—and in this instance, Hinduism.

In chapter six, I develop this theological vision to relate to other disciplines, with philosophy, as mediator, and pay particular attention to physics and cosmology, to see whether fragmentation can be overcome. I chose physics and cosmology as they are often presented as totally unrelated to theology, a discipline that many might think would look entirely similar were it in a secular liberal university or a Catholic university. I hope to show otherwise. Thus, I try to avoid two usual intersections between these subjects: points of conflict, and the need for an ethical or religious stance regarding the use of technology. I also take this test case, not in a search for an overarching philosophy or ideology, but to see whether the unity of all creation, assumed theologically, might promote health, interconnectedness, and developments between different disciplines. In chapter three I had touched on this issue with specific reference to the vision of a "Catholic university" set forth by Pope John Paul II. Chapter six fleshes that out a little, testing papal documents in terms of a specific discipline. If the results look promising, then there are further good reasons to argue for a Catholic university. What can be said of this relationship obviously cannot simply be applied to other disciplines. Carrying out this long meticulous and complex task belongs to the Catholic university and has hardly been started. Such a university's existence would be invaluable to the Church as it would provide the intellectual life-blood permitting a rich description of what all creation looks like from a Christian perspective. To facilitate this, alongside different views and practices of knowledge (postmodern, modern, Buddhist, Jewish, don't knows, and so on) will structurally supports real plurality. Only then can we have the debates that are necessary to deal with pluralism, peace, truth, and justice. Without such diversity, there will be little new progress, little challenge from really different alternatives, and in Christian terms, the stifling of a theological voice in the public square.

Acknowledgments

I have been encouraged, helped, and challenged by many people in the writing of this book, only some of whom I mention below. Clifton Cathedral, Bristol, has continued to inspire and nourish me, especially those who work in the Children's Liturgy Team, as has the Bristol Steiner School. Special thanks also to my colleagues at the University of Bristol in the Department of Theology and Religious Studies, especially Drs. Rupert

Gethin and Carolyn Muessig who generously took over as Acting Heads of Department while I had study leave to complete this manuscript. The University of Bristol also awarded me an extra period of study leave to complete this book. I am grateful to the Dean, Dr. Liz Bird, for her support.

Many read or commented on individual chapters that were presented at various universities in Bristol, London, Oxford, Cambridge, Manchester, Exeter, Texas, Boston, Leuven, Rome, and Utrecht. I'm grateful to those who arranged and attended those seminars. I'd like to particularly thank Professor Lewis Ayers, Dr. Tina Beattie, Revd. Barry Chapman, Professor David Conway, Revd. Dr. Philip Endean SJ, Professor Gavin Flood, the late Professor Colin Gunton, Professor Peter Hampson, Dr. Jackie Hirst, Dr. David Jones, the late Dr. I. Julia Leslie, Professor Julius Lipner, Professor David F. Ford, Mr. Davy Machin, Professor George Marsden, Professor Ian Markham, Professor Ernan McMullin, Revd. Dr. Arthur Peacocke, Professor Alvin Plantinga, Professor Sir John Polkinghorne, Dr. Gaynor Pollard, Dr. Sr. Bernadette Porter, Mr. Patrick J. Reilly, Professor Alan Torrance, Dame Janet Trotter, Revd. Professor Keith Ward and Revd. Professor John Webster for their help, often despite strong disagreement. Others read the entire manuscript and made invaluable suggestions and were generous even when in deep opposition. I'd like to thank Canon Professor Edward Bailey, Revd. Catherine Coster, Ms Ann Fowler, Professor Sinclair Goodlad, Professor Paul Griffiths, Revd. Dr. Laurence Hemming, Mrs Tessa Kuin, Dr. Gerard Loughlin, Revd. Dr. Andrew Moore, Dr. Susan Frank Parsons, Professor William L. Portier, Revd. John Sargant, Dr. Chris Sinkinson, Dr. Daniel Strange, Professor Paul Williams, and Revd. Graham Woods. Inevitably, all errors, omissions, and other failings in this book are entirely mine. There would have been many more were it not for such thoughtful critics and friends.

Finally, thank you to Beryl my wife and to Roshan and Sachin our children. To the latter, a new generation, I dedicate this book with gratitude and hope.

(Feast of All Saints, 2004)

Chapter One

Theology's Babylonian Captivity in the Modern University

I Should "Theology" and "Religious Studies" Be Terminated?

Since this book is concerned with the health of theology and the Church's engagement with cultures, it might seem rather odd to begin with a question that intimates the termination of theology within the university, the very place that is central to the future of Anglo-American theology. But as the Israelites found out, living in Babylon can have the effect of purifying the faith as well as destroying it. In what follows I shall be suggesting that theology's location within the modern western secular liberal university is not unlike the Israelite captivity within Babylon. Theology, properly understood, cannot be taught and practiced within the modern university. This is not a view shared by all Christians, but is held by a number of post-liberal theologians and philosophers, such as Stanley Hauerwas, John Milbank, and Alasdair MacIntyre.[1]

One way of noticing this Babylonian captivity is in the arguments that are conducted in the modern university about the role of theology. The view

---

[1] See Stanley Hauerwas, *Christian Existence Today*, The Labyrinth Press, Durham, North Carolina, 1988, esp. the two chapters, "Truth and Honor" and "How the Universities Contribute to the Corruption of Youth"; "On Witnessing our Story: Christian Education in Liberal Societies" in eds. Stanley Hauerwas and John H. Westerhoff, *Schooling Christians: "Holy Experiments" in American Education*, W. B. Eerdmans, Grand Rapids, Michigan, 1992, pp. 214–36; John Milbank, "The Conflict of the Faculties: Theology and the Economy of the Sciences" in eds. Mark Thiessen Nation and Samuel Wells, *Faith and Fortitude: In Conversation with the Theological Ethics of Stanley Hauerwas*, T. & T. Clark, Edinburgh, 2000, pp. 39–58; Alasdair MacIntyre, *After Virtue*, Duckworth, London, 1985 (2nd edn.), *Whose Justice? Which Rationality?*, Duckworth, London, 1988, and *Three Rival Versions of Moral Enquiry*, Duckworth, London, 1990.

expressed by some scientific atheists (Richard Dawkins, for example) is that theology has no place in the modern university. It is a vestige of a religious world and society which has long since crumbled and been discredited. It is a disservice to a modern research university to include such a subject in the curriculum.[2] A similar voice is heard from some who teach in departments of religious studies. Donald Wiebe, for example, argues that a scientific, objective, rational study of "religion," without any privilege being granted to any one religion, is the only intellectually respectable practice in the modern university.[3] Dawkins and Wiebe have one presupposition in common, which I shall be calling into question: that there is such a thing as neutral objectivity in any mode of research, either science, Dawkins's own area, or religious studies, Wiebe's specialism. However, in another sense I agree with Dawkins's and Wiebe's conclusions, but for very different reasons. What are these reasons? In the next section of this chapter I want to look at the process of secularization, as it has affected both the university and the discipline of theology. Secularization is a much debated topic, and I use the word to connote two specific historical processes.[4] The foundation of the universities took place in a universe with a sacred canopy, whereby people understood their practices to relate to an organic and cosmic pattern participating in the nature of reality. This reality was divinely created for the good of men and women, for the flourishing of human society, and for participation in truth and love. The modern university, with some exceptions, in contrast, develops its programs and practices without any reference to a sacred canopy. Often finance is the chief criterion, without any organic vision of the relation of the different disciplines, without any shared values regarding the good of men and women, or concerning what truth might possibly be. Augustine, well before the universities were founded, carried out a scathing critique of pagan institutions of learning: their main purpose being vanity in so far as they served purely to gain better employment, and self-promotion.[5]

[2]   Richard Dawkins, Professor of the Public Understanding of Sciences at the University of Oxford, contributes to popular discussion on the matter in English newspapers. For one example, among many other debates and discussions, see *The Daily Telegraph*, March 16, 2002.

[3]   See Donald Wiebe, *The Politics of Religious Studies: The Continuing Conflict with Theology in the Academy*, Macmillan, Basingstoke, 1999.

[4]   Most helpful on the secularization debate and its impact on theology are Kieran Flanagan, *The Enchantment of Sociology: A Study of Theology and Culture*, Macmillan, London, 1996, pp. 52–99; Peter Berger, *The Heretical Imperative: Contemporary Possibilities of Religious Affirmation*, Collins, London, 1980; and ed. Steve Bruce, *Religion and Modernisation: Sociologists and Historians Debate the Secularisation Thesis*, Clarendon Press, Oxford, 1992.

[5]   Augustine, *Confessions*, trans. Maria Boulding OSB, New York City Press, New York, 1997, 4.1.1, 4.2.1, 4.16.30 and more trenchantly, *Teaching Christianity*, trans. Edmund Hill OP, New York City Press, New York, 1996, 2.26.40, 2.13.20, 2.61.

This removal of the sacred canopy in institutional terms is one definition of secularism and it is one reason why I believe Dawkins and Wiebe are correct. The attendant sense denotes the way in which the process of secularization both creates and is created by various intellectual presuppositions embedded in our intellectual institutions. Of course, institutions do not have ideas, people do. But, through their organization and processes, institutions always reflect ideas about the good, the true, and the worthwhile. By briefly examining the secularizing of the university and the discipline called theology, I hope at least to indicate why Dawkins is correct: theology cannot flourish in the modern university. However, I think Dawkins is also wrong for two reasons. The modern university, like modern secular societies in England and the United States, has a strong commitment to liberal pluralism: cultural, intellectual, and religious diversity. In principle, it should be committed to facilitating real diversity, as opposed to Dawkins's impulse to be rid of it. Further, if theology can argue that it is a real intellectual discipline and requires a different sort of university for its health, and, if it were healthy, would be a contributor to the common good, then in principle, liberals should be willing to entertain funding this alternative university for the common good, and the flourishing of real pluralism. In chapter three I shall be pursuing this argument in some depth, facing a number of serious objections to such a "sectarian" proposal, not least the question of funding, and the problem of the authority under which such a university is finally accountable. In much of this I draw on the experience of Roman Catholic universities in the United States. Every country is different and internally diverse.[6] However, because I happen to be a Roman Catholic Christian, I

---

[6]   I deal only with universities in England, as the university system in Scotland and Wales has originated and evolved in differing circumstances. Furthermore, the Colleges of Higher Education have a different history from that of the universities, even though both are part of "higher education." Because of this, I exclude them from consideration, despite their now forming the "new universities." See "Religious Studies in the Universities," covering England (Adrian Cunningham), Scotland (Andrew F. Walls), Wales (Cyril Williams), and the Open University (Terence Thomas), in ed. Ursula King, *Turning Points in Religious Studies*, T. & T. Clark, Edinburgh, 1990, pp. 21–67. Ireland is also excluded from this study although it presents a most interesting contrast. The university has developed very differently in Europe and North America. See on this: ed. Sheldon Rothblatt, *The European and American University Since 1800: Historical and Sociological Essays*, Cambridge University Press, Cambridge, 1993; and for the period before that: ed. James M. Kittelson, *Rebirth, Reform, and Resilience: Universities in Transition, 1300–1700*, Ohio State University Press, Columbus, 1984; and the two-volume work edited by Hilde de Ridder-Symoens, *Universities in Early Modern Europe, 1500–1800*, vol. 1, Cambridge University Press, Cambridge, 1992, and vol. 2, 1996. Antonio García y García traces the history of the faculty of theology during this period in volume 1. The practice of theology in the developing world is contextually so different that I do not attempt to engage with this important field.

have focussed more on Catholic universities. This is not intended as an un-ecumenical gesture, and I do believe that in England there is more chance of a Christian university than a Catholic university, but it is necessary to work out ideas and practice with some sensible focus. I very much hope that Christians of all denominations can find something in this exploration and bring their rich heritage to bear on the question and further the discussion.

But what of Wiebe's proposals? At least, unlike Dawkins, he wishes to retain the place of religion in the university. In the third section of this chapter, I shall be arguing that his type of position is called into question because of its methodological assumptions, shared by Dawkins: that a neutral, objective, rational study is the only method permissible in the uni-versity. In fact, I would wish to go further and argue that the discipline of "religious studies," as conceived by some of its major theoreticians, is intel-lectually flawed, such that it, not theology, has a contestable place in the modern research university. I want to argue that the legitimate place for the study of religions is within a theological religious studies, such that world religions are part of a theological curriculum. As it exists under Wiebe's model, it is a secular study of religions, privileging secularism, over against the objects of study. Wiebe's desire to escape from ideology is utterly ideo-logical. I should make it very clear that I am not contesting religious studies' role in the modern university; rather, I contest some forms of it, regarding their self-description.

Two further clarifications before proceeding with my argument. In this first chapter I shall be making apparently sweeping comments about the modern university. I beg the reader's patience, as in chapter two I attempt to check these comments against empirical studies of universities in the United States and England. For certain readers, it may be worth reading chapter two first if they are unconvinced that there is a problem with the health of theol-ogy. Such a reader might say two things: there are Christian universities in the United States, so what is all the fuss about? They may add: Christians, like yourself, argue that it is impossible to do in the modern university pre-cisely what you are doing. Does that not show that the modern university encourages pluralism far more than is admitted in the arguments of this book? To the first question, I respond in chapter two that American Christ-ian research universities have already lost their salt, or are in the process of doing so. They retain their Christian character primarily by having a Mass on holy days, having well-resourced chaplaincies, and being actively involved in social work to the poor and less privileged. These features are very impor-tant, and I think they are a vital element of a Christian university, but they are not enough to constitute a Christian university. Many secular universities might boast all three of these features. Further, the deeper question is, how does the Mass, or prayer meeting, affect the curriculum, the interrelationship of the disciplines, or the research methodologies utilized not only in theology but other disciplines? Very few universities, hardly any among those studied, can answer these questions in any form of thick description. I argue, with a number of significant American scholars, that Christian universities are dying or dead in the United States. The second question is admittedly uncomfortable. Yes, I write this book with research leave from my own secular liberal university, Bristol, and my colleagues generously tolerate my writing suggesting that our department be closed down. I also enjoy good rigorous conversation with colleagues within the university who come at issues from very different angles. I am not arguing that the modern liberal university be closed, but rather that alternative universities be encouraged alongside it, to facilitate long-term serious intellectual pluralism. Such universities can train new generations in alternative intellectual traditions of theory and practice, rather than perpetuating a single non-sacred intellectual canopy. Currently there is a worrying (although predictable) homogeneity, and a real commitment to pluralism is better served by training those who are different (from the secularist) to develop their traditions rigorously. This issue will be dealt with both at the end of this chapter and in the first section of chapter three.

II On (Not) Doing Theology in the Modern University

Let me now turn to plotting the narrative of theology in its pre-university days and then from the thirteenth century, its university career, which has lasted until today. Theology became deeply transformed from the fourteenth century on, with particular seismic movements in the Reformation of the sixteenth century and the Renaissance, and the earthquake of the seventeenth century with the rise of the new natural sciences. The nineteenth century was the decisive turning point, although the seeds for that moment had been planted much earlier, with the new Enlightenment research university founded in Berlin. Theology lived under a very dark cloud.

The four aspects that I shall focus on are as follows. First, I will show how the discipline of theology becomes separated from the practices that are required for its undertaking: prayer, sacraments, and virtue. Second, in rough tandem, but not with exact parallels, I will trace how university theology became prised from ecclesial life so that it now often succumbed to alien philosophies, methodologies, and models for its very life-blood, a blood that would subsequently infect Church life. Admittedly, this has happened throughout the history of the Church. Third, I will focus on theology's role as queen of the sciences. It provided patterns for the unity of the disciplines and argued that the *telos* of all knowledge was the glorification of God. I shall chart the massive eclipse of this role so that theology now struggles to retain a place in the modern research university. Fourth, and due to the above pressures, I will (in the next section) see how this history eventually led to the Oedipal configuration between theology and religious studies, so that the latter claimed Enlightenment privileges and sought to exclude theology from the university.

The parameters of this survey require emphasis. The history of theological education is complex and vast and all I can do is provide snapshots, making observations and illustrating an argument.[7] Further, I only draw from the Latin tradition—and the rich history of the eastern churches cannot be examined at all, and nor can the wider tradition of the universities within the Muslim, Buddhist, and Hindu contexts.[8]

The history of institutional theology is tied to the patronage of the Church. However, "theology" had pre-Christian roots in Greek culture. The Greek word θεολογια (the "science of God," or "words about God") is found in both Plato (427–347 BC) and Aristotle (384–322 BC) pertaining to gods or eternal principles. Plato, in the *Republic* (379A), gives an ordered account of the gods, and in Aristotle's *Metaphysics* (XI, 1, 1025 a. 19; 1026 a 19–22), he explains the principle of the cosmos's existence in terms of an unmoved mover. Christians would rework these accounts, sometimes not successfully. The role of the unifying power of the gods in relation to other disciplines (curriculum structure) and the role of knowledge was also subject to intense debate in Greek culture. These issues would also be

---

[7]   I am indebted to: Aidan Nichols, *The Shape of Catholic Theology*, T. & T. Clark, Edinburgh, 1991; R. Latourelle, *Theology: Science of Salvation*, trans. Sr. Mary Dominic, St. Paul's, Slough, 1969 [1968]; G. VanAckeren, "Theology" in the *New Catholic Encyclopaedia*, vol. 14; P. De Letter, "Theology, History of" in the *New Catholic Encyclopaedia*, vol. 14; Yves Congar, *A History of Theology*, trans. Hunter Gutherie, Doubleday, Garden City, New York, 1968; David Kelsey, *Between Athens and Berlin: The Theological Education Debate*, W. B. Eerdmans, Grand Rapids, Michigan, 1993; and Arthur F. Holmes, *Building the Christian Academy*, W. B. Eerdmans, Grand Rapids, Michigan, 2001.

[8]   For instance, Muslim universities started with the University of Cairo in 970 and were also established with theology as the organizing subject (with the important exceptions of Ma'mūn in Baghdad and the Fātimids in Cairo). See F. E. Peters, *Aristotle and the Arabs: The Aristotelian Tradition in Islam*, New York University Press, New York, 1968. The positive role of Islam in the development of the western university cannot be underestimated. But the question is relevant in contemporary western society. For example, Peter Steinfels reports briefly on the existence of Jewish, Muslim, and Buddhist forms of higher education in the United States, in *A People Adrift*, Simon & Schuster, New York, 2003, p. 145.

central concerns for the Christian tradition. Positions repeated to the present day are often to be found in Greek culture. Hence, Gorgias' emphasis on rhetoric and speech being all-important, or Protagoras' argument that man is the measure of all, or Socrates' scathing criticism of the Sophists' relativism and his concerns for virtue and truth, or Plato's emphasis on learning as wisdom, necessary for a just society and a just ruler, or Isocrates' "humanism," or Aristotle's "liberal" (*eleutheros*) education, indicating its necessity for "freemen," not slaves. Hence, the question of education for utility, aestheticism, liberalism, its own sake, the good of society, and truth (all in different hues) was thoroughly debated.[9]

The earliest Christian theologians were the New Testament writers, not conducting their work from any institutions of learning but from communities of practice, with varying educational backgrounds. In the patristic period (first to eighth century), the nearest thing to the university was the Nestorians in the Persian city of Nisibis in the fifth century, forming an institute of learning, teaching, and research, that is reputed to have inspired Cassiodorus' monastic school at Vivarium.[10] In this period, three strands emerge regarding the relation of theology to other disciplines. The first stresses that all truth and salvation is to be found in the Bible, therefore pagan knowledge is fundamentally useless. What has Jerusalem to do with Athens? This view is often associated with Tertullian (c.160–225), although in his writings he is far more nuanced.[11] The second, containing rich internal diversity, sees the Greek philosophical heritage as *preparatio* (preparation) and *paidagogos* (an education finally aiming at Christ). Origen (c.185–254) uses the metaphor of the ransack of the Egyptians for the future of Israel, so that all learning could in principle be turned to the service of God.[12] Earlier, Justin Martyr (c.100–165) had understood the seed of the logos as explaining such knowledge, after abandoning the position that the Greeks had read Moses or met some of the Old Testament prophets. The later giants Augustine, less so, and Aquinas, more so, belong to this strand. The third strand, at least in the eyes of the first and second, adopted Greek philosophy uncritically, so that it shaped the Christian message, rather than the Christian message critically employing conceptualities and categories from the Greeks and thereby transforming them. This led to heresy. Origen

---

[9] See Henri Marrou, *A History of Education in Antiquity*, Sheed & Ward, New York, 1956, and Werner Jaeger, *Paideia: The Ideals of Greek Culture*, trans. Gilbert Highet, 3 vols., Oxford University Press, New York, 1944.

[10] See George Every, *Early Eastern Christianity*, SCM, London, 1980, pp. 77–9.

[11] For Tertullian and the Fathers, see Henri de Lubac, *The Church: Paradox and Mystery*, trans. James R. Dunne, Alba House, Staten Island, New York, 1969 [1967], ch. 4.

[12] Origen, *Commentarium in Joannem*, I. 24; II. 34.

was considered guilty of this, as was Arius, and in Aquinas's time, the Latin Averroësists and indeed Aquinas himself. After surveying the patristic period, Aidan Nichols writes that "in the ancient Church there were almost no theological academies dedicated to the systematic study of the subject."[13] Clearly, this does not mean that theology was in any way stifled; indeed, the opposite is true.

Augustine's (354–430) complex dialectical position would be a major shaper of the educational tradition.[14] On the one hand, he despised much of his own classical education, arguing that the academies led to self-glorification and self-advancement, and pagan knowledge itself was un-truth.[15] On the other, he was to embark on an unfinished project to show how all of the seven liberal arts were important in exemplifying eternal archetypes in the mind of God. He only partly completed his study *On Music*. His *On Christian Doctrine* exemplified the usefulness of liberal arts in the reading of scripture, thereby turning all knowledge toward praise of God, a theme that would be central to Christian visions of knowledge. Augustine would be claimed by strands one and two, perhaps most power-fully by Aquinas in his synthesis of Augustine with Aristotle. The Emperor Justinian's closure of all pagan institutions in 529 "cleared" the field for Christian institutions of learning, and from the eighth century on, monas-teries, convents, and cathedrals were to be the site of this new knowledge.

The Carolingian Renaissance, in the reign of Charlemagne (768–814), with brilliant educational advisors like Alcuin and Theodulf of Orléans, saw the emergence of education within monastic or convent settings, and also in the cities, under the wing of the cathedrals. Charlemagne's Palace School was probably the first school to give a classical education to significant numbers of laity, and involved the seven liberal arts, the learning of psalms, chanting, and grammar. These schools represented the first major institu-tional move that would later, in part, transmute into the university, widening the curriculum, but losing the monastic context. This new site of production had a number of strengths and weaknesses. Its greatest strength was the unity of theology with prayer and practice. While some monastic theologians were little interested in life outside the monastery or in the

---

[13]   Nichols, *Shape*, p. 282.

[14]   See the very nuanced accounts of Kevin L. Hughes, "The 'Arts Reputed Liberal': Augus-tine on the Perils of Liberal Education" in eds. Kim Paffenroth and Kevin L. Hughes, *Augustine and Liberal Education*, Ashgate, Aldershot, 2000, pp. 95–110; and Fredrick van Fleteren, "St. Augustine, Neoplatonism, and the Liberal Arts: The Background to *De doctrina christiana*" in eds. Duane W. H. Arnold and Pamela Bright, "*De doctrina christiana*": *A Classic of Western Culture*, Notre Dame University, Notre Dame, Indiana, 1995, pp. 14–24.

[15]   *Confessions* 4.1.1; 4.2.1.

liberal arts of the classical world, most of its best theologians, such as Aelred, William of Auberive, and Geoffrey of Auxerre, utilized the disciplines and traditions of the pagan world, while Christianizing them through this process (strand two above). A second strength was that the monastic site of theology allowed a limited theological education to women in some of the convents and schools, whereas the creation of the university excluded women from the institutions of theological learning.[16] It was in a cathedral school that Abelard taught Heloïse. It has been noted that the convents were a "refuge for female intellectuals, as the monastery was for the male. Although the majority of nuns were at best literate, most of the learned women of the Middle Ages—the literary, artistic, scientific, and philosophical stars were nuns."[17] Such stars, bringing together many branches of learning in theological wisdom, were women such as Roswitha of Gandersheim, Hildegard of Bingen, and Herrad of Landsberg. Of course, whether women were admitted to the sacred discipline or not, it was still a clerical monopoly. The canonical definition of "clerical" in 1231 excluded women from being considered clerics, as they had been up until then, and further, only permitted masters and students of the universities to be clerics. A third strength, according to Jean Leclercq, was that the monastic setting allowed theologians to discern more quickly the abuses in the employment of dialectics in *university* theological reflection, an employment that was considered a hallmark of university scholasticism.[18] Leclercq goes so far as to say that scholastic university theology, being wedded to the form of disputation and dialectics, eventually "lost contact with the life of prayer."[19] This loss would eventually lead to the slow divorce between "knowledge and love, science and contemplation, intellectual life and spiritual life" and it would then become necessary to construct categories of mystical and spiritual theology, the worse for their separation from dogmatic theology.[20] While there was admittedly what Grabmann has called "hyperdialectic" in university scholasticism, it would be wrong to characterize scholasticism in such

---

[16] On the contribution of women to theology in this period, see Caroline Walker Bynum, *Fragmentation and Redemption: Essays on Gender and the Human Body in Medieval Religion*, Zone Books, New York, 1992.

[17] Frances Gies and Joseph Gies, *Women in the Middle Ages*, Thomas Y. Crowell, New York, 1978, p. 65.

[18] See Jean Leclercq, *The Love of Learning and the Desire for God: A Study of Monastic Culture*, trans. Catherine Misrahi, Fordham University Press, Fordham, New York, 1960 [1957], esp., pp. 189–231, 202, for a masterly overview of the background to the medieval monastic context of the study of theology.

[19] Leclercq, *Theology and Prayer*, St. Meinrad Seminary, Indiana, 1962, p. 13.

[20] Ibid., p. 13.

manner, as we shall see shortly.[21] However, Leclercq's point is still pertinent to my argument, rather because of the *telos* of the institutional setting, than of any inherent quality of scholasticism or dialectics, a point that Leclercq admits elsewhere.[22]

The twelfth century saw theology slowly moving out of the monastery and cathedral school into the university. By the thirteenth century, the University of Paris was ecclesiastically established, with what is often called the Magna Carta of the university, Gregory XI's bull *Parens Scientiarum* (1231). Soon the new *studium generales* took root across Europe. The curriculum at the University of Paris was very significant, both in its vision of the relation of the disciplines, with theology as queen of the sciences, and in its actual failure to provide the unity of knowledge. The division of the faculties in the University of Paris generated complex cross-currents. The faculties were structured into the "inferior": arts (made up of the *trivium*, where three roads meet, grammar, rhetoric, and logic; and the *quadrivium*, made up of arithmetic, music, geometry, and astronomy), followed by the "superior": canon law, medicine, and theology. The benefit of such division was the assumption that all the disciplines were founded on a common unifying principle: that creation was from God, ordered, for the good of man, and to be used as such. Each discipline's methods and objects of study were carefully defined and developed. All the disciplines were subject to theological unification, and sometimes, theological correction. The latter was not always fruitful, and sometimes misused.

However, in the division of faculties lay also the seeds of the fragmentation of knowledge. Prudence Allen argues that the University of Paris's experiment would lead to a disastrous outcome, despite its own intentions. She argues that the fragmentation of the disciplines actually resulted from the poor implementation of a rich vision of an organic whole. In the practices of the University of Paris the parts were not held together. The four faculties of arts, theology, medicine, and law were designed to operate in harmony, in the service of God, the Church, and civic society. All students would start with the seven liberal arts and then proceed to an equivalent postgraduate study in theology, medicine, and law (divided into civil and canon law), with students often studying in faculties other than their own. Hence, the key role of philosophy (embedded in the arts) was central to the training and development in the three other faculties. However, Allen argues that

---

[21] Grabmann, *The Spirit of the Scholastic Method*, 1911, pp. 98–100, cited in Leclercq, *Theology and Prayer*, p. 202.
[22] Leclercq, *Love of Learning*, pp. 212, 218.

once the institutional separation of branches of knowledge was made, a slow but steady rupture in the unity of knowledge began to occur. Controversial questions began to bring the different faculties into conflict with one another. Ultimately, university education became more and more fragmented until philosophy became cut off from theology, medicine, or law.[23]

Theology became detached from the other faculties, thereby instigating the currents that led to the modern university. The circumstances that brought about these effects are complex. For example, the fact that revelation was the proper object of theology led to laws in the 1270s, prohibiting philosophers from discussing God. A law, it should be added, passed by the Faculty of Arts.[24] The same happened with medicine, with a law prohibiting clerics from studying medicine, based on the distinction between the soul (the province of theology) and the body (the province of medicine). Clerics, it was argued, should not be led away from their proper area of concern. The same happened with civil law and theology. Allen concludes:

> This process of fragmentation has continued to the present time. Universities now consist of a plethora of disciplines all vying for the central place in the determination of truth. Aristotle had correctly argued for the need to make significant distinctions in the search for truth. However, the institutionalization of Aristotle turned these distinctions into rigidly defined areas of knowledge that made a unified approach to the person nearly impossible. The shadow of the institutionalization of Aristotle haunts the corridors of the contemporary academic world like a ghost from the thirteenth-century University of Paris.[25]

This fragmentation of the person, and of the spheres of human and divine reality, was to remain embedded in the institutions that transmitted knowledge, with some exceptions. This *telos* would evolve, with the addition of new factors, into the Enlightenment university.

A second development in the university was the development and flowering of Scholasticism. Scholasticism can be traced back to Augustine, who stressed the need of dialectics in studying Christian doctrine. It ran through some of the "Schools" and received important formulation from Anselm (c.1033–1109), who inspired the *Sentences*, the first really systematic arrangement of theological questions, citing biblical and patristic authorities

---

[23] Prudence Allen RSM, *The Concept of Woman: The Aristotelian Revolution 750 BC–AD 1250*, Eden Press, Quebec, 1985, p. 417.
[24] See John F. Wippel, "The Condemnation of 1270 and 1277 at Paris," *The Journal of Medieval and Renaissance Studies*, 7, 1977, pp. 169–201.
[25] Allen, *The Concept of Woman*, p. 419.

(*auctoritas*) on a question, followed by rational disputation (*ratio*) to settle conflicts and create harmonization. Abelard (1079–1142) refined the *quaestio*, *interrogatio*, and *disputatio* methods and Albert the Great and his pupil Thomas Aquinas (c.1225–74) probably represent the high point of Scholasticism. Scholasticism is important in my narrative for two reasons. First, dialectics becomes firmly established as part of Christian education, giving an important role to *ratio*, thereby providing a bridge between all forms of knowledge and learning and Christian revelation. This was embodied in Aquinas's great synthesis of the Aristotelian and Augustinian traditions in Thomism, providing an important role for philosophy, adequately Christianized, to expound doctrine. It also allowed Aquinas to relate the different disciplines and show the role of the virtues (both intellectual and moral) in education.[26] It also showed in practice how all knowledge can be integrated, critically, into the Christian vision. Aristotle, Islamic appropriations of Aristotle, and Greek philosophy are all brought to the aid of Christian theology in Aquinas. My own book flows out of this tradition.

Second, Aquinas offers an alternative to Nominalism, although historically Nominalism was very influential. Many argue that Nominalism sowed the seeds of secularism and atheism. Ockham's (c.1285–1347) version of Nominalism (rather than Roscellinus's) asserts that no universal can actually be found in reality, but only in the human mind. This would mean that God could not be conceptually understood, and was solely a reality based on revelation. But this sundering of reason, reality, and deity would eventually lead to fideism and its opposite, atheism. The role of Nominalism, as Francis Martin points out, is of course key to the transmission of the idea of a secular universe, with Duns Scotus's attempt to show that being was univocal, a property shared by both God and the creature. The consequence of this was that being could eventually be explained without recourse to God and seen as entirely autonomous.[27] Milbank sees Scotus as central to the *telos* of modernity.[28] In contrast, Milbank extols Aquinas's analogical understanding of

---

[26] See *Summa contra Gentiles*, Bk II, chs 2–4; *Summa Theologiae*, I–1, q. 1; a. I–10, q. 57.

[27] Francis Martin, *The Feminist Question: Feminist Theology in the Light of Christian Tradition*, T. & T. Clark, Edinburgh, 1994, pp. 49–52.

[28] See John Milbank, *Theology and Social Theory*, Blackwell, Oxford, 1990, pp. 302–6, and Gillian Rose, *Dialectics of Nihilism: Post-Structuralism and Law*, Blackwell, Oxford, 1984, pp. 104–7. However, note the important reading of Scotus by Richard Cross, "Where Angels Fear to Tread: Duns Scotus and Radical Orthodoxy," *Antonianum*, 76, 2001, pp. 7–41, who rightly questions Scotus's attributed role. Hans Urs von Balthasar also positions Ockham as key to the fragmentation of the disciplines and the internal implosion of theology, which now could only be "practical" and "fideistic" as it is removed from all other forms of knowledge. See *The Glory of the Lord: The Realm of Metaphysics in the Modern Age*, vol. V, trans. Oliver Davies et al., Ignatius Press, San Francisco, California, 1991 [1965], pp. 9–47, esp. pp. 19–21.

being, a strategy that allows for the radical difference between God and creation, and at the same time, the participation of creation with God. However, this Thomist line with which I agree (and there are of course many Thomisms[29]) is contested, as is the question as to whether Ockham, rather than Scotus, is really the villain. It is unnecessary to settle these questions here, except to point out that Scholasticism is often falsely associated with hyperdialectic and rationalism, when in fact its best representatives mark a brilliant Christian integration of the role of reason in relation to revelation. Leclercq's emphasis on disputation alone in his criticism of Scholasticism conceals the critical-confessional enterprise of Thomism.[30] Of course, there were problems with Scholasticism in its emphasis on logic and dialectics, rather than languages and literature, on reason rather than metaphor and poetry, the emphasis favoured in the Renaissance, and by Reformers like Luther.

Nevertheless, despite a very complex reality, at the beginnings of the European university, *both* those who taught and those who learnt in the university believed their task was in service to God, Church, and society.[31] Despite all these swirling cross-currents set in motion with the creation of the university, there are three important positive elements that followed from thirteenth-century Paris. First, the university would be a place of considered disputation, a location for rational argument, embedded within a tradition, to flourish and develop in engagement with rival traditions. A distorted fragment of this tradition is developed in the modern secular university, a place of rational discussion, without adequate attention to tradition-specific forms of enquiry or the *telos* of *ratio*. I will develop this point below. Second, even though university theology was the preserve of male clerics, the location of theology in the university meant that eventually in the Enlightenment university, lay theological education could develop, which would also be gender-inclusive. Third, theology was given a prime place in harmonizing and integrating the other three faculties of arts, medicine, and law. At least the vision of a proper relation between the disciplines

[29] See Fergus Kerr, *After Aquinas: Versions of Thomism*, Blackwell, Oxford, 2002.

[30] See MacIntyre's insistence that Thomism was both confessional and dialectical, in *Three Rival Versions*, p. 201. Colin Gunton misreads Aquinas in *The One, the Three and the Many: God, Creation and the Culture of Modernity*, Cambridge University Press, Cambridge, 1993, pp. 138–42; and for a persuasive defense, see Milbank, *Theology and Social Theory*, pp. 380–438.

[31] See Hastings Rashdall, *The Universities in the Middle Ages*, 3 vols., new edn., Clarendon Press, Oxford, 1963, esp. vol. 1, ch. 5. See also Stephen C. Ferruolo, *The Origins of the University*, Stanford University Press, Stanford, California, 1985, and for the parallel origins in the UK, see Alan B. Cobban, *The Medieval English Universities: Oxford and Cambridge to c.1500*, Scolar Press, Aldershot, 1988, esp. pp. 209–38.

had become institutionally embedded. However, as Allen, Martin, and Leclercq have argued, a price was to be paid on all three fronts: theology became disassociated from prayer and contemplation, it was eventually possible to do theology without any Christian commitment, and the establishment of the Aristotelian divisions provided the possibility for the modern fragmentation of the disciplines.

The Reformation was to shake the structures of university theology in limited ways. First, theology faculties and universities were now divided along Protestant and Catholic lines. Hence, ancient universities such as Oxford and Cambridge, from their Catholic foundations, came explicitly to exclude Roman Catholics, just as Catholic institutions excluded Protestants. When such exclusions were eventually repealed at Oxford and Cambridge in the nineteenth century, with exceptions for the Faculties of Divinity, they reflected the structural implementation of secularism, not an ecumenical renewal with an open Christian university. There were both advantages and problems with this Reformation divide. One such advantage, noted by MacIntyre, is that such exclusions "provided some of the necessary preconditions for the Thomistic revival and thereby for the reappropriation of Aquinas's dialectical enterprise."[32] These exclusions allowed for the flowerings of the distinct Protestant and Roman Catholic theological traditions, even if the Calvinists remained essentially scholastic following Calvin's own Catholic tradition. It was Luther who was to steer the Reformation into a very different mold, with Catholicism initially reacting defensively, and only in the modern period taking on and developing some of Luther's positive themes (theology as salvation, theology of the cross), while robustly rejecting the anti-metaphysical tradition generated from Luther.[33] If these denominational universities contained mixed blessings, they both began to have something in common, which brings me to the second point.

Nichols writes that "perhaps the most lasting result of the period from 1500 to 1700 was the rise of theological specialization."[34] This was a result of many factors: rapidly expanding knowledge through the age of discovery (by Europeans) of new worlds, the emergence of the natural sciences, the rise of Humanism, and eventually, with the emergence of the middle classes in the nineteenth century, the growth of professionalism within the universities.[35]

---

[32] MacIntyre, *Three Rival Versions*, p. 224.
[33] The Lutheran tradition is well served and rehabilitated in the excellent work of Gerhard Ebeling, *The Study of Theology*, trans. Duane A. Priebe, Collins, London, 1979 [1975].
[34] Nichols, *Shape*, p. 318.
[35] This latter is perceptively traced in American culture by Burton J. Bledstein, *The Culture of Professionalism: The Middle Class and the Development of Higher Education in America*, W. W. Norton, New York, 1976.

But specialisms would have a huge effect on the internal disintegration of theology, as of other disciplines that were undergoing rapid internal diversification. For example, the sixteenth century sees, for the first time, distinct treatises on moral theology written mainly by Jesuits for priests. In themselves, they represent remarkable achievements, but their form dictated a focus on morals divorced from grace and dogmatics. In Thomas's *Summa Theologiae*, morals and grace were dealt with together. The result of such specialism is that morality would eventually be given the aura of autonomy, separate from grace and God, a move that was consolidated through the Enlightenment. Of course no Jesuit author would have intended such a trajectory, but the institutional settings could easily work against individual intentions.

The earthquake of the seventeenth century with the development of the natural sciences cannot be underestimated, although the hostility between religion and science is often overestimated. I will return to this theme in chapter six, but for the moment it is worth noting three important effects of the growing dominance of science on the development of theology. First, as Michael Buckley has argued, theologians too often tried to defend theology from scientific criticism on scientific grounds or in purely philosophical terms, rather than Christological or experiential grounds.[36] This eventually assimilated theology to science, and in this process, theology lost sight of its different method and object: "Theology gives way to Cartesianism, which gives way to Newtonian mechanics. The great argument, the only evidence for theism, is design, and experimental physics reveals that design."[37] This is a version of what I called the third strand. The roots of atheism were partly planted by theologians, who failed to be theological enough. Second, this assimilation also ran in tandem with the mathematization of the disciplines, whereby subjects strove to be "scientific" (in a natural scientific sense), eventually finding institutionalization in the University of Berlin, the model of the Enlightenment research university. Third, this process across the disciplines, and within theology itself, led to the phenomena whereby the New Testament would become subject to positivist sciences, initially historical-critical methods. This, when employed as the major hermeneutical tool, would further erode the recovery of theology's unique object of study: God, as revealed in history. Nicholas Lash discussing both Buckley's thesis and Hans Frei, writes that in the seventeenth-century context

---

[36]   Michael J. Buckley, *At the Origins of Modern Atheism*, Yale University Press, New Haven, Connecticut, 1987, pp. 65–6 makes clear how theologians like Lessius and Mersenne rebutted atheism as if it were a "philosophic stance towards life" rather than a "rejection of Jesus Christ as the supreme presence of god [sic] in history."

[37]   Ibid., p. 202.

we are evidently already in the presence of what Hans Frei called the "great reversal," that shift in interpretative strategy as a result of which theological interpretation became "a matter of fitting the biblical story into another world" (namely, the world now taken to be constituted by those ranges of experience deemed open to any human being) "rather than incorporating that world into the biblical story." In the self-assured world of modernity, people seek to make sense of the Scriptures, instead of hoping, with the aid of Scripture, to make some sense of themselves.[38]

Hans Frei sees the "great reversal" which shifted theology out of its ecclesial context embedded in the design of the University of Berlin at the beginning of the nineteenth century. Berlin was designed to reflect the "research university" along the lines of the Enlightenment vision of education.[39] In this respect, it intentionally defined itself against the earlier model of *paideia* which had characterized ecclesial forms of education (and dominant forms of pre-Christian Greek education) and instead emphasized a critical, orderly, and disciplined science of research. That is, no texts or ways of reading them were to be seen as authoritative because of spiritual authority or traditions deeming them so. Rather, all texts were to be critically scrutinized, using methods that were accessible to all rational men, and methods that could allow the repetition of tests to authenticate and establish results. In this sense, theology, whose authority rested on revelation, was an obvious problem for the University of Berlin and there was considerable controversy about its inclusion in the new research university.

It was only through the genius of Schleiermacher (1768–1834) that theology made it into the university, but on the easily corrosive grounds that it was important for professional training, rather than arguing its status as a "science," let alone queen of the sciences.[40] In this sense Schleiermacher conceded the most important point. He argued that just as medicine and law

---

[38] Nicholas Lash, *The Beginning and End of "Religion,"* Cambridge University Press, Cambridge, 1996, pp. 147–8. He cites Hans W. Frei, *The Eclipse of Biblical Narrative: A Study in Eighteenth and Nineteenth Century Hermeneutics*, Yale University Press, New Haven, Connecticut, 1974, p. 130 (citations), and see also pp. 51, 325.

[39] For the situation of the German universities at the time, see Daniel Fallon, *The German University*, Colorado University Press, Boulder, 1980.

[40] In 1808 Schleiermacher published (the untranslated) *Thoughts on German Universities from a German Point of View* and in 1810, *Brief Outline on the Study of Theology*, trans. Terrence N. Tice, John Knox Press, Richmond, Virginia, 1966 [1811]. For the historical context, see Martin Redeker, *Schleiermacher: Life and Thought*, trans. John Wellauser, Fortress Press, Philadelphia, Pennsylvania, 1973 [1968], III. 2 and IV. B. See also Hans Frei, *Types of Christian Theology*, Yale University Press, New Haven, Connecticut, 1992, where he carefully charts aspects of the debate generated by Schleiermacher's proposals in "Appendix A: Theology in the University," pp. 95–132.

were included in the university, the historical and philosophical study of theology was also justified, for these disciplines provided the materials for a theological training that was required for ministers of the Church. However, there were strong criticisms of theology from the very disciplines to which it sought to ally itself: history and philosophy. Kant, like Fichte after him, could only tolerate theology as the practical working out of the truths available in philosophy via universal reason in a transcendental mode (Kant), or in an idealist philosophy (Fichte).[41] Later philosophies would replicate this pattern: Marxism, feminism, postmodernism. Likewise, positivist history demanded theology be reined in by its methods and findings (Harnack and Strauss) and to this would be added postmodern reading strategies.[42] It is not that theology cannot learn from these disciplines, but that it cannot be ruled and made to conform to them. Judging the dividing line is a complex matter. Nevertheless, the Enlightenment university began the process of translating theology into its own philosophical, natural scientific, or social analysis modalities. The Enlightenment *Wissenschaft* dictated to theology the preconditions and limits of its enquiry and also regulated its agenda. The question of the subservience of theology to secular disciplines would not be resolved formally, although the increasing secularity of the university institutionally favored one party over the other in subsequent debates.

The genealogical picture is extremely complicated, but there are two main points I wish to emphasize as an outcome of the above. First, the secularization of theology was a process that reached its culmination in the nineteenth century and we now live in the shadow of the "great reversal" embodied in the history of the Enlightenment, such that institutional university theology bears many of the marks of this secularized process. As we shall see in a later chapter, one such mark was the ascendance of alien methods and disciplines as the definitive interpreters of scripture, tradition, and authority. The ascendancy of historical positivism also explains the inevitable rise of the history of religions school, transferring its hermeneutical strategies designed for

---

[41] See Kant, "The Conflict of the Faculties" in *Religion and Rational Theology*, trans. Allen W. Wood and George di Giovanni, Cambridge University Press, Cambridge, 1996, pp. 233–9.

[42] See Stephen F. Fowl, "Introduction" in ed. Stephen F. Fowl, *The Theological Interpretation of Scripture*, Blackwell, Oxford, 1997, pp. xii–xxx with good reference to US scholarship in this field. See also the excellent overview of New Testament scholarship as falling into three camps: (1) historical critical (Philip Davies, Heikki Räisänen, Werner Jeanrond); (2) Christian theological (Peter Stuhlmacher, Brevard Childs, Francis Watson); and (3) postmodern (David Clines, Anthony Thiselton, Stephen Moore), with an argument similar to my own, regarding the shortcomings of the first and third: Markus Bockmuehl, "'To Be or Not to Be': The Possible Futures of New Testament Scholarship," *Scottish Journal of Theology*, 51, 1998, pp. 271–306. However, at the last moment Bockmuehl steps back from the implications of his argument, fearing sectarianism (p. 291).

reading ancient texts to interpret texts used in living traditions, such as the New Testament, but without reference to its traditional forms of exegesis like the multiple senses of scripture and the role of the Holy Spirit for proper exegesis. This was of course one of the major contentions between Karl Barth and Adolf Harnack.[43] Harnack's historical positivist reading of theology would eventually result in the emergence of "religious studies," as we shall see in the next section.

Second, while various intellectuals within the university have constantly alerted theologians to this situation, the significance of this crisis in requiring a new type of university has been less fully explored. This is in part due to very pragmatic pressures: university culture in England and the United States is in deep recession, with funding ever tighter and a market-led economy becoming pervasive, even in the Ivy League institutions; departments of theology being a major casualty, such that for theologians to argue for alternative universities might almost seem tragi-comic, or aptly, farce. Without minimizing these pressures, it must be said that one of the reasons for this crisis in funding and support of university education is precisely that large numbers of the general public and the intelligentsia schooled in such institutions can see very little use for the universities. Apart from professional training (law, medicine, engineering, and so on), and scientific research where results are tangible, produce revenue, and finance themselves, the Arts are seen increasingly as a luxury. In 2003 the Minister for Education in Tony Blair's British Labour government publicly said that the study of medieval texts was a luxury that could not be justified from public funding.[44] This is hardly surprising, for when the university becomes part of the instrumentalist culture of modernity and the fragmentation of the disciplines is so complete, their importance and interrelation are not even debated by the British government. Later, I shall turn to the major exploration of the question of the need for a post-liberal university, in the work of MacIntyre.

Hence, to draw this story to a provisional conclusion, we have seen how theology started as part of the ecclesial practice within small communities, then engaged with the great currents of Hellenistic philosophy, not from any organized institutional base, but in an *ad hoc* manner. Later, in the monasteries and cathedral schools it was wedded to prayer and the practice of contemplation and love, and later it became established as the "queen of the sciences" in thirteenth-century Paris, faith taking on a positive and constructive relation to reason and the other disciplines, even if this synthesis was not always achieved well and the university emphasis on dialectics

---

[43] See their exchanges in James M. Robinson, *The Beginnings of Dialectical Theology*, John Knox Press, Richmond, Virginia, 1968, pp. 165–87.

[44] See *The Guardian*, Monday, May 12, 2003.

sometimes lost its ecclesial moorings. The Reformation saw denominational flowerings, although perpetuating the scandal of disunity among Christians. However, in an increasingly secularized culture, theology was finally symbolically toppled at the University of Berlin, so that it would, if fortunate, eventually be part of the liberal arts, not a faculty on its own, and then be eclipsed by religious studies. In brief: from Queen of the Sciences to the laughing stock of the Arts Faculty.[45]

In relation to my four concerns, I hope to have traced the historical context for the following. First, the way in which the discipline of theology became separated from the practices that are required for its proper undertaking: prayer, sacraments, and virtue. It would be correct to say that the epistemological precondition for theology was the community of the Church and the Spirit.[46] Second, the way university theology became assimilated to alien methodologies, philosophies, and sciences, so that the very intellectuals who might safeguard the Church from de-Christianization often accelerated the process. Rather than "incorporating the world into the biblical story," theology became more and more a "matter of fitting the biblical story into another world" (which was constructed by secular modernity and "policed" by its rules and methodology).[47] Third, the way in which theology and philosophy's mediating role to discern the *telos* and unity of the different disciplines has almost totally disappeared, so that fragmentation, competitive professionalism, and utilitarianism in the universities have no check. Fourth, this scenario would not only relegate theology to the margins, but also threaten its very existence with the Enlightenment discipline of "religious studies."

Many readers will of course breathe a sigh of relief at these changes, and I do not want to turn the clock back—for that is in one sense impossible.[48]

---

[45] See the English Catholic novelist, David Lodge, *Paradise News*, Secker & Warburg, London, 1991.

[46] See Aidan Nichols OP, "The Habit of Theology, and How to Acquire It," *The Downside Review*, 105, 1987, pp. 247–59; and the aptly entitled, *Instruction on the Ecclesial Vocation of the Theologian*, CTS/Veritas, London/Dublin, 1990, issued by the Congregation for the Doctrine of the Faith. I shall return to this latter document in the next chapter.

[47] See Frei, *Eclipse*, p. 130; and John Milbank's critical reconstruction of this process in *Theology and Social Theory*, esp. Part II: "Theology and Positivism," pp. 51–143, which accounts for my reference to "policing."

[48] See Dorothy L. Sayers, "The Lost Tools of Learning," *National Review*, January 19, 1979, pp. 90–9, who wants to go "back to the Middle Ages," for we must distinguish, "Does 'go back' mean a retrogression in time, or the revision of an error? The first is clearly impossible *per se*; the second is a thing which wise men do every day" (p. 93). Sayers's argument is persuasive except that she minimizes the many good things that modernity has introduced into education (including opportunities for women, like herself), and oddly abandons theology's synthesizing role at the end of the trivium for no apparent reason (see p. 99).

Instead, I only want to suggest that what masquerades as theology cannot intellectually and historically meet the description. What now exists is simply a study of texts that are concerned with religious matters. Strictly speaking, one cannot claim that theology departments are there to help teach people to theologize better and become virtuous. What is denied to theology departments is allowed to many others. History departments can claim to produce good historians, and English departments will often actively encourage "creative writing" within the academic curriculum. However, it is difficult to find a theology prospectus in England that claims to produce "good theologians."

III On the Secular Respectability of Doing Religious Studies

In England, as in the United States and Europe, a number of factors are worth noting in tracing the production of religious studies as both bed-fellow and successor to theology in the 1960s. In what follows I will refer to England to avoid generalizations. My contention is that religious studies in England adapted secular methodologies (positivist history and neutral enquiry) as key to the study of religion, contesting that it, not theology, was the proper subject to be embedded in the emerging modern university. Clearly, while the contexts are very different, some of the points here will be applicable more widely. The Oedipal configuration of "bed-fellow" and "successor" is not random, for religious studies explicitly claims to cohabit the academic territory with theology, but if taken seriously, implicitly seeks its destruction for it must rightly claim Christianity as its object of investigation, in the same manner as it claims Buddhism or Islam as its objects. Hence, at best, religious studies subconsciously desires to seize and control the academic territory regarding the "divine" from theology. As a prominent religious studies supporter notes: the "theological establishment is therefore, a problem in that it is a kind of conceptual albatross around the neck of religious studies."[49] The albatross became extinct! Despite this claim, it would be intriguing to know what would change in the practice

[49] Ninian Smart, "Religious Studies in the United Kingdom," *Religion*, 18, 1988, p. 8. For a more militant North American version of Smart, see Donald Wiebe, *The Politics of Religious Studies*, Macmillan, Basingstoke, 1999. Wiebe considers Smart to be a collaborator with theology in suggesting empathy is compatible with objectivity (p. 66), and likewise criticizes the American Academy of Religion (p. 248). Wiebe, like Smart, also exalts science, neutrality, and objectivity. See Kieran Flanagan's powerful critique of "Religious Studies" in "Theological Pluralism: A Sociological Critique" in ed. Ian Hamnett, *Religious Pluralism and Unbelief: Studies*

and curriculum in theology departments were they to metamorphose overnight to religious studies departments. I suspect very little.

The increasing secularity of theology in the 1960s, both institutionally and methodologically, produced a situation where many felt that what actually existed in the practice of theology was the study of religion. Historical accidents meant that the religion so selected was Christianity. In the context of England's multi-religious nature, its colonial conquests, and the growth of Indology, many argued that religions other than Christianity should be taught. If the study of religion was an academic specialty, it seemed right and obvious that to limit the menu to Christianity was parochial, to say the least. This trajectory was predictable in the Enlightenment's resistance to the particularity of Christian revelation. By this, I do not mean that the proper study of theology can be done in isolation from engagement with world religions, nor that other religions should not mount analogous arguments to the ones here presented. I am simply outlining the manner in which modernity came to homogenize the university. Furthermore, students in the period of the introduction of religious studies to the universities, in the late 1960s, were increasingly from secularized backgrounds. The attraction of Buddhism and Hinduism to these consumers, aligned with the Romantic European idealization of these traditions, meant that the market was right for religious studies.[50]

The final factor worth mentioning, and perhaps the most significant in the English context, was the introduction of an allegedly scientific, objective, and academic method appropriate to the study of religion: phenomenology. It is no accident that the main supporter of such a method in this country was also the founder of the first Department of Religious Studies in England, at

---

Critical and Comparative, Routledge, London, 1990, pp. 81–113, esp. pp. 88–90. While few today follow Smart, his influence is deeply imprinted upon the academy; and universities, like the Church, take time to shift.

[50] For the appropriation of the "east" by the "west," see, for example, Raymond Schwab, *The Oriental Renaissance*, Columbia University Press, New York, 1984; Wilhelm Halbfass, *India and Europe: An Essay in Understanding*, State University of New York, Albany, New York, 1988; Paul Hacker, "Aspects of Neo-Hinduism as Contrasted with Surviving Traditional Hinduism" in ed. Lambert Schmithausen: *Paul Hacker: Kleine Schriften*, Harrassowitz, Wiesbaden, 1978, pp. 580–608. For the domestication of these differing construals of power (for that is what Buddhism, Hinduism, and Islam are, like Christianity) within the (colonial) western academy, see Talal Asad, *Genealogies of Religion: Discipline and Reasons of Power in Christianity and Islam*, Johns Hopkins University Press, Baltimore, Maryland, 1989; and Timothy Fitzgerald, *The Ideology of Religious Studies*, Oxford University Press, Oxford, 2000, esp. chs. 6–10. Fitzgerald's critical analysis is helpful in showing how religions are cultural construals of power, but he brazenly caricatures theology as a "misleading obsession with superhuman beings and related notions that cluster around 'religion'" (p. 224). He is of course right in terms of modernity's shaping of theology.

Lancaster in 1967, and the author of the albatross statement quoted above. While Lancaster was the first department with this name, the study of "comparative religion" goes back to 1904, when Manchester University had the first Department of Comparative Religion, chaired by the Pali scholar, T. W. Rhys Davids. Nevertheless, Ninian Smart's *The Phenomenon of Religion* (1973) is central for understanding the Oedipal relations between theology and religious studies.[51] It is important to note that the understanding of the "phenomenological" method and approaches to "religious studies" are increasingly multifarious, and have a history going back to 1873, when the founding father of comparative religions, Friedrich Max Müller, published his famous study, *Introduction to the Science of Religion*. Eric Sharpe calls this the "foundation document of comparative religion."[52] Sharpe's study is one of the best in charting the emergence of religious studies, both in the UK and also worldwide. A constellation of titles describes this general approach: comparative religion, history of religions, religious studies. The first fell from grace due to its evolutionary associations; the second, based on the German *Religionsgeschichte*, is still found in Germany, Sweden, and Finland.[53] Note too, the term religious studies in its phenomenological sense has an entirely different genealogy in Europe to that in the UK.[54]

[51] Macmillan, London, 1973, and his *The Science of Religion and the Sociology of Knowledge*, Princeton University Press, Princeton, New Jersey, 1973, pp. 158ff. It would be churlish to question Smart's outstanding contribution academically and institutionally. I use him purely as a symbol in what follows. See also Wiebe's assessment of the US and Canada, in *The Politics of Religious Studies*. For a criticism based on avoiding Christianity's political influence, rather than exalting objectivity in the academy, see David A. Hollinger, "Enough Already: Universities Do Not Need More Christianity" in ed. Andreas Sterk, *Religion, Scholarship, and Higher Education: Perspectives, Models, and Future Prospects*, University of Notre Dame Press, Notre Dame, Indiana, 2002, pp. 40–50.

[52] Eric J. Sharpe, *Comparative Religion: A History*, 2nd edn., Duckworth, London, 1986 [1975], p. 35. See also Walter H. Capps, *Religious Studies: The Making of a Discipline*, Fortress Press, Minneapolis, Minnesota, 1995.

[53] See Sharpe, *Comparative Religion*, pp. xii–xiv, 294–319: "From Comparative Religion to Religious Studies."

[54] See Smart's characterization of the differences between himself and Husserl in *The Science of Religion*, pp. 49ff. See, also for example, the survey in ed. Michael Pye, *Marburg Revisited: Institutions and Strategies in the Study of Religion*, Diagonal Verlag, Marburg, 1989. This volume neglects developments in gender studies in religion. See the entry on "Phenomenology of Religion" for a good overview by Douglas Allen, in eds. M. Eliade et al., *The Encyclopedia of Religion*, Macmillan, London, 1987, vol. 11, pp. 272–85. The theological study of religions that I am proposing needs to be worked out in closer engagement with differing approaches such as feminism, structuralism, psychoanalysis, materialism, constructivism, and so on. Clearly, one cannot essentialize "Religious Studies." However, what is common to the differing types (history of religions, comparative religion, religious studies) is the basic presupposition that the discipline can be conducted and practiced by Christian and non-Christian alike. Theology, properly speaking, cannot.

In explicit contrast to the memory of the dead mother (theology), whose distorted image masqueraded in the universities, the emerging prince of the religious academy proposed a method that definitely and distinctively should not and could not involve faith as its starting point. Faith as a starting point was both unscientific and unscholarly, according to the canons then acceptable to the secular academy and the cultured despisers of Christianity. Hence, the phenomenological method started with *epochē* or bracketing. *Epochē* meant the suspension of one's own beliefs, attitudes, and values, in order to avoid contaminating objective description with personal prejudice such as one's own personal religious commitment. It was allegedly only in this fashion that the enquirer could really attain the object of enquiry and understand it correctly, be it Hinduism, Buddhism, or Christianity.

However, the very notion of different "religions," related to each other as species of a common genus, was itself a seventeenth-century invention, as Peter Harrison has so persuasively argued.[55] The construction of such a field ("religion") is a project that is partly located in the Enlightenment's refusal to acknowledge the particularity of Christian revelation. Consequently, there followed the creation of a single secular history whereby different religions were organized within the Enlightenment's own over-arching narrative, rather than taking seriously the different organizations of time, space, and history within the various religions. Such a taxonomy also failed to attend to the epistemological pre-requisites required for comprehension specified by some of the religions under examination.

John Milbank makes an interesting connection between the growth of comparative religion in the discipline of religious studies and the assumption that all religions are equal paths to the one divine. He suggests this connection because in the very creation of the field of "religion" there is an in-built assumption of different species of a common genus, and with this assumption, the idea that the common genus is our "own" religion of which others are various manifestations. Milbank writes:

> The usual construals of religion as a genus, therefore, embody covert Christianizations, and in fact no attempt to define such a genus (or even, perhaps,

[55] Peter Harrison, *"Religion" and the Religions in the English Enlightenment*, Cambridge University Press, Cambridge, 1990, and also Timothy Fitzgerald, *The Ideology of Religious Studies*, Oxford University Press, Oxford, 2000. Wilfred Cantwell Smith, *The Meaning and End of Religion*, Macmillan, New York, 1962, pp. 15–30, also shows the modern construction of the notion of "religion." However, Smith perpetuates this reification of modernity in his problematic notion of "faith" as the common generic "essence" of each tradition. See my: "A Christian Reflection on Some Problems with Discerning 'God' in the World Religions," *Dialogue and Alliance*, 5, 1, 1991, pp. 4–17.

delineation of an analogical field of "family resemblances") will succeed, because no proposed common features can be found, whether in terms of belief or practice (gods, the supernatural, worship, a sacred community, sacred/secular division, etc.) that are without exceptions. The most viable, because most general definitions ("What binds a society together," and so forth) turn out to be so all-encompassing as to coincide with the definition of culture as such.[56]

It is no mere coincidence that Smart's phenomenological methodology bears striking resemblance to Descartes's and Locke's stripping down process to get to the foundations of knowledge; nor is its similarity to Hume's empiricist positivism insignificant.[57] In one sense the new scientific methodology of religious studies that was emulated by theology in its attempt to remain within the academy, was clearly a child of the Enlightenment. Admittedly, there has been much debate about Smart's model by practitioners of religious studies in England, but the point I wish to make is this. While the methodology and subject matter of religious studies in its institutional setting were increasingly successful (there are now a number of Religious Studies departments, while prior to 1967 there were none in this country), intellectually the presuppositions of Smart's approach are deeply problematic. Its problematic nature lies in its Enlightenment marriage to objectivity and scientific neutrality. Hence, and I must make this clear, my argument is in no way directed against the study of Buddhism and Hinduism and other religious traditions in the academic curriculum (far from it), but rather against the assumptions about how such subjects are studied and how they are related to theology within the curriculum.

There are important objections against *epochē* as a method and consequently all that follows from it.[58] As mentioned above, the success of the phenomenological method was in part due to the social context which looked favorably upon such an enterprise. Such consensus, though certainly not unanimous, is coming to an end, and the episteme is shifting in our times, in a period that is often described as "postmodern." The natural and

---

[56] John Milbank, "The End of Dialogue" in ed. Gavin D'Costa, *Christian Uniqueness Reconsidered*, Orbis, New York, 1990, pp. 174–91: pp. 176–7. Milbank's point is precisely that of Fitzgerald, *The Ideology of Religious Studies*, that religion is power and cultural construction. Milbank, however, argues that theology has lost its sense that this is its proper concern.

[57] See Gavin Flood's brilliant criticisms of the Cartesian roots of phenomenalism in religious studies: *Beyond Phenomenology: Rethinking the Study of Religion*, Cassell, London, 1999. Flood's own approach typifies the new diversity within the discipline. Smart is not unaware of the sort of objections Flood and I are advancing. See his *The Science of Religion*, p. 58.

[58] See António Barbosa da Silva, *The Phenomenology of Religion as a Philosophical Problem*, Gleerup, Lund, 1982.

social sciences have tended to move away from the positivist assumptions they shared at the turn of the century—and which were imitated by Smart's religious studies. Both the former disciplines have tended to eschew objectivity and neutrality, and increasingly acknowledge that the role of the investigator and his or her socio-political location is crucial to the production of knowledge.

For instance, Thomas Kuhn's notion of scientific paradigms is widely, though certainly not unanimously or uncritically, accepted in the natural sciences.[59] Kuhn challenged the idea of some kind of neutral objectivity whereby the scientist can make judgements from a universally acceptable neutral starting point as the Enlightenment episteme assumed. There would be few contemporary scientists who would deny that the language of investigation, the methods and controls of experimentation, and the very questions asked in scientific exploration, are profoundly shaped by the paradigm inhabited by the research scientist. And there is no scientist who is not operating within a paradigm. This insight need not lead to relativism (as some argue), for the very fact of paradigm shifts suggests that the quest for truth is still maintained, even with the recognition that all enquiry proceeds from a particular epistemological and ontological tradition. *Epochē*, in this view, is not only epistemologically impossible (for how could one suspend one's beliefs?), but actually undesirable, for it both masks the operative set of beliefs held by the investigator (thinking they are neutral), and obscures the forceful eviction of contenders for intellectually respectable methods of study (in my case, the dead mother—theology).

IV MacIntyre and the Criticisms of Liberalism and Postmodernism

Kuhn's point can be seen to have its counterpart in moral philosophy and the social sciences. For example, Alasdair MacIntyre has argued persuasively against the possibility of neutral enquiry or a universal rationality, and has tried to show the tradition-specific nature of all moral and philosophical intellectual enquiry. In his three major books, MacIntyre has confined himself to western Christian and secular culture and generally ignored the pressures exerted on western culture from other religions. This is hardly a

---

[59] Thomas Kuhn, *The Structure of Scientific Revolutions*, 2nd edn., Chicago University Press, Chicago, 1970. The more radical positions held by Paul Feyerabend (non-realist and relativist) and Mary Hesse (instrumentalist) are paralleled in theology by Don Cupitt and Richard Braithwaite respectively.

failing, given his mammoth achievement, but we should keep this in mind in what follows. MacIntyre's argument in his third main book *Three Rival Versions of Moral Enquiry* (1990) is particularly germane to my own argument, but it needs to be placed in the context of the other two.

In *After Virtue* (1981) MacIntyre helps to highlight the problems and persuasiveness of modernity, or as he calls it, the Enlightenment project. MacIntyre argues that the Enlightenment project was doomed to failure. John Horton and Susan Mendus provide a lucid summary:

> The Enlightenment project which has dominated philosophy during the past three hundred years promised a conception of rationality independent of historical and social context, and independent of any specific understanding of man's nature or purpose. But not only has that promise in fact been unfulfilled, the project is itself fundamentally flawed and the promise could never be fulfilled. In consequence, modern moral and political thought are in a state of disarray from which they can be rescued only if we revert to an Aristotelian paradigm, with its essential commitment to teleology, and construct an account of practical reason premised on that commitment.[60]

The Enlightenment project, in so much as it has dominated philosophy and moral and political thought, has inevitably affected religious thought and the intellectual institutions in which they developed (the universities). John Milbank's work is a complement to MacIntyre's in charting the impact of modernity on Christian theology and practice in two particular ways. First, the Enlightenment trajectory in part accounts for the demise of trinitarian theology and Christian practice in rendering and reconstructing the world within the grand narratives of philosophy (Kant, Hobbes, Locke, Rousseau, and eventually Marx and Hegel), sociology (Comte, Durkheim, Weber), and science (both the natural and social sciences). Within these narratives the world is best understood and analyzed without God, who is always positioned as moral authorizer, social cement, and expedient but ultimately redundant explanatory principle. Deism was the initial home for this vaporized God, but redundancy was inevitable. As noted earlier, Milbank sees nominalism as a major factor in this process, and, like MacIntyre, sees Aquinas as a major resource to counter modernity.

Second, the relationship between morality and deity underwent a radical shift. The Christian *telos* was ousted, in that universal reason and freedom became both the ethical means and ends. The Kantian move toward a uni-

---

[60] Eds. John Horton and Susan Mendus, *After MacIntyre: Critical Perspectives on the Work of Alasdair MacIntyre*, Polity Press, Oxford, 1994, p. 3.

versal ethics, which would be grounded in pure reason and fleshed out in practical reason, was inevitable. Kant could view the religions, with Christianity as the unsurpassable best, as more or less embodying the ethical universals he was able to arrive at through reason alone. This form of ethical thinking required an impartial state to arbitrate political, social, and ethical matters. Christianity would have to align itself with these ethical universals or lose social credibility and privilege, wherever it still had any. This narrative, by Milbank and MacIntyre, provides the canvas on which the brief history of theology I have been narrating can be painted. The emergence of modernity would not only erode Christianity intellectually, while admittedly providing the resources for many resurgences, it would shape the very intellectual institutions within which Christian theology might flourish.

After Virtue (1985) had many failings, the major one, in my opinion, being that its Aristotelianism required fuller explication and grounding in a community of practice (as opposed to an idealized past, based on heroic violence, as Milbank so pertinently points out), from which it might create an alternative society of virtue.[61] This was slightly remedied in his second work, *Whose Justice? Which Rationality?* (1988), but would have to await *Three Rival Versions* (1990) to be most fully explicated. *Whose Justice?* contains a defense by MacIntyre against the charge of relativism, a charge also aimed at Kuhn. MacIntyre tries instead to show that different positions might be able to engage in rational debate so that there may be a successful outcome. His example is the debate that takes place in thirteenth-century Paris between Aquinas and the Aristotelian and Augustinian traditions, with Thomism emerging the victor. Stanley Hauerwas and Charles Pinches summarize the argument succinctly:

> Crucial to [MacIntyre's] position is the possibility that the Christian account of the virtues can be successfully grafted onto the Greek heritage. Hence, he attempts to demonstrate how Augustine was able to resolve antinomies intrinsic to and yet unresolvable within the Greek account of virtue, and how Aquinas, revising and extending Augustine's insights, did the same, producing the most satisfactory version of morality we have had so far.[62]

---

[61] See Stout's balanced and thoughtful critique of MacIntyre's earlier work, much of it rectified in MacIntyre's later work: Jeffrey Stout, *Ethics after Babel: The Languages of Morals and their Discontents*, James Clarke, Cambridge, 1988, pp. 191–220; and Milbank's charged differentiation between the Christian and antique *polis* (which was written before *Three Rival Versions*), *Theology and Social Theory*, pp. 326–76.

[62] Stanley Hauerwas and Charles Pinches, *Christians Among the Virtues: Theological Conversations with Ancient and Modern Ethics*, University of Notre Dame Press, Notre Dame, Indiana, 1997, p. 62.

One might say that MacIntyre's intellectual search was driving him into Roman Catholic Thomism, as the only intelligible intellectual moral position on offer. This is confirmed in *Three Rival Versions*, which finally takes more seriously the socio-political context that nourishes such practices: the Church.

Three Rival Versions continues MacIntyre's project and his final chapter addresses the question of the university specifically. MacIntyre argues that western European society is confronted by three rival versions of moral enquiry, each with its own epistemological, ontological, ethical, and methodological assumptions. While they may seem incommensurable, MacIntyre also seeks to show that there may be the possibility of an historically narrated rational debate between them, so that one might emerge the superior.[63]

What are the three rival versions? There is, of course, the Enlightenment project, which MacIntyre here calls the "Encyclopaedic," for he characterizes it in its embodiment in the ninth edition of the *Encyclopaedia Britannica*. The second tradition, which has always been on the horizon of MacIntyre's project, is that of the "Genealogical," or the postmodern, typified by Nietzsche's *Genealogy of Morals*. The postmodern is parasitic upon the Enlightenment. To understand how, we must briefly return to MacIntyre's critique of Enlightenment morality. In the words of Kelvin Knight, MacIntyre argues that, despite all their important differences,

> [what] united Hume, Kant and others in a single project was . . . their agreement that the prerequisite for Enlightenment was the rejection of their Aristotelian heritage. A central part of what they thereby rejected was a syllogistic way of justifying the rules of morality on the basis not only of an apprehension of "man-as-he-happens-to-be" but also of "human-nature-as-it-could-be-if-it-realised-its-*telos*." In so doing, claims MacIntyre, they [such Enlightenment thinkers] rejected the only way of coherently moving from an apprehension of what is to an apprehension of what ought to be. Only when approached as the only means by which to move from one's present self to one's *telos*, to one's true good in society with others, can it be concluded that the rules of morality are categorical. What followed from Enlightenment philosophers' rejection of teleology was their interminable disagreement about how the rules of morality might be justified, insoluble problems in the proposals of each being identified by others.[64]

---

[63] *Three Rival Versions*, p. 5.
[64] Kelvin Knight, "Editor's Introduction," *The MacIntyre Reader*, Polity Press, Oxford, 1998, p. 8.

Eventually all that could be agreed was that people ought to be free to agree or disagree, and the birth of the modern nation state and liberal democracy was its social and political counterpart. However, with no common *telos*, even this minimal consensus would eventually come into question. Nietzsche was inevitable, given the unresolvable lacunae within the Enlightenment project that replaced the *telos* of the common good with the formal requirement of human freedom. Nietzsche saw that there could be no real foundation for ethics in this stance and consequently celebrated the will to power, which was always the repressed truth within the Enlightenment matrix. For MacIntyre's own argument to work, he develops a further critique of the postmodern or Nietzschean Genealogical "tradition" which focuses on its internal contradictions regarding the continuities of a narrative self.[65]

The third position from which MacIntyre can reveal and narrate the shortcomings of the Encyclopaedic and Genealogical traditions is Thomism, mediated by Pope Leo XIII's *Aeterni Patris*. Finally, MacIntyre has found his flicker of light; the vague gesticulation at the end of *After Virtue* turns out not to be neo-Benedictine, but a neo-Thomism.[66] My own project can be thus located within this position identified by MacIntyre, although I am not a Thomist as such, but write out of a fluid and complex "tradition": Roman Catholicism.

In the final chapter, MacIntyre calls for a postliberal university. He notes three characteristics vital to the premodern university, essential to healthy intellectual enquiry. First, the emergence of agreement upon standards of rational justification through the work of enquiry itself, not only in the explicit discussion of the philosophers but also through the intellectual practice of professors of mathematics and history and law and theology.[67] MacIntyre recognizes that such agreements are never static, but some shared consensus is important. Second, were "enforced exclusions from the universities and colleges of points of view too much at odds with the consensus underpinning both enquiry and education."[68] Of course, this system led to losses, and even grave injustices. MacIntyre bemoans the systematic injustice spawned, most notably toward Jews. Nevertheless, such exclusion was also

---

[65] Admittedly, this criticism is only focussed upon Foucault and Deleuze, and de Man's unmasking, and cannot be said to be an exhaustive engagement with postmodern texts. Milbank, in this respect, is more thorough: *Theology and Social Theory*, pp. 278–326.

[66] His final plea was for a neo-Benedict who might construct "new forms of community within which the moral life could be sustained so that both morality and civility might survive the coming ages of barbarism and darkness." *After Virtue*, p. 263.

[67] *Three Rival Versions*, p. 223.

[68] Ibid., p. 223.

the precondition of great success in building traditions of enquiry, and as MacIntyre wryly notes, the natural sciences have always best succeeded with "quiet, informal, characteristically unstated policies of enforced exclusion, unacknowledged and unnoticed except by sociologists of science."[69] Third, a counterpart to such exclusions was "the use of preferments and promotions to ensure that upholders of the consensus, including those who extended, corrected, and otherwise improved the standards of rational justification embodied in it, occupied the relevant professorial chairs."[70] Again, he is fully aware of "error and abuse," but notes that this sort of abuse is present in every system. MacIntyre concludes, repeating my earlier arguments:

> For those who require sufficient resolution of fundamental disagreements in morals and theology in order that rational enquiry in those areas may proceed, the liberal university can provide no remedy. And by providing no remedy it has successfully excluded substantive moral and theological enquiry from its domain. . . . the dethronement of moral philosophy, like the dethronement of theology in an earlier period, would in any case have deprived the curriculum of any but pragmatic principles of ordering.[71]

In one sense moral philosophy had already lost the plot with the dethronement of theology, a point that takes MacIntyre some time (three volumes) to recognize, but the significance of this loss of ordering, vision, and orientation is all-important.[72] It is precisely why there is no ability to argue for the "flourishing of the whole."[73] It is also precisely why the Great Books curriculum, suggested by intellectuals who realize the depths of the catastrophe in the modern university, is ineffectual. Alan Bloom, for example, clearly sees the closing of the "American mind" and berates the universities in a manner not unlike MacIntyre.[74] However, his proposed study of great books, the great classics of western civilization from Homer, Plato, and Aristotle, through Augustine, Chaucer, Shakespeare, to Austen and Mark Twain, cannot really restore any cultural tradition, as it bypasses the double question: how are we to read these texts, and how is their eurocentrism to be justified? Paul Griffiths sums up many of these issues nicely:

---

[69] Ibid., p. 225.

[70] Ibid., p. 224.

[71] Ibid., pp. 226–7.

[72] This lack of theological sensibility is raised in a balanced manner by David Fergusson, *Community, Liberalism and Christian Ethics*, Cambridge University Press, Cambridge, 1998, pp. 135–7.

[73] *Three Rival Versions*, p. 227.

[74] Alan Bloom, *The Closing of the American Mind*, Simon and Schuster, New York, 1987. William J. Bennet is another example.

Pedagogically, modernity is the cafeteria-style university catalog of courses from which consumers (provided they have paid their tuition fees) can choose what most pleases them; it is the row of paperback editions of sacred works from a dozen religious traditions jostling one another on the bookstore's shelves. Religious pedagogy, by contrast, is the single curriculum, identical for all, like that in place in Nālandā in India in the eighth century, or at Clairvaux in France in the twelfth; and it is a single set of sacred works that cannot be placed on a par with (much less on the same shelf as) others. Religious learning therefore requires explicit appeal to authority in ways that consumerist pedagogy does not. The former wants to make choices for its learners, while the latter wants to equip them to choose for themselves . . .[75]

MacIntyre finally makes clear the implication of his proposals in seeing that real plurality, apparently sought after by liberal moderns, might best be promoted by "rival universities":

each modelled on, but improving upon, its own best predecessors, the Thomist perhaps upon Paris in 1272, the genealogist upon Vincennes in 1968 [and one might add, the modern, upon Berlin in 1810]. And thus the wider society would be confronted with the claims of rival universities, each advancing its own enquiries in its own terms and each securing the type of agreement necessary to ensure the progress and flourishing of its enquiries by its own set of exclusions and prohibitions, formal and informal. But then also required [sic—according to whom?] would be a set of institutionalized forums in which the debate between rival types of enquiry was afforded rhetorical expression.[76]

These conclusions and MacIntyre's reasons for arriving at them account for my extended attention to his work, both in my indebtedness and also in our different emphases. In chapters two and three, I try and deal more seriously than MacIntyre does with the objection of utopianism and sectarianism. He argues that these objections may be "best understood more as a symptom of the condition of those who level it than an indictment of the projects against which it is directed."[77] While this may well be true, it is not an entirely adequate response.

There are two particular intersections between MacIntyre's and my own argument that I would like to highlight. First, religious studies, as I have been charting it above, is part of the Encyclopaedic tradition and is properly

[75] Paul J. Griffiths, *Religious Reading: The Place of Reading in the Practice of Religion*, Oxford University Press, Oxford, 1999, p. 68.
[76] *Three Rival Versions*, p. 234, my additional brackets.
[77] Ibid., p. 235.

located within that mode of enquiry. In this sense its murderous Oedipal desire toward theology can now be located within a wider picture. Theology must rightly contest religious studies' autonomous existence and its claim to objective production; although any sensible theologian would also recognize that there are invaluable skills, tools, methods, and insights present within the phenomenological approach of Smart's religious studies. The only point I am contesting is Smart's epistemological claims for religious studies. It is not an objective and dispassionate methodology by which to approach "religions," but an historically and philosophically situated enterprise, just like theology. Second, MacIntyre's material account lacks attention to the intellectual traditions of enquiry within other religions. Rather than MacIntyre's isolation of three traditions of enquiry (liberal modernity, parasitic genealogical criticism, and neo-Thomism), each requiring their own institutions of learning as their conceptions of education vary so profoundly (even if genealogy can only exist parasitically on the other two and, in this sense, could not exist on its own), there are good reasons to consider further traditions for institutional developments within the formal, rather than material, terms of MacIntyre's discussion.

Indeed, a sympathetic Muslim critic of MacIntyre, Muhammad Legenhausen, has made this very point. He notes Islam's relationship to the Aristotelian tradition upon which MacIntyre is so dependent, and therefore criticizes MacIntyre's inexplicable omission of Islam in the debate. Furthermore, Legenhausen, writing in Iran, also suggests that Islam can account for the aporia within MacIntyre's argument in *After Virtue*, whereby MacIntyre's espousal of the necessity of small sectarian communities to counter barbarism, after the order of St. Benedict, fails entirely to engage with the problem of nation states that MacIntyre identifies as one of the roots of the malaise. Susan Mendus and John Horton make the same point: "Moreover, given the importance which MacIntyre attaches to the social embeddedness of thought and enquiry, his largely negative view of modernity continually threatens to undermine any attempt to root his positive proposals in the contemporary world of advanced industrial societies."[78]

According to Legenhausen, Islam, on the other hand, is able to offer a theocratic solution, allegedly avoiding both "nationalism and liberalism," an alternative that is "not taken seriously by Western theorists."[79] Hence, Legenhausen takes up MacIntyre's critique of modernity, but points to the same

---

[78] Horton and Mendus, *After MacIntyre*, pp. 13–14.

[79] Muhammad Legenhausen, extended book review of *Whose Justice? Which Rationality?*, *Al-Tawhid*, 14, 2, 1997, pp. 158–76: p. 169. See also H. H. Bilgrami and S. A. Ashraf, *The Concept of an Islamic University*, Hodder & Stoughton, The Islamic Academy, Cambridge, 1985, esp. pp. 16–39 for a helpful perspective on the matter. Islamic universities were important influences on the development of Christian universities, in part through their shared Aristotelian heritage.

weakness located by Horton and Mendus within MacIntyre's alternative, and at that point thereby commends Islam. In institutional terms, given MacIntyre's premises, this would amount to an argument for an Islamic university. Certainly the existence of such an entity within western Europe and the United States might better facilitate systematic theology's rigorous engagement with a living religious intellectual tradition other than Judeo-Christianity. It may also have many other important benefits and consequences. The Jewish community has already established higher educational institutions within western Europe, the USA, England, and of course, Israel. Whether and how these arguments and considerations should be related to the various religions and whether such institutions would even be desirable is a question that would have to be pursued by intellectuals within those communities. For example, it seems clear that Tibetan Buddhism presupposed a very precise epistemological and pedagogical set of assumptions in its construction of the four major Tibetan universities operating in Tibet—prior to the Chinese occupation.[80] In my own desire to see the true flourishing of pluralism, rather than domesticated plurality regulated by modernity, I can see many advantages in encouraging such alternative universities. However, I cannot go further with this suggestion here, as it would take me well beyond my remit.

Admittedly, the above discussion does not address the question of how religious studies would be taught within "sectarian" theology departments. I shall address this issue in chapter five below.

To return to my main argument, to show that the crisis in the liberal Enlightenment project runs across the disciplines, I want finally to turn to the social sciences and anthropology. Bernard McGrane has argued that anthropologists and ethnologists should eschew their desire for objectivity and neutrality, for it simply masks forms of ethnocentrism that can only be discerned properly when the location of the studying subject is taken into consideration. McGrane's survey of ethnographic work from the sixteenth to the twentieth centuries is provocative and he argues that the construal of objects of study always takes place within a definite and specific horizon and in this sense is historically tradition-specific, and cannot assume a universal neutral platform for enquiry.[81] While McGrane tends toward too neat a

---

[80] Anne Klein, *Knowledge and Liberation: Tibetan Buddhist Epistemology in Support of Transformative Religious Experience*, Snow Lion, New York, 1986, p. 49.

[81] Bernard McGrane, *Beyond Anthropology: Society and the Other*, Columbia University Press, New York, 1989. Foucault is of course the inspiration behind McGrane's project and Edward Said's. See Edward Said, *Orientalism: Western Conceptions of the Orient*, Routledge & Kegan Paul, London, 1978. See a fuller discussion of these writers in my "Trinitarian Différance and World Religions" in ed. Ursula King, *Faith and Praxis in a Postmodern Age*, Cassell, London, 1998, pp. 28–46.

schematized catalog, it is worth considering his findings. He begins at the Renaissance and argues that during that period, non-Christian western European cultures and religions were always:

> interpreted on the horizon of Christianity. It was Christianity which funda-
> mentally came between the European and the non-European other. Within
> the Christian conception of Otherness anthropology did not exist; there was,
> rather, demonology. It was in relation to the Fall and to the influence of Sin
> and Satan that the Other took on his historically specific meaning.[82]

According to McGrane, after the Enlightenment, ignorance and error replaced sin. With the slow erosion of religious belief, there developed a "psychology of error and superstition, an ontology of ignorance, and an epistemology of all the forms of untruth and unenlightenment."[83] Demonization was replaced by ignorance, by a lack of enlightenment. Defoe's *Robinson Crusoe* (1719) emblematically reflects both these periods and anticipates the next in the representation of Friday: partly fallen, clearly ignorant, and definitely uncivilized. In the nineteenth century the influence of geology (George Lyell), evolutionary theory (Charles Darwin), and anthropology (Edward Tylor) provides the horizon of interpretation, so that the non-European Other is organized in terms of stages of development, "between the prehistorically fossilized 'primitive' and the evolutionary advancement of modern Western science and civilization."[84] The evolutionary ladder of savage, primitive, civilized is established and different groups positioned along its rungs with the European at the top. Finally, when McGrane comes to the twentieth century, he fiercely contests the predominant episteme of cultural relativism in which difference is rendered as cultural difference alone, thereby masking the real challenge that the Other poses.

McGrane rehearses the arguments against such relativizers: their absolute claim that all is relative must itself be relative, and their hidden imperialism in assuming a non-relative vantage point from which to make this observation about all cultures.[85] McGrane argues that culture becomes the dominant

---

[82]   McGrane, *Beyond Anthropology*, p. ix. McGrane's use of "his" ironically adds to the occlusion of the feminine Other.

[83]   Ibid., p. ix.

[84]   Ibid., p. x.

[85]   See such arguments in their more developed forms: Hilary Putnam, *Reason: Truth and History*, Cambridge University Press, Cambridge, 1981; Peter Berger, *A Rumour of Angels*, Penguin, London, 1970; and more recently Ernst Gellner, *Postmodernism: Reason and Religion*, Routledge, London, 1992. While these three make similar criticisms of relativism, they defend very different notions of rationality and tradition.

paradigm for interpreting the Other. Cultural relativity becomes the grand text into which difference is encoded; the non-European Other is seen as "fundamentally and merely, culturally different."[86] Ironically, in this modernist mode of portrayal, difference is reduced to sameness and inoculated from any real interaction. So while in the sixteenth to nineteenth centuries there was a tendency to portray the Other in metonymic mode, a distorted mirror image of the European, in the twentieth century, the Other is simply a mirror of the European, homogenized by assimilation, culturally relative, made same, rendered safe, and thereby able to "achieve" the respect of secular liberalism.

The roll-call of figures to support my argument could be extended (to include Michel Foucault, Edward Said, Donald Davidson, and others) to show the crisis in liberal modernity's intellectual assumptions and the institutions that enshrine and perpetuate this tradition (especially the university and the nation state).[87] Of course, there are supporters of all positions lodged within the university. Nevertheless, notions of *epochē* and neutral objectivity have been radically questioned in just those citadels that the method of religious studies sought to emulate. In this respect, it is theology that can offer religious studies (of an admittedly different kind) a home and proper role within a postliberal Christian university.

The fact that these different disciplines can be called upon to support my case is not in itself a decisive argument, but part of a cumulative case against the epistemological basis of religious studies relying as it does on *epochē* and the subsequent belief in the objective production and examination of the subject of study.[88] Another argument that could be deployed which is not dissimilar to the above, but derives from a different provenance while contesting the same institutional territory, comes through the voice of the nearly

---

[86] McGrane, *Beyond Anthropology*, p. x.

[87] Against the relativist difficulties often imputed to the perspectivalism advanced here, see W. V. O. Quine, *Pursuit of Truth*, Harvard University Press, Cambridge, Massachusetts, 1990, pp. 37–59, and Donald Davidson, "On the Very Idea of a Conceptual System" in *Inquiries into Truth and Interpretation*, Oxford University Press, Oxford, 1984, pp. 183–98.

[88] A similar assault has been made on religious studies and theology by feminist and liberation theologians. See, for example, Elisabeth Schüssler Fiorenza, "Commitment and Critical Enquiry," *Harvard Theological Review*, 82, 1, 1989, pp. 1–11; Jon Luis Segundo, "Capitalism Versus Socialism: Crux Theologica" in ed. Rosino Gibellini, *Frontiers of Liberation Theology in Latin America*, trans. John Drury, SCM, London, 1980 [1975], pp. 240–59. The concerns of liberation and feminism come together in María Clara Bingemer, "Women in the Future of the Theology of Liberation," and Mercy Amba Oduyoye, "Reflections from a Third World Woman's Perspective: Women's Experience and Liberation Theologies"—both in ed. Ursula King, *Feminist Theology from the Third World: A Reader*, SPCK, London, 1994, pp. 308–17, and 23–34 respectively.

dead mother (theology). The theologian could rightly argue that the study of religions is only properly located within the horizons of Christian theology precisely because all creation was made for praise and worship of the triune God. This would also be the basis for arguing more widely for the transfiguration of different disciplines within a Christian university, a matter with which I shall deal later in the book.

For the moment, let me recall the second stage of my argument. Religious studies was born into English universities: partly because of the anachronism of theology being located within the secular academy; partly owing to the search for scientific and objective ways of carrying out research in religions to avoid theological sectarianism (but nevertheless creating another form); and to gain the approval of the secular academy (which has, in many other disciplines, moved on). Put together with part one of my argument, the cumulative case will require, if it is accepted, at least one of three possible responses, only the third of which I support. One would be to abolish both theology and religious studies departments altogether and integrate them into history, literature, politics, and so on. On secular grounds, this seems to be logical and possibly inevitable. Second, one could rename theology and religious studies as the historical critical study of religion and continue what went on previously. On secular grounds this option is attractive for two reasons. First, no hermeneutical privilege is given to any one religion in the study of "religions." Second, the world is full of religions and therefore justifies a field related to this social reality. Clearly, both these options are not attractive to theology as presented here. Or third, one might allow specific starting points to flourish, label them clearly, and allow them to interact. Within this third option, many different models are possible.[89] My own specific theological option would be to argue for a Roman Catholic university (in principle, the first step before being able even to argue for a Christian university) within a pluralist academy on the lines advanced by Alasdair MacIntyre.[90] This is not in any way supposed to privilege,

---

[89]   See, for instance, Alan Wolfe, "The Potential for Pluralism: Religious Responses to the Triumph of Theory and Method in American Academic Culture" in ed. A. Sterk, *Religion, Scholarship, and Higher Education*, pp. 22–39. My own position actually embodies elements from all three of Wolfe's options, no single one of which I would identify with exclusivists. His options are rejectionism (returning "religious institutions to a position of instruction in the faith"—p. 31; a necessary part of the discipline); parallelism ("the existence of more than one kind of academic culture within an institution"—p. 32; or, as I would argue, within different institutions) and his own preferred pluralism or "opportunism," whereby institutions encourage the practice of differing approaches (p. 34). Wolfe gives no theological reasons for why this approach "ought" to be attractive to Christians, let alone others.

[90]   Such "plurality" already exists in the USA, but the extent to which it represents real "plurality" is called into question in the next chapter.

ghettoize, or sanctify Roman Catholics, but to recognize that tradition-specific forms of enquiry should be facilitated on good intellectual grounds. However, before proceeding with the theoretical argument, it is time to turn to a brief historical inspection, to see if my thesis relates to US and English university institutions.

Chapter Two

Babylon in the Church:
The United States and England

I A Brief Review of the United States:
The Secularization of the Christian University

In what follows I shall briefly examine some key studies of Christian universities in the United States, with a special focus on Roman Catholic institutions. This special focus is justified because it repeats the story of Protestant universities, as well as allowing a slightly more manageable field of material to be covered in such brief compass. I shall then turn to England to see if there are any significant parallels with my findings in the United States. Admittedly, in England there is nothing quite comparable to the numbers and denominational diversity of Christian universities in the United States. The contexts and histories of England and the United States are quite different, but I hope to highlight three common themes: (1) the secularization of the university, with minor exceptions; (2) the fragmentation of the curriculum so that specialisms flourish with little sense of any Christian vision relating and harmonizing these different fields; and (3) the secularization of the study of theology, so that it resembles its secular counterpart—religious studies. This overall picture, painted with a broad brush, misses out many counter *individual* practices, or *groupings* within institutes, but this is inevitable and necessary, as I am focussing on the institutional dimensions of the question. We need not only counter-cultural individual scholars, or in some cases, groups of scholars, but counter-cultural universities—and many of them, for real plurality.

Turning to the United States, I shall explore my three themes through three important studies. To explore the process of the secularization of Catholic universities and the impact on the curriculum I shall begin with a close reading of Philip Gleason's influential work, published in 1995,

Contending with Modernity: Catholic Higher Education in the Twentieth Century.[1] The first attempt at such a survey had been Edward J. Power's *Catholic Higher Education in America: A History* (1958),[2] but analytically it did not advance any major thesis, nor obviously could it account for the watershed of the 1960s which so drastically changed the face of Catholic higher education in the United States when many Catholic universities slowly became indistinguishable from secular universities except that Mass was regularly celebrated.[3] Gleason's book is probably the most comprehensive study of the topic to date (even though the intervening years since its publication have brought about further changes—which, however, do not call Gleason's analytical argument into question). Gleason surveys the period 1900–95, covering many aspects of institutional, organizational, curricular, personal, international, socio-political, ideological, theological, and philosophical issues. Even given the bewilderingly complex patterns and shifts he charts, it would still be possible to summarize his thesis under two headings: institutional/organizational, and curricular/ideological. The first refers to issues of management, mission statements, institutional character, and aims, and the second refers to detailed questions of how the curriculum reflects mission statements, and how it implements an ideology, possibly at variance with a mission statement. The title of his study (*Contending with Modernity*) brings those two foci together, so that the overall argument can be summarized nicely in Gleason's own words:

> what happened in the 1960s climaxed the transition from an era in which Catholic educators *challenged* modernity to one in which they *accepted* modernity. This too oversimplifies because modernity means many different things, and Catholics' new readiness to accept it was not altogether uncritical. But this formulation comes closer to capturing the fundamental shift that took place in Catholic higher education when the assimilative tendencies that had been gathering strength since World War II met and intermingled with the seismic forces unleashed by Vatican II and the social, political and cultural crisis of the 1960s.[4]

[1]   Oxford University Press, Oxford/New York, 1995. The page numbers in the text refer to this work. Gleason's account is taken to the present, in part supported and in some details contested, in Alice Gallin, *Negotiating Identity: Catholic Higher Education since 1960*, University of Notre Dame Press, Notre Dame, Indiana, 2000. I shall return to her (and David O'Brien's) differences below.

[2]   Macmillan, London, 1973 [1958].

[3]   Power's work was so obsolete as not to be discussed in any detail in Gleason's magisterial study, *Contending with Modernity*, with minor exceptions, e.g. p. 405, note 20.

[4]   Gleason, *Modernity*, p. 318.

In a word: Catholic higher education institutions were increasingly indistinguishable from their secular counterparts after the 1960s. Prior to this time, Gleason shows that there was a sustained attempt, even if never centrally orchestrated and certainly not without deep internal factions, to establish and sustain Catholic universities which at least attempted to contend with modernity, and represent an alternative practice and vision to both its Protestant and (later on) its secular counterparts.

American higher education began primarily in terms of Christian denominational institutions. The single most comprehensive study of Christian institutions in American higher education is, without question, James Tunstead Burtchaell, *The Dying of the Light. The Disengagement of Colleges and Universities from their Christian Churches*.[5] The first, Congregationalist Harvard, was founded in 1636 and was followed by at least 16 other denominational foundations (counting only those that still survive) including William and Mary (1693: Church of England/Episcopalian), Yale (1701: Congregationalist), Princeton (1746, originally called "The College of New Jersey": Presbyterian), Dartmouth (1769: Congregationalist), and Rutgers (1766, originally called Queens: Dutch Reformed). The first Catholic institution, Georgetown, appeared in 1789, founded by John Carroll SJ also the first American Catholic bishop (1788). He had been educated by Jesuits, became a Jesuit and taught for them in Europe under the Jesuit-devised *Ratio Studiorum* (plan of studies).[6] This Continental model of the curriculum was central in initially distinguishing Catholic higher education, as we shall see. By 1885 many of the major Catholic institutions had been founded: Saint Louis University (1818), Xavier University, Cincinnati (1831), Fordham University, New York (1841), Villanova University (1842), University of Dayton (1850), Boston College (1863), Marquette University (1881), and the Catholic University of America (1885). The last was the fourth institution sponsored by the Holy See in Rome or by the local See, therefore called Pontifical institutions. Catholic University is the largest of all, representing the first united actions by the American bishops in the sponsoring of Catholic higher education. Between 1920 and 1970 Catholics founded 76 institutions that are still extant, while during this same period all the other denominations taken together opened 32 comparable institutions. Burtchaell observes the steep decline after the 1960s: "One Catholic

[5]   W. B. Eerdmans, Grand Rapids, Michigan, 1998.
[6]   Two helpful studies on the *Ratio* are: Thomas Hughes, *Loyola and the Educational System of the Jesuits*, Heinemann, London, 1982, and Robert Schwickerath, *Jesuit Education: Its History and Principles, Viewed in the Light of Modern Educational Problems*, Herder, Freiburg im Breisgau, 1903.

observer recalls that in the early 1970s the mortality rate (through closing or merger) was about one per week."[7] Gleason's book is an attempt to examine this chronic decline.

Gleason, to return to the title of his book, is very clear that there is no simple or singular definition of "modernity" as applied to Catholicism as it was historically unravelling. It is associated at different times with Americanism (the assimilation of Catholicism to American ideals and culture), biblical studies, Vatican II, and Scholasticism in various ways, with different consequences. In Gleason's book it might be better construed as the "secularization" of Catholicism, indicating the assimilation of key features of American secular society: emphasis on freedom for the individual; repudiation of authorities external to the individual; favoring Christian action in terms of social service.[8] Gleason is also critical of the manner in which church institutions sometimes acted in response to these shifts in society.[9] For example, there are three cases of turbulent disputes over "academic freedom" where staff at Catholic institutions were eventually dismissed.[10] The first, and the only one I shall mention here, exemplifies the powerful tensions *within* ecclesial circles and also the growing expression of hostility in non-Catholic circles to certain aspects of Catholic polity.

In 1965, at St. John's University in New York, 31 professors were fired abruptly for their unorthodoxy. They were not even able to finish teaching their courses that semester. The entire faculty boycotted teaching, the institution was severely censured by the American Association of University Professors, and St. John's came to represent to many Catholics and non-Catholics, old-fashioned pre-Vatican II authoritarian high-handedness, disregard for human rights and due process, and a failure to take intellectual integrity seriously. Some faculty members made it clear that the problem resided in the "highly paternalistic" Vincentian administrators (earlier called the Congregation of the Mission) who also controlled the board of trustees.

---

[7]   Burtchaell, *Dying*, p. 562.

[8]   See especially Gleason, *Modernity*, pp. 283–323.

[9]   This is also true of Burtchaell, whose rhetoric is "cantankerous" (*Dying*, p. 850) at times, but he is equally critical of some members of the Curia, e.g. pp. 587–90.

[10]   See Gleason, *Modernity*, pp. 308–16 for all three cases; and also Joseph Scimencca and Toland Damiano, *Crisis at St. John's: Strike and Revolution on the Catholic Campus*, Random House, New York, 1967, for more on St. John's. Scant evidence was produced to justify the unorthodox doctrinal beliefs or immoral actions of the dismissed staff. Despite St. John's being one of the largest and "more tradition-oriented" Catholic universities, Frank D. Schubert has shown in his sociological analysis of its religious curriculum, that it too has been deeply secularized. See Frank D. Schubert, *A Sociological Study of Secularization Trends in the American Catholic University: Decatholicizing the Catholic Religious Curriculum*, Edwin Mellen Press, Lewiston, New York, 1990, quote above from p. 45; see Part II (pp. 49–129; and pp. 136–9).

In turn, the administrators defended their action in terms of the need to preserve the basic religious character of the institution. It should be noted that only a year before, as reported in John Donovan's *Academic Man in the Catholic College*, Catholic academics in the US were reporting job satisfaction in terms of "catholic environment," "faculty cordiality," and "academic freedom"—in that order.[11] Quite suddenly, this freedom was called into question. The number of such cases increased in the late 1960s and after, indicative of one of two views, depending on where one stands. For liberals, these struggles were generated from the angry flailings of the authoritarian mentality of a conservative rear-guard shocked by the modernizing influences of Vatican II. For conservatives, even if inelegantly executed, these actions were required for a Church aware that if it did not reclaim its higher educational institutions from secularism and modernity there would be no intellectual resource to regenerate Catholicism. The issues are of course more complex, and the labels "conservative" and "liberal" hopelessly inadequate, but the St. John's case is indicative of the complex nature of Catholic identity in terms of institutional/organizational and curricular/ideological issues.

To further illustrate this, I will take examples of each of these two foci to give some detail to Gleason's argument. His book contains multiple detailed descriptions, and Burtchaell complements this in his finely textured narrative that follows the same tracks regarding non-Catholic Christian institutions of higher education.[12] The institutional/organizational and curricular/ideological issues can in this instance be taken together if we look at the role of the *Ratio Studiorum* in early Catholic education. It was the backbone for the pioneers of American Catholic (Jesuit) universities, especially in the Missouri Province under the very traditional provincial Rudolph Meyer SJ, who requested a "Course of Studies" be drawn up in 1887 so that the *Ratio* could be implemented.

This Jesuit education plan of study had been canonically set forth in 1599 and was employed, with various changes, in Georgetown, Fordham, and other Catholic Jesuit institutions in the pre-war period when such institutions were developing. It is worth focussing on, for it indicates an ancient pedagogic pattern that saw the unity of all branches of knowledge being related definitively through philosophy and theology. Hence, this was a distinct Catholic vision that affected the curriculum and also indicated a

---

[11]   Sheed and Ward, New York, 1964, pp. 181–2.

[12]   Burtchaell argues that the broader picture (Christian colleges, denominations other than Catholic) is the same, although Protestant colleges went down the secularizing road at least 20 to 30 years in advance of their Catholic counterparts—*Dying*, pp. 561–3, 715–16.

theological and philosophical position regarding the very meaning of all the disciplines taught at the different levels of education. The *Ratio* consisted of a period of around seven years of studies taken in three stages (or cycles): humanistic, philosophical, and theological. The humanistic goal was *eloquentia perfecta*, a command of Latin and training in the classics, rhetoric, grammar, and logic. Some American Jesuits would later argue that this first stage was central to developing the virtues of the intellect and self-discipline, and criticized the "utilitarian" demands of contemporary education in America (such as commercial studies). Ironically the first stage had been historically formulated, in part, to help the advancement of a number of elite career paths that required Latin, such as law, medicine, government, and theology (pp. 51–5). The second cycle required three years of study of philosophy, followed by the queen of the sciences, theology, allowing for all these different branches of knowledge to be interrelated and seen as a reflection of God's glory in man's knowledge. This latter stage was envisaged for clerics.

Implementing the *Ratio* faced severe difficulties. First, the demands of a student group eager for vocational training meant that when, for example, Fordham dropped its commercial courses in the early 1890s "a severe decline in enrolment led to its reinstatement and the creation of a six-year, non-classical program leading to the Bachelor of Science degree" (p. 54). Likewise, such a program meant that many of the Jesuit institutions were "in most cases well nigh deserted" (p. 55).[13] The need for Catholics to advance themselves in American society meant that professional and vocationally oriented degrees were in demand. The aristocracy (or the wealthy in the US) and the Church were not the main clients of these new universities, as in early Europe, but often incoming immigrant populations, sometimes from poorly educated backgrounds.[14] Second, during and after the First World War, disagreements about the *Ratio* in Catholic circles began to call its authority into question for some educators. Its implementation in different countries with different resources, needs, and academic timetables and expectations presented innumerable problems. In the United States, for example, it did not fit into the normal distinctions between high school education and university education. Hence, the world assembly of Jesuits in 1906 ruled that it was no longer possible to draw up a universally binding *Ratio*, so each province could adapt it to local conditions. In the face of such

[13] Citing Roman Benert, "A Study of the Responses of Jesuit Educators in Theory and Practice to the Transformation of Curricular Patterns in Popular Secondary Education between 1880 and 1920," PhD thesis, University of Wisconsin, 1963, p. 243.
[14] Donovan, *Academic Man*, pp. 191–2 focuses on the Irish factor, arguing that the Irish carried on in their pattern of being "intellectually incurious"!

changes, when Meyer was replaced by Alexander J. Burrowes SJ, a moderate progressive, the Committee he set in motion in 1914–15 produced a new Course of Studies, yet another attempt at implementing the *Ratio*, and hailed as a "landmark in Jesuit educational modernization" (p. 56). Changes followed as Jesuit institutions (at various levels of education) accepted the notion of standardization of curriculum which required compatibility with the state's standards and goals. In the words of Burrowes: "we shall have to follow" the state (p. 57). The result was a reduced number of courses, less time required to complete a cycle, and options and choices (electives) at each stage of the cycle that reflected economic and commercial needs.

Gleason argues that by 1920 the Missouri Province practiced "effective abandonment of the *Ratio*" (p. 57), although not without many Jesuit traditionalists regarding these moves as "foolish and a betrayal of their heritage" (p. 59). This is a small case study of one province, Missouri, and the point to be gleaned from Gleason is that a once distinct Catholic vision that united both curriculum and the theology and philosophy of education was dismantled to be replaced by a secularized model dictated by financial and educational authorities outside the Church. One might speculate about the outcomes had the Jesuits of Missouri gone in a different direction.[15] One possibility, of course, is that Jesuit educational institutions would have been virtually empty. The more significant point is that many within the Church did not see this process as a falling away from the distinctness of a Catholic vision undergirding education, even though they were hard-pressed to defend what exactly was Catholic about the newer institutions apart from their personnel and their board of governors and trustees.

This curriculum example is echoed throughout Gleason's account, but there are also examples of refusal to assimilate, and indeed for nearly 50 years until the 1960s, a Catholic intellectual revival took place, with multiple tributaries feeding into it. Gleason argues that the dual effects of Pope Leo XIII's *Aeterni Patris* (1897), calling for a revival of Thomism, and Pope Pius X's *Pascendi Dominici Gregis* (1907) condemning Modernism, meant that energies were channeled into the development of neo-Scholasticism which "furnished the cognitive foundation for American Catholic intellectual and cultural life—including higher education" (p. 16).[16] Jacques Maritain's move

---

[15]   On Jesuit trajectories in American higher education, see the highly critical overview by Burtchaell, *Dying*, pp. 563–634; and for a more complex, because more detailed, assessment, but one nevertheless not in contradiction to Burtchaell, see William P. Leahy SJ, *Adapting to America: Catholics, Jesuits, and Higher Education in the Twentieth Century*, Georgetown University Press, Washington, DC, 1991.

[16]   Gleason, *Modernity*, chs. 5 and 6 trace this flourishing history, and chs. 11 and 12 its decline.

to the United States and Etienne Gilson's chair in Toronto meant that two of the greatest Thomists of the Scholastic revival were "local." Further influences in this counter-modernist move included "developments in the religious sphere—the liturgical movement and the theology of the Mystical Body of Christ—meshed beautifully with the understanding of Catholicism as a culture," as well as the understanding of history championed by Christopher Dawson, who helped also establish the idea of a "Catholic culture."[17] There were of course tensions between the neoscholastic philosophical and theologically oriented syntheses and Dawson's more historical project, but a joint vision was still possible (even if only in very general terms). Hence, in 1935 the Committee on Educational Policy and Program of the National Catholic Educational Association was able to affirm the following:

> The Catholic college will not be content with presenting Catholicism as a creed, a code, or a cult. Catholicism must be seen as a culture; hence, the graduates of the Catholic college of liberal arts will go forth not merely trained in Catholic doctrine, but they will have seen the whole sweep of Catholicism, its part in the building up of our western civilization, past and present . . . They will have before them not merely the facts in the natural order but those in the supernatural order also, those facts which give meaning and coherence to the whole of life.[18]

However, what was being produced in Catholic higher education during these years was also severely questioned, not only in terms of the 1960s' liberal movements, but also from within by those who, while holding to the importance of a Catholic university, found that it failed to emulate the non-Catholic universities of America, or match up to the best medieval traditions. After all, so it was argued: if one hired on the basis of faith commitment, the field of top academics was substantially reduced; if one sought to provide a wide-based liberal arts program oriented toward the development of the whole person, specialisms and higher research often suffered as a consequence—and this was supported by empirical research between the 1920s and 1950s indicating low levels of achievement of excellence of both staff and students at Catholic institutions.[19] If a Catholic culture was confident that it had all the resources for the future, it inevitably generated a smug, insular, ghetto-like culture failing to interact with the best and most

---

[17] Gleason, *Modernity*, p. 148, and ch. 7 for these developments.

[18] Gleason, *Modernity*, p. 149; citing NCEAM 32, November 1935, pp. 70–1.

[19] See John Tracy Ellis, *American Catholics and the Intellectual Life*, Heritage Foundation, Chicago, 1956; and for further reference to empirical studies: Thomas F. O'Dea, *American Catholic Dilemma: An Inquiry into the Intellectual Life*, Mentor, New York, 1962.

challenging currents in non-Catholic culture. Just such charges were leveled in 1955 at Catholic universities by one of the most distinguished Catholic historians from the Catholic University of America, Professor John Tracy Ellis.[20] Ellis was not seeking to challenge the idea of a Catholic university, just its falling short of such an ideal. His arguments were widely, though of course not universally, accepted.

Twelve years later, in 1967, one of the most high-powered Catholic educational meetings presided over by Father Theodore Hesburg, who held the presidency of Notre Dame University for a record 35 years, produced the Land O'Lakes Statement.[21] It opened with a resounding claim that expressed the drive for institutional independence from the Church, which had already been increasingly established in universities by the growth of lay people and non-Catholics on boards of trustees, governors, and academic staff. However, it is striking in its clear clarion call: "To perform its teaching and research function effectively the Catholic university must have a true autonomy and academic freedom in the face of authority of whatever kind, lay or clerical, external to the academic community itself."[22] This was a vision of the Catholic university cut adrift from the Church, from society, and only accountable to "the academic community itself." If Ellis had wanted Catholic universities to better their secular counterparts, then as a charter, the Land O'Lakes Statement could not have been more apt. Of course, in the context of the heated debates and practices regarding academic freedom and tenure, touched on above, the open (and loyal) theological dissent by some Catholic theologians, and the climate of the 1960s, such a statement was welcomed by many for good reason. However, Gleason rightly says the Land O'Lakes Statement was "a declaration of independence from the hierarchy and a symbolic turning point" (p. 317) from opposition to modernity to cohabitation with it. Here, after all, were the presidents and leaders of the Catholic university community insisting that their organizational structures and powers of accountability be cut adrift from the ecclesia. It is in this context that the

---

[20] John Tracy Ellis, "American Catholics and the Intellectual Life," *Thought*, 30, 1955, pp. 351–88; and Powers, *Catholic Higher Education in America*, pp. 382–94 for an alternative (positive) assessment of Ellis's speech.

[21] The meeting represented seven Catholic universities in the United States, four from Canada and Latin America, and the document is to be found in the appendix in ed. Neil G. McCluskey SJ, *The Catholic University: A Modern Appraisal*, University of Notre Dame Press, Notre Dame, Indiana, 1970, pp. 336–41, with participants on p. 336, history and background to this meeting on pp. 3–8, and subsequent involvement of the Roman Curia in response on pp. 8–28, 342–65.

[22] In ed. McCluskey, *Catholic University*, p. 336. See also David Schindler's elegant critique of Hesburg's idea of a Catholic university in Schindler, *Heart of the World, Center of the Church*, T. & T. Clark, Edinburgh, 1996, pp. 143–76.

subsequent American debate as well as the 1990 Apostolic Constitution, *Ex Corde Ecclesiae* (trans. *On Catholic Universities*, subsequently *CU*), from Pope John Paul II, on the Catholic university is to be understood.

Gleason's study concludes with a lucid diagnosis. The diagnosis, penned in 1995, notes that while Catholic institutions are still there, and still managed by Catholics (by and large), they are unable clearly to articulate a curriculum and ideology that is distinctly Catholic:

> Most Catholic institutions have, to be sure, survived; indeed, they have, in most cases, improved their academic standing, or at least kept pace with improvements elsewhere. Only an insignificant handful have outrightly abandoned their Catholic character. The identity problem that persists is . . . not institutional or organizational, but ideological. That is, it consists in a lack of consensus as to the substantive content of the ensemble of religious beliefs, moral commitments, and academic assumptions that supposedly constitute Catholic identity, and a consequent inability to specify what that identity entails for the practical functioning of Catholic colleges and universities. More briefly put, the crisis is not that Catholic educators do not want their institutions to remain Catholic, but that they are no longer sure what remaining Catholic means.[23]

In one sense, Gleason's conclusions as cited, though not his text as a whole, minimize the crisis of authority in the organizational running of Catholic institutions. The papal constitution on Catholic universities, *CU*, for instance, implicitly connects the lack of Catholic vision or ideology in Catholic universities with the question of how the institutional management is formed. Crudely put, it expresses a view that unless there is centralized management (the Holy See in Rome, mediated via the local bishops, although always answerable to Rome) overseeing curriculum and ideology, and administration in terms of governing charters, Catholic universities will often fail to live up to their potential. *CU* is important as it puts the correct issues back on the agenda. A Catholic university is not just a matter of liturgical celebrations on feast days, social work oriented to the poor, or a large number of faculty as Catholics. While these are all important, the vital intellectual relation of the disciplines unified under a theological

---

[23] Gleason cites, at this point (p. 320), a 1975 doctoral thesis that studied 25 Catholic institutions, reporting that their presidents confessed "inability to articulate properly their religious objectives today, even though they want the college to have a strong religious orientation." See Edward F. Maloney SJ, "A Study of the Religious Orientation of the Catholic Colleges and Universities in New York State from 1962 to 1972," PhD thesis, New York University, 1973, abstract page.

vision is central to the nature of a Catholic university (see below). That is, in Gleason's terms, it is the ideological component that makes the Catholic university salt to the intellectual world, or in MacIntyre's terms, a light in the darkness. However, it is a moot question whether subsidiarity is properly attained in supposing that Roman management is vital to the regeneration of Catholic universities.

To pursue Gleason's findings further I want briefly to look at my second important study: James Tunstead Burtchaell, *The Dying of the Light: The Disengagement of Colleges and Universities from their Christian Churches* (1998), with subsequent page references referring to this book. Here we will see Gleason's thesis verified and given further concrete specification in terms of three Catholic institutions sponsored by three of the more experienced Catholic teaching congregations that are trailed in detail: the Jesuit-run Boston College, the Ursuline-run College of New Rochelle, and the Brothers of the Christian Schools-run Saint Mary's College of California. I will not summarize any of Burtchaell's detailed stories. Burtchaell's findings are remarkable in two ways. First, they fully corroborate Gleason's major study, a point acknowledged by Burtchaell (p. ix). Like Gleason, Burtchaell isolates a number of factors that led to the "dying of the light": a decline of religious orders in the 1960s, so that personnel were not available to staff universities; an increasingly secular society, leading to the decline of Catholic students and their loyalties to Catholic institutions; financial crises in these institutions requiring them both to change the curriculum to recruit students and also to change their forms of governance quickly to ensure massive state aid when the question of their religious nature was questioned as being in conflict with the First Amendment (an issue only resolved in the mid-1970s, after most institutions had already changed); the low level of excellence achieved, leading to emulation of secular (latterly Protestant) rivals; a movement in the curriculum away from rigorous confessional theology to academic historically oriented study of Christianity, followed by the growth of religious studies (known by various names); the decline of worship and Catholic praxis being central to all staff and students; the decline in religious having key positions as presidents;[24] and finally, the acceptance of modernity within lay and ecclesial circles. Here Burtchaell works with a different and overlapping notion of modernity. It has at least two strands running through it.

---

[24]   This is a curious indicator, as Burtchaell is extremely sensitive to the way in which some "religious" orders and individuals were central to promoting secularism (*Dying*, pp. 563–634, 826–7). It was the policy of the president, not their belonging to a religious order, that was central. Land O'Lakes was drafted mainly by "religious," not lay people.

Philosophically, Burtchaell analyzes modernity in terms of the growth of piety initially in Protestant Christianity. Priorities here were "the primacy of the spirit over letter, commitment over institution, affect over intellect, laity over clergy, invisible over visible, and they [Pietists] looked to the earliest Christian communities for their models" (p. 839). He sees in this move the growth of individualism as the tripos of history, tradition, and community became less and less valued, leading eventually into either liberal pietism, where ecclesial form is very secondary, or another version of this, rationalism, where ecclesial forms are seen to be the cause of violence, conflict, and strife. Faith is put in the nation state and its laws as the arbiter of such petty disputes. Rationalism produced Deism, "the religious equivalent of safe sex" (p. 842) and the resultant impact on institutions was "indifferentism and rationalism" (p. 843), whatever the rhetoric in some catalogs and brochures advertising such institutions. In other catalogs a concerted attempt was made to erase all reference to religious foundations. Burtchaell is not laying blame on the university *per se*, for "it must be repeated, this self-destructive pathology arose first within the churches, not within the colleges" (p. 847). Soon however, the pathological condition would be rife within both university and Church. Burtchaell bitterly outlines such a case:

> Jesuit father William Byron, who presided over both Scranton and Catholic Universities, has also argued on behalf of diversity: "It would not be a good thing to have an all-Catholic board, an all-Catholic administration, faculty, staff and student body." No one cautions against a board composed entirely of Americans, or a faculty composed only of publishing scholars, or a student body in which every member could write effectively. A shared faith seems to be the only hazardous affinity (p. 831).[25]

Rationalistic modernity would eventually affect Catholics as much as Protestants, although here Gleason's analysis is more subtle in differentiating the impact of modernity upon American Catholics and American Protestants. The other sense of modernity that Burtchaell employs concerns the manner of institutional formation and management, a key theme in Alasdair MacIntyre's analysis of modernity.[26] Two particular factors account for the

---

[25] Burtchaell is citing William J. Byron SJ, *Quadrangle Considerations*, Loyola University Press, Chicago, 1989, p. 22.

[26] See A. MacIntyre, *Three Rival Versions of Moral Enquiry*, Duckworth, London, 1990; although Burtchaell does not refer to this work. He cites MacIntyre's argument (pp. 335–6) against liberal models of education in "Values and Distinctive Characteristics of Teaching and Learning in Church-Related Colleges" in *Institutional Integrity and Values: Perspectives on United Methodist Higher Education*, Division of Higher Education/Board of Higher Education and Ministry, Nashville, Tennessee, 1989, pp. 12–35.

growing darkness in Burtchaell's account, forces not so highlighted by Gleason, although certainly not ignored: the importance of a single president in running large institutions; and the increase in specialisms and professionalism, leading to the fragmentation of learning, and the emergence of career academics. The former allowed that changes could be made rapidly, while the latter meant that faculty members were generally less and less interested in anything other than their career prospects and resources to support their research. In brief, the universities had become their own worst enemy.

The second remarkable finding in Burtchaell's study is, as we have already begun to see, that what happened to the Catholics in the 1960s had been happening to the Protestants since the 1890s (p. x). Burtchaell's study examines Congregationalist, Presbyterian, Methodist, Baptist, Lutheran, and Evangelical denominations and his analysis leads him to the conclusions outlined above. Admittedly, he omits the Mennonites, Mormons, Quakers, Disciples of Christ, Episcopalians, and Seventh Day Adventists as they have founded only a small number of institutions. Therefore, any vast generalizations resulting from his study must be carefully limited. Nevertheless, his conclusions about Protestant universities in America are echoed in two further major studies on the issue: George Marsden's *The Soul of the American University: From Protestant Establishment to Established Nonbelief* (1994) and Douglas Sloan's *Faith and Knowledge: Mainline Protestantism and American Higher Education* (1994).[27] Marsden's argument is interesting in that it too accords secularism a leading role in transforming major universities. Christian theology was not part of the general curriculum and, indeed, would eventually be removed from the faculty altogether. This caused some Church institutions that were sponsors of the universities to found alternative theological establishments in their dismay at such changes. Princeton and Andover at Harvard are two examples and Marsden examines Johns Hopkins, Chicago, Yale, Columbia, Michigan, and others.

Sloan's study grounds the analysis more clearly in terms of the theological roots of modernity already mentioned above that are analyzed by Burtchaell, and will be strongly focussed in Schubert's study (see below). Sloan sees the process of secularization as central and charts it as beginning in the nineteenth century, rather than at the Reformation where some put the blame for the prising apart of intellect and faith. He attributes to secularism the undermining of the rationale for a Christian university. Sloan

---

[27] Oxford University Press, New York, 1994; and Westminster John Knox, Louisville, Kentucky, 1994, respectively. Marsden has edited a companion volume with Bradley J. Longfield which is also helpful: *The Secularizing of the Academy*, Oxford University Press, New York, 1992.

examines various theological attempts to reunite the two orders of secular and sacred, natural, and supernatural, but argues that most Protestant divines in the twentieth century viewed "knowledge" in terms of the findings of the faculties of the natural and social sciences and the humanities. Theology, based on faith, was of a different, but less secure, order of knowledge. Thus, theology was secularized in the very process through which it was being allegedly rejuvenated. In my attempt to focus on just one element (Catholic universities) in this wide canvas of America, I will not pursue the analysis regarding Protestant universities, except to note that the major studies in this field point to the same outcome: the disengagement of these institutions from their ecclesial roots, the secularizing of the curriculum, and the demise of any uniting role that theology and philosophy might play.

Burtchaell's view of the recovery of the light lies quite simply in relocating the university in the heart of the Church (*ex corde ecclesiae*):

> the gospel within the church has continually been at the centre of intense and critical dialectic: textual, hermeneutical, historical, intercultural, philosophical, theological. Further, the church has steadfastly recognized the revelatory powers of inspiration, witness, repentance, and communal conflict within and without, as a stimulant to continuous redefinition and purification. These are the intellectual resources about which the contemporary academy, for the most part, has only crude and tendentious intimations.[28]

Burtchaell overstates his case regarding "redefinition and purification" and his own brief sections on heavy-handed and anti-intellectual Curial interventions regarding Catholic institutions should have tempered his claims. But a more serious objection to his and my basic argument is to be found in David J. O'Brien and Alice Gallin. O'Brien contests Burtchaell's and Gleason's reading that Catholic institutions followed the same road as those of Protestants, in Avery Dulles' words, from "denominational to generic Christianity, then to vaguely defined religious values and finally to total secularisation."[29] He cites Gallin's study to show that there were significant differences between the Catholic and Protestant stages of change and also differing social forces at play within and external to the ecclesial communities in question.[30] Furthermore, Gallin argues that secularism can act as a

---

[28] Burtchaell, *Dying*, pp. 850–1.

[29] Avery Dulles, *The New York Times*, May 1, 1991, cited in David J. O'Brien, *From the Heart of the American Church: Catholic Higher Education and American Culture*, Orbis, New York, 1994, p. 97.

[30] Alice Gallin, "American Church-Related Higher Education: Comparison and Contrast," paper delivered at Convention of American Historical Association, December 29, 1992; discussed by O'Brien, *Heart*, pp. 103ff.

scapegoat for the lack of coherence in disciplines like theology and philosophy and can mask the lack of confidence on the part of administrators and faculty in clearly presenting their own faith and values. While Gallin's qualifications are appropriate, her study, and indeed Henry C. Johnson's work also cited by O'Brien in contesting the appropriateness of "secularization" as the last step in the process, do not really call into question the secularization that took place.[31] Rather, it indicates that this "secularization" was identical with what certain Christians regarded as "Christian," a faith commitment that makes no intellectual difference to intellectual enquiry, and a faith that is primarily hermeneutically answerable to wider society, rather than normatively to its own traditions—and then only, secondarily, to society. Indeed, Gallin concedes this point some eight years later when she writes of the period 1965–80: "The university presidents regarded the changes they had made and were making as adaptation to American academic culture, not an acceptance of godless "secular" values. This distinction was a hard one to maintain."[32] Hence, while there may be grounds for a more nuanced understanding of "secularism," I would contend that this term is both helpful and accurate. Importantly, both Gallin and O'Brien are agreed on the need for curriculum changes to make Catholic universities more clearly Catholic, and in this at least, both "liberals" and "conservatives" have something in common.

Before concluding this overly brief section on the United States, I want to turn to my third study that closely examines the relationship of theology to religious studies, to see if Burtchaell's argument on this one aspect bears closer scrutiny. Clearly, if it does, then my own argument gains strength. Frank D. Schubert's sociological study of the curriculum in the religion faculty of three Catholic universities during the period 1955–85 strongly supports Burtchaell's and Gleason's findings and my argument about the relationship between theology and religious studies. (All subsequent page references in the main body of the text are to Schubert.) Schubert chooses

---

[31] See Henry C. Johnson, "Down from the Mountain: Secularization and the Higher Learning in America," *Review of Politics*, 54, 1992, pp. 551–8; discussed by O'Brien, *Heart*, pp. 104–7.
[32] Gallin, *Negotiating Identity*, p. 161. This is not to say that "Americanism" or American culture, to use O'Brien's term, is thoroughly secular, but to note that in this instance of Higher Education identity, this tends to be the case. See my chapter three regarding further objections by O'Brien and Gallin. Some go even further. William Shea, "Catholic Higher Education and the Enlightenment: On Borderlands and Roots," *Horizons*, 20, 1993, pp. 99–105, argues that Catholic identity is determinate upon discovering the identity of the "Other." While his concern for the "Other" is germane to my concerns, he makes the "Other" falsely "determinate," thereby replicating the problem with secularism, but replacing secularism with other religions.

the Catholic University of America (Washington, DC), St. John's University (New York) and Boston College (Chestnut Hill, MA) for his study on the basis of their location in major metropolitan centers, and because of their cross-section of religious foundations: the collective effort on the part of the American Bishops with no religious order in charge, the Vincentians, and the Jesuits respectively.[33] He looks at their curricula in terms of two categories: theology and religious studies. He defines theology as the investigation of the sacred order of the sponsor, that is, as an intra-Catholic exposition, development, and critical reflection on the Catholic "sacred order," whereby the world is seen through this lens (pp. 10–13). He defines "religious studies" as the outsider examination of any particular sacred order (pp. 5–10). He suggests an analytical framework to help isolate the possible secularization of the curriculum and tabulates it in a helpful manner on page 14.

The distinctive orders of "theology" and "religious studies"

Theological	Religious	Secular
Sacred history	Historical foundations of religions	History
Sacred morality	Moral systems of religions	Morality
Sacred scripture	Literature study of religions	Literature
Sacred polity	Polity of religions	Politics
Sacred apologetics	The study of world religions	Culture

It is worth quoting Schubert's use of this table, for upon these assumptions his entire argument rests:

> The items within these columns can be understood as polar points between which a particular curricular item might fall. Characterizing the items under theological, then, one notes a certain givenness to the order which is under investigation, while the items under religious retain a sense of inclusiveness among major world perspectives. If such an understanding is allowable, it is clear that any movement in the above categories from theological to religious

---

[33] It is worth reading Schubert in parallel with Burtchaell, *Dying*, pp. 563–92 who looks at Boston College in some detail, showing *administrative* changes that paralleled the *curriculum* changes, whereby the Jesuits relinquished executive control so that Boston would not be disqualified from State funding, as well as a theology of lay and pluralist (non-Catholic) involvement in the formation of the Church.

and beyond is also a movement toward greater secularization in this sense: *The categories under religious can equally appear in a traditionally secular curricula [sic] (such as history, literature or social studies), while the reverse (towards theological) is not the case.* (pp. 14–15)

It is important to note that Schubert develops his secularizing theory based on sociological work ranging from Weber, Durkheim, Parsons, Bellah, Berger, and Luckmann, and in this sense his is not, like mine, a theological argument, but a sociological observation.[34] Schubert is also out to test how resistant Catholicism is, as is suggested by some of his sociological sources, to modernity and secularization. While there is obviously room for questioning elements of Schubert's reading of curriculum catalogs,[35] a point of which he is well aware, his findings are well documented from the primary source materials and he tracks three periods regarding his data. First, through 1955–65 (although this period is during the Second Vatican Council, the effects of the Council are not felt until after the mid-1960s) Schubert finds the sacred order of theology "promulgated." Then in 1965–75 this order is "questioned," and finally, during the period 1975–85, this order is "dissolved."[36] His summary of the third period isolates the main factors leading to his analytical conclusion:

> Perhaps the most distinctive change in these courses as opposed to the earlier courses, then, remains that of the proliferation of courses beyond the traditional range of Roman Catholicism, and even the slightly wider range of Christianity as a whole. In the introduction of courses concerning world religions from every type of source and background and means of investigation, it is clear that the most documentable change within the curricula of the entire period of our study is the move from theology (the study of religion from *within* a particular sacred order) to religion (the study of *all* sacred orders). (p. 128)

The key factor to isolate in Schubert's study is not the introduction of world religions into the curriculum *per se*, but rather the way in which these religions were studied: from the viewpoint of religious studies, rather than a theological or sacred viewpoint; that is, "*the authoritative sway of secular disciplines has within this period eclipsed the authority of the traditional Roman*

---

[34] Schubert's work was a doctoral dissertation supervised by Peter Berger.

[35] For instance, one might have a very "sacred view" analysis of secularization in the classroom (due to the teacher's approach), although the curriculum data might simply indicate a study of secularization. Burtchaell makes this point in *Dying*, p. 729, note 151.

[36] The citations are the thematic summaries of the three chapters that deal with each period: chs. 4–6.

Catholic sacred order itself" (p. 131). While Schubert draws six conclusions from his study, I am particularly interested in his fifth and sixth as they illuminate aspects of my own argument:

> 5. The order of Roman Catholicism in the present day has taken its place within the curricula [*sic*] chosen for investigation only as one possible order among the many *orders* of religion.

> 6. In order to incorporate the study of world religions into a curriculum previously reserved for one sacred order, it is necessary to rely upon a common language. Such common languages, unavoidably, are those of secular disciplines. (p. 132)

Schubert argues that this process began in the middle period of his investigation, in Catholic attempts to include Protestantism in the curriculum. This form of ecumenism required the search for common points of agreement so that respectful engagement and co-operation might result. For instance, the hiring of scholars from outside the Catholic Church increased during this period. Consequently scholars could rely less on the particularities and authority of their specific sacred order if they were in conflict, and the eventual inclusion of world religions meant that the only common order that all could refer to were secular disciplines. It is important not to force this pattern into too neat a schematization, nor is Schubert blind to the limitations of his study: it "is regional, not exhaustive; second, it is limited to catalogued data and not to classroom access, and third, it is limited to religious curricula and does not evaluate the curricula of other fields" (p. 130). We might draw two conclusions from Schubert's work.

First, while it is clear that there are grounds for the study of religions to take place in the university, there are also good grounds to suggest that a *theological* study of religions is much more necessary than a positivist "religious studies." Three further points sustain this first. The approach of religious studies has an inbuilt *telos* toward secularization and in that sense, one might argue, there is no justice done to any of the sacred canopies, except the new one of secularism. Schubert's mentor, Peter Berger, suggests that "secularization fosters the civic arrangements under which pluralism thrives, while the plurality of world-views undermines the plausibility of each one and thus contributes to the secularizing tendency."[37] Further, within a particular sacred viewpoint, it is entirely legitimate to examine

---

[37] Peter L. Berger, "From the Crisis of Religion to the Crisis of Secularity" in eds. Mary Douglas and Steven Tipton, *Religion and America: Spiritual Life in a Secular Age*, Beacon Press, Boston, 1983, pp. 8–24: p. 15.

"the world" from that viewpoint according to the methods and presuppositions of that viewpoint. This is the burden of my argument throughout this book. Third, if there is to be any public funding and interest in such scholarship, then there may be a requirement that these viewpoints articulate their world-view in critical engagement with pluralism (other world-views). How this will be done is clearly unpredictable and a point to which I will later return. The second conclusion that might be tentatively drawn from Schubert's study is that despite the institutions' clear commitment to upholding a sacred order in the very place in which one might expect to see it most clearly, in their departments of theology, it is barely discernible. Hence, regardless of the institutional control of Catholic universities, the curriculum bears the power of transmitting a pedagogy, ontology, and epistemology that may be at variance with the intended aims of the institution.

I do not want to end this section as if the overall picture is relentlessly unitary regarding all Christian universities in the United States. I have already commented on the fact that there are many individuals who lament this situation and are engaged in counter-cultural practices within the liberal university. Many of the authors I have drawn on in this section are examples. Furthermore, recent studies show that although the light might be nearly extinguished in institutional terms, there are places where it is burning bright.[38] This should not be forgotten as we turn to look briefly at the situation in England.

II A Brief Review of England and the Secularization of the Christian University

In this section I shall first look at the way in which the two ancient English universities, Oxford and Cambridge, became exclusivist Anglican universities for the most part of their history, despite their Roman Catholic foundations. However, currently they must be reckoned as secular universities (with

---

[38] For a slightly more optimistic reading of the current situation in the USA, see especially Robert Benne, *Quality with Soul: How Six Premier Colleges and Universities Keep Faith with Their Religious Traditions*, W. B. Eerdmans, Grand Rapids, Michigan, 2001, and ed. Joseph M. O'Keefe, *Catholic Education at the Turn of the New Century*, Garland, New York, 1997. See also the reports of important changes: O'Brien, *From the Heart*, pp. 74–6, 79–92, 180–2; Gallin, *Negotiating*, pp. 158–9, 181–3; Peter Steinfels, *A People Adrift*, Simon & Schuster, New York, 2003, pp. 142–4. For England, see Sinclair Goodlad, "Christian Universities and Colleges: A Conceptual Inquiry," being The St. Matthias Lecture: September 12, 2002, unpublished ms. Clearly, there are institutions, especially non-research intensive, that keep the light burning, including the recently created Christian Academic Network in the UK.

interesting exceptions—see below). Second, I shall look at the contemporary situation of Christian universities in England. Admittedly, in the mainstream traditional research universities, there are no Christian universities as in the United States. We have to look at the new universities created in the 1990s to find two "Christian universities," although this is not how they advertise themselves. There are a small number of "University Colleges" or "Higher Education" colleges which I will not examine as, technically, they are not universities.[39] In these two Christian universities I shall be focussing on my three questions regarding: the institutional vision; the manner of integration of curriculum within a Christian vision; and the teaching of theology and religious studies. Third, given the paucity of Christian universities in England, I shall briefly look at the curriculum in English universities in general regarding their teaching of "theology" and "religious studies." Historically, we will see some very close parallels to the US situation, where theology as a subject is now widely taught *with* religious studies, with very little attempt made to articulate the difference between the two except in terms of subject matter: the former being the study of Christianity, the latter being the study of Judaism, Islam, Buddhism, Hinduism, and other religions. The manner in which these religions are studied is, I shall be arguing, indistinguishable. Finally, I shall end this section on English universities with a brief comment on two recent inaugural lectures given by Professors in the Divinity Faculties at Oxford and Cambridge, charting their own visions for the future of the discipline.

The situation in England has important similarities to that in the United States, although there are significant differences regarding Church–State relations, and consequently, state funding. The prising apart of State and Church in the US through the First Amendment of the Constitution is not mirrored in England where the Queen is currently both head of state and head of the Anglican Church.[40] However, the effect of the Reformation and the Protestant monopoly over the universities in England and some of

[39] These two categories reflect institutions that did not gain university status, although not all tried. My exclusion is technical and not a comment on the level of teaching and research that exists within such institutions. I do not include Heythrop College, University of London, as it only teaches theology (as I understand the word) rather than other disciplines, or the Catholic colleges at Oxbridge since they are not, properly speaking, university departments or faculties as such, even though they might act as microcosms of Catholic universities in their interdisciplinary membership.

[40] However, the two decision-making legislatures, the House of Commons and the House of Lords, while formally loyal to the Queen, have become secularized and pluralist (with the sole exception in the Lords of including Anglican bishops), reflecting English society at large. The current Archbishop of Canterbury, Rowan Williams, has publicly favored dis-establishment and so have some other senior Anglican figures.

Europe until around the last part of the nineteenth century had its impact in the United States. For example, the earliest university in the States, Harvard, was founded by pioneers from the Congregationalist elements of Emmanuel College, Cambridge. Emmanuel was itself originally built on the site of a former Dominican house, but soon became a favorite for Puritans. The fact that many of America's pioneering intellectuals were educated at Berlin also meant that the model of the Enlightenment university had deep roots in American soil.[41] The Catholic influence in the United States came mainly through immigrants from Ireland and continental Europe.

However, in England the oldest universities are Oxford and Cambridge. Both relied heavily on Roman Catholic orders for the setting up of their colleges in the thirteenth to fifteenth centuries.[42] Cambridge was proclaimed a *studium generale* in 1318 by Pope John XXII. To all intents and purposes, they were Catholic universities, even though Cambridge alone was given formal papal approval. It was under the Elizabethan statutes of 1570 and the Laudian statutes of 1636 that both universities eventually required subscription to the Acts of Supremacy and Uniformity.[43] This meant that not only Catholics but also Non-Conformists were excluded. Oxbridge did not then teach theology. They only did when the complaint was made that the curriculum had lost its Christian character and the University was doing nothing to preserve it.[44] The Reformation in England was a state affair, as was the persecution of Catholics. Most of the major cultural institutions were seized by the crown and only varying traces of Catholicism were left, even though it was powerful at the grass roots level.[45] Even when the exclusionary statutes were finally revoked three

[41] In *Between Athens and Berlin*, David Kelsey offers a very careful reading of the debate that started in the 1980s in the United States regarding theological education, showing how it might be located in Athens or Berlin. He is clear that the dominant model was Berlin, only because it was the model which the earliest American research institutions imitated, with virtually all of Johns Hopkins faculty in 1884 coming from German universities. Since theological education needed to imitate "respectable education," Berlin permeated the theological schools as well (see pp. 18–19).

[42] The Colleges are listed in the *New Catholic Encyclopaedia*, 1st edn. (eds. Staff of Catholic University of America), Palatine, Illinois, and McGraw-Hill, 1981, under "Oxford" and "Cambridge."

[43] For histories of Oxbridge, see S. Rothblatt, *The Revolution of the Dons: Cambridge and Society in Victorian England*, Faber, London, 1968; V. H. Green, *Religion at Oxford and Cambridge*, SCM, London, 1964; and Arthur Jason Engel, *From Clergyman to Don: The Rise of the Academic Profession in Nineteenth Century Oxford*, Clarendon Press, Oxford, 1983.

[44] See David Bebbington, "The Secularization of British Universities Since the Mid-Nineteenth Century" in eds. G. Marsden and B. J. Longfield, *The Secularisation of the Academy*, Oxford University Press, New York, 1992, pp. 259–77: p. 266.

[45] See Eamon Duffy, *The Stripping of the Altars: Traditional Religion in England 1400–1580*, Yale University Press, New Haven, Connecticut, 1992.

hundred years later (in 1858 for the BA, with the MA following in 1871),
owing to pressures of a Royal Commission and Parliamentary support, the
Divinity Faculty in Oxford remained immune from the changes instituted
by Parliament. In Oxford, all masters and students of the Divinity Faculty
had to be Anglicans right into the twentieth century. The struggle to establish a Grace in 1898 for St. Edmund's House in Cambridge, my own
college, to be a recognized college of the University was defeated at Senate,
exemplifying stark levels of anti-Catholicism. For example, Revd. J. Ellis
MacTaggard wrote to the editor of the *Cambridge Anti-Popery Gazette* that
the fight for "the Pure Gospel for which Cranmer and Ridley offered their
saintly lives" was on:

> That the Roman Church should venture in this age of enlightenment to
> attempt this assault on the liberties of the University is to some a matter of
> surprise; but those who look at the past history of this Great Apostasy will, I
> think, feel that the conduct of Cardinal Vaughan and his satellites is consonant
> with all the traditions of Rome. What is really surprising is that, within the
> precincts of the University, there should be found Members of the Senate
> who are willing to prostrate themselves before the pretensions of an Italian
> bishop.[46]

However, it is fair to say that after the 1850s there was a real attempt at separation between Church and State in the ancient universities, and this
obviously affected the subsequent foundations of the second wave of universities in England.[47] This also meant that theology in the new universities
(1850s onward), when it was taught, was no longer designed for ordinands
and increasingly became non-denominational (although mainly taught by
Anglicans). In line with this, methodologically it inevitably became secularized, depending on disciplinary procedures that were "acceptable" to secular
colleagues in the Arts faculties. Historical critical studies of the Bible and
early Church history flourished, as did languages, but systematic theology
did not. In Oxbridge, at the turn of the millennium the situation was such
that only four Chairs in Oxford are still reserved for Anglicans (but two of
these are now open to members of churches that have ecumenical relations
to the Church of England), and Cambridge has repealed all such canonical

---

[46] *Cambridge Anti-Popery Gazette*, May 1898. For a good discussion of the St. Edmund's House
struggle, see Vincent Alan McClelland, *English Roman Catholics and Higher Education: 1830–
1903*, Clarendon Press, Oxford, 1973, pp. 409–26. It was only in 1964 that it was formally
approved as a Graduate Society.
[47] See Bebbington, "The Secularization of British Universities." He argues that the two
major periods of change were 1850–1920, where rival Christians resolved their antagonisms
through a secularization process, and 1920–90 where wider society became secularized.

requirements for its Divinity Chairs.[48] The Regius Chair of Divinity in Cambridge was the last to be uncoupled from its ecclesial moorings in 1997. The current holder of the Regius Chair, David F. Ford, at the time of writing (2003) is the first non-clergyman to hold the Chair in its 452 years. Nicholas Lash, the retired Norris-Hulse Professor, was the first Roman Catholic to hold that Chair in the Theology Faculty at Cambridge and has been followed by another lay English Roman Catholic, Denys Turner. Hence, we might say that while the Anglican monopoly has ended at Oxbridge, with tiny vestiges lingering in tied Chairs at Oxford's Divinity Faculty, the two universities have not instead become ecumenically Christian but, rather *in institutional terms*, secular, so that the religious profession of a teacher is deemed insignificant. That is, the religious beliefs of those who teach theology are institutionally irrelevant. In this respect, other than in the college chapels, we find that all Christian intellectual activity has no proper place *institutionally* within Oxford and Cambridge, except perhaps in the Divinity Faculties (by circumstances rather than design), but that too is questioned—even by those listed within those Faculties.[49]

The first university to open its doors to Catholics and other non-Anglicans was King's College, London in 1827. A little later, Durham was founded by an Act of Parliament in 1832, and, like London was designed for students of limited means. However, it was endowed with the revenues of Durham cathedral and diocese, which explains why still today a Chair in the Divinity School is reserved exclusively for an ordained Anglican. The spate of universities that followed, however, were distinctively non-religious and non-denominational: Manchester (Owens College) in 1851, Leeds (Yorkshire College of Science) in 1874, and University College of Bristol in 1876. The Redbrick universities of the twentieth century were utterly secular without exception, even to the extent that some forbade the teaching of religion. This was not only due to secularism, but to Christians who had previously experienced exclusion. For example, John Owens, a Non-Conformist, founded Owens College, banning any theological subject

---

[48] Durham is the only other research university with an Anglican Chair.

[49] Professor Richard Gombrich is listed in the "Association of University Departments of Theology and Religious Studies Handbook 2001" Leeds, AUDTRS, 2001, under Oxford University, although in the Oriental Institute at Oxford. In a public lecture on the question of universities pursuing truth, Gombrich asks whether they alone do this, and turns to religions: "religious bodies may claim to, but they are only interested in a few issues and perfectly indifferent to most of the questions asked in academia; moreover, they are not prepared to question absolutely anything or to follow the truth wherever it leads them." Ms. of lecture delivered on January 7, 2000 in Tokyo at the Graduate Institute of Policy Studies, p. 14, privately circulated by Gombrich. See also Gombrich's liberal "tolerance" in "Reflections of an indologist" in ed. Hamnett, *Religious Pluralism*, pp. 243–61.

"which shall be reasonably offensive to the conscience of any student." Thus Colleges like Firth (1879; later University of Sheffield) and University College, Liverpool (1881) prohibited religious tests.

It should be said that with the expulsion of Catholics from mainstream university education at Oxford and Cambridge, Catholic higher education in England (and Ireland) took on complex twists and turns, with constantly failing attempts to set up Catholic equivalents to Oxbridge, the most famous perhaps, being Newman's Catholic University for Ireland. This, and the collegiate link with London and the attempt to re-enter Oxford, are all carefully charted in Vincent Alan McClelland's *English Roman Catholics and Higher Education, 1830–1903*. McClelland argues that there were three main phases during this period:

> a period of withdrawal, isolation, and dogged self-help, characterized by efforts to provide enlightened collegiate education and by a realization of the need for professional qualifications recognized by the State; a period of compromise and modification, typified by attempts to erect denominational university institutions for English Catholics in Ireland, Oxford, and London; and thirdly, a period of gradual assimilation, combined with efforts to retain a recognizable community identity. The process of gradual absorption has not yet been fully completed.[50]

In many respects our investigation of Christian universities, their curricula, and their valuing of theology is nearly at an end, and that appropriately reflects the situation in England. However, there are two new universities that are in limited senses "Christian universities." They deserve brief attention as does the only research that I am aware of that is being undertaken in this area, that by Sinclair Goodlad.[51] In this section all three of our research

---

[50] Vincent A. McClelland, *English Roman Catholics, and Higher Education, 1830–1903*, Clarendon Press, Oxford, 1973, p. i. At the time of writing, the process is complete, with the exception of Heythrop College, University of London, and Maryvale Institute, Birmingham. See the judicious review of "Catholic Theology in Britain: the Scene since Vatican II," *New Blackfriars*, 80, 1999, pp. 451–71, by Aidan Nichols. Nichols does not extend his argument to the university itself.

[51] See Goodlad, "Christian Universities and Colleges," p. 9. See also his "The Bear's Hug: Hazards and Opportunities for Church Universities and Colleges in accommodating to secular society," *Prologue*, 3, 2002, pp. 46–60. Goodlad's work also calls into question whether the exclusion of church colleges (they are not technically universities) from my study skews my findings. Presently (2004) the Council of Church Colleges encompasses 16 institutions, two of which have university status. This Council has produced a number of publications showing their collective vital interest in pursuing their Christian identity, often against difficult market forces. On the extent of such market forces in the USA, see Mark Schwehn, *Exile from Eden: Religion and the Academic Vocation in America*, Oxford University Press, New York, 1993, ch. 1.

questions can be partly addressed: have Christian universities been secular-ized? What is the vision of the broad curriculum in Christian terms, the connection between the disciplines, and their relation to theology in such institutions? And, finally, what is the role of theology departments in such institutions?

The two new universities in question are the Universities of Gloucester-shire and Surrey, Roehampton. Gloucestershire has its roots in the evangeli-cal freethinker Francis Close who founded a teacher training college in 1847 with a Church Foundation Trust, which according to the University "influences the governance of the University today and provides a frame-work for its mission."[52] One-third of the governing Council of 200 derives from the Trust and these members sign a document stating their active sym-pathy with the Trust Deed of 1847 which states that "the Religious Educa-tion to be conveyed in the Colleges shall always be strictly SCRIPTURAL, EVANGELICAL AND PROTESTANT and in strict accordance with the ARTICLES and LITURGY of the CHURCH OF ENGLAND AS NOW ESTABLISHED BY LAW." The evidence of this in institu-tional publicity documents is the Mission Statement that reads, quite uniquely for English universities (apart from Roehampton):

> Our aim is to provide for our stakeholders accessible high quality learning environments that are innovative, challenging and enterprising.
>   We achieve this by working in partnership with individuals, organizations and communities to develop their full potential within a culture which is:
>
> Excellent but not inaccessible
> Christian but not exclusive
> Supportive but not constraining
> Proactive locally but not parochial.[53]

While such a high level visibility is significant, it is also significant that there is no ecclesial sense of this non-exclusive "Christian" identity in any of its documents. Clearly, there was an important transition from a staunchly evangelical Protestant scriptural outlook to that of non-exclusive Christian-ity. This non-exclusive Christian identity is absent from any of the program publicity for any of the courses offered by the institution, including the

---

[52] All quotations from the University webpages, accessed December 2003: A New Univer-sity with a history. Basic web page reference: gloucester.ac.uk. I have relied exclusively on the image presented of themselves by these two institutions, via their web pages and their under-graduate and postgraduate prospectuses. This type of information is of course tendentious and limited, but important for discerning the image that the institution wishes to project to the public.

[53] Webpage: Mission Statement.

fare available in the School of Theology and Religious Studies. When, in 2003, the previous Archbishop of Canterbury, Lord Carey of Clifton, was appointed Vice-Chancellor, the University and its new Chancellor made clear that it was ecumenical, a phrase which included an inter-religious dimension.[54] Regarding the latter, the School of Theology and Religious Studies offers an undergraduate pathway in "Theology" which is described entirely in terms of a study of Christianity and its doctrines, not in any "theological" sense in the way I have been using the word, and certainly making no reference to the university mission statement. It also offers a pathway in "Religious Studies" that includes some of the same units making up the Theology program, plus others on philosophy and the religions of India. In one sense the inclusion of so many units from the Theology program in the Religious Studies program highlights my point about there being no real difference between the two fields methodologically, and here the distinction in content has begun to dissolve. Significantly, in 2003, a move was made to change the nature of the department of Theology and Religious Studies, turning toward long-distance learning and developing a new program in "Religion, Philosophy and Ethics." The outcome is unresolved at the time of writing. If we utilize Burtchaell or Gleason's criteria, Gloucestershire might count as a "dying light," a thinly Christian, but really secularized university in all three respects that I am investigating, despite its mission statement. However, and none of this should be minimized, it should also be noted that in England, it does represent an institution that is at least keeping the light burning in terms of its governing body, its directorate, and disparate theological projects with which it is involved. For example, it is collaborating with three Church Institutions in two projects related to education/church schools and Christian theology under the title "strengthening the mission." Given the financial pressures on the new universities, Gloucester should also be congratulated.

What of Roehampton? At the time of writing (2003), the University of Surrey, Roehampton is at least headed by a religious: the Rector of the University is Sister Dr. Bernadette Porter. This is actually unique in contrast to all the other Christian institutions in the University, University College, and Higher Education sector.[55] Roehampton was created as a result of the

54 See glos.ac.uk/uog/content.asp?pid=369 (accessed December 2003).
55 All quotations from the University webpages, accessed December 2002. Basic web page reference: roehampton.ac.uk. Checking the webpage prior to submission of this ms. in 2004, the website has been modified considerably. One interesting shift is that the Christian nature of the institution is further hidden, including the erasure of the fact that the Rector and Chief Executive is a member of a religious order. See "Welcome from the Rector" (address as above, plus: /about/index/asp.). In 2005 Sister Porter was replaced by a layman.

merger of three church colleges: Digby Stuart, Whitelands, and Southlands (Catholic, Anglican, and Methodist respectively) with a secular college, Froebel, to become Roehampton Institute. In the late 1970s it entered into association with the University of Surrey, awarding, through validation, University of Surrey degrees from 1982. In 2000 it attained university status as a partner in the Federal University of Surrey. Roehampton is like Gloucestershire in terms of institutional mission statements, and equally inclusive:

> Roehampton has a strong Christian tradition. Three of the Colleges are Christian foundations (Catholic, Anglican and Methodist) and have their own chapels, while the University also has Muslim Prayer Rooms and an active Jewish Resource Centre. Religion is not compulsory but it's there to help you make sense of life when you need to.[56]

This indicates the unifying vision that "religion" (not Christianity) might offer, but like Gloucestershire there is no return to this Christian or religious dimension outside of the pages about the chaplaincies and chapels at the different sites, except for a brief cross-reference to the history of the foundation in the theology and religious studies prospectus. Indeed, the statement quoted above is not to be found on the web pages of Roehampton, but only in the published prospectus. Certainly there is no trace of it in any of the undergraduate programs on offer. Roehampton's "theology and religious studies" program, which is offered both as a single honors and a joint-honors pathway, is part of the School of Humanities and Cultural Studies. When presenting this pathway, the Christian background is noted and given description in two ways: "Theology and Religious Studies (TRS) has always been one of the core subjects offered at Roehampton; and the religious foundations have a long tradition of providing pastoral care and a congenial environment for students."[57] These two latter claims are undoubtedly true, but cannot be distinctive Christian claims as such, for pastoral care and congenial environments are found mentioned in most university catalogs. The advertising goes on to emphasize that the program is not "geared only toward students with a faith" (again, wide generic cover) "but toward all those interested in religion as a spiritual, cultural, and social phenomenon." It is clear that Christian theology is not given any high visibility, but a general religious ethos is. However, Roehampton's Theology and Religious Studies program does offer a student the chance to be trained in a number of units in Christian studies, as well as undertake religious studies in a non-

---

[56] Roehampton Institute Prospectus, 2001, p. 4.
[57] All these statements came from Roehampton's webpage in November 2002.

theological fashion, comparative studies, and languages—a remarkably wide range, given its size. The institution has also formed a theological forum in the South West that actively explores issues of Christian identity and co-operation among like-minded institutions. These latter features are important sparks to the light, despite the strong market winds working against the flames. There is an apparent market un-attractiveness to institutional Christian identity.[58] In conclusion: despite important individual and structural efforts to the contrary, on Burtchaell or Gleason's criteria both institutions represent the secularization of the Christian university.

Sinclair Goodlad, a far more optimistic interpreter than I am, says of his more wide-ranging investigation of English Christian universities' and colleges' prospectuses:

> Christian institutions in England take great pains to stress that they welcome students of all faiths or none. Indeed, so strongly is this message of inclusiveness purveyed that it is really quite difficult in some cases to discern from prospectuses which are Christian institutions and which are not. Even within the covers of their prospectuses, some institutions simply mention their Church roots but without indicating what the church affiliation might signify.[59]

It is also worth commenting briefly on Goodlad's research on the wider English picture, even though his study primarily takes into consideration institutions I have not included above, in the University College and Higher Education sector.[60] Goodlad makes a very pertinent comparison in his research, which certainly relates to my minor findings about English Christian universities: "The UK [church] colleges' histories . . . paint very similar pictures of change within the colleges to that chronicled by Burtchaell in the American ones."[61] Goodlad isolates five factors of Burtchaell's analysis to establish this similarity: (1) reductions in staff and students from a particular denomination thereby changing the nature of the institution; (2) a movement from the inculcation of religious beliefs and practices toward academic

---

[58] Roehampton's Marketing Director, Tricia King, reports: "Research conducted with prospective students demonstrates that the Christian nature of our colleges is of low interest" (March 2004, letter to author).

[59] Goodlad, "Christian Universities and Colleges," p. 9.

[60] In my research for this section, Liverpool Hope was the most striking example of integration at the institutional level in terms of presentation of a Christian inclusive vision that amounted to more sustained detailed description than any other comparable institution. However, it failed to relate any of its provisions to this vision/mission statement, except marginally in its theology and religious studies offerings which are akin to those of Roehampton.

[61] Goodlad, "Christian Universities and Colleges," p. 6.

theology, and eventually toward religious studies so that the curriculum becomes detached from the institution's Christian aims; (3) compulsory worship giving way to optional worship, thereby changing the nature of communal unity; (4) the lifting of restrictions on student behavior so that "moral" and "religious" forms of life become independent of intellectual activity; and, finally, (5) a move from clergy or religious to lay presidents (principals or rectors).[62] Goodlad's important study shows that all these five factors (isolated in Burtchaell) were pervasive in English church colleges. These and other important factors (such as rapid and abrupt changes in government policies regarding the training of teachers) precipitated the collapse of the majority of them in the twentieth century, the initial wave after the First World War, and the next more severe wave, almost tidal, after the Second World War.[63]

Goodlad goes on to assess the remaining Christian institutions in terms of three criteria: (1) institutional integrity (meaning their explicit sense of mission and purpose, understood as encouraging a Christian ethos and culture); (2) research; (3) college life, curriculum, and teaching methods.[64] His findings under the first and third of these categories (which are closest to my own concerns) lead him to be cautiously optimistic, and he highlights a number of impressive features, although Goodlad's use of his criterion are far more minimally applied than I would wish.[65] He pays little attention to the wider curriculum issue in relation to mission statements.[66] He only tests whether theology and religious studies is offered, rather than the nature of

---

[62] Goodlad's attitude to modernity is quite different to that of Burtchaell and Gleason. See his "Bear's Hug."

[63] Goodlad, "Christian Universities and Colleges," p. 6. This pattern is also close to the US one. Finance also plays a major role, as it did in the US For a chronicle of cuts in the higher education sector see, for the early period, M. Lofthouse, *The Church Colleges 1918–1939: The Struggle for Survival*, J. Billings, Leicester, 1992; for post-1939 cuts, see D. Hencke, *Colleges in Crisis*, Penguin, London, 1978, and, up to 1982: M. Locke, J. Pratt, and T. Burgess, *The Colleges of Higher Education: 1972–1982*, Critical Press, Croydon, 1985.

[64] Goodlad, "Christian Universities and Colleges," pp. 6–11.

[65] Regarding research he notes that while "most church institutions in England now have respectable portfolios of research," 75% of research award monies go to the 20 largest universities in England (Goodlad, "Christian Universities and Colleges," p. 8). I would add that in terms of current government research assessment ratings (2001), no Christian institution (in all three sectors) attained a top mark (5★) or second highest (5) in theology/religious studies, but the two universities (and two others) attained 4. The two lowest ratings in the subject were to church colleges, and a church college that had been absorbed into a new university.

[66] Admittedly, on the wider curriculum front, Goodlad does note the development of a collaborative project by the Council for Church and Associated Colleges entitled "Engaging the Curriculum," which has produced three very helpful books exploring theology's interaction with different areas of the curriculum (sociology, English literature, and a more general

that offering, and he places strong emphasis on chapel provision and social work projects that he calls "service learning." I have not focussed explicitly on this latter significant dimension in my own study, and would not want to exclude it as an important indicator, although I am at pains to discern what is specifically Christian about Goodlad's proposals regarding service learning.[67] Despite his many good findings (according to his criteria), which are grounds for real optimism, on my criteria using Goodlad's work, one might conclude that what Burtchaell said about US institutions is also true of English institutions: Christian institutions are dying, although there are embers glowing and sparking. I should make it clear that these are not Goodlad's conclusions.

In this penultimate section, I want to comment briefly on the shift in English universities from theology to religious studies.[68] I want to do this to see if there is any distinctive sense in which the universities distinguish

---

look at spirituality and the curriculum). See: ed. Leslie J. Francis, *Sociology, Theology and the Curriculum*, Cassell, London, 1999 (as for all the volumes); ed. Liam Gearon, *English Literature, Theology and the Curriculum*; and ed. Adrian Thatcher, *Spirituality in the Curriculum*. Disappointingly, only Mary Grey and Adrian Thatcher really address issues concerning the entire curriculum in the third book. These volumes indicate that thinking is going on regarding this issue, but there is no evidence of institutional implementation of any of these curriculum issues in these institutions, at least from the web pages and prospectuses Goodlad or I have examined.

[67] In email response to this question Goodlad wrote: "No: service learning is not a specifically Christian activity . . . It is an area in which people who are not Christians can experience the agapeic dimension of Christianity. What chaplains might do is to celebrate with and for Christians the Christian dimensions of the work." September 25, 2002.

[68] It is worth mentioning that three of the four ancient Scottish universities, St. Andrews, Glasgow, and Aberdeen all had divinity faculties that undertook the entire training for the ministry of the national Church and were therefore confessional, professional, and postgraduate in the early twentieth century. Scotland did not undergo the separation of university and Church that happened in England and Wales in the 1850s, and as late as 1962, legislatively, this situation persisted. In this respect, my arguments about the secularization of theology and the emergence of religious studies require careful nuance in the Scottish context. Nevertheless, Andrew Walls argues that the profound changes in society (secularization, end of empire, pluralism in society, internal changes within the Church in Scotland—and world-wide) precipitated radical changes such that during 1960–75 religious studies emerged in Scottish universities and the ancient universities began to change (alongside the emergence of the new Scottish universities). This change was consolidated during the expansion of the universities so that in "1980 Religious Studies in Scotland appeared to be thriving" (Walls in ed. U. King, *Turning Points in Religious Studies*, T. & T. Clark, Edinburgh, 1990, p. 45). Walls shows that in the 1980s all the expansion tended to be in religious studies, but ten "years later [after radical cuts to funding for the universities] all its bases except Edinburgh had contracted, the Glasgow presence had ceased, and Aberdeen had lost departmental status" (ibid.). Despite Walls's pessimistic tone, in 2000 all of the ancient four except St. Andrews offer study of non-Christian religions within their degree programs, and undergraduate theology degrees are no longer designed for ordinands. Stirling, the only other Scottish university offering either theology or religious studies, offers a religious studies program, with virtually no Christian theology. Some

these two disciplines, and if anything like confessional theology exists. In no published prospectus or website of the 23 English universities offering theology or religious studies is there a single definition which distinguishes between method in "theology" and "religious studies" (or religion, study of religion, cultural studies), and no single public affirmation that theology is basically a confessional discipline involving an ecclesial context. Even though this is hardly surprising, it is worth noting. Clearly, in these 23 institutions, there are scholars, including myself, who would distinguish the disciplines and see theology as an ecclesial activity but institutionally this registers a simple conclusion: there is no discernible *public difference* between method in "theology" and "religious studies" in English universities. Furthermore, while "theology" tends usually to refer to the study of Christianity, there are theology departments that offer units from their own teachers or outside the departments that would clearly be deemed religious studies in another department. This is true of all the Theology or Divinity departments, which do not (yet) include Religious Studies in their name: Birmingham, Durham, Exeter, Heythrop, Hull, Nottingham, and Oxford.

We can also see the shift from theology to religious studies in terms of the naming of departments. In 1990, Adrian Cunningham noted:

> In the mid-1950's there were no more than sixteen people in English universities teaching religions other than Christianity. In 1990, all of the sixteen relevant departments include at least an option in another tradition, either taught within the department or drawing upon a cognate department or school of, say, Middle Eastern or oriental studies. While there are only two departments described simply as "Religious Studies" (Lancaster and Newcastle), another eight now have "Religious Studies" as part of their title.[69]

Updating this information, given the increase of the (new) universities, of the relevant 23 departments, all offer at least an option related to a religion

---

of the posts in world religions from Glasgow and Aberdeen were taken up by Edinburgh, so were not lost but regionally centralized. This is not to deny that Scotland, like England, has been seriously hit by education cuts and that the *development* of the new field of religious studies was certainly a casualty. I have briefly digressed to note that Scotland's situation initially seems more favorable to confessional theology. Nevertheless, the development of religious studies has been significant as well as the secularization of the university. This analysis is certainly confirmed in George Newlands, "Theology and Cultural Change: A Variety of Students" in eds. Martien E. Brinkman et al., *Theology between Church, University and Society*, Royal Van Gorcum, Assen, 2003, pp. 164–74.

[69] Adrian Cunningham, "Religious Studies in the Universities: England" in ed. U. King, *Turning Points*, pp. 22–31, p. 21.

other than Christianity,[70] and in title only seven are called "Theology" or "Divinity," with Sheffield as an exception, called Department of Biblical Studies, but its fare might well be assimilated within Theology (or Cultural Studies?). This is in stark contrast to the fact that before 1967 there were no departments of Religious Studies (although admittedly Manchester University had the first Department of Comparative Religion back in 1904). Hence a further conclusion is that religious studies is advancing and gaining ground, statistically and ideologically. Admittedly, these are conclusions based on limited findings. For example, gender studies and political theologies are calling into question the neutrality of religious studies and these issues do not necessary register in the prospectuses I have been examining, for they have no institutional force, just as there are many Christians teaching theology with a lively faith commitment, but this too does not show through a prospectus, possibly as it is not ideologically acceptable. Faculties might keenly advertise such wares if they were thought to attract students.

So far I have been conducting this enquiry from an official public relations angle: prospectus and web pages tell only a limited amount. In this final section, I want to turn to two leading theologians at two ancient English universities, to examine their vision of theology, its role, function, and purpose as presented in their inaugural lectures: Professor John Webster (Lady Margaret Professor of Divinity at Oxford—delivered in 1997) and Professor David F. Ford (Regius Professor of Divinity at Cambridge—delivered in 1992).[71] The titles of the two lectures are particularly pertinent to my concerns. Webster's is called "Theological Theology," and Ford's, "A Long Rumour of Wisdom. Redescribing Theology." Page numbers for these lectures subsequently appear in the text. They indicate that the questions I am asking are vibrantly alive in England's academic institutions, despite the slightly bleak picture above.

Webster wants to argue that theology has been assimilated into the Enlightenment *Wissenschaft*. He draws heavily on thinkers like Alasdair MacIntyre, Eberhard Jüngel, and Michael Buckley to argue that in this new *Wissenschaft* the inner self is privileged, in either its instrumentalist or representational ideologies. Rational instrumentalism means that

[70] This is a difficult area to press, as Jewish Studies sometimes contains what in pre-war departments would have been viewed as Christian Studies (Old Testament, Hebrew Bible). Also, as with Gloucestershire, we saw that much offered in the Religious Studies program was to be found in the Theology program.

[71] John Webster, *Theological Theology*, Clarendon Press, Oxford, 1998; see also "Hermeneutics in Modern Theology: Some Doctrinal Reflections," *Scottish Journal of Theology*, 51, 1998, pp. 307–41; David F. Ford, *A Long Rumour of Wisdom: Redescribing Theology*, Cambridge University Press, Cambridge, 1992; and further elaborated, *Theology: A Very Short Introduction*, Oxford University Press, Oxford, 2000. Webster has since moved to Aberdeen.

[the] modern research university is dominated by ideals of procedural rationality, context- and conviction-independence, and representation and judgement. The effect of this anthropology is to isolate and then privilege an ideal
of rational competence: "human rationality is such and the methods and
procedures which it has devised and in which it has embodied itself are such
that, if freed from external constraints and most notably from the constraints
imposed by religious and moral tests, it will produce not only progress in
enquiry but also agreement among all rational persons as to what the rationally justified conclusions of such enquiry are."[72]

Instead, Webster wants to reassert the authenticity of a tradition-specific
discipline, a *Bildung* where

[the] goal of schooling is the cultivation of a particular kind of person who
has acquired certain habits of mind and will, a certain cast or temper of the
soul, and so is oriented to what is considered to be the good and the true.
Schooling is transformation, and involves the eradication of defects and limitations, as well as the fostering of skills which are learned through engagement in common intellectual practices.[73]

This schooling has an ontological and noetic dimension. Here Webster strat-
egically draws on the seventeenth-century Reformer, Johannes Wollebius.
His argument continues that such a schooling is ontological:

giving priority to the object immediately calls into question any notion that
methods of enquiry are set by the subjective conditions of enquirers and not
by that to which they direct their loving attention. For theology as Wollebius
envisages it, the being of God is not simply a hypothesis into which theology
enquires, but rather the reality which actively constitutes and delimits the
field of theological activity. Talk of God and God's actions will not just
describe theology's ultimate horizons, as it were the furthest boundaries of
the field, within which theologians go about their business unconstrained.
Rather, the field of theology and the activities which theologians perform
within that field—its texts, its modes of interpretation, its standards of assessment, its rhetoric and modes of persuasion—will be described by talk of
God. What Wollebius calls "the principle of the being of theology," what we
might call its intellectual ontology, has priority over anthropology and epistemology. Theology is simply not a free science.[74]

---

[72] Webster, *Theological Theology*, p. 6, citing MacIntyre, *Three Rival Versions*, p. 225. See
further Webster, *Theological Theology*, pp. 16–17.
[73] Ibid., p. 6.
[74] Ibid., pp. 18–19.

Clearly, this is utterly inimical to the Enlightenment university, but this is not all. Noetically, this object of theology for Wollebius and Webster is:

> nothing less than the eschatological self-presence of God in Jesus Christ through the power of the Holy Spirit . . . In a very important sense, the notion of the Word of God undertakes the duty which in later theology will be performed by epistemology and anthropology: it shows how it is that knowledge of God is possible and real.[75]

Webster is acutely aware that this vision of theology sits uncomfortably with Oxford University's view that "theology's place in the university is to be won by its conformity to an ideal of disengaged reason."[76] He suggests that theology's voice should be a deeply critical presence in today's secular university, an articulation of "Christian difference," a kind of thorn in the flesh.[77]

I have quoted from Webster in some detail for his inaugural indicates some very important points in relation to my argument—and I have learnt much from him. First, Webster's voice presents a very similar challenge (as articulated in this book) to the discipline of theology, although he develops his argument in a profoundly Barthian and Reformed manner, rather than in a Catholic fashion. Prayer, practice, and communal-ecclesial context are vital to Webster, even though his ecclesia is different from my own.[78] Clearly, the implications of Webster's picture of a theological theology as found here, and in other writings, have no place for a "theological religious studies" as I have been proposing, as this would be assimilated to "apologetics" which is ascetically rejected, or seen as a form of "correlation."[79] I think they need be neither. The exclusive focus of interest for Webster's project is theology as *explication* of the Bible, and dogmatics as the same. This has the strength of fully relating biblical studies and dogmatics. David Ford criticizes

---

[75] Ibid., p. 18.

[76] Ibid., p. 20. Here he cites the views of the 1850 University Reform Commission.

[77] Ibid., p. 20, here supportively citing Milbank, *Theology and Social Theory*, p. 381.

[78] See *Holiness*, SCM, London, 2003, pp. 8–30, where Webster argues: (1) theological reason is under the Church's authority; (2) because the Church is under the authority of truth; (3) only in so much as the Church lives in deference to the claim of the gospel. Surely this means that ecclesia has a much more central role in dogmatics for the gospel is canonically formed through the authority of the Church deciding its texts, and in this process there is therefore an interaction between Bible–tradition–authority in more circular a manner than Webster's hierarchically descending order of these three.

[79] I am drawing on his review of Ford's *Self and Salvation: Being Transformed* in *Scottish Journal of Theology*, 54, 2001, pp. 548–59. See also Webster, "Discovering Dogmatics" in ed. Darren C. Marks, *Shaping a Theological Mind*, Ashgate, Aldershot, 2002, pp. 129–36.

Webster for severely downplaying the value of culture as a mode of theology's practice, and in a very limited sense Ford is correct.[80] Nevertheless, Webster's argument here indicates that despite differences he and I might have, there are important similarities in our argument. There are of course others in England with similar disquiet.[81]

Second, Webster does begin to relate his argument about theology to the other disciplines in the university. Webster's theological theology would require that other subjects, both their methodologies and objects of study, are called into question by his critique. He writes: "what is needed is a renewed 'conflict of the faculties,' though not one driven by [citing Richard Rorty] 'the quest for commensuration,' but by a confident sense of the importance of nonconformity."[82] Given the context of Webster's remarks, it would be wrong to criticize their allusiveness, but clearly the theological sense in which other disciplines may be affected requires further fleshing out. Webster's highlighting "nonconformity" might be taken in a theological sense (to be unpacked further by him?) or a colloquial sense (that requires the faculties to do the unpacking, Christian or otherwise?), or it might imply some joint action between theologians and Christian academics.

Third, Webster registers the institutional impact on the university of his view of theology, which again bears fruitful relation to my own argument. Given Webster's own background (prior to Oxford) at Christian institutions in Toronto, Canada, it is odd that his notion of theology as "critical presence" goes no further than to suggest that theology be a constant thorn in the flesh of the secular university. He does not push his own argument to its logical conclusion: theology can only flourish in a theological (Christian) university. Webster is probably too realistic to suggest this, but he does seem to encourage utopian thinking, to the degree that "the function of utopias is to encourage ironic distance from prevailing conceptions, and to recount the past and envisage the future from a different point of view."[83]

[80] See David Ford's reply to Webster's review in *Scottish Journal of Theology*, 54, 2001, pp. 559–63.

[81] For English theologians see, for example, from a Reformed perspective, Colin Gunton, "Doing Theology in the University Today" in eds. Colin E. Gunton, Stephen R. Holmes, and Murray A. Rae, *The Practice of Theology: A Reader*, SCM, London, 2001, pp. 441–55; for a more Thomistic perspective from the Anglican theologian, John Milbank, "The Conflict of the Faculties: Theology and the Economy of the Sciences"; and the irenic synthesis of Daniel D. Hardy, *On Being the Church*, SCM, London, 2002.

[82] Webster, *Theological Theology*, pp. 22–3. See also Richard Rorty, *Philosophy and the Mirror of Nature*, Princeton University Press, Princeton, New Jersey, 1979, p. 317. Milbank more fully explores this conflict in Milbank, "The Conflict of the Faculties."

[83] Webster, *Theological Theology*, p. 24.

Let us now compare Webster's inaugural to the inaugural of one of England's foremost theologians, David Ford. Like Webster, Ford did his doctoral work on Barth, but very little of that influence can be seen in Ford's irenic inaugural. Ford's strategy (which is usefully carried through in other writings) is to dissolve many disciplinary boundaries,[84] thereby conflating theology and religious studies (perhaps reflecting Cambridge's more diverse faculty and funding sources) into a practice called "public theology" which is said to exist in the academy. Ford notes the decision in 1969 to change the Cambridge Theological Tripos to the Theology and Religious Studies Tripos. "Public theology" is then fleshed out in relation to three groups: the university, the religious communities, and wider society. The ordering of these three groups is Ford's, and it is significant. It compares interestingly to Webster's where the ecclesial is prioritized.

For Ford, theology is an enterprise that is undertaken by anyone, from any religious group or none, and proceeds according to intellectually respectable and pluriform criteria in the university. While he acknowledges that the subject matter(s) of theology are to be studied with methods "appropriate to them" (p. 7) he fails to explore the possible irreconcilable methodological tensions that I explored in the previous chapter, let alone those raised by Muslim theology or Buddhist practice. Admittedly, Ford does not deny that there are problems in his proposal, but he does not address them in the terms that I am urging. However, in so much as this entire discussion regarding theology's relation to the university is carried on with a very broad sense of the subject matter, Ford implicitly seems to assimilate different "religions," which he must if he is to use the umbrella term "public theology."

When Ford gets to the next question of "Responsibilities to religious communities," similar unresolved tensions emerge. First, he really only addresses Christian concerns, never once indicating that the concerns of a Muslim, Hindu, or Buddhist might be quite radically different.[85] At one point he adopts a magisterial position as spokesperson for all religions (which I am sure is far from his intention): "What are the theological needs of the main religious communities? I would suggest that they are for a high quality of engagement with what comes from the past, for discernment

---

[84] See Ford's *Self and Salvation: Being Transformed*, Cambridge University Press, Cambridge, 1999.

[85] Admittedly Ford (p. 24) is sensitive to this criticism: "You may have sensed a certain abstraction, the inability of that level of talk [his lecture so far] to come to grips with many of the most urgent and interesting issues. The main reason is that one does not have to press far before one comes upon the deep particularity of concepts such as responsibility or wisdom." Indeed!

and judgement about the present and future significance of their traditions, and for the provision of 'ordered learning.'" (p. 13).[86] It may well be the case that this articulation is empirically correct, although I imagine it is open to question. What is significant is that Ford, a Christian, by force of his rhetorical strategy unwittingly becomes the spokesperson for the "main religious communities" without citing a single authority to support this contention.

Second, Ford does nevertheless grant that each community should "play a full part in the discipline," (p. 12) and happily criticizes those concerned to maintain neutrality and objectivity. He responds to charges that religious commitment entails improper advocacy, by arguing that this affects not only theology, but also economics, law, history, architecture, and all the disciplines. Further, rather than banning advocacy in the university, it must "take place in a setting [the university] where rigorous argument and consideration of alternatives are normal" (ibid.). Again, this general setting of the rules of academic study is resistant to, let us say, a Websterian picture, where theology's advocacy is *not* accountable to the "considerations of alternatives" as a "normal" theological procedure, for this normality according to Webster is the Enlightenment's normality.

Finally, when Ford does come to address the Church's role in academic theology, he refers to the ecumenical Cambridge Federation of Theological Colleges and his comments are telling. These colleges differ from the university Faculty "not necessarily in content, standards or even in personnel; but simply, I suggest, in the priority the theological colleges must give to the welfare of the particular faith communities they represent and to preparing their students for one type of vocation" (pp. 13–14). The difference is not to be found in the curriculum or methodology or intellectual presuppositions. In this sense, university theology is removed from its ecclesial basis, or rather this ecclesial basis is privatized, so that a Muslim and Christian student can both do Christian theology at Cambridge and publicly they are said to do the same thing.[87]

My reading of Ford is that quite subtly, in trying to accommodate theology and religious studies under the umbrella of "public theology" he has

---

[86] Here he refers to Edward Farley, *The Fragility of Knowledge: Theological Education in the Church and the University*, Fortress Press, Philadelphia, Pennsylvania, 1988, ch. 5. Farley is not discussing religious communities, but specifically the Christian community.

[87] I think this is what leads Kieran Flanagan in *The Enchantment of Sociology*, Macmillan, London, 1996, p. 94 to say of Ford's proposals that they are "vague in a liberal Anglican way. The denominational responsibilities of such a theology and the issue of its authority are hardly sketched. Little attention is given to the issue of the way an academic theology disembodied from spiritual practice and ecclesial accountability is a contradiction in terms."

instead replaced it with an imaginative, rich, and creative form of religious studies. That this form of religious studies is not explicitly secular shows the limitations of my own analysis regarding "religious studies," as well as calling into question whether Ford's harmonious marriage between the two can be sustained. Certainly, Webster's theological theology can have no place in Ford's redescription, for if Webster's Trojan horse were admitted, the Fordian project would surely collapse.

In the final part on "Responsibilities to society," Ford makes some very significant points, insightfully fleshing out certain aspects of Webster's thesis. In his refusal to allow theology to be a private interest, Ford calls for high-level engagement with other disciplines, while being painfully aware of the general lack of such publicly acknowledged engagement. "On the whole it is hard to think of theological treatments of the legal system, the economy, education, science, technology, medicine and the formation of our culture that have entered the mainstream of debate" (p. 17). Ford calls for collaboration across disciplines, and in this respect he, like Webster, avoids an argument for a Christian university. However, unlike Webster, Ford forges instead a vision of a rich religiously pluralist university, which is probably far more likely than a Christian university.

Having now viewed the complex and rich picture that actually exists in England, and equally if not more so in the United States, we can finish this section with some basic generalizations. First, Christian universities (by name or mission statement or foundation) have generally been secularized, with little real institutional evidence of what makes the university Christian. Second, in such institutions there is very little evidence of any Christian vision affecting the different disciplines, either in their intellectual practices or procedures, or in their being related to theology or philosophy in some sort of holistic manner.[88] Third, theology in such institutions has been increasingly secularized, admittedly in differing degrees, but in terms of public self-presentation it is very difficult to tell the difference between theology and religious studies except in their different fields and subject matters. The methods of study and the anthropological presuppositions of study are usually the same for both subjects. Fourth, in both the US and England there are staunch critics of this process, with varying counter-strategies: those who want a thorough reform of theology (Webster), those who call into question the fragmentation of study and the isolation of the disciplines (Ford, Burtchaell, Gleason), those who call for the importance of

---

[88]   This is true of English church school education, and of course, much of this debate relates to earlier pre-university years. See, for example, Trevor Cooling, *A Christian Vision for State Education: Reflections on the Theology of Education*, SPCK, London, 1994.

worship and religious practice as central to intellectual enquiry (Goodlad, Burtchaell, Webster), and, finally, those who call for a new sort of university (Burtchaell, Gleason, Webster, and MacIntyre). I suggest that all these strands have to be pursued together for any one of them to be pursued intelligibly. To push for one alone means that in the long run all will probably fail, and certainly to ignore the last is to seriously imperil the others. I acknowledge that this last judgement is contentious, but intellectually I see no alternative, even if in England it smacks of utopia. In England, due to resources, an ecumenical Christian university is perhaps more practical, although more complicated regarding questions of authority and accountability.

In the next chapter I turn to the defense of such a utopian idea. Critics see this "utopia" as an undesirable "sectarianism."

Chapter Three

Cyrus Returns:
Rebuilding the Temple in Babylon

I Desirable Sectarianism

At the end of chapter one, we saw Alasdair MacIntyre's not quite sufficient rebuttal of the charge of sectarianism and utopianism. He argues that the charge reflects the fact that moderns "insist upon seeing only what it [modernity] allows them to see," hence they cannot even "identify, let alone confront the problems which will be inscribed in their epitaphs."[1] It is not quite a matter of who writes such epitaphs, or that MacIntyre's response is not without truth, but rather that his response needs to engage more closely with the very real concerns expressed by the best thinkers, both modernists and those who are in varying degrees critical of modernity, but who see that there is much to salvage, much to be grateful for, and much to learn from.[2] He also needs to face more squarely the concerns of those who have witnessed the ravages of sectarian societies, where separate education has become a form of apartheid and segregation, creating economic and political injustice. In this chapter I want to face squarely some of these critics and argue for a desirable "sectarianism," for there are good theological reasons to

---

[1] MacIntyre, *Three Rival Versions of Moral Enquiry*, Duckworth, London, 1990, p. 235.

[2] The best examples of such critics would be Charles Taylor, *Sources of the Self: The Making of the Modern Identity*, Harvard University Press, Cambridge, Massachusetts, 1989, and *Ethics of Identity*, Harvard University Press, Cambridge, Massachusetts, 1992; Jeffrey Stout, *Ethics After Babel*; and Martha Nussbaum, *The Fragility of Goodness*, Cambridge University Press, Cambridge, 1986. Nussbaum, however, is the most hostile to MacIntyre: "Recoiling from Reason," *New York Times Review of Books*, 19, 1989, pp. 36–41. Taylor is rightly questioned for his Christian orientation by George Marsden, in "Matteo Ricci and the Prodigal Culture" in ed. James L. Heft, *A Catholic Modernity? Charles Taylor's Marianist Award Lecture*, Oxford University Press, New York, 1999, pp. 83–94, 88–92; and for the vagueness and lack of specificity of his key notion of "transcendence" by Rosemary Luling Haughton, "Transcendence and the Bewilderment of Being Modern" in ed. Heft, *Catholic Modernity?*, pp. 65–82.

be a sectarian committed to the common good. I also want to address the attendant questions of the public funding and differing forms of account-ability of such sectarian enterprises, focussed as they are, at least in terms of a Catholic university, on the "common good." As such, I am not attempting to justify all forms of sectarianism, but simply this tradition-specific form in terms of a Catholic university, although much of the argument would equally apply to an ecumenical Christian university, or indeed other denominational foundations. There may well be some types of sectarianism that the liberal modern state should not fund or even encourage.

Roman Catholic, Methodist, Muslim, Buddhist, Hindu, and Jewish higher education institutions have a long and complex international history and it would be futile to essentialize these projects, or deal with their dynamics outside their specific historical and political contexts. Here I simply want to concentrate on a dilemma posed by two critics of MacIn-tyre's postliberal university proposal. John Horton and Susan Mendus call MacIntyre's proposal "interestingly Janus-faced":

> On the one hand, his recognition that there is a variety of traditions in the modern world, each with legitimate claims to serious investigation, intimates a pluralism which, if not straightforwardly liberal, is at least an embodiment of mutual toleration between proponents of different traditions. On the other hand, his insistence on the role of authority within traditions and his apparent acceptance of the idea that the guardians of a tradition can, for example, legitimately exclude from their own universities those who do not share the basic assumptions of their tradition seem potentially more authoritarian and socially divisive.[3]

Janus was the gate keeper to heaven and the two faces of the dilemma are vital. Let us take the second face first. There is a curious irony that this same criticism could be directed at the present liberal monolithic university system that MacIntyre is criticizing. The "guardians of tradition" can pre-sently exclude those who do not share their liberal assumptions in a plethora of ways, all of which would be thought of as respectable and perfectly legit-imate. For instance, the whole notion of specific entry requirements that must be possessed before entering the university is firmly established, and exclusion of those who do not possess such training and abilities is enshrined to help safeguard the standards and quality of these institutions. And one might recall MacIntyre's point about how the natural sciences have always operated with "unstated policies of enforced exclusion," often only

---

[3]   Horton and Mendus, *After MacIntyre*, Polity Press, Oxford, 1994, p. 13.

noticed by sociologists of science.[4] Of course, such exclusions are sometimes relaxed for ideological reasons related to political quotas for intake of
students. Why is it that Horton and Mendus do not see this as "authoritarian and socially divisive"? Or again, it is usually assumed that what is
required for gaining a good university degree is the acquisition of skills and
abilities that are possessed in a higher degree by the guardians and teachers
within the universities, than in the students whom they seek to teach. It is
precisely by successfully imparting these skills to these students through a
long apprenticeship that they are deemed to "succeed." The guardians of
tradition within the secular university constantly exclude those who are not
worthy of their traditions and this is seen as "maintaining standards," not
authoritarianism and social divisiveness. Of course, in many student-based
learning programs there is an abandonment of the model of teacher as wise
person who is deeply immersed in a tradition of learning and enquiry, who
needs mimicking, rather than being a pure facilitator of students making up
their own education. One could elaborate upon this point with reference to
the entire set of epistemological and ontological presuppositions that under-
pin the secular university.[5]

In this second face of Janus, Mendus and Horton rightly focus upon the
unresolved question of the "role of authority" within different traditions
and therefore within different universities. For instance, we are faced with
the question of how these different authorities might envisage the task of
engaging in controversy with rival traditions that is required by MacIntyre's
tradition-specific Thomistic model.[6] Here indeed, we touch upon a serious
objection to the "sectarian" proposal, for the requirement to engage with
rival traditions is a tradition-specific requirement, that may well be unacceptable to all the traditions in question, or mean quite different things. I
do not think a theoretical resolution to this problem is possible. One would
first have to see what type of universities were being proposed, and what
type of universities do exist and how they operate in terms of this issue.
Only then could one explore possible responses to the theoretical and practical difficulties that are raised. However, I hardly think this weakens Mac-
Intyre's case *per se*, as his Thomism is committed to engagement with all
forms of different traditions, as his work clearly exemplifies. So does the
historical narrative of Thomism's engagement with rival traditions since the

[4]   MacIntyre, *Three Rival Versions*, p. 225.
[5]   One very perceptive accounting of these differences is to be found in Paul J. Griffiths,
Religious Reading, Oxford University Press, Oxford, 1999, and see chapter one above.
[6]   This specific type of argument would help Wolfe defend his pluralist position in "The
Potential for Pluralism" in ed. A. Sterk, *Religion, Scholarship and Higher Education*, University of
Notre Dame Press, Notre Dame, Indiana, 2002, pp. 22–39.

thirteenth century, with some exceptions. After Leo XIII's encyclical in 1897, Thomism has begun to flourish in differing schools within the Roman Catholic tradition. Indeed, the entire argument of MacIntyre's trilogy is that liberalism cannot really promote radical pluralism, as the liberal university is incapable of fostering real difference.

The first Janus-face of MacIntyre located by Mendus and Horton is his inadvertent, if not "straightforwardly liberal" promotion of peaceful pluralism. However, such a charge is strangely ahistorical and monopolist in assuming that it is only liberal modernity that can claim to provide the social, political, and intellectual conditions whereby difference and pluralism can flourish.[7] The burden of MacIntyre's argument has been to show otherwise, and to challenge just such a claim. Horton and Mendus must dislodge MacIntyre's basic argument against liberal modernity before they can assume liberalism's ownership of the conditions that might foster real diversity. Their very suspicion of a proposal that takes pluralism seriously, in suggesting the development and support of different intellectual institutions of enquiry, betrays the weakness of their criticism that MacIntyre is an inadvertent liberal. Might it be that precisely MacIntyre's Thomism is capable of supporting a social and intellectual plurality in a radical way hardly even imagined by liberal modernity? John Milbank, for one, has forcefully argued that Augustinian Christianity is capable of constructing the social and political conditions within which real difference is allowed to flourish, for difference and relationship is seen as the form of creation's original goodness.[8] Vatican II's *Declaration on Religious Freedom* also suggests a question mark against the suspicions of Horton and Mendus that fostering, within limits, and valuing pluralism must be equated with "liberalism."[9] Horton and

---

[7] For a nice turning of the tables regarding the accusation of religion as the greatest cause of European wars, see William T. Cavanaugh, "'A Fire Strong Enough to Consume the House': the Wars of Religion and the Rise of the State," *Modern Theology*, October 1995, pp. 397–420.

[8] See John Milbank, *Theology and Social Theory*, Blackwell, Oxford, 1980, pp. 380–438, even if Milbank is committed to out narrating all difference! See the perceptive critique of Milbank advanced by Gerard Loughlin, "Christianity at the End of the Story or the Return of the Meta-Narrative," *Modern Theology*, 8, 1992, pp. 365–84, and also Gillian Rose, *The Broken Middle*, Blackwell, Oxford, 1992, pp. 277–96, registering similar disquiet at Milbank's violent peace.

[9] See the "Declaration" and the introduction by John Courtney-Murray SJ in ed. Walter M. Abbott, *The Documents of Vatican II*, Guild Press, New York, 1966, pp. 672–4 for Murray's introduction. All citations from Vatican II will be taken from Abbott. However, it should be acknowledged that the influence of modernity upon Vatican II's documents is undeniable, and its consequences much debated and it is precisely the *Declaration on Religious Freedom* that is seen as modernity's Trojan horse. See Michael Davies, *The Second Vatican Council and Religious Liberty*, Neumann Press, Minnesota, 1992. Davies is right to see this document as an about-turn on earlier positions, such as held by Pius VII (p. 56).

Mendus's criticisms tend to show that objections to such a postliberal pluralism within the universities reflect the very liberal presuppositions that are being called into question. These very criticisms undermine their allegedly tolerant stance and unveil just the type of authoritarianism that MacIntyre exposes and questions.

There would be a problem, such as Horton and Mendus envisage, were MacIntyre's Thomism to be replaced by a religious view that desired perfect hegemony and monolithic ideological control over all society. Ironically, this precise situation is structurally enforced by the hegemony of the liberal university. Of course, the desire for social hegemony and control is hardly foreign to the history of Christianity. But until specific proposals for different intellectual establishments are examined in detail, the charge by Mendus and Horton does not really fit MacIntyre's Thomism, nor can it be applied *a priori* to non-liberal approaches.

A comment on the word "sectarian." The *Oxford English Dictionary* relates some interesting definitions showing that the word's earliest written usage goes back to 1649, conjuring up both schism and heresy, as well as denoting irrational or bigoted beliefs. It was initially used by Presbyterians against Independents and later by Anglicans against Non-Conformists, or those in power against minorities with less power. The *OED* indicates that more recent usage applies it to zealous allegiance to any party or group, although more often to religious groups. From this a couple of preliminary comments are in order, in the light of my employment of "sectarian" to denote my own position. The word can be retained as a sign of struggle, in the way in which some groups employ the words used pejoratively of them, such as "black," "gays," and so on. Alternatively, given the complex freight of the word, it might be better to leave it now as it obscures the real issues that are of concern to my project. I am sympathetic with this latter alternative, but still more needs to be said before leaving this term aside and moving forward in the argument.

When "sectarianism" is employed in the modern period by non-religious people to denote the activity of religious people, it usually betrays the former's own allegiance to modernity. This amounts to one (usually powerful) sect (modernity) calling the other (religious) group a "sect." The label can easily, and perhaps more appropriately, be reversed, especially in the light of the critique of modernity that we have suggested above. This point is well made, although in a different context, by Walter Brueggemann. He nicely turns the tables, in his commentary on the exchanges between Hezekiah, Isaiah, and the Assyrian ambassadors in II Kings 18–19, when he suggests that we might profitably think of "empire as sect," rather than seeing the numerically smallest group as deviant. Israel's formation *behind* the walls (thus traditionally accused of sectarianism) gives it the very resources to criticize the language of the Assyrians *at* the wall, to expose their self-seeking interests.

> The Assyrian negotiators at the wall are not offering a policy in the general interest, but under such a guise are pursuing Assyrian policy at the expense of all those behind the wall. Then the dominant conversation partner acts and speaks only from a narrow interest that is sectarian. We are not accustomed to thinking of the voice of the empire as a sectarian voice. But so it is when it serves only a narrow interest. *Empire as sect* is a theme worth pursuing in our own situation [Brueggemann is writing in the USA] because it may be suggested that the voice of American power, for example, claims to be the voice of general well-being and may in a number of cases be only the voice of a narrow range of economic and political interest. The ideological guise is effective if large numbers of people can be kept from noticing the narrow base of real interest. That narrow base will not be noticed unless there is another conversation behind the wall which gives critical distance and standing ground for an alternative assessment. In ancient Israel, the prophets are the ones who regularly expose the voice of the empire as a sectarian voice not to be heard as a comprehensive, disinterested voice.[10]

Brueggemann's point is enormously helpful in reversing the spotlight: small cultic groups are now not the dangerous sectarians, but rather, the empire, state, or ruling powers that wish them to conform, are exposed as the partisans. It also nicely highlights the way in which the particularity of the gospel is not a hindrance to its universality; it is open to all, meant for all, and draws all creation into the universal covenant. Of course, we are potentially a few steps away from verbal abuse, each side calling the other the dreaded "sectarian." But Brueggemann's story is also interesting, as the metaphor of "behind the wall" conjures up a fortress or siege mentality, in contrast to Pope John XXIII's image of opening the windows to the world, when announcing the Second Vatican Council, and embracing the modern world in *aggiornamento*.[11] And here we encounter an intra-Christian controversy, which takes us a step away from the modernity versus religion debate. This also moves us closer to the interesting epicenter of the debate over "sectarianism" in Christian circles.

---

[10] Walter Brueggemann, "II Kings 18–19: The Legitimacy of a Sectarian Hermeneutic," *Horizons in Biblical Theology*, 7, 1985, pp. 1–41, 22–3.

[11] For an historical contextualization of Catholicism and "modernity," see ed. Darrell Jodcock, *Catholicism Contending with Modernity: Roman Catholic Modernity and Anti-Modernism in Historical Context*, Cambridge University Press, Cambridge, 2000, esp. pp. 1–27, 88–112, and 308–36.

The substantive issues connected with the use of the word sectarian are nicely exposed in a modern instance of the Lutheran ethicist and theologian, James Gustafson, accusing the Methodist Stanley Hauerwas (and the Lutheran George Lindbeck) of sectarianism.[12] In examining this exchange, I will suggest that one very important theological issue related to the use of this term revolves around the centrality of Christology for epistemology and ontology, and that this is perhaps the heart of the intra-Christian debate on sectarianism. To put it differently, it is a debate between Christians who believe they share a common world with non-Christians, although one group believes that by virtue of being human, all people encounter a common "world," which offers the basis for common discourse, the common good, and a "public theology" on social, ethical, and other issues (e.g. Gustafson, David Tracy, Richard McCormick—and to include some non-Christian philosophers, Martha Nussbaum and Edith Wyschogrod). The other group believes that the "worlds" encountered by different groups are culturally and religiously shaped, hence no such presumption of public discourse is *a priori* possible (e.g. Hauerwas, Lindbeck, Michael Banner, Oliver O'Donovan, John Milbank—and philosophers like MacIntyre and Alvin Plantinga). There is no shared moral language, although this need not mean that public discourse is not possible. In theological terms, the first group believes that by the use of reason all people can discern and use common "natural" ethical laws, Christian or otherwise; the second group believes that such laws may exist, but are related to and properly disclosed in the self-revelation of God in Christ. For the second, Christology is central to epistemology and ontology, but not so for the first. This distinction serves only to highlight the issues, not to suggest that all those named would subscribe to what has been stated without various qualifications.

Before turning to the Hauerwas–Gustafson exchange, it is worth also noting Ernst Troeltsch's observations on sectarianism. He defines it as:

> a voluntary society, composed of strict and definite Christian believers bound to each other by the fact that all have experienced "the new birth." These "believers" live apart from the world, are limited to small groups, emphasise the law instead of grace, and in varying degrees within their own circle set up

---

[12] Gustafson, "The Sectarian Temptation: Reflection on Theology, the Church, and the University," *Proceedings of the Catholic Theological Society of America*, 1985, 40, pp. 83–94; and see Hauerwas's response: in "Why the 'Sectarian Temptation' is a Misrepresentation: A Response to James Gustafson" in eds. John Berkman and Michael Cartwright, *The Hauerwas Reader*, Duke University Press, Durham, North Carolina, 2001, pp. 90–110; in relation to Lindbeck see the very incisive piece by William C. Placher, "Revisionist and Postliberal Theologies and the Public Character of Theology," *The Thomist*, 49, 1985, pp. 392–417.

the Christian order, based on love; all this is done in preparation for the expectation of the coming Kingdom of God.[13]

Troeltsch opposed "sect" with the "church type," the latter characterized by its all-embracing and "universal" outlook, open to all. Thus "sect" is made derivative, in so much as it is a breaking away from the Church in order to maintain the sect's distinctiveness from the world. In this sense, the sect often sees the Church as conforming to the world (and therefore the state). Far from Troeltsch's definitions being sociologically descriptive, Duane Friesen has carefully shown that it was normatively balanced, containing many hidden assumptions about the normative nature of the "church type."[14] Be that as it may, the sect's *alleged* disregard for the "universal" is seen in its living apart from society and lack of concern for those outside its walls. This has been interpreted as a disregard for the common good of humanity and a self-centered concern for the sect's self-privileging and self-perpetuation. Interestingly, these are precisely the characteristics attributed to Hauerwas by Gustafson.

Gustafson's critique suggests that Hauerwas's position is established without recourse to non-theological discourse (social, human, and natural sciences) and as such it has little to say to these discourses, insulating itself from them, and is thus sectarian. It is ideologically closed, as it is impenetrable to criticism from non-theological discourse. It therefore does not belong in the university. Further, it isolates the Church from the world, and fails to provide any serious engagement with civic and public life, as it has cut off this interdependency, the very life-blood for a real theology. Gustafson suggests that this sectarian option is tempting, given Christianity's crumbling self-identity and its lack of public support due to secularism. Hence the title of his piece: "The Sectarian Temptation." Gustafson's own alternative relies on creating an ethics that does not depend on Christ or Christianity, but on "theism," rationally established:[15]

> Faithful witness to Jesus is not a sufficient theological and moral basis for addressing the moral and social problems of the twentieth century. The theologian addressing many issues—nuclear, social justice, ecology, and so forth—must do so as an outcome of a theology that develops God's relation

[13] Ernst Troeltsch, *The Social Teaching of the Christian Churches*, trans. O. Wyon, Macmillan, New York, 1931, vol. 2, p. 993.
[14] Duane Friesen, "Normative Factors in Troeltsch's Typology of Religious Association," *Journal of Religious Ethics*, 3, 2, 1975, pp. 271–83.
[15] See Gustafson's sectarian theocentricism, hardly helpful to Buddhists and Advaitin Hindus, let alone humanists and atheists: *Ethics from a Theocentric Perspective*, vols. 1 and 2, Chicago University Press, Chicago, 1981, 1984, respectively.

to all aspects of life in the world, and develops those relations in terms which are not exclusively Christian in a sectarian form. Jesus is not God.[16]

Hauerwas's response is very helpful as it shows that he is not guilty of many of the charges made by Gustafson. Hauerwas does engage in all sorts of public debates and sees Christian engagement with secular powers as necessary, sometimes harmonious, other times deeply contentious, but inevitably *ad hoc*: he does not hold that theological discourse is unanswerable to other forms of discourse, but rather questions the normative status given to scientific discourse (and therefore modernity?) in Gustafson's approach. Further, Hauerwas strongly believes that theology has a critical place in the university, precisely as critique. Hauerwas also notes, as I have, the potential superficiality of the use of "sectarian" in theological debate: "Show me where I am wrong about God, Jesus, the limits of liberalism, the nature of the virtues, or the doctrine of the Church—but do not shortcut that task by calling me a sectarian."[17] However, Hauerwas also helpfully locates the most basic theological disagreement: Gustafson's desire for public discourse in terms of commonly accepted premises, his claim for a doctrine of creation in natural-law terms, and Hauerwas's refusal of these terms of engagement with the world. That is, for Gustafson, Christians must address non-Christians *on grounds that are acceptable to non-Christians*. In effect, those who eschew apologetics are sectarian, and here we have located the theological underpinning of the charge.[18]

In answer to Gustafson's charge, I think a decisive response is possible. Hauerwas dismantles Gustafson's criticisms into three basic issues: truth versus fideism; Christian social engagement versus irresponsibility; creation versus a theological tribalism (meaning the claim: my group is right, and that's it, there is no need to account for this claim). It is the third of these which is most important to me, although it is important to note pre-emptively that under the first, Hauerwas makes it clear that he is not a postmodernist nihilist, but rather, "Christian theology has a stake in a qualified epistemological realism."[19] It is not that Hauerwas denies God as creator of a good and blessed order, which is narrated Christologically and ecclesiologically,

---

[16]   Gustafson, " The Sectarian Temptation," p. 93.

[17]   Hauerwas, "Why the 'Sectarian Temptation' is a Misrepresentation," p. 97.

[18]   This is also the position held by David Tracy and Richard McCormick in their criticisms of sectarianism: see Tracy, *The Analogical Imagination*, SCM, London, 1981, pp. 3–46, McCormick, *Notes on Moral Theology: 1981 Through 1984*, University Press of America, Lanham, Maryland, 1984, pp. 23–6, 123–6.

[19]   *Hauerwas Reader*, p. 99; and Hauerwas cites Sabina Lovibond's, *Realism and Imagination in Ethics*, University of Minnesota Press, Minneapolis, 1983, as spelling out the realism to which

but rather "I have refused to use that affirmation [God as creator] to under-write an autonomous realm of morality separate from Christ's lordship."[20] He writes elsewhere, "appeals to creation too often amount to legitimating strategies for the principalities and powers that determine our lives," forget-ting that eschatologically the Fall still means that we deceive ourselves rather easily.[21] For Hauerwas the order of creation is only understood in terms of its *telos*, understood eschatologically, and therefore Christologically.[22] Ethics cannot be separated from its Christological and ecclesiological base and *telos*, and, therefore, neither can Christian discourse. Hauerwas is not arguing that Christians cannot engage with other forms of discourse. Rather, the warrants for Christian discourse are necessarily Christian, based on revelation, and thereby *sui-generis*. They nevertheless can make a claim on non-Christians both by their truthfulness and by their ability to call the non-Christian into question. The latter is precisely why Hauerwas spends much of his time attacking the presuppositions of liberalism. This histori-cally mediated and negotiated sense of universality does not constrain the universality of Christian ethics but rather, takes the negotiation of such uni-versality with difference, utterly seriously. This is precisely the point that is missed by McCormick, writing from a rationalist, natural law, Thomist position, when he criticizes postliberal ethics. McCormick claims that Hauerwas's methodology must commit him to thinking that Christian moral claims are "limited in application to a particular historical commu-nity—as if it were wrong to abort Catholic babies but perfectly all right to do so with Muslim, Protestant or Jewish babies."[23] Michael Banner rightly criticizes McCormick's serious misunderstanding:

---

he would subscribe. Lindbeck is also defended against non-realism very convincingly by Bruce Marshall, "Aquinas as Postliberal Theologian," *The Thomist*, 53, 1989, pp. 353–402. Hauerwas is similarly charged with non-realism by David Fergusson, *Community, Liberalism*, Cambridge University Press, Cambridge, 1998, pp. 68–72, clearly a common perception of the post-liberal school with its caution against some models of truth as correspondence.

[20] *Hauerwas Reader*, p. 109.

[21] Hauerwas, *Dispatches from the Front: Theological Engagements with the Secular*, Duke Univer-sity Press, Durham, North Carolina, 1994, p. 56.

[22] Michael Banner is right to call Hauerwas to task for his over-hasty dismissal of Oliver O'Donovan's *Resurrection and the Moral Order*, Inter Varsity Press, Leicester, 1986. Hauerwas wrongly claims that O'Donovan "seeks an account of natural law which is not governed by the eschatological witness of Christ's resurrection."—*Dispatches*, p. 175. See Banner, *Christian Ethics and Contemporary Moral Problems*, Cambridge University Press, Cambridge, 1999, pp. 16–19. Gustafson is therefore wrong when he says that "Nature is . . . of no ethical signifi-cance as a source of direction in Hauerwas' ethics. Hauerwas becomes a twentieth century Marcion," in James Gustafson, "A Response to Critics," *Journal of Religious Ethics*, 13, 1985, pp. 185–209: p. 191.

[23] McCormick, *Notes*, p. 127.

Here McCormick misses the point that the universality of the Christian story, and thus the universality of the demands it makes on human action, are logically quite distinct from the universality of knowledge of that story and its demands; thus, while denying the universality of knowledge of the Gospel, we may still say with Bonhoeffer (*Ethics*, 322) that "the whole law and the whole Gospel belong equally to all men."[24]

The decisive issue, in my opinion, is this. The charge of sectarianism when theologically related to the question of the autonomy of the created order, serves to show the assimilation of the accusers to a form of rationalist modernity. McCormick, in this instance, and Gustafson in his project, presume to read creation *neutrally*, and then relate this reading to one that fulfils the natural reading supernaturally in the gospel, or for Gustafson in rational theism. The reason why I have spent some time on this issue is critically to focus on the problematic assumption of a neutral, and therefore universally shared, sense of the order of creation. My main argument in this chapter and book calls into question the assumption that any neutral reading of creation such as this is epistemologically possible, and in this respect Gustafson and McCormick rely on presuppositions that can be criticized theologically.[25] Hence, on their own criteria, they are covert sectarians, in so much as their assumptions are not universally shared. Rather than continuing the name calling, it would be better for both sides of the debate actually to focus on the theological issues at stake, and this brief excursus on the word "sectarian" has at least tried to make clear why this is a necessity.

Before returning to the MacIntyre and Mendus/Horton debate, it will be worth briefly looking at a *theological* attempt to find a middle ground between communitarianism and modernity, advanced by a neo-Barthian, David Fergusson, in *Community, Liberalism and Christian Ethics* (1998). This work is significant as it comes out of the postliberal camp, but maintains "a

---

[24] Banner, *Ethics*, p. 33, n. 101. I do not think Banner's criticism of Hauerwas is sustainable (p. 19) where he assimilates Hauerwas and Moltmann, and criticizes him for lack of *present* discernment regarding God's presence in his creation, emphasising only *future*. See Arne Rassmusson, *The Church as Polis: From Political Theology to Theological Politics as Exemplified by Jürgen Moltmann and Stanley Hauerwas*, University of Notre Dame Press, Notre Dame, Indiana, 1995, who shows the wide gulf of difference between Moltmann and Hauerwas on precisely this point. There is a sense in which this debate perennially replays itself in many forms: Barth versus Brunner, corrected by Balthasar on analogy versus Barth: see Hans Urs Von Balthasar, *The Theology of Karl Barth*, trans. Edward T. Oakes, Ignatius Press, San Francisco, 1992 [1951], being another recent replay.

[25] O'Donovan, *Resurrection*, p. 19 puts it nicely: "the *epistemological* program for an ethic that is 'natural,' in the sense that its contents are simply known to all, has to face dauntingly high barriers."

commitment to a residual liberalism," based on the theological insight that
moral goodness and true moral reasoning can be found outside the
Church.[26] The latter is founded, according to Fergusson, on the Barthian
"understanding of human action as determined by the prior, ongoing, and
future action of the triune God" that results in the possibility "of human
action outside the church also being determined by God."[27] Hence, apart
from various interesting criticisms of each, his main criticism of both Mac-
Intyre and Hauerwas is that they resist any possibility of contributing to a
common moral consensus, which is the basis of a democratic society. Fergusson carefully nuances his position, so that he is arguing neither for
neutral natural law ethics, nor for a common consensus based on "common
moral theory."[28] I find two main problems with Fergusson's position. First,
and negatively, his criticisms of Hauerwas and MacIntyre on this particular
issue are surely misplaced? Both, in different circumstances, are willing to
argue for joining non-Christians in fighting some common ethical cause, as
does Hauerwas about abortion or non-violent resistance to war. And both
are willing to recognize that modernity and other cultures have, to utilize a
phrase from Vatican II, "rays of light and truth" within them, as does Mac-
Intyre about neo-Confucianism. It is precisely *as a whole*, as a political,
philosophical, and moral project that modernity is rejected, for in these
basic respects the project rests on deeply problematic assumptions. Neither
has given any sustained attention to non-western religious traditions, so
they cannot be found guilty in this respect either. If Fergusson is realistic
that no common moral theory can be found, then his criticism of Hauerwas
and MacIntyre on this point begins to dissolve. They can accept *pragmatic*
co-operation and joint social action, and in this sense common *consensus*,
but they resist the notion that such common action will be generated from
common moral theory in the case of modernity and Christianity. However, at
times Fergusson's proposal seems to edge further toward the possibility of a
common moral theory, despite his rejection of this possibility. This happens
when he draws on Michael Walzer's account of thick and thin moralities.[29]

---

[26] Fergusson, *Community*, p. 172.
[27] Ibid., p. 162.
[28] Ibid., pp. 72–9. He notes, with typical fairness, that some of MacIntyre's most recent work
seems to advance a version of natural law theory requiring "some minimal rules requiring
truthfulness and justice from all participants" (p. 164). In my view, this is a predictive stipula-
tion, not one describing an actual state of affairs. It is the necessary requirement, discovered *ad
hoc* and *a posteriori*, that these minimal rules allow for real moral exchange, not that they imply
or require shared moral theory.
[29] See ibid., pp. 75–9, 142, 162–5. See also Michael Walzer, *Thick and Thin: Moral Argument
at Home and Abroad*, University of Notre Dame, Notre Dame, Indiana, 1994.

The latter are:

> minimal standards and practices which should be demanded of all people and societies. They are a function of thicker and culturally determined moral understandings, but the convergence of these on minimal common ground provides some basis for the maintenance of pluralist societies.[30]

This then leads Fergusson in his drive to find common ground, to argue tentatively that the "only plausible candidate for a universal moral discourse is that of human rights." To abandon this "is to leave one without the moral vocabulary for making common cause with agencies and forces whose goals are not wholly antithetical to those of the church."[31]

This line of argument is open to a number of objections. First, Walzer's research has only shown that there can be overlap *pragmatically* between thick description in terms of some thin description. This does not mean there is moral consensus, except negatively: a general agreement that "thou shalt not kill" is a good moral maxim. However, if we unpack what this might mean, in terms of both moral consensus and social action, we would see all sorts of problems, with some strongly opposing others, while both share the thin description. Hence, anti-abortionists, pacifists, and vegetarians might argue for legislation against "killing," while those who would oppose them would argue that all these examples do not constitute "killing" properly speaking, but preserving the rights of a woman, the legitimacy of self-defense, and that animals are not part of the remit of such an injunction. The point I am making is that the very notion of agreement on thin description implicitly requires thick description, or narrative specificity, to test whether there is agreement. So thin description is both uninteresting and uninformative regarding real moral agreement in society.[32] This is not to say that there may be sufficient overlap between thick description so as to attain moral consensus *pragmatically* (say, on abortion), but that would not require endorsing the other person's moral theory *in toto*. Second, there is within Catholic theology in modern times the central social doctrine of the "common good," which requires that Catholic morality serves the common good, and should be interpreted in that context. Hence, a communitarian Catholic like MacIntyre or a high Anglo-Catholic like Milbank, or a high

---

[30] Fergusson, *Community*, p. 75.

[31] Ibid., p. 78.

[32] I have pursued this further in reference to Hans Küng's use of Walzer for his global ethics project in my "Postmodernity and Religious Plurality: Is a Common Global Ethic Possible or Desirable?" in ed. Graham Ward, *The Blackwell Companion to Postmodern Theology*, Blackwell, Oxford, 2001, pp. 131–43.

Methodist like Hauerwas may still strive in their communitarianism to serve the common good, without recourse to shared moral theory with non-Christians or the language of human rights. This leads to my third difficulty here. I think that Fergusson is right in arguing that human rights may be compatible with Christian ethics, and Pope John Paul II has certainly developed this language during his pontificate with much effect. However, Fergusson is surely wrong in arguing that it is the "only contemporary candidate for a universal moral discourse."[33] Not only are there severe objections to the language of rights from Judaism, Islam, Buddhism, and Hinduism but genealogically, as MacIntyre has shown, they arise out of the project of modernity. It is surely only modernity's global pretensions that would suggest this as a "universal moral discourse," over-riding complex multifarious thick descriptions, especially religious thick description. For example, the great Indian legal historian P. V. Kane critically comments on the Indian Constitution of 1950, after conducting a magisterial survey of traditional Hindu legal ethics. Kane argues that in one stroke, the new Constitution erased India's historical traditions:

> The Constitution makes a complete break with our traditional ideas. *Dharma-śātras* and *Smritis* begin with the dharmas ("duties") of the people (*varnas* and *āśramas*). Prime Minister Pandit Nehru himself says in his Azad Memorial Lectures on "India today and tomorrow" (1959), "All of us now talk of and demand rights and privileges, but the teaching of the *dharma* was about duties and obligations. Rights follow duties discharged." Unfortunately this thought finds no place in the Constitution . . . The Constitution engenders a feeling among common people that they have rights and no obligations whatever and that the masses have the right to impose their will and to give the force of law and justice to their own ideas and norms formed in their own cottages and tea shops. The Constitution of India has no chapter on the duties of the people to the country or to the people as a whole.[34]

It should be noted that Kane was a Brāhmin. Many lower caste groups rejoiced at the Constitution for the very reason that Kane criticizes it. Nevertheless, Kane's point still stands: the Indian Constitution is inimical to Hindu ethics, which is based primarily on duties, not rights. The Buddhist Craig K. Ihara makes a very similar point regarding the introduction of the notion of rights within Buddhism:

---

[33] Fergusson, *Community*, p. 129.
[34] P. V. Kane, *History of the Dharmaśāstras*. 2nd rev. edn., Bhandarkar Oriental Research Institute, Poona, 1968, pp. 1664–5.

In my view there is a much more significant change being proposed and which I fear [some] are overlooking. The change to a modern concept of rights is one from conceptualising duties and obligations as the role-responsibilities of persons in a cooperative scheme to seeing them as constraints on individuals in their interactions with other individuals all of whom are otherwise free to pursue their own objectives.[35]

Kane and Ihara reflect the rights/duties, individual/communitarian, divide that runs across most traditional religions in their relation to modernity. In this respect, these brief illustrations will have at least indicated that there are, in the discourse of rights, the pretensions of modernity to replace the thick descriptions variously provided by the different religions. Fergusson is perhaps optimistic in his estimate of rights providing the "only" universal discourse on which moralities might overlap or come together in common concern.

What I have been trying to show is that the mid-ground construed between communitarianism and modernity by Fergusson sometimes unwittingly slides into modernity's camp. To suggest a mid-ground is perhaps already to capitulate to modernity. Of course, there can be shared actions and overlapping theoretical agreements, but that should not assume that the truth of the gospel is compatible, *in toto*, with other "truths." It is not. And even when there is a strong appreciation of the abundance of goodness and truth found in all cultures and societies, such that the Church has admittedly much to learn, there is still a sense in which this recognition and learning is subject to and required by the gospel, and not any specific demands of modernity or other religions. The point is really a methodological one.

To return to the MacIntyre and Mendus/Horton debate, the unresolved question raised is very important as to "how traditions are to be individuated and, in matters of policy, whose interpretation of what counts as a tradition is to be treated as authoritative."[36] There is no easy answer for any tradition-specific community, for even within Roman Catholicism there is a contested understanding of "authority." Forms of Babylonian captivity can also exist within the Church. It is precisely because such questions of authority are so central to real pluralism within the university that I must now turn to the question of the funding and governing of sectarian universities.

---

[35] Craig K. Ihara, "Why There Are No Human Rights in Buddhism: A Reply to Damien Keown" in eds. Damien V. Keown, Charles S. Prebish and Wayne R. Husted, *Buddhism and Human Rights*, Curzon, London, 1998, p. 49.

[36] Horton and Mendus, *After MacIntyre*, p. 13.

II Funding and Accountability: A Clash of Authority?

In the case of a Roman Catholic model, the theologian's accountability to the magisterium and the university's accountability to the bishops raise a host of questions, some related, many distinct, and all horribly complex. This complexity is, in part, due to the different funding arrangements of Catholic universities in different areas of the world. As Catholic nation states are a thing of the past, the variety of civil legislation bearing upon the question of funding Church or sectarian universities ranges from total prohibition of state funding to Catholic universities or educational institutions, to degrees of funding, with various qualifications, such as in Germany, the United States, England, Italy, and France. For instance, in England all universities currently receive government funding, but in the United States, only state universities are recipients, although private universities gain huge indirect funding from federal and state sources, funding that is also open to state universities. And in proportion to the largesse of state funding, the "problem" about "outside" interference (from the Vatican, local bishops, other ecclesial authorities) sometimes increases.

In the following discussion I want to isolate and explore three questions, using the United States as a test case. Such a test case method clearly limits any conclusions, but it allows some of the theological issues to be laid bare, and such questions apply outside the United States. The first regards the nature of ecclesial accountability: to whom are American Catholic universities accountable, regarding the nature of their "Catholic" character? The second question is linked, but distinct: to whom are Catholic theologians, within such universities, accountable? The third question follows on from the previous two: is the idea of a Catholic university, understood maximally or minimally (given the spectrum of answers), compatible with public funding in a democratic, modern, secular society? Or to phrase it differently, can a sectarian institution be publicly funded? The answer to this question will be, to summarize: a sectarian institute might not be publicly funded under certain maximal models, although this is not certain; and it will almost certainly qualify for state and federal funding under minimal models. The point of such a limited conclusion is simply to strengthen my argument that a Catholic university and a theological theology (as well as other disciplines) are not only theologically desirable, but also attainable in practice in a secular and pluralist society, using the funds of that state. If a state is committed to a non-pluralist society, clearly the situation will be entirely different, but since we are only concerned with the US and England, two countries committed to religious tolerance and healthy pluralism, we can proceed.

As we have seen earlier, the necessity of state and federal funding was a major factor in driving American Catholic institutions into an inadvertently secularizing process, in terms of their governance and subsequent curriculum and hiring policies. These institutes wanted to compete with the best and it is better to exist with compromise than not to exist at all. Admittedly, this way of putting it clashes with the good faith of the many religious communities involved, who believed that such moves were consolidating their establishment, and therefore Catholic identity, in American society. The long and complex history prior to *Ex Corde Ecclesiae*, 1990[37] in the United States, is well told in a number of sources, and in part in the previous chapter.[38] It results fundamentally from a tension that developed from the mid-twentieth century between Catholic universities (institutions chartered directly by the Holy See when Pius XII formed the International Federation of Catholic Universities, and broadened in 1963 to include non-ecclesiastical universities) and the Vatican as to the role of the Catholic university, especially its theologians and general accountability and Catholic character. In 1973 changes were put in place by Cardinal Garronne to establish these three factors, eventually resulting in canon laws in 1983, and *CU*, which combines both the intellectual rationale for the Catholic university and canon law.

The Apostolic Constitution *CU* (from the Latin opening words, very significantly: "Born from the heart of the Church," *ex corde ecclesiae*) is a succinct summary of recent papal and Vatican thinking about the nature of the university in the modern world, following on from Vatican II's *Declaration on Catholic Education* (1966) that contained two specific paragraphs on the Catholic university. *CU* does not address ecclesiastical universities and faculties, that is, universities entirely organized and controlled by the Holy See and addressed in an earlier papal allocution, *Sapientia Christiana* (1979). Instead it addresses those universities that consider themselves Catholic, and those that were established and/or owned by dioceses and religious orders. The first part, devoted to the identity and mission of such universities, is a powerful vision of the nature and role of the Catholic university, and the second part contains general norms (or regulations) building upon canons 807–14, to secure the implementation of the Apostolic Constitution. (Canon laws are ecclesiastical rules regarding matters of faith, morals, and disciplines. Canons 807–14 pertain to Catholic universities and other

---

[37] Paragraph references given in the main body of my text, abbreviated *CU*.

[38] For a "liberal" telling of the narrative see ed. McCluskey, *The Catholic University*, University of Notre Dame Press, Indiana, 1970, and for a more "conservative" account, see James Jerome Conn, *Catholic Universities in the United States and Ecclesiastical Authorities*, Editrice Pontifica Universita Gregoriana, Rome, 1991.

institutions of higher education. Later, we will return to these canons.) Here, I will briefly summarize only section one of part one, dealing with the nature and objectives of the university, for this is the main concern of my book. A Catholic university is certainly no less than the best of the secular universities in so much as it is "an academic community which, in a rigorous and critical fashion, assists in the protection and advancement of human dignity and cultural heritage through research, teaching and various services offered to the local, national and international communities" (12). But it has a special vocation and character, best summarized in four ways:

> 1. a Christian inspiration not only of individuals but of the university community as such; 2. a continuing reflection in the light of the Catholic faith upon the growing treasury of human knowledge, to which it seeks to contribute by its own research; 3. fidelity to the Christian message as it comes to us through the Church; 4. an institutional commitment to the service of the people of God and of the human family in their pilgrimage to the transcendent goal which gives meaning to life. (13)

In this respect, the university has its mission from the "heart of the Church" (*ex corde ecclesiae*): the promotion of the good and true in close critical engagement with the "treasury of human knowledge," oriented toward a single vision of the meaning of human life as fulfilled in praise to God. This is not a pragmatic or economic *telos* or rationale, and the special character of the Catholic university is further specified in terms of four requirements permeating all research (understood as "studies," thereby including teaching and learning), not just theological, but in every faculty and discipline. It offers the possibility of slowly ending the fragmentation of knowledge, not by having Mass on campus, or taking part in good works, both of which are central to the document, but in terms of an intellectual enterprise.

The first requirement nicely frames the awesome task: "the search for an integration of knowledge" (16). It is necessary to work toward "a higher synthesis of knowledge" on theological grounds, for in this "alone lies the possibility of satisfying that thirst for truth which is profoundly inscribed on the heart of the human person" (ibid.). There is no attempt actually to spell out any particular model of integration, except to denote that theology and philosophy have a vital role in developing this integration: "Aided by the specific contributions of philosophy and theology, university scholars will be engaged in a constant effort to determine the relative place and meaning of each of the various disciplines within the context of a vision of the human person and the world that is enlightened by the Gospel" (ibid.).

There is no attempt to deny the *proper* autonomy of disciplines and their varying methods in making this claim, but the insistence that their overall place and meaning be defined in terms of a Christian vision.

The second requirement for all research is the promotion of the "dialogue between faith and reason." This section is vital, for it indicates that there can be no improper interference with the proper autonomy of different disciplines, and academic research is in one sense the free pursuit of truth. However, there is a confidence, born out of the theological insight that God is creator, that there is a genuine harmony between reason properly exercised and faith correctly understood. Hence such a dialogue demonstrates that "methodological research within every branch of learning, when carried out in a truly scientific manner and in accord with moral norms, can never conflict with faith. For the things of the earth and the concerns of faith derive from the same God" (17). This is not to deny that historically this tension has been explosive at times, and a particular conception of faith has sometimes blindly resisted the force of graced reason, but then to imagine otherwise is surely naive. However, to imagine that there is no real harmony between faith and reason (understood as graced reason, not pure reason or pure rationality) falls short of the Christian vision here presented.

Third, and dependent on the truth of the first two, is that all research must bear a "concern for the ethical and moral implications both of its methods and of its discoveries" (18). That both methods and discoveries are highlighted, reflects concern with both means and ends in all research, with a single abiding priority, especially relevant to the natural sciences: "It is essential that we be convinced of the priority of the ethical over the technical, of the primacy of the person over things" (ibid.). What is important about this is that all human endeavor is constrained by a moral purpose, which cannot be divorced from the intellectual. Research for its own sake is not possible, unless it conform to this questioning.

The final point returns to the "theological perspective" underpinning all research, one of the major concerns of my own work. In contrast to the one-way traffic of the University of Paris, where theology dictated to the other disciplines, the theological understanding suggested here, although not unpacked in minute detail, envisages mutual conversations and enrichment, with theology as the initiator, as it is able to straddle the disciplinary boundaries of each subject. Theology:

> serves all other disciplines in their search for meaning, not only by helping them to investigate how their discoveries will affect individuals and society but also by bringing a perspective and an orientation not contained within

their own methodologies. In turn, interaction with these other disciplines and their discoveries enriches theology, offering it a better understanding of the world today, and making theological research more relevant to current needs. Because of its specific importance among the academic disciplines, every Catholic university should have a faculty, or at least a chair, of theology. (19)

The latter is in stark contrast to the demise and even prohibition of theology in many universities. What is significant about this part of the document is its refusal to leave any corner of human knowledge untouched by the gospel, and a refusal to inhibit the university in any inappropriate manner. As we shall see, the practice and the theory are not always one, but then it would be impossible to judge one without the other.

The document then attends to the university community (21–6) specifying the necessity of its Catholic character, without being exclusive, and the vital role of lay Catholics in the current and future development of the Catholic university. It also addresses the Catholic University "in the Church" (27–9), in terms of local, national, and universal loyalty. The institutional fidelity of the University means a "recognition of and adherence to the teaching authority of the Church in matters of faith and morals." It is worth noting the special mutual respect called for in regard to non-Catholic members: "Non-Catholic members are required to respect the Catholic character of the University, while the University in turn respects their religious liberty" (28). The role of the theologian will be addressed in chapter four of this book, while also addressing another 1990 Vatican document, referred to in *CU*, issued by the Congregation for the Doctrine of the Faith, *Instruction on the Ecclesial Vocation of the Theologian* (subsequently *IEVT*). Here I will only say that theologians are asked to be involved in "creative research" and enjoy the same freedom as other researchers within the bounds of their employing appropriate methods and principles. They must also "respect the authority of the Bishops, and assent to Catholic doctrine according to the degree of authority with which it is taught" (29). Obviously, all Catholics require this respect of authority, but the theologian's role is particularly significant. As to the travails this may involve, see chapter four. The document then attends to the mission and service of the university to Church and society (31–7). To the former it gives the tools to engage with the world, with full intellectual seriousness, thus helping in the Church's mission, as well as the complex task of cultural dialogue (43–7): extending to dialogue with the modern sciences, ecumenical, and inter-religious dialogue. To society, the Church is most concerned with the promotion of "social justice" (34), even if this requires speaking "uncomfortable truths," and the promotion of the "emerging nations" (34). No one can accuse a Catholic university of not being concerned with the common good, as this section of the document makes clear that the purpose of the university is precisely in promoting the common good, which constantly attends especially to the poor and minority groups (34), as well as advancing human culture. The next section is on pastoral ministry (38–42), followed by cultural dialogue (43–7), and ends with evangelization (48–9), stressing that the university's existence, like the Church, is primarily to proclaim the gospel.

The background of *CU* in the United States can be briefly summarized, with considerable loss of nuance, as the American Catholic Church defending its universities from what was perceived as "outside" interference from Rome, not in a desire to be unaccountable, but in the belief that their accountability was, for the most part, already well established in a number of ways and was delicately related to state and federal funding.[39] The view of the American bishops and the American Catholic universities, at the highest structural levels, was that a good relationship existed between university and Church and that the American situation demanded freedom from canon law requirements, regarding issues related to governance, staffing, curriculum, and academic processes so that universities did not violate the legal requirement for funding that they be not "*pervasively* sectarian."[40] From the viewpoint of the Congregation for Seminaries and Universities, the issue was quite different.[41] The 1917 code of canon law was often interpreted to mean that Catholic universities were under the canonical jurisdiction of the Congregation, and therefore, while answerable to their local and national

---

[39] Michael Buckley puts it well: "Many in the Catholic academy have been alienated by what they see as an excessive centralization in the church and more particularly in the fields of education—by the impositions of mandates, professions of faith, and oaths of fidelity and by repeated reports of the unwarranted use of the present powers of the Holy See to inhibit academic appointments or promotions or public recognition through honorary degrees. This is admittedly a very serious situation, but to cite it as grounds for denying the central summons of *Ex corde Ecclesia* a sympathetic hearing would be tragic." in ed. John P. Langan, *Catholic Universities in Church and Society: A Dialogue on Ex Corde Ecclesiae*, Georgetown University Press, Washington DC, 1993, p. 87.

[40] See Philip R. Moots and Edward McGlynn Gaffney Jr., *Church and Campus: Legal Issues in Religiously Affiliated Higher Education*, Notre Dame University Press, Notre Dame, Indiana, 1979, pp. 21–5, covers the three landmark decisions on this issue regarding whether Catholic universities are "pervasively sectarian." See also the legal discussion in ed. Langan, *Catholic Universities*, pp. 153–96. Conn, *Catholic Universities*, pp. 185–242 examines episcopal and university responses to Roman curial attempts to resolve outstanding issues.

[41] In 1967 Pope Paul VI gave it the name 'Sacra Congregatio pro Institutione Catholica.' Today's name, the Congregation for Catholic Education (in Seminaries and Institutes of Study), was established in 1988 under Pope John Paul II.

bishops, were finally answerable to, and could be directed by, the Congregation.[42] There was recognition of the complex funding issue by the
Congregation, but it was felt that this did not necessarily bear upon the
canonical jurisdiction under which the university was obliged. These two
differing views were pronounced on from the Congregation when it officially disagreed with the widely influential view of a canon and civil lawyer
at the Catholic University of America, John J. McGrath.[43] McGrath had
argued that American universities were exempt from canonical regulation as
they were not ecclesial juridic persons. They were constituted through the
state by federal authority and were therefore "governed by the American
law and not by canon law."[44] McGrath was clear that those in religious
orders, who worked in the university, were obliged by canon law, but the
institution *per se* was not. The Congregation responded in 1974 clearly
stating that the "so called 'McGrath thesis' . . . has never been considered
valid by our Congregation and has never been accepted."[45] The Congregation's view was that even if a university was not canonically founded
(instituted by the Holy See directly, or by its mandate) by virtue of being
founded by religious, the body thus founded was an ecclesial juridic person.
Two questions were central: first, were Catholic universities, as institutions,
bound by canon law? That is, were they or were they not ecclesial juridic
persons? And if so, second, to whom were they bound? Resistance to the
first was strong, and even when the first was conceded, the subsequent
binding was then often understood in terms of the local and national hierarchy and not to the Roman See.

In some respects, as with this entire issue, there was a simple underlying
issue at stake: *ecclesiology*. The Americans tended toward subsidiarity (the
principle of allowing decisions to be made at the lowest appropriate level),
helped here by the non-juridical and pastorally oriented Vatican II—hence
their emphasis lay on universities working together with the US bishops,
not with the Roman Congregations. On the other hand the Congregation

---

[42] Canon 1376, s. 1 was contested from the outset regarding its scope. See Alexander F.
Sokolich, *Canonical Provisions for Universities and Colleges: A Historical Synopsis and Canonical
Commentary*, Catholic University of America Press, Washington DC, 1956, who traces the
debate.

[43] McGrath's position was not unopposed from within the US, see for example Adam J.
Maida, *Ownership, Control and Sponsorship of Catholic Institutions*, Pennsylvania Catholic Conference, Harrisburg, Pennsylvania, 1975, who cites other important objectors to McGrath's
thesis. Maida also notes the wide acceptance of McGrath's position, pp. 7–9.

[44] Cited in an interview: Carl Balcerak, "Path to Institutions' Autonomy"; *The National
Catholic Reporter*, 20 December, 1967, p. 9; cited in Conn, *Catholic Universities*, p. 196.

[45] Ed. William A. Schumacher, *Roman Replies 1982*, Canon Law Society, Washington DC,
1982, pp. 7–8.

was not bypassing subsidiarity, but rather wanting to see it through to its apparent logical conclusion: answerability to Rome, and the provision of channels for this to take place. In this sense James Provost's comments are most germane: "The difficulty with subsidiarity is that it means different things to different people. What is one person's 'appropriate level of responsibility' may be seen by another as inappropriate intervention."[46]

The revision of the code of canon law in 1983 simply raised these questions again, specifying further definition to controversial questions, which in turn were further controverted. However, they represent a significant step in terms of the issues we are examining, and *CU* and *IEVT* advance no further than restating these canons as determinative for understanding the nature of a Catholic university, but they do help clarify what counts as a Catholic university. I shall look at three issues in canons 807–14 dealing with "Catholic Universities and Other Institutes of Higher Education."[47] These canons are found in *The Code of Canon Law*, Book III, dealing with "The Teaching Office of the Church." Canon law reflects the laws germane to the Church as a social body and it is binding upon members of that body. The code of 1917 was revised after the Second Vatican Council, with a draft of the revision in 1980, the revision in 1983, and then subsequent clarifications in *CU* and *IEVT* in 1990. This examination will allow us to identify minimal and maximal models, although these labels are loose and the field is far too complex to yield such a clear spectrum of answers. This will, nevertheless, allow us to address the three issues of this section.

On the first issue regarding ecclesial juridic persons (institutions who act as official representatives of the Church), Conn nicely summarizes a number of significant US responses to these canons: "These commentators essentially argued that the canons did not apply to US universities since most of them were not juridic persons and were therefore not subject to rights and obligations within the Church."[48] This focuses the first of the three issues of this section in a helpful manner. The accountability of a Catholic university is determined by whether it is an ecclesial juridic person. If it is, then canon law clearly specifies the manner in which accountability is to take place. Admittedly, the interpretation of canons 810–14, and especially 810 and 812,

---

[46] James Provost, "A Canonical Commentary on 'Ex corde Ecclesiae'" in ed. Langan, *Catholic Universities*, pp. 105–36: p. 129.

[47] See *The Code of Canon Law*, New Revised English translation, HarperCollins, London, 1997; and see Conn's commentary in *Catholic Universities*, on "US Catholic Universities and the 1983 Code of Canon Law," pp. 243–90, and James A. Coriden, "Book III, The Teaching Office of the Church" in eds. Coriden, Thomas J. Green, and Donald E. Heintschel, *The Code of Canon Law: A Text and Commentary*, Paulist Press, New York, 1985, pp. 574–5.

[48] Conn, *Catholic Universities*, p. 288.

has been subject to extensive debate (see below). However, in principle, the canons (and *IEVT* and *CU*)[49] stipulate that the local bishops and the episcopal conference are one important locus of ecclesial accountability for Catholic universities. How this relationship is implemented is left unclear in the canons, but made more concrete, although no less problematic in *CU*. *CU* requires that canons 810 and 812 (included in the general norms of *CU*, Part II) "be applied concretely at the local and regional levels by episcopal conferences and other assemblies of Catholic hierarchy . . . taking into account the statutes of each university or institute and, as far as possible and appropriate, civil law" (Pt. II, art. 1, s. 2). Provost's commentary on this explication is important. He rightly argues that "This provision is a clear example of healthy subsidiarity within the church," acknowledging that the differences of situation make "a precise law for application to all Catholic universities . . . impossible."[50] The same section of *CU* continues that of these new ordinances: "After inspection (*inspectio*) by the Holy See [note 44], these local or regional 'ordinances' will be valid for all Catholic universities and other Catholic institutes of higher studies in the region." There is considerable debate as to whether *inspectio* implies *recognita* "reviewed," such that the Holy See would have the power to amend and change episcopal decrees, or simply that *inspectio* means that they be submitted to the Holy See before being enacted. The problem lies in footnote 44 of *CU*, referring to canon 455, section 2, where *recognita* is used, and grants the power of revision. However, some lawyers maintain that in so far as *inspectio* is used in the main body of the text rather than *recognitio* the former interpretation should hold.[51]

Hence, despite all these problems, it would be right to conclude that even were a university an ecclesial juridic person, the manner of its relation to the national episcopacy and its relation to Rome in terms of the governance of Catholic universities is still open to differing legal interpretation and national variations. A maximal position would require *recognitio* authority for Rome. A minimal position must at least hold *inspectio*, but a minimal position may also avoid inspection by deeming the university a non-juridic person. It would also be correct to say that in so much as a university were

[49]   *IEVT*, 37; *CU*, pt. II, art. 1, s. 1; art. 5, s. 2.
[50]   Provost, in ed. Langan, *Catholic Universities*, p. 109; the second quote is a citation from the official commentary on the 1985 draft of the 1990 document found in *Origins*, 15, 43, 1986, p. 708.
[51]   James Provost for example. See in contrast, Conn, *Catholic Universities*. It should be noted that the Holy See employed both *recognita* and *inspectio* in their review of the US bishops' first draft of *CU*'s Application (1966), rejecting it, and then requiring significant revisions to the second draft (1999), then finally approving the third version (2000). I am grateful to Patrick J. Reilly for alerting me to this "resolution" of the debate. The published version of the Application can be found at: www.usccb.org/bishops/mandatumguidelines.htm

not an ecclesial juridic person the precise manner in which they are Catholic universities is left to individual institutions to pursue with the appropriate ecclesial authorities (local and national bishops), without change of statutes or introduction of ordinances.[52] While the debate is unresolved, the minimal position is sometimes viewed as incoherent and illogical by supporters of the maximal. For example, the maximalist Conn proposes that:

> if the argument is correct that the lack of juridic personality frees the institu-
> tions from legal obligations and from any relationship with ecclesial authority,
> it would follow that those same institutions would also be deprived of certain
> rights, most significant of which is the right to present themselves as
> Catholic.[53]

The problem for Conn's argument is that the minimal model does not break free from "any relationship" with "ecclesial authority," but only a juridical canonical one. Conn is entirely correct, in my view, as is the dominant minimal view, that some "relationship" to the episcopacy is required for an institution to be deemed "Catholic."

As a statement of fact it must be said that both the minimal and maximal positions currently exist within the Roman Catholic communion without a definitive pronouncement excluding either. *CU*, following seven years after the revision of the Code of Canon Law in 1983, still failed to resolve the question of whether American Catholic universities were ecclesial juridic persons.[54] Finally, in 2000, after a six-year consultation process with repre-sentatives of the American university presidents and other bodies, the National Conference of Catholic Bishops published *Ex Corde Ecclesiae: An Application to the United States*. This took effect from 2001, and, despite many concerns, has not (yet) resulted in lawsuits against Catholic institutions or a brain drain away from them. The *Application*, with careful qualifications that possibly allow ample room for maneuver, makes five definite moves, without, however, fully resolving issues discussed above or below on certain

---

[52] See Frederick R. McManus, "'The Canons on Catholic Higher Education' prepared for the Association of Catholic Colleges and Universities," April 1983 (ACCU)—cited frequently by Conn. I have not consulted this document myself. See also Ladislas Orsy, "The Mandate to Teach Theological Disciplines: Glosses on Canon 812 of the New Code," *Theological Studies*, 44, 1983, pp. 476–88; and Coriden's "Book III," for legal interpretations of the 1983 code.

[53] Conn, *Catholic Universities*, p. 288.

[54] None of the respondents calls into question James Provost's canonical commentary on Pt. II, art. 1, s. 1 of *CU*, where he says that "This norm does not determine which institutions of higher learning are included as 'Catholic universities' and 'Catholic institutes of higher studies.' It merely asserts that whatever institutions fall within these categories are bound by these norms." in ed. Langan, *Catholic Universities*, p. 109.

points of canon law. First, university presidents should be Roman Catholic and are obliged to make a profession of faith to the local bishop or his delegate. If the person is not a Catholic, they must make a commitment to the university's Catholic mission and identity. Second, the majority of boards of directors should be Catholic, whenever possible, and be informed of their responsibilities for the Catholic character of the university. Third, the same applies to university professors. Fourth, academic freedom is proper to research and teaching, within the confines of "the truth and the common good." Fifth, and most contentiously, it agrees that all those teaching theological disciplines must receive a mandate from the local bishop, but it is up to the local bishop to pursue this matter. It is too early to see whether the *Application* will help restore the character of Catholic universities.

The second interesting issue of the revised code was the responsibility of the university to oversee hiring and firing in line with Catholic doctrinal and moral teaching. Canon 810, s. 1 and s. 2 state:

> s. 1: In catholic universities it is the duty of the authority which is competent in accordance with the statutes to ensure the appointment of teachers who are suitable both in scientific and pedagogical expertise and in integrity of doctrine and uprightness of life, and if these qualities are lacking, to ensure that they are removed from office, in accordance with the procedure determined in the statutes.

> s. 2: The Bishops' Conference and the diocesan Bishops concerned have the duty and the right of seeing to it that, in these universities, the principles of catholic doctrine are faithfully observed.

These two sections raise a crucial question: what is the relationship of the local bishop and the national bishops' conference to the process of assessing the credentials of staff appropriate in a Catholic university? The maximal position tends to see a strong and important role for the episcopacy in these matters, so that the Catholic identity of the institution is safeguarded. Perhaps Francisco Javier Urrutia, writing before *CU*, expresses the strongest maximalist position. Urrutia argues for the bishops' right of vigilance, as operative within the concept of canonical mission (that is, the university as a whole is carrying out the work of the Church, and therefore are representatives of the bishops), such that the *entire* teaching staff of the institution be bound to obedience to the bishop in their academic role.[55] Conn, more cautiously, and with greater textual fidelity, argues that only theologians are

---

[55]   Conn, *Catholic Universities*, p. 263.

required to gain a formal mandate from the local bishop (see below), but Conn is in agreement (in spirit) with Urrutia, viewing all members of a Catholic university as under the jurisdiction of the local bishop. The way the local or national bishops oversee the Catholic nature of the university must be discreet and prudent, but the overseeing role must be exercised—and can be legitimately required.

Obviously, section 2 does make it clear that no Catholic university can be Catholic without some episcopal oversight. Interestingly enough, and not surprisingly, the minimal model would also share this position. It would differ on the legal nature and scope of this "overseeing" role. Hence, James Coriden admits to the importance of the episcopal "influence," but not to any legal involvement in due process sanctioned by the university's statutes. In his commentary on s. 1, he argues that this canon grants full autonomy in hiring and firing to the competent university authority.[56] This reading, contrary to Conn and Urrutia (admittedly, writing pre-CU),[57] does not minimize the final sentence of s. 1, regarding removal from office, but rather interprets that process, as with hiring, as part of the "standards of fairness and good practice which are accepted in the academic community of the country or culture."[58] (In US universities there are usually a number of clauses for "termination of cause" such as "acts of moral turpitude" or "unbecoming conduct.") We will return to this issue in a moment, but the point to be made here is that s. 1 can be interpreted, in the light of the revisions of the earlier draft of s. 2 in 1980 (see below), and the fact that s. 2 is made distinct from s. 1, to emphasize that the Catholic university is free from legal intervention from bishops into its due process, unless its ordinances or statutes require or allow for this. The way in which national episcopates implement CU will vary and it is too early to make any judgement as yet.

It is important to note that the resistance to the 1980 draft of s. 2, regarding the authority of bishops, came not from those who opposed any episcopal influence whatsoever. This was taken for granted in a Catholic university. The resistance was to the form in which the canon expressed this. It stated that the episcopal conference and appropriate diocesan bishop had the "right and obligation" to "likewise demand that, if faith and morals

---

[56] Coriden, "Book III," pp. 574–5. But, even if universities were not ecclesial juridical persons, were they to implement this, they would require massive legal resources to change the contractual terms of employment, so as not to be vulnerable to damaging litigation: see Philip Burling and Gregory T. Moffatt, "Notes from the Other Side of the Wall" in ed. Langan, Catholic Universities, pp. 158–62.

[57] Conn, Catholic Universities, pp. 261–2.

[58] Coriden, "Book III," p. 574.

require it, teachers be removed from their office."[59] This draft was strongly opposed by American Catholic universities and some American bishops for failing to acknowledge the appropriate autonomy of the university and the laity, affirmed in Vatican II, and for being utterly inapplicable in the US context.[60] Significantly, it was dropped and revised with the present wording.

Hence regarding the question: "What is the role of the bishops' conference in overseeing the university?' canon 810 can be interpreted minimally and maximally, with both minimal and maximal positions assenting to the necessary "relationship" of university with episcopacy, while the manner of this relationship in exact legal terms is open to considerable variation. This canon therefore simply raises the same issues as above: if ecclesial intervention takes on a maximal form, this could jeopardize the autonomy of the university in the view of the general public and of state or federal funding bodies. It need not, but it might. If episcopal relations take no form at all, then strangely "Catholic universities" would be totally unrelated to the hierarchic Church. This latter stance would fall below a minimal relation. Between minimal and maximal positions there is considerable variety and it is important to note that the Association of Catholic Colleges and Universities (ACCU) never once suggests that there be no relationship with bishops, local or national, and thus never strays below the minimal position (as I have defined it). *CU* does not clarify this matter further, except requiring the "local bishop" to resolve any concerns with the "competent university authorities in accordance with established procedures, and, if necessary, with the help of the Holy See" (art. 5, s. 2). However, since "established procedures" only relate to "ecclesial juridical bodies," a category denied by most American Catholic universities (relating to art. 3, s. 3 of *CU*), the only advance here is putting the initiative for resolving differences with the local bishop.

Even if a maximal reading of canon law were held, there are important unresolved questions regarding the potential clash between civil and canon law as to hiring and firing. This factor is central to the US debate. In so much as staff are chosen or dismissed on religious grounds, the university begins to stray into the territory that might constitute "pervasive sectarianism" and disqualify it from funding, as well as make it vulnerable to costly litigation. The civil law issues are complex and untested. Philip Burling and Geoffrey Moffatt make a strong case for avoiding reliance on canon law regarding hiring and firing, given the high probability of litigation and

---

[59]   Canon 765, 1980 draft, recalling can. 1381, s. 3 of the 1917 code.
[60]   Conn, *Catholic Universities*, pp. 259–60 citing the ACCU and the Canon Law Society of America.

possible disqualification from state and federal funding.[61] On the other hand, David Thomas Link and Patrick J. Reilly are confident that these are surmountable problems.[62] What is clear is that both maximal and minimal positions are agreed that hiring and firing are legitimately related to ecclesial identity, but they differ concerning the manner of implementing this in relation to "outside" intervention. Episcopal "influence" is uncontested.[63]

Maximalists and minimalists on the relationship of the episcopal influence on understanding and utilizing right belief and practice in the hiring and firing of staff both agree that maintaining a Catholic character in staff is a legitimate enterprise, requisite for the intellectual character of the institution, not just for pastoral duties. Some minimalists would construe "influence" extremely vaguely and argue implementation is both impracticable and undesirable. Such is the position of David J. O'Brien, but in my construal of the matter it would be difficult to see what constitutes a Catholic university for such a minimalist.[64] Some ultra-maximalists, like Francisco Urrutia, seem to see the university as almost identical to the Church, and entirely in terms of "canonical mission," such that it be granted no appropriate autonomous character and thus be understood as an ecclesial university, fully subject to the episcopate. Intellectually, Urrutia's position is at least cogent in refusing autonomy to the secular order, and seeing the entire intellectual processes of the university as bearing upon its Catholic character. The main problem with such a maximalist position is its non-conformity to episcopal teaching in *CU*!

The third issue about the revised code concerns canon 812, one of the shortest but most contentious, and reiterated and cited in *CU* and in *IEVT* in 1990: "Those who teach theological subjects in any institute of higher studies must have a mandate [mandatum] from the competent ecclesiastical authority." This canon was entirely new and not found in the earlier 1917 code of canon law. During the drafting of the 1983 code, it aroused serious protest on three grounds: well-qualified faculty and students would not be

---

[61] In ed. Langan, *Catholic Universities*, pp. 153–75.

[62] Link, "Comments," in ed. Langan, *Catholic Universities*, pp. 187–92. See also Patrick J. Reilly, "Funding for Faith-Based Higher Education," *Capital Research Center: Foundation Watch*, March 2002, pp. 1–7.

[63] I have left untouched a host of other questions related to this canon, such as: who is to determine, and in what manner, the doctrinal orthodoxy and uprightness of life of academic staff; how are these to be defined in legal contracts if they are to be binding? Leaving these untouched does not indicate their unimportance, but I am presently attending to specific questions that do not require us to address such questions here.

[64] O'Brien in ed. Langan, *Catholic Universities*, pp. 20–8, and Michael J. Buckley, *The Catholic University as Promise and Project: Reflections in a Jesuit Idiom*, Georgetown University, Washington DC, 1998, ch. 3.

attracted to Catholic institutions on the grounds that this canon would "immediately render suspect the legitimate freedom of professors";[65] the reputation among other American institutions would be diminished; and funding (around $500 million per annum) would be jeopardized. The Canon Law Society of America also commented quite sharply that "Rather than safeguard the orthodoxy of Catholic teaching . . . this legislation would, in fact, destroy the ability of the American Catholic collegiate enterprise to survive."[66] The protests were submitted but did not lead to any revision of canon 812.

In one sense, there was no real question that those teaching Catholic theology were accountable for what they taught, and had a responsibility to the Church and the faithful. There was concern about the impact of this requirement in terms of its apparent conflict with academic freedom. Despite maximalist criticisms of sections of the American Church, this point is often overlooked. The real dispute was whether this responsibility was part of the institutions' canonically legal responsibility. When the revisions were published and included canon 812, Ladislas Orsy formulated a response that was representative of the response of most American institutions.[67] Given that they had interpreted canons 807–14 as not applying to American universities as they were not ecclesial juridic persons, Orsy interpreted the canon as a requirement upon an individual theologian to gain from his or her own local bishop, the "mandate." This reading overcame the serious reservations aired in the drafting period. Every term of Orsy's conclusion was open to contention. Who was responsible for seeking the mandate? Who could grant it? And what indeed was a "mandate"? In so much as a "mandate" was not a "canonical mission," the term dropped from the 1980 draft of the 1983 revisions, there was considerable debate about the very meaning of "mandate."[68] Why did this situation arise?

"Mandate" was a term used in Vatican II's *Decree on the Apostolate of the*

---

[65] Conn, *Catholic Universities*, p. 267. Note the use of "suspect." There is concern about its public relations effects, not *per se* a question against the importance of accountability.

[66] Michael C. Cannily, OSFS, "De Munere Docendi: Some Observations" in *Proceedings of the Forty-fourth Annual Convention, Hartford, Connecticut, October 18–21, 1982*, Canon Law Society of America, Washington DC, 1983, p. 231.

[67] Ladislas Orsy, "The Mandate to Teach"; see also the more detailed interpretation by Robert P. Deeley, *The Mandate for Those Who Teach Theology in Institutes of Higher Studies: An Interpretation of the Meaning of Canon 812 of the Code of Canon Law*, Pontifical Gregorian University, Rome, 1986.

[68] See Orsy, "The Mandate"; Deeley, *The Mandate*; John J. Strynkowski, "Theological Pluralism and Canonical Mandate," *The Jurist*, 43, 1983, pp. 524–33; Sharon A. Euart, "Comment" in ed. Langan, *Catholic Universities*, pp. 137–46; and the essays in ed. Leo J. Donovan SJ, *Cooperation between Theologians and the Ecclesiastical Magisterium*, Canon Law Society of America, Washington DC, 1982.

Laity, para. 24, to describe the hierarchy's closer association with legitimate forms of lay activity, which have their own autonomy, but as being related to the mission of the Church. "Canonical mission" in the same paragraph denotes functions "which are more closely connected with pastoral duties" normally undertaken by ordained priests or religious, such as the teaching of doctrine, certain liturgical functions, and the care of souls. Here the laity are proper representatives of the hierarchy and therefore subject to supervision. Nevertheless, subsequent interpretations of "mandate" vary enormously. Conn, for example, acknowledges that it should *not* be conflated with canonical mission:

> The teacher of theology who has such a mandate teaches in his own name and not in the name of the bishop, for the roles of the two are distinct. Still, the theologian does his teaching, writing, and research on behalf of the Church, that is, for the Church's benefit and within its communion. The bishop's mandate is an attestation that the theologian is in ecclesial communion. That a theologian needs no canonical mission suggests that he holds no ecclesiastical office.[69]

It is interesting that he distinguishes his position from that of his teacher, Urrutia, who sees the terms as interchangeable. In this respect the CDF's use of the terms "canonical mission" and "mandate" in its interpretation of canon 812 in *IEVT*, para. 37, does not clarify the matter, for canonical mission would clearly apply to ecclesiastical universities and could thus be discounted as an interpretation of "mandate."

John Strynkowski interprets it as an "expression of communion" between theologians and hierarchy in so much as a Catholic theologian is required clearly to present the teaching of the Church, and identify his or her own private opinions and views that depart from those teachings.[70] Ladislas Orsy reads it as a specific commission to teach, clearly "less ponderous than a canonical mission, which suggests that an ecclesiastical office is being conferred, but more significant than a simple permission since mandate involves the notion of the deputy teaching in a name other than his own alone."[71] Conn tries to avoid this implication, and a minimalist like Orsy, in some situations, adopts a more maximalist view of mandate. John Alessandro gives a similar reading, but defines the specific role of the theologian in terms of the hierarchy's "deputation" or "agency."[72] McManus denies to it any specific

---

[69] Conn, *Catholic Universities*, 278.
[70] Strynkowski, "Theological Pluralism."
[71] See note 18 in Orsy, "The Mandate," p. 480.
[72] See note 17 in ibid., p. 480.

legal, juridical, or ecclesiastical force, based on the fact that "canonical mission" was dropped from the text and "mandate" used instead. In his view "mandate" allows a "degree of recognition and perhaps attestation of one's role within the church community."[73] This amounts to a purely administrative gesture. Coriden seems also to give this minimal (and legitimate) reading when he says the mandate is "not a formal association with the Church's mission or ministry of teaching."[74]

It is not possible to adjudicate between these views, although it seems clear, at least in a negative definition, that a mandate cannot be seen to entail the work normally undertaken by a bishop. Nevertheless, it is more than simply carrying out duties appropriate to the laity's status which relate to the purely "secular" realm. Furthermore, negatively, it does not seem to be interchangeable with "canonical mission"; otherwise this would make nonsense of the latter term being dropped and replaced by "mandate." For the purpose of my argument, the important point is that there is agreement between the minimalists and maximalists on one very important issue.[75] It is nicely summarized by Sharon Euart, who writes as a member of the National Conference of American Catholic Bishops, after a very helpful survey of the variety of definitions of mandate: "What is common to the various interpretations is that some ecclesiastical authorization is required for those who teach theological disciplines in Catholic colleges and universities. The implications of that authorization continue to be explored."[76]

---

[73] As cited by Conn, *Universities*, p. 276, from McManus, "The Canons," p. 14.

[74] Coriden, "Book III," p. 576.

[75] It would be accurate to say that most American academic theologians have resisted the "imposition" of the mandate on pragmatic grounds. O'Brien and Gallin, for example, contest the need for juridical reform, while nevertheless calling for serious reforms in curriculum and personal orientation among faculty and administrators. See Alice Gallin, *Negotiating Identity*, University of Notre Dame Press, Indiana, 2000, pp. 162–74; David J. O'Brien, *From the Heart of the American Church*, Orbis, New York, 1994, 69–95; and also Peter Steinfels, *A People Adrift*, Simon & Schuster, New York, 2003, pp. 131–61, who is also very critical of juridical reform. All three are committed to developing the project of a Catholic University. Theirs is a "bottom-up" approach, based on sensitivity to the importance of inner and organic rather than imposed changes from outside, to the different populations and social contexts of each institutions rather than a centralized and universalized model serving all contexts. However, their ecclesiologies oddly minimize the institutional and juridical aspects of being an ecclesial community, citing the American context rather than theological arguments for this lacuna.

[76] Euart, "Comment," p. 141. See the US Conference of Bishops "Guidelines Concerning the Academic *Mandatum* in Catholic Universities (Canon 812)," 2001, currently (2004) in force: www.usccb.org/bishops/mandatumguidelines.htm. The two issues particularly pertinent at the time of writing (2004) are: should universities and/or bishops make public the names of those who have received the *mandatum*; and should a Catholic university require the *mandatum* for theology professors as a condition of hiring and tenure? In current practice, both are not the case. William L. Portier makes the pertinent point that the heated and

In this bewildering pluralist context the achievement of canon 812, for both maximalist and minimalist, is to stress the ecclesial context of theology—such as I have been arguing for in this book, while leaving it an open and complex question as to the institutional arrangements of this practice.[77] This inspection of canon 812 has also addressed the question: to whom are Catholic theologians responsible? The answer by both minimal and maximal positions is: Catholic theologians are accountable to academic colleagues properly trained in the discipline, and to the magisterium of the bishops.[78] This answer clearly leaves open the exact and appropriate channels of this relationship. However, it does allow us tentatively to resolve the questions of this section.

We might draw an initial conclusion: the models of ecclesial accountability for a Catholic university can be understood both minimally and maximally. The minimal understanding certainly allows for a Catholic university (in a non-juridic canonical sense) that qualifies for state or federal grants and funding as is the current situation in the US, and regards accountability to variously understood forms of ecclesial authority as part of its purpose. This might be in terms of its relationship either to its local bishop, or the episcopal conference, or the religious congregation that relates to its foundation, and the practical manner in which these relationships are institutionally embedded might vary enormously. While this approach is not centrally controlled, or uniform, it relies on an ecclesiology that emphasizes the local and national Church's responsibility for its institutions. Its ecclesiology emphasizes subsidiarity. Its alleged benefits are twofold: Catholic universities can compete with the best, and can retain their character while retaining state and federal funding. Without the latter, they could not achieve their purpose. In contrast, the maximal position holds that canonical requirements upon an institution would not compromise funding as the US Constitution also

---

protracted debate on the mandatum has sadly distracted Catholic institutions from focussing on the wider and deeper question: the transformation of the curriculum. His use of *Fides et Ratio* and *Ex Corde Ecclesia* to show how both the mandatum and curriculum changes are deeply compatible with academic freedom is most instructive. See William L. Portier, "What Does it Mean to be *Ex Corde Ecclesiae*? Toward an Alternative Academic Culture," *Delta Epsilon Sigma Journal*, 42, 3, 1997, pp. 77–84; and "Reason's 'Rightful Autonomy' in *Fides et Ratio* and the Continuous Renewal of Catholic Higher Education in the United States," *Communio*, 26, 1999, 541–56.

[77] In researching this chapter, I wrote to my own bishop seeking a mandate, as I interpreted canon 812 along with Conn and Deeley to oblige an individual theologian working in a non-Catholic institution to seek the mandate if they were teaching Catholic theology. He did not share my interpretation and I was released from this obligation.

[78] In this sense, *IEVT*, para. 30 makes out a very legitimate case for the limits of absolute freedom self-imposed by a Catholic theologian.

safeguards the rights, privately and institutionally, to practice one's religion.[79] The issue of "pervasively sectarian" has never been properly defined in US legal history, but once that fuzzy line has been crossed, funding would be at stake. Many argue that keeping the line fuzzy is of enormous benefit for Catholic universities. However, maximalists are confident that they would not be trespassing over the line. In this sense, for them, the future of US Catholic universities is not at stake, but simply their refusal to be juridically accountable to the ecclesia, understood in terms of the appropriate Roman Congregation and the magisterium, notwithstanding the role of the local and national US Church. I am not concerned to adjudicate on this complex matter. In terms of my own argument, there is no guarantee that a minimal model would withstand the secularizing process I have been lamenting, and indeed, may accelerate it. But, of course, it may not.[80] The maximal model, as portrayed above, is concerned to safeguard the character of Catholic universities through canon law. In one sense, without resolving the thorny question of ecclesial juridic persons, this concern is entirely legitimate. However, neither the minimal nor the maximal position succeeds if it is not driven by a vision of what constitutes a Catholic university, and in this respect, there is no better guide than CU.

We have also seen that the theologian requires a special mandate, and that this mandate is not really objectionable, but intrinsic to the vocation of the theologian. The ACCU's and the Canon Law Society of America's objections to canon 812 were never against either the requirement of the theologian's ecclesial accountability, or that it strictly contravened academic freedom. The objections were concerned with the adverse legal-financial and recruitment-publicity effects of such a public requirement. Hence, despite the chasms between minimalists and maximalists, there is some theological agreement that is germane to my argument. In this respect, my limited conclusion is that extra-ecclesial funding and proper ecclesial accountability (both minimal and maximal) are not incompatible in our test case scenario. The requirement for theologians to be especially accountable is also not incompatible with academic freedom, proper research methods, and genuine research. Thus, their Catholic character need not hinder the best research universities. Indeed, the opposite could be true. My argu-

---

[79] See especially David Thomas Link's legal comments in ed. Langan, *Catholic Universities*, pp. 187–92; and the nuanced commentary from civil and ecclesial lawyers Burling and Moffatt, ibid., pp. 153–75, and especially their constructive suggestions, pp. 174–5.

[80] Buckley, *Catholic University*, argues a minimal position in full accord with *CU*, relentlessly criticizing the secularizing process. See also his optimistic reading of *CU* in ed. Langan, *Catholic Universities*, pp. 74–89.

ment only required me to establish this possibility—and I believe I have established it using my test case scenario. It is clear that such a conclusion could not be applied to other ecclesial traditions until tradition-specific investigations were concluded. Further, it is clear that other countries with different funding assumptions will reach different outcomes. In this section I have sought to show why public non-ecclesial funding is compatible with a maximal and a minimal understanding of a Catholic university.

This chapter will by no means have convinced readers who are in basic opposition to my proposals. However, what I have sought to do is provide both a practical and theoretical argument for the desirability of a Christian (Catholic) university, which by its very nature is open to engagement with culture (in the broadest sense), and that such an institution is deserving of public monies in societies that are officially either unaligned to any religion (US) or, in some constitutional manner, aligned to Christianity (England). This is the case in the latter even though the majority of people in England are not church attenders.

In the next chapter I continue my argument by attending to the role of prayer. The Babylonian exiles often turned to prayer in their despair. The modern exiled Christians should join their ancient ancestors.

Chapter Four

Why Theologians Must Pray for Release from Exile

I A New Context for University Theology: Ecclesial Prayer

If theology needs to break free from its Babylonian captivity within the confines of the secular university, then theologians need to learn to pray, as part of their vocation as theologians. Such advice may sound impotent in the light of the structural power of modernity, and the type of postliberal university being advocated here is going to require a lot more than prayer. However, I shall be arguing that the type of tradition-specific theology that I am advocating requires prayer as its epistemological presupposition, precisely because theology is primarily concerned with a communal love affair with the living God. Its communal location involves taking seriously, at an epistemological level, much that is involved in prayer: the community of saints, the concept of liturgical time, and the importance of cultivating the virtues. Without prayerfulness in students and teachers of theology, the university cannot produce theologians. I have chosen this specific focus for a number of reasons that should become evident as the argument unfolds. However, by specifying prayer as a "qualification" for being a theologian, I am advancing a vision of theology that might break free from the homogeneous secularization of the disciplines that currently predominates, and offer to students within the university an intellectually rigorous alternative. If I am told that I should teach in a Roman Catholic seminary—a frequent response to my argument—I suggest that one vocation of the Roman Catholic Church requires the rigorous and careful educating of the lay faithful—not just a priestly elite.

> You must be made new in mind and spirit, and put on the new nature. (Eph. 4: 23–4)

Have mercy on me, O God, in your kindness, In your compassion blot out my offence.

O wash me more and more from my guilt and cleanse me from my sin . . .

Indeed you love truth in the heart; then in the secret of my heart teach me wisdom . . .

A pure heart create for me, O God, put a steadfast spirit within me. Do not cast me away from your presence, nor deprive me of your holy spirit. (Psalm 51: 1–2, 6, 10–11)

Quoting biblical texts like this might irritate historical-critical biblical scholars, for I have snatched verses out of historical context and stitched them together in an unchronological fashion. But this is not all. I might also offend those concerned with Jewish-Christian issues, in suggesting an imperialist anti-Jewish hermeneutic, whereby the "New" Testament, placed first, interprets the "Old." And worst of all, some readers may now wonder if this is a pious tract, indistinguishable from a sermon. However, other readers will recognize, if they cultivate certain sectarian habits, that they have prayed these scriptures, perhaps today if they are reading this text on a Friday, from their *Divine Office*. The rest of this chapter works with the specificity of the prayers for Friday, week four, when I began on this chapter. It seems most appropriate to argue for the importance of prayer in the professional training of the theologian by using a communal set of prayers prayed by the universal Church. This is not to privilege the saying of the *Office*, but one has to start somewhere.

The *Divine Office* is a series of prayers, probably dating back to the fourth century, and continuously modified. It is dependent on the psalms, also called the *Liturgy of the Hours*, originating within a monastic setting—sanctifying the different times of the day through prayer and meditation. The Office was sung in Latin until 1963, when Vatican II's *Constitution on the Sacred Liturgy* allowed for the vernacular, and for the first time encouraged lay participation in this prayer cycle. The *Office* was fully revised in Latin by 1971, and the English authorized version that I am using was completed in 1974. A new revision is being prepared. Besides the Proper of the Seasons (Advent, Christmas, Lent, Easter) and Special Solemnities (such as the feasts of the Sacred Heart of Jesus, the Body and Blood of Christ, the Trinity), there is a four-week cycle of prayer, and optional and non-optional feast days celebrating saints, sites, and ceremonies.[1]

[1]   On the *Divine Office* in the modern Church, see Vatican II's *Constitution on the Sacred Liturgy*, ch. IV, paras. 83–101, and Commentary by Josef Andreas Jungmann, in ed. H. Vorgrimler, *Commentary on the Documents of Vatican II*, vol. 1, Burns and Oates, London, 1967, esp. pp. 57–69.

However, those readers disposed toward the martyrs may have used a different set of prayers in their optional celebration of Saint Januarius whose feast day occurs on 19 September (Friday at the time of writing). Perhaps I should have celebrated him, for he was persecuted for not giving due honor to worldly authorities and was beheaded after the wild beasts "could not be provoked" to devour him.[2] Alternatively, I could have celebrated the dour and troubled Saint Emily de Rodat, whose feast day also occurs "today." She was the founder of the Congregation of the Holy Family of Villefranche. Her celebration would have required an alternative Common. The use of either would have raised different questions in their emphases upon the different charisms of our two saints. However, in what follows I shall stick to week four.

To return to my argument: the reader may ask, why cite prayers from the Friday morning *Divine Office* in an "academic" discussion on the nature of theology? Because, as I have been arguing, theology, if it is to be done with full intellectual rigor, cannot be done outside the context of a love affair with God and God's community, the Church. And one cultivated habit of the greatest lovers (and the best theologians) within the Church, is that of prayer. I shall be arguing that good, intellectually rigorous, theology within the university can only be done within the *context of a praying community*, not just nourished by prayer as if an optional and private extra, but also *guided* and *judged* by prayer. These are three distinct epistemological functions.

As a lay Roman Catholic in a secular university, one of these preconditions (a confessional praying communal starting point) is structurally problematic. This involves me in some odd anomalies, such that I could only do my job well if I suggested, which I cannot, that my students take prayer as seriously as their reading lists (although some might fare better with prayer than their reading lists). This is not to argue for either a pietist or a fideist theology department where intellectual rigor and accountability are surrendered, so that bad arguments or poorly researched materials can be acceptable because those who have produced them pray. Nor is it an argument for some magical status for prayer, whereby the painful, laborious slog of research evaporates, and the complex intellectual questions dealt with are miraculously answered. The opening line of this morning's Psalm: "Have mercy on me, O God, in your kindness," indicates that prayer, if anything, should remind us of our creatureliness and our propensity to forget this. Rowan Williams translates this penitence in terms of a warning against theological idolatry when he writes that a prayerful theology "declines the

---

[2]   Rev. Alban Butler, *The Lives of the Fathers: Martyrs and Other Principal Saints*, edited for daily use by Rev. Bernard Kelly, Virtue & Company Ltd, London, vol. 3, 1936, p. 1123.

attempt to take God's point of view (i.e. a 'total perspective')."[3] Likewise, I shall be arguing that prayer, as part of a disciplined love affair with God, has profound epistemological and methodological consequences for the practice of theology.

In 1990 the Vatican Sacred Congregation for the Doctrine of the Faith (CDF), in an interesting and contentious document, addressed the role of the theologian. The title of the document is telling, for it indicates the proper location of theology: *Instruction on the Ecclesial Vocation of the Theologian*,[4] subsequently *IEVT*. What is especially startling in this document, at least for those like myself who inhabit secular university theology departments, is the claim that other than the absolutely vital and necessary academic skills (philology, geography, history, philosophy, and so on), prayer and a commitment to virtue and holiness are *equally* vital and necessary for the academic to be a theologian. Imagine the University of Bristol or Cambridge or Harvard putting into its theology prospectus: "candidates are required to have three very good A levels (or whatever equivalent academic qualifications), and need to be committed to prayer, virtue, and holiness. Frequenting the sacraments is encouraged, sinners are especially welcome—as is a sense of humor."[5]

Let me return to the *IEVT* document and cite a key paragraph:

> Since the object of theology is the Truth which is the living God and His plan for salvation revealed in Jesus Christ, the theologian is called to deepen his own life of faith and continuously unite his scientific research with prayer, [as explained in footnote]. In this way, he will become more open to the "supernatural sense of faith" upon which he depends, and it will appear to him as a sure rule for guiding his reflections and helping him assess the correctness of his conclusions.[6]

There are three very specific claims being made here about prayer, all of which run counter to the institutional presuppositions of secular theology

3 Rowan Williams, "Theological Integrity," *New Blackfriars*, 72, 847, 1991, pp. 140–51: p. 143.

4 Also pertinent as a backcloth to this discussion are the Apostolic Constitution, *Ex Corde Ecclesiae* (1990) and the joint document from the Congregation for Catholic Education and the Pontifical Councils for the Laity and for Culture: *The Presence of the Church in the University and in University Culture* (1984)—in *Briefing*, July 21, 1994, pp. 2–9.

5 I add the latter qualification of humor in memory of the dead body in Umberto Eco's *The Name of the Rose*, trans. William Weaver, Harcourt Brace, San Diego, 1994, and the danger of idolatry ever present in the proposals I am defending. See Karl Josef Kuschel, *Laughter*, SCM, London, 1994 [1993], pp. 22–32 on the dead body in the novel.

6 *IEVT*, para 8; after the word prayer, there is a reference to John Paul II, "Discorse in occasione della consegna del premio internazionale Paulo VI a Hans Urs von Balthasar," June 23, 1984: Insegnamenti di Giovanni Paolo II, VII, 1 (1984), 1911–17. Balthasar is the only modern theologian mentioned in this document and is a significant role model of the ecclesial theologian, not least in terms of method and style.

departments: first, that it facilitates cohabitation with the "object" of study—the triune God, second, that it guides this study, and third, that it helps theologians assess the truthfulness of their study. In this chapter I briefly explore the first two claims, which are not as fully developed in the document.

IEVT attends to the third claim in considerable detail (paragraphs 13–42), and some very important questions regarding "accountability" and "authority" are raised in that section (some of which were discussed in the previous chapter). As we have seen, the precise structural relations between a Christian department of theology and its ecclesial community are open to many possibilities and historically have taken no one single form. Even within one ecclesial group, such as Roman Catholicism, there can be very different university structures within which authority is exercised and accountability practiced. Compare, for example, the Catholic University of America, Boston College in Massachusetts, the Pontifical Gregorian University in Rome, Nijmegen University in the Netherlands, and the University of Leuven in Belgium. These institutions exemplify very differing forms of practice and structural organization and forms of accountability. Were a department to be ecumenical, as would be highly desirable in certain contexts, the question of accountability and authority would be further complicated, but not in principle irresolvable. These questions cannot be addressed here but they are clearly important. In what follows I stay with the issue of prayer, for the notion of prayerful theology is structurally absent from the academy and is required in the revival of theology. Without prayer, worshipping the triune God will remain an increasingly marginalized concern and not the heart of theological endeavor. If indeed a pure heart and steadfast spirit are required for the wisdom that is theology (Ps. 51), am I asking for Jerusalem in Bristol? Is a postliberal university system a dream?

II Cohabiting with One's Beloved

He showed me the holy city of Jerusalem and it had all the radiant glory of God. (Rev. 21: 10–11)

How blessed are those who love you! They will rejoice in your peace. Blessed are those who grieved over all your afflictions, for they will rejoice for you upon seeing all your glory, and they will be made glad for ever. (Tob. 13: 14) (Part of the "Old Testament Canticle," following the "Morning" Psalm from Friday, week four, *Divine Office.*)

Let me turn to the first claim, that cohabitation with God through prayer is a prerequisite for doing theology. Besides the vital technical skills required by the student of theology (languages, drama, art history, music, literary criticism, abstract thought and reasoning, and so on), there is a need to know the "object" of study via cohabitation. Here theology has similarities and differences with other disciplines. Regarding the most profound difference, the "object" of study is unique. The formal "object" of all other disciplines is, part of the created order. The formal "object" of theology is the living God, creator of all things, dissimilar to and different from the entire created order, but who nevertheless reveals Himself in flesh and blood, in time and place, and in narrative particularity: that is, within the created order of signs. Hence, in a very real sense, faith is a necessary prerequisite for theology, because without faith as a gift, God cannot be known. However, despite these differences, theology is not without analogy to other disciplines in two very important respects. I employ these analogies to indicate that all forms of enquiry require different skills and disciplines and that theology should not conform itself to, nor be defined by, norms essentially alien to its nature. Conversely, nor is theology able to adjudicate between methods and skills related to other disciplines which have their own limited degree of autonomy. However, theology is able to relate the other disciplines to one another in its analysis of their functions, limitations, and co-operative possibilities toward helping co-create God's kingdom.

Let me explore the two analogical similarities between theology's requirement of prayer and other disciplines requiring appropriate practices to make two related points regarding prayer. First, theology, like other disciplines, requires the student to inhabit a tradition of enquiry which is a *living tradition* characterized by various *dogmas* and *practices* that facilitate a structured and disciplined co-habitation with the object of study, appropriate to that object.[7] This has been argued for in a variety of disciplines. For example, both Michael Polanyi and Thomas Kuhn, in different ways, have shown that the successful scientist is one who is trained and apprenticed so that he or she eventually inhabits a paradigm or outlook which is constructed and sustained by numerous presuppositions, both in regard to intellectual sets of beliefs (analogically: dogmas), and appropriate and

---

[7] See Aquinas, *Summa Theologiae*, la. 1. Aquinas, following Aristotle, realizes that method and skills can only be formulated in the light of the proper object of study. All references to the *Summa* are from the Blackfriars translations published by Blackfriars/Eyre and Spottiswoode, London/McGraw-Hill Book Co., New York. Victor White OP and Thomas Gilby OP are co-responsible for the appendices to the first volume which have been invaluable, especially appendix 10: "Dialectic of Love in the *Summa*" (pp. 124–33), and appendix 6: "Theology as Science" (pp. 67–88).

corresponding experimental and empirical practices (analogically: liturgy and ethics). The scientist always operates from within a world-view with more or less established sets of dogmas and practices that are assumed, so that the living tradition might develop and explore new questions. If the established dogmas and practices come under severe strain and such tensions cannot be resolved, there may be a "revolution" followed by a paradigm shift.[8] That is, the scientist might then inhabit another tradition, and analogically the Roman Catholic might become an atheist, or Buddhist. They may even radically shift within the Roman tradition, but this may be at the limits of the analogy. The point is that there are no non-traditioned scientists, just as there are no non-traditioned theologians. Hans-Georg Gadamer, likewise, has developed an analogous argument in the liberal arts to suggest that every reader always interprets texts within a particular framework of aesthetic, moral, and philosophical presuppositions. The good reader, in Gadamer's view, is one who both questions the text's world and allows that textual world to question his or her own presuppositions. In this sense every reader, as every scientist, inhabits a tradition of enquiry with specific dogmas and practices as epistemological requirements for intellectual engagement.[9]

We have already seen similar arguments in the previous chapter, advanced by MacIntyre (in moral enquiry) and McGrane (in anthropology). There is no naïve *epoché* being proposed within these different approaches, but instead, the recognition that living traditions of enquiry form the epistemological preconditions of all types of enquiry. And a "living tradition" is just that: dynamic, and to that extent unpredictable, while also being part of a structured set of beliefs and practices. But the notion of "living tradition" will mean very different things to different research communities. Hence, if the formal subject matter of theology is God, then appropriate cohabitation for the disciplined enquiry into this subject matter will surely involve prayer, especially since, as Rowan Williams puts it, "if theology is the untangling of the real grammar of religious practice, its subject matter is, humanly and specifically, people who pray."[10]

To be specific, prayer, according to the 1994 *Catechism of the Catholic Church*, "is the habit of being in the presence of the thrice-holy God and in communion with him."[11] This is stated despite the immense variety of

---

[8]   See Michael Polanyi, *Knowing and Being*, Routledge & Kegan Paul, London, 1969 and *Personal Knowledge: Towards a Post-Critical Philosophy*, Harper & Row, New York, 1962; and Thomas Kuhn, *The Structure of Scientific Revolutions*, Chicago University Press, 1970.

[9]   See Hans-Georg Gadamer, *Truth and Method*, Sheed and Ward, London, 1975 (trans. of 2nd German edn.).

[10]   Williams, "Integrity," p. 149.

[11]   Geoffrey Chapman, London, 1994, para. 2565.

prayers and traditions that constitute Christian history. Communing in God's presence is precisely what constitutes the living tradition, an ongoing love affair with the loved one of Eve, Sarah, Mary, Adam, Abraham, Joseph, Hildegard, Teresa of Avila, Mother Teresa, Aquinas, and Padre Pio, along with many ordinary everyday Christian men and women. It is the developing dogmas and practices of this particular community, called "Christians," that form the context of theology.[12] But we can only explore and understand these dogmas in the practices of those who lived them, for they were forming an embodied community, the "body of Christ." The point I am making is that prayer facilitates a complex cohabitation and participation with a "living tradition" of saints, sinners, fasts and feast days, dogmas and doctrines, the repressed and the explicit emblems of what communing with God might mean. Praying the *Office* illustrates the praying theologian's necessary (critical) dependence on this complex living tradition and its detailed descriptive character. A Methodist and a Baptist and a Roman Catholic pray differently and inhabit different, even though significantly overlapping, worlds. In joining this prayer, the theologian participates in and contributes to this on-going, unfinished tradition. The theologian becomes part of a tradition-specific community by participating in its central practice.

The polymorphous complexity of tradition that prayer allows us to cohabit also alerts us to the sometimes impoverished training received by graduating theologians. University theology, which has become so detached from the life of prayer, tends to structure the study of theology as if it were concerned solely with three types of texts: biblical, philosophical, and theological. Many university theology courses pay little attention to poetry, rhetoric, art and music, festivals and pilgrimages, liturgy, or lives of the saints. All these cognate disciplines, areas of study, and traditions, are central to the Church's living tradition that forms the theologian and his or her sensitivity, judgement, and skills. Praying the *Office* is a dramatic experience of engagement with pluriform modes and genres that constitute the lives of "people who pray," as Williams puts it.

One important feature of the liturgical calendar is that it actually challenges the time–space constructs imposed by different regimes of power. Cohabiting the living tradition means living in a different world from those who do not live within this tradition, where the liturgical calendar determines the diachronic and synchronic context of our existence. To put this point theologically, one might say that the liturgy continues the action of the incarnation, and the incarnation is the alpha and omega of all history. If

---

[12] See John Henry Newman, *An Essay on the Development of Christian Doctrine*, Longman, London, 1890, for a rich theological exploration of the complexity and historicism of tradition.

theology is nothing but a reflection upon this event of the Word made flesh, then theology cannot actually take place outside a liturgical context in so much as it is subject to God in Christ, the action made present at the heart of the liturgy, the eucharist, the transubstantiation of the human into the divine.[13] Catherine Pickstock has made this point very well in her book *After Writing: On the Liturgical Consummation of Philosophy*.[14] Her work helps relate the Office, as liturgical prayer, to the Mass's transformation of creation, instigating a new time and space through this eucharistic event. Pickstock's argument is also important as she too is concerned with the way in which modernity (and its mirror, postmodernity) has misformed liturgy, and because of this, theology. Pickstock's argument, to summarize, is that liturgical action is the consummation of Plato's understanding of orality. Plato in the *Phaedrus*, contrary to Derrida's reading of him, actually did not institute "presence" as the correlate of the sign—and the beginning of western metaphysics. Rather, "Plato favours orality because of its temporality, open-endedness, and link with physical embodiment."[15] Ironically, it is Derrida's own focus on writing rather than orality (hence the title of the book, *After Writing*) that unwittingly pushes Derrida into the mirror opposite of modernity's metaphysic of presence, that of absence, the *nihil*. The endless deferral of language in postmodernity is the reverse side of modernity's fetish that the sign delivers the real. Hence postmodernity's focus on ambiguity and absence. Pickstock's positive contribution comes in the second part of her book where she argues that the liturgy challenges both modernity's and postmodernity's understanding of writing and orality, space and time, the real as given and the real as gift, the empty subject and the liturgically constructed subject, death and life, presence and absence, as well as consummating Plato's understanding of orality. She argues that in the eucharist, the sign (the bread and wine) and the signified (Jesus Christ) are both coincidental and contrary, identificatory, and dissimilating, thereby making Christ present in the breaking of bread, transforming not only the nature of the eucharistic elements or signs, but of all creation. An extended quote of Pickstock nicely summarizes this part of her argument regarding the eucharist within the liturgy:

> The circumstance of the greatest dereliction of meaning [speaking of bread as "This is my body"] is here read as the promise of the greatest plenitude of

---

[13] This type of argument is also to be found in the work of Jean-Luc Marion, Jean-Yves Lacoste, Gerard Loughlin, and John Milbank.

[14] *After Writing: On the Liturgical Consummation of Philosophy*, Blackwell, Oxford, 1998.

[15] Pickstock, *After Writing*, p. xiii, and see also pp. 3–118, for the textuality of this argument.

meaning. However, if we do trust this sign, it cannot be taken simply as a dis-
crete miraculous exception, if we are true to a high medieval and Thomistic
construal of the Eucharist. First of all, we have seen how Aquinas sees bread
and wine as the most common elements of human culture. Hence, if these
become the signs of promise, they pull all of human culture along with them.
Second, "This is my body" cannot be regarded as a phrase in isolation any
more than any other linguistic phrase. Here, the Saussurean point holds true,
that every phrase of language in some sense depends for its meaningfullness
upon the entire set of contrasts which forms the whole repertoire of language, such that, for example, "this" only makes sense in contrast to "that,"
"my" in contrast to "your" and "his," "is" in contrast to "is not" and "was" and
the other verbs, and so forth *ad infinitum*.

For this reason, if this phrase is guaranteed an ultimate meaningfulness, it
draws all other phrases along with it.

In the third place, these words and events only occur in the Church. And
we only accept real presence and transubstantiation because the giving of
Body and Blood in the Eucharist gives also the Body of the Church.[16]

Pickstock's liturgical point then, is that the time–space regime instituted
by the liturgy, and more specifically by the Roman rite, constitutes a different world through which the believer is shaped and formed. (Her concern
with the Roman rite is related to her criticism of the reforms of Vatican II
and the argument that much subsequent liturgy was inculturated into
modernity, a point with which I am in some agreement, but a point that
should not detain us at this stage of my argument.[17]) It is not just a pious
sense in which theologians must pray, but an epistemological requirement
for proper engagement with the subject of study. I started this chapter with
the praying of the office, but it is central, at least to the Catholic tradition,
that the eucharist forms the heart of the world, the heart of an alternative
community.[18]

---

[16] Pickstock, "Thomas Aquinas and the Quest for the Eucharist" in ed. Sarah Beckwith,
Catholicism and Catholicity: Eucharistic Communities in Historical and Contemporary Perspective,
Blackwell, Oxford, 1999, pp. 47–68: 65–6. While this is specifically on Aquinas, it also sum-
marizes aspects of her argument in *After Writing*, pp. 259–61.

[17] A moderate position, with which I find myself in agreement, is found in Eamon Duffy's
"Rewriting the Liturgy: The Theological Implications of Translation" in ed. Stratford Caldecott, *Beyond the Prosaic: Renewing the Liturgical Movement*, T. & T. Clark, Edinburgh, 1998,
pp. 97–126. I have learnt much from Kieran Flanagan's analysis of the liturgy in *Sociology and
Liturgy: Re-presentations of the Holy*, Macmillan, London, 1991, although Flanagan is uncritical
about some of the cultural norms embedded in his alternative proposals.

[18] It is for this reason that I find David Fergusson's Barthian criticisms of Hauerwas both
unconvincing and misdirected. He writes, criticizing Hauerwas' ecclesiocentricism: "The
church is not the extension of the incarnation, but exists to bear witness and to live faithfully

Another feature of this liturgical calendar is that of the celebration of saints' days that act as the disciplined recalling of our indwelling the different narrated lives that construct the tradition of which we are part. Saints Januarius and Emily are two models of holiness among many thousands, both sung and unsung. Another feature of celebrating the saints is in our learning the parts that the saints took in the drama of salvation. In so much as we inhabit the dramatic *personae* of the saints, say in the praying of the *Benedictus* every morning and the *Magnificat* every evening (the dramatic "lines" of Zechariah and Mary), and through familiarity with their differing roles in the one drama of salvation which we quite literally act out in ecclesial prayer, we are called to improvise and continue the story of God's dealing with men and women through our own "acts" and "speech." The learned and holy improvisation in the drama of redemption is liturgically celebrated by the Church's recognition of a *saint* as also a *doctor* of the Church (*doctores ecclesiae*). These doctors are "virtuoso" in their learning and sanctity. It is this unity between the intellectual and the practical, the life lived and the textual writing and teachings of the doctor, that is occluded in the Encyclopedic university where rationality and disembodied reason alone are extolled. That the actual lives and practices of women and men are so important for intellectual enquiry is a facet increasingly noticed in the academy. We have already seen MacIntyre's exploration of this matter in the previous chapter. Edith Wyschogrod's *Saints and Postmodernism: Revisioning Moral Philosophy* is a rich and interesting Jewish and allegedly "universal" turn toward the lives of "saints" as the source and method of moral philosophy. However, Wyschogrod still maintains a form of positivism (and therefore modernism) in failing to recognize that the accounts of the saints are tradition-mediated and not historically and conceptually self-present, as she methodologically assumes.[19]

The necessity of prayer for cohabiting with this tradition of enquiry, in this polymorphous manner, opens up various neglected areas in the current theology curriculum. It also calls into question the assumptions

---

in the light of this unrepeatable and unsubstitutable event." See Fergusson, *Community, Liberalism and Christian Ethics*, Cambridge University Press, Cambridge, 1998, p. 69. Surely it only bears witness to this event, if it is able to re-present this event, which also in Catholic theology is "'a once for all' achievement" (Fergusson, *Community*, p. 69). Christ's presence in the eucharist is an extension of the incarnation in the sense that the incarnation is the continuing transformation of all creation (see 2 Cor. 5: 14–21, Rom. 5: 6ff.).

[19] See Edith Wyschogrod's *Saints and Postmodernism: Revisioning Moral Philosophy*, University of Chicago Press, Chicago, 1990 who recovers the importance of saints for the discipline of moral philosophy. See also David McCarthy Matzo's criticism of Wyschogrod in "Postmodernity, Saints and Scoundrels," *Modern Theology*, 9, 1993, pp. 19–36.

regarding who is an appropriate teacher, and who are appropriate students of theology. The answer I am suggesting is that besides the necessary academic requirements, there are also necessary ecclesial requirements for a theology department actually to be engaged in theology, rather than in a positivist examination of Christian history. Secular history departments are the appropriate place for that activity. I am certainly not suggesting that only saints be allowed to teach and study theology. The universities would be virtually empty—and I certainly would be out of a job. What I am stressing is the very real ecclesial epistemological requirements for the study and teaching of theology, that are properly facilitated by prayer.

The second point of analogy between theology and other disciplines concerns my point regarding saintly or "virtuoso" lives. Within scientific communities, or indeed within other communities of enquiry, respect is often given to those skilled and highly able practitioners who have inhabited the living tradition of enquiry. They have cohabited with the paradigm, with both heart and intellect, so that they may be looked to as wise role models whose intuition, judgement, and learning are especially valued. It is not by chance that innovation within a tradition is usually brought about by those most schooled in it. It is for this reason that the line between heresy and genuine doctrinal development is sometimes so thin, and heresy advanced by sometimes saintly figures. Newman rightly says that it is "almost a definition of heresy, that it fastens on some one [correct] statement as if the whole truth, to the denial of all others," thereby "erring rather in what it rejects, than in what it maintains."[20] Such skilled and highly able theological practitioners within the Church are seen as "doctors" and "saints": "doctors" because the only role of the intellect is to minister truthfully to the ailing body of Christ, of which the saint is a part; "saints" because the criterion of excellence in theology is inseparable from the holiness of life. These two virtues are inseparable for the theologian. If the greatest practitioners of the discipline of theology enjoin the practice of prayer for the discipline, then it is surely appropriate seriously to entertain this claim.

We need to be careful here regarding the cult of saints, for all sorts of reasons. History testifies to the fact that bishops and churchmen, and also the theologians of the University of Paris, can deliver negative judgements on saints and even send them to the stake, as was the case with Joan of Arc,

---

[20] In "Sermon XV: The Theory of Development" in *Fifteen Sermons Preached Before the University of Oxford Between AD 1826 and 1843*, University of Notre Dame Press, Notre Dame, Indiana, 1996, p. 296.

who was only retrospectively recognized as a saint.[21] Nor do I want to idealize, for some were probably insufferable. Hagiography is a complex genre. One of the greatest doctors of the western tradition, St. Jerome, whose portrait adorns the front of the English translation of the *IEVT*, was renowned for his intemperateness in controversy and savage invective. Some try to excuse this in terms of classical rhetorical models, but Pope Sixtus V may have been closer to the truth. He is reported as saying, when looking at a picture of Jerome beating his breast with a stone, "You do well to use that stone: without it you would never have been numbered among the saints."[22] Furthermore, some great theologians and even "doctors"—such as Aquinas—were silenced or condemned by the Church and being declared a doctor does not mean that all the person's writings are free of error. And the process of saint selection is far from unproblematic. For example it has taken nearly two thousand years to proclaim women officially as doctors of the Church—Catherine of Siena and Teresa of Avila were named by Pope Paul VI only in 1970, and Thérèse of Lisieux in 1997 by Pope John Paul II. This lack of female doctors of the Church only partially reflects the crisis mentioned in chapter one, whereby women have been excluded from the universities since the thirteenth century. It also reflects some intellectual misogyny that runs through the Christian tradition.

Clearly, given the vastly complex notion of the living tradition that I have been exploring above, the analogy between theology and other disciplines begins to break down a little. Of course, in one sense, the analogies have already broken down, for the living tradition in question is (and is sometimes not), testimony to the triune God, who is like no other object of study. However, prayer keeps this similarity and difference in appropriate

---

[21] Michel Foucault reminds us of the power of "tradition" to persecute, tyrannize, and marginalize, so as to sustain itself—and this we should not forget. See Foucault, *The Archaeology of Knowledge*, Tavistock Publications, London, 1972. *IEVT* is remarkably sensitive to this complex issue (paras. 32–41). Certain elements within the Church, especially within the feminist tradition, have painfully struggled to negotiate tensions between fidelity and critique. See, for example, the work of Roman Catholic feminists such as Janet Martin Soskice, "Can a Feminist Call God 'Father'?" in ed. Alvin F. Kimel Jnr, *Speaking the Christian God: The Holy Trinity and the Challenge of Feminism*, W. B. Eerdmans, Grand Rapids, Michigan, 1992, pp. 81–94; Anne Carr, Elizabeth Johnson, and Catherine Mowry LaCugna in the collection edited by Catherine Mowry LaCugna, *Freeing Theology: The Essentials of Theology in a Feminist Perspective*, Harper, San Francisco, 1993 (pp. 5–30, 115–38, and 83–114 respectively), and Tina Beattie, *God's Mother, Eve's Advocate*, University of Bristol, Bristol, 1999.

[22] Donald Attwater, *Dictionary of Saints*, Penguin, London, 2nd edn. revised and updated by Catherine Rachael John, 1983, p. 182. Steven M. Oberhelman, *Rhetoric and Homiletics in Fourth-Century Christian Literature: Prose Rhythm, Oratorical Style, and Preaching in the Works of Ambrose, Jerome, and Augustine*, Scholars Press, Atlanta, Georgia, 1991, contextualizes Jerome's language in the terms of fourth-century rhetorical style.

tension, for it both enjoins a living relationship with God and gestures toward a major site of enactment, its mediated ecclesial culture. Tradition, in this sense, cannot be understood as a static deposit. The theologian is entrusted with this "deposit" of faith, which requires endless recovery and re-presentation, and in doing so the theologian adds to and enriches the deposit of faith.

This very point can be nicely illustrated in terms of *The Divine Office*. It is not atemporal, and has had a long history, with some major revisions at the Council of Trent, and then again at Vatican II, where it was especially modified and shortened to facilitate lay participation. Presently it fails to reflect many ancient prayers and traditions that employ feminine metaphors for the divine, and prayers or poems from women saints and mystics. Furthermore, the official English translation employs exclusive language in the intercessionary prayers—which is quite unnecessary. One hopes (perhaps vainly) that at the next revision these points will be addressed, as well as the lack of artistic images for meditation. Nevertheless, the praying of the *Office* is quite an unpredictable experience, for the different contexts and concerns of the various users will affect the manner in which the prayers are prayed. Hence, the *Office*'s use in daily prayer constantly invites re-readings, fresh insights and practices, and non-identical repetition of the life of Christ, for there is never a single stable context of interpretation. As the Church is also a constructed, concretized set of social practices, its readings and the practice of its texts cannot be atemporal or essentialized.[23] Every day in the life of the Church represents the negotiation of the gospel within culture. Hence, we recall "today" that after the emergence of a saint like Emily de Rodat, her theology and practice give further shape to the "body of Christ," in the emergence of the congregation she founded, the Holy Family of Villefranche, a type of spirituality and social formation not so formalized until her opening of a free school in Villefranche-de-Royergue.[24] This kaleidoscopic and developing canon called "tradition" allows for theological plurality in a quite extraordinary manner, as well as for plurality in practice—without succumbing to relativism or indifferentism. This internal

---

[23] See Joseph Ratzinger's insightful "Commentary on the *Dogmatic Constitution on Divine Revelation*" in ed. Herbert Vorgrimler, *Commentary on the Documents of Vatican II*, vol. 3, Herder & Herder, New York, 1969, esp. p. 197. He criticizes Pope Pius XII's *Humani Generis* (1956) for advocating a regressive understanding of tradition, whereby it is seen as a fixed unambiguous deposit. See also Karl Rahner's extremely helpful exploration of the organic relationship between theologian, magisterium, and tradition in "Magisterium and Theology," *Theological Investigations*, vol. 18, Darton, Longman & Todd, London, 1984, pp. 54–73.

[24] See Doris Burton, *Saint Emilie de Rodat: Foundress of the Sisters of the Holy Family*, Paternoster, London, 1951, for an account of her life.

pluralism is often played down in criticisms that theologically tradition-specific forms of enquiry are univocal and monolithic. They rarely are.

In conclusion, regarding my two points of analogy between theology and other disciplines, I have been arguing that prayer, and the accompanying call to virtue, are indispensable prerequisites to the study and practice of theology. It is one form of cultivated habitual practice that constitutes cohabitation with theology's proper object of study: the triune God and His community, the Church.[25] Theology can demand this from its students as justly and legitimately as geologists can demand attendance at field trips from theirs, or musicologists can demand competent practice of one musical instrument and attendance at various recitals from their students.

My argument so far has been to show how prayer helps us in our cohabitation with the triune God and His community, the Church. I now want to develop this argument a little further such that it will act as a bridge to the second claim made by *IEVT*, which I will explore later.

The second claim is that prayer *guides* theological study. The point I now want to press is that by virtue of cohabitation with the living and triune God through prayer and all that it involves and the life of virtue, the theologian increases in love, and love is the lamp of knowledge. Prayer, one might recall, is finally and only worthwhile in so much as it gives glory to God: adoration for its own sake. But in this slow laborious process of learning to pray, learning to let go, learning to discern and check our constant use of prayer toward other ends (pious self-image, public status, and so on), we are learning to love. As the Catechism puts it, prayer "is the habit of being in the presence of the thrice-holy God and in communion with him." This is no easy process. We should recall that a major symbol of prayer is Jacob's wrestling with the strange and unnamed figure—who blesses him after putting his thigh out of joint! (Gen. 32: 22–32).

I now want to push the argument, to claim that the disciplined habits of prayer can engender love—and love is the lamp of knowledge, such that prayer can properly be said to guide study. In *IEVT* it is noted that: "The theologian's work thus responds to the dynamism found in the faith itself" (para. 6). This "dynamism" is trinitarian love. The next paragraph of the document continues:

> Obedient to the impulse of truth which seeks to be communicated, theology also arises from love and love's dynamism. In the act of faith, man knows God's goodness and begins to love Him. Love, however, is ever desirous of a

---

[25] The *Divine Office* as an example of ecclesial prayer is one point within the liturgical tradition. The eucharist is another, as are the six other sacraments.

better knowledge of the beloved. From this double origin of theology, inscribed upon the interior life of the People of God and its missionary vocation, derives the method with which it ought to be pursued in order to satisfy the requirements of its nature. (para. 7)[26]

This is a startling claim: that theology's *method* is dictated by love's dynamism. I want to focus on this in terms of the "double origin," this restless movement between love and knowledge, by briefly looking at Aquinas.[27] In the *Summa Theologiae*, 2a. 2ae. q. 45, Aquinas discusses "The gift of wisdom," which should, for the purpose of our discussion, be read with the *Summa* 1a. 1. 6, where he argues that theology is "wisdom." In 2a. 2ae, he makes two very important points concerning our question. First, in article 2 he argues that theological wisdom is a gift of the Holy Spirit, precisely because it arises from cohabitation with the divine life which facilitates right judgement. Note, Aquinas's stress is on judgement: it is presupposed that the technical skills required of the theologian are gained by long, hard, and rigorous training. He writes:

So it is with divine things. A correct judgment made through rational investigation belongs to the wisdom which is an intellectual virtue. But to judge aright through a certain fellowship with them [divine things] belongs to that wisdom which is the gift of the Holy Spirit. Dionysius [*De Divinis Nominibus* 2. PG 3, 648.] says that Hierotheus is perfected in divine things for he *not only* learns *about* them but *suffers* them as *well*. Now this sympathy, or connaturality with divine things, results from charity which unites us to God [compassio

---

[26] After the word "beloved," the document cites St. Bonaventure, *Prooem: in I Sent.*, q.2, ad. 6. I shall, however, follow Aquinas to illuminate this point. There are many ways in which this avenue could be explored, for instance, in comparing Benedictine, Dominican, and Jesuit understandings and practices related to "love of God." See, for instance, Jean Leclercq, *The Love of Learning and the Desire for God*, Fordham University Press, Fordham, New York, 1960 [1957].

[27] One might equally use Augustine. His first book, *On Christian Doctrine*, makes it clear that Christians are schooled within the Church of love (Christian *paideia*), rather than by pagan education—and that love is both the prerequisite (within seven steps) which teaches us how to read the scripture, as well as being the goal of scripture. See Augustine, *On Christian Doctrine*, The Liberal Arts Press, New York, 1958, esp. pp. 7–34. See also Andrew Louth, *Discerning the Mystery*, Clarendon Press, Oxford, 1989, ch. 4, esp. pp. 76–84. 1 am deeply indebted to Louth's book, although his generous ecumenical approach sometimes obscures the importance of locating the tradition-specific starting point for which he argues. Louth's own later denominational shift from Anglicanism to the Orthodox Church may be significant in accounting for such textual ambivalence. One might also use Augustine's *Confessions* to show his critique of secular *paideia*; one not dissimilar to the critique of modernity's *paideia* and its monstrous consequences in the Holocaust—see Zygmunt Bauman, *Modernity and the Holocaust*, Polity Press, Cambridge, 1991.

sive connaturalitas ad res divinas fit per caritatem, quae quidem unit nos Deo]; *he who is joined to the Lord is one spirit with him* [1 Corinthians 6: 17]. [28]

Aquinas makes it clear that love is central to the process of theological judgement and that this quality is a gift given to us. Hence, any notion that prayer automatically attains various goals and qualities within the theologian must be countered and rightly criticized. Prayer does not act magically, but is a major formative practice of love. Aquinas also makes a related distinction between two types of wisdom: first:

> [when a] "wise person" comes to a correct judgment, arrived at from a bent that way, as when a person who possesses the habit of a virtue rightly commits himself to what should be done in consonance with it, because he is already in sympathy with it. Hence Aristotle's remark that the virtuous man himself sets the measure and standard for human acts. (*Ethics* X, 5. 11 76a 17) Alternatively, the judgment may be arrived at through a cognitive process, as when a person soundly instructed in moral science can appreciate the activity of virtues he does not himself possess. [29]

Hence, being in "sympathy with" is precisely what is referred to in *IEVT* as a "supernatural sense of faith," for Aquinas is clear to point out that the first type of wisdom is classed among the gifts of the Holy Spirit, and the second is primarily the hard workings of the intellect, with requisite training. My argument above has been concerned with the first type. This first type, according to Aquinas, works through cohabitation, or in his words, through "sympathy" or suffering with; and this amounts to a gift of wisdom by the Holy Spirit, a point that our opening prayer-psalm from the Friday *Office* also labors. Aquinas writes:

> The first way of judging divine things belongs to that wisdom which is classed among the Gifts of the Holy Ghost; so St. Paul says, *The spiritual man judges all things* [1 Corinthians 2.15], and Dionysius speaks about *Hierotheus being taught by the experience of undergoing divine things, not only by learning about them.* [*De Divinis Nominibus* 11, 9] The second way of judging is taken by sacred doctrine to the extent that it can be gained by study; even so the premises are held from revelation. [30]

This reiterates the requirement both of correct training and knowledge, but also of virtue, which allows for greater receptivity to the Holy Spirit. This

---

[28] *Summa*, 2a. 2ae. 2.
[29] *Summa*, la.1.6.
[30] *Summa*, la. 1. 6, a. 3.

connaturality with divine things, according to Aquinas, results from a life of love and contemplation, a life of prudence, justice, fortitude, and temperance which is both affected by, and results in, continuous participation with the life of God—a gift of the Holy Spirit. Striving after the virtues requires the will, but attaining them is finally a gift. For Aquinas, the acquisition of the virtues is a slow process that takes a lifetime; although it does not always develop in a straightforward, evolutionary line. The process can be violently disrupted and derailed by mortal sin: a serious infidelity to God whereby one prefers "sin to the divine friendship" (*Summa* 2a. 2ae. 24.12). In Thomas R. Heath's commentary on question 45, Heath implicitly attends to what *IEVT* calls the "double origin" of theology. Heath argues that Aquinas's basic insight is this:

> knowledge of the goodness of an object causes us to love it; love then brings about a different and a better kind of knowledge; this new appreciation deepens the love which, in turn, intensifies the appreciation, and so on. In the life of grace the first kind of knowledge about God comes through faith; the love is charity; the second kind of knowledge comes through the gifts of the Holy Spirit.[31]

The seriousness of Aquinas's contention that sound theological judgement is predicated upon the "gift of the Holy Spirit" and requires "sympathy, or connaturality with divine things" resulting from, and leading to, a life of contemplative love of God, entirely accords with, and illuminates, *IEVT*'s focus on this "double origin" of theology. And this indwelling within love means that the Holy Spirit is properly present, guiding and leading all believers, including theologians, into a deepening indwelling with God, through increased knowledge (faith), through tireless struggle (hope), and most vitally, through the practice of charity (love). Needless to say, this process is fragile and to invoke infallibility for any saintly theologian (or straightforwardly, for the Church) would be folly. As Nicholas Lash puts it, "To believe in the 'infallibility' of the Church is not to suppose that we are reliable, but that God is."[32] Love thus plays this central part in Aquinas because of the three theological virtues of faith, hope, and charity. For Aquinas it is only love that endures, for in our final rest with God, faith and hope (which are always mediated in this life) are required no longer, whereas love endures, and in our present state has no intermediary; for it is only through and with the love of God that we learn to love God and our neighbor properly. In another context Aquinas explains:

[31] *Summa*, vol. 34, p. 200.
[32] Nicholas Lash, "The Difficulty of Making Sense," *New Blackfriars*, 70, 824, 1999, pp. 74–84: p. 74.

we have to say that love, which is an act of an appetitive virtue, even in our present state tends first to God, and from him follows to other things: in this way charity loves God without any intermediary. The case is directly the opposite with knowledge, since it is through other things that we come to know God.[33]

Love's dynamism, flexibility, and kenotic nature are startlingly brought out in Aquinas's subtle discussion of the four proximate effects of love: melting, pleasure, languor, and fever. Of melting he writes:

> The opposite of this is *freezing*, for frozen things are so tight-packed that they cannot easily let other things penetrate them. But with love, the orexis [appetitus] is quick to take into itself the object loved: this is how that object "dwells" in the lover, as we have seen [referring to art. 2]. Coldness or hardness of heart is therefore a state incompatible with love; whereas "melting" or warmth suggests a certain softness which means that the heart will be quick to let the object loved enter into it.[34]

Aquinas's metaphor of the transformation required by love, what he calls a "certain softness," is echoed in the second reading from Tobit this morning, that reminds us how those who have "grieved," who have shared Christ's sufferings, as Paul puts it (Col. 1: 24), will find in this "softness" a rejoicing, for they will find life in God: "How blessed are those who love you. They will rejoice in your peace" (Tob. 13: 14).

It is, I hope, now more clear how the second claim (that prayer is a key "method" in theology) is intrinsically related to the first and third claims. It is related to the first, for by cohabitation with God, through prayer, the theologian's enquiry may be guided by love. And it is related to the third claim, for the correctness of the theologian's conclusions is assessed by a traditioned and disciplined love—that starts and ends in communal prayer. This does not obscure the importance, autonomy, and integrity of the various critical tools and methods employed by the theologian. Rather, it suggests a discernment, a judgement, and guidance that are required in their utilization. To put flesh on this, let me further explore the second claim of prayer guiding study and being an appropriate theological method. Such a claim belongs within the logic of understanding theology as an offspring of a passionate love affair with God and God's world.

---

[33] *Summa*, 2a. 2ae. 27. 4. See also 2a. 2ae. 26. 1 and 2. See also, Brian Davies, *The Thought of Thomas Aquinas*, Clarendon Press, Oxford, 1992, pp. 288–96.

[34] *Summa*, 1a. 2ae. 28. 5. See vol. 19, p. 105. For "orexis" see *Summa*, vol. 19, p. xxiv for Eric D'Arcy's helpful notes on this term.

III The Nuptial Love Affair

Come and I will show you the bride that the Lamb has married. (Rev. 21: 9)

He sends out his word to the earth and swiftly runs his command. He showers down snow white as wool, he scatters hoar-frost like ashes.

He hurls down hailstones like crumbs. The waters are frozen at his touch; he sends forth his word and it melts them: at the breath of his mouth the waters flow.[35]

The marriage of the bride and the Lamb generates the momentum of the love affair, upon which theological method is based, a rhythm and momentum characterized by both joy and affliction (Tob. 13), guilt and mercy (Ps 51), in which we pray that a "pure heart" be created within us so that we might be taught "wisdom" (Ps 51); but a wisdom that is attentive to the reality of God's action which cannot be controlled or predicted. Thus He will choose to "send forth his word" and melt the icy waters, and thaw out our frozen hearts so that united with Christ our head, our blood may quicken and our bodies may be rightly animated.

This biblical metaphor might illuminate the significance of the well-attested liquefying of St. Januarius's blood, going back to 400. It is said that when St. Januarius's dry blood, which is kept in an old glass vial, is brought into the presence of his head, which is kept separately, the blood becomes volatile. Christ as the head, gives his body life, through his blood—without him the Church is lifeless.[36] Might this tradition emblematically embody the profound Pauline metaphor of Christ's life-giving power as head of the body?

However, to return to prayer being the guide and method for an intellectually rigorous theology, we might first note an important insight by Newman who places the theologian within a Marian typology. In his *University Sermons*, Newman perceptively recognized that Mary is a prime model of the theologian, for her life is a clue to theological method; something alluded to in the final paragraph of *IEVT*.[37] Newman writes:

---

[35] Psalm 147: 15–18; taken from a "Psalm of Praise," following the previous two from the Friday week four *Office*.

[36] This particular genre of miracle is a Southern Italian specialty—see Attwater, *Saints*, p. 181, and Butler, *Lives*, p. 1124.

[37] Para. 42; although an allusion is all that it remains. See further Hans Urs von Balthasar, *Mary for Today*, St. Paul's, Slough, 1977, pp. 33–41. However, his Marian ecclesiology is potentially problematic in identifying the feminine as primarily passive, with all the attendant

[Mary] is our pattern of Faith, both in the reception and in the study of Divine Truth. She does not think it enough to accept, she dwells upon it; not enough to possess, she uses it; not enough to assent, she develops it; not enough to submit to reason, she reasons upon it; not indeed reasoning first, and believing afterwards, with Zacharias, yet believing without reasoning, next from love and reverence, reasoning after believing. And thus she symbolizes to us, not only the faith of the unlearned, but of the doctors of the Church also.[38]

Newman sees Mary as the prime theologian, displaying the theologian's organic dependency on the Church, in both Mary's responsiveness to God and her co-creative activity with God, as Church. This dynamic corresponds to the theologian's accountability (third claim) to the living tradition; and the theologian's being guided (second claim) by the multiple impulses within this never fully explored tradition as it interacts with contemporary culture.[39] Admittedly, the notion of watertight and separate "contemporary" and "ecclesial" cultures interacting is highly artificial. Nevertheless, let me take one feature of today's *Office* to further my exploration of the manner in which the theologian is *guided* by prayer: how God's love is the dynamism that dictates method.

If theology's method is dictated by love's dynamism, then this is to say that *God's own trinitarian love should dictate the method* by which God is known and loved. Theology requires to develop its shape critically from the liturgical life of the Church. This does not mean that prayer in its different forms has any privileged ahistorical position, free from critical engagement, exemplified by the passionate debate on the liturgy since Vatican II. That theology's method be prayerfully mediated is a point too often neglected in Anglo-Saxon academic circles.[40] Even some writers who stress the ecclesiological grounding of theology sometimes neglect the liturgical heart constituting the Church.

---

socio-political-sexual ramifications. See further, my "Queering the Trinity" in ed. Gerard Loughlin, *Queer Theology*, Blackwell, Oxford, 2005, forthcoming. *Faith and Reason* (1998), 108, identifies Mary with philosophy and right reason; and this allusion is richly explored by David Vincent Meconi, "*Philosophari in Maria: Fides et ratio* and Mary as the Model of Created Wisdom" in eds. D. R. Foster and J. W. Koterski, *The Two Wings of Catholic Thought*, Catholic University of America Press, Washington, DC, 2003, pp. 69–90. Koterski also downplays the active social role played by Mary. Her actions in John 2: 1–12 are overlooked.

[38] "Sermon XV: The Theory of Development" in *Fifteen Sermons*, p. 313.

[39] It is vital that tradition be seen as "living," for otherwise there would be no resources to draw upon by which it develops and criticizes itself. For a more dynamic Catholic appropriation of Lindbeck and Frei's category of narrative, see Gerard Loughlin, *Telling God's Story: Bible, Church and Narrative Theology*, Cambridge University Press, Cambridge, 1996.

[40] For some of the many exceptions, see: Rowan Williams, *The Wound of Knowledge*, Darton, Longman & Todd, London, 1979; David Ford and Dan Hardy, *Jubilate: Theology in Praise*,

Vatican II was instrumental in emphasizing the role of liturgy in the study of theology. In the *Constitution on the Sacred Liturgy*, it is stated:

> The study of sacred liturgy is to be ranked among the compulsory and major courses in seminaries and religious houses of studies; in theological faculties it is to rank among the principal subjects. It is to be taught under its theological, historical, spiritual, pastoral, and juridical aspects. Moreover, other professors, while striving to expound the mystery of Christ and the history of salvation from the angle proper to each of their own subjects, must nevertheless do so in a way which will clearly bring out the connections between their subjects and the liturgy, as also the unity which underlies all priestly training.[41]

Bringing out the connections between the different disciplines that constitute theology and the Church's liturgy needs more careful exploration and I shall pursue my point here with one example: biblical studies. I also use this example for it helps to illustrate my wider argument that theology critically utilizes various and contextually autonomous disciplines in an *ad hoc* manner, rather than theology itself being determined by such disciplines. To a limited extent, I have already hinted how the useful disciplines involved in religious studies (languages, sociology, history, philosophy, and so on) can be turned into a theological religious studies and in chapter five I will show this in operation. Here I shall focus on the Bible due to its partial capture by historical biblical criticism and the secular presuppositions embedded within that discipline.

One important aspect of praying the *Office* is its intriguing deployment of scripture, as is seen, for example, in the configuration of texts from the Old and New Testaments and the tradition. This has profound implications for biblical studies within the university. Consider two points. First, scripture is constantly mediated via tradition. For example, in this morning's *Office* we have Ephesians (4: 23–4) and Revelation (21: 10–11 and 21: 9) guiding our prayerful reading of the Psalms (51, 147) and the Old Testament Canticle

---

Darton, Longman & Todd, London, 1984; Geoffrey Wainwright, *Doxology: The Praise of God in Worship. Doctrine and Life: A Systematic Theology*, London, Epworth, 1980; Webster, *Holiness*, SCM, London, 2003; A. Nichols, *The Shape of Catholic Theology*, T. & T. Clark, Edinburgh, 1991; Pickstock, *After Writing*; Flanagan, *The Enchantment of Sociology*, Macmillan, London, 1996, esp. chs. 3 and 6. All these offer a sociological argument for the liturgical importance of determining theology's method. There are many others who could be included. The fact that only two writers in this list are Roman Catholic indicates both the specificity and the shared sense of the task I am proposing.

[41] Josef Andreas Jungmann points out in his "Commentary" how this paragraph relates to *Deus Scientiarum* (1930) which placed Christian archaeology and patrology as compulsory principal subjects. See also *Decree on Priestly Formation*, ch. 5, esp. para. 16, in ed. Abbott, *Documents of Vatican II*.

(Tob. 13), which in turn guides our reading of the New Testament passages. Had we instead used the Common of Pastors celebrating Saint Januarius, or the Common of Women Saints celebrating Saint Emily, we would not only have had scriptural co-mediation, but also spiritual writers from varying moments within the tradition prefixing the psalmody: Hesychius today, but it could equally be Cassiodorus, Irenaeus, Augustine, or Athanasius (although, sadly and shamefully, always men). In the English translation of the *Office*, the poets Gerard Manley Hopkins and John Donne are also allowed to sing in this sublime, albeit all-male, choir. Furthermore, the scriptures today are actually mediated via the lives of St. Emily or St. Januarius, inviting us to read both their lives in terms of the scriptures and the scriptures in terms of their lives. This is well reflected in the scripture reading for St. Januarius's Common today:

> Remember your leaders, who preached the word of God to you, and as you reflect on the outcomes of their lives, imitate their faith. Jesus Christ is the same today as he was yesterday and as he will be for ever. Do not let yourself be led astray by all sorts of strange doctrines (Heb. 13: 7–9a).

Note the endless possibilities of non-identical repetition included within the idea that St. Januarius, Paul, and those who imitate Christ's faith, actually reproduce, in very different lives and contexts, the reality of Jesus Christ in the world.[42] Leaders, thank goodness, are never the same, nor are the saints, yet they are all in various and historically differing fashions possible "imitations of Christ." The point I am making is that reading the scriptures as scripture is a profoundly ecclesial activity.

This can be further developed in a number of ways, two of which I will briefly outline. First, reading and praying with scripture require us to examine how it has been read and used in the life of the Church over two thousand years, not in a slavish desire to reproduce ancient procedures and methods, but rather to allow those past readings to call us into question and to incorporate what might be useful and illuminating into our current practices. Stephen E. Fowl writes that with "a few notable exceptions, modern biblical scholars have paid little attention to premodern biblical interpretation," except to "treat it as a form of error."[43] While there is cer-

---

[42]   See John Milbank, "The Name of Jesus" in *The Word Made Strange: Theology, Language and Culture*, Blackwell, Oxford, 1997, pp. 145–70.

[43]   Ed. Stephen F. Fowl, *The Theological Interpretation of Scripture*, Blackwell, Oxford, 1997, p. xvii. He cites Brevard Childs as a prominent American exception, only then to comment that after 1979 there is a decreasing interest in premodern exegesis in Childs's work (ibid., p. xxviii).

tainly a move away from a univocal notion of meaning within biblical texts (the premise of historical-critical exegesis), Fowl observes that the current challenge to historical-critical forms of reading often comes from those who drink from postmodern, not premodern, wells. One very significant exception, included in Fowl's collection, is the great Catholic scholar, Henri de Lubac, who pioneered a recovery of the patristic and medieval tradition precisely as a form of richer engagement with scripture than that offered by the modern historicist perspective.[44] David Steinmetz develops this in his argument for "The Superiority of Pre-Critical Exegesis" on epistemological grounds, the focus of much of my argument in this chapter. He argues that medieval exegetes had a sober middle way between extreme subjectivism (such as some literary theory has spawned, whereby the meaning of the text is entirely a function of the reading community) and historical-critical positivism (which ties the text purely to the authorial intention). While medieval exegesis is not without its faults and problems, it at least rescues the Bible, for it holds "that the meaning of scripture in the mind of the prophet who first uttered it is only one of its possible meanings and may not, in certain circumstances, even be its primary or most important meaning."[45] Steinmetz is thus able to conclude, after trawling through various patristic and medieval materials to substantiate his point:

> The medieval theory of levels of meaning in the biblical text, with all its undoubted defects, flourished because it is true, while the modern theory of a single meaning, with all its demonstrable virtues, is false. Until the historical-critical method becomes critical of its own theoretical foundations and develops a hermeneutical theory adequate to the nature of the text which it is interpreting, it will remain restricted—as it deserves to be—to the guild and the academy, where the question of truth can be endlessly deferred.[46]

Hence, in contrast to the positivist readings advanced by a strict application of the historical-critical method we might well find that critically returning to the allegorical, moral, and typological forms of earlier times has much to

---

[44] Henri de Lubac, *The Sources of Revelation*, trans. J. O'Neill, Herder & Herder, New York, 1968, speaks of the "spiritual understanding" of scripture (ch. 1), and see also his masterly *Medieval Exegesis*, four volumes; two of which have been translated and published by T. & T. Clark, Edinburgh, vol. 1 trans. Mark Sebanc, 1998; and vol. 2 trans. E. M. Macierowski, 2000.

[45] In "The Superiority of Pre-Critical Exegesis" in ed. Fowl, *The Theological Interpretation of Scripture*, pp. 26–38: p. 27.

[46] Ibid., p. 37.

say to current hermeneutics.[47] Postmodern approaches to the Bible like those of David Clines, Anthony Thiselton, and Stephen Moore are problematic for different reasons. I cannot pursue that matter here.[48]

A second way of reading the scripture through tradition is via the lives of the saints and its explication through the production of lives of virtue. It is curious and encouraging that this emphasis on "performativity" is being recovered from both the so-called "liberal" and "postliberal" wings of the Christian community.[49] From the liberal side, liberation and feminist theologies have insisted on the socio-political liberating strategies opened up in reading the scriptures in regard to the poor and women respectively.[50] Likewise, both groups have reflected on life histories of key figures central to furthering their cause. For instance, the Brazilian Leonardo Boff uses the Virgin Mary as an icon of women and liberation, thereby combining both feminist and liberationist hermeneutics.[51] Often, feminists are more sensitive to the problem that the primary text is sometimes resistant to their strategies, while both feminists and liberationists are more confident that it is the history of exegetical strategies rather than the Bible itself that has caused the problem of recovering its proper meaning in respect to the poor and women.

---

[47] See James S. Preus, *From Shadow to Promise: Old Testament Interpretation from Augustine to the Young Luther*, Harvard University Press, Cambridge, Massachusetts, 1969, who offers a survey of medieval exegesis and relates it to the modern historical project. See also Neil B. MacDonald, "The Philosophy of Language and the Renewal of Biblical Hermeneutics" in eds. C. Bartholomew et al., *Renewing Biblical Interpretation*, Paternoster Press, Cumbria, 2000, pp. 123–40 for an interesting recovery of "typology." The Roman Catholic notion of the "Sensus Plenior" has sadly been little developed. However, see Raymond E. Brown, "The History and Development of a Sensus Plenior," *Catholic Biblical Quarterly*, 15, 1953, pp. 141–62, and in the same journal, "The Sensus Plenior in the Last Ten Years," 25, 1963, pp. 262–85, and his book, written in between these two pieces: *The Sensus Plenior of Sacred Scripture*, St. Mary's College, Baltimore, Maryland, 1955.

[48] See Bockmuehl, "'To be or not to be': The Possible Futures of New Testament Scholarship," *Scottish Journal of Theology*, 51, 1998, pp. 271–306, for a superb criticism of postmodern strategies.

[49] See David Fergusson's excellent outline of these two camps in: *Community, Liberalism and Christian Ethics*, pp. 161–73. He rightly questions the boundaries of such definitions.

[50] See, for instance, ed. Letty Russel, *Feminist Interpretation of the Bible*, Westminster Press, Philadelphia, 1985; Elisabeth Schüssler Fiorenza, *Bread Not Stone: The Challenge of Feminist Biblical Interpretations*, Beacon Press, Boston, Massachusetts, 1984. For liberation theology, a good overview can be found in ed. Rosino Gibellini, *Frontiers of Liberation Theology*, SCM, London, 1980 [1975]; and third world perspectives: ed. Deane William Ferm, *Third World Liberation Theologies*, Orbis, New York, 1986.

[51] Leonardo Boff, *The Maternal Face of God: The Feminine and its Religious Expressions*, trans. Robert R. Barr, Harper & Row, San Francisco, 1987; as do Mara Clara Bingemer and Ivone Gebara, "Mary—Mother of God, Mother of the Poor" in ed. Ursula King, *Feminist Theology from the Third World*, SPCK, London, 1994, pp. 275–83.

On the postliberal side, George Lindbeck, Stanley Hauerwas, and John Milbank are clear examples of those requiring that the Bible interpret the world, emphasizing "performativity" and "narrative" as the categories that help the Bible unfold via the practices of the Church.[52] While they advance quite different positions between them, they commonly differ from the liberals in arguing that the Bible interprets the world, rather than its use for supporting various political or hermeneutical fashions. Hence they are often critical of feminism and liberation theologies for their ideological control over Christian discourse. It is not that they are unsympathetic to socialism (Hauerwas is strongly anti-capitalist and Milbank is more explicitly a Christian Socialist) or to feminism (Hauerwas indicating a sympathy), but rather they want to state that the meanings and practices of liberation cannot be decided in advance of its multi-layered sense within the Bible and tradition, and its application is primarily ecclesial, this latter practice acting as a critique of secular or multi-religious society.[53] This is a complex field and while I am sympathetic to both socialism and feminism, I am more inclined to engage with these issues on postliberal terms. I simply want to gesture to the significance of the Bible being read within a very different context—performativity—to highlight another way in which the Bible can be recovered from the absolute control by historical-criticism. That these varied strategies have emerged within the academy in close engagement with ecclesial practices is significant.

Another feature reiterating that we are not simply speaking of texts interpreting other texts (so that the Church is like an interactive on-line library), but are engaged with living texts interpreting our lives and practices and vice versa, and presenting God to the world—is the fact that the scripture in the *Office* is contextualized by "Intercessions." For example, one formal intercession for this Friday morning reads:

---

[52] See Lindbeck, *The Nature of Doctrine: Religion and Theology in a Postliberal Age*, SPCK, London, 1984, or more succinctly, "The Story-Shaped Church" in ed. Fowl, *The Theological Interpretation of Scripture*, pp. 39–52; Stanley Hauerwas, *Unleashing the Scripture: Freeing the Bible from Captivity to America*, Abingdon Press, Nashville, Tennessee, 1993; and John Milbank, *Theology and Social Theory*, Blackwell, Oxford, 1990.

[53] For Hauerwas's stringent critique of liberation theology, see "Some Theological Reflections on Gutiérrez's Use of 'Liberation' as a Theological Concept," *Modern Theology*, 3, 1, 1986, pp. 67–76; and for Hauerwas's sympathy with feminism, which is somewhat underdeveloped, see his response to Linda Woodhead, "Can Women Love Stanley Hauerwas? Pursuing Embodied Theology" in eds. Mark Thiessen Nation and Samuel Wells, *Faithfulness and Fortitude: In Conversation with the Theological Ethics of Stanley Hauerwas*, T. & T. Clark, Edinburgh, 2000, pp. 161–88; and Hauerwas's reply: pp. 327–9. For Milbank's critique, see chapter 8, "Founding the Supernatural" in *Theology and Social Theory*, and "The End of Dialogue" in ed. D'Costa, *Christian Uniqueness Reconsidered*, Orbis, New York, 1990, pp. 174–91.

"You continue to work in your faithful people: create through them a new world where injustice and destruction will give way to growth, freedom and hope."

Response: "Lord Jesus, come to us today."

Each local church avoids saying its prayers seriously if in reading its scriptures it is not moved to the practice of justice and hope, even if it never fully knows what these terms mean, apart from continuously engaging with scripture and tradition. Praying and reading the scripture are a profoundly practical activity as well as an intellectually complex and rigorous one, as Augustine so well explains in Book One of *On Christian Doctrine*. It takes a lifetime of schooling to learn how to read, pray, and live. The life of the Church today is part of the continuing tradition that forms the complex contexts of pluriform scriptural interpretation. This hermeneutical plurality also has the delightful consequence of entailing that the meanings of scripture are never exhausted, otherwise praying the *Office* would be like reading and re-reading the telephone directory rather than being washed in the cyclical rhythms of sacred time. Closure of meaning is precluded, for as long as the Church continues to pray its scripture, it expands the endless contexts of interpretation, and the complex, murky, and moving love affair (called tradition) is fueled, nourished, and critically re-appropriated while remaining an open-ended project.

These features that I have been charting have profound implications for biblical study within university theology departments. My own limited biblical studies as a student were shaped exclusively in the Germanic Anglo-Saxon historical-critical tradition. In many respects this tradition still dominates in many countries, though by no means uniformly and there are many hopeful signs of change. What I would suggest is that the dominance of historical-critical biblical studies is radically called into question by a theology whose methodology is generated by prayer. This, for a number of reasons.

First, while philological and historical investigations into scriptural texts are absolutely necessary for an understanding of the text within the remit of such disciplines, to exalt this single way of reading as *the* way of reading the scripture is a form of hermeneutical myopia.[54] Not only has the historical-

---

[54]   1 would characterize Edward Sanders's type of approach to the Bible as precisely the sort that I am criticizing. See, for example, *Jesus and Judaism*, SCM, London, 1985, and especially his criteria for establishing what count as "valid" materials (pp. 3–22). Even so, his historical theses and reconstructions are not without importance. For an opposite approach in practice, see Stanley Hauerwas, *Unleashing the Scripture*.

positivist approach been challenged hermeneutically within the Humanities by Gadamer, Foucault, de Certeau, and others, the exclusivist exaltation of this approach seriously marginalizes an open ecclesial tradition as the appropriate context for reading and practicing scripture. Keeping this allegedly hard-science reading strategy in place was part of theology's gaining respectability in the secular academy. Hence, strictly speaking, this was the hermeneutical strategy of secular positivism.

George Lindbeck argues this point forcefully in relation to North America in the late 1980s:

> If anything controls Scripture today, it is the exegetical establishment. The exegetical establishment in North America consists of the institutions which train the overwhelming majority of the people who teach Scripture in a vast array of colleges and universities—some church schools, some Catholic, some Protestant. But the majority of them are secular institutions. Most of the people who currently receive doctorates in biblical studies in this country end up teaching in institutions which are secular. The American Academy of Religion (AAR) is the establishment. This establishment is unified. That is to say, confessional boundaries make very little difference. One teaches in the prestigious graduate schools in such a way as to prepare people who will be viewed as reputable academic scholars everywhere. So, what one emphasizes has very little to do with personal faith.[55]

Training students to imagine that the historical-critical method is the proper way to read the Bible today does not allow for the deconstruction of the historical-critical method's own theological and philosophical presuppositions. In this way secular theology departments exclusively utilizing historical-critical methods exalt one moment of the modern world as the unexamined Archimedean point from which to read all history.[56] I am not suggesting that interpretation can or should be premodern or that it can avoid contemporary

---

[55]   Ed. Richard John Neuhaus, *Biblical Interpretation in Crisis: The Ratzinger Conference on Bible and Church*, W. B. Eerdmans, Grand Rapids, Michigan, 1989, p. 120. Lindbeck's claim about the A.A.R. is disputed by some—see pp. 120–2. It is ironic that Donald Wiebe castigates the A.A.R. as a "religious association" that "does not wish to be a scientific or academic society," in Wiebe, *The Politics of Religious Studies*, Macmillan, Basingstoke, 1999, p. 248. See also the Roman Catholic theologian, Francis Martin, *The Feminist Question: Feminist Theology in the Light of Christian Tradition*, T. & T. Clark, Edinburgh, 1994, pp. 50ff, who also argues that the historical-critical method is partially responsible for prising theology out of its proper ecclesial context. See also eds. Carl Breaten and Robert Jenson, *Reclaiming the Bible for the Church*, W. B. Eerdmans, Grand Rapids, Michigan, 1995, which makes out a similar case to mine from a broadly Lutheran perspective.

[56]   For some searching examinations into the philosophical presuppositions of historical criticism, see Cardinal Joseph Ratzinger, "Biblical Interpretation in Crisis: On the Question of

hermeneutical issues. These are not options for theology. Rather, contemporary hermeneutical strategies need also to be questioned by alternative and past interpretative strategies—and finally, by revelation itself, which is only accessible to us as mediated through the Church. *IEVT* notes that all the tools, concepts, and disciplines adopted by theology are judged by revelation, "which itself must furnish the criteria for the evaluation of these elements and conceptual tools and not *vice versa*" (para. 10). However, in *IEVT*, revelation is at times invoked in an almost positivist fashion, as if it were not itself subject to mediation through culture. In contrast to such a position, in another context, Cardinal Joseph Ratzinger (now Pope Benedict XVI) argues against both a biblical fundamentalism (the Bible interprets itself without mediation, or is seen in a purely positivist manner, not requiring ecclesial mediation), and an ecclesiological fundamentalism or positivism (the Church owns and controls the meaning of the text). He writes:

> Certainly texts must first of all be traced back to their historical origins and interpreted in their proper historical context. But then, in a second exegetical operation, one must look at them also in the light of the total movement of history and in light of history's central event, Jesus Christ. Only the *combination of both* these methods will yield understanding of the Bible. If the first exegetical operation by the Fathers and in the Middle Ages is found to be lacking, so too is the second, since it easily falls into arbitrariness.[57]

Ratzinger's point is important for it rightly locates the ecclesial context of reading scripture, without suggesting closure as a result. In a rather nicely balanced fashion he expresses the future-oriented dynamic between the Church and the Bible when he says: "The Bible interprets the church, and the church interprets the Bible. Again, this must be a mutual relationship. We cannot seek refuge in an ecclesiastical positivism. Finally, the last word

---

the Foundations and Approaches of Exegesis Today" in ed. Neuhaus, *Biblical Interpretation*, pp. 1–23; and John Coventry's excellent critique of this method with specific reference to *The Myth of God Incarnate*: "The Myth and the Method," *Theology*, 81, 682, 1978, pp. 252–61; and Gerard Loughlin, *Telling God's Story*, pp. 149–52. Questioning the very notion of "writing" history and its interpretation—see Robert Young, *White Mythologies: Writing History and the West*, Routledge, London, 1990 .

[57] Ratzinger, "Biblical Interpretation in Crisis," pp. 20–1. However, Ratzinger never specifies how the Fathers and Medievals were "lacking" and some participants within the subsequent conference rightly question this claim: e.g. pp. 117, 155–60. Avery Dulles, rather briefly, but very provocatively, suggests the rehabilitation of the medieval threefold spiritual sense of scripture married to the three theological virtues: ed. Neuhaus, *Biblical Interpretation*, p. 154. See also Louth's defense of allegory over against the historical critical method—in Louth, *Discerning*, esp. ch. 3.

belongs to the church, but the church must give the last word to the Bible."[58]

Such considerations make it clear that within confessional Christian departments of theology there may be radically different ways of construing biblical studies. For example, and these are crude generalizations, some Protestant departments may not give such a role to tradition, while most Roman Catholic and Orthodox departments would certainly wish to locate biblical studies *within* the engagement of traditioned readings. Some Roman Catholic departments may require prompting from Orthodox departments to focus more rigorously on the significance of liturgy in exegesis. I say this, as in the conference from which I have been quoting Ratzinger, it took Thomas Hopko, from St. Vladimir's Orthodox Theological Seminary, to remind Ratzinger that the "hermeneutical key [to biblical exegesis] is liturgy," not tradition.[59]

Locating biblical studies within the context of traditioned readings results in a dangerous and delicate destabilizing of existing disciplinary boundaries, rather than shoring up any pious conservatism. For instance, there could be no such discipline as biblical studies that is in any way isolated from patristic, medieval, reformation, historical, structural, and postmodern reading strategies (to name a few). Biblical scholars, who cannot of course be experts in all these areas, will nevertheless have to be sensitive and alert to these different forms of reading if they are to be competent readers themselves. But this blurring of disciplinary boundaries does not stop here, for it also requires that the biblical scholar be a moral theologian, for if the Bible has a moral sense, as Augustine, Aquinas, Barth, and others have rightly insisted, then biblical scholarship must relate to moral practice. This near-divorce from moral theology and biblical theology was subtly registered at Vatican II: "Special attention needs to be given to the development of moral theology. Its scientific exposition should be more thoroughly nourished by scriptural teaching."[60] In briefly outlining the implications of my argument both for

[58] Ratzinger, "Biblical Interpretation in Crisis," p. 23. Ratzinger's balance can be seen as developing Vatican II's *Dogmatic Constitution on Divine Revelation*, para. 12, which suggests both the necessity of technical exegesis and its insufficiency and inadequacy apart from tradition: see Ratzinger's commentary on this point, in ed. Vorgrimler, *Commentary*, vol. 3. See also his criticisms of Pius XII, in ibid., p. 197.

[59] Ed. Neuhaus, *Biblical Interpretation*, p. 118. Ratzinger is of course well aware of this. Elsewhere he writes: "The Church's liturgy being the original interpretation of the biblical heritage has no need to justify itself before historical reconstructions: it is rather itself the standard, sprung from what is living, which directs research back to the initial stages." Joseph Ratzinger, *Church Ecumenism and Politics*, trans. Robert Nowell, St. Paul Publications, Slough, 1988 [1987], pp. 84–5.

[60] *Decree on Priestly Formation*, para. 16. Cardinal Ratzinger also makes the point well: "I am against the reduction of orthodoxy to orthopraxy, but without concrete Christian action,

"biblical studies" here and for "religious studies" (in chapter one) within a freshly reconceived "theology," one begins to see just some of the profound institutional ramifications.

To conclude: I want briefly to situate my own position in relation to that which is sometimes called "postliberal" theology. The interpretation of the tensions between the three implicit poles that I have been discussing above (Bible, tradition, authority) is also related to the context of the Church's engagement with its own living traditions while being situated in a pluralistic culture. In this sense, every engagement with the contemporary, pluralistic world is already and always an engagement with the biblical world, and the tradition-specific history out of which Christianity operates. Unless the Church has become so assimilated to the world's cultures, it will constantly explore its own traditions while *simultaneously* engaging with the Other. It is for this reason that I have reservations regarding George Lindbeck's notion that the biblical text "absorbs" the world. In a key (and oft-quoted) passage, Lindbeck writes: "Intratextual theology redescribes reality within the scriptural framework rather than translating scripture into extrascriptural categories. It is the text, so to speak, which absorbs the world, rather than the world the text."[61]

Both Lindbeck and Hans Frei, as with what has been termed "postliberal" theology, seek to instigate a counter-"reversal" in common with my own proposed project.[62] While I may well be pressing Lindbeck's metaphor about "absorbing" the world, too far, it worryingly suggests a rather unilateral process whereby the world has nothing to offer to the Church and does not in any way disrupt and challenge the narrative traditions of the Church, its reading and practice of scripture. The Church simply makes sense of and interprets the world within its "framework." Both the singular and the impersonal nature of this latter metaphor ("framework") give cause for disquiet. (Admittedly, Lindbeck is talking about scripture, not the Church, but the concern still applies.) Rowan Williams registers a similar worry.[63]

---

biblical interpretation will be found wanting" in ed. Neuhaus, *Biblical Interpretation*, p. 188. I would suggest that John Paul II's encyclicals are one possible model of this re-marriage between ethics and biblical scholarship, as is the work of John Howard Yoder. See, for example, *The Politics of Jesus*, W. B. Eerdmans, Grand Rapids, Michigan, 1972.

[61] George A. Lindbeck, *The Nature of Doctrine: Religion and Theology in a Postliberal Age*, SPCK, London, 1984, p. 118.

[62] For a good introduction to postliberal theology, see William C. Placher, "Postliberal Theology" in ed. David F. Ford, *The Modern Theologians*, Blackwell, Oxford, 1997 (2nd edn.), pp. 343–56.

[63] Rowan Williams, "Postmodern Theology and the Judgement of the World" in ed. Fredrick Burnham, *Postmodern Theology: Christian Faith in a Pluralistic World*, Harper & Row, San Francisco, 1980, pp. 92–112: p. 93.

In contrast, he stresses the messy, two-way process that takes place in the interpretative interaction, for "the very act of interpreting affects the narrative as well as the world, for good and ill."[64] Furthermore, the notion of *the* text absorbing the world also raises a further question. It concerns the way Lindbeck specifies rules that are embedded within doctrines, but then utilizes these rules so that they become almost atemporal and ahistorical constructs for determining doctrinal development, in the time-bound need for the constant re-presentation of Christian truth. For example, the various doctrinal statements about the incarnation are said to exemplify three rules that must always be observed in all Christological discussion.[65] While there is an important insight in Lindbeck's example, which is derivative from Lonergan in regard to a very specific analysis of a particular Church council, what is problematic is the ahistorical manner in which these rules and narratives are proposed as guides to how Christian history should develop. John Milbank presses this point with incisive force:

> Thus [for Lindbeck] Christians are seen as living within certain fixed narratives which function as schemas, which can organize endlessly different cultural contents. These "hypostasized" narratives are not seen as belonging within the sequence of history itself, but instead as atemporal categories for Christian understanding. . . . There is no real possibility here for Christianity to exert a critical influence on its cultural receptacles, nor for these in turn to criticize Christianity. This possibility is occluded by Lindbeck, not because he is a good postmodern relativist, but rather because he has artificially insulated the Christian narrative from its historical genesis. A narrative that is falsely presented as a paradigm is seen as over and done with, and easy to interpret.[66]

Milbank overstates a tendency or danger within Lindbeck's project, but it highlights the formalist manner of Lindbeck's hermeneutics. In contrast, by using prayer as the key to deal with the notion of "living tradition" (which is analogous to Lindbeck's concept of "framework"), I have tried to emphasize the shifting relationships that constitute my tradition-specific approach. Prayer at least guards against atemporal and ahistorical notions, for it points to a living, struggling relationship that has taken on endless forms between ecclesial persons and God. It, should therefore also help to counter abstract

[64] Ibid., p. 94.

[65] George Lindbeck, *The Nature of Doctrine*, pp. 92–6.

[66] John Milbank, *Theology and Social Theory*, Blackwell, Oxford, 1990, p. 386. See also in a similar vein, Geoffrey Wainwright, "Ecumenical Dimensions of George Lindbeck's *The Nature of Doctrine*," *Modern Theology*, 4, 1988, pp. 121–33: esp. 125–6. Ironically, Milbank is criticized similarly by Rowan Williams for assuming an ahistorical ecclesia in, "Saving Time: Thoughts on Practice, Patience and Vision," *New Blackfriars*, 73, 861, 1992, pp. 319–26.

and system-oriented approaches, which Lindbeck inadvertently perpetuates by using "text" as his key metaphor.

One final minor reservation. Lindbeck's apparent emphasis on the biblical text as providing all categories of interpretation, rather than the living reality of Jesus Christ in his community, is in danger of emphasizing scripture as the norm for "Christianity."[67] This outlook neglects the fact that the very notion of scripture is *dependent* on a Church which judges and names what it takes to be scripture. Furthermore, this notion of Church also requires the concept of authority (in making a decision) and tradition (in making subsequent such decisions) to be taken as part of an interconnected organic historical reality within which interpretation takes place. In my use of the *Office* in this chapter I have sought to show how the very notion of "living tradition" is constantly reconfigured and developed (or mutilated and disfigured) within the historical project called the Church. Hence, to put it sharply, Lindbeck's approach is perhaps too biblical and formalist and insufficiently ecclesial.[68]

In this chapter I have been outlining the importance of prayer and a life of virtue and discipline for academic ecclesial theology within a postliberal university system. It is an implication of this argument that such a theology may structurally and institutionally be more successful, in the long run, for returning theology to its proper task that is still unfinished: appropriately focussed, intellectually and practically, upon worship of the triune God who reveals Himself in the particularity of a complex narration of the life of Jesus and his companions, the Church. In developing the picture of what this theology might look like, I turned to the traditions of prayer, saints' days, liturgical feasts, and the practice of charity and virtue as some of the prerequisite skills necessary for the university theologian—whose only task is to worship God truthfully. The argument so far has been that theology is in danger of becoming assimilated to modernity. This is inevitable within the context of theology as a discipline within the secular university. In engagement with MacIntyre, I called for a postliberal plurality of universities with differing traditions of enquiry, and within such institutions, the renewal of tradition-specific ecclesial forms of theological enquiry. The study of religions finds its proper home within theology and it is to this that we now re-turn.

---

[67]   This is seen in the way "church" is produced from the "biblical texts" in Lindbeck's "The Story-Shaped Church"; whereas, in contrast, Loughlin indicates the priority of ecclesia—see Gerard Loughlin, *Telling God's Story*, pp. 38–42, 46–51, 56–61.

[68]   See Reinhard Hütter, *Suffering Divine Things: Theology as Church Practice*, trans. Doug Scott, W. B. Eerdmans, Grand Rapids, Michigan, 2000, pp. 35–54, where Hütter develops this point.

Chapter Five

The Engagement of Virtue: A Theological Religious Studies

I An Example of Theological Religious Studies: A Methodological Note

I now want to draw together some of the theological threads and themes of the previous four chapters and focus specifically on the question, what might a theological religious studies look like? This was a major concern running through chapter one. I now want to demonstrate what a theological religious studies might look like. If virtue is required for the study of theology, what precisely is the shape of virtue, exemplified in a Christian saint? In the context of a theological religious studies we add another question: how does Christian virtue engage with Hindu "virtue," presuming for a contentious moment that there is some common ground between the two traditions? And if prayer is required for the study of theology, what of those theologians who have devoted themselves to prayer, such as a good Carmelite nun? A further question arises in the context of a theologized religious studies: how does Christian prayerful practice engage with Hindu prayerful practices? I have chosen the subject of this chapter—a Christian saint and Carmelite nun who died for the Jewish people under the Nazis, and a modern Hindu *sati*, who (allegedly) died to atone for the sins of others—to show how a theological reading is often able to understand what modernity cannot: religious self-sacrifice as a means of winning merit through grace. I shall also engage with gender issues, again to call into question many of the assumptions that moderns or positivist historians bring to these issues, while also learning from them. This work is done in the footnotes, so as not to disturb the flow of the narrative. If the theologian working in a Christian university is accused of sectarianism, of being inward turning, unconcerned with non-Christians, this chapter serves to illustrate that the theologian's work is nothing but rigorous openness to the Other, to

critical and sympathetic engagement with every other discipline possible—
in this instance, "religious studies."

As this chapter illustrates my criticisms of Ninian Smart's non-theological
phenomenology of religious studies, it is worth noting what we have in
common, given my previous emphasis on what divides us. I am deeply
indebted to aspects of Smart's approach in at least two ways. First, in contrast to Marxist or feminist or psychoanalytical reductionist readings of
"religion" (when they are reductionist), I want theologically to presume that
in encountering "religion" one may be encountering something that calls
into question these various methodological approaches. This is a presumption I have argued for in terms of Christianity, and now I extend this
presumption, open-endedly, without any *a priori* judgements, in engaging
with Hinduism.[1] In this respect, Smart's type of openness to otherness can
stem from theological principles rather than being inimical to such principles, as Smart always assumes. Second, to facilitate this encounter I stand
back from judgement in the process of trying to uncover the deep structural
religious logic within the Hindu ritual acts that I shall be inspecting. This is
not to ignore socio-economic, gender, and other interests that vie together
in the production of "religion," but it is a refusal to render that which is
examined purely in such terms. Smart and I have something in common.
However, the difference between us will be apparent as the chapter develops, for my primary interest in the Hindu events inspected is theological,
allowing Christian theology to engage with the materials to transform religious studies into a theological religious studies.

While this chapter serves to develop the argument of the previous chapters as well as draw together some of their themes and concerns, it is the first
of two chapters that illustrate the positive engagement of an ecclesial theology with other disciplines within the curriculum, indicating the possible
fruitfulness of a Christian university. In the next chapter I will be turning to
the question of a theological physics. Here I deal with a theological religious studies. Clearly, a Barthian, a Roman Catholic liberal, or a Southern
Baptist might approach these questions differently. I want to illustrate what
one Catholic approach actually looks like.

A final word on method. Following the growth of the history of religions
one finds numerous books and studies that assume saintliness and holiness
are "trans-religious" concepts, or "cross-religious" concepts.[2] By "trans-

---

[1]   I have argued for this approach in *The Meeting of the Religions and the Trinity*, Orbis Books,
New York, 2000, pp. 99–142.

[2]   See, for example, ed. John Stratton Hawley, *Saints and Virtues*, University of California
Press, Berkeley, 1987; and from a Hindu perspective, *Women Saints: East and West*, editorial
advisors Swami Ghanananda and Sir John Stewart-Wallace, Vedanta Press, California, 1955.

religious," I mean a concept of holiness that the researcher creates, or at least assumes as universal, and then finds among many different religions, thereby often running against the self-interpretation of the said saint and their tradition. This is true of Rudolf Otto and William James, as it is of John Hick, and even postmodernist writers who should know better, such as Edith Wyschogrod.[3] In a previous book I have argued against such an approach.[4] By "cross-religious," I mean a tradition-specific notion of holiness, such as found in neo-Hinduism or liberal Roman Catholicism, which then seeks parallels or reflections within other traditions. Karl Rahner supported such a theological history of religions.[5] While I am far more sympathetic to the "cross-religious" approach, it still faces the problem of running into conflict with the self-description of the valorized saint and his or her community. It is worth recalling the Buddhist scholar Edward Conze's remarks: "I once read through a collection of the lives of Roman Catholic saints, and there was not one of whom a Buddhist could fully approve . . . They were bad Buddhists though good Christians."[6] However, it is sometimes the case that a Catholic saint-*type* might be found within Hinduism, and that person would also be seen as a saintly example of holiness within his or her own tradition. Alternatively, that which Hindus might proclaim saintly may be found to be deeply questionable by some Roman Catholics. It is at this metaphoric conjunction of two different streams of "holiness" that some of the most interesting flotsam appears.

I shall be examining the life of a Hindu *devi* and a Christian *saint*, Roop Kanwar and Saint Edith Stein respectively, remembering that such designations—"*devi*" or "saint"—are contested from within and from outside each particular tradition.[7] Roop Kanwar, a Hindu housewife, is a *devi*, a female goddess, according to many. Nevertheless, the Government of India and the State of Rajasthan have outlawed veneration to Kanwar. Our Roman Catholic "good wife," Edith Stein, is officially a saint. She was beatified on May 1, 1987 in Germany and canonized by Pope John Paul II in Rome on October 11, 1998. Nevertheless, some Jews and various Catholics were outraged by the canonization of Edith Stein. Being "holy" has always been

---

[3] See Rudolf Otto, *The Idea of the Holy*, trans. John W. Harvey, Oxford University Press, London, 1928; William James, *The Varieties of Religious Experience*, Simon & Schuster, New York, 1997; John Hick, *An Interpretation of Religion*, Macmillan, London, 1989; Edith Wyschogrod, *Saints and Postmodernism*, University of Chicago Press, Chicago, 1990.

[4] See my *The Meeting of Religions*, pp. 1–15.

[5] Karl Rahner, "Christianity and the non-Christian religions" in *Theological Investigations*, Darton, Longman & Todd, London, vol. 5, 1966, pp. 115–34, esp. p. 132.

[6] Edward Conze, *Thirty Years of Buddhist Studies*, Bruno Cassirer, Oxford, 1967, p. 47.

[7] I have omitted diacritics throughout to ease reading for non-specialist readers, and because there is more than one convention regarding transliterated terms.

offensive for it touches our deepest fears, taboos, and fantasies, and calls into question the complex ways in which we construct our world. Let me turn to each woman in sequence.

II Roop Kanwar—A Hindu *Devi*?

Roop Kanwar, an 18-year-old Rajput woman, is venerated by many Hindus as a saint, indeed technically something more: a female goddess (*devi*)[8] capable of showering blessings upon those who visit the site of her "heroic" death which took place in Rajasthan on September 4, 1987. Kanwar was, by the majority of eye-witness accounts, and by those who knew her, a woman who *voluntarily* became a *sati*. Sati, starkly defined, is the self-immolation of a woman with her (dead) husband on his funeral pyre. I say starkly, for the exact rules defining *sati* vary enormously. That there should be such controversy over her veneration is hardly surprising. Kanwar, according to the post-Christian feminist, Mary Daly, was burnt and mutilated by patriarchal Hinduism and could only be valorized by a religion exalting cruelty toward women.[9] Daly is not alone in seeing *sati* as the cultural embodiment of terrifying misogyny.[10] First, however, a word on the term *sati*.

---

[8] *Devi* is the general term for a goddess: the feminine form of *deva*, a god or celestial power. In the earliest texts (*Rig Vedas*) the term is used to refer to the wives of the gods, or to parts of religious worship personified as goddesses (see II, 1; II, 11 for example). Only in the post-Vedic period does the term come to be used for *the* goddess and also for the many local goddesses of the Śaivite pantheon. *Satimata* (literally: truth/virtuous mother, or living *sati*) is an alternative appropriate term, although there are gradations even within this state—see ed. John Stratton Hawley, *Sati: The Blessing and the Curse*, Oxford University Press, Oxford, 1994, pp. 81–2.

[9] Mary Daly, *Gyn/Ecology: The Metaethics of Radical Feminism*, The Women's Press, London, 1987, ch. 3.

[10] For a good overview of feminist responses see Veena Tahwar Oldenberg, "The Roop Kanwar Case: Feminist Responses" in ed. Hawley, *Sati*, pp. 101–30. These responses come from secular Indian and European feminists (the majority) as well as Hindu feminists and non-feminist orthodox and liberal Hindus. For those who would contest such readings, ranging from orthodox Hindus (the Shankaracharya of Puri), cosmopolitan Indian Hindus (Ananda Kentish Coomaraswamy), non-Hindu Indians (Ashis Nandy), and European indologists (Katherine K. Young and Catherine Weinberger-Thomas) see respectively: Sakuntala Narasimhan, *Sati: Widow Burning in India*, Anchor Books, Doubleday, New York, 1990, pp. 24–7, reporting on the Shankaracharya's comments; Ananda Kentish Coomaraswamy (the distinguished art historian), "Sati: A Vindication of the Hindu Woman," *Sociological Review*, 6, 2, 1913, pp. 117–35; and more vigorously, "Status of Indian Woman" in *The Dance of Shiva*, Noonday Press, New York, 1957, 2nd edn., 1957 [1948], pp. 115–39; Ashis Nandy, "Sati. A Nineteenth Century Tale of Women, Violence and Protest" in *The Edge of Psychology: Essays*

The common translation of *sati* as "widow burning" is an incorrect rendition, as the *sati* chooses other than "widowhood," for she is not technically a widow until the funeral pyre is lit. Further, according to some pandits, her husband is not technically dead until his soul (*atman*) leaves the body when his skull is cracked for this purpose at the cremation. In both instances, the *sati* is never a widow. Etymologically, *sati* is the feminization of the Sanskrit word, *sat*, which means "true, real, good" and therefore "virtuous," which is used to characterize the divine reality in the term *sat-cit-ananda* (loosely translated as being/real, consciousness, bliss). *Sati* has numerous semantic contexts. Most commonly in English it has been rendered as a (verbal) noun, something that is done, the act of burning. This colonial sense is nicely captured in the Anglo-Indian dictionary, *Hobson-Jobson*: "the rite of widow-burning; i.e. the burning of the living widow along with the corpse of her husband, as practiced by people of certain castes among the Hindus, and eminently by the Rajputs."[11] In Hindi, Marathi, and Sanskrit sources, and in a minority of colonial accounts, *sati* is applied to the person, not the action.[12] It is the woman who is the truthful, good wife, and her manner of death is then secondarily derived from this primary definition. Some writers insist on this second usage alone, while others do not. I shall use *sati* in both senses, which does justice to the multiple manners of construing it. Third, *sati* is also connected etymologically and emblematically with the goddess *Sati*, wife of *Siva*, who immolates herself to avenge an insult upon her husband. It has been noted that her death precedes her husband's and is undertaken as a result of her father's insult by his occluding *Siva* from an important ritual. David Kinsley concludes, "It is not altogether clear, however, that *Sati*'s suicide provides the mythological paradigm for suttee [i.e. *sati*]."[13] However, Catherine Weinberger-Thomas provides a more

---

in *Politics and Culture*, Oxford University Press, Delhi, 1980, pp. 1–31, and the controversial "Sati as Profit Versus Sati as Spectacle: The Public Debate on Roop Kanwar's Death" in ed. Hawley, *Sati*, pp. 131–48 (with responses from Ainslee T. Embree and Veena Tahwar Oldenberg); Katherine K. Young and Alaka Hejib, "Sati, Widowhood and Yoga" in Arvind Sharma with Ajit Ray, Alaka Hejib, and Katherine K. Young, *Sati: Historical and Phenomenological Essays*, Motilal Banarsidass, Delhi, 1988, pp. 73–85; and Catherine Weinberger-Thomas, *Ashes of Immortality: Widow-Burning in India*, University of Chicago Press, Chicago, 1999, trans. Jeffrey Mehlman and David Gordon White [1996].

[11] Henry Cole and A. C. Burnell, *Hobson-Jobson*, [rev. edn.], Munshiram Manoharlal, New Delhi, 1979, p. 878. Cited in Hawley, *Sati*, p. 12.

[12] See Hawley, *Sati*, pp. 12–13; Weinberger-Thomas, *Ashes*, pp. 11–18.

[13] David Kinsley, *Hindu Goddesses: Visions of the Divine Feminine in the Hindu Religious Tradition*, University of California Press, Berkeley, 1986, p. 40. For a fuller account of the variant myths, see Wendy Doniger O'Flaherty, *Siva: The Erotic Ascetic*, Oxford University Press, Oxford, 1973. O'Flaherty properly makes the connection that Kinsley misses: incest.

imaginative reading in this regard, as well as in tracking other *sruti, smriti,* legal, and folk sources.[14]

To return to the Kanwar story. Briefly, Kanwar, an educated (up to tenth grade) 18-year-old, was married to a Rajput, Maal Singh, a 23-year-old graduate living in Deorala, Rajasthan. After eight months of their marriage, Singh fell ill and died. That much is clear. According to Singh's parents, Kanwar prepared the body for cremation, refusing any help from relatives, and then insisted she would be a *sati*. Her father-in-law tried to dissuade her, to no avail, as did some of the village elders and local Brahmin priests who were summoned. However, Kanwar would brook no opposition. Her own parents testify to her frequent devotional visits to the *sati* shrines, especially the major *Satimata* Narayani Devi temple at Jhunjhunu, of which there are 110 other shrines and temples in India. Further, and in keeping with tradition, a miracle displaying her power was performed. Mark Tully relates this story:

> Then a senior member of the family held up both her hands and said, "Stop, stop! I'll find out whether she is a sati. I have an illness. I will bathe and put on clean clothes. If the bleeding stops, I will know she is a sati. If it does not, she is not." The singing petered out, the arguments died down and everyone waited for the woman to return. Roop Kanwar sat by her husband's body muttering, "*Om sati, om sati, om sati.*" When the relative returned, she walked over to Roop Kanwar, took her chin in her hands and said, "I accept that you are a sati."[15]

Kanwar led the procession through the streets of Deorala to the pyre, where under a nearby sacred pipal tree were three small shrines commemorating three previous *satis* belonging to the village. Between 1943 and 1987 there have been at least thirty *satis* in the Rajput/Shekavati region.[16] Upon the pyre, Kanwar placed her husband's head in her lap and "Villagers maintain that Roop Kanwar continued to pray right up to the moment her body slumped forward and was consumed by the flames."[17] From that moment on, Kanwar as *sati* was to be venerated, deified, protested, pitied, and contested.

[14] See Weinberger-Thomas, *Ashes,* esp. pp. 160–9. A very precise list of sources is to be found in Sharma, *Sati,* pp. 31–9; and for the most careful and comprehensive commentary on the legal texts see P. V. Kane, *History of the Dharmaśastras,* Bhandarkar Oriental Research Institute, Poona, 1968, vol. 2, pt. 1.

[15] Mark Tully, *No Full Stops in India,* Viking, London, 1991, p. 212.

[16] Catherine Weinberger-Thomas, *Ashes,* pp. 182–5, who points out that the number is probably higher, given that this is the officially recorded number, plus two extra discovered in her field work.

[17] Tully, *No Full Stops,* p. 213.

One way in which her death might be understood would be via the orthodox defense of *sati* in the eighteenth-century text, *Strīdharmapaddhati: Guide to the Religious Status and Duties of Women*, written by the Hindu orthodox pandit, Tryambakayajvan, who employs scripture, tradition, and law to show why *sati* makes a woman truly virtuous. Tryambakayajvan's treatise was written for the royal court of Thanjavar (Tanjore), South India.[18] In what follows I present *one* reading of Kanwar's death through the constructs of Tryambakayajvan, recognizing throughout that this is a contested and perilous reading. There are no first-hand accounts from Kanwar. Her relatives, family, and eye-witnesses to her death all testify to Kanwar's voluntary self-immolation. I shall assume this to be so, at least for the purpose of the comparison that I undertake.

Five qualifications are necessary before outlining Tryambakayajvan's arguments. First, the politics of describing this tradition has been rightly criticized: both as potentially defamatory to Hinduism; and in its misogynistic voyeurism. Mary Daly suggests that this type of hagiography is pornography. I cannot claim any detached status in writing this. I have great respect for aspects of Hinduism, as well as many questions. I find *sati* deeply abhorrent and believe that Daly is partly right in her analysis: it reflects Hindu patriarchy's destruction of women; but is there something more to be explored? I do not believe that the practice can be dismantled until the full power of its religious vision is understood. Second, the history of the practice is extremely complex, as is the question of the number of women who have died in this manner.[19] It is a dangerous form of scholarship to pretend that this religious saintly "ideal" for women can be divorced from forced *sati*, for which there is ample horrific evidence, or that it is not sometimes related to dowry murders, female infanticide, child brides, and abortions of female fetuses. Nor can it be divorced from the fact that men have constructed the Hindu legal tradition, as in most religions including Christianity. Third, *sati* is now illegal in India (since the 1829 Suttee Regulation Act), and was strongly opposed by some orthodox Hindus throughout Indian history, as also in the present day. Fourth, in modern India there are many women and men who still regard *sati* as an act of heroic virtue. Julia Leslie writes: "[S]*ati* remains as an ideal. While the numbers of women who

---

[18]   See I. Julia Leslie's translation of Tryambakayajvan in: *The Perfect Wife: The Orthodox Hindu Woman According to the Strīdharmapaddhati Tryambakayajvan*, Oxford University South Asian Series, Oxford University Press, Delhi, 1989. Admittedly, a Rajput text would be more appropriate, but there is none comparable to Tryambakayajvan, except through oral history— see Lindsey Harlan, *Religion and Rajput Women: The Ethic of Protection in Contemporary Narratives*, University of California Press, Berkeley, 1992; and Weinberger-Thomas, *Ashes*, pp. 175–96.

[19]   The best guides on this are: Weinberger-Thomas, *Ashes*; Sharma, *Sati*; Hawley, *Sati*.

died in this way have always been statistically small, the ideal of such women and such a death is reverenced throughout traditional India today."[20] Roop Kanwar's case is a clear example. Many Hindus from all castes claimed she was a goddess (*devi*). However, soon after her death, 3,000 women marched in Jaipur in protest with banners proclaiming: "A woman's murder is a challenge to the entire sex." Some weeks later at a pro-*sati* rally in Jaipur 70,000 men, women, and children marched together, proclaiming Kanwar a *devi*, and an estimated $3 million were collected at the meeting for a shrine to venerate Kanwar. *The Times of India*[21] estimated that over 200,000 people all over India defied the government ban to honor her death and deification. My exploration is into the logic of the *dharma* (the moral and religious duties of a Hindu) that is behind such veneration, or to put it differently, an attempt to understand *sati* intra-textually. This is not an attempt to justify it. Fifth, I have chosen the most difficult example of "saintliness" within Hinduism that I could think of, because it raises such complex questions and makes for some painful comparisons.

In as brief and non-technical a manner as possible, I will outline the basic argument advanced by Tryambakayajvan, who cites numerous older legal Sanskrit texts and scriptures, and whose methodology is not unlike that of the medieval disputation. The work is extremely orthodox both in the authorities cited and the methodology employed. It is divided into five sections: introduction and parameters to the study; a detailed list of the daily duties of the Hindu wife (the only path of sanctification for women in Tryambakayajvan's view); an outline of the inherent nature of women; the general duties applicable to all women (regarding menstruation, property, and so on)— where the discussion of *sati* takes place; and finally, stories and quotations about women. The basic position is contextualized in terms of cosmic righteousness, the *dharma*, which, if followed by men and women in their different roles, will result in social and cosmic harmony. Things were once in such harmony, and the stories of the virtuous wives of gods are set in this golden epic period, before human history began. The proper role of a woman is being a devoted wife (*pativrata*), and that of the man, a devoted and righteous husband—until his wife dies. Admittedly, he has many other social roles, while his wife does not, and he can include, in these, another marriage. He is then able to pursue his *dharma* as a forest-dwelling ascetic (*vanaprasthya*), prior to the final stage of total renunciation (*sannyasi*). *Sati* comes into play as one of the two paths open to a woman if her husband dies

---

[20] I. Julia Leslie, "Suttee or Sati: Victim or Victor?" in ed. I. Julia Leslie, *Roles and Rituals for Hindu Women*, Pinter Publishers, London, 1991, pp. 175–93: p. 176.
[21] September 17, 1987.

first. His life can be defined without his wife, if she dies first. Egalitarian symmetry is not relevant.

Hindu *dharma* entails an extremely complicated number of duties set out for every caste group and each sex in all stages of development. Tryambakayajvan outlines two possibilities for the woman whose husband dies before her: *sati*, dying with one's husband, which he sees as the preferable route; or widowhood (*vidhavadharma*), which has numerous duties analogous to the celibate ascetic first stage of the man (*brahmacarya*).[22] In his advocation of *sati* Tryambakayajvan makes some very important points so that *sati* can be understood appropriately. First, *sati* is to be distinguished from suicide, and therefore does not break the legal prohibition against suicide in Hindu law. It is distinguished along the same lines as the warrior who fights in a righteous battle knowing that he will be killed. He is not thereby guilty of suicide, but is virtuously following his proper *dharma*. The warrior, like the widow, must not fear death, for in doing their duty courageously they will be reborn in a higher form, to be eventually released from the *karmic* cycle. At the Roop Kanwar rally, Kalyan Sing Kalvi, a spokesman for the demonstration, criticized those who oppose only *sati*, and not other religious forms of "suicide": "Jains are known to die by fasting. Buddhists are known to immolate themselves. So why apply this law only to us?"[23] He was referring to a byelaw introduced in Rajasthan (1987) after the Kanwar case, to fine and imprison surviving *satis*, and apply the death penalty to those abetting the practice.

Second, all ritual actions accrue merit, normally for the one undertaking the action. There are three types of ritual action: obligatory (*nitya*) ones that are performed daily—e.g. praying; occasional ones that must be performed (*naimittika*) such as on the day of one's marriage; and optional (*kamya*) ones that need not be performed, except to gain the merit accorded to that action.[24] For Tryambakayajvan, *sati* is in the last category. Any

---

[22] Young and Hejib, "Sati, Widowhood and Yoga" in Sharma, *Sati*, pp. 73–85 make out an excellent case for the ends of *sati* as parallel to that of the *yogi* (p. 82), hence relating it to the male *yogi*'s final stage of life, with the crucial difference that the male *yogi*'s final goal is *moksha* (liberation from rebirth), whereas the woman's is an analogical equivalent, given her womanly status, of union with her husband, her *pati* (god husband) (p. 83). For the asymmetry of male and female in this respect, see Katherine Young, "Why Are Hindu Women Traditionally Oriented to Rebirth Rather Than Liberation (*Moksha*)?," *Third International Symposium on Asian Studies*, Asian Research Service, Hong Kong, 1981. This is contested, based on fieldwork, by Lynn Teskey Denton, "Varieties of Hindu Female Asceticism" in ed. Leslie, *Roles*, pp. 211–31.

[23] I. Badhwar, "Kalyan Sing Kalvi: Beliefs Cannot be Repressed," *India Today*, October 31, 1987, p. 20.

[24] There is a great deal of debate on these classifications and how they should be interpreted. See, for example, Weinberger-Thomas, *Ashes*, pp. 197–214.

forced *sati* would not be *sati* at all. While Tryambakayajvan is pessimistic about the widow's ability to live properly as a widow, due to the supposedly ill-disciplined and licentious nature of women, he is clear that only those who aspire toward the ideal will be capable of *sati*. The alleged voluntarism of the act has been severely criticized: "If a woman does not have the right to choose whether she wants to marry, and when, and whom, how far she wants to study, whether she wants to take a particular job or not, how is it that she suddenly gets the right to take such a major decision as whether she wants to die?"[25] This criticism misses one important point—that a woman's choice is not a right, but a matter of following one of two possible duties. Within the *dharma* there is no place for rights outside of these duties. The important difference between men and women here is that a husband has no such *sati* option (although a very small number of men have immolated themselves on their wives' pyres). This asymmetry works both ways, for the male warrior is also called to accept death, when appropriate, as part of his ritual duty, as Krishna reminds Arjuna.[26] However, one should remember that consistently within the *dharma* there is no attempted "equality" between caste or genders, for righteousness is served in following the duties prescribed to each as members of their group. Equality is an extremely modern ideology. Hence, *intra-systematically*, *sati* is an optional ritual to which is ascribed considerable merit, both for the woman and through her actions, for her husband, and both their families.

Third, it is this unique transferential merit that gets us to the *dharmic* core of *sati* and it is an important exception to the Hindu understanding of *karma* or merit, that normally holds that all actions can reap good or bad merit by one who undertakes the action. Normally, one must undergo the consequences of such action, and only through compensation and reparation for one's wrong actions (through fasting, doing ritually meritorious acts, etc.) can one eventually attain release (*moksha*).[27]

The merit due to the *sati* is three-fold. First, her ritualized act of righteous devotion releases her from all bad merit that she has accrued during her life. Clearly, the good wife who is defined by doing her duties, which include obeying her husband, will have less incentive to atone for her own

[25]   Madhu Kishwar and Ruth Vanita, *In Search of Answers: Indian Women's Voices from Manushi*, Zed Books, London, 1984, p. 21.

[26]   Nandy, "Sati as Profit" turns the warrior analogy on its head, and asks why journalists who are up in arms about *sati* do not similarly protest about the structural self-destruction tied up with the army (pp. 145–6), and the hypocritical valorization of immolation in the cause of revolution and liberation movements (p. 136).

[27]   This should be qualified in two ways. First, knowledge, not action can lead to *moksha* in some strands of the tradition. Second, from Vedic times, priests offered sacrifices on "behalf" of a donor, who might offer these on behalf of another.

wrong-doings. On the other hand, and second, a bad wife has every reason to perform *sati*, for this will be a definitive chance to purify herself. Tryambakayajvan puts it clearly, indicating that intentionality and consequence are not unilaterally identified:

> Women who, due to their wicked minds, have always despised their husbands (while they were alive) and behaved disagreeably towards them, and who none the less perform the ritual act of dying with their husbands when the time comes—whether they do this of their own free will, or out of anger, or even out of fear—all of them are purified of sin.[28]

The latter two causes (anger and fear) can certainly conspire toward forced *sati*, but it is clear that Tryambakayajvan is not intending to support these forms of *sati*, for his argument is precisely to extol the free choice of *sati* because it is *dharmically* coherent and attractive in securing righteousness in the world. For Tryambakayajvan, *sati* has the quality of "sufficient atonement" (*prayascitta*) for the deeds of the bad wife. As one of the epic husbands puts it, in a dialogue cited by Tryambakayajvan: "it is through the merit of being a devoted wife that a woman attains the highest heaven. If she does not do this, even if she has bathed in all the sacred places, she will go to hell."[29] The ritual efficacy of this atoning act is extremely powerful, for it easily outdoes the ritual efficacy of bathing in sacred places, usually enough to cancel many serious shortcomings.

The third and most significant meritorious aspect is the transferential merit gained for the husband and his family as well as the *sati*'s own ancestral family. Merit is usually accrued by the one who undertakes the ritual act, although there is a long tradition going back to the Vedas, whereby merit can be attained for another. The *sati atones* for the sins of her husband and has the power, in her action, to release him from the fires of hell (a provisional, not eternal hell). In some texts, it is clear that this atoning power also applies to the wider families in the marriage and to those who visit the shrines of the *satimata* (lit. truth/virtuous mother). Tryambakayajvan cites many texts. Here is one showing the extent of the *sati*'s atoning power. One begins to

---

[28] Leslie, *The Perfect Wife*, 43r. 7–9; Leslie, *Roles*, p. 186. In this Tryambakayajvan crosses a line that is contested by other jurists, some of whom argue that *only* the *sativrata*, the good wife, can follow this course as her decision to do so (*samkalpa*) must be immediate and without deliberation, an expression of her virtuous character that has been practiced throughout her married life. A bad wife would not come to such a decision spontaneously and immediately. Admittedly, the weight of the tradition paradoxically imputes the death of a husband prior to his wife as the fault of the wife who should have looked after him better; obviously not applicable to a warrior.

[29] Leslie, *The Perfect Wife*, 44.3–6; Leslie, *Roles*, p. 187.

understand why the Rajput crowd (who support *sati*) want to venerate Kanwar as a *devi*. Her self-sacrificial love of duty breaks the bounds of hell, as through her free act she liberates her husband, even if he committed the most heinous crime, such as murder of a Brahmin:

> Even in the case of a husband who has entered into hell itself and who, seized by the servants of Death and bound with terrible bonds, has arrived at the very place of torment; even if he is already standing there, helpless and wretched, quivering with fear because of his evil deeds; even if he is a brahmin-killer or the murderer of a friend, or if he is ungrateful for some service done for him—even then a woman who refuses to become a widow can purify him: in dying, she takes him with her.[30]

Or with more dramatic and succinct force, Tryambakayajvan cites another verse: "Just as the snake-catcher drags the snake from its hole by force, even so the virtuous wife (*sati*) snatches her husband from the demons of hell and takes him up to heaven."[31] It is this force of virtue that defies the demons of hell that make the *sati* capable of bestowing blessings upon those who visit her shrine. As one Indian woman is reported to have said, when attending the Kanwar pro-*sati* rally: "*Sati* is not possible for all women, only those who are very blessed. I have come here for the blessings of this holy place."[32]

Tryambakayajvan touches on lots of other interrelated matters that I cannot pursue here. What is so startling about the intra-textual logic of his exposition of the *dharma* is the positioning of *sati* as heroic virtue, whereby the freely undertaken self-sacrifice of a woman is able to atone for her sins, for the sins of her husband, and for the sins of others, both her family and relatives who know her, and her devotees, most of whom will never have known her. The good woman has soteriological power. This transferential merit, which breaks most normal *karmic* rules, is what constructs the ideal holy and good woman. In the midst of an apparently horrific misogyny, women suddenly are able to be saviors, victors, saints, and not victims— even if tragically, only in their willingness to die. For one single moment, the woman becomes (in Julia Leslie's words) "victor"; in *sati* "victims find a path through a maze of oppression, a path that to them spells dignity and power."[33] Leslie refuses to glorify this dignity, holiness, and power; but nor does she simply dismiss it, as do Mary Daly and so many others.

---

[30]   Leslie, *The Perfect Wife*, 43r.4–5; Leslie, *Roles*, p. 185.
[31]   Leslie, *The Perfect Wife*, 43r.4–5; Leslie, *Roles*, p. 185.
[32]   *The New York Times*, September 19, 1987. Harlan's study *Rajput Women* indicates very strong support for attitudes such as these.
[33]   Leslie, *Roles*, p. 177.

What is so disturbing, although quite different, is an analogous intra-textual logic of transferential merit displayed in the life of some Christian saints. It is not accidental that the Jesuit missionary, Roberto de Nobili, witnessing 404 *sati* at the great funeral of Nayak Muttu Krishnappa in 1606, "rued the fact that they were not his coreligionists, since such would have further heightened the glories of Christian martyrology."[34] Among the canonized we see women within a predominantly male-constructed theological tradition, attaining sainthood, often via death—which is at some level, "freely" chosen, and reflects the soteriological power of the good woman, the faithful bride of Christ.

III Edith Stein—A Catholic Saint

As with *sati*, the veneration of saints is not unanimously accepted by all Christians, and within Roman Catholicism there is much dispute about the manner of canonization, the gender problems within the canon, and the various historical constructions of virtue and sanctity at different times in the Church's history.[35] However, there are four significant formal, not material, overlaps between the *sati* tradition as outlined above and modern notions of sainthood. I introduce these to help focus my argument. First, both celebrate a life lived virtuously, not a single act at the end of a life. Second, such lives are identified in so much as there is conformity to doctrinal orthodoxy. Third, miracles accompany the identification of the candidate, and these are not seen to be anything other than a manifestation of the holiness of the person. Fourth, each is seen as a mediator of divine power, the *sati* in terms of her *sat* quality, and the saint in terms of being an imitation of Christ. None is formally worshipped in themselves. The *sati* cult relies on a prior mythology and cosmology of divine power that the *sati* embodies in her life, and saints are venerated, not worshipped; there is a gulf of difference between *dulia* and *latria*.[36]

One of the most controversial elements of Edith Stein's canonization was the transferential merit she accorded to her death. If Kanwar died for her

---

[34] Weinberger-Thomas, *Ashes*, pp. 119–20.

[35] Kenneth L. Woodward, *Making Saints: How the Catholic Church Determines Who Becomes a Saint, Who Doesn't, and Why*, Simon & Schuster, New York, 1996, is a good guide regarding most of these issues, especially for the modern period. See also Richard Kieckhefer, "Imitators of Christ: Sainthood in the Christian Tradition" in eds. Richard Kieckhefer and George D. Bond, *Sainthood: Its Manifestations in World Religions*, University of California Press, Berkeley, 1988, pp. 1–42, for a masterly overview.

[36] *Dulia* is to be distinguished from *hyperdulia* reserved for Mary alone, that is distinguished from worship proper, *latria*, due to God alone.

own sins, her husband's, and their families', the Jewish convert Carmelite nun Edith Stein viewed her death, which she did not desire, but possibly could not avoid, as an atonement for her own sins, the sins of the Church, the German people—and the sins of the Jewish people (of whom she was one). Many Jews objected to Stein's remarks about Jewish sinfulness and their need for atonement, and that the Church seemed to celebrate her "martyrdom" when in fact she died primarily for being Jewish, and only secondarily for being Catholic.[37] But first, let me briefly outline the relevant contours of Edith Stein's life which allow us to see the significant analogies between Stein and Kanwar. Then I will sketch the cosmology out of which she operated. She, like Roop Kanwar, was claimed to exemplify orthodox doctrine and practice to an extraordinary degree, was venerated by some groups, and seen as a shining example of a woman mediating soteriological power. On all these three counts, there was, as with Kanwar, intra-tradition dissent as well as dissent from outside the tradition.

I shall sketch some biographical moments within Stein's life, using Stein's own writings. Edith Stein was the seventh child of a well-to-do practicing Jewish family born in 1891. She was born on Yom Kippur, the Jewish day of atonement, which Stein's mother saw as auspicious, as did Stein. Later, Stein would see her life as an atonement for Jewish disbelief—among other sins of the world. Her father died when she was three. At the age of 15 she declared herself an atheist, without religion. She was intellectually outstanding among her peers. From 1913–15 she studied at the University of Göttingen, under Husserl. Husserl's young colleagues, Adolf Reinach, Roman Ingarden, and Max Scheler, were Jews who became Roman Catholics. (Pope John Paul II, who canonized Stein and declared her a woman doctor of the Church, had discussed Scheler in his doctoral work and was a personal friend of Ingarden.) Stein recalls that what impressed her most about Catholicism was its teachings on marriage. She very much desired to be married, and eventually would be: as a bride of Christ, by taking sacred vows and holy orders in the Carmelite tradition. She, like Roop Kanwar, would find in her husband the image of God, and seek to follow him everywhere, even through death, although unlike Kanwar, Stein's husband was God. Two important events happened during World War I. The first was her doctoral dissertation under Husserl, written on empathy. Writing as an atheist, she was able to empathize with the notion of religious sacrifice: "I myself may be an infidel and yet understand that someone else may sacrifice all his earthly possessions for his faith. Thus I acquire by empathy the concept of *homo religiosus*, and though it

---

[37]   For example, see ed. Harry James Cargas, *The Unnecessary Problem of Edith Stein*, University Press of America, Lanham, Maryland, 1994.

is alien to my thinking, I understand him."[38] The second event was the death of Reinach on the Western Front. His widow Anna Reinach's consolation in the cross shook Stein, who had gone to sort out Reinach's philosophical papers at the request of his widow. Stein notes this as her turning point: "This was my first encounter with the Cross and the divine strength it imparts to those who carry it. It was the moment when my unbelief collapsed. Judaism paled and Christ shone forth; Christ in the mystery of the cross."[39] The transferential merit of the cross, and the participative redemptive suffering undertaken freely by those who follow the bridegroom, would become increasingly central for Stein.

On January 1, 1922, Stein was baptized into the Roman Catholic Church taking the name of Teresa, after Teresa of Avila, for it was the Carmelite life that attracted her greatly. Her mother was devastated, and Stein was advised not to enter the order in deference to her mother's hurt. Stein lived with nuns and continued a formal philosophical education, turning to the study of Aquinas, women's education, and spirituality. In 1933 the Nazis enacted anti-Semitic laws and Stein's teaching position at Münster ended. Seeing the course of anti-Semitic currents, she sought an audience with Pius XII, but failed. Instead she wrote to him urging that he publicly denounce anti-Semitism. He did not directly reply to her questions but, instead, sent her his blessing. In 1933, she writes that during the Holy Hour at the Carmel of Cologne-Lindenthal:

> I spoke to our Saviour and told Him that I knew that it was His Cross that was being laid on the Jewish people. Most did not understand it, but those who did understand must accept it willingly in the name of all. I wanted to do that. Let Him only show me how. When the service was over I had an interior conviction that I had been heard. But in what the bearing of the Cross was to consist I did not yet know. I was almost relieved to find myself now involved in the common fate of my people.[40]

Stein always considered herself Jewish, so it is clear that she felt this cross as hers in a double manner: being Jewish, and being Catholic. This is most important for a proper sense of her understanding of transferential merit. Eventually, the pull of Carmel was too strong, and she applied for admission, was accepted, and returned to tell her family—and mother. This was to prove at least as painful as sharing the news of her conversion to

---

[38] Edith Stein, *On the Problem of Empathy*, trans. Waltraut Stein, 3rd ed., Institute of Carmelite Studies Publications, Washington, DC, 1989, p. 114.

[39] *Inside the Vatican*, October 1998, p. iv.

[40] Ibid., p. vii.

Catholicism. After going to the synagogue together on October 12, 1933 (which Stein always did when she visited her mother), she agreed with her mother that the sermon was "beautiful" and that Jews can be pious and devout—if they have not yet learnt about Jesus. Stein wrote that her decision to enter Carmel was incomprehensible to her mother and most of the family, but not to her sister Rosa. Rosa was eventually baptized and became a Third Order Carmelite, to perish together with Edith. In her clothing ceremony on April 15, 1934, Edith took on the name: Teresa Benedicta of the Cross. Of this name, she writes retrospectively in 1938:

> By the cross I understood the destiny of God's people which, even at that time, began to announce itself. I thought that those who recognized it as the Cross of Christ had to take it upon themselves in the name of all. Certainly, today I know more of what it means to be wedded to the Lord in the sign of the Cross. Of course, one can never comprehend it, for it is a mystery.[41]

The theme of Stein taking on suffering for the atonement of others, especially the Jews, becomes stronger and stronger as Nazi anti-Semitism grew around her. This understanding is also connected with her marriage to Christ, for the cross was the seal of the marriage. She must follow her groom into death if necessary, and her death will then be atonement for others, especially the Jewish people. In 1938 she uses the image of Queen Esther from the biblical book of Esther to construct her own self-image. Esther pleads for all the Jewish people to her husband, King Ahasuerus— and reveals that she too is Jewish, in an attempt to save them from the pogrom instituted by the king's advisor, Haman. (In the Bible story, Esther does not actually die on behalf of her people, but changes their destiny through her intervention.) Stein writes of the "shadow of the Cross which is falling on" her people. She trusts:

> in the Lord's having accepted my life for all of them. I keep having to think of Queen Esther who was taken from her people precisely that she might represent them before the king. I am a very poor and powerless Esther, but the King who chose me is infinitely great and merciful.[42]

Three years before she was murdered in Auschwitz on Thursday August 9, 1942, she wrote on June 9, 1939 a passage that further elaborates this theme.

---

[41] Edith Stein, *Self-Portrait: In Letters 1916–1942*, trans. Josephine Koeppel, O.C.D., ICS Publications, Washington, DC, 1993 [1987], letter 287 (subsequent reference: *Letters*, each letter numbered as in book, rather than page numbers).
[42] *Letters* 281.

One should note in this quotation three important points: first, that her marriage to Jesus means her joyful acceptance of her own death as she, like the *sati*, can only find her fulfilment in terms of her relationship to her husband; second, that her own death will be redemptive to others; third, these others will be Christians and Jews. The bride's death ensures transferential merit:

> Even now I joyfully accept the death which God has destined for me, in total submission to His most holy will. I beg the Lord to accept my life and my death for His honour and glorification, for all desires of the most holy hearts of Jesus and Mary and the Holy Church, and especially for the preservation, sanctification and perfection of our Holy Order, particularly the Carmel in Cologne and in Echt, *for the atonement* of the unbelief of the Jewish people and for this: that the Lord may be accepted by his own people and that His Kingdom may come in glory, for the salvation of Germany and for world peace, and finally for my relatives both living and dead, and all those who God has given me: that none of them may perish.[43]

Many critics have (falsely) found in this passage evidence of her alleged anti-Semitic attitude and her replication of the myth of Jewish hard-heartedness. Yet her incomplete autobiography *Life in a Jewish Family* gives an account of her own Jewish family life in an attempt to present the normal human face of ordinary Jews in the light of the "horrendous caricature" that drives Hitler and the Nazi Party.[44] For those who think that Stein was negative about Judaism, her comment on her mother is instructive:

> Her faith and trust in God remained unshaken from her earliest childhood and was her last support in her hard struggle with death. I am confident that she has found a most merciful Judge, and that she is now my most faithful helper on my own journey toward my homeland.[45]

Stein is simply concerned to take upon herself, like her husband, the sins of the world, specified in terms of her own historical context.

By 1936 Stein completed two important works: one on Husserl and Aquinas; and the other on *Life in a Jewish Family*. In 1936 her mother died at the very moment when Stein renewed her vows in the Cologne Carmel;

---

[43] *Inside the Vatican*, p. x, my emphasis.

[44] Edith Stein, *Life in a Jewish Family: Her Unfinished Autobiographical Account*, trans. Josephine Koeppel, ICS Publications, Washington, DC, 1986, p. 23 She neither romanticizes nor defames the community she knew through her childhood, and her mother's piety is both revered and respected; see also *Letters* 146b, 160.

[45] *Letters* 227.

and after her mother died, Rosa joined Edith and was baptized. In 1938 Stein took her final vows, and in December of that year moved to Holland, concerned for the safety of the other nuns in Cologne because of her Jewish roots. Above, I have cited a vital passage from 1939, where we see Stein connecting her death and atonement. This theme became very central in these last years.

On July 26, 1942, after the Archbishop of Utrecht ordered a denunciation of the Nazi treatment of Jews to be read in all Dutch Roman Catholic churches, the Nazis ordered a round-up of all Jewish converts. Records show that the Nazis promised not to hurt Jewish converts if bishops, from all denominations, did not interfere with their action toward the Jews. Protestant Churches were going to join in the protest but eventually refrained. Consequently, only Catholic Jews were rounded up. It was this aspect that allowed Stein eventually to be accelerated through the procedures of canonization, as the *relator* for her cause was able to argue that she was a "blood martyr" (a person who dies for their faith).[46] Rosa and Edith were arrested on the evening of 2 August. Her last reported words as she left with her sister were: "Come, let us go for our people."[47] On 9 August Edith and Rosa were gassed at Auschwitz. Their bodies, as with so many others, were never recovered.

Stein's letters and writing demonstrate the following themes:

(a) In her view she was to carry the cross, destined for the Jewish people, as well as all humanity. In the first sense, she would share the fate of her people.

(b) With respect to the Jewish people, Stein viewed her role as analogous to that of Queen Esther, who undertook to represent her people.

(c) Stein chose her married name at her formal profession, Teresa Benedicta of the Cross, to indicate this vocation.

(d) It was Stein's marriage to her spouse, Christ, that required her to carry this cross.

(e) Stein interpreted her death as expiatory, as voluntarily undertaking the penance due to others for their sinfulness, a penance required for their atonement.

---

[46] See Woodward, *Saints*, pp. 138–42, especially on the fact that her original process did not involve her being claimed a martyr. It took 21 years to change the claims within the process: from confessor to martyr. Exceptionally, she was proclaimed both.

[47] There is some controversy as to the source and authenticity of this quote. Dutch Carmelites attribute it to Maria Desling, a lay volunteer in the extern quarters of the Carmel in Echt, where Desling worked with Rosa Stein and who witnessed the arrest.

From this, and the knowledge of the Catholic culture out of which Stein grew, we can assemble a cosmological framework within which these themes fall into a coherent pattern. Stein does not present an explicit cosmos in her writings; rather, she assumes it, not unlike Kanwar. Given her close readings of Thomas Aquinas, Teresa of Avila, and John of the Cross we can speculatively construct the following world-view in which the action of the good wife enacts an extraordinary transferential merit, a rent in the fabric of the moral order, allowing a terrifying entry of the divine Word.

Aquinas drew heavily on Anselm's *Cur Deus Homo?*, what Gustav Aulén calls the Latin theory of atonement (expressed in terms of an objective satisfaction or expiation), as well as incorporating certain themes from Abelard's moral theory (which tends to emphasize the subjective change that is facilitated in following the example of Christ).[48] Aquinas agrees with Anselm that we are freed from sin by "Christ's satisfaction," that is, the proper restitution of God's just order, broken by human sin. Of course, God could simply forgive the sin without requiring anything of humankind, which in fact He does in the order of charity. However, God's justice also requires "punitive restitution" that will restore the order of justice.[49] Neither Anselm nor Aquinas envisage a vindictive God desiring punishment, but rather they employ and transform terminology from their social and legal contexts to provide models to elucidate revelation and illuminate the moral order created by God for our good and God's glory. Sin requires satisfaction, enacted in penance, that has two effects: curative or healing grace (*curat*) restoring the person to their proper relationship; and the grace of preservation (*preservat*) that strengthens them from future falling away. Aquinas thus arrives at exactly the same solution as Anselm, best captured in the *Compendium theologiae*:

> Justice demands satisfaction for sin. But God cannot render satisfaction, just as he cannot merit. Such a service pertains to one who is subject to another [which God cannot be to Himself]. Thus God was not in a position to satisfy for the sin of the whole of human nature; and a mere human being was unable to do so . . . Hence divine Wisdom judged it fitting that God should become human, so that thus one and the same person would be able both to restore the human race and to offer satisfaction.[50]

---

[48] See Gustav Aulén, *Christus Victor*, SPCK, London, 1931, for this typology, which Aulén insists should not be pressed sharply.
[49] *Summa Theologiae* (subsequently: ST) 1a. 2ae. 87. 6.
[50] Ch. 200.

As Christ is without sin, he alone among men and women is able to offer proper satisfaction. Aquinas differs from Anselm in two important respects. First, he does not insist that Christ's death is necessary, a point that need not detain us here.[51] Second, Christ's satisfaction is not only sufficient, but superabundant, by virtue of: the greatness of Christ's love, exemplified in the greatness of his suffering; the worth of his life, as God-man; and the universal significance of the passion. Hence, Aquinas concludes: "And so Christ's passion was not only a sufficient but also a superabundant satisfaction for the sins of mankind."[52] One weakness in Anselm's work was his failure to explain how we might find the resources to follow Christ's obedience. This same problem is found in Abelard's moral theory. Aquinas again develops the tradition to present a solution to this problem, in a manner that particularly helps us understand the case of Stein. It is an ingenious and important move—and is utterly simple: the resources are there, in the body of Christ.

Purely knowing about Christ's death does not bring about our own satisfaction, for a person may well continue a life of sin. Aquinas posits an ordinary mystical union that generates the sinner's transformation. It is "ordinary," in the sense that it is open to all through baptism, their enjoyment of the sacraments, and following the disciplines of the Christian life; it is the inclusion into Christ's body, the Church. This is so that first, we may enjoy the merit attained for us and grow in grace and virtue; and second, that we may continue the actions of Christ:

> Grace was in Christ . . . not simply as in an individual human being, but as in the Head of the whole Church, to whom all are united as members to the head, forming a single mystic person. In consequence, the merit of Christ extends to others in so far as they are his members. In somewhat similar fashion in individual human beings the action of the head belongs in some measure to all their bodily members.[53]

This second point is important and is also acknowledged by Anselm: as one person (like Christ) can undergo the punishment due to another, likewise Christians can undergo for others the penance due to them, such as to effect

---

[51]   Brian Davies carefully qualifies Aquinas's difference from Anselm in *The Thought of Thomas Aquinas*, Clarendon Press, Oxford, 1992, pp. 330–2.

[52]   ST 3a. q. 48.4. L. W. Grensted, *A Short History of the Doctrine of the Atonement*, University Press of Manchester, Manchester, 1920, p. 153 is surely wrong to see this as an "inferior commercial conception," for the superabundance indicates, rather, the unqualified gratuity of the gift of grace, it is *sui generis* beyond every merit of human action.

[53]   ST 3a. 19.4.

healing grace for the other. This of course requires that the other is well disposed toward this grace. Aquinas was clear that preservative grace could not be applied to another, as it was only effected through and in the actual action undertaken (e.g. fasting):

> Satisfactory punishment has a twofold purpose, viz. to pay the debt, and to serve as a remedy for the avoidance of sin. Accordingly, as a remedy against future sin, the satisfaction of one does not profit another, for the flesh of one person is not tamed by another's fast; nor does one person acquire the habit of well-doing through the actions of another, except accidentally . . . On the other hand, as regards the payment of the debt, someone can satisfy for another, provided that the person in question is in a state of charity.[54]

Scotus and Ockham would contest Aquinas's construction, and later scholastics would refine Aquinas's corpus, but this is basically the cosmological framework that Stein inhabits. It is developed in conjunction with Stein's Carmelite spirituality in two particular ways.[55] First, central to inclusion into the life of Christ is the nuptial metaphor found in Teresa's *The Interior Castle*.[56] Second, the two basic themes of Carmelite life in Stein's Germany were prayer and penance, and these allow us to understand how the virtuous wife of Christ must act. The seven chambers of Teresa's interior castle are progressive stages whereby mystical union is attained, and Teresa employs the image of the bridal chamber for the sixth and seventh chambers whereby this union becomes a spiritual (and erotic) marriage.[57] Eight years after her baptism and three before Stein entered the Carmelites, she lectured to Catholic professional women. In these remarkable lectures Stein elaborates the nuptial link:

> To the nun, in place of the marriage sacrament, the liturgy of *virginal consecration* is granted as a particular means of grace for the strengthening of her vocation; at the least, it is the solemn vow by which she is wedded to the Lord for always . . . If the married woman is obliged to be subject to her husband as to the Lord, so is the nun obligated to honour her legitimate superior as Christ's proxy . . . By partaking in this ceremony [entering the religious life], she receives the blessing by which to live as the *Spouse of Christ* . . . Perhaps,

---

[54] *Sentences*, 4, 20, d.2.

[55] For a helpful background on Carmelite spirituality after St. Teresa, see W. Nevin, *Heirs of Saint Teresa of Avila*, Bruce Publishing Co., Milwaukee, Wisconsin, 1959.

[56] See *Complete Works of Saint Teresa of Jesus*, 3 vols., trans. and ed. E. Allison Peers, Sheed & Ward, London, 1946.

[57] See the most helpful reading of this book offered by Alison Weber, *Teresa of Avila and the Rhetoric of Femininity*, Princeton University Press, Princeton, New Jersey, 1990, pp. 98–122.

hidden from all human eyes, she intercedes for endangered souls by expiatory prayer and vicarious works of reparation in God.[58]

Here, the two themes of Carmelite life are closely linked to nuptial union, both of which are ways in which the religious life is one form of entry into the "single mystic person" of Christ's mystical body, the Church. Stein, like Kanwar, chooses to follow her husband, and in her virtuous action brings about transferential merit for the sake of others. For Kanwar, it is the ritualized death of *sati*; for Stein, the ritualized death of martyrdom.[59]

Is Kanwar a "saint"; and is Stein a "*satimata*"?

IV Virtuous Women as Emblems of Gratuitous Grace or Victims of Patriarchy?

To recount Edith Stein's life and Roop Kanwar's is grueling in different ways: the odor of patriarchy is never far away, as women's bodies continue to be used by men for their own purposes. The German bishops and the German *Relator* handling Stein's case had much to prove, especially in response to Jewish criticisms of the Catholic Church.[60] The long history of Catholic anti-Semitism also runs close to the surface of the narrative. Both pride and politics were at stake in Stein's beatification, along with the issue of holiness. Kanwar's death was certainly used to bolster the caste interests of Rajputs (once proud warriors, now with crumbling identity), the Brahmin priests (with decreasing religious power), and the Marwaris (powerful businessmen, also called *banias*, who are religiously deeply conservative and patrons of the Jhunjhunu temple).[61] Furthermore, there are counter-stories—of Kanwar being drugged, forced into *sati*, and that her screams

---

[58]   Edith Stein, "Spirituality of the Christian Woman" in *Essays on Woman*, trans. Freda Mary Oben, ICS Publications, Washington, 1987 [1959], pp. 122–3, my addition in brackets. It is sometimes facile to straightforwardly relate this bridal imagery to the continuation of patriarchy—as is done by some writers—for, on the contrary, convents often allowed women varying degrees of escape from patriarchy. See Deirdre Green, *Gold in the Crucible: Teresa of Avila and the Western Mystical Tradition*, Element Books, Dorset, 1989, pp. 156–64.

[59]   The martyrdom cause in Stein's case is a complex one, especially in the light of her attempts to move to neutral Switzerland, even during her internment in Drente-Westerbork Barracks on August 4—see *Letters* 340, and earlier 331. Her sharing the fate of her people is qualified. For the best discussion on this point, see Woodward, *Making Saints*, pp. 138–44.

[60]   See Woodward, *Making Saints*, pp. 137–44.

[61]   As reported in Tully, *No Full Stops*, p. 223; and see Sharada Jain, Nirja Mesra, and Kavita Srivastava, "Deorala Episode: Women's Protest in Rajasthan," *Economic and Political Weekly*, 22, 45, 1987, pp. 1891–4.

from the flames were protest rather than blessings.[62] Nevertheless, I have tried to explore an alternative reading of both lives. Further, in viewing Stein as a saint, I am pressed into re-assessing my repugnance at *sati*, given the startling similarity in the logic of their transferential merit. Indeed, if I must re-assess *sati*, am I called to re-assess Stein? Before proceeding I re-iterate that amidst asking the question of whether analogically there is holiness and sanctity to be found in Kanwar's life, one should recall that, theologically, analogy is always found within a greater and more fundamental dissimilarity when talking about God. This certainly applies to the present case, and should be kept in mind in what follows for I do not wish to detract from the intra-textual logic of either of our two traditions. Let me turn to exploring a theological historical-studies approach by way of analogy.

First, by marrying men, both women apparently understood that the occasion of the death of their husband would seal their own lives. Both, in different ways, saw in their husband "the image of God", *patideva*, so that their own death in following their husband would not now hold any fear. The "image of God" has very different senses. For Tryambakayajvan the husband is "like a god," so that the wife be dutiful and serve him, always putting his will first, given that his will reflects the *dharma*. Tryambakayajvan holds the dubious misogynist view that women were better off trusting in a man than in their own capacities, which would usually lead them astray. For Stein, her spouse "is God," so that dutiful obedience to Him leads to salvation. However, for Stein, His will is mediated by her vow of obedience to her mother superior, "Christ's proxy."[63] The gender fluidity within the marriage arrangements is startling, as actual submission for Stein is to another woman, as well as a man.[64] For both, marriage entailed following a path upon which redemption for themselves and others might mean voluntarily accepting an early death, due to circumstances entirely beyond their control.

Regarding the nuptial imagery, we would do well to recall certain "feminist" and "queer" criticisms of marriage in Christian theology. Elizabeth Stuart writes of nuptial images employed in the celibate religious life, criticizing the valorization of the virgin martyr:

---

[62] See the harrowing alternative constructions: Tully, *No Full Stops*, pp. 213–15; Oldenburg, "Kanwar Case," pp. 119–26; and Jain et al., "Deorala Episode."

[63] *Woman*, p. 122.

[64] Admittedly, one would then have to face the objection that the mother superior is submissive to a male-dominated Church.

she rejects marriage to a human husband in order to become the bride of Christ; one form of marriage is exchanged for another. One form of submissiveness to men is exchanged for another which demands renunciation, pain and death. Complete autonomy for women is simply not an option.[65]

Lisa Isherwood also writes of marriage as "institutional torture," a structure that legitimates relentless violence upon women (and children) through an ideology of submissive obedience. She offers considerable empirical evidence.[66] These criticisms, however overstated, cannot be ignored. However, the issues Stuart and Isherwood raise about "submission" require critical inspection.[67] It is always in danger of being framed within an alien choice: submission *or* autonomy, when in fact both Stein and Kanwar construe the world differently other than in these options.

Stein, for example, is very wary about submissiveness to unjust powers, be they in a husband or the Nazis. We have seen her urging Pius XII publicly to denounce Nazi anti-Semitism. Of a bad husband, she says he is an "unworthy spouse" who "makes her [the wife's] life an ordeal . . . in this terrible distortion of the marriage ideal," but the wife must nevertheless "stand firmly before the souls of her children, guarding the life of grace begun in them by holy baptism."[68] Furthermore, Stein also overturns the usual nuptial metaphors of women's submissiveness to man (like St. Paul), arguing that both the man's and woman's nuptial roles are predicated upon a full "surrender to the Lord wherever it is purely and freely observed" by both.[69] In this sense, if both men and women act "properly," submissiveness entails true freedom to follow God—as in marriage, or in the celibate religious life. Of course, there is a constant tension between this "ideal" and social realities and Stein never sanctions social realities that fall short of such ideals. In this sense Stuart's criticism misses its target. It is not that one form

---

[65] Elizabeth Stuart, *Spitting at Dragons: Towards a Feminist Theology of Sainthood*, Mowbray, London, 1996, p. 16.

[66] Lisa Isherwood, "Marriage: Heaven or Hell? Twin Souls and Broken Bones" in ed. Adrian Thatcher, *Celebrating Christian Marriage*, T. & T. Clark, Edinburgh, 2001, pp. 201–17.

[67] Sarah Coakley raises such pertinent questions in her excellent book, *Powers and Submissions: Spirituality, Philosophy and Gender*, Blackwell, Oxford, 2002.

[68] *Woman*, p. 122.

[69] Ibid., p. 123. In this instance, she is discussing the priest and the nun, and draws from this a rather ingenious conclusion about women's exclusion from the priesthood: pp. 123–4, that they, unlike men, are called into a direct union with Christ, rather than via a "delegated authority." We saw that Teresa of Avila also developed this view implicitly. Stein also considers the valid and "difficult" role of the "unmarried woman" seeking to "fulfill her destiny apart from life in the convent" (p. 124). Stein's answer, original and refreshing, is still thoroughly ecclesial: such a woman still lives her life for Christ, in his Church, for "the Lord's method is to form a person through other persons" (p. 126).

of submissiveness is exchanged for another (marriage for the religious life), nor that "complete autonomy" is removed from the woman's choice, but rather for Stein real autonomy is only attained through her marriage, and submissiveness brings about the real freedom to love. Stein's world, not without recognition of the pain and suffering indicated by Stuart's and Isherwood's critiques, is simply not captured in their critiques. I shall turn to the question of pain and violence later.

Kanwar, if we employ Tryambakayajvan's interpretative grid, also calls Stuart and Isherwood into question, at least at the level of theory. Stuart and Isherwood would point out that in both cases male theological constructs are interpreting women's lives. This is truer of Kanwar than of the intellectually independent Stein, although it is true that in the Hindu tradition, the fiercest public critics of *sati* have included many men. Admittedly, historically, this could not have been otherwise. Nevertheless, we find a similar logic to Stein's in Tryambakayajvan in so much as Tryambakayajvan argues the good husband must carry out all his duties toward his wife and carefully follow the *dharma*. In this sense *only*, the woman must obey her husband, for in obeying her husband she is obeying the *dharma*. In practice, it is difficult to see how the husband is "monitored," although in theory the good husband is required to reflect on his own life and seek constant guidance through prayer, sacrifice, and brahminical advice. However, as with Stein, the intra-textual logic is such that the wife's submissiveness is not *per se* to her husband as husband, but only in so much as he is "like God," or for Stein, "is God."[70] It would be unconvincing to suggest that this logic entirely addresses the matter raised by such critics, but too often such a logic is hardly even acknowledged.

Admittedly, there is an issue that after a husband's death the high-caste orthodox widow who does not die with her husband should undergo a very difficult and austere life. She should fast, abstain from all pleasures, cannot remarry, and is traditionally despised for outliving her husband. However, here too, matters are complex, and from an intra-textual view a rather convincing case has been made by Katherine Young and Aleka Hejib that the life of the widow is akin to the male yogi and therefore structured toward maintaining the *dharma*, even while acknowledging the complex social realities.[71] Hence, the widow is still properly following a prescribed *dharmic* path. And to the rightful question: "but is this only so for women, while men can remarry?" there are two answers. First, there is no logically required

---

[70] Some Hindus would claim that he "is" God for that woman in this life, but that would not be a claim that he was a *sui generis* incarnation of God, as in traditional Christianity.

[71] Young and Hejib, "Sati, Widowhood and Yoga."

intra-textual gender symmetry, and second, there is the gender-fluid answer that the soul is finally neither male nor female. The good wife will eventually return to the *samsaric* life as a man. Then "s/he" can attain final release, *moksha*, in which there is no gendered identity.[72]

In both traditions, Christian and Hindu, there is little sense of women's or men's "autonomy" *apart from* their vocational callings (for woman as wife, celibate religious, non-religious celibate, professional person—inclusive within the previous three roles) or in their *dharmic* roles (wife, and more controversially, celibate or non-celibate religious), respectively.[73] In both traditions, marriage and procreativity are highly valued, although in Christianity there is a long history of women following the celibate religious life, and a more recent tradition valuing the single woman who chooses neither of the above two paths. Admittedly, in both traditions there is no religious role for same-sex nuptial-like unions. In conclusion, marriage can be hell for women, but equally, it can lead to heaven. In the case of Stein and Kanwar, there are grounds to argue that it led to the latter (even if different "heavens").[74]

But there is another feature in the narratives of Stein and Kanwar that makes their cases so troubling. It is the apparent glorification of sacrifice, even violent sacrifice. Both believed that their violent deaths would have atoning value, to themselves, and more so to others. Death, and the suffering it entailed, were a means by which transferential merit could be enacted. For Kanwar, being the "good wife" (*pativrata*) allowed her to atone for her own sins, for her husband's sins, and their families, and the devotees who would subsequently flock to the site of her death. Tryambakayajvan calls the *sati* sufficient atonement: *prayascitta*. For Stein, being the good wife and accepting death allowed her to atone for her own sins, for her family, for the sins of Jewish disbelief, and for the sins of the German people. Clearly, she does not atone for her husband's sins, as does Kanwar. But for both, their families by blood and by marriage are positively affected by the violent atoning death that both women accepted.

---

[72] Among the main *acaryas* the exception on this point is Madhva.

[73] On Stein's exploration of these three, see *Woman*, pp. 118–28. On the religious roles in Hinduism, admittedly exceptional and marginal, see the remarkable field work of Lynn Teskey Denton, "Varieties of Hindu Female Asceticism" in Leslie, *Roles*, in which she explores three ascetical types: renouncing asceticism, celibate asceticism, tantric asceticism. The last is important in allowing non-celibate single women *moksha*.

[74] Kanwar's fate as the good wife is to enjoy heaven with her husband for various amounts of time, depending on their *karma*, after which time they both return in different incarnations. There is a tradition that after seven marriages to the same person, incarnated differently of course, the man attains *moksha* and the woman then returns as a man. For Stein, heaven means the beatific vision in eternity.

The criticisms of this sacred violence can be developed in two ways, drawing on the work of René Girard and Luce Irigaray. Girard has relentlessly tried to uncover the allegedly universal religious sanctioning of ritual violence whereby the scapegoat mechanism allows for the periodic and collective murder of a victim, who is both feared, but also then glorified, to cover up the nature of the crime. This is Freud's Oedipal and sexual origins of religion, rewritten in terms of mimetic rivalry. This rivalry is generated by the conditions of learning through mimetic desire, which then produces rivalry for the object of desire, followed by violence against a rival who seeks the same object. Once the rival is defeated and expelled, there is a partial but temporary and fragile peace. The cycle is doomed to turn again. Girard's researches led him to discover that Christianity is the only tradition that unmasks the scapegoat mechanism, for Christ reveals the innocence of the victim and the guilt of the tribe, and in his refusal to enter into violence offers a different order of desire, mimetically practicing peace and reconciliation.[75] While Girard does not inspect Hinduism, his analysis can be fruitfully applied to a *sati*. Her glorification at the time of her destruction conceals the desire for, as well as hatred and fear of, women. She is destroyed as she is the cause of her husband's untimely death, and she is vindicated and venerated, in her willing acceptance of this ritual violence, which once more restores the *dharmic* order.[76] It is slightly more difficult to apply Girard's analysis to the virgin martyr except in so much as such martyrdom is encouraged from within the tradition. However, someone like Stuart would obviously argue for a tight parallel case as she sees virgin martyrs as analogous to wives, who are the sacrifice of such male religions. Gender is obviously vital.

Luce Irigaray challenges Girard precisely on gender grounds. She criticizes Girard's influential thesis in two ways. First, she suggests that the foundational model of religion Girard employs "seems to correspond to the masculine model of sexuality described by Freud: tension, discharge, return to homeostasis."[77] In this sense, Girard never envisages or engages with women's religion(s). Whether the latter indeed exists anywhere in pristine

---

[75] See René Girard, *Violence and the Sacred*, trans. Patrick Gregory, Johns Hopkins University Press, Baltimore, Maryland, 1977 [1972]; and ed. James G. Williams, *The Girard Reader*, Crossroad Publishing Co., New York, 1996.

[76] See, for example, Nandy, "Sati: A Nineteenth Century Tale," p. 9: "Sati was therefore an enforced penance, a death penalty through which the widow expiated her responsibility for her husband's death. Simultaneously, it reduced the sense of guilt in those confronted with their rage against all women . . . It perpetuated the fantasy of feminine aggression toward the husband, bound anxiety by giving substance to the vague fears of women, and contained the fear of death in a region where death struck suddenly."

[77] Luce Irigaray, "Women, the Sacred and Money" in *Sexes and Genealogies*, trans. Gillian C. Clark and Carolyn Burke, Athlone Press, London, 1993 [1987], pp. 77–88: p. 76.

uncontaminated form is a subject for debate, but Irigaray's point is important. Girard masks the fact that he is dealing with "male constituted religion" in defining violence and the sacred. This should not be overlooked. Further, Irigaray is critical of Girard's failure to focus on gendered violence, instead of employing, as he does, "sacred" violence as a universal trans-gendered category. The victims of religious violence are nearly always women. Girard, without mentioning Irigaray, has convincingly defended himself on this latter point.[78]

It seems to me that the strictures of Girard and Irigaray cannot be ignored, but nor do they comprehensively deconstruct the sacred universe that I have sought to illuminate, although they rightly call into question aspects of these universes, in theory and in practice. In the case of Stein, it is important to highlight two points. First, there is an ambiguity in Aquinas's account of redemption that can lead to readings valorizing suffering and pain. Aquinas veers between emphasizing that it was Jesus' loving obedience *even unto death* that makes the passion fruitful, and the view that it was the *extent of his pain and suffering* that demonstrate this loving obedience. This delicate balance is seen in the following: "And this very work, the voluntary endurance of the Passion, was especially acceptable to God, as *springing especially from love; whence it is clear* that Christ's Passion was a true sacrifice."[79] It is possible to argue that since Aquinas was clear that we merit eternal salvation from the moment of Christ's conception, which seems to make the Passion secondary, the only reason why his Passion happens is regarding us: "on our part there were important obstacles which prevented us from enjoying the result of his previously acquired merits. In order to remove these obstacles, then, it was necessary for Christ to suffer."[80] Hence, suffering is not important for its own sake, but necessarily because in the Passion Christ embodies "obedience, humility, constancy, justice, and the other virtues displayed in the passion, which are requisite for human salvation."[81] These virtues are infused into the body of Christ through grace, and therefore available to the baptized. Stein writes on the subject with the same delicate balance:

And whoever is penetrated by the meaning of the sacrifice of the Mass, it were as if he had grown into Christ's redemptive action. The small and great offerings asked of him daily are no longer compulsory, inflicted, overwhelming

---

[78]   Ed. James G. Williams, *The Girard Reader*, pp. 275–7.
[79]   Grensted, pp. 154ff; ST 3a. q. 48. 4, my emphasis.
[80]   ST 3a. 48.1.2.
[81]   ST 3a. 46.3.

burdens. Rather, they become true sacrifices, *freely and joyfully offered*, through which he wins a share in the work of redemption as a co-suffering member of the Mystical Body of Christ.[82]

Sin, both our own and that of others, causes endless obstacles, thus "Christ's redemptive action" inevitably entails taking on the effects of sin: death, suffering, and pain. The aim of doing this is "true sacrifice, freely and joyfully offered," not the desire for pain and death, although this has too often been present in models of holiness.[83] It is perhaps this same balance that is reflected in Stein's saying to Rosa: "Come, let us go for our people" when arrested by the Nazis at Echt, which seemingly entails a death drive, and her constant attempt to get Rosa and herself into Switzerland, out of Westerbork Camp. Matthew Monk's claim that Stein chose not to hurry her arrangements to escape to Switzerland so that she could face death in solidarity with her people is perhaps indicative of this valorization of suffering. It implies that proof of real love is pain and suffering. Admittedly, this may well be required in the course of real love, but to make it proof and evidence of such love is problematic. Further, Monk makes this claim without offering evidence.[84]

Second, Stein's understanding of sacrifice and transferential merit is not unique to her gender or her religious order. In the history of Roman Catholic spirituality it is to be found in many epochs and transforms the lives of both men and women, although admittedly there is something particularly interesting in the parallels evoked in the marriage imagery that Stein herself employs, and Kanwar's situation as a recent bride. Nevertheless, Stein's martyrdom still stands, even precariously, as a culmination of redemptive love. Does Kanwar's?

In many respects Kanwar's case is metaphysically complex from a gender and sacrificial point of view. While the application of Girard and Irigaray's analysis to *sati* provides dark and disturbing fruit that should not be dismissed, there are still features of the Hindu cosmology that call into question some of the more basic assumptions in such an analysis. To begin with, there is the gender fluidity of the cosmology: *karma* and *samsara*, universal principles of justice and cosmic order, determine that a person is born

---

[82] *Woman*, p. 121, my emphasis.

[83] Stuart, *Dragons*, pp. 11–49; and see Elizabeth Johnson, *Friends of God and Prophets: A Feminist Theological Reading of the Communion of Saints*, SCM, London, 1998, pp 27–30, 73–6, 151–6.

[84] Matthew Monk, *Edith Stein*, Catholic Truth Society, CTS Twentieth Century Martyrs Series, London, 1997, p. 26. Her correspondence counters this claim: see *Letters* 331, 337, 339, 340.

low caste or a woman as a result of their previous lives. While this may clearly indicate a "low" valuation of women from outside the cosmology, intra-textually, each and every figure has its place in the *dharmic* order. Nevertheless, there is a hierarchy within Hinduism that means it is better to be born a male brahmin than a woman. Furthermore, from within the *dharmic* scheme, justice and order can be used to argue for three points—showing there is no injustice involved in *sati*. Indeed, the contrary is the case. First, there is no essentialism to being a woman, it is only a *samsaric* moment in a long process that will also involve being a man, and finally a genderless released soul (*atman*), which is the real ontological state of the self. This is the real state of the self, both prior to becoming entangled in birth and rebirth, as well as after such entanglement is complete and *moksha* attained.[85] Second, women are not excluded from *moksha* for, in following their temporal role they will eventually be reincarnated as men and can then attain full liberation. Third, there is no "violence" upon the *sati* for she must choose this course (*samkalpa*) freely, whereas Girard's thesis requires violence *upon* the victim by the group. It is worth pausing on this matter, as it is a complex one.

The argument is in danger of being very circular at this point, both for those who oppose and those who support *sati*. At a legal level it brings about a curious contradiction. Those who argue that there is no choice for women for they are forced into *sati* culturally must reconcile the new law against *sati* (The Commission of Sati (Prevention) Act, 1987, No. 3 of 1988)[86] that makes the woman (and all her accomplices) liable to punishment for *sati*. In this case, she is conceptualized as both free and not-free in one and the same act. It is little wonder that many against *sati* found the law most unsatisfactory in this respect, for the woman, the victim, is doubly punished. On the other hand, for those defending *sati* the Act is a clear case of legal interference with women's religious freedom. The question of women's agency is further complicated as the cosmology requires that the act only be undertaken freely and is optional. Oldenberg also observes a further complexity:

> even when agency can be forensically established, can the woman's act of self-immolation be judged to be a product of her own will, or must it be judged

---

[85] Ironically, Madhva supports *sati* and believes that souls will not be genderless, but the Madhvacharayas of Pejewar and Admar both opposed *sati*; and Sankara opposes *sati* and believes the self is genderless, but the head of the Sankara Puri order supports *sati*. See Narasimhan, *Sati*, p. 25.

[86] The Act is reproduced in Narisimhan, *Sati*, pp. 175–83, see esp. pt. II, 3, 4.

as a product of the very studious socialization and indoctrination of women (particularly for the role of wife) that shape her attitudes and actions from girlhood?[87]

But if this argument is employed, and in one limited sense it is a very valid argument, the question of agency itself become increasingly irrelevant. If a person acts freely but is indoctrinated, then it is not important to establish their acting freely, for it proves nothing either way. Stuart's demand for "complete autonomy" for women is almost a non-sequitur and the Indian feminist Lata Mani quite incisively argues:

> The example of women's agency is a particularly good instance of the dilemmas confronted in simultaneously attempting to speak within different historical moments and to discrepant audiences. What might be a valuable pushing of the limits of the current rethinking of agency in Anglo-American feminism, may, if not done with extreme care, be an unhelpful, if not disastrous move in the Indian context.[88]

Such a stalemate on this very traditional avenue for western feminists causes Veena Oldenberg to suggest that it "might be better to settle for a provisional view of woman as victim until some way is found to resolve the question of woman's agency in this particular setting."[89] But Oldenberg's option answers the problem prematurely by settling *a priori* against *sati*. Ironically, it enacts colonial discourse that stands in superior judgement against *sati*, constructing it from outside, an approach that both Oldenberg and Mani oppose.[90] Does theological discourse end up as colonial discourse in opposing *sati* extra-textually, or is it able to reach deep into the Hindu tradition employing an analogical imagination, not affirming or criticizing it (as yet), but seeking an understanding that touches, even obliquely, the divine? To claim a clear answer here would be perilous, for it could so easily be a matter of one patriarchal cosmology giving a nod and wink to another. However, I think that Weinberger-Thomas's conclusion to her study of *sati* is worth quoting in full as a way of closing this particular chapter, but not this question:

---

[87]   Oldenberg, "Kanwar Case" in ed. Hawley, *Sati*, p. 124.

[88]   Lati Mani, "Multiple Mediations: Feminist Scholarship in the Age of Multinational Reception," *Feminist Review*, 35, 1990, pp. 24–41: p. 38.

[89]   In Hawley, *Sati*, p. 124.

[90]   Ibid., p. 124; and Mani, *Contentious Traditions: The Debate on Sati in Colonial India*, University of California Press, Berkeley, 1998, pp. 158–90, 192–4.

one sees that men and women wound and sacrifice themselves, individually or together, in isolation or en masse, in accordance with rules of conduct that are constantly being reinvented. In other words, one gauges a phenomenon that, when viewed in its totality, transcends issues of gender and social hierarchy. And so we are led to see that the constant in all of this, which plays the role of catalyst for both individual motivations and social constraints, is the idea that violence consented to and used knowingly—after the model of the primordial act and basis for all acts, sacrifice—that this violence alone releases a charge of energy such that he or she who accepts its *fatum* and knows how to benefit from it may, by shattering the circuits of the phenomenal world, of that ineluctable series of rebirths and redeaths, at last cross over the ford that leads to immortality.[91]

Both Kanwar and Stein apparently followed a path, sanctioned by their religious traditions, whereby their own death brings redemption to others. To gloss it: they die selflessly on behalf of others, in a way that scandalizes many and causes others to proclaim their special value and venerate them. If as a Roman Catholic and despite the numerous objections, I affirm Stein to be a saint (which I do), can I really be so horrified, as I was and still am, that Kanwar was proclaimed a *devi*? I still cannot answer this question, but have tried to show why unambiguously opposing *sati* is problematic from a theological religious studies point of view. Equally, from the same point of view, any uncritical support of *sati* is out of the question. I have tried to make out a case whereby Kanwar's death is seen to have analogical similarities to that of Stein such that Kanwar is rescued from the claims that her death was futile, tragic, and a product of patriarchy. In fact, if one is able to navigate these counter-claims (and I am not sure that I am entirely successful), then one might even glimpse in the midst of such deaths, horrific as they are, an insight into holiness, a glimpse of love that knows no bounds, even unto death. Such holiness is disturbing and troubling for it "shatters the circuits of the phenomenal world," the world of sin, such that divinity enters, disrupting the social and cosmic order. That the spring and well of all holiness is Christ is not at issue, but rather the way in which God's grace works in the religious world outside Christianity.[92]

---

[91] Weinberger-Thomas, *Ashes*, pp. 218–19.
[92] I attend to this more general question in *The Meeting of Religions*.

Chapter Six

The Marriage of the Disciplines: Explorations on the Frontier

I Walking Down the Aisle?

Given the analysis of the first two chapters, it needs to be said that in exploring the possible marriage of the disciplines within a Christian university, there is a mixture of both realism and idealization in what follows. The realism bears some relation to practices currently found in different Catholic and Protestant universities. The harmony envisaged within a Catholic university is founded on theological arguments present in the documents of Vatican II, and developed in the writings of Pope John Paul II.[1]

In this chapter I have two aims. First, I examine some general propositions regarding the unity of the disciplines deriving from the writings of John Paul II cited in note one. Second, I want to explore some of these general propositions in engagement with a disciplinary area usually thought to be independent and unrelated to the ecclesia, except when moral opinions on the use of technology are sought: the natural sciences, with special attention to physics and cosmology. This second part, which is perhaps the most illuminating, is also the most tendentious for a number of reasons. The most obvious is my ignorance. I have drawn heavily on secondary literature and cannot claim any special expertise in these fields. I would also hope that this work is a discussion platform, for clearly those in the different disciplines are the most able to formulate alternatives and criticize what is

---

[1]   See Vatican II: GS, 36, 59; GE, 10–12; the most important of John Paul II's works: *CU* (1990); Motu Proprio: "Socialism scientiarum investigations," 1994; "Letter to the director of the Vatican Observatory, George V. Coyne SJ, on the 300th anniversary of Newton's *Philosophiae Naturalis Principia Mathematica*," subsequently "Letter," 1989; *Faith and Reason*, subsequently *FR*, 1998; "Address to the Pontifical Academy of Sciences," 2000. *FR* can rightly be read as an elaboration of *CU*.

being advanced here. But there is a mitigating circumstance. I shall be arguing that unless those in other disciplines have some degree of training in theology and philosophy, the enterprise of a Catholic university is doomed. In analogous manner, theologians need to have some conversation with disciplines other than theology and philosophy. It is impossible to envisage this taking place except with very careful long-term institutional support. Hence, it may be that economics and political science departments carry out specific programs concerned with the Church's social teaching; physics departments explore the interface of cosmology and religious claims concerning creation; and philosophy departments explore the interface between theology, philosophy, and the natural sciences. Another reason for caution here is the rapid change at the cutting edge of research areas. Most of the literature I am surveying was written in the last decade of the twentieth century, and some of it will already be out of date. Hence, I want to emphasize the tentative nature of any conclusions drawn. However, this second section is the most illuminating because one begins to see the complexity of the general propositions, as they are applied to a single context. I can only intimate, in a brief final section, the way these general propositions do in fact illuminate other disciplinary areas. Here, the tensions and unresolved lacunae come into view, inevitably, and I hope, productively. I cannot hope to resolve any of these issues, but bringing them to light is my main aim, to indicate the rich paths that open once we begin to walk down *this* aisle.

Before proceeding I should note two significant issues that are not addressed in what follows. First, the telling of the story of the history of the different intellectual disciplines is required for the full exposition of any envisaged marriage of the disciplines; a wide-ranging genealogy of knowledge.[2] What is common to these different stories is this. There was once a time when Aristotle's vision of the harmony of the different disciplines allowed for creative relations between them, where the fundamental supposition was that each discipline had its own proper autonomy, related to the object of its enquiry. In relation to this object, appropriate methods and questions were thus generated, and the different disciplines were subse-

---

[2]   For the natural sciences (and other disciplines), see entries in *Encyclopaedia Britannica* and *Catholic Encyclopaedia*, both registering significant changes with the various editions. For the natural sciences, see also Ian Barbour, *Issues in Science and Religion*, Prentice Hall, New York, 1966, pp. 15–136; Edward Grant, *The Foundations of Science in the Middle Ages: Their Religious, Institutional and Intellectual Contexts*, Cambridge University Press, Cambridge, 1996; Amos Funkenstein, *Theology and the Scientific Imagination from the Middle Ages to the Seventeenth Century*, Princeton University Press, Princeton, New Jersey, 1986; and Stephen Shapin, *Leviathan and the Air Pump: Hobbes, Boyle, and the Experimental Life*, Princeton University Press, Princeton, New Jersey, 1985. For a history of philosophy, see *FR*, pp. 36–48, and MacIntyre's works cited in note 1, ch. 1 of this book.

quently arranged along a hierarchy related to their status as a "science" (*scientia*: knowledge).[3] Theology was the highest science as it related to the unchangeable, and was thus also the basis of physics. The natural world, concerned with contingency, therefore subsumed what we would today call the humanities and the sciences, those subjects whose object of study lay within the realm of change and mutability. This was the basis of the divisions in the university of Paris, where the Arts (including philosophy, science [*sic*], and literature) were required before one specialized in Theology, Medicine, or Law.

This harmony eventually broke down, initially in the fourteenth century, and then especially with the rise of the empirical sciences in the seventeenth century, the weakening of the Aristotelian world-view, and the various changes charted in chapter one. Three crucial disruptions that characterize this fragmentation relate also to the creation of new disciplinary "sciences." The first relates to the fourteenth century when Ockham and later Biel began to prise apart creation and God for theological motives. However, this inadvertently helped to establish the next nearest most immutable Archimedean point: mathematics. Hence mathematics supplanted the divine overarching principle of unity and harmony. Amos Funkenstein summarizes thus:

> Within the Aristotelian and Scholastic tradition, it was forbidden to transplant methods and models from one area of knowledge to another, because it would lead to a category-mistake. This injunction suited the social reality of medieval universities well, separating theology from philosophy to the benefit of both; but it eroded considerably from the fourteenth century, when mathematical consideration started to be heavily introduced into physics, and even into ethics and theology. What was a methodological sin to Aristotle became a recommended virtue in the seventeenth century . . . The ideal of a system of our entire knowledge founded on one method was born.[4]

Note, Aristotle's unity of the disciplines, and the differing but related Scholastic concept of unity after it, did not lie in the assumption of a single method. It could not, as the objects of study were different. The shift to a single method signified the slow emergence of the Enlightenment. Furthermore, the closed mechanistic universe inaugurated through many of

---

[3] Aristotle, *Metaphysics*, 1026a, 1064b. See also Giovanni Reale, *The Concept of First Philosophy and the Unity of the Metaphysics of Aristotle*, trans. John R. Catan, State University of New York, Albany, New York Press, 1979.

[4] Funkenstein, *Theology*, p. 6, and see also pp. 31–41, 290–9. See also Michel Foucault, *The Order of Things: An Archaeology of the Human Sciences*, Tavistock, London, 1970 [1966], p. 346.

Newton's followers, not Newton himself, consolidated two processes. The method of experiment, deduction from repeatable phenomena, and knowledge based on testable mathematical probability became increasingly normative. Second, the closed mechanistic universe was seen by many as perfectly explicable without the action of God, either as creator or as actor in terms of secondary causality.[5] This meant that some began to (falsely) typify a continuous battle between religion and science.[6] There is no single position among scientists, but certainly with the rise of quantum physics (of the Copenhagen variety), which called into question the Newtonian mechanistic closed universe as well as the limits of what physics might know, the alleged conflict between science and religion has begun to dissolve. Further, epistemologically, the focus on the knower/knowing community in science, from sociological, historical, and philosophical angles, has called into question the neutral objectivity of science claimed by some earlier traditions.[7] Admittedly, these claims are contested, but I only want to indicate the outlines of a narrative. It suggests that the natural sciences are in part an invention of the seventeenth century, inaugurating a mathematical and experimental positivism that was used to standardize all disciplines according to its methods and presuppositions, and for nearly three hundred years this project was dominant. Today, it is crumbling.

The second shift is located within the first: the emergence of the *social sciences* and their *fundamental positivism*. Significantly, as John Milbank has argued, the social "scientific" attempt to explain humans from various

[5]   See I. Bernard Cohen, *The Newtonian Revolution*, Cambridge University Press, Cambridge, 1980; and the insightful piece by J. W. Garrison, "Newton and the Relation of Mathematics to Natural Philosophy," *Journal of the History of Ideas*, 48, 1987, pp. 609–27. See also Hans Blumenberg, *The Legitimacy of the Modern Age*, trans. Robert M. Wallace, MIT Press, Cambridge, Massachusetts, 1986, esp. pp. 77–88.

[6]   The historical picture is of course more complicated. See, for instance, John Hedley Brooke, "Science and Theology in the Enlightenment" in eds. W. M. Richardson and W. J. Wildman, *Religion and Science*, Routledge, New York and London, 1966, pp. 7–28; and Claude Welch, "Dispelling Some Myths about the Split between Theology and Science in the Nineteenth Century" (pp. 29–40) in eds. W. Mark Richardson and Wesley J. Wildman, *Religion and Science*. Michael Buckley, *At the Origins of Modern Atheism*, Yale University Press, New Haven, Connecticut, 1987 is also clear that it was theologians aping science, in both method and content, that led to atheism.

[7]   Philosophically, see Thomas Kuhn, *The Structure of Scientific Revolutions*, 2nd. edn., reprinted with postscript, Chicago University Press, Chicago, 1970; and most influentially, Michael Polanyi, *Personal Knowledge*, Harper & Row, New York, 1962. Sociologically, see Barry Barnes, *Scientific Knowledge and Sociological Theory*, Routledge & Kegan Paul, London, 1974 and *Interests and the Growth of Knowledge*, Routledge & Kegan Paul, London, 1977; and the very helpful collection, eds. Barry Barnes and Stephen Shapin, *Natural Order: Historical Studies of Scientific Culture*, Sage, London, 1979.

reductive angles refused, methodologically, to take seriously the reality of a trinitarian, let alone transcendent, creator. This leads Milbank to unmask the anti-theology of sociology, from Malebranche through Durkheim to Weber, even if he misses the traditions within contemporary sociology that aid theology rather than strangle it, precisely in their reflexivity and their concerns for the site of the production of knowledge(s).[8] This positivism characterized the development of psychology, political science, and other branches of social sciences, which have often been methodologically dominated by the exclusion of the divine. Hence, Freud turns the divine into wish-fulfilment and infantile regression, and Marx likewise into the instrument of bourgeois control of the proletariat. These disciplines have of course developed and precisely these assumptions have been challenged from within, but it is the nature of these challenges and their logic that is the concern of this chapter.[9]

The third shift relates to the Humanities as *Arts*. Nicholas Boyle argues that the notion of literature and arts in Germany during the eighteenth and nineteenth centuries was crucial for it was exported throughout Europe and to the United States through the mimicking of Berlin as the exemplary research university.[10] Boyle's thesis, concurring with my arguments in chapter one, shows how initially philosophy supplanted theology, followed by the Romantic notion of Art also supplanting theology, so that Art became the medium of universal access to truth, beauty, and the divine. Schiller, Novalis, and Schlegel were at the forefront of this movement and developed the "Great Books" tradition, such that "the universality of literature transcends the particularities of religion" and "has become received

---

[8] See Kieran Flanagan, *The Enchantment of Sociology*, Macmillan, London, 1996. Flanagan's use of Bourdieu is exemplary in calling into question Milbank's wholesale critique of sociology, see especially pp. 59–60. Similarly, Richard Roberts, *Religion, Theology and the Human Sciences*, Cambridge University Press, Cambridge, 2002, pp. 190–266, although his attempt to define sociology (p. 206) grants it a questionable neutrality. Both Flanagan and Roberts minimize the role of philosophy. See also the complex debate in eds. David Martin, John Orme Mills, and W. F. S. Pickering, *Sociology and Theology: Alliance and Conflict*, Harvest Press, London, 1980. In this, Antoine Lion's essay (pp. 163–82) interestingly and problematically calls into question the continuing distinction between these two disciplines.

[9] One such challenge to Marx, while learning greatly from him is Nicholas Lash, *A Matter of Hope? A Theologian's Reflections on the Thought of Karl Marx*, Darton, Longman & Todd, London, 1981; and my engagement with psychoanalysis, *Sexing the Trinity*, SCM, London, 2000; also Paul Ricoeur, *Freud and Philosophy: An Essay in Interpretation*, trans. Denis Savage, Yale University Press, New Haven, Connecticut, 1970. This is to mention only a tip of a huge and complex set of icebergs.

[10] Nicholas Boyle, "'Art,' Literature, Theology: Learning from Germany" in ed. Robert E. Sullivan, *Higher Learning and Catholic Traditions*, University of Notre Dame Press, Notre Dame, Indiana, 2001, pp. 87–111.

wisdom in universities throughout the English-speaking world."[11] The construction of a pagan Greek utopia was also central to the emphasis on the Arts in German Romanticism. All this was premised on the displacement of theology as queen of the sciences. These changes, as we shall see, were also central in forcing wider the split between the arts and sciences. Foucault likewise traces these same themes.[12] Of course, Foucault privileges psychoanalysis and ethnology, for in his view they keep open a constant suspicion, but in so doing, they also become the nihilist platform of his project. Plantinga rightly traces a movement in method in the Arts from realism supplanted by "structuralism to poststructuralism and deconstruction" that "nicely recapitulates the move from Kantian anti-realism to relativism."[13]

The point of these comments is to note that the "methods" and "assumptions" guiding the various disciplines operating in the modern university must be theologically scrutinized, not taken for granted, regardless of their prestige with academic elites. This, *per se*, does not call into question the particular autonomy that these disciplines rightly possess, but does raise the question whether the assumptions and methods operating in such disciplines as currently practiced are inimical to Christian belief, and whether they need be that way. And one must insist at the same time, this engagement cannot be one-way traffic. The formulations of Christian theology are also a cultural process. Thus theology will be challenged in all sorts of unpredictable ways, as we shall see below, as it is (hopefully) self-critically enculturated. The case of Galileo should be kept in mind, reminding the Church of its possibility of *erring* in non-doctrinal matters. While the Galileo story is not a straightforward case of backward and superstitious theologians, for there were indeed theologians who sided with Galileo (Foscarini being the most important, and Castelli, Ciampoli, and Dini were others), his case may well concern issues of methods in biblical exegesis and the established place of Aristotelian philosophy (see further below).[14] Nevertheless, it was only in 1983 that Church officials acknowledged that Galileo's condemnation in 1616 may have been problematic. In 1984 they

---

[11] Boyle, "'Art,' Literature, Theology," p. 96.

[12] See one important conclusion: Michel Foucault, *The Order of Things*, p. 345.

[13] Alvin Plantinga, "On Christian Scholarship" in ed. Theodore M. Hesburg, *The Challenge and Promise of a Catholic University*, University of Notre Dame Press, Notre Dame, Indiana, 1994, pp. 267–96: p. 282. George Steiner's examination of the contents of literature, as opposed to critical hermeneutics, mirrors this point. See George Steiner, *The Death of Tragedy*, Faber & Faber, London, 1995, and *Real Presences: Is There Anything in What We Say?*, Faber, London, 1989.

[14] Ernan McMullin, *Galileo: Man of Science*, Basic Books, New York, 1967; and "The Conception of Science in Galileo's Work" in ed. Robert E. Butts and Joseph Pitt, *New Perspectives on Galileo*, Dordrat, Boston, Massachusetts, 1978, pp. 209–57; and Richard J. Blackwell, *Galileo, Bellarmine and the Bible*, University of Notre Dame Press, Notre Dame, Indiana, 1991.

conceded that "Church officials had erred in condemning Galileo."[15] In 1992, as we shall see shortly, John Paul II made very favorable statements about Galileo.

In conclusion, the first area requiring extensive investigation that I cannot pursue here is the task of tracing the genealogy of the intellectual disciplines that presently constitute the modern university. This would properly contextualize the envisaged marriage of the disciplines within a Christian university. This task would also call for a second genealogical investigation, my second area requiring further attention. This needs the writing of the story of the Church's relation to these disciplines as they have developed. Such a narration would allow Christians to understand their own responsibility for the current crisis and to appreciate the many and complex causal factors that have configured the modern university. For instance, returning to Galileo, his condemnation basically concerned a question of hermeneutics and philosophy. In the first case, Galileo's claims about the movement of the earth contradicted various biblical passages, calling into question their literal meaning. The reluctance of the Church to employ its own complex modes of exegesis so that Christians might discriminate between literal, allegorical, symbolic, moral, and eschatological statements in the Bible was a reluctance bred from its struggle with the Reformers. This reluctance was not found four centuries earlier in its attempt to come to terms with Aristotelian physics and psychology. Regarding philosophy, Galileo's findings called into question Aristotle's physics, and it was Aristotelians who denounced Galileo to the Holy Office, claiming he was "treading under foot the entire philosophy of Aristotle, which had been of such service to scholastic theology."[16] From this example, we can see that the two issues generate different questions. The first might have been avoided were it not for the defensiveness of the Church regarding the Reformation. The second was far more substantial, as Galileo's theory seemed to undermine long-held convictions regarding Aristotle. Nevertheless, history shows how the Church is able to discriminate regarding the various elements of its Aristotelian heritage. More pertinently, it must constantly be vigilant so that theology does not make judgements in fields where it has no proper competence or where it violates the rightful autonomy of the field's methods. For example, in the

---

[15] *Origins*, Documentary Service, 16, 1986, p. 122.

[16] Cited from the complaint to the Holy Office lodged by the Dominican, Niccolò Lorini, in Maurice Finocchiaro, *The Galileo Affair: A Documentary History*, 1989, p. 135 in Ernan McMullin, "Science and the Catholic Tradition" in ed. Ian G. Barbour, *Science and Religion: New Perspectives on the Dialogue*, SCM, London, 1968, pp. 30–42: p. 31. I am grateful to McMullin for providing the source of his quote.

science–religion debate, John Paul II writes that the "hylomorphism of Aristotelian natural philosophy, for example, was adapted by the medieval theologians to help them explore the nature of the sacraments and the hypostatic union. This did not mean that the Church adjudicated the truth or falsity of the Aristotelian insight, since that is not her concern" (M10–11). The principle stated by John Paul II is important: theology cannot adjudicate on truth in matters proper to another discipline, but it can certainly adapt and employ such findings to explore further God's salvation in the world. Applying this principle is always going to be fraught.

II A Banquet in Sight: The Possibilities of a New Harmony

There are three general statements that can be distilled from the various documents cited in note one that help establish an orientation to the question of the relationship between theology, philosophy, and the intellectual disciplines, and more importantly, how they might be re-visioned within a Catholic university. In what follows I necessarily presume a relation between theology and philosophy whereby each cannot proceed without the other, while each is independent of the other, as outlined in the encyclical *Faith and Reason*. There are many questions regarding the portrayal of philosophy in the encyclical and its precise relation to theology, but I abstain from these questions so as to focus on the issue of the wider relationship between the disciplines, a question rarely addressed. I shall state the propositions, offer a brief commentary regarding their implications, and then develop them in the next section in the light of an engagement with the specific discipline of physics and cosmology. The first proposition is as follows:

> *All creation is God's creation, so that, in principle, no form of authentic knowledge properly gained from any discipline will contradict the truth of Christianity. Indeed, all such knowledge will in fact illuminate, deepen, and develop our understanding of both the created world and the Creator.*

CU succinctly expresses the dialectical tension within this claim:

> A Catholic University's privileged task is to unite existentially by intellectual effort two orders of reality that too frequently tend to be placed in opposition as though they were antithetical: the search for truth, and the certainty of already knowing the fount of truth.[17]

---

[17] *CU*, p. 1, citing a papal discourse from 1980.

Clearly, while the truths of the disciplines are not revealed truth, their fount is. Put like this, the distinction between theology and the other disciplines is properly highlighted, but not in terms of affording theology special knowledge properly due to biologists, physicists, and economists. Hence the dialogue between the disciplines takes place with a proper confidence of their respective integrities and fields:

> While each academic discipline retains its own integrity and has its own methods, this dialogue demonstrates that methodological research within every branch of learning, when carried out in a truly scientific manner and in accord with moral norms, can never truly conflict with faith. For the things of the earth and the concerns of faith derive from the same God.[18]

It is in the relationship between theology and such disciplines that many interesting questions arise, rather than whether there is any such relationship. There are thus a number of important points that result from this proposition.

First, it allows for a confidence that the intellectual search for truth, properly undertaken, in whatever discipline, should not and need not be feared by the Church. The Church's own mission is advanced through the university's learning, and without such learning the Church's incarnation in all aspects of human life, analogically following the full incarnation of the Word in flesh and social reality, is compromised. In this respect, the intellectual defense and elaboration of Christianity and its relation to all human culture is entrusted to intellectuals within Christianity, and there is no better structural gathering for such a task than a Christian university. Clearly, those who are not Christian are often as "good" if not better economists, biologists, and so on—technically and in terms of research productivity. And in so much as they properly pursue their disciplines, there should be no conflicts between their work and the truth of Christianity. This leads to a second point.

Whenever there are conflicts between theology and other disciplines, and proper legitimate conflicts, one critical issue is this: should either pole of the tension have priority in determining the outcome? Put differently, is there any priority or normativity given to truth, theologically understood, when it comes into conflict with the findings of any discipline? Or does each discipline, including theology, have equal standing, given that each discipline is acting properly within its remit? At this level of generality, it

---

[18]   *CU*, p. 18, citing *Church in the Modern World*, 61; and two addresses by John Paul II, interestingly including reference to his 1983 address on Galileo.

might be said that properly speaking, no such conflict is possible if each discipline is legitimately pursued, for it would not make claims outside its proper limitations and contexts. Those within the discipline are usually best at spotting tendentious claims. However, this dramatically highlights the question as to who defines the legitimate object of study, the appropriate methods of enquiry, and the research questions within that field. This question is sharply raised by our brief genealogical forays, and part of a Christian university's task is to pay attention to these issues in a systematic manner. Alvin Plantinga puts the matter well when he argues that in any discipline:

> [S]hould we not take for granted the Christian answer to the large questions about God and creation and then go on from that perspective to address the narrower questions of that discipline? . . . To what sort of premises can we properly appeal in working out the answers to the questions raised in a given area of scholarly or scientific inquiry? Can we properly appeal to what we know as Christians? . . . Must the Christian community accept the basic structure and presuppositions of the contemporary practice of that discipline in trying to come to an understanding of its subject matter? Must Christian psychologists appeal only to premises accepted by all parties to the discussion, whether Christian or not? I should think not. Why should we limit and handicap ourselves in this way?[19]

Theology has a priority or normativity when it comes to a legitimate clash between itself and other disciplines. But this normativity is not one that can question the competence and findings of a scientist or sociologist within the parameters of their legitimate discipline. This point requires elaboration if such researchers are not to complain against inappropriate interference. Hence, it is necessary to clarify the possible contexts of these clashes and the very limited cases where normativity can obviously be affirmed. J. G. Hagen makes three important distinctions:

> When a religious view is contradicted by a well-established scientific fact, then the sources of revelation have to be re-examined, and they will be found to leave the question open. When a clearly-defined dogma contradicts a scientific assertion, the latter has to be revised, and it will be found premature. When both contradicting assertions, the religious and scientific, are nothing

---

[19] Plantinga, "On Christian Scholarship," in ed. Hesburg, *The Challenge and Promise of a Catholic University*, p. 292. Similarly, Nicholas Wolterstorff, "Scholarship Grounded in Religion" in ed. A. Sterk, *Religion, Scholarship and Higher Education*, University of Notre Dame Press, Notre Dame, Indiana, 2002, pp. 3–15.

more than prevailing theories, research will be stimulated in both directions, until one of the theories appears unfounded.[20]

Hagen's model has porous lines, but one might still cite the current understanding of the Galileo case to be an example of the first category. The second might instance a scientist claiming on scientific grounds [sic] that there was no creator of the world. Admittedly, but not in this case, the understanding of a dogma may develop so as to later allow for a scientific view that was earlier excluded. The third category might relate to a very wide field indeed, and here matters are left rightly open. Hagen, writing in 1912, cites Copernicus, Kepler, and Galileo as examples of conflict in this category. Hence, a scientist, sociologist, or psychologist who is a Christian should, in principle, find these distinctions reassuring as they indicate no abuse of academic freedom and a position to which they probably implicitly subscribe. These same principles are rather bluntly stated in Vatican I's canons.[21]

The third and final point is to note that the first principle assumes a metaphysics, epistemology, and historical character that all require further elaboration. *Faith and Reason* begins this task. If I were asked to outline in more detail my own presuppositions here, they can best be described as Thomistic "integral humanism."[22] Some of the assumptions embedded in this approach (which are clearly not exclusive to Thomism) are that God's creation is intelligible, rational, and indirectly reflects God. Properly investigating this creation can therefore indirectly lead to God, can never exclude God, and within a Christian context, the existence of God harmonizes all forms of knowledge, for *a priori*, there is a unity to creation for it was created for a single purpose: to give glory to God. Further, this means that belief in God is an appropriate context for the proper and fullest understanding of the various objects of study not always necessarily in terms of the objects themselves (as this would compromise the genuine autonomy of each discipline), but certainly in relation to discerning when a discipline has illegitimately made claims, and also in relating the discoveries of each discipline to moral, epistemological, and ontological issues. This is precisely what

---

[20] J. G. Hagen, *Catholic Encyclopaedia*, 1912, entry: "Science and the Church," p. 21 of 27 (www.newadvent.org/cathen/13598b.htm).

[21] See canons 4.2, 4.3 promulgated by the third session, in eds. J. F. Clarkson et al., *The Church Teaches*, Herder, St. Louis, Missouri, 1955, 82–3.

[22] See Jacques Maritain, *Integral Humanism: Temporal and Spiritual Problems of a New Christendom*, trans. Joseph W. Evans, University of Notre Dame, Notre Dame, Indiana, 1973 [1936], and Etienne Gilson, *The Christian Philosophy of Saint Thomas Aquinas*, trans. L. K. Shook, Victor Gollancz, London, 1957. See further note 29 below.

Plantinga's comment above proposes. Wolfhart Pannenberg in the context of a specific science–religion debate puts this strongly, nicely drawing out these implications:

> If the God of the Bible is creator of the universe, then it is not possible to understand fully or even appropriately the processes of nature without any reference to that God. If, on the contrary, nature can be appropriately understood without reference to the God of the Bible, then that God cannot be the creator of the universe, and consequently he could not be truly God and could not be trusted as a source of moral teaching either. To be sure, the reality of God is not incompatible with all forms of abstract knowledge concerning the regularities of natural processes, a knowledge that abstracts from the concreteness of physical reality and therefore may also abstract from the presence of God in his creation. But neither should such abstract knowledge of regularities claim full and exclusive competence regarding the explanation of nature, and if it does so, the reality of God is thereby denied by implication. The so-called methodological atheism of modern science is far from pure innocence.[23]

The *second* general proposition that follows on from the first and its various implications is this:

> *All knowledge should be pursued primarily out of love for the world as an object of God's creation, and only secondarily for instrumental or functional ends. Only through the primary can the secondary be best determined. In this sense, the primary end of all forms of knowledge is contemplation of and glory to God, and love of God. Likewise, the means of pursuing these different sciences, while determined by the object of enquiry, should never be in conflict with the ends of all enquiry.*

This proposition might initially sound both pious and useless, but its operation can be impressively discerned in Oliver O'Donovan's profound theological critique of modernity's technological instrumentalism leading to constructivism and atheism.[24] This proposition offers a platform from which to criticize the trend to harness universities to industrial and economic ends, thereby judging all disciplines in terms of economic productivity. It also is

---

[23] W. Pannenberg, "Theological Questions to Scientists" in ed. A. R. Peacocke, *The Sciences and Theology in the Twentieth Century*, Oriel Press, Henley and London, 1981, pp. 3–16: p. 4. Torrance, in the same collection, makes clear that "modern science" cannot be so homogeneously characterized viz. methodological atheism. Indeed, Torrance, like John Paul II, envisages a new tide in the scientific world: see Torrance, "Divine and Contingent Order," pp. 81–97; John Paul II, "Letter."

[24] Oliver O'Donovan, *Begotten or Made?*, Clarendon Press, Oxford, 1984; and see also Jacques Ellul, *The Technological Society*, trans. J. Wilkinson, Jonathan Cape, London, 1965.

able to question the liberal's defense of the university as preserving knowledge for knowledge's sake, which in the end fails hopelessly to identify
what that "sake" is, given that the conceptions of knowledge are so diverse
in the modern arena. Such liberalism eventually relates (and often leads to)
postmodernism's love of endless play and plurality which is late capitalism's
hidden exaltation of knowledge for *its* own sake, the production of culture
for the enjoyment of the bourgeoisie.[25] Of course, the liberal and the utilitarian both hold important elements of what is being asserted here. The
utilitarian is right in seeing that knowledge is power to be harnessed, but the
telos of the good and the *means* of securing that *telos* are "questions" always
requiring the help of the social sciences and natural sciences. This is precisely why *CU* specifies as one of the essential characteristics of a Catholic
university, the ethical dimensions to all knowledge.

> Because knowledge is meant to serve the human person, research in a
> Catholic University is always carried out with a concern for the *ethical* and
> *moral implications* both of its method and of its discoveries. This concern,
> while it must be present in all research, is particularly important in the areas of
> science and technology.[26]

Note that the ethical concerns are not simply about the use of discoveries
and the fruits of knowledge, but also the means and methods employed.
The former is too often emphasized at the cost of the latter, which is intellectually as important in the envisaged marriage. Also to be noted is the
cyclical nature of the purpose of knowledge: its serves the human family
and the natural and cultural world within which it subsists, but it *only* does
so because God's redemption is concerned with the human person, and also
therefore, the natural and cultural world. Rather than human ends at the
center, we have God's glory, and from that follows the purpose of
humankind. In *Faith and Reason* (subsequently *FR*, with page references in
the text) this is given specification when Pope John Paul II writes: "In the
field of scientific research a positivistic mentality took hold which not only
abandoned the Christian vision of the world, but more especially rejected
every appeal to a metaphysical or moral vision." This led, in some scientists,
to the exaltation of "market-based logic" and also "the temptation of a
quasi-divine power over nature and even over the human being" (*FR*,
p. 46). The need is for scientists to work again within "the *sapiential*
horizon" (*FR*, p. 106).

---

[25] See Fredric Jameson, *Postmodernism, or, the Cultural Logic of Late Capitalism*, Verso, London,
1990.
[26] *CU*, p. 18.

Hence, only when we affirm the glory of God in prayer and praise can the purpose of the human family be fully discerned, and thus the ethical criteria by which to judge the methods and contents of the various disciplines. In this respect, the liberal is right to value knowledge for its own sake, for the truth discovered in genuine intellectual enquiry is to be honored as truth; but finally it is truth about the world God has created, loves, and draws toward himself. The valuing of knowledge for its own sake requires further grounding, and a developed justification, and this is where Nietzsche's critique unmasks the encyclopaedic project which exalted knowledge for its own sake, yet constructed knowledge in an entirely ideological manner as MacIntyre and others have shown. It is precisely when power is replaced by love, understood as service to the powerless, that the Church's sense that all knowledge is at the service of the kingdom of God enters the contemporary debate about the university. Put bluntly, the purpose of the university is to find love at the heart of all things, for love is the cause of the world. There is a strong Christian tradition in the Bible, later developed by Augustine, Aquinas, and others, that the Creator's image is analogically reflected in creation. This does not mean that the study of atoms is going to show that love rather than neutrons and protons are to be found, or that the meaning of *pi* is love rather than approximately 3.14159. Rather, once the atomic structure has been explicated, or the structure of mathematical formulae, the question of how such ordering analogically facilitates the possibilities of love, harmony, beauty, and truth is vital, and is another way of recognizing the ethical and methodological dimensions of the disciplines.

Historically, Christian universities have often fallen short of this task and even perverted it, but that would be no argument against the basic vision being advanced here. David Schindler makes the point very incisively when he writes that the task of the Catholic university is twofold:

> (1) to show, from within each discipline and in the terms proper to each discipline, how that discipline is being guided by a worldview—in the case of liberalism, by mechanism and subjectivism; and (2) to show how a Catholic worldview (of the cosmos as created in the image of Christ's [eucharistic] love, hence of a cosmos wherein order and love are mutually inclusive) leads to a more ample understanding of evidence and argument, already within the terms proper to each discipline.[27]

Hence, to summarize this second general proposition, within the context of a Christian university, knowledge is first about contemplation, wonder, and

---

[27] Schindler, *Heart of the World*, T. & T. Clark, Edinburgh, 1996, p. 171.

awe, and only then, because its proper context is situated within God's creation and creative purposes, can its instrumental value be judged. In both method and conclusions, all disciplines must value and protect the dignity of the human person. The ethical context of the intellectual enterprise is properly regarded only within the overall religious framework of the university.

The *third* proposition is already in part implied in the first and related to the manner of the second's operation:

> *Theology has a central role to play in the Christian university and must function as a servant "queen of the sciences."*

Rather than feathering my own discipline's nest, I hope the argument of the book contextualizes this claim, and further distinguishes it in three ways. First, the integration of knowledge central to the Catholic university, in contrast to the modern research university, requires the Catholic intellectual vision to be articulated in some detail by theologians in harmony with natural scientists, social scientists, and the human sciences. This is clearly a collaborative and long-term task. Since the truth of God is the center of this unification, theology with philosophy is central to this attainment. *CU* puts it succinctly, and is worth quoting in detail:

> Integration of knowledge is a process, one which will always remain incomplete; moreover, the explosion of knowledge in recent decades, together with the rigid compartmentalization of knowledge within individual academic disciplines, makes the task increasingly difficult. But a University, and especially a Catholic University, 'has to be a *"living union"* of individual organisms dedicated to the search for truth . . . It is necessary to *work towards a higher synthesis* of knowledge, in which alone lies the possibility of satisfying that thirst for truth which is profoundly inscribed on the heart of the human person.' [note 19] Aided by the specific contribution of philosophy and theology, university scholars will be engaged in a constant effort to determine the relative place and meaning of each of the various disciplines within the context of a vision of the human person and the world that is enlightened by the Gospel, and therefore by a faith in Christ, the *Logos*, as the centre of creation and of human history.[28]

Here, a considerably complex issue arises. Philosophy, and not only theology, is privileged as essential to attain this unity. At this point we enter a very specific understanding of philosophy. In *Faith and Reason*, John Paul II

---

[28]   *CU*, p. 16. Note 19 in the document cites John Paul II in 1989, *Church in the Modern World*, 61; and Newman's *The Idea of a University*, p. 457: the University "professes to assign to each study which it receives, its proper place and its just boundaries; to define the rights, to establish the mutual relations and to effect the intercommunion of one and all."

outlines what has been argued to be a form of Thomism, and specifically, "Existential Thomism" associated with Maritain and Gilson.[29] However, it is important to note that he underlines that the Church is not committed to any one philosophy (FR, p. 49) and only intervenes when certain philosophies come to illegitimate conclusions due to their employing premises or methods that disfigure the rightful autonomy of their own discipline (FR, pp. 49–56). The issue is this: the object of theology is God, and in this sense, theology requires a mediating discipline to engage with other disciplines, for their objects of proper knowledge are other than God. The function of philosophy is multi-directional. Theology cannot proceed without philosophy (FR, p. 65) and neither can philosophy operate properly without an openness to the truths known by revelation (those that are exclusively known in revelation and those that might be arrived at through right reason). But philosophy is also able to form the bridge between theology and the disciplines. This mediating function is found in philosophy, not in any specific school of philosophy, such as existentialism, phenomenology, analytic, or postmodern, but in philosophy's rightful concern with epistemological, ontological, metaphysical, and ethical questions as with "the structures of knowledge and personal communication, especially the various forms and functions of language" (FR, p. 65).

This concept of reason in philosophical thinking must be distanced from two particular models that are not being envisaged. First, the Enlightenment model of the power of reason alone to arrive at truth is not commended.[30]

---

[29] See John F. X. Knasas, "*Fides et Ratio* and the Twentieth Century Thomistic Revival," *New Blackfriars*, 81, 955, 2000, pp. 400–8, who argues that of the three forms of twentieth-century Thomism (Aristotelian—the River Forest School; Existential—Gilson and Maritain; and Transcendental—Rahner, de Lubac [*sic*], Lonergan), only one conforms to the encyclical, the Existential. Admittedly, he draws from non-encyclical materials to fully establish his point (pp. 407–8). Steven Baldner, "Christian Philosophy, Gilson, and *Fides et Ratio*" in ed. Timothy L. Smith, *Faith and Reason*, St. Augustine's Press, Chicago, 2001, pp. 153–66 also comes to the same conclusion but with less tendentious arguments than Knasas. However, in the same book, the River Forest theologian, Benedict M. Ashley, "The Validity of Metaphysics: The Need for a Solidly Grounded Metaphysics," pp. 67–89, suggests otherwise. Avery Dulles suggests de Lubac is the key influence; see his "Can Philosophy be Christian? The New State of the Question" in eds. D. R. Foster and J. W. Koterski, *Two Wings*, Catholic University of America Press, Washington, DC, 2003, pp. 3–21, p. 18. It is not essential to settle this argument here, and it would have been odd for John Paul II to publicly favor one particular school in such a debate, even if in private he did. While he might publicly criticize one, if in grave error, I think these arguments, at best, suggest a compatibility with a particular type of Thomism and John Paul II's position.

[30] See Joseph W. Koterski, "The Challenge to Metaphysics in *Fides et Ratio*," pp. 22–5; and Timothy Sean Quinn, "Infides et Unratio: Modern Philosophy and the Papal Encyclical," pp. 177–92—both in eds. Foster and Koterski, *Two Wings*.

Reason, in Pope John Paul II's model, operates within the context of faith, within a tradition-specific set of assumptions and concepts, even though the latter are highly pluriform. Second, reason reflects the mind's inherent power to transcend the particular, to conceptualize, to universalize from the particular, and to relate the many particulars into a synthetic whole, constantly being open to a development of this synthesis in the light of new particulars. Hence, Pope John Paul II's critique of eclecticism, relativism, and nihilism (*FR*, pp. 82, 85, 90). This critical realism has to be defended philosophically. It is also defended from the perspective of Christianity, based on the claims of revelation. *FR* is finally a plea for philosophy's proper autonomy and recovery after its deformation, its "fateful separation" from the "late Medieval period onward" (*FR*, p. 45).[31] The Encyclical is a recognition of the way that the whole enterprise of knowledge (the university) has been divorced from its proper roots in wisdom and God.[32] It is the fundamental power of speculative reason that is open to God, able to reflect on all particulars and their differing structures, and move toward the universal that is being extolled. Hence, this contentious second point is that theology, with the aid of philosophy (so understood), has a privileged place within a Catholic university. *CU* thus sees theology as an essential dimension to any Catholic university:

> *Theology* plays a particularly important role in the search for a synthesis of knowledge as well as in the dialogue between faith and reason. It serves all other disciplines in their search for meaning, not only by helping them to investigate how their discoveries will affect individuals and society but also by bringing a perspective and an orientation not contained within their own methodologies. In turn, interaction with these other disciplines and their discoveries enriches theology, offering it a better understanding of the world today, and making theological research more relevant to current needs. Because of its specific importance among the academic disciplines, every Catholic University should have a faculty, or at least a chair, of theology.[33]

Admittedly, the quotation does not adequately bring out the role of philosophy, but should be read with *Faith and Reason* for a more balanced picture. It would logically also require a faculty, or at least a chair, in philosophy in every Catholic university. However, the quotation does show that

---

[31] See also *FR*, pp. 45–8, covering this period until postmodernity. See eds. Laurence Paul Hemming and Susan Frank Parsons, *Restoring Faith in Reason*, SCM, London, 2002, esp. the commentary by James McEvoy, pp. 175–98.

[32] *FR*, p. 9, and also pp. 16–20.

[33] *CU*, p. 22.

a Catholic university is impossible without theology, for it facilitates the intellectual co-ordination (and sometimes questioning) of the methods and findings of the disciplines, while never questioning the legitimate autonomy of any. This "servant" status is an important qualifier to the title "queen of the sciences" which might at other times imply theology as a petulant interventionist. This intervention should logically never happen if disciplines are true to their subject. Hence, the quotation underscores theology's servant role in terms of bringing to a discipline a perspective and orientation "not contained within their own methodologies." And this servant status is further highlighted by such dialogue allowing theology to be more alert to "current needs."

The third implication, not explicitly stated or developed in any of the Church documents inspected, is that all students *and* teachers in *every* discipline should at least have some training in theology and philosophy. This is important for a number of reasons. Theologians are simply not competent to develop this integration from their side alone, and while there are some very able intellectuals who were or are trained to a high degree in both theology and another discipline (Teilhard de Chardin, Wolfhart Pannenberg, Thomas F. Torrance, Arthur Peacocke, and John Polkinghorne are examples regarding the natural sciences), one cannot rely on such individuals alone. Whole research communities need to be working within such a paradigm, where highly trained physicists, economists, and psychologists are already thinking about these issues themselves, rather than theologians in any way policing matters, be they servants or queens. Alasdair MacIntyre emphasizes that all students in a Catholic university need more (and at the very least, some) training in theology and philosophy, or else the curriculum will simply replicate the best secular research universities.[34] He oddly fails to extend this to all academic staff.

There is a correlative requirement upon theologians. All theologians should gain some grounding in the social, human, and natural sciences, as well as philosophy at least to an elementary level if they are able to contribute to the task of a Catholic university. If these difficult demands are not structurally implemented, Catholic universities will revert to what many of them are at present: places where liturgies and social service characterize the campus, but the intellectual scene is no different from its secular counterparts.

Having briefly outlined these three general propositions regarding a Catholic university, it is now time to explore how they might be developed in regard to a specific disciplinary practice: physics and cosmology. This will

---

[34] Alasdair MacIntyre, "Catholic Universities: Dangers, Hopes, Choices" in ed. R. E. Sullivan, *Higher Learning and Catholic Traditions*, University of Notre Dame Press, Notre Dame, Indiana, 2001, pp. 1–22: pp. 6–10.

allow us to identify what is unrealistic or misinformed about these three propositions as well as identify various tensions in them in relation to this specific discipline.

III Sharing the Feast? Theology, Physics, and Cosmology

In what follows I concentrate on three issues raised by John Paul II in a "Letter to the director of the Vatican observatory, George V. Coyne SJ, on the 300th anniversary of Newton's *Philosophiae naturalis principia mathematica*" (subsequently called "Letter," page numbering in text, preceded by M).[35] The "Letter" was so remarkable in the eyes of three scientists, that together they published a book collecting reflections on it from top-ranking scientists, theologians, and philosophers, not all explicitly Christian, nor Catholic. First, let me summarize the "Letter" which obviously has no authoritative ecclesial status regarding any matters of science.

John Paul II cites the recent "movement for union" with Christian Churches, and then the wider move toward unity of cultures and religions (M4). Hence, the Church's relationship with science is seen as a natural development: the Church reaching out to the world. He also situates this within the "historic animosities" that exist in cultures and especially within the academic community where "the separation between truth and values persists, and the isolation of their several cultures—scientific, humanistic and religious" (M2). Knowledge harnessed to power requires to be used in the context of a vision of all things united in Christ (M5). John Paul II then notes how forces within each of the disciplines propel this closer relationship. He suggests that contemporary science seems to reflect this "correlative unity" that relates all things, which is found in Jesus Christ (M6). Contemporary physics exemplifies this in its quest for the unification of all four fundamental physical forces: gravitation, electro-magnetism, and strong and weak nuclear interactions. This convergence in physics is hopeful in a world of such detailed specialization and fragmentation. Here we have a movement toward convergence (M6).[36] Second, there is a philosophical and

---

[35] In eds. Robert John Russell, William R. Stoeger SJ, and George V. Coyne SJ, *John Paul II on Science and Religion: Reflections on the New View from Rome*, Vatican Observatory Publications, Rome, 1990, numbered M1–M14.

[36] This convergence is noted by many scientists. See, for example, Barbour, *Issues*, pp. 283–98. The bibliography and issues are updated in the following: Torrance, "Divine and Contingent," pp. 82–91, and "Comments," pp. 106–8; Pannenberg, "Theological Questions," pp. 3–16; Polkinghorne, "Christian Faith," in ed. Sullivan, *Higher Learning*, p. 46.

theological dimension to convergence. "Unity involves the drive of the human mind toward understanding and the desire of the human spirit for love." The theme of knowledge and love is central here, and he applies this analogy on both the personal level and the level of the sciences: "If love is genuine, it moves not towards the assimilation of the other but towards union with the other" (M9). With this double convergence in mind, he then turns to the question of the relationship between theology and the natural sciences, especially physics.

First, the relationship is not to be regarded as a "disciplinary unity," for the "Church does not propose that science should become religion or religion science" (M7). Hence, this is not a relationship of "regressive . . . unilateral reductionism." Oneness in theology is relationship between three, the trinity, preserving distinctness and unity at the same time. This model of loving relationship and unity is analogically applied to the disciplines. "We are asked to become one. We are not asked to become each other" (M8). Each discipline, positively, can "enrich, nourish and challenge the other to be more fully what it can be and to contribute to our vision of who we are and who we are becoming" (M7). Both "must preserve their autonomy and their distinctiveness . . . Each should posses its own principles, its patterns of procedures, its diversities of interpretation and its own conclusions . . . neither ought to assume that it forms a necessary premise for the other" (M9). Admittedly here, and throughout the letter, John Paul II seems to give all disciplines, including theology, an equal status in the mutual dialogue. However, read in the context of other papal documents, this balance requires more nuanced specification.

Finally, John Paul II outlines two areas of importance in this dialogue. First, in the light of the mutual antagonisms present in the history of these two disciplines he attempts to highlight the foundations for a different future. Theology, after all, also concerns the human world, the object of study for the sciences, and thus will learn in a whole arena concerning "the intelligibility of nature and history" and the "human person" (M10). This new learning cuts deeply:

> If the cosmologies of the ancient Near Eastern world could be purified and assimilated into the first chapters of Genesis, might contemporary cosmology have something to offer to our reflections upon creation? Does an evolutionary perspective bring any light to bear upon theological anthropology, the meaning of the human person as the *imago Dei*, the problem of Christology—and even upon the development of doctrine itself? What, if any, are the eschatological implications of contemporary cosmology, especially in the light of the vast future of our universe? Can theological method fruitfully

appropriate insights from scientific methodology and the philosophy of science? (M11)

These questions open a quite radical agenda for theology, and with it the memory of Teilhard de Chardin (1881–1955) who did employ an evolutionary perspective to reflect on theological anthropology, Christology, and eschatology. Rome's criticism of him is worth recalling, but it is also clear that one theologian's contribution is not to the point. The point is that the contents of science (evolution) and the methods and philosophy of science may have much to teach theology, even though this process of learning from science can be very problematic if science attempts to shape and determine theology. Andrew Moore has shown very thoroughly the problems involved in the latter process.[37] Moore argues that too many theologians (Braithwaite originally, then Soskice, Peacocke, Murphy, and Barbour) have defended theological realism on the basis of scientific realism. Moore criticizes their assumptions of a positive analogical relationship between the two disciplines on methodological, epistemological, and ontological grounds. In highlighting significant differences he shows how theology becomes alien to itself in conforming itself to science, rather than revelation.[38] He is not arguing *per se* that conceptual models from the sciences and other disciplines have nothing to teach theology. Indeed, he is indebted to a number of philosophers in developing his theological position.

To return to the "Letter." We see theology's learning from physics. It is significant that the question of what physics has to learn from theology is kept to the end, and this order is indicative of the real attempt at re-building trust between theologians and scientists, stressing what theology has to learn, and the autonomy of the natural sciences. However, this learning can only be based on tried and tested findings. Theology should only take seriously those findings that eventually "become part of the intellectual culture of the time," and theologians must "test their value in bringing out from Christian belief some of the possibilities which have not yet been realised" (M10). In this instance, John Paul II is not as suspicious of contemporary intellectual culture as in *FR* or earlier in *The Splendour of Truth Shines* (*Veritatis Splendor*), 1993, but the point is that only well-established scientific

---

[37] Andrew Moore, *Realism and Christian Faith: God, Grammar, and Meaning*, Cambridge University Press, Cambridge, 2003, pp. 40–72.

[38] Moore's arguments are persuasive in principle, but I would question his analysis of Soskice and her use of Aquinas (and Moore's reading of Aquinas) in suggesting they both are guilty of using causal analogies of being such that "God is regarded as a member of the same ontological kind as his creation" (p. 141). This is true of neither. See my discussion of Clouser below.

findings are significant in this engagement. Otherwise, enculturation can become whimsical and shallow. To illustrate this process he cites as an example, the "hylomorphism of Aristotelian natural philosophy" that was "adopted by the medieval theologians to help them explore the nature of the sacraments and the hypostatic union" (M10–11). This did not mean that the "Church adjudicated the truth or falsity of Aristotelian insight" (M11). Of course, it did in the Galileo trial, and in other instances. Nevertheless, he challenges contemporary theologians to integrate their work "with respect to contemporary science, philosophy and the other areas of human knowing" asking "if they have accomplished this extraordinarily difficult process as well as did these medieval masters"? (M11). We find here an acceptance of the possibility of a radical change of world-view, whereby the Aristotelian paradigm might be replaced by new scientific paradigms that could transform the face of theology. Note, there is no judgement on this matter, just an openness.

Second, while theologians clearly have their agenda full, what of scientists? Interestingly, in the "Letter" their learning from theology concerns the recognition of the limits of their discipline. That is, theology can help different sciences recognize their limitations and rightful parameters so that they do not make false claims about absolutes, the meaning of life, and ethics, determined purely from within the context of these limited disciplines. In this sense Pannenberg's comment cited earlier is germane: "The so-called methodological atheism of modern science is far from pure innocence." While this theme of critical engagement is pursued rigorously in FR, it is not in the "Letter." However, the "Letter" is an invitation to scientists to reflect on their methodologies, assumptions, and contexts to purify their own practice. This mutual process is nicely summarized. "Science can purify religion from error and superstition; religion can purify science from idolatry and false absolutes" (M13). Or put another way, theology does "not profess a pseudo-science and science does not become an unconscious theology" (M14).

The "Letter" closes with comments on the necessary training of theologians and scientists for this task, and the citation of the Pontifical Academy of Sciences as a structural example of this bridge building. Given the many papal documents on the university, we might take it for granted that the university is indeed the main structural force for implementing this program. It is also important to note that John Paul II did not dwell on the usual issue of ethics in the uses of science, and that he also stresses the gains for theology in this dialogue far more than for science. Hence, the scientist editors are surely correct in saying "This message is unique in that it is the first major papal statement in almost four decades specifically focused on the substantive and constructive relation of theology and science."[39]

Arising from the subsequent discussion around this document, and in relation to the wider field of science and religion, I would now like to pursue four questions simultaneously. First, in the literature concerning the relation of science to religion, where might we locate John Paul II's comments? Second, what are some of the critical issues raised for theology in this document, and are any in dissonance with the document or the three general propositions I have articulated? Third, what are some of the critical issues raised for the sciences from this document, and are any in dissonance with the document or the general statements I have articulated? Fourth, drawing two and three together, what light does this discussion throw on the general statements developed above, either in confirming, disconfirming, or problematizing them. These questions of course represent the tip of more than one iceberg, and possibly an entire continent!

The literature on the relationship between science and theology is replete with differing models.[40] I choose the typology of Ted Peters in what follows for it is helpful in locating John Paul II's position as well as indicating problems in Peters's typology, which allows the process of location to be both creative and critical. Furthermore, Peters's typology is constructed on developing and refining earlier typological offerings and he offers eight positions regarding the differing relationship between the two disciplines, some being mutually incompatible and others not.

First comes scientism that seeks war, with victory for the scientist alone. Examples are Richard Dawkins, Stephen Hawking, Carl Sagan, Fred Hoyle, and Bertrand Russell (who while not a scientist, was a mathematical and logical reductionist). In terms of John Paul II's analysis, scientism is clearly a pseudo-or unconscious theology dealing with false absolutes. Whether the atheism of these thinkers determines their scientific positions is a moot point. However, it is worth noting that this factor cannot be discounted on either logical or contingent grounds. Logically, the critique mounted by Reformed Calvinists such as Alvin Plantinga following the works of Abraham Kuyper, and Roy A. Clouser influenced by Herman Dooyeweerd, are most impressive. They take an aspect of the Catholic insight and develop

[39] Eds. Russell et al., *John Paul II on Science and Religion*, p. vi.

[40] See, for example, the typologies of ed. A. R. Peacocke, *The Sciences and Theology in the Twentieth Century*, Oriel Press, Henley and London, 1981; Ted Peters, "Science and Theology" in ed. David F. Ford, *The Modern Theologians*, 2nd edn., Blackwell, Oxford, 1997, pp. 649–68, and ed. T. Peters, *Cosmos as Creation: Science and Theology in Consonance*, Abingdon, Nashville, Tennessee, 1989; Barbour, *Science and Religion*, pp. 3–29, and *Religion in an Age of Science*, HarperSanFrancisco, San Francisco, 1990.

it to its logical conclusion.[41] Both argue that every world-view has an implicit "metaphysics," formally identified by Clouser as that which is regarded as "self-existent and unconditionally trustworthy." (p. 194).[42] Clouser then argues that all theories are open to being judged as pagan in so much as their self-existent element is part of creation. He then ranges over the fields of maths, physics, and psychology, showing this to be the case with various theories. For example, in maths he argues that Plato's and Leibniz's number-world theory, whereby the laws dictating the ways numbers behave are eternal and invisible, making all observable things possible, leads to a false divine. "The truths we obtain are supposed to be eternal, and not affected by the experienced universe. But by regarding this hypothetical realm as having independent existence they [Plato and Leibniz] accord it the status of divinity!" (pp. 122–3). That is:

> It is only when someone regards the hypothetical entities and laws as existing independently of *all* other reality, so that mathematical truths would be the same whether *anything* else existed or not, that the person has ascribed utterly non-dependent self-existence to the hypothetical realm, and has thereby regarded them as divine. (p. 123)

Clouser also outlines John Stuart Mill's theory, controlled by the assumption that "reality is exclusively sensory" (p. 115), a kind of absolute subjectivism in contrast to Plato's objectivism. He shows that Bertrand Russell's theory of logical classes, of which maths is one instance, and that logic is the ultimate nature of things upon which all other aspects depend, is also thereby pagan (pp. 114–16). Finally, Dewey's instrumentalism is analyzed. Clouser shows there is no ultimate reality being described, just pragmatic success or lack of it (pp. 116–19). This Clouser calls a "biological perspective," which is also deemed pagan (p. 118).

---

[41] See Alvin Plantinga, "On Christian Scholarship"; "Advice to Christian Philosophers (With Special Preface for Christian Thinkers from Different Disciplines)," www.leaderu.com/truth/1truth10html, pp. 1–19; *The Twin Pillars of Christian Scholarship*, The Stob Lectures of Calvin College and Seminary, 1989–90, Calvin College and Seminary, Grand Rapids, Michigan, 1990; and his inspiration Abraham Kuyper, *Calvinism: Six Stone Foundation Lectures*, Eerdmans, Grand Rapids, Michigan, 1932, and more concisely, *Encyclopaedia of Sacred Theology*, Charles Scribner, New York, 1898, esp. pp. 59–181. See also Roy A. Clouser, *The Myth of Religious Neutrality: An Essay on the Hidden Role of Religious Belief in Theories*, University of Notre Dame Press, London, 1991, whose inspiration is Herman Dooyeweerd, *A New Critique of Theoretical Thought*, 4 vols., Peideia Press, Ontario, 1983. Unsurprisingly Plantinga is at home in a Catholic university. Clouser, on the other hand, totally misunderstands Catholic analogy—see below in main text.

[42] Page references to Clouser, *The Myth*.

In physics Clouser notes that Ernst Mach's sensory hypothesis regarding atoms (i.e. they do not exist, but are postulated to explain what can be experienced), requires that it is a theory that there are physical objects at all (p. 131). Einstein went a step further, holding that sensory perception was in fact dependent upon logical/mathematical properties and laws (p. 133), and these laws were therefore more fundamental. Hence, despite others finding in Einstein a religious spirit, Clouser argues that in his theory he is not. Heisenberg navigates between the two, arguing that they are "mathematical possibilities" (p. 135) and that all things real are mathematically calculable. As above, Clouser sees these fundamental rules determining each world-view as the elevation of a created quality to that of the divine in so much as they are deemed "self-existent" (p. 139). Hence, Clouser wants to argue that certain forms of theoretical physics are founded on atheist presuppositions.

Clouser's analysis is forceful and insightful, although it has two major shortcomings. First, he fails to distinguish between relative absolutes that legitimately exist in relation to a specified limited field and metaphysical absolutes, discernible through theology and philosophy. For instance, it may be held within a discipline that the fundamental truth of sense perception is that it is dependent upon logical and mathematical properties and laws. It is only when this fundamental truth is applied beyond its competent sphere and taken as the single normative absolute that it is erroneous. Hence, for Einstein, his law regarding sense perception technically has no necessary bearing upon the fact that our sense perception is ultimately dependent on a Creator (who may well reflect logical and mathematical properties). This lack of contextualization drives Clouser to condemn as pagan many theories that *can* be pagan if held in an absolutist manner, but can also operate within a broader theistic context, or indeed an agnostic context. In short, Clouser fails to make the distinction between faith's and reason's proper arenas.

Second, Clouser also offers a critique of Roman Catholicism based on an erroneous understanding of analogy. At first, he rightly notes that when "religious language speaks of God, therefore, it must do so by *analogy* so that the meaning of our terms is partly the same but also partly different from when they are used of creatures" (p. 175). However, the difference is then ignored when a few lines later he writes of Aquinas: "Traditional theology's account of both God's nature and the possibility of religious language require that there are qualities possessed by creatures which are uncreated" (p. 175). But this is never claimed by Aquinas, and the quotes given from *Summa* 1a. q.13, a.2–3, fail to appreciate that Aquinas is clear in the overall context, rather than from these two quotes alone, that God's *dissimilarity* is greater than the similarity.[43] Hence, Clouser misunderstands Aquinas and subsequently also develops his otherwise very illuminating theory on the basis that the attributes of God are not divine, not uncreated, and God's own uncreated being is never known to us. This totally severs the relation between God as He is in Himself and in relation to us. It leaves Clouser ironically unable to ground any statement on revelation as the real analogical disclosure of God. However, Clouser's attempts to subject all theories to such analysis, deriving from Dooyeweerd's work, is to be applauded, even if flawed in certain respects.

Plantinga offers a more sophisticated and less systematic set of examples than Clouser, ranging from the sociobiology of E. O. Wilson to Dawkins's defense of evolution, and the dominance of creative anti-realism in the humanities (in MacIntyre's terms, modernism and postmodernism). He also insightfully notes how the religious beliefs of a scientist can affect their openness to contrary positions. He cites Francisco Ayala, Richard Dawkins, Stephen Jay Gould, William Provine, and Philip Spieth as all declaring the truth of evolution as a fact, as much a fact as that the earth is round and revolves around the sun. He cites Dawkins's telling comment that if someone contested evolution they would be either "ignorant, stupid or insane (or wicked, but I'd rather not consider that)."[44] The only way to explain Dawkins's and others' attitude, as it is patently not the case that the scientific evidence is absolutely certain, is to see that

> If you reject theism in favour of naturalism, this evolutionary story is the only visible answer to the question Where did all this enormous variety of flora and fauna come from? Even if the fossil record is at best spotty and at worst disconfirming, even if there are anomalies of other sorts, this story is the only answer on offer (from a naturalistic perspective) to these questions; so objections will not be brooked . . . From a naturalistic perspective evolution is the only game in town.[45]

---

[43]   The two quotations are "'God is good' . . . means that what we call goodness in creatures exists in God in a higher way. Thus God is not good (merely) because he causes a goodness, but rather goodness flows from him because he is good." And second: "God is known from the perfections that flow from him and are to be found in creatures yet which exist in him in a transcendent way." See David Burrell on Aquinas and analogy: *Aquinas: God and Action*, Routledge & Kegan Paul, London, 1979. This misreading of Aquinas was initiated by Barth, and repeated by Moore and Clouser.

[44]   Plantinga, "On Christian Scholarship," p. 283, with no reference for the Dawkins quote. For references to all the scientists cited, see p. 294, n. 11. One could also add Fred Hoyle—see McMullin, "How Should Cosmology Relate to Theology?" in ed. Peacocke, *The Sciences and Theology*, p. 33.

[45]   Plantinga, "On Christian Scholarship," pp. 284–5.

Plantinga slightly overstates his case as there are non-theistic scientists who raise problems with orthodox Darwinism.[46] Nevertheless, what both Clouser and Plantinga demonstrate is that there are logical and contingent grounds to challenge scientific atheism, and this takes two directions. Negatively, in terms of a critique of atheist science based on metaphysical methodological naturalism, and constructively, in terms of working within scientific paradigms that keep the religious question properly open, such as the scientific "view of the universe as a unitary open system."[47]

Peters's *second* position seeks to make scientific language the normative language for belief, such that all theological statements should be understood purely and exclusively in scientific terms. Peters calls this scientific imperialism. He cites Paul Davies and Frank Tipler as examples. Tipler claims that the Big Bang and thermodynamics can provide a better explanation of the resurrection and defense of Christianity, and that theology should become a branch of physics.[48] In John Paul II's analysis, this is also an instance where science fails to respect the limited autonomy of theology, in excluding the validity of theological discourse, as well as overstepping science's own proper boundaries. As it stands, it is an unacceptable position. However, in a very limited sense it pursues what John Paul II urges, a rethinking of theology in terms of scientific conceptuality, akin to the use of Aristotelian physics. But Tipler would be criticized for failing to contextualize his own project, *absolutizing* and *prioritizing* scientific discourse in an analogous manner to scientism, but not for pursuing an understanding of resurrection in terms of the Big Bang and thermodynamics. The latter type of exploration is certainly encouraged by John Paul II, even if there are issues that require further clarification in this type of approach.[49]

The *third* position depicted by Peters is called ecclesiastical authoritarianism and is exemplified in Pius IX's *Syllabus of Errors* where item 57 stated that it is an error that science and philosophy can withdraw from ecclesial control. Peters argues that Vatican II and post-Conciliar Catholic thought reverses this, allowing instead for "autonomous disciplines" (citing *Pastoral*

---

[46] According to McMullin, Plantinga also fails to distinguish between what McMullin calls this historical fact of evolution (descent with modification) and the theory of evolution explaining why evolution occurred. See Ernan McMullin, "Evolution and Special Creation," *Zygon*, 28, 1993, pp. 229–335.

[47] Torrance, "Divine and Contingent," p. 91, where Torrance argues that the post-Newtonian paradigm has created a new hospitality toward religion. This kind of position is also held by various "new age" scientists such as Fritjof Capra (and David Bohm—see below).

[48] Frank J. Tipler, *The Physics of Immortality. Modern Cosmology, God and the Resurrection of the Dead*, Pan, London, 1996.

[49] See my comments on Moore above.

Constitution on the Church in the Modern World (*Gaudium et Spes*), 59, and "Letter"). It is clear that Pope John Paul II is able to recognize the Church erring, as it did with Galileo and in other instances, but can Peters be correct in placing Pope John Paul II in opposition to Pius IX and earlier authoritative tradition? I think not, for four reasons. First, condemnation 57 is in keeping with Vatican I's position on faith and reason. In fact it is cited in paragraph 59 of Vatican II's *Church in the Modern World* quoted by Peters to show a difference between Pius and Vatican II! Vatican I's position on faith and reason is also central to *FR*, p. 13, and therefore hardly in tension with John Paul II's position. Vatican I held the "two orders of knowledge" which are distinct, namely faith and reason, and from this derived the teaching of the proper autonomy of the sciences.[50] Pius IX simply reiterated that in principle when science or philosophy overstepped its legitimate autonomy and made claims regarding matters of dogma or morals, the Church had a duty and authority to point this out. In practice, this may sometimes lend itself to "ecclesiastical authoritarianism," but in principle, the issue of the Church's final and circumscribed authority is not contested by either Vatican II or John Paul II.

Second, the context of the legitimate autonomy of the intellectual disciplines, and especially the sciences, in Vatican II, in *Church in the Modern World* (p. 59) (and also in the *Declaration on Christian Education* (*Gravissimum Educationis*) (pp. 10–12), and *Declaration on Religious Freedom* (*Dignatatis Humanae*) (p. 1), regarding other religions and non–religious civil freedoms) is always in the context of "the rights of the individual and of the community, whether particular or universal" and that of the "common good." Hence, there is no absolute sense of "autonomy," but only a legitimate and contextual autonomy *within* the wider narrative of truth, which is of Christ, and therefore truth entrusted to the Church. Hence, in a proper sense, despite abuse and misuse, the Church does have an intellectual duty to speak authoritatively in regard to philosophy and the sciences when they conflict with revelation.

Third, in *FR* there is an explicit defense of the magisterium's authority over philosophy, in one limited sense: "It is the task of the Magisterium in the first place to indicate which philosophical presuppositions and conclusions are incompatible with revealed truth, thus articulating the demands which faith's point of view makes of philosophy" (*FR*, p. 50). That this is not ecclesiastical authoritarianism is evident in the fact that the magisterium's competence is not extended into the field of philosophy *per se*,

---

[50] See canons 4.2 and 4.3, cited above.

which rightly has its own autonomy, but only in so much as that discipline has lost "*recta ratio*" (*FR*, p. 50), teaching that which is contrary to revelation. This point specifically made about philosophy, is legitimately extended to any other discipline in so much as it makes claims beyond its methods, limits, and competencies.

Fourth, and finally, Peters reads the words "autonomous disciplines" uncontextually, importing a liberal political notion of the term, rather than recognizing that his own favoured position, hypothetical consonance, also calls into question some notions of "autonomy" (see below). In sum, Peters seems falsely to construct ecclesiastical authoritarianism as a binary opposite in principle to the legitimate autonomy of the sciences.[51] I have questioned this primarily in principle. The practice supplies examples of illegitimate authoritarianism as well as legitimate authority. Hence, if we remove the derogatory note to "authority," John Paul II's position does fit this category along with that of Reformed Calvinist philosophers like Clouser and Plantinga. This position may well be negatively exemplified by the opposite to scientism, or various Protestant groups that simply claim the literal truth of the Bible as determinative over all scientific claims, but not by Peters's illustration and type.

The *fourth* position is that of scientific creationists. Although these writers' grandparents were biblical fundamentalists, today's scientific creationists "are willing to argue their case in the arena of science . . . They assume that biblical truth and scientific truth belong to the same domain."[52] Roger E. Timm is one of this new breed, that Peters characterizes as "soldiers within the science army."[53] The war analogy only operates when there is "a battle between atheistic science and theistic science."[54] John Paul II's "Letter" would also allow him to occupy this type, for there is no question about the proper autonomy of science in this position, and also no question that properly conducted science never contradicts Christian truth, but always rather supports it, directly or indirectly.

However, this position raises one question regarding the priority of truth in theology that it is important to clarify. Roger E. Timm, for instance, makes it clear that if there is a clash between a biblical truth and a scientific truth, the latter should be called into question, given that the former has

---

[51]   Peters is not a Catholic, but Karl Schmitz-Moorman is, and assumes this same erroneous understanding of autonomy as well as John Paul's distance from earlier teachings in "Science and Theology," in eds. Russell et al., *John Paul II on Science and Religion*, pp. 99–106.

[52]   Peters, "Science," p. 651.

[53]   Ibid.

[54]   Ibid., p. 665, note 11.

prior authority. In this instance, because Genesis is true, then it must be the case that: God fixed the distinct kinds of organisms and species at the original point of creation and they did not evolve; there is a separate ancestry for apes and humans; creation is out of nothing; mutation and natural selection cannot explain the process of evolution, and so on.[55] Two very specific issues are raised at this point. First, priority is given to the authority of revelation in the Catholic position so far outlined, and this makes it fit, in principle, with this fourth model. Second, the Catholic position does not have any uniform or accepted methodological way of working out which propositions of biblical revelation and doctrine translate themselves into specific scientific claims, such that counter-claims made by scientists might be called into question by the magisterium. This area is left open, and the magisterium's intervention is only called upon when there is a question of false doctrines or morals being propounded by *any* discipline, including theology.

Duane T. Gish, in contrast, at least presents a position of biblical literalism analogous to the persecutors of Galileo, while Timm's position is more flexible. Hence, it is important to say that Catholic scientific and theological opinions may vary enormously on the issue, even within the parameters so specified. For example, there is no reason why Timm's and Gish's position could not be held (at least in principle) by a Catholic exegete or scientist (although I know of none), while at the same time, some of the implications of either biblical or doctrinal statements are more complexly related to scientific statements. For instance, Gish and Timm hold that creation out of nothing and the Genesis story mean that the world has a "beginning in time." Once it was not, then it was.

However, the Roman Catholic Ernan McMullin, past director of the Program in History and Philosophy of Science at the University of Notre Dame, and a philosopher, notes that the issue of whether or not the universe can be said to have had a beginning in time depends on the choice of time-scale in cosmology. This may well respond to John Paul II's question as to whether contemporary cosmology has "something to offer to our reflections on creation." Besides, an implicit assumption is being made that the Big Bang was not preceded by a "Big Squeeze."[56] Thus, McMullin questioned one feature of Pius XII's allocution in 1951 to the Pontifical Academy

---

[55]   Roger E. Timm, "Scientific Creationism and Biblical Theology" in ed. Peters, *Cosmos as Creation*, pp. 247–64. See also Duane T. Gish, *Evolution: The Challenge of the Fossil Records*, Creation Life Publishers, California, 1985; and *Evolution: The Fossils Still Say NO!*, Institute for Creation Research, California, 1999.

[56]   See McMullin, "How Should?," pp. 28–40.

of Sciences, namely that the Big Bang theory should lead the unprejudiced scientific mind to acknowledge the enigma of a cosmic beginning and could thus bring the scientist to see "the work of creative omnipotence, whose power set in motion by the mighty *Fiat* pronounced billions of years ago by the Creating Spirit, spread out over the universe." Pius continued, carefully:

> It is quite true that the facts established up to the present time are not an absolute proof of creation in time, as are the proofs drawn from metaphysics and Revelation in what concerns simple creation, or those founded on Revelation if there be a question of creation in time.[57]

McMullin also notes that although Sir Edmund Whittaker, a member of the Pontifical Academy, agreed with Pius's assumption that the theory had, in effect, validated belief in the beginning of time, this assumption was strongly opposed by another member of the Academy, the Belgian priest-cosmologist Georges Lemaître, as well as by George Gamow, a leading physicist of the day. Furthermore, there is the much discussed exegetical issue of how literally the Genesis story should be taken. McMullin recalls here Augustine's assurance that the story of the "six days" were not to be taken literally. Does the Genesis text require us to suppose that the universe began in time or only that it depends for its existence on a Creator, whether it began in time or not? The text does imply that God has had a special care for mankind whose temporal history assuredly did have a beginning. But our universe? Is that part of the point the author of Genesis was making?[58] There is clearly a variety of strategies open to theologians and scientists who are intent on finding the appropriate ways to relate Scripture or more broadly, theology, to the sciences. Clearly, this type of discussion is encouraged by John Paul II's question as to whether "contemporary cosmology" has "something to offer to our reflections upon creation" (M11).

One further question here relates to "realism." There is an assumption in the position I'm defending that both science and theology are ontologically "realist," that is they describe the way things are—in the actual structures of nature, or in God's relation to the world. But in practice, in both disciplines we have non-realists, and complex debates on defining "realism." Nevertheless, while theological realism is presupposed in John Paul II's theological position, is it theologically required in the scientific approach? *FR* would

---

[57] Cited by McMullin, "How Should?," p. 53, from *Bulletin of the Atomic Scientists*, 8, 1952, pp. 143–65: pp. 145–6.

[58] McMullin, "How Should?," p. 36.

imply yes, in so much as it criticizes modernity's loss of confidence in reason's ability to grasp truth in all fields, including science, but of course it does not develop this discussion in any detail. Hence, it is still debatable between theologians, philosophers, and scientists as to what precisely constitutes "realism," and what degrees and differing types of "realism" might operate. It is not possible to develop this further here, except to state summarily that I would side with McMullin's moderate realism and his critique of the Catholic philosopher of science, Bas van Fraassen's non-realistic "empiricism," all argued by McMullin on scientific grounds.[59] Further, there is also scope to develop theological arguments against non-realism in science, although those who do, such as Pannenberg, Torrance, and Swinburne, all argue their case on both fronts: scientific and theological-philosophical.[60]

The *fifth* position is the two-language theory that accepts the sovereign and incommensurable territories of both science and theology. This has been recently defended by Langdon Gilkey and Stephen Jay Gould (who, however, denies any ontological referent to theological language), and it results in a truce between the two disciplines. This approach, which can be located in the seventeenth-century divide between scientific and theological method, is in part a theological response to the attempts by science to control and even eradicate theology. In Torrance's words:

> Some theologians, in accepting the Kantian and Laplacian rationalization of Newton's system of the world into a self-containing and self-explaining deterministic framework, have gone to great lengths in seeking to detach understanding of the Bible and Christian theology from any world-view and indeed to cut off faith from any empirical correlates in physical space-time reality. Thereby, however, they have replaced a God-centred and objective outlook with a radically man-centred and subjective outlook.[61]

---

[59] See their essays in ed. Jan Hilgevoord, *Physics and Our View of the World*, Cambridge University Press, Cambridge, 1994: McMullin (pp. 79–114), van Fraassen (pp. 114–34), and their discussion, pp. 255–94; and subsequent debate: McMullin, "Van Fraassen's Unappreciated Realism," *Philosophy of Science*, 70, 3, 2003, pp. 455–78; and Van Fraassen's reply: "On McMullin's Appreciation of Realism Concerning the Sciences," *Philosophy of Science*, 70, 3, 2003, pp. 479–92.

[60] See Pannenberg, Torrance, and Swinburne in ed. Peacocke, *The Sciences and Theology*, pp. 297–304. However, this view is contested by the nuanced argument advanced by Moore, who suggests that scientific realism is not logically or theologically required by Christianity, for non-realists like van Fraassen are *not* pure constructivists, acknowledging a "reality" that is creation. However, they are legitimately agnostic as to whether scientific theories are capable of ontological realism. See Moore, *Realism*, pp. 183–95.

[61] Torrance, "Divine and Contingent," p. 82.

The two-language position is not in keeping with John Paul II's orientation, which assumes the unity of all reality. Yet the proper limits of the disciplines thus require a patient dialogue to discover the interrelationship and connections between them. It is true, as Torrance argues, that the recognition of this proper autonomy can also promote "a methodological secularism in natural science which through an orientation in inquiry away from God runs the risk of over-reaching itself in dogmatic secularism or atheism."[62] Peters is critical of the two-language model, for it gains "peace through separation, by establishing a demilitarized zone that prevents communication." He also asks, why not start with the assumption that "there is but one reality and sooner or later scientists and theologians should be able to find some areas of shared understanding?"[63] However, there is a truth in this two-language approach that needs to be retained. It is the recognition that not all theological or scientific statements necessarily bear upon each other. Which do and which do not can only be determined *a posteriori* through the dialogue of theologians and scientists.

The *sixth* model, the one favored by Peters, is named hypothetical consonance. Peters attributes it to Ernan McMullin and defines it as the exploring of "those areas where there is a correspondence between what can be said scientifically about the natural world and what the theologian understands to be God's creation."[64] Consonance indicates that "Accord or harmony might be a treasure we hope to find, but we have not found it yet."[65] Stated thus, this is certainly in keeping with John Paul II's position, although it is important to recognize strong and weak forms of consonance, neither of which he comments on. The difference is exemplified in the clash between McMullin (weak consonance) and Pannenberg (strong, and better called "direct implication"). McMullin suggests that Pannenberg's position can be read in two ways. The first, that he criticizes, would take Pannenberg "as saying that Christian faith is specific enough in its affirmations in these areas to lead to a critique of the scientific theories involved."[66] This is also the position of Clouser and Plantinga, and my own. McMullin criticizes it as "rash" because all scientific theories are so fragile, contested, and provisional as well as there being "no agreement as to what truth-status *ought* to be assigned to well-supported scientific theory and most especially to the speculative theories of the cosmologists" (p. 49). While both points are true, in

---

[62] Ibid., p. 87.
[63] Peters, "Science," p. 652.
[64] Ibid.
[65] Ibid.
[66] McMullin, "How Should?," p. 51.

my opinion, they need not call into question the *principle* upheld by Pannenberg, which does not absolutely fix where these possible overlaps and indirect implications lie. However, when they are identified, they must be taken seriously, even if three hundred years later the theologian's or scientist's assumptions might be entirely discredited, or be differently understood. McMullin's own weak version calls us:

> [to] look harder at the theories of physics and biology, not to alter them, but to find interpretations that will be maximally acceptable from the Christian standpoint. This would be to take theology not as an autonomous source of logical implication capable of affecting scientific theory-appraisal, but as one element in the construction of a broader view. The aim would be consonance rather than direct implication. (p. 51)

I think McMullin is entirely correct in saying that theology cannot *per se* alter theories of physics and biology, just as it cannot change empirical evidence, and should seek to find scientific theories which are "maximally acceptable" to faith.[67] Nevertheless, there is no historical or philosophical justification to exclude examples where there are "logical implications" arising from theology that do affect "scientific theory-appraisal." Torrance, Pannenberg, Plantinga, and others give many examples where scientific views have direct implications upon theology and vice versa. Thus, Torrance writes in his survey of cosmologies:

> Undoubtedly faith in God finds itself restricted, if not altogether suffocated, in some cosmologies rather than in others, which implies that it cannot disregard views of the universe within the society or culture in which faith arises and seeks to take root. Likewise, theology functions more freely in some cosmologies than in others, and the fact that it may find itself in conflict—as has often happened in the past—with conceptions governing a particular outlook upon the universe, reveals that theology operates with basic cosmological conceptions of its own which it cannot give up.[68]

Insomuch as John Paul II's position implies that both science and theology are embedded within a critical realism, the view clearly defended in *FR*, it is reasonable to suppose that hard consonance, or direct implication, is to be preferred to Peters's or McMullin's soft consonance. However, such a point does not affect placing John Paul II squarely within this sixth position.

---

[67]   Admittedly evidence as "fact" is problematic, as "facts" are constructed within some paradigms of knowledge. Even Pannenberg, who asserts that theology cannot change facts, later admits this claim is problematic—see Pannenberg, "Comments," p. 78.
[68]   Torrance, "Divine and Contingent," p. 82.

However, Peters draws various inferences from this position regarding theology, only some of which John Paul II would share. For Peters this model means a new method in theology whereby theological statements are not inviolable, but are deemed hypothetical (here he draws on Pannenberg and Popper), and so subject to confirmation or disconfirmation.[69] Drawing on Wentzel van Huyssteen, he argues that theology would "progress" through continuous "illumination," not by appeal to ecclesia or some other indisputable authority.[70] Theology, on a Roman Catholic model, can make no "progress" without reference to scripture, tradition, and ecclesial authority, even if in practice "progress" may sometimes be hampered by the latter authority, or probably more often, wisely guided.[71] But the notion of theology simply sailing past such a port replicates liberal theology's lack of ecclesia that I have been questioning. Further, the view that theology can learn from scientific method, its contents, and the philosophy of science opens up the question of precisely how this learning may take place. Discerning those methods and their findings that are compatible with Christian faith is a matter for the ongoing community of theologians and scientists and the magisterium. At face value, there need be no *a priori* restrictions, except to recognize that the principle of analogy will be central to this process, for theology's subject matter is quite other than that of science's subject matter, and thus its methods and presuppositions, while possibly having some analogical parallels, will always be principally determined by the object of study. Polkinghorne and Barbour each make some pertinent points about the differences and why they require caution in any attempt to assimilate methods.[72]

One further clarification in contrast to Peters's position is required. In his portrayal he puts theological statements on a par with scientific, and this admittedly is even found in John Paul II's "Letter." However, given that the basic viewpoint of the researcher is founded on a religious optimism regarding science (see general principle one above), then it must also be granted that while each discipline makes its distinct contribution to the unity, there will necessarily be a priority given to theology because its "data" are revealed. Schindler puts it thus:

> the contributions, respectively, of theology and science intrinsically affect each other. The distinctness of the respective contributions is not merely a

[69] Peters, "Science," p. 652.
[70] Ibid., p. 656.
[71] See Moore, *Realism*, pp. 50–2, who argues convincingly that "progress" is not an appropriate term for theology.
[72] Barbour, *Issues*, pp. 137–71, 207–37; Polkinghorne, "Christian Faith," pp. 49–55.

matter of addition (e.g., "harmonizing"), which would presuppose exactly the sort of primitive autonomy (or extrinsicism) of the disciplines that must be rejected. At the same time, theology, in the construction of the broader worldview to which both theology and science must contribute, nonetheless maintains a (logically) prior and normative status within this mutuality of distinct contributions.[73]

Thus modified and challenged, John Paul II's position can be understood as operating in what Peters calls the hypothetical consonance model, even if it is more accurately called the harmonious direct implication model.

Peters's *seventh* model is unproblematic, and he notes how it can be allied with most of the other models. This is the ethical overlap position, which requires that theology address the questions of the common good and the purpose of creation, within which technology can then be appropriately utilized. Peters does not touch on the way in which science has so deeply transformed culture, not only desacralizing it, but also as John Paul II puts it, introducing "the temptation of a quasi-divine power over nature and even over the human being" (*FR*, p. 46). Man is God, no longer made in God's image.[74] O'Donovan pertinently notes:

> The technological transformation of the modern age has gone hand in hand with the social and political quest of Western man to free himself from the necessities imposed upon him by religion, society, and nature. Without this social quest the development of technology would have been unthinkable; without technology the liberal society as we know it would be unworkable.[75]

For John Paul II, technology is only there to serve God's kingdom and can help transform humankind's existence for the better, if properly employed.

Peters's *eighth* model is that of New Age spirituality, characterized by holism, integration, and a unifying of the disciplines. He distinguishes two strands. The first is exemplified by Fritjof Capra and David Bohm. Bohm argues for an explicate order in the natural world, behind which and

---

[73] Schindler, *Heart of the World*, p. 172, note 48. He also sides with Pannenberg against McMullin.

[74] In this instance, I use "man" as differentiated from women, in the light of the significant reflections of Jean Bethke Elshtain, *Public Man, Private Women: Women in Social and Political Thought*, Princeton University Press, Princeton, New Jersey, 1993; and in the specific field of science: Jean Barr, *Common Science? Women, Science, and Knowledge*, Indiana University Press, Bloomington, Indiana, 1998, and T. O. Gornez and G. B. Conde, *Women in Science: Women, Feminism and Natural, Experimental and Technological Science*, Oxford University Press, Oxford, 1998.

[75] O'Donovan, *Begotten*, p. 6.

presupposing it, is an implicate order, a realm of "undivided wholeness in flowing movement."[76] If we focus on either the subjective or objective poles within this knowing process, reality is incomplete and abstracted. Bohm does not explicitly identify his position with any one religious world-view, and Peters dismisses him (along with the second group composed of Brian Swimme and Thomas Berry, who attribute to the earth itself the characteristics of deity: morality, the ability to teach, govern, heal, and sanctify) as endorsing a "metareligious naturalism."[77] I agree that Swimme and Berry be thus characterized, even though there is immense wisdom and insight in their positions. However, Bohm's position is open to alternative reading, and has in fact been creatively employed by Schindler to challenge the dominant Cartesian dualism and reductionism in so much science and to provide a framework for what I have called harmonious direct implication.[78] Schindler is not uncritical of Bohm, but whether he can be simply dismissed as endorsing "metareligious naturalism" is perhaps premature and unappreciative of his significance. Nevertheless, Peters's rejection of this position, thus characterized, is shared by John Paul II, in so much as any form of pantheism or naturalism is inadequate.[79]

The reason I have tried to locate John Paul II's orientation toward science within Peters's typology is primarily to show that a Catholic engagement with physics and cosmology leaves many avenues *radically open*, while signaling, in very general terms, many dead-end routes, or scientific paradigms incompatible with Christian faith. Rather than imagine the caricatured old warfare between the two disciplines, one might instead see a rich and creative mixture, each benefiting the other. Furthermore, John Paul II's theological orientation has also called into question Peters's exact typology: seeing a positive note in scientific imperialism; transforming ecclesiastical authoritarianism into legitimate ecclesial direction and intervention; recognizing important truths in scientific creationism, two-language theory, and

[76] David Bohm, *Wholeness and the Implicate Order*, Routledge & Kegan Paul, London, 1980, p. 11. See also (with B. J. Hiley) *The Undivided Universe: An Ontological Interpretation of Quantum Theory*, Routledge, London, 1993.

[77] Peters, "Science," p. 654.

[78] David Schindler, "David Bohm on Contemporary Physics and the Overcoming of Fragmentation," *International Philosophical Quarterly*, Fall, 1982, pp. 315–27, and Bohm's very positive response in the subsequent pages: "Response to Schindler's Critique of my *Wholeness and the Implicate Order*," pp. 329–39. See also their further collaboration in ed. Schindler, *Beyond Mechanism: The Universe in Recent Physics and Catholic Thought*, University Press of America, Lanham, Maryland, 1986.

[79] Whether Teilhard de Chardin is guilty of pantheism is a moot point. See R. B. Smith, "God and Evolutive Creation" in ed. Hanson, *Symposium on Teilhard de Chardin*, Darton, Longman & Todd, London, 1970, pp. 41–58.

new age science-spirituality; and challenging features of Peters's major position, hypothetical consonance. Hence, John Paul II's extrapolated position is broad and Catholic in a double sense, allowing for legitimate plurality in both sciences and theology, yet seeking their unity, with full respect for their legitimate autonomy, not understood as utterly unrelated or unrestrictedly free in method or presuppositions.[80]

There was a fourth question. Do any of the micro findings call into question the general propositions guiding the investigation? In principle, I would not expect this, in part owing to their level of generality, and in part, due to my conviction of their truthfulness. There have been tensions and unresolved lacunae, such as the *a priori* or *a posteriori* assumption of biblical statements bearing literal import, the debate between hypothetical consonance and direct implication, the extent of the priority given to truth derived from faith when there are conflicts of truth, the extent and limits of the analogical (or otherwise) transferability of methodology from science to theology, and so on. However, none of these have invalidated the three general statements. In this respect the three general statements are indeed helpful in orienting us to see how the complex area of inter-relation between the disciplines can prove fruitful, both methodologically and regarding conclusions. The sustained programmatic attention to these issues can be nourished only within a Christian university.

What we have seen so far regarding physics might analogically be applied to other disciplines such as history, sociology, law, medicine, and so on. Of course, each particular discipline presents very specific issues and problems and different histories in relation to theology. But there is an important commonality: they are all disciplines bounded within creation, whose proper object of study is part of God's good creation, and whose proper object of study is finally and only fully understood within the light of God's overall purpose for all creation, the coming of God's kingdom. Knowledge is in this important sense both worship and praise, as well as profoundly pragmatic, vital to social action.

---

[80] The actual questions raised in eds. Russell et al., *John Paul II on Science and Religion* by Elizabeth Johnson (no history of allowing such theological plurality), Rosemary Ruether (a patriarchal power critique of both theology and science is required), Wolfhart Pannenberg (the downplaying of philosophy and of Aristotelianism philosophical categories that are still valid) are important, but do not affect my main argument here.

Epilogue

Theology: The Church at the Heart of the Christian University Proclaiming the Word to the World

It is not unusual for authors to make exaggerated claims in a rousing conclusion. I claim that Christian culture and civilization are at stake if we do not attend to the nature of the university, a major institution that fosters the cultural and intellectual life of nations and trains the intelligentsia of the ecclesia. No doubt, governments and big business are important as are civic societies (like churches, mosques, temples, baseball clubs, music societies, and so on), but all these groups get their intelligentsia from the universities and in this sense the intellectual life of nations finds its primary nourishment in its universities. That is why the university must lie in the "heart of the church." Not all universities, and clearly, not all churches—but my argument has been tradition-specific: the Catholic university must serve the Church, so that it can serve society. This is found in microcosm in the discipline of theology but is true, in differing ways, for all the disciplines. Let me briefly rehearse the plot of the book to draw together the various stands of the argument that have led to this conclusion.

I began by showing how theology is held captive within the Berlin-Babylonian university. In the modern research Enlightenment university, the ecclesial nature of theology is suppressed and policed as a crumbling liberalism lisps its concerns for pluralism in all fields of life, while denying the genuine methodological pluralism that might call its own existence into question (chapter one). As a matter of fact, the ideological control is never quite so tight, indicative of my writing this book while being granted study leave from my own secular Bristol University—and being able to teach my students why they (and I) are prisoners to mammon. Nevertheless, I wanted to focus on important intellectual currents that could alert us to the dark future for theology as it is slowly transformed into religious studies, a discipline that serves positivist historians, sociologists, literary scholars, feminists, psychoanalysts, almost anyone and everyone apart from ecclesial Christians.

If theology is to be theology, it must be ecclesial, and this involves prayer and careful attention to various polyphonic sources of authority, along with the highest intellectual standards (chapter four). If the university cannot recognize and facilitate the unique character of this intellectual discipline, indeed the queen of the sciences, then the university must be called into question, not the discipline. Hence, my argument for a Christian university, and in this case, a Roman Catholic university. In such a university, not only can theology be theology, but also the transformation of all the disciplines can begin. In the latter part of the book I show how this might look in the case of a theological religious studies keeping the theme of the scandal of holy lives within Christianity and Hinduism in focus (chapter five), and also in relation to theology, philosophy, and cosmology (chapter six). Both these chapters open up numerous avenues for further research and both, I believe, exemplify the enormous richness of this alternative construal of traditional terrains. In these chapters I show that contrary to being inward-turning, a Christian university such as I envisage would be engaged with *every* aspect of created reality. If the Christian university is worth its salt, it requires a transformation of the curriculum so that the Christian vision can illumine every aspect of created reality, both natural and cultural. The Christian university requires campus social action, liturgies, upright lives and committed staff, but without curriculum changes, Christian intellectual culture will continue to be impoverished.

I try and answer two types of critics: the ones who argue that we already have religious universities as in the United States—so what's all the fuss? (chapter two); and those who have serious objections against aspects of a Christian university (chapter three). To the first I suggest that there is a "dying of the light" to use Burtchaell's imagery of the health of church colleges in the United States, with almost no sustained attention to the intellectual curriculum as central to what constitutes Catholic identity. In England, my own country, I chart the secularization of the universities and the Herculean pressures against two remaining Christian universities, showing how the light is almost extinguished—but not quite. Roman Catholics need to revisit their universities in the United States, promoting a genuine difference in scholarship and curriculum so that in five generations a Catholic intellectual culture might possibly be present and transformative of society. The Christian Church at the heart of the university will facilitate such genuine developments that can only enrich intellectual and cultural life, facilitate real pluralism and dialogue, and serve the common good. Liberal society owes itself religious universities. American Catholics owe it to their Church and their nation. There are already beacons burning on this front in old-established universities and in some newly founded ones—may these fires continue to blaze. In England the possibilities are more fragile, but nonetheless present. It would be impossible demographically and geographically to have denominational universities, but an ecumenical university is very possible (and opaquely present in two institutions). It requires the churches, educational administrators, academic staff, and students to work together over a sustained period to develop such institutions. In the meantime, Christians can be missionaries within the secular universities. The image of Troy can be exchanged for Babylon.

The other group of critics, those against "sectarian" projects such as mine, and those against outside interference (the Church) in the university, are to be found in strength—within the churches, as well as from non-religious camps. I argue that such criticisms are misplaced and even self-deluding. Since all enquiry and methods of enquiry are tradition-specific, all forms of education are sectarian in certain ways. There is no high ground in this debate, only differing forms of sectarianism, be they liberal, religious, feminist, psychoanalyst, and so on. But there is an advantage to Catholic sectarianism: its conviction, founded in revelation and beautifully expounded by Thomas Aquinas, that reason has a rightful autonomy. MacIntyre has shown why Thomism is superior to modernity and postmodernity. What is at stake is either the fostering of a homogenous voice (when the liberal and totalitarian sing from the same hymnal) or the nourishing of genuinely plural voices within the public square, so that real debate and exchange might take place. The Christian university, such as I defend, is deeply concerned with the common good because it is concerned with truth—in the academic disciplines and most importantly, in their interrelationships and in their practices. Hence, its commitment to the public square is obvious for all to see. Further, the Roman Catholic Church is theoretically committed to intellectual freedom (within legitimate parameters) and cannot logically be seen as "outside" interference in the university, given reason's graced autonomy. That the same church has sometimes abused its position is not at stake or in question; but what I do contest is the claim that intellectual freedom in theology or any of the disciplines is incompatible with an ecclesial university. Funding should not therefore be a matter of dispute for institutions of intellectual excellence committed to the common good, keeping within the law and inculcating true academic freedom, even when pluralistically conceived and practiced.

The reader who has got this far might well ask the question: does the argument in this book serve as an ideal type, simply stirring debate? Surely it is an impractical and impossible ideal? I think my argument can serve this "ideal-type" function and that is for the good. However, whether it is an impossible ideal remains to be seen and one can see all levels of the theoretical argument fragmentarily embedded in actual institutions. Hence, I do not think it either impractical or impossible. It may appear utopian, but so does the gospel. Mine is an argument offered to the Church, the university, and to the world (or less grandly, to a handful of readers) with the knowledge that education is central to the development of civilization and if the Church fails to transform education at every level, then the future of the Church and the world are in deep trouble. If the North American and English public cannot see this, then they should drop all the rhetoric about fostering genuine pluralism and admit the ideological nature of their secularism. This would involve suppressing history—as the recent contested European constitution exemplifies, where the Christian heritage of Europe is passed over in silence. It is up to the churches in North America and England to take up this challenge, to bring the light of God to shine through the portals of the university, to allow for a revitalization of Christian culture so that God may be given glory and the common good thereby served.

To conclude, we would do well to recall Saint Bonaventure's wise and challenging words (introducing his *Itinerarium Mentis in Deum* in *Prologus*, 4, cited in *FR*, p. 105), inviting the reader to recognize:

> [the inadequacy of] reading without repentance, knowledge without devotion, research without the impulse of wonder, prudence without the ability to surrender to joy, action divorced from religion, learning sundered from love, intelligence without humility, study unsustained by divine grace, thought without the wisdom inspired by God.

We can but weep by the rivers of Babylon, but we cannot despair, for there is much to be done, not least our prayers.

Bibliography

ed. Walter M. Abbott, *The Documents of Vatican II*, Guild Press, New York, 1966

Douglas Allen, "Phenomenology of Religion" in eds. M. Eliade et al., *The Encyclopedia of Religion*, vol. 11, 1987, pp. 272–85

Prudence Allen, *The Concept of Woman: The Aristotelian Revolution 750 BC–AD 1250*, Eden Press, Quebec, 1985

Thomas Aquinas, *Summa Theologiae*, Blackfriars translations, published by Blackfriars/Eyre and Spottiswoode, London/McGraw-Hill Book Co., New York, 1963–6

—— *Summa contra Gentiles*, trans. Anton C. Pegis, Notre Dame Press, Indiana, 1975

Aristotle, *Metaphysics*, trans. Hugh Lawson-Tancred, Penguin, London, 1998

—— eds. Duane W. H. Arnold and Pamela Bright, *"De doctrina christiana": A Classic of Western Culture*, Notre Dame University Press, Notre Dame, Indiana, 1995

Talal Asad, *Genealogies of Religion: Discipline and Reasons of Power in Christianity and Islam*, Johns Hopkins University Press, Baltimore, Maryland, 1989

Benedict M. Ashley, "The Validity of Metaphysics: The Need for a Solidly Grounded Metaphysics" in ed. T. L. Smith, *Faith and Reason*, St. Augustine's Press, Chicago, Illinois, 2001, pp. 67–89

Donald Attwater, *Dictionary of Saints*, 2nd edn. revised and updated by Catherine Rachael John, Penguin, London, 1983

Augustine, *On Christian Doctrine*, trans. D. W. Robertson Jr., The Liberal Arts Press, New York, 1958

—— *Teaching Christianity*, trans. Edmund Hill OP, New York City Press, New York, 1996

—— *Confessions*, trans. Maria Boulding OSB, New York City Press, New York, 1997

Gustav Aulén, *Christus Victor*, trans. A. G. Hebert, SPCK, London, 1931 [1931]

I. Badhwar, "Kalyan Sing Kalvi: Beliefs Cannot be Repressed," *India Today*, October 31, 1987, p. 20

Steven Baldner, "Christian Philosophy, Gilson, and *Fides et Ratio*" in ed. T. L. Smith, *Faith and Reason*, St. Augustine's Press, Chicago, Illinois, 2001, pp. 153–66

Hans Urs von Balthasar, *Mary for Today*, trans. Robert Nowell, St. Paul's, Slough, 1987 [1977]

—— *The Glory of the Lord: The Realm of Metaphysics in the Modern Age*, vol. V, trans. Oliver Davies et al., Ignatius Press, San Francisco, California, 1991 [1965]

—— *The Theology of Karl Barth*, trans. Edward T. Oakes, Ignatius Press, San Francisco, California, 1992 [1951]

Michael Banner, *Christian Ethics and Contemporary Moral Problems*, Cambridge University Press, Cambridge, 1999

Ian Barbour, *Issues in Science and Religion*, Prentice Hall, New York, 1966

—— *Science and Religion: New Perspectives on the Dialogue*, SCM, London, 1968

—— *Religion in an Age of Science*, HarperSanFrancisco, San Francisco, California, 1990

Barry Barnes, *Scientific Knowledge and Sociological Theory*, Routledge & Kegan Paul, London, 1974

—— *Interests and the Growth of Knowledge*, Routledge & Kegan Paul, London, 1977

—— eds. Barry Barnes and Stephen Shapin, *Natural Order: Historical Studies of Scientific Culture*, Sage, London, 1979

Jean Barr, *Common Science? Women, Science, and Knowledge*, Indiana University Press, Bloomington, Indiana, 1998

eds. Craig Bartholomew, Colin Greene, and Karl Möller, *Renewing Biblical Interpretation*, Paternoster Press, Cumbria, 2000

Zygmunt Bauman, *Modernity and the Holocaust*, Polity Press, Cambridge, 1991

Tina Beattie, *God's Mother, Eve's Advocate*, CCSRG Monograph Series 3, University of Bristol, Bristol, 1999

David Bebbington, "The Secularization of British Universities Since the Mid-Nineteenth Century" in eds. G. Marsden and B. J. Longfield, *The Secularisation of the Academy*, Oxford University Press, New York, 1992, pp. 259–77

ed. Sarah Beckwith, *Catholicism and Catholicity: Eucharistic Communities in Historical and Contemporary Perspective*, Blackwell, Oxford, 1999

Robert Benne, *Quality with Soul: How Six Premier Colleges and Universities Keep Faith with Their Religious Traditions*, W. B. Eerdmans, Grand Rapids, Michigan, 2001

Peter Berger, *A Rumour of Angels*, Penguin, London, 1970

—— *The Heretical Imperative: Contemporary Possibilities of Religious Affirmation*, Collins, London, 1980

—— "From the Crisis of Religion to the Crisis of Secularity" in eds. Mary Douglas and Steven Tipton, *Religion and America: Spiritual Life in a Secular Age*, Beacon Press, Boston, Massachusetts, 1983, pp. 8–24

eds. John Berkman and Michael Cartwright, *The Hauerwas Reader*, Duke University Press, Durham, North Carolina, and London, 2001

H. H. Bilgrami and S. A. Ashraf, *The Concept of an Islamic University*, Hodder & Stoughton, The Islamic Academy, Cambridge, 1985

María Clara Bingemer, "Women in the Future of the Theology of Liberation" in ed. Ursula King, *Feminist Theology from the Third World*, SPCK, London, 1994, pp. 308–17

María Clara Bingemer and Ivone Gebara, "Mary—Mother of God, Mother of the Poor" in ed. Ursula King, *Feminist Theology from the Third World*, SPCK, London, 1994, pp. 275–83

Richard J. Blackwell, *Galileo, Bellarmine and the Bible*, University of Notre Dame Press, Notre Dame, Indiana, 1991

Burton J. Bledstein, *The Culture of Professionalism: The Middle Class and the Development of Higher Education in America*, W. W. Norton, New York, 1976

Alan Bloom, *The Closing of the American Mind*, Simon & Schuster, New York, 1987

Hans Blumenberg, *The Legitimacy of the Modern Age*, trans. Robert M. Wallace, MIT Press, Cambridge, Massachusetts, 1986 [1966]

Markus Bockmuehl, "'To Be or Not To Be': The Possible Futures of New Testament Scholarship," *Scottish Journal of Theology*, 51, 1998, pp. 271–306

Leonardo Boff, *The Maternal Face of God: The Feminine and its Religious Expressions*, trans. Robert R. Barr, Harper & Row, San Francisco, California, 1987 [1966]

David Bohm, *Wholeness and the Implicate Order*, Routledge & Kegan Paul, London, 1980

—— "Response to Schindler's Critique of My *Wholeness and the Implicate Order*," *International Philosophical Quarterly*, Fall, 1982, pp. 329–39

—— (with B. J. Hiley) *The Undivided Universe: An Ontological Interpretation of Quantum Theory*, Routledge, London, 1993

Nicholas Boyle, "'Art,' Literature, Theology: Learning from Germany" in ed. R. E. Sullivan, *Higher Learning and Catholic Traditions*, University of Notre Dame Press, Notre Dame, Indiana, 2001, pp. 87–111

eds. Carl E. Breaten and Robert Jenson, *Reclaiming the Bible for the Church,* W. B. Eerdmans, Grand Rapids, Michigan, 1995

eds. Martien E. Brinkman et al., *Theology Between Church, University and Society*, Royal Van Gorcum, Assen, 2003

John Hedley Brooke, "Science and Theology in the Enlightenment" in eds. W. M. Richardon and W. J. Wildman, *Religion and Science*, Routledge, New York and London, 1996, pp. 7–28

Raymond E. Brown, "The History and Development of a Sensus Plenior," *Catholic Biblical Quarterly*, 15, 1953, pp. 141–62

—— *The Sensus Plenior of Sacred Scripture*, St. Mary's College, Baltimore, Maryland, 1955

—— "The Sensus Plenior in the Last Ten Years," *Catholic Biblical Quarterly*, 25, 1963, pp. 262–85

ed. Steve Bruce, *Religion and Modernisation: Sociologists and Historians Debate the Secularisation Thesis*, Clarendon Press, Oxford, 1992

Walter Brueggemann, "II Kings 18–19: The Legitimacy of a Sectarian Hermeneutic," *Horizons in Biblical Theology*, 7, 1985, pp. 1–41

Michael J. Buckley, *At the Origins of Modern Atheism*, Yale University Press, New Haven, Connecticut, 1987

—— *The Catholic University as Promise and Project: Reflections in a Jesuit Idiom*, Georgetown University, Washington, DC, 1998

Philip Burling and Gregory T. Moffatt, "Notes from the Other Side of the Wall: A University Counsel's Reflection on Potential Interactions between the Civil Law and the Apostolic Constitution" in ed. J. P. Langan, *Catholic Universities in Church and Society*, Georgetown University Press, Washington, DC, 1993, pp. 158–62

ed. Fredrick Burnham, *Postmodern Theology: Christian Faith in a Pluralistic World*, Harper & Row, San Francisco, California, 1980

David Burrell, *Aquinas: God and Action*, Routledge & Kegan Paul, London, 1979

James Tunstead Burtchaell, *The Dying of the Light: The Disengagement of Colleges and Universities from their Christian Churches*, W. B. Eerdmans, Grand Rapids, Michigan, 1998

Doris Burton, *Saint Emilie de Rodat: Foundress of the Sisters of the Holy Family*, Paternoster, London, 1951

Alban Butler, *The Lives of the Fathers: Martyrs and Other Principal Saints*, edited for daily use by Bernard Kelly, Virtue & Company Ltd., London, vol. 3, 1936

eds. Robert E. Butts and Joseph Pitt, *New Perspectives on Galileo*, Dordrat, Boston, 1978

Caroline Walker Bynum, *Fragmentation and Redemption: Essays on Gender and the Human Body in Medieval Religion*, Zone Books, New York, 1992

ed. Stratford Caldecott, *Beyond the Prosaic: Renewing the Liturgical Movement*, T. & T. Clark, Edinburgh, 1998

Michael C. Cannily OSFS, "De Munere Docendi: Some Observations" in *Proceedings of the Forty-fourth Annual Convention, Hartford, Connecticut, October 18–21, 1982*, Canon Law Society of America, Washington, DC, 1983, pp. 222–39

Walter H. Capps, *Religious Studies: The Making of a Discipline*, Fortress Press, Minneapolis, Minnesota, 1995

ed. Harry James Cargas, *The Unnecessary Problem of Edith Stein*, University Press of America, Lanham, Maryland, 1994

Catechism of the Catholic Church, Geoffrey Chapman, London, 1994

The Catholic Encyclopedia, ed. Charles G. Herbermann et al., Caxton Publishing Company, London and New York, 1907

William T. Cavanaugh, "'A Fire Strong Enough to Consume the House': The Wars of Religion and the Rise of the State," *Modern Theology*, October 1995, pp. 397–420

eds. J. F. Clarkson et al., *The Church Teaches*, Herder, St. Louis, Missouri, 1955

Roy A. Clouser, *The Myth of Religious Neutrality: An Essay on the Hidden Role of Religious Belief in Theories*, University of Notre Dame Press, Notre Dame and London, 1991

Sarah Coakley, *Powers and Submissions: Spirituality, Philosophy and Gender*, Blackwell, Oxford, 2002

Alan B. Cobban, *The Medieval English Universities: Oxford and Cambridge to c.1500*, Scolar Press, Aldershot, 1988

I. Bernard Cohen, *The Newtonian Revolution*, Cambridge University Press, Cambridge, 1980

Henry Cole and A. C. Burnell, *Hobson-Jobson*, [rev. edn.] Munshiram Manoharlal, New Delhi, 1979

Yves Congar, *A History of Theology*, trans. Hunter Gutherie, Doubleday, Garden City, New York, 1968 [1938]

Congregation for Catholic Education and Pontifical Councils for the Laity and for Culture, *The Presence of the Church in the University and in University Culture* (1994)—in *Briefing*, July 21, 1994, pp. 2–9

Congregation for the Doctrine of the Faith, *Instruction on the Ecclesial Vocation of the Theologian*, CTS/Veritas, London/Dublin, 1990

James Jerome Conn, *Catholic Universities in the United States and Ecclesiastical Authorities*, Editrice Pontifica Universita Gregoriana, Rome, 1991

Edward Conze, *Thirty Years of Buddhist Studies*, Bruno Cassirer, Oxford, 1967

Trevor Cooling, *A Christian Vision for State Education: Reflections on the Theology of Education*, SPCK, London, 1994

Ananda Kentish Coomaraswamy, "Sati: A Vindication of the Hindu Woman," *Sociological Review*, 6, 2, 1913, pp. 117–35

—— "Status of Indian Woman" in *The Dance of Shiva*, Noonday Press, New York, 2nd edn., 1957 [1948]

James A. Coriden, "Book III, The Teaching Office of the Church" in eds. J. A. Coriden et al., *The Code of Canon Law*, Paulist Press, New York, 1985, pp. 574–5

eds. James A. Coriden, Thomas J. Green, and Donald E. Heintschel, *The Code of Canon Law: A Text and Commentary*, Paulist Press, New York, 1985

John Coventry, "The Myth and the Method," *Theology*, 81, 682, 1978, pp. 252–61

Richard Cross, "Where Angels Fear to Tread: Duns Scotus and Radical Orthodoxy," *Antonianum*, 76, 2001, pp. 7–41

Adrian Cunningham, "Religious Studies in the Universities: England" in ed. U. King, *Turning Points in Religious Studies*, T. & T. Clark, Edinburgh, 1990, pp. 22–31

Mary Daly, *Gyn/Ecology: The Metaethics of Radical Feminism*, The Women's Press, London, 1987

António Barbosa da Silva, *The Phenomenology of Religion as a Philosophical Problem*, Gleerup, Lund, 1982

Donald Davidson, *Inquiries into Truth and Interpretation*, Oxford University Press, Oxford, 1984

Brian Davies, *The Thought of Thomas Aquinas*, Clarendon Press, Oxford, 1992

Michael Davies, *The Second Vatican Council and Religious Liberty*, Neumann Press, Minnesota, 1992

Gavin D'Costa, *Christian Uniqueness Reconsidered*, Orbis, New York, 1990

—— "A Christian Reflection on Some Problems with Discerning 'God' in the World Religions," *Dialogue and Alliance*, 5, 1, 1991, pp. 4–17

—— "Trinitarian Difference and World Religions" in ed. Ursula King, *Faith and Praxis in a Postmodern Age*, Cassell, London, 1998, pp. 28–46

—— *The Meeting of the Religions and the Trinity*, Orbis Books, New York, 2000a

—— *Sexing the Trinity*, SCM, London, 2000b

—— "Postmodernity and Religious Plurality: Is a Common Global Ethic Possible or Desirable?" in ed. Graham Ward, *The Blackwell Companion to Postmodern Theology*, Blackwell, Oxford, 2001, pp. 131–43

—— "Queering the Trinity" in ed. Gerard Loughlin, *Queer Theology*, Blackwell, Oxford, 2005, forthcoming

Robert P. Deeley, *The Mandate for Those Who Teach Theology in Institutes of Higher Studies: An Interpretation of the Meaning of Canon 812 of the Code of Canon Law*, Pontifical Gregorian University, Rome, 1986

Lynn Teskey Denton, "Varieties of Hindu Female Asceticism" in ed. I. J. Leslie, *Roles and Rituals for Hindu Women*, Pinter Publishers, London, 1991, pp. 211–31

John Donovan, *Academic Man in the Catholic College*, Sheed & Ward, New York, 1964

ed. Leo J. Donovan SJ, *Cooperation Between Theologians and the Ecclesiastical Magisterium*, Canon Law Society of America, Washington, DC, 1982

Herman Dooyeweerd, *A New Critique of Theoretical Thought*, 4 vols., Peideia Press, Ontario, 1983 [1935]

Eamon Duffy, *The Stripping of the Altars: Traditional Religion in England 1400–1580*, Yale University Press, New Haven, Connecticut, 1992

—— "Rewriting the Liturgy: The Theological Implications of Translation" in ed. S. Caldecott, *Beyond the Prosaic*, T. & T. Clark, Edinburgh, 1998, pp. 97–126

Avery Dulles, "Can Philosophy Be Christian? The New State of the Question" in eds. D. R. Foster and J. W. Koterski, *Two Wings of Catholic Thought: Essays on Fides et ratio*, Catholic University of America Press, Washington, DC, 2003, pp. 3–21

Gerhard Ebeling, *The Study of Theology*, trans. Duane A. Priebe, Collins, London, 1979 [1975]

Umberto Eco, *The Name of the Rose*, trans. William Weaver, Harcourt Brace, San Diego, California, 1994

eds. M. Eliade et al., *The Encyclopedia of Religion*, Macmillan, London, 1987

John Tracy Ellis, "American Catholics and the Intellectual Life," *Thought*, 30, 1955, pp. 351–88

—— *American Catholics and the Intellectual Life*, Heritage Foundation, Chicago, Illinois, 1956

Jacques Ellul, *The Technological Society*, trans. J. Wilkinson, Jonathan Cape, London, 1965

Jean Bethke Elshtain, *Public Man, Private Women: Women in Social and Political Thought*, Princeton University Press, Princeton, New Jersey, 1993

Arthur Jason Engel, *From Clergyman to Don: The Rise of the Academic Profession in Nineteenth Century Oxford*, Clarendon Press, Oxford, 1983

Sharon A. Euart, "Comment" in ed. J. P. Langan, *Catholic Universities in Church and Society*, Georgetown University Press, Washington, DC, 1993, pp. 137–46

George Every, *Early Eastern Christianity*, SCM, London, 1980

Daniel Fallon, *The German University*, Colorado University Press, Boulder, Colorado, 1980

Edward Farley, *The Fragility of Knowledge: Theological Education in the Church and the University*, Fortress Press, Philadelphia, Pennsylvania, 1988

David Fergusson, *Community, Liberalism and Christian Ethics*, Cambridge University Press, Cambridge, 1998

ed. Deane William Ferm, *Third World Liberation Theologies*, Orbis, New York, 1986

Stephen C. Ferruolo, *The Origins of the University*, Stanford University Press, Stanford, California, 1985

Timothy Fitzgerald, *The Ideology of Religious Studies*, Oxford University Press, Oxford, 2000

Kieran Flanagan, "Theological Pluralism. A Sociological Critique" in ed. I. Hamnett, *Religious Pluralism and Unbelief*, Routledge, London, 1990, pp. 81–113

—— *Sociology and Liturgy: Re-presentations of the Holy*, Macmillan, London, 1991

—— *The Enchantment of Sociology: A Study of Theology and Culture*, Macmillan, London, 1996

Gavin Flood, *Beyond Phenomenology: Rethinking the Study of Religion*, Cassell, London, 1999

David F. Ford, *A Long Rumour of Wisdom: Redescribing Theology*, Cambridge University Press, Cambridge, 1992

—— *Self and Salvation: Being Transformed*, Cambridge University Press, Cambridge, 1999

—— *Theology: A Very Short Introduction*, Oxford University Press, Oxford, 2000

—— "Reply to Webster's Review," *Scottish Journal of Theology*, 54, 2001, pp. 559–63

ed. David Ford, *The Modern Theologians*, Blackwell, Oxford, 1997, 2nd edn

David F. Ford and Dan Hardy, *Jubilate: Theology in Praise*, Darton, Longman & Todd, London, 1984

eds. David Ruel Foster and Joseph W. Koterski, *Two Wings of Catholic Thought: Essays on Fides et ratio*, Catholic University of America Press, Washington, DC, 2003

Michel Foucault, *The Order of Things: An Archaeology of the Human Sciences*, Tavistock, London, 1970 [1966]

—— *The Archaeology of Knowledge*, trans. A. M. Sheridan Smith, Tavistock Publications, London, 1972 [1969]

ed. Stephen F. Fowl, *The Theological Interpretation of Scripture*, Blackwell, Oxford, 1997

ed. Leslie J. Francis, *Sociology, Theology and the Curriculum*, Cassell, London, 1999

Hans W. Frei, *The Eclipse of Biblical Narrative: A Study in Eighteenth and Nineteenth Century Hermeneutics*, Yale University Press, New Haven, Connecticut, 1974

—— *Types of Christian Theology*, Yale University Press, New Haven, Connecticut, 1992

Duane Friesen, "Normative Factors in Troeltsch's Typology of Religious Association," *Journal of Religious Ethics*, 3, 2, 1975, pp. 271–83

Amos Funkenstein, *Theology and the Scientific Imagination from the Middle Ages to the Seventeenth Century*, Princeton University Press, Princeton, New Jersey, 1986

Hans-Georg Gadamer, *Truth and Method*, 2nd edn., trans. William Glen-Doepel, Sheed and Ward, London, 1975 [1965]

Alice Gallin, "American Church-Related Higher Education: Comparison and Contrast," paper delivered at Convention of American Historical Association, December 29, 1992

—— *Negotiating Identity: Catholic Higher Education Since 1960*, University of Notre Dame Press, Notre Dame, Indiana, 2000

J. W. Garrison, "Newton and the Relation of Mathematics to Natural Philosophy," *Journal of the History of Ideas*, 48, 1987, pp. 609–27

ed. Liam Gearon, *English Literature, Theology and the Curriculum*, Cassell, London, 1999

Ernst Gellner, *Postmodernism: Reason and Religion*, Routledge, London, 1992

ed. advisors Swami Ghanananda and Sir John Stewart-Wallace, *Women Saints: East and West*, Vedanta Press, California, 1955

ed. Rosino Gibellini, *Frontiers of Theology in Latin America*, trans. John Drury, SCM, London, 1980 [1975]

Frances Gies and Joseph Gies, *Women in the Middle Ages*, Thomas Y. Crowell, New York, 1978

Etienne Gilson, *The Christian Philosophy of Saint Thomas Aquinas*, trans. L. K. Shook, Victor Gollancz, London, 1957

René Girard, *Violence and the Sacred*, trans. Patrick Gregory, Johns Hopkins University Press, Baltimore, Maryland, 1977 [1972]

Duane T. Gish, *Evolution: The Challenge of the Fossil Records*, Creation Life Publishers, California, 1985

—— *Evolution: The Fossils Still Say NO!*, Institute for Creation Research, California, 1999

Philip Gleason, *Contending with Modernity: Catholic Higher Education in the Twentieth Century*. Oxford University Press, Oxford/New York, 1995

Richard Gombrich, "Unpublished Ms. of Lecture Delivered on January 7, 2000, in Tokyo at the Graduate Institute of Policy Studies"

—— "Reflections of an Indologist" in ed. I. Hamnett, *Religious Pluralism and Unbelief*, Routledge, London, 1990, pp. 243–61

Sinclair Goodlad, "The Bear's Hug: Hazards and Opportunities for Church Universities and Colleges in Accommodating to Secular Society," *Prologue*, 3, 2002a, pp. 46–60

—— "Christian Universities and Colleges: A Conceptual Inquiry," being The St. Matthias Lecture, September 12, 2002b, unpublished ms., pp. 1–24

T. O. Gormez and G. B. Conde, *Women in Science: Women, Feminism and Natural, Experimental and Technological Science*, Oxford University Press, Oxford, 1998

Edward Grant, *The Foundations of Science in the Middle Ages: Their Religious, Institutional and Intellectual Contexts*, Cambridge University Press, Cambridge, 1996

Deirdre Green, *Gold in the Crucible: Teresa of Avila and the Western Mystical Tradition*, Element Books, Dorset, 1989

V. H. H. Green, *Religion at Oxford and Cambridge*, SCM, London, 1964

L. W. Grensted, *A Short History of the Doctrine of the Atonement*, University Press of Manchester, Manchester, 1920

Paul J. Griffiths, *Religious Reading: The Place of Reading in the Practice of Religion*, Oxford University Press, Oxford, 1999

Colin Gunton, *The One, the Three and the Many: God, Creation and the Culture of Modernity*, Cambridge University Press, Cambridge, 1993

—— "Doing Theology in the University Today" in eds. Colin E. Gunton et al., *The Practice of Theology: A Reader*, SCM, London, 2001, pp. 441–55

eds. Colin E. Gunton, Stephen R. Holmes, and Murray A. Rae, *The Practice of Theology: A Reader*, SCM, London, 2001

James Gustafson, *Ethics from a Theocentric Perspective*, vols. 1 and 2, Chicago University Press, Chicago, Illinois, 1981, 1984, respectively

—— "The Sectarian Temptation: Reflection on Theology, the Church, and the University," *Proceedings of the Catholic Theological Society of America*, 1985a, 40, pp. 83–94

—— "A Response to Critics," *Journal of Religious Ethics*, 13, 1985b, pp. 185–209

Paul Hacker, "Aspects of Neo-Hinduism as Contrasted with Surviving Traditional Hinduism" in ed. Lambert Schmithausen, *Writings of Paul Hacker: Kleine Schriften*, Harrassowitz, Wiesbaden, 1978, pp. 580–608

J. G. Hagen, "Science and the Church," *The Catholic Encyclopedia*, 1912, ed. Charles G. Herbermann et al. (transcribed by Douglas J. Potter) www.newadvent.org/cathen/13598b.htm

Wilhelm Halbfass, *India and Europe: An Essay in Understanding*, State University of New York Press, Albany, New York, 1988

ed. Ian Hamnett, *Religious Pluralism and Unbelief: Studies Critical and Comparative*, Routledge, London, 1990

ed. Anthony Hanson, *Symposium on Teilhard de Chardin*, Darton, Longman & Todd, London, 1970

Daniel D. Hardy, *On Being the Church*, SCM, London, 2002

Lindsey Harlan, *Religion and Rajput Women: The Ethic of Protection in Contemporary Narratives*, University of California Press, Berkeley, 1992

Peter Harrison, *"Religion" and the Religions in the English Enlightenment*, Cambridge University Press, Cambridge, 1990

Stanley Hauerwas, "Some Theological Reflections on Gutierrez's Use of 'Liberation' as a Theological Concept," *Modern Theology*, 3, 1, 1986, pp. 67–76

—— *Christian Existence Today*, The Labyrinth Press, Durham, North Carolina, 1988

—— *Unleashing the Scripture: Freeing the Bible from Captivity to America*, Abingdon Press, Nashville, Tennessee, 1993

—— *Dispatches from the Front: Theological Engagements with the Secular*, Duke University Press, Durham, North Carolina, 1994

—— "Why the 'Sectarian Temptation' is a Misrepresentation: A Response to James Gustafson" in eds. J. Berkman and M. Cartwright, *The Hauerwas Reader*, Duke University Press, Durham, North Carolina, and London, 2001, pp. 90–110

Stanley Hauerwas and Charles Pinches, *Christians Among the Virtues: Theological Conversations with Ancient and Modern Ethics*, University of Notre Dame Press, Notre Dame, Indiana, 1997

eds. Stanley Hauerwas and John H. Westerhoff, *Schooling Christians: "Holy Experiments" in American Education*, W. B. Eerdmans, Grand Rapids, Michigan, 1992

Rosemary Luling Haughton, "Transcendence and the Bewilderment of Being Modern" in ed. J. L. Heft, *A Catholic Modernity?*, Oxford University Press, New York, 1999, pp. 65–82

ed. John Stratton Hawley, *Saints and Virtues*, University of California Press, Berkeley, 1987

ed. John Stratton Hawley, *Sati: The Blessing and the Curse*, Oxford University Press, Oxford, 1994

James L. Heft, *A Catholic Modernity? Charles Taylor's Marianist Award Lecture*, Oxford University Press, New York, 1999

eds. Laurence Paul Hemming and Susan Frank Parsons, *Restoring Faith in Reason*, SCM, London, 2002

D. Hencke, *Colleges in Crisis*, Penguin, London, 1978

ed. Theodore M. Hesburg, *The Challenge and Promise of a Catholic University*, University of Notre Dame Press, Notre Dame, Indiana, 1994

John Hick, *An Interpretation of Religion*, Macmillan, London, 1989

ed. Jan Hilgevoord, *Physics and Our View of the World*, Cambridge University Press, Cambridge, 1994

David A. Hollinger, "Enough Already: Universities Do Not Need More Christianity" in ed. Andreas Sterk, *Religion, Scholarship, and Higher Education: Perspectives, Models, and Future Prospects*, University of Notre Dame Press, Notre Dame, Indiana, 2002, pp. 40–50

Arthur F. Holmes, *Building the Christian Academy*, W. B. Eerdmans, Grand Rapids, Michigan, 2001

eds. John Horton and Susan Mendus, *After MacIntyre: Critical Perspectives on the Work of Alasdair MacIntyre*, Polity Press, Oxford, 1994

Kevin L. Hughes, "The 'Arts Reputed Liberal': Augustine on the Perils of Liberal Education" in eds. Kim Paffenroth and Kevin L. Hughes, *Augustine and Liberal Education*, Ashgate, Aldershot, 2000, pp. 95–110

Thomas Hughes, *Loyola and the Educational System of the Jesuits*, Heinemann, London, 1982

Reinhard Hütter, *Suffering Divine Things: Theology as Church Practice*, trans. Doug Scott, W. B. Eerdmans, Grand Rapids, Michigan, 2000 [1997]

Craig K. Ihara, "Why There are no Human Rights in Buddhism: A Reply to Damien Keown" in eds. D. Keown et al., *Buddhism and Human Rights*, Curzon, London, 1993, pp. 43–51

Luce Irigaray, "Women, the Sacred and Money" in *Sexes and Genealogies*, trans. Gillian C. Clark and Carolyn Burke, Athlone Press, London, 1993 [1987], pp. 77–88

Lisa Isherwood, "Marriage: Heaven or Hell? Twin Souls and Broken Bones" in ed. A. Thatcher, *Celebrating Christian Marriage*, Cassell, London, 2001, pp. 201–17

Werner Jaeger, *Paideia: The Ideals of Greek Culture*, trans. Gilbert Highet, 3 vols, Oxford University Press, New York, 1944

Sharada Jain, Nirja Mesra, and Kavita Srivastava, "Deorala Episode: Women's Protest in Rajasthan," *Economic and Political Weekly*, 22, 45, 1987, pp. 1891–4

William James, *The Varieties of Religious Experience*, Simon & Schuster, New York, 1997 [1902]

Fredric Jameson, *Postmodernism, or, the Cultural Logic of Late Capitalism*, Verso, London, 1990

ed. Darrell Jodcock, *Catholicism Contending with Modernity: Roman Catholic Modernity and Anti-Modernism in Historical Context*, Cambridge University Press, Cambridge, 2000

Pope John Paul II, *Ex Corde Ecclesiae* (trans. *On Catholic Universities*), 1990a, all papal texts, apart from "Letter" below, available from www.vatican.va/holy_father/john_paul_ii/apost_constitutions/documents/hf_jp-ii_apc_15081990_ex-corde-ecclesiae_en.html

—— "Letter of His Holiness Pope John Paul II to the Reverend George V. Coyne SJ, Director of the Vatican Observatory 'On the Occasion of the Three Hundredth Anniversary of the Publication of Newton's *Philosophiae Naturalis Principia Mathematica*,'" 1989, in eds. R. J. Russell et al., *John Paul II on Science and Religion*, Vatican Observatory Publications, Rome, 1990b, numbered M1–14

—— Motu Proprio: "Socialium Scientiarum Investigations," 1994

—— *The Code of Canon Law*, New Revised English translation, HarperCollins, London, 1997 [1983]

—— *Fides et Ratio* (trans. *Faith and Reason*), 1998

—— "Address to the Pontifical Academy of Sciences," 2000

Elizabeth Johnson, *Friends of God and Prophets: A Feminist Theological Reading of the Communion of Saints*, SCM, London, 1998

Henry C. Johnson, "Down from the Mountain: Secularization and the Higher Learning in America," *Review of Politics*, 54, 1992, pp. 551–8

Josef Andreas Jungmann, "Commentary on *Constitution on the Sacred Liturgy*" in ed. H. Vorgrimler, *Commentary on the Documents of Vatican II*, trans. Lalit Adolphus, Kevin Smyth, and Richard Strachan, vol. 1, Burns & Oates, London, 1967 [1966], pp. 1–87

Pandurang Vaman Kane, *History of the Dharmaśāstras*, 2nd rev. edn., Bhandarkar Oriental Research Institute, Poona, 1968

Immanuel Kant, "The Conflict of the Faculties" in *Religion and Rational Theology*, trans. Allen W. Wood and George di Giovanni, Cambridge University Press, Cambridge, 1996, pp. 233–9

David Kelsey, *Between Athens and Berlin: The Theological Education Debate*, W. B. Eerdmans, Grand Rapids, Michigan, 1993

eds. Damien V. Keown, Charles S. Prebish, and Wayne R. Husted, *Buddhism and Human Rights*, Curzon, London, 1998

Fergus Kerr, *After Aquinas: Versions of Thomism*, Blackwell, Oxford, 2002

Richard Kieckhefer, "Imitators of Christ: Sainthood in the Christian Tradition" in eds. Richard Kieckhefer and George D. Bond, *Sainthood: Its Manifestations in World Religions*, University of California Press, Berkeley, 1988, pp. 1–42

ed. Alvin F. Kimel Jnr, *Speaking the Christian God: The Holy Trinity and the Challenge of Feminism*, W. B. Eerdmans, Grand Rapids, Michigan, 1992 ed. Ursula King, *Turning Points in Religious Studies*, T. & T. Clark, Edinburgh, 1990

ed. Ursula King, *Feminist Theology from the Third World: A Reader*, SPCK, London, 1994

ed. Ursula King, *Faith and Praxis in a Postmodern Age*, Cassell, London, 1998

David Kinsley, *Hindu Goddesses: Visions of the Divine Feminine in the Hindu Religious Tradition*, University of California Press, Berkeley, 1986

ed. James M. Kittelson, *Rebirth, Reform, and Resilience: Universities in Transition, 1300–1700*, Ohio State University Press, Columbus, 1984

Anne Klein, *Knowledge and Liberation: Tibetan Buddhist Epistemology in Support of Transformative Religious Experience*, Snow Lion, New York, 1986

John F. X. Knasas, "*Fides et Ratio* and the Twentieth Century Thomistic Revival," *New Blackfriars*, 81, 955, 2000, pp. 400–8

ed. Kelvin Knight, *The MacIntyre Reader*, Polity Press, Oxford, 1998

Joseph W. Koterski, "The Challenge to Metaphysics in *Fides et Ratio*" in eds. D. R. Foster and J. W. Koterski, *Two Wings of Catholic Thought*, Catholic University of America Press, Washington, DC, 2003, pp. 22–5

Thomas Kuhn, *The Structure of Scientific Revolutions*, 2nd edn., Chicago University Press, Chicago, 1970

Karl Josef Kuschel, *Laughter: A Theological Essay*, trans. John Bowden, SCM, London, 1994 [1993]

Abraham Kuyper, *Calvinism: Six Stone Foundation Lectures*, W. B. Eerdmans, Grand Rapids, Michigan, 1932

—— *Encyclopaedia of Sacred Theology: Its Principles*, Charles Scribner, New York, 1898

Catherine Mowry LaCugna, *Freeing Theology: The Essentials of Theology in a Feminist Perspective*, Harper, San Francisco, California, 1993

ed. John P. Langan, *Catholic Universities in Church and Society: A Dialogue on Ex Corde Ecclesiae*, Georgetown University Press, Washington, DC, 1993

Nicholas Lash, *A Matter of Hope? A Theologian's Reflections on the Thought of Karl Marx*, Darton, Longman & Todd, London, 1981

—— "The Difficulty of Making Sense," *New Blackfriars*, 70, 824, 1989, pp. 74–84

—— *The Beginning and the End of "Religion,"* Cambridge University Press, Cambridge, 1996

René Latourelle, *Theology: Science of Salvation*, trans. Sr. Mary Dominic, St. Paul's, Slough, 1969 [1968]

William P. Leahy SJ, *Adapting to America: Catholics, Jesuits, and Higher Education in the Twentieth Century*, Georgetown University Press, Washington, DC, 1991

Jean Leclercq, *The Love of Learning and the Desire for God: A Study of Monastic Culture*, trans. Catherine Misrahi, Fordham University Press, Fordham, New York, 1960 [1957]

—— *Theology and Prayer*, St. Meinrad Seminary, Indiana, 1962

Muhammad Legenhausen, "Book Review of *Whose Justice? Which Rationality?*," *Al-Tawhid*, 14, 2, 1997, pp. 158–76

I. Julia Leslie, *The Perfect Wife: The Orthodox Hindu Woman According to the Strīdharmapaddhati of Tryambakayajvan*, Oxford University South Asian Series, Oxford University Press, Delhi, 1989

—— "Suttee or Sati: Victim or Victor?" in ed. I. Julia Leslie, *Roles and Rituals for Hindu Women*, Pinter Publishers, London, 1991, pp. 175–93

George A. Lindbeck, *The Nature of Doctrine: Religion and Theology in a Postliberal Age*, SPCK, London, 1984

—— "The Story-Shaped Church" in ed. S. F. Fowl, *The Theological Interpretation of Scripture*, Blackwell, Oxford, 1997, pp. 39–52

David Thomas Link, "Comment" in ed. I. Langan, *Catholic Universities in Church and Society*, Georgetown University Press, Washington, DC, 1993, pp. 187–92

M. Locke, J. Pratt, and T. Burgess, *The Colleges of Higher Education: 1972–1982*, Critical Press, Croydon, 1985

David Lodge, *Paradise News*, Secker & Warburg, London, 1991

M. Lofthouse, *The Church Colleges 1918–1939: The Struggle for Survival*, J. Billings, Leicester, 1992

Gerard Loughlin, "Christianity at the End of the Story or the Return of the Metanarrative," *Modern Theology*, 8, 1992, pp. 365–84

—— *Telling God's Story: Bible, Church and Narrative Theology*, Cambridge University Press, Cambridge, 1996

Andrew Louth, *Discerning the Mystery*, Clarendon Press, Oxford, 1989

Henri de Lubac, *The Sources of Revelation*, trans. J. O'Neill, Herder & Herder, New York, 1968 [1967]

—— *The Church: Paradox and Mystery*, trans. James R. Dunne, Alba House, Staten Island, New York, 1969 [1967]

—— *Medieval Exegesis*, vol. 1 trans. Mark Sebanc, T. & T. Clark, Edinburgh, 1998 [1959]; and vol. 2 trans. E. M. Macierowski, T. & T. Clark, Edinburgh, 2000 [1959]

Neil B. MacDonald, "The Philosophy of Language and the Renewal of Biblical Hermeneutics" in eds. C. Bartholomew et al., *Renewing Biblical Interpretation*, Paternoster Press, Cumbria, 2000, pp. 123–40

Alasdair MacIntyre, *After Virtue*, Duckworth, London, 1985 (2nd edn.)

—— *Whose Justice? Which Rationality?*, Duckworth, London, 1988

—— "Values and Distinctive Characteristics of Teaching and Learning in Church-Related Colleges" in *Institutional Integrity and Values: Perspectives on United Methodist Higher Education*, Division of Higher Education/Board of Higher Education and Ministry, Nashville, Tennessee, 1989, pp. 12–35

—— *Three Rival Versions of Moral Enquiry*, Duckworth, London, 1990

—— "Catholic Universities: Dangers, Hopes, Choices" in ed. Robert E. Sullivan, *Higher Learning and Catholic Traditions*, University of Notre Dame Press, Notre Dame, Indiana, 2001, pp. 1–22

Madhu Kishwar and Ruth Vanita, *In Search of Answers: Indian Women's Voices from Manushi*, Zed Books, London, 1984

Adam J. Maida, *Ownership, Control and Sponsorship of Catholic Institutions*, Pennsylvania Catholic Conference, Harrisburg, Pennsylvania, 1975

Lati Mani, "Multiple Mediations: Feminist Scholarship in the Age of Multinational Reception," *Feminist Review*, 35, 1990, pp. 24–41

—— *Contentious Traditions: The Debate on Sati in Colonial India*, University of California Press, Berkeley, 1998

Jacques Maritain, *Integral Humanism: Temporal and Spiritual Problems of a New Christendom*, trans. Joseph W. Evans, University of Notre Dame Press, Notre Dame, Indiana, 1973 [1936]

ed. Darren C. Marks, *Shaping a Theological Mind*, Ashgate, Aldershot, 2002

Henri Marrou, *A History of Education in Antiquity*, Sheed & Ward, New York, 1956

George Marsden, *The Soul of the American University: From Protestant Establishment to Established Nonbelief*, Oxford University Press, New York, 1994

—— *The Outrageous Idea of Christian Scholarship*, Oxford University Press, New York, 1997

—— "Matteo Ricci and the Prodigal Culture" in ed. J. L. Heft, *A Catholic Modernity? Charles Taylor's Marianist Award Lecture*, Oxford University Press, New York, 1999, pp. 83–94

—— and Bradley J. Longfield, *The Secularisation of the Academy*, Oxford University Press, New York, 1992

Bruce Marshall, "Aquinas as Postliberal Theologian," *The Thomist*, 53, 1989, pp. 353–402

eds. David Martin, John Orme Mills, and W. F. S. Pickering, *Sociology and Theology: Alliance and Conflict*, Harvest Press, London, 1980

Francis Martin, *The Feminist Question: Feminist Theology in the Light of Christian Tradition*, T. & T. Clark, Edinburgh, 1994

David McCarthy Matzo, "Postmodernity, Saints and Scoundrels," *Modern Theology*, 9, 1993, pp. 19–36

Vincent Alan McClelland, *English Roman Catholics and Higher Education, 1830–1903*, Clarendon Press, Oxford, 1973

ed. Neil G. McCluskey SJ, *The Catholic University: A Modern Appraisal*, University of Notre Dame Press, Notre Dame, Indiana, 1970

Richard McCormick, *Notes on Moral Theology: 1981 Through 1984*, University Press of America, Lanham, 1984

Bernard McGrane, *Beyond Anthropology: Society and the Other*, Columbia University Press, New York, 1989

Ernan McMullin, *Galileo: Man of Science*, Basic Books, New York, 1967

—— "Science and the Catholic Tradition" in ed. Ian G. Barbour, *Science and Religion: New Perspectives on the Dialogue*, SCM, London, 1968, pp. 30–42

—— "The Conception of Science in Galileo's Work" in eds. Robert E. Butts and Joseph Pitt, *New Perspectives on Galileo*, Dordrat, Boston, Massachusetts, 1978, pp. 209–57

—— "How Should Cosmology Relate to Theology?" in ed. A. R. Peacocke, *The Sciences and Theology in the Twentieth Century*, Oriel Press, Henley and London, 1981, pp. 17–57

—— "Evolution and Special Creation," *Zygon*, 28, 1993, pp. 229–335

—— "Enlarging the Known World" in ed. J. Hilgevoord, *Physics and Our View of the World*, Cambridge University Press, Cambridge, 1994, pp. 79–114

—— "Van Fraassen's Unappreciated Realism," *Philosophy of Science*, 70, 3, 2003, pp. 455–78

John Milbank, "The End of Dialogue" in ed. Gavin D'Costa, *Christian Uniqueness Reconsidered*, Orbis, New York, 1990a, pp. 174–91

—— *Theology and Social Theory*, Blackwell, Oxford, 1990b

—— *The Word Made Strange: Theology, Language and Culture*, Blackwell, Oxford, 1997

—— "The Conflict of the Faculties: Theology and the Economy of the Sciences" in eds. Mark Theissen Nation and Samuel Wells, *Faith and Fortitude: In Conversation with the Theological Ethics of Stanley Hauerwas*, T. & T. Clark, Edinburgh, 2000, pp. 39–58

Matthew Monk, *Edith Stein*, Catholic Truth Society, CTS Twentieth Century Martyrs Series, London, 1997

Andrew Moore, *Realism and Christian Faith: God, Grammar, and Meaning*, Cambridge University Press, Cambridge, 2003

Philip R. Moots and Edward McGlynn Gaffney Jr., *Church and Campus: Legal Issues in Religiously Affiliated Higher Education*, Notre Dame University Press, Notre Dame, Indiana, 1979

Ashis Nandy, "Sati: A Nineteenth Century Tale of Women, Violence and Protest" in *The Edge of Psychology: Essays in Politics and Culture*, Oxford University Press, Delhi, 1980, pp. 1–31

—— "Sati as Profit Versus Sati as Spectacle: The Public Debate on Roop Kanwar's Death" in ed. J. S. Hawley, *Sati*, Oxford University Press, Oxford, 1994, pp. 131–48

Sakuntala Narasimhan, *Sati: Widow Burning in India*, Anchor Books, Doubleday, New York, 1990

eds. Mark Theissen Nation and Samuel Wells, *Faithfulness and Fortitude: In Conversation with the Theological Ethics of Stanley Hauerwas*, T. & T. Clark, Edinburgh, 2000

ed. Richard John Neuhaus, *Biblical Interpretation in Crisis: The Ratzinger Conference on Bible and Church*, W. B. Eerdmans, Grand Rapids, Michigan, 1989

W. Nevin, *Heirs of Saint Teresa of Avila*, Bruce Publishing Co., Milwaukee, Wisconsin, 1959

New Catholic Encyclopaedia, 1st edn. (eds. Staff of Catholic University of America), Palatine, Illinois and McGraw-Hill, USA, 1981

George Newlands, "Theology and Cultural Change: A Variety of Students" in eds. Martien E. Brinkman et al., *Theology Between Church, University and Society*, Royal Van Gorcum, Assen, 2003, pp. 164–74

John Henry Newman, *An Essay on the Development of Christian Doctrine*, Longman, London, 1890

—— *Fifteen Sermons Preached Before the University of Oxford Between AD 1826 and 1843*, University of Notre Dame Press, Notre Dame, Indiana, 1996

Aidan Nichols, "The Habit of Theology, and How to Acquire It," *The Downside Review*, 105, 1987, pp. 247–59

—— *The Shape of Catholic Theology*, T. & T. Clark, Edinburgh, 1991

—— "Catholic Theology in Britain: The Scene Since Vatican II," *New Blackfriars*, 80, 1999, pp. 451–71

Martha Nussbaum, *The Fragility of Goodness*, Cambridge University Press, Cambridge, 1986

—— "Recoiling from Reason," *New York Times Review of Books*, 19, 1989, pp. 36–41

Steven M. Oberhelman, *Rhetoric and Homiletics in Fourth-Century Christian Literature: Prose Rhythm, Oratorical Style, and Preaching in the Works of Ambrose, Jerome, and Augustine*, Scholars Press, Atlanta, Georgia, 1991

David J. O'Brien, *From the Heart of the American Church: Catholic Higher Education and American Culture*, Orbis, New York, 1994

Thomas F. O'Dea, *American Catholic Dilemma: An Inquiry into the Intellectual Life*, Mentor, New York, 1962

Oliver O'Donovan, *Begotten or Made?*, Clarendon Press, Oxford, 1984

—— *Resurrection and the Moral Order*, Inter-Varsity Press, Leicester, 1986

Mercy Amba Oduyoye, "Reflections from a Third World Woman's Perspective: Women's Experience and Liberation Theologies," in ed. U. King, *Feminist Theology from the Third World*, SPCK, London, 1994, pp. 23–34

Wendy Doniger O'Flaherty, *Siva: The Erotic Ascetic*, Oxford University Press, Oxford, 1973

ed. Joseph M. O'Keefe, *Catholic Education at the Turn of the New Century*, Garland, New York, 1997

Veena Tahwar Oldenberg, "The Roop Kanwar Case: Feminist Responses" in ed. J. S. Hawley, *Sati: The Blessing and the Curse*, Oxford University Press, Oxford, 1994, pp. 101–30

Ladislas Orsy, "The Mandate to Teach Theological Disciplines: Glosses on Canon 812 of the New Code," *Theological Studies*, 44, 1983, pp. 476–88

Rudolf Otto, *The Idea of the Holy*, trans. John W. Harvey, Oxford University Press, London, 1928 [1923]

Wolfhart Pannenberg, "Theological Questions to Scientists" in ed. A. R. Peacocke, *The Sciences and Theology in the Twentieth Century*, Oriel Press, Henley and London, 1981, pp. 3–16

—— "Comments" in ed. A. R. Peacocke, *The Sciences and Theology in the Twentieth Century*, Oriel Press, Henley and London, 1981, pp. 297–9

ed. A. R. Peacocke, *The Sciences and Theology in the Twentieth Century*, Oriel Press, Henley and London, 1981

F. E. Peters, *Aristotle and the Arabs: The Aristotelian Tradition in Islam*, New York University Press, New York, 1968

Ted Peters, "Science and Theology" in ed. David F. Ford, *The Modern Theologians*, 2nd edn., Blackwell, Oxford, 1997, pp. 649–68

ed. Ted Peters, *Cosmos as Creation: Science and Theology in Consonance*, Abingdon, Nashville, Tennessee, 1989

Catherine Pickstock, *After Writing: On the Liturgical Consummation of Philosophy*, Blackwell, Oxford, 1998

—— "Thomas Aquinas and the Quest for the Eucharist" in ed. S. Beckwith, *Catholicism and Catholicity*, Blackwell, Oxford, 1999, pp. 47–68

William C. Placher, "Revisionist and Postliberal Theologies and the Public Character of Theology," *The Thomist*, 49, 1985, pp. 392–417

—— "Postliberal Theology" in ed. David F. Ford, *The Modern Theologians*, Blackwell, Oxford, 1997 (2nd edn.), pp. 343–56

Alvin Plantinga, "Advice to Christian Philosophers (With Special Preface for Christian Thinkers from Different Disciplines)," 1984, www.leaderu.com/truth/1truth10html, pp. 1–19

—— *The Twin Pillars of Christian Scholarship*, The Stob Lectures of Calvin College and Seminary, 1989–90, Calvin College and Seminary, Grand Rapids, Michigan, 1990

—— "On Christian Scholarship" in ed. Theodore M. Hesburg, *The Challenge and Promise of a Catholic University*, University of Notre Dame Press, Notre Dame, Indiana, 1994, pp. 267–96

Plato, *The Republic*, trans. Tom Griffiths, Cambridge University Press, Cambridge, 2000

Michael Polanyi, *Personal Knowledge: Towards a Post-Critical Philosophy*, Harper & Row, New York, 1962

—— *Knowing and Being: Essays*, Routledge & Kegan Paul, London, 1969

John Polkinghorne, "Christian Faith in the Academy. The Role of Physics" in ed. R. E. Sullivan, *Higher Learning and Catholic Traditions*, University of Notre Dame Press, Notre Dame, Indiana, 2001, pp. 39–59

William L. Portier, "What Does it Mean to be *Ex Corde Ecclesiae*? Towards an Alternative Academic Culture," *Delta Epsilon Sigma Journal*, 42, 3, 1997, pp. 77–84

—— "Reason's 'Rightful Autonomy' in *Fides et Ratio* and the Continuous Renewal of Catholic Higher Education in the United States," *Communio*, 26, 1999, 541–56

Edward J. Powers, *Catholic Higher Education in America: A History*, Macmillan, London, 1973 [1958]

James S. Preus, *From Shadow to Promise: Old Testament Interpretation from Augustine to the Young Luther*, Harvard University Press, Cambridge, Massachusetts, 1969

James Provost, "A Canonical Commentary on 'Ex Corde Ecclesiae,'" in ed. J. P. Langan, *Catholic Universities in Church and Society*, Georgetown University Press, Washington, DC, 1993, pp. 105–36

Hilaŕy Putnam, *Reason: Truth and History*, Cambridge University Press, Cambridge, 1981

ed. Michael Pye, *Marburg Revisited: Institutions and Strategies in the Study of Religion*, Diagonal Verlag, Marburg, 1989

Willard Van Orman Quine, *Pursuit of Truth*, Harvard University Press, Cambridge, Massachusetts, 1990

Timothy Sean Quinn, ""Infides et Unratio": Modern Philosophy and the Papal Encyclical" in eds. D. R. Foster and J. W. Koterski, *Two Wings of Catholic Thought*, Catholic University of America Press, Washington, DC, 2003, pp, 177–92

Karl Rahner, "Christianity and the Non-Christian Religions" in *Theological Investigations*, trans. H. Kruger, Darton, Longman & Todd, London, vol. 5, 1966, pp. 115–34

—— "Magisterium and Theology" in *Theological Investigations*, trans. Edward Quinn, vol. 18, Darton, Longman & Todd, London, 1984, pp. 54–73

Hastings Rashdall, *The Universities in the Middle Ages*, 3 vols., new edn., Clarendon Press, Oxford, 1963

Arne Rassmusson, *The Church as Polis: From Political Theology to Theological Politics as Exemplified by Jürgen Moltmann and Stanley Hauerwas*, University of Notre Dame Press, Notre Dame, Indiana, 1995

Joseph Ratzinger, "Commentary on the *Dogmatic Constitution on Divine Revelation*" in ed. H. Vorgrimler, *Commentary on the Documents of Vatican II*, trans. William Glen-Doepal et al., vol. 3, Herder & Herder, New York, 1969 [1967], pp. 155–98, 262–71

—— *Church Ecumenism and Politics*, trans. Robert Nowell, St. Paul Publications, Slough, 1988 [1987]

—— "Biblical Interpretation in Crisis: On the Question of the Foundations and Approaches of Exegesis Today" in ed. R. J. Neuhaus, *Biblical Interpretation in Crisis*, W. B. Eerdmans, Grand Rapids, Michigan, 1989, pp. 1–23

Giovanni Reale, *The Concept of First Philosophy and the Unity of the Metaphysics of Aristotle*, trans. John R. Catan, 3rd edn., State University of New York, Albany, 1979 [1967]

Martin Redeker, *Schleiermacher: Life and Thought*, trans. John Wallhauser, Fortress Press, Philadelphia, Pennsylvania, 1973 [1968]

Patrick J. Reilly, "Funding for Faith-Based Higher Education," *Capital Research Center: Foundation Watch*, March 2002, pp. 1–7

eds. W. Mark Richardson and Wesley J. Wildman, *Religion and Science: History, Method and Dialogue*, Routledge, New York and London, 1996

Paul Ricoeur, *Freud and Philosophy: An Essay in Interpretation*, trans. Denis Savage, Yale University Press, New Haven, Connecticut, 1970 [1965]

ed. Hilde de Ridder-Symoens, *Universities in Early Modern Europe, 1500–1800*, Cambridge University Press, Cambridge, vol. 1, 1992; vol. 2, 1996

Richard Roberts, *Religion, Theology and the Human Sciences*, Cambridge University Press, Cambridge, 2002

James M. Robinson, *The Beginnings of Dialectical Theology*, John Knox Press, Richmond, 1968

Richard Rorty, *Philosophy and the Mirror of Nature*, Princeton University Press, Princeton, New Jersey, 1979

Gillian Rose, *Dialectics of Nihilism: Post-Structuralism and Law*, Blackwell, Oxford, 1984

—— *The Broken Middle*, Blackwell, Oxford, 1992

Sheldon Rothblatt, *The Revolution of the Dons: Cambridge and Society in Victorian England*, Faber, London, 1968

—— ed. Sheldon Rothblatt, *The European and American University Since 1800: Historical and Sociological Essays*, Cambridge University Press, Cambridge, 1993

ed. Letty Russel, *Feminist Interpretation of the Bible*, Westminster Press, Philadelphia, Pennsylvania, 1985

eds. Robert John Russell, William R. Stoeger SJ, and George V. Coyne SJ, *John Paul II on Science and Religion: Reflections on the New View From Rome*, Vatican Observatory Publications, Rome, 1990

Edward Said, *Orientalism: Western Conceptions of the Orient*, Routledge & Kegan Paul, London, 1978

Edward P. Sanders, *Jesus and Judaism*, SCM, London, 1985

Dorothy L. Sayers, "The Lost Tools of Learning," *National Review*, January 19, 1979, pp. 90–9

William Shea, "Catholic Higher Education and the Enlightenment: On Borderlands and Roots" *Horizons*, 20, 1993, pp. 99–105

David Schindler, "David Bohm on Contemporary Physics and the Overcoming of Fragmentation," *International Philosophical Quarterly*, Fall, 1982, pp. 315–27

ed. David Schindler, *Beyond Mechanism: The Universe in Recent Physics and Catholic Thought*, University Press of America, Lanham, Maryland, 1986

—— *Heart of the World, Center of the Church*, T. & T. Clark, Edinburgh, 1996

Friedrich Schleiermacher, *Brief Outline on the Study of Theology*, trans. Terrence N. Tice, John Knox Press, Richmond, Virginia, 1966 [1811]

Karl Schmitz-Moorman, "Science and Theology" in eds. R. J. Russell et al., *John Paul II on Science and Religion*, Vatican Observatory Publications, Rome, 1990, pp. 99–106

Frank D. Schubert, *A Sociological Study of Secularization Trends in the American Catholic University: Decatholicizing the Catholic Religious Curriculum*, Edwin Mellen Press, Lewiston, New York, 1990

ed. William A. Schumacher, *Roman Replies 1982*, Canon Law Society, Washington, DC, 1982

Elisabeth Schüssler Fiorenza, *Bread Not Stone: The Challenge of Feminist Biblical Interpretations*, Beacon Press, Boston, Massachusetts, 1984

—— "Commitment and Critical Enquiry," *Harvard Theological Review*, 82, 1, 1989, pp. 1–11

Raymond Schwab, *The Oriental Renaissance: Europe's Rediscovery of India and the East, 1680–1880*, trans. Gene Patterson-Black and Victor Reinking, Columbia University Press, New York, 1984 [1950]

236   BIBLIOGRAPHY

Mark Schwehn, *Exile from Eden: Religion and the Academic Vocation in America*, Oxford University Press, New York, 1993

Robert Schwickerath, *Jesuit Education, Its History and Principles, Viewed in the Light of Modern Educational Problems*, Herder, Freiburg im Brisgau, 1903

Joseph Scimencca and Toland Damiano, *Crisis at St. John's: Strike and Revolution on the Catholic Campus*, Random House, New York, 1967

Jon Luis Segundo, "Capitalism Versus Socialism: Crux Theological" in ed. Rosino Gibellini, *Frontiers of Theology in Latin America*, SCM, London, 1980, pp. 240–59

Stephen Shapin, *Leviathan and the Air Pump: Hobbes, Boyle, and the Experimental Life*, Princeton University Press, Princeton, New Jersey, 1985

Arvind Sharma with Ajit Ray, Alaka Hejib, and Katherine K. Young, *Sati: Historical and Phenomenological Essays*, Motilal Banarsidass, Delhi, 1988

Eric J. Sharpe, *Comparative Religion: A History*, 2nd edn., Duckworth, London, 1986

Douglas Sloan, *Faith and Knowledge: Mainline Protestantism and American Higher Education*, Westminster John Knox, Louisville, Kentucky, 1994

Ninian Smart, *The Phenomenon of Religion*, Macmillan, London, 1973a

—— *The Science of Religion and the Sociology of Knowledge*, Princeton University Press, Princeton, New Jersey, 1973b

—— "Religious studies in the United Kingdom," *Religion*, 18, 1988, pp. 1–9

R. B. Smith, "God and Evolutive Creation" in ed. A. Hanson, *Symposium on Teilhard de Chardin*, Darton, Longman and Todd, London, 1970, pp. 41–58

ed. Timothy L. Smith, *Faith and Reason*, St. Augustine's Press, Chicago, Illinois, 2001

Wilfred Cantwell Smith, *The Meaning and End of Religion*, Macmillan, New York, 1962

Alexander F. Sokolich, *Canonical Provisions for Universities and Colleges: A Historical Synopsis and Canonical Commentary*, Catholic University of America Press, Washington, DC, 1956

Janet Martin Soskice, "Can a Feminist Call God 'Father'?" in ed. A. F. Kimel, *Speaking the Christian God*, W. B. Eerdmans, Grand Rapids, Michigan, 1992, pp. 81–94

Edith Stein, *Life in a Jewish Family: Her Unfinished Autobiographical Account*, trans. Josephine Koeppel, ICS Publications, Washington, DC, 1986 [1933]

—— *Essays on Woman*, trans. Freda Mary Oben, ICS Publications, Washington, DC, 1987 [1959]

—— *On the Problem of Empathy*, trans. Waltraut Stein, 3rd edn., Institute of Carmelite Studies Publications, Washington, DC, 1989 [1917]

—— *Self-Portrait: In Letters 1916–1942*, trans. Josephine Koeppel OCD, ICS Publications, Washington, DC, 1993 [1987]

George Steiner, *Real Presences: Is There Anything in What We Say?*, Faber, London, 1989

—— *The Death of Tragedy*, Faber & Faber, London, 1995

Peter Steinfels, *A People Adrift*, Simon & Schuster, New York, 2003

David Steinmetz, "The Superiority of Pre-Critical Exegesis" in ed. S. F. Fowl, *The Theological Interpretation of Scripture*, Blackwell, Oxford, 1997, pp. 26–38

ed. Andreas Sterk, *Religion, Scholarship, and Higher Education: Perspectives, Models, and Future Prospects*, University of Notre Dame Press, Notre Dame, Indiana, 2002

Jeffrey Stout, *Ethics after Babel: The Languages of Morals and their Discontents*, James Clarke, Cambridge, 1988

John J. Strynkowski, "Theological Pluralism and Canonical Mandate," *The Jurist*, 43, 1983, pp. 524–33

Elizabeth Stuart, *Spitting at Dragons: Towards a Feminist Theology of Sainthood*, Mowbray, London, 1996

ed. Robert E. Sullivan, *Higher Learning and Catholic Traditions*, University of Notre Dame Press, Notre Dame, Indiana, 2001

Charles Taylor, *Sources of the Self: The Making of the Modern Identity*, Harvard University Press, Cambridge, Massachusetts, 1989

—— *Ethics of Identity*, Harvard University Press, Cambridge, Massachusetts, 1992

—— "A Catholic Modernity?" in ed. J. L. Heft, *A Catholic Modernity?*, Oxford University Press, New York, 1999, pp. 13–38

Teresa of Avila, *Complete Works of Saint Teresa of Jesus*, 3 vols., trans. and ed. E. Allison Peers, Sheed & Ward, London, 1946

ed. Adrian Thatcher, *Spirituality in the Curriculum*, Cassell, London, 1999

—— *Celebrating Christian Marriage*, T. & T. Clark, Edinburgh, 2001

Roger E. Timm, "Scientific Creationism and Biblical Theology" in ed. T. Peters, *Cosmos as Creation*, Abingdon, Nashville, Tennessee, 1989, pp. 247–64

Frank J. Tipler, *The Physics of Immortality: Modern Cosmology, God and the Resurrection of the Dead*, Pan, London, 1996

T. F. Torrance, "Divine and Contingent Order" in ed. A. R. Peacocke, *The Sciences and Theology in the Twentieth Century*, Oriel Press, Henley and London, 1981, pp. 81–97

—— "Comments" in ed. A. R. Peacocke, *The Sciences and Theology in the Twentieth Century*, Oriel Press, Henley and London, 1981, pp. 302–3

David Tracy, *The Analogical Imagination*, SCM, London, 1981

Ernst Troeltsch, *The Social Teaching of the Christian Churches*, vol. 2, trans. O. Wyon, Macmillan, New York, 1931

Mark Tully, *No Full Stops in India*, Viking, London, 1991

United States Conference of Bishops, "Guidelines Concerning the Academic *Mandatum* in Catholic Universities (Canon 812)," 2001: www.usccb.org/bishops/mandatum guidelines.htm

Fredrick van Fleteren, "St. Augustine, Neoplatonism, and the Liberal Arts: The Background to *De doctrina christiana*" in eds. Duane W. H. Arnold and Pamela Bright, *De doctrina christiana*, Notre Dame University Press, Notre Dame, Indiana, 1995, pp. 14–24

Bas C. van Fraassen, "The World of Empiricism" in ed. J. Hilgevoord, *Physics and Our View of the World*, Cambridge University Press, Cambridge, 1994, pp. 114–34

—— "On McMullin's Appreciation of Realism Concerning the Sciences," *Philosophy of Science*, 70, 3, 2003, pp. 479–92

ed. Herbert Vorgrimler, *Commentary on the Documents of Vatican II*, vols. 1–3, Herder & Herder, New York, 1969

Geoffrey Wainwright, *Doxology: The Praise of God in Worship. Doctrine and Life: A Systematic Theology*, London, Epworth, 1980

—— "Ecumenical Dimensions of George Lindbeck's The Nature of Doctrine," *Modern Theology*, 4, 1988, pp. 121–33

Michael Walzer, *Thick and Thin: Moral Argument at Home and Abroad*, University of Notre Dame, Notre Dame, Indiana, 1994

ed. Graham Ward, *The Blackwell Companion to Postmodern Theology*, Blackwell, Oxford, 2001

Alison Weber, *Teresa of Avila and the Rhetoric of Femininity*, Princeton University Press, Princeton, New Jersey, 1990

John Webster, *Theological Theology*, Clarendon Press, Oxford, 1998a

—— "Hermeneutics in Modern Theology: Some Doctrinal Reflections," *Scottish Journal of Theology*, 51, 1998b, pp. 307–41

—— "Review of David Ford, *Self and Salvation*," *Scottish Journal of Theology*, 54, 2001, pp. 548–59

—— "Discovering Dogmatics" in ed. Darren C. Marks, *Shaping a Theological Mind*, Ashgate, Aldershot, 2002, pp. 129–36

—— *Holiness*, SCM, London, 2003

Catherine Weinberger-Thomas, *Ashes of Immortality: Widow-Burning in India*, trans. Jeffrey Mehlman and David Gordon White, University of Chicago Press, Chicago, Illinois, 1999 [1996]

Claude Welch, "Dispelling Some Myths about the Split Between Theology and Science in the Nineteenth Century" in eds. W. M. Richardon and W. J. Wildman, *Religion and Science*, Routledge, New York and London, 1996, pp. 29–40

Donald Wiebe, *The Politics of Religious Studies: The Continuing Conflict with Theology in the Academy*, Macmillan, Basingstoke, 1999

ed. James G. Williams, *The Girard Reader*, Crossroad Publishing Co., New York, 1996

Rowan Williams, *The Wound of Knowledge*, Darton, Longman & Todd, London, 1979

—— "Postmodern Theology and the Judgement of the World" in ed. F. Burnham, *Postmodern Theology*, Harper & Row, San Francisco, California, 1980, pp. 92–112

—— "Theological Integrity," *New Blackfriars*, 72, 847, 1991, pp. 140–51

—— "Saving Time: Thoughts on Practice, Patience and Vision," *New Blackfriars*, 73, 861, 1992, pp. 319–26

John F. Wippel, "The Condemnation of 1270 and 1277 at Paris," *The Journal of Medieval and Renaissance Studies*, 7, 1977, pp. 169–201

Alan Wolfe, "The Potential for Pluralism: Religious Responses to the Triumph of Theory and Method in American Academic Culture" in ed. A. Sterk, *Religion, Scholarship, and Higher Education*, University of Notre Dame Press, Notre Dame, Indiana, 2002, pp. 22–39

Nicholas Wolterstorff, "Scholarship Grounded in Religion" in ed. A. Sterk, *Religion, Scholarship and Higher Education*, University of Notre Dame Press, Notre Dame, Indiana, 2002, pp. 3–15

Linda Woodhead, "Can Women Love Stanley Hauerwas? Pursuing Embodied Theology" in eds. M. T. Nation and S. Wells, *Faithfulness and Fortitude*, T. & T. Clark, Edinburgh, 2000, pp. 161–88

Kenneth L. Woodward, *Making Saints: How the Catholic Church Determines Who Becomes a Saint, Who Doesn't, and Why*, Simon & Schuster, New York, 1996

Edith Wyschogrod, *Saints and Postmodernism: Revisioning Moral Philosophy*, University of Chicago Press, Chicago, Illinois, 1990

John Howard Yoder, *The Politics of Jesus*, W. B. Eerdmans, Grand Rapids, Michigan, 1972

Katherine K. Young, "Why are Hindu Women Traditionally Oriented to Rebirth Rather than Liberation (*Moksha*)?," *Third International Symposium on Asian Studies*, Asian Research Service, Hong Kong, 1981

—— and Alaka Hejib, "Sati, Widowhood and Yoga" in A. Sharma et al., *Sati*, Motilal Banarsidass, Delhi, 1988, pp. 73–85

Robert Young, *White Mythologies: Writing History and the West*, Routledge, London, 1990

Index

DIE FRAU IM URCHRISTENTUM

DIE FRAU
IM URCHRISTENTUM

JOSEF BLANK
CLAUS BUSSMANN
MAGDALENE BUSSMANN
GERHARD DAUTZENBERG
RUTHILD GEIGER
GERHARD LOHFINK
ROBERT MAHONEY
HELMUT MERKLEIN
KARLHEINZ MÜLLER
HUBERT RITT
ALFONS WEISER

HERAUSGEGEBEN VON
GERHARD DAUTZENBERG
HELMUT MERKLEIN
KARLHEINZ MÜLLER

HERDER
FREIBURG · BASEL · WIEN

SONDERAUSGABE VON BAND 95 DER REIHE
„QUAESTIONES DISPUTATAE"

Vorwort

Als sich der Schülerkreis Rudolf Schnackenburg für seine Herbsttagung 1980 zum Thema „Die Frau im Urchristentum" entschloß, geschah dies unter dem Eindruck der Anfragen, welche die moderne Frauenbewegung an die Theologie und an die Exegese des Neuen Testaments richtet. Das Ziel der Tagung bestand weniger in einer unmittelbaren Auseinandersetzung mit aktuellen Themen oder Thesen feministischer Theologie als in der Sammlung und Interpretation jener neutestamentlichen Text- und Traditionszusammenhänge, welche sowohl die Stellung der Frauen im Urchristentum spiegeln als auch in der Kirchengeschichte für die Bestimmung der Rollen von Männern und Frauen in Kirche und Gesellschaft bestimmend wurden.

Für die sachkundige Vermittlung der Anliegen und Anfragen einer sich formierenden feministischen Theologie bei unserer Tagung konnten wir Frau Dr. Magdalene Bußmann gewinnen, die uns dankenswerterweise ihren Beitrag für diesen Band zur Verfügung gestellt hat. Zwischen den Problemstellungen und der Sprache der Exegese und der von Frau Bußmann vorgestellten feministischen Theologie bestehen zweifellos hermeneutische Differenzen, die aber kaum unüberbrückbar sein dürften.

In der Sache zeichnet sich in den neutestamentlichen Schriften – und dies ist ein übereinstimmendes Ergebnis der Untersuchungen dieses Bandes – ein Doppeltes ab: Das Verlangen der Frauen nach voller Gleichberechtigung von Männern und Frauen im kirchlichen und gesellschaftlichen Leben findet neutestamentlich eine im Christusgeschehen gründende Rechtfertigung; zugleich wird aber auch deutlich, daß bereits in neutestamentlicher Zeit gesellschaftliche Tendenzen und Mechanismen wirksam wurden, welche eine zunehmende Verdunkelung der Gleichheit von Männern und Frauen in Christus und ein Zurückdrängen der Frauen in die Ordnungen einer patriarchalischen Gesellschaft zur Folge hatten.

Es traf sich gut, daß Prof. Dr. Gerhard Lohfink zur Zeit unserer Tagung einen Artikel über das Amt der Diakonin mit weiterführenden Überlegungen zur Gestaltung der kirchlichen Ämter für die Zeitschrift Diakonia ausgearbeitet hatte. Er ergänzte die Themen unserer Tagung, und wir sind ihm und den Verlagen Grünewald und Herder (Wien) dankbar, daß wir diesen Artikel in unsere Sammlung übernehmen dürfen.

Alle übrigen in diesem Band vorgestellten Beiträge wurden in einer ersten Fassung auf der Tagung vorgetragen und diskutiert. Für die Veröffentlichung wurden sie teils in der Vortragsform belassen, größtenteils aber erheblich überarbeitet. Mancher Beitrag hat dabei einen Umfang erreicht, der die einem Vortrag gesetzten Grenzen sprengt, der aber in einem Band zum Thema „Die Frau im Urchristentum" erforderlich ist, wenn eine begründete Darstellung des neutestamentlichen Befundes vermittelt werden soll.

Allen Mitarbeitern dieses Bandes dürfen wir an dieser Stelle herzlich danken, ebenso auch den Herausgebern der Quaestiones Disputatae und dem Verlag Herder für die bereitwillige Aufnahme dieser Untersuchungen in die Reihe. Ein besonderes Wort des Dankes gebührt Herrn Dr. Rolf Busemann und Herrn Reinhold Then für das Mitlesen der Korrekturen.

Gießen/Bonn/Würzburg, im Oktober 1982   *Gerhard Dautzenberg*
Helmut Merklein
Karlheinz Müller

Inhalt

I

Frauen in den Jesusüberlieferungen*

Von Josef Blank, Saarbrücken

1. Frauenbewegung und Jesustradition

Neue Probleme führen häufig zu neuen Anfragen an die altüberlieferten Traditionen und Texte; dies wiederum führt zu einer neuen Lektüre (relecture) dieser Texte, bei der manches, was man früher nicht so gesehen hatte, in einem neuen Licht erscheint. Die moderne Frauenbewegung scheint solche Impulse zu vermitteln oder auch zu provozieren. Da wird nicht nur nach den weiblichen Zügen im biblischen Gottesbild gefragt, oder nach dem neuen Selbstverständnis der Frau in der „Männerkirche", dem endlich auch ein neues Rollenverständnis entsprechen müsse. Vielmehr stellt sich die Frage, ob nicht gerade Jesus einen neuen Umgang mit der Frau gebracht hätte, eine neue Hochachtung, wie sie es weder in der damaligen jüdischen noch in der hellenistisch-römischen Gesellschaft gab, und in Rückwirkung dazu auch ein neues Verständnis des Mannes. Besonderes Aufsehen hat in jüngster Zeit das Buch der Psychotherapeutin und Theologin *Hanna Wolff*, Jesus der Mann, erregt, die Jesus als den

---

* *Allgemeine Literatur: P. Billerbeck,* Kommentar zum Neuen Testament aus Talmud und Midrasch, 4 Bde. (München ²1956); *S. Safrai – M. Stern,* (ed.), The Jewish People in the First Century (CRJ ad NT) I, 1–2 (Assen – Amsterdam 1974/76); *R. Bultmann,* Die Geschichte der synoptischen Tradition (Göttingen ³1957); *M. Dibelius,* Die Formgeschichte des Evangeliums (Tübingen ²1933); *E. Moltmann-Wendel* (Hrsg.), Menschenrechte für die Frau. Christliche Initiativen zur Frauenbefreiung (Mainz – München 1974); *P. Ketter,* Christus und die Frauen. Frauenleben und Frauengestalten im Neuen Testament (Düsseldorf 1933); *K.-H. Schelkle,* Der Geist und die Braut. Die Frau in der Bibel (Düsseldorf 1977); *H. Wolff,* Jesus der Mann. Die Gestalt Jesu in tiefenpsychologischer Sicht (Stuttgart ³1977); ferner: Concilium 12 (1976) Heft 1: Die Frauen in der Kirche; 16 (1980) Heft 4: Frauen in der Männerkirche; 14 (1978) Heft 5: Neue Orte des Theologietreibens; Una Sancta 32 (1977), H. 4: Frau – Kirche – Ökumene.

„nicht animosen Mann", als den „voll integrierten Menschen" beschreibt:

„Jesus hingegen war ein wahrer Mann, ein Mann von hochentwickelter anima, ein Mann von exzeptioneller Integration oder Individuation. Er war ein Mann mit schöpferischem, gültige Werte setzendem Gefühl. Er stellt alle inflatorische Scheinmännlichkeit durch sein bloßes Selbstsein bloß. Er ist exemplarisch für alle Zeit, der hominine Anruf zur nicht destruktiven, sondern schöpferischen Männlichkeit jeder Zukunft[1]."

Ähnliche Aussagen, welche die innere Freiheit Jesu im Umgang mit Frauen betonen, seine Fähigkeit der Zuwendung, der Aufmerksamkeit und des Ernstnehmens von Frauen finden sich immer wieder[2]. Es scheint, daß Jesus darin anders war als die meisten seiner Zeitgenossen in der jüdischen und hellenistischen Welt[3].

Inwieweit sind solche Aussagen berechtigt? Oder handelt es sich um moderne Überzeichnungen, wie sie immer wieder dann entstehen, wenn ein bestimmtes Thema en vogue ist? Wir wollen dazu die Texte der vier Evangelien befragen, die Frauen erwähnen und von Begegnungen Jesu mit Frauen berichten. Dabei werden allerdings jene Texte ausgeklammert, die von Maria, der Mutter Jesu, handeln oder von den Frauen in den Passions- und Ostergeschichten, da diesen eigene Beiträge gewidmet sind.

---

[1] *Wolff*, Jesus der Mann 174.
[2] Vgl. *L. Swidler*, Jesu Begegnung mit Frauen: Jesus als Feminist, in: *Moltmann-Wendel*, Menschenrechte 130–146, hier 132: „Was ist das Modell für die Begegnung Jesu mit Frauen? Wenn wir die Evangelien einmal nicht durch die Augen des maskulinen Chauvinismus oder des ewig Weiblichen betrachten, werden wir sehen, daß das Modell, das Jesus uns gibt, das eines Feministen ist – Jesus war Feminist! Ein Feminist ist ein Mensch, der die Gleichheit von Mann und Frau bejaht und zu verwirklichen sucht, ein Mensch, der sich dafür einsetzt, Frauen als menschliche Personen zu behandeln (wie Männer selbstverständlich behandelt werden) und der bewußt durch seine Handlungen gesellschaftlichen Bräuchen entgegenwirkt."
[3] Vgl. dazu die entsprechenden Abschnitte bei *Wolff*, Jesus der Mann 75–79; *Swidler*, aaO. 133 ff.

2. Zur Diskussion stehen die folgenden Texte:

2.1. Aus der Markusüberlieferung:

1. Die Heilung der Schwiegermutter des Petrus, Mk 1,29–31 (par. Mt 8,14–15; Lk 4,38–39).
2. Die Heilung der blutflüssigen Frau und die Auferweckung der Tochter des Jairus, Mk 5,21–43 (par. Mt 9,18–26; Lk 8,40–56).
3. Die Syrophönikierin, Mk 7,24–30 (par. Mt 15,21–26).
4. Die antipharisäische Scheltrede und das Vorbild der armen Witwe, Mk 12,38–40.41–44 (par. Lk 20,47; 21,1–4).
5. Die Salbung Jesu in Betanien, Mk 14,3–9 (Mt 26,6–13; Joh 12,1–8; vgl. Lk 7,36–50).

2.2. Aus der Matthäusüberlieferung:

1. Gleichnis vom Sauerteig, Mt 13,33.
2. Das Gleichnis von den zwei Söhnen, Mt 21,28–32.
3. Das Gleichnis von den klugen und törichten Jungfrauen, Mt 25,1–13.

2.3. Aus der Lukasüberlieferung:

1. Die Auferweckung des Jünglings von Nain, Lk 7,11–17.
2. Jesus und die Sünderin, Lk 7,36–50.
3. Die dienenden Frauen, Lk 8,1–3.
4. Martha und Maria, Lk 10,38–42.
5. Heilung einer verkrüppelten Frau am Sabbat, Lk 13,10–17.
6. Gleichnis von der verlorenen Drachme, Lk 15,8–10.
7. Das Gleichnis vom bösen Richter und der Witwe, Lk 18,1–8.

2.4. Aus der Johannesüberlieferung:

1. Jesus und die Samariterin am Jakobsbrunnen, Joh 4,1–42.
2. Der „erratische Block" im Johannesevangelium: Jesus und die Ehebrecherin, Joh 7,53 – 8,11.

Wie man auf den ersten Blick sieht, sind die Traditionen, in welchen von Frauen oder von Begegnungen Jesu mit Frauen die Rede ist, recht unterschiedlich; dies gilt auch von den verschiedenen Textsorten und literarischen Gattungen. Die ausführlichsten Erzählungen finden sich bei Lukas und bei Johannes; aber gerade hier dürfte es sich um relativ späte Fixierungen der Überlieferung handeln, so daß

11

eine historische Skepsis nicht ausgeschlossen werden kann. Gerade jene Geschichten, die am häufigsten als Belege für den neuen Umgang Jesu mit der Frau herangezogen werden, sind im Hinblick auf ihre historischen Grundlagen relativ unsicher, es sei denn, was im Prinzip durchaus möglich ist, man rechnet damit, daß sich in der lukanischen und johanneischen Überlieferung einige Sondertraditionen erhalten haben, in denen die besondere Art Jesu im Umgang mit Frauen festgehalten wurde. Möglicherweise war man an solchen „Frauenüberlieferungen" in der Urkirche (oder in manchen urchristlichen Gemeinden) nicht allzu stark interessiert, weil die gegenläufigen Tendenzen, der Frau in den christlichen Gemeinden eben doch wieder eine untergeordnete Rolle zuzuweisen, unter dem Druck der allgemein herrschenden patriarchalischen Vorstellungen und Verhältnisse damals[4] eben doch stärker waren. Die „Irrfahrten" der Perikope von der Ehebrecherin (Joh 7, 53 – 8, 11), bis sie im Johannesevangelium an ihrer jetzigen Stelle unterkam, sprechen in dieser Hinsicht doch eine recht deutliche Sprache; ähnlich könnte es sich mit anderen Überlieferungen verhalten haben.

Die Frauengeschichten in der Markustradition handeln weitgehend von Heilungswundern, die man der entsprechenden literarischen Gattung der Wundergeschichten zuordnen muß. Sodann fällt das öftere Vorkommen von Witwen auf, die, wie die „arme Witwe" (Mk 12, 41–44), auch als Vorbild hingestellt werden können. Ist das Markusevangelium vielleicht schon ein Vertreter einer „patriarchalischen" Richtung, dem sich dann auch Matthäus mit seinen stark judenchristlichen Traditionen angeschlossen hätte? Bedenkt man, welch großen Einfluß das Matthäusevangelium in der werdenden und dann in der Geschichte der etablierten Großkirche ausgeübt hat, und zwar gerade was die Kirchenverfassung und die Kirchenzucht angeht, dann wird man diesen Gesichtspunkt wohl kaum außer acht lassen können. Umgekehrt könnte man dann in den Frauengeschichten der lukanischen und der johanneischen Tradition eine Richtung erblicken, in der sich die „neue Bewertung der Frau durch

---

[4] Vgl. *Ch. Munier*, L'Église dans l'Empire Romain (IIe–IIIe siècles) (Paris 1979) 3–72: „Le Chrétien et la vie familiale". Leider fehlt in diesem sonst sehr gut informierenden Buch ein eigener Beitrag über die Stellung der Frau in der alten Kirche.

Jesus" deutlicher erhalten hätte. Diese Traditionen könnten der urchristlichen Missionsbewegung (Heidenmission) näher gestanden haben, in Verbindung mit dem profetischen Element, das ja auch Frauen als namhafte Vertreterinnen kennt. Ebenso könnte hier eine Linie zu den gnostischen, später auch montanistischen Bewegungen des 2. und 3. Jahrhunderts gezogen werden, wo Frauen ebenfalls eine führende Rolle spielten.

Die lukanischen Geschichten wurden in der kirchlichen Auslegungstradition häufig durch Allegorisierung ihrer ursprünglichen Brisanz beraubt, wie am deutlichsten die Auslegungstradition der Erzählung von Maria und Martha zeigt (vgl. Lk 10,38–42): die beiden Frauen sind Typen des asketisch-beschaulichen und des weltlich-aktiven Lebens; Martha steht für die „vita activa", Maria dagegen für die „vita contemplativa", wobei diese den fraglosen Vorrang vor jener hat.

3. Aus der Markusüberlieferung[5]

Bei Markus dominieren zunächst *die Wundergeschichten, in denen Frauen vorkommen*. Bei ihrer Analyse kann weitgehend auf die vorliegenden Kommentare und Monographien verwiesen werden; hier geht es vor allem um den die Frauen betreffenden Aspekt.

3.1. Die Heilung der Schwiegermutter des Petrus, Mk 1,29–31 (par. Mt 8,14–15; Lk 4,38–39)

Die Erzählung ist eine Kombination von „Wundergeschichte" und „Personallegende"[6], in deren Mittelpunkt die Schwiegermutter des Simon Petrus steht. Sie war vom Fieber(-Dämon) befallen und

---

[5] Zum Folgenden vgl. *K. Kertelge*, Die Wunder Jesu im Markusevangelium (München 1970); *G. Theißen*, Urchristliche Wundergeschichten (Gütersloh 1974); *R. Pesch*, Das Markusevangelium, 2 Bde. (HThK II/1–2) (Freiburg i. Br. 1976/77); *J. Gnilka*, Das Evangelium nach Markus, 2 Bde. (EKK II/1–2) (Neukirchen-Vluyn – Zürich 1978/79); *R. Schnackenburg*, Das Evangelium nach Markus (Geistliche Schriftlesung 2/1–2) (Düsseldorf 1966/71); *E. Klostermann*, Das Markusevangelium (HNT 3) (Tübingen ⁴1950); *M. J. Lagrange*, Évangile selon Saint Marc (Paris 1966); *V. Taylor*, The Gospel according to St. Mark (London 1963); *E. Schweizer*, Das Evangelium nach Markus (NTD 1) (Göttingen ¹⁴1975).
[6] Vgl. dazu *Pesch*. Markus I 128ff.

wurde durch Jesus, „der sie, indem er ihre Hand ergriff, aufrichtete", geheilt. Damit ist zum Ausdruck gebracht, daß die heilende und helfende Zuwendung Jesu allen Menschen beiderlei Geschlechts gilt (Mk 1,23–28 war von der Heilung eines besessenen Mannes die Rede). Bemerkenswert ist vielleicht noch der Hinweis, daß die gesund gewordene Frau Jesus „bedient". Damit ist nicht nur der Heilungserfolg sichergestellt, sondern wohl auch ein neues, besonderes Verhältnis der geheilten Frau zu Jesus. „Denn der Tischdienst einer Frau gegenüber Männern oder gar gegenüber einem Rabbi war im Judentum sonst nicht üblich."[7]

3.2. Die Heilung der blutflüssigen Frau und die Auferweckung der Tochter des Jairus, Mk 5,21–43 (par. Mt 9,18–26; Lk 8,40–56)

Die vorliegende Fassung der Wundergeschichte stellt zwei Frauen in den Mittelpunkt des Heilshandelns Jesu, eine ältere Frau, die an Blutfluß leidet[8], und ein Mädchen, die Tochter des Synagogenvorstehers Jairus, die vom kurz zuvor eingetretenen Tode auferweckt wird. Die Frage, ob es sich um zwei ursprüngliche Einzelerzählungen handelt, die nacheinander zu dieser kunstvoll gestalteten Doppelgeschichte verbunden wurden, oder ob diese Verbindung ursprünglich vorgegeben war, braucht uns hier nicht weiter zu beschäftigen[9]. Im vorliegenden Text bewirkt der Einschub der Erzählung von der Blutflüssigen eine Verzögerung in der Rahmengeschichte von der Auferweckung des Mädchens.

Für die Heilung der Blutflüssigen ist nicht nur der Umstand wichtig, daß die Frau schon 12 Jahre an ihrer Krankheit leidet und keine Heilung hatte finden können[10], sondern auch, daß es sich dabei um

---

[7] Nach *Billerbeck* I 480 (zu Mt 8,25) war das Dienen der Frau bei Tisch verpönt. Die jüdischen Rabbinen waren der Auffassung: „Man läßt sich überhaupt von keiner Frau bedienen, sie mag erwachsen oder klein sein".

[8] „Blutfluß (hebr. *zôb*, auch für den Eiterfluß des Mannes) ist der genorrhöische Blut-Eiter-Ausfluß der Frau (Lev 15,19.25 f.28.30). Die Flußbehaftete (hebr. *zābā*; griech. *haimorroûsa*) ist unrein …"; so *W. Bunte*, Art Blutfluß, in: BHHW I 260.

[9] Vgl. dazu die Diskussion bei *Kertelge*, Wunder 110 ff.

[10] Hier handelt es sich um den Topos der „Charakterisierung der Not", vgl. *Theißen*, Wundergeschichten 61 f.

den Zustand permanenter Unreinheit handelt[11]. Jesus kommt, und dies ist ein zusätzliches, erschwerendes Moment, nicht nur mit einer Frau in Berührung, sondern mit einer „Unreinen", wodurch er selber nach jüdischer Auffassung unrein wurde. Aber Jesus überwindet nicht nur diesen Anstoß, sondern er heilt die Frau und befreit sie auf diese Weise zugleich von ihrer Unreinheit. Wichtig ist darüber hinaus das Schlußwort, mit welchem Jesus die geheilte Frau entläßt: „Tochter, dein Glaube hat dich gerettet, gehe hin in Frieden!" (Mk 5,34). Die Anrede „Tochter" ist freundlich und zeigt eine persönliche Zuwendung Jesu zu der Frau. „Jesu Schlußwort stiftet tiefere Gemeinschaft zwischen der Frau und ihm; er redet sie als ‚Tochter' an (vgl. 2,5), benützt also eine vertrauliche Anrede (vgl. Ri 2,8; 3,10; Ps 45,11)."[12] Gerühmt wird auch der Glaube der Frau, dem Jesus die Heilung zuschreibt; gerade dies, daß sie als „Glaubende" erscheint, bewirkt ihr Heil und macht sie in den Augen Jesu bedeutsam. Hier wird auch das Besondere der neutestamentlichen Wundergeschichten offenbar, nämlich ihr Charakter als „Glaubens-Geschichten". Zieht man die Erzählung vom „Hauptmann von Kafarnaum" (Q, Mt 8,5–13; Lk 7,1–10) zum Vergleich heran, dann ist es jedenfalls der Glaube, die πίστις, die das ausschlaggebende Moment im Vorgang des Heilungswunders bildet. Daraus darf man den Schluß ziehen: *Im Glauben gewinnen Mann und Frau, theologisch gesehen, ihre volle Gleichheit. Wenn der Mensch die Dimension der πίστις erreicht, dann gewinnt er das Heil, und dieser Vorgang ist von der geschlechtlichen Differenz völlig unabhängig.*

Bei der „Tochter des Jairus" geht es in der Totenerweckungsgeschichte letztlich um ein Zeichen der Teilhabe am vollen Endheil[13]. Die Erzählung ist stark von den Totenerweckungsgeschichten aus dem alttestamentlichen Elija/Elischa-Zyklus (vgl. 1 Kön 17,17–24; 2 Kön 4,8–37) mitgeprägt. Man darf jedenfalls damit rechnen, daß hier, wie bei den übrigen Totenerweckungsgeschichten (Jüngling von Nain, Lk 7,11–17; Auferweckung des Lazarus, Joh 11,1–44), die Verkündigungsabsicht leitend gewesen ist, Jesus als den „Überwin-

---

[11] Diesen Umstand betont mit Recht *Pesch*, Markus I 301; vgl. ferner *Gnilka*, Markus I 214f.
[12] *Pesch*, Markus I 304.
[13] Zum Gesamtverständnis vgl. *Pesch*, Markus I 295–314; *Gnilka*, Markus I 208–211.

der der Todesmacht" darzustellen. In der markinischen Erzählung steht auch hier wieder das Glaubensmotiv im Zentrum, wo Jesus zu dem Vater des Mädchens sagt: „Fürchte dich nicht; glaube nur" (Mk 5,36; bei Lk 8,50 noch ergänzt durch: „... und sie wird gerettet werden"; dagegen fehlt bei Matthäus die Aufforderung zum Glauben). Es geht auch hier um den Glauben an die Krankheit und Tod überwindende Macht Jesu. In der Schilderung des Auferweckungswunders zeigt sich wieder die persönliche Zuwendung Jesu zu dem Mädchen. Jesus faßt das tote Mädchen bei der Hand und spricht zu ihr: „Talita kum", „Mädchen, ich sage dir, stehe auf! Und sogleich stand das Mädchen auf und ging umher, denn es war zwölf Jahre" (Mk 5,41 f). Auch in dieser Erzählung wird deutlich, daß das von Jesus vermittelte Heil allen Menschen gilt, ohne Rücksicht auf Geschlecht und Alter.

3.3. Die Syrophönikierin, Mk 7,24–30 (par. Mt 15,21–28)[14]

Die Pointe dieser Geschichte, die manche Ähnlichkeiten mit der Erzählung vom „Hauptmann von Kafarnaum" (Mt 8,5–13; Lk 7,1–10) zeigt, liegt darin, daß Jesus es hier mit einer nichtjüdischen, „heidnischen" Frau zu tun hat, mit einer „hellenistischen Frau, einer Syrophönikierin", wie Markus sie bezeichnet (Mk 7,26). Damit ist aber auch das Problem der Heidenmission berührt. „Die Markus vorgegebene Geschichte ... setzt sich mit dem Problem der Heidenmission, die noch nicht unangefochten war, auseinander. Sie beantwortet die Frage der Heidenmission so, daß sie sich bei der Wahrung der Privilegien Israels mit dem Hinweis auf die Glaubensbereitschaft der Heiden, die schon Jesus erfahren konnte, für die Mission entscheidet. Dabei spielt die Erkenntnis, daß das Heil Gottes immer ein Geschenk ist, eine entscheidende Rolle."[15]

Die Frau, die Jesus für ihre kranke Tochter um Hilfe bittet, zeigt einen rückhaltlosen Glauben, der sich durch keinen Widerstand aus der Fassung bringen läßt, sondern der im Gegenteil aus einem Wort, das nicht gerade freundlich lautet – „Es geht nicht an, den Kindern das Brot wegzunehmen und es den Hündlein hinzuwerfen" – noch

---

[14] Zum folgenden *Pesch*, Markus I 385–421; *Gnilka*, Markus I 289–295.
[15] *Gnilka*, Markus I 290.

einen Vorteil zieht: „Richtig Herr; aber auch die Hündlein unter dem Tisch kriegen von den Krümeln der Kinder noch etwas ab" (Mk 7,27f). Daraufhin gibt sich Jesus überwunden und heilt die von einem Dämon besessene Tochter. Schon Matthäus hat das Wort der Frau als „Glauben" verstanden, wenn nach ihm Jesus sagt: „Frau, dein Glaube ist groß; dir geschehe nach deinem Willen" (Mt 15,28).

Ein Problem der Geschichte ist *die Frage nach ihrer Historizität.* Nach *R. Pesch* handelt es sich um eine symbolische Erzählung, die die Heidenmission, die Jesus selbst nicht eröffnet, ja nicht einmal gefordert hatte, auf den Willen bzw. auf das Beispiel Jesu zurückführen will[16]. Daß die Urkirche, vor allem die christlichen Gemeinden in Galiläa mit dieser Geschichte die Öffnung zur Heidenmission begründet haben, dürfte ohne Zweifel richtig sein. Damit ist jedoch die Annahme, daß diese Geschichte auch einen historischen Kern haben kann, keineswegs ausgeschlossen, zumal da es sich um eine Dämonenaustreibung handelt, die bekanntlich zu den gut bezeugten Jesuswundern gehören. Auch daß Jesus – vielleicht um Nachstellungen des Herodes Antipas zu entgehen[17] – sich in heidnisches Gebiet begab, ist nicht unmöglich. „Heidenmission" hat er dort sicher nicht betreiben wollen, wie die Geschichte selber zeigt und Matthäus noch einmal eigens unterstreicht. Daß später die Urkirche dann auf solche „zufällige Begegnungen Jesu mit Heiden" zurückgriff, um damit ihre neue Praxis von Jesus her zu begründen, erscheint jedoch einleuchtend.

Was unsere Fragestellung angeht, so ist auch hier wieder zu unterstreichen, daß es Jesus bei dieser Frau in erster Linie um das Glauben geht, ja daß sie einen „großen Glauben" hat. Auch hier könnte das Wort Jesu an den Hauptmann von Kafarnaum gelten: „Wahrlich ich sage euch, bei keinem in Israel habe ich einen so großen Glauben gefunden" (Mt 8,10; vgl. Lk 7,9). Hier geht es um das

---

[16] Vgl. *Pesch,* Markus I 390. Ähnlich, wenn auch zurückhaltender, urteilt *Gnilka,* Markus I 294. Vgl. dagegen *Kertelge,* Wunder 153ff.

[17] *H. Kraft,* Die Entstehung des Christentums (Darmstadt 1981) 115, meint: „Mindestens zweimal konnte Jesus sich den Nachstellungen nur dadurch entziehen, daß er weit über die Grenze ging. Die Züge nach Norden ebenso wie in die Dekapolis werden durch die Gefahr erzwungen worden sein, die ihm in Galiläa drohte ... Die Wanderungen in rein heidnische Gebiete können schon darum nicht freiwillig gewesen sein, weil Jesus unter den Heiden nicht wirken konnte noch wollte."

Glauben im Sinne eines einfachen, radikalen Vertrauens auf die Wunder- und Heilsmacht Jesu. Für solch umfassendes Vertrauen steht diese hellenistische Frau als „Zeichen". Darüberhinaus, das Glauben überwindet nicht nur den Unterschied zwischen Juden und Heiden, sondern relativiert auch für Jesus den Unterschied der Geschlechter. Wo Jesus Menschen findet, die glauben, wird für ihn alles andere nebensächlich und sekundär. In der Zeit der beginnenden Heidenmission wird man diese Erzählung schon deshalb gerne überliefert haben, weil der Anteil der Frauen an der urchristlichen Mission anerkanntermaßen groß gewesen ist[18]. Jesus seinerseits hat diese Frau angenommen und sich durch ihren ungebrochenen Glauben aus der Reserve den Heiden gegenüber einmal herauslocken lassen. Das hat durchaus historische Wahrscheinlichkeit.

3.4. Die antipharisäische Scheltrede und das Vorbild der armen Witwe, Mk 12, 38–40.41–44 (par. Lk 20, 47; 21, 1–4)[19]

Was die beiden, wohl ursprünglich selbständigen Texte Mk 12, 38–40 und 12, 41–44 miteinander verbindet, ist das Stichwort „Witwe/χήρα"[20]. In der markinischen Redaktion wird den Schriftgelehrten, welche „die Häuser der Witwen verzehren und zum Schein lange Gebete hersagen" (Mk 12, 40) die aufrichtige und von reiner Hingabe erfüllte Frömmigkeit einer armen Witwe gegenübergestellt.

Die Stellung der Witwe in der antiken Welt, auch im Judentum, war ziemlich unsicher, vor allem, wenn sie kein Vermögen besaß und keine Söhne hatte, bei denen sie ihr Unterkommen und Auskommen finden konnte. „Solange eine Frau ihre Söhne hatte, war sie auch als Witwe nicht ganz mittellos. Deshalb war die Aussicht, ihre Söhne zu verlieren, besonders bitter (2 Sam 14, 5; 1 Kön 17, 20)."[21] Das Gegenbeispiel einer „reichen Witwe" und ihrer Möglichkeiten zeigt das Buch Judit; aber das waren Ausnahmen. Der Normalfall

---

[18] Vgl. dazu *E. Schüssler-Fiorenza,* Die Rolle der Frau in der urchristlichen Bewegung, in: Concilium 12 (1976) 3–9.

[19] Vgl. *Pesch,* Markus II 257–264; *Gnilka,* Markus II 173–178; *Schnackenburg,* Markus II 179–183.

[20] *G. Stählin,* Art. χήρα, in: ThWNT IX 428–454; *Hoffner,* Art 'almanah, in: ThWAT I 307–313; *R. de Vaux,* Das Alte Testament und seine Lebensordnungen I (Freiburg i. Br. 1960) 75 ff.

[21] *Hoffner,* aaO. 311.

dürfte eher die Notlage gewesen sein; daher werden Witwen und Waisen dem besonderen Rechtsschutz Gottes unterstellt. So heißt es bereits im „Bundesbuch":

„Eine Witwe oder Waise sollt ihr nie bedrücken. Wenn du sie bedrückst und sie ruft zu mir, dann werde ich ihr Rufen erhören und mein Zorn wird entbrennen. Ich werde euch durch das Schwert umkommen lassen, so daß eure Frauen zu Witwen und eure Kinder zu Waisen werden" (Ex 22,21–23)[22].

„Zweierlei bedurfte eine Witwe: Schutz gegen Ausbeutung und Unterstützung in der Not. Diese Pflichten der Frau gegenüber, die unter normalen Umständen dem Mann oder dem Vater oblagen, wurden, wenn beide fehlten, von der Gesellschaft im allgemeinen übernommen. Religiös ausgedrückt hieß es aber, daß Gott diese Verantwortung übernahm und sie der Gesellschaft auferlegte. Er war der Hüter der Witwe und der Vater ihrer Kinder (Ps 68,6)."[23]

In der markinischen Streitrede gegen die Schriftgelehrten (Mk 12,38–40), die wohl vormarkinische Traditionen verarbeitet[24], begegnet nun die Aussage: „Sie verzehren die Häuser der Witwen" (V. 40 a). Was ist mit diesem Vorwurf gemeint? In einer wohl antipharisäisch gemeinten Scheltrede in der „Himmelfahrt des Mose" heißt es u. a.:

---

[22] Der besondere Rechtsschutz von „Witwen und Waisen" findet sich auch im altorientalischen Recht. So heißt es in den Gesetzen des Königs Urnammu von Ur (um 2111–2094 v. Chr.): „Den Waisen überantwortete ich keineswegs dem Reichen, die Witwe überantwortete ich keineswegs dem Mächtigen ..." (Nr. 162 ff); vgl.: Texte aus der Umwelt des Alten Testaments (hrsg. von O. Kaiser), Bd. 1, Rechts- und Wirtschaftsurkunden. Historisch-chronologische Texte, Lieferung 1 (Gütersloh 1982) 19.

Oder im Epilog zum „Codex Hammurapi": „Damit der Starke den Schwachen nicht schädigt, um der Waise und der Witwe zu ihrem Recht zu verhelfen, habe ich in Babel ... meine überaus wertvollen Worte auf meine Stele geschrieben": CH XLVII, 59 ff; vgl. TUAT I, 1, 76.

Zur Situation von Witwen vgl. die Elija- und Elischageschichten 1 Kön 17,8–24; 2 Kön 4,1–7.

Zum besonderen Rechtsschutz der Witwen vgl. noch Dtn 10,18; 24,17–21; 26,12 f; 27,19; Jes 1,17; Jer 22,3; dagegen heißt es Jes 1,23: „Deine Fürsten sind Aufrührer und eine Bande von Dieben, sie lassen sich gerne bestechen, alle jagen dem Geld nach. Sie verschaffen den Waisen kein Recht, die Sache der Witwen kümmert sie nicht"; vgl. auch Jer 7,6; Ijob 29,13; Ps 146,9: „Der Herr beschützt die Fremden und verhilft den Waisen und Witwen zu ihrem Recht."

[23] Hoffner, aaO. 312.

[24] Pesch, Markus II 257, meint, „daß die mk Tradition ein Exzerpt aus umfangreicherer antipharisäischer Polemik bietet, die vormk wohl in der Gattung der Weheesprüche überliefert war und von Markus in die Form der Warnrede umgegossen wurde."

„Es herrschen über sie Verderbliche und Gottlose, die lehren, daß sie selbst gerecht seien. Und sie verbreiten ihrer Lehre Gift; sie sind betrügerische Leute und leben nur sich selber zu Gefallen, und sie verstellen sich in ihrem ganzen Wandel und schmausen gern zu jeder Tageszeit und schlemmen unersättlich … *Der Armen Güter fressen sie,* und sie behaupten, sie täten dies nur aus Gerechtigkeit; in Wirklichkeit verderben sie" (Ass. Mos. 7,3–6)[25].

Auch an die sogenannten „Sikhem-Pharisäer" könnte man denken: „Wie Sikhem sich beschneiden ließ, um die Dina zu erlangen (Gen 34,1ff), so ist ein Sikhem-Pharisäer ein solcher, der mit seinem frommen Gebaren selbstische Zwecke verfolgt, also aus der Religion ein Gewerbe macht[26]." Dagegen meint *Stählin:* „Sie" (die Schriftgelehrten) „befolgen scheinbar die prophetische Forderung ..., den Witwen zum Recht zu verhelfen, lassen sich aber ihre Anwaltstätigkeit so hoch bezahlen, daß die Witwen ihr Eigentum ... an ihre Rechtshelfer verlieren."[27] Vielleicht sollte man den Vorwurf allgemeiner verstehen: die Schriftgelehrten und Pharisäer scheuen nicht davor zurück, auf Kosten armer Witwen zu leben[28]. Das Wort gehört dann in die urchristliche, von Jesus inspirierte Sozialkritik, die an diesem Punkt eine traditionell alttestamentlich-prophetische Einstellung aufgreift, wenn sie für den Schutz der Witwen eintritt. Wahrscheinlich war die erneute, intensive Zuwendung zu den Unterdrückten und Armen, zu denen zahlreiche Witwen gehörten, auch ein besonderes Anliegen der Urgemeinde (vgl. Apg 6,1).

Die Erzählung vom „Scherflein der Witwe" (Mk 12,41–44; par. Lk 21,1–4) zeigt am Verhalten einer armen Witwe, die ihren letzten Pfennig opfert, wie hoch die Frömmigkeit dieser einfachen Frau derjenigen der selbstsüchtigen Schriftgelehrten überlegen ist.

Jesus sitzt der Schatzkammer des Tempels im Frauenvorhof gegenüber und schaut zu, wie die Leute ihre Geldopfer dem Priester

---

[25] *M. J. Lagrange,* Le Judaisme avant Jesus Christ (Paris 1931) 239 meint: „Wir können darin die Pharisäer erkennen"; so auch *Billerbeck* IV/1, 334–352 (14. Exkurs: „Die Pharisäer u. Sadduzäer in der altjüdischen Literatur"), hier 336. – Anders *R. H. Charles,* The Apocrypha and Pseudepigrapha of the Old Testament, 2 Bde. (Oxford 1969) II 419; er denkt vor allem an die Sadduzäer.

[26] *Billerbeck* IV/1 338.

[27] *Stählin,* aaO. 437.

[28] „Aber Jesu Anklage geht weiter: Sie zehren die Häuser der Witwen auf, das heißt, sie lassen sich für ihre Auskünfte und Ratschläge gut honorieren und verbrauchen skrupellos das Gut der Witwen", *Schnackenburg,* Markus II 180.

übergeben. „Und viele Reiche legten viel hinein." Da kommt eine arme Witwe und legt „zwei Lepta, das ist ein Quadrans" (etwa einen Pfennig) hinein. Daraufhin ruft Jesus seine Jünger herbei und sagt zu ihnen: „Diese arme Witwe hat mehr hineingelegt als alle andern, die in die Schatzkammer Spenden gaben; denn alle andern haben aus ihrem Überfluß gespendet; diese aber hat aus ihrem Mangel alles, was sie besaß, gespendet, ihren ganzen Lebensunterhalt."

Dazu sagt *Schnackenburg*: „Im Frauenvorhof des Tempels befand sich eine Halle (Schatzkammer), in der 13 posaunenförmige Geldbehälter aufgestellt waren. Die Behälter dienten für Gaben zu verschiedenen Zwecken, auch für freiwillige Gaben ohne besondere Zweckangabe. Die Tempelbesucher warfen das Geld nicht wie in unsere Opferstöcke selbst ein, sondern übergaben es dem damit beauftragten Priester, der es je nach der Bestimmung in die Geldbehälter legte. Das erklärt, warum Jesus die Gabe der armen Witwe beobachten konnte: Sie nannte den Betrag und seinen Zweck dem Priester, und Jesus konnte es hören."[29]

Im Unterschied zu den „Reichen", die sich mit ihren Opfergaben keineswegs völlig verausgaben, sondern aus ihrem „Überfluß" heraus fromme Gaben spenden, gibt die arme Witwe das Letzte, was sie hat. Ihre Opferspende ist darum ein Zeichen ihrer völligen Hinabe an Gott; bei ihr ist das „Opfer" wirklich das, was es vor Gott eigentlich sein soll, ein Zeichen wahrer Frömmigkeit. „All die Opfer erfreuen dich nicht; wollte ich Brandopfer bringen, du nimmst sie nicht an. Mein Opfer ist ein reuiger Sinn; ein Herz voll Demut und Reue wirst du nicht verschmähen" (Ps 51,18 f) Hier ist die Opfergabe einmal keine Ersatzleistung, oder ein Sich-Loskaufen von ethischen und sozialen Verpflichtungen; vielmehr sind „die Gabe" und „das Herz" bei dieser armen Witwe völlig identisch. So wird diese einfache Frau zum Symbol aufrichtiger Frömmigkeit[30].

Diese Frömmigkeit der Armen und Lauteren kann freilich auch immer wieder ausgenützt werden. Der Vorwurf gegenüber den Schriftgelehrten: „Sie verzehren die Häuser der Witwen", gilt freilich auch dann, wenn solches Verhalten, wie sehr oft im Lauf der Kirchengeschichte, innerhalb der christlichen Kirche vorkommt; wenn etwa die Spendenfreudigkeit des Kirchenvolkes schamlos aus-

---

[29] *Schnackenburg*, aaO. 182.
[30] An der Historizität der Geschichte braucht man nicht zu zweifeln; vgl. *Pesch*, Markus II 263.

genützt wird. Und wie oft sind es nicht gutgläubige, fromme Frauen, die auf solche Weise ausgenützt werden.

3.5. Die Salbung in Betanien, Mk 14,3–9
(par. Mt 26,6–13; Joh 12,1–8; Lk 7,36–50)[31]

Die Erzählung von der „Salbung Jesu in Betanien" durch eine ungenannte Frau (erst bei Joh 12,3 wird diese Frau mit Maria, der Schwester des Lazarus, identifiziert, was sicher sekundär ist) ist eine der wichtigsten Frauengeschichten im Markusevangelium. Sie hat ihren Platz am Beginn der Leidensgeschichte. Der Grund dafür ist, daß die Erzählung ihre Funktion im Rahmen der markinischen Passionsgeschichte darin hat, auf das Begräbnis und die Auferstehung Jesu vorauszuweisen, was V. 8 auch mit aller Deutlichkeit gesagt wird: „Sie hat vorweggenommen, zu salben meinen Leib zum Begräbnis." Damit stimmt es dann auch zusammen, daß nach Markus bei der Kreuzesabnahme Jesu keine Zeit mehr bleibt, um den Leichnam Jesu vor dem Begräbnis zu salben. Dies wiederum wird zum Motiv für den Gang der Frauen zum Jesusgrab am Ostermorgen (vgl. Mk 15,42–47; 16,1ff)[32]. Man kann deshalb die „Salbung in Betanien" als einen vorweggenommenen symbolischen Hinweis auf Ostern verstehen, wenigstens in dem Sinne, daß schon am Beginn der Passionsgeschichte auf die Bedeutung der Passion Jesu und ihren siegreichen Ausgang hingewiesen werden soll. Auch für Markus ist die Passion Jesu kein „blindes Schicksal", das Jesus dumpf zu erleiden hätte; vielmehr ist sie auch für ihn vom österlichen Morgenlicht überstrahlt.

Gegen die Annahme einer historischen Grundlage der Erzählung

---

[31] Vgl. *Pesch*, Markus II 328–336; *Gnilka*, Markus II 221–228; *Schnackenburg* II 228–233; zur johanneischen Fassung vgl. *J. Blank*, Das Evangelium nach Johannes (Geistliche Schriftlesung 4/1 b) (Düsseldorf 1981) 290–294; *J. Jeremias*, Die Salbungsgeschichte Mk 14,3–8, in: *ders.*, Abba (Göttingen 1966) 107–115.

[32] Anders ist die johanneische Darstellung. Nach Joh 19,38–42 wird der Leichnam Jesu vor seinem Begräbnis ordnungsgemäß mit Öl eingesalbt. Entsprechend lautet auch die Weisung Jesu an „Maria": „Laß sie, damit sie es für den Tag meines Begräbnisses aufbewahre" (Joh 12,7). Man muß also sowohl bei Mk wie bei Joh die sachliche Verbindung zwischen der „Salbung in Betanien" und den Grablegungs- und Ostergeschichten beachten.

bestehen keine durchschlagenden Einwände[33]. Ihre Einfügung in den Rahmen der Passionsgeschichte scheint relativ früh erfolgt zu sein, wie insbesondere die johanneische Parallele zeigt, wo die Erzählung freilich noch vor dem Einzug Jesu in Jerusalem steht (Joh 12, 1–8). Schwieriger dürfte die sachliche Interpretation sein. Nach *J. Jeremias* ist für das Verständnis von Mk 14, 3–8 grundlegend die Unterscheidung von „Almosen und Liebeswerk": *„Das Almosen* wird durch drei Merkmale vom Liebeswerk unterschieden: es wird den Armen gegeben, erstreckt sich nur auf Lebende und besteht in der Geldgabe. *Das Liebeswerk* dagegen umfaßt neben den Armen auch die Reichen, neben den Lebenden auch die Toten. Und es erfordert neben der Geldaufwendung zugleich den persönlichen Einsatz. *Darum steht das Liebeswerk über dem Almosen.*"[34] Nach dieser Unterscheidung wäre also das Tun der Frau gegenüber Jesus als „Liebeswerk" zu bezeichnen, und zwar als Liebeswerk, zu dem bald keine Gelegenheit mehr sein wird. Näherhin soll es sich um das „Liebeswerk der Totenbestattung" handeln, das proleptisch an einem vollzogen wird, der vor der Hinrichtung steht[35]. Doch so hilfreich auch diese Unterscheidung für das Verständnis der Geschichte ist, so liegt darauf nicht der entscheidende Akzent. Dieser liegt vielmehr, wie *J. Gnilka* richtig gesehen hat, in seiner „christologischen Relevanz"[36]. Es geht darum, am Beginn der Passionsgeschichte die überragende Bedeutung der Person Jesu selbst hervorzuheben.

Jesus hält sich in Betanien im Hause Simons des Aussätzigen auf, wo er mit diesem zusammen ein Mahl einnimmt. Der Ortsname Betanien (vgl. Anm. 33) ist fest mit der Erzählung verbunden (vgl. Joh

---

[33] „Die Geschichte von der Salbung in Betanien ist früh in der Gemeinde erzählt worden. Sie ist fest mit dem schon beim Einzug Jesu in Jerusalem genannten Ort verbunden (vgl. 11, 1.11 f), der etwa 3 km entfernt auf dem östlichen Abhang des Ölbergs lag. Der Stil weist semitische Spracheigentümlichkeiten auf, und die Anschauungen erklären sich ebenfalls aus der jüdischen Mentalität. So besteht kein Grund, an ihrer Geschichtlichkeit zu zweifeln", *Schnackenburg*, Markus II 229. Nach *Pesch*, Markus II 328, gehört die Erzählung „in den Horizont der Passionsgeschichte ..., der sie literarkritisch nicht abzusprechen ist", vgl. auch ebd. 335 Abs. IV. *Gnilka*, Markus II 22: „Am nächsten kommt das Urteil: biografische Szene."
[34] *Jeremias*, aaO. 109 f; *Pesch*, Markus II 333, hat diesen Vorschlag übernommen und arbeitet damit.
[35] *Jeremias*, aaO. 114.
[36] *Gnilka*, Markus II 224.

12, 1); auch der Name des Hausherrn scheint auf guter Tradition zu beruhen. Der Beiname „der Aussätzige" deutet wohl auf eine frühere Lepraerkrankung hin, von der Simon inzwischen wieder geheilt worden war; ob von Jesus, geht aus der Geschichte nicht hervor. Während des Essens kommt eine Frau herein, mit einem Alabastergefäß voll kostbaren Nardenöls. Das Nardenöl[37] wird aus Wurzeln der Narde (zugehörig der Pflanzengattung Valeriana), die in Indien und Ostasien vorkommt, gewonnen und gilt als ganz besonders köstlich. Sie zerbricht das Gefäß und gießt das kostbare Öl über dem Haupt Jesu aus. Zweifellos ist dies eine verschwenderische Geste, ein Luxus ohnegleichen; kein Wunder, daß Überraschung und Widerspruch laut werden. Einige der Tischgenossen murren: „Wozu diese Verschwendung des Salböls? Man hätte doch dieses Öl für mehr als 300 Denare verkaufen und den Erlös den Armen geben können." Die Reaktion der Leute, die selber auch nicht zu den Reichen gehörten, ist verständlich; es regt sich das „soziale Gewissen"; man geht soweit, die Frau zu inkriminieren (καὶ ἐνεβριμῶντο αὐτῇ, V. 5 b). Geht man rein vom „sozialen Gesichtspunkt" (Almosen) aus, dann haben die Kritiker durchaus recht. Jesus jedoch nimmt die Frau in Schutz und verteidigt ihr Handeln: „Laßt sie; was belästigt ihr sie? Sie hat ein gutes Werk an mir getan" (V. 6). Danach interpretiert Jesus das Handeln der Frau als „Liebeswerk" (καλὸν ἔργον), das die Frau an Jesus selbst (ἐν ἐμοί) getan hat. Die Handlung gilt also der Person Jesu selbst; es handelt sich um einen Ausdruck der Zuneigung und Verehrung gegenüber Jesus, was von Jesus ausdrücklich bestätigt wird. V. 7 wird die „soziale Bedeutung", auf der die Kritiker insistieren, zurückgewiesen und eher als Scheinheiligkeit dekuvriert, wenn Jesus sagt: „Die Armen habt ihr allezeit bei euch und könnt ihnen Gutes tun, wenn ihr wollt; mich aber habt ihr nicht allezeit." Auch darin kommt der „jesuanische Bezug" der Salbung zum Ausdruck. Jesus wird nicht mehr lange da sein; seine irdische Anwesenheit ist begrenzt und wird durch seinen Kreuzestod ein baldiges Ende finden. Die Frau hat also ein Gespür für die Bedeutung der „Gegenwart Jesu"; Jesus ist für sie ein Gegenstand der Verehrung; sie „treibt mit ihm einen Kult". Da gelten andere Maß-

---

[37] E. Segelbach, Art. Narde, in: BHHW II 1288.

stäbe[38]. Dazu kommt die positive Aussage: „Was sie tun konnte, hat sie getan; sie hat vorweggenommen zu salben meinen Leib zum Begräbnis" (V. 8). Auch diese Frau hat alles, was in ihren Kräften stand, getan. Ihr Verhalten ist, was die innere Einstellung, ihre Hingabe, ihre Liebe zu Jesus angeht, durchaus mit dem der „armen Witwe" vergleichbar. Auch sie gab rückhaltlos und aus vollem Herzen. Zugleich aber hat sie ein „Zeichen" gesetzt im Hinblick auf das Begräbnis Jesu; sie hat gleichsam die „Totensalbung" vorweggenommen. Genau darin aber liegt der Hinweis auf den Ostermorgen, wo die Frauen Maria Magdalena, Maria Jacobi und Salome Salben kaufen und ans Grab gehen, um den Leichnam Jesu zu salben; doch das ist nicht mehr nötig (Mk 16, 1 ff). Erst so wird auch die abschließende, mit dem feierlichen „Amen" bekräftigte Verheißung voll verständlich: „Amen ich sage euch: Wo immer man in der ganzen Welt das Evangelium verkündigen wird, da wird man auch erzählen, was sie getan hat, ihr zum Gedächtnis" (V. 9). „Das Evangelium" ist ja zunächst die Heilsbotschaft von Jesus Christus, und zwar im markinisch-narrativen Sinn als „die Heils-Geschichte von Jesus". In diese Geschichte gehört nun aber auch diese Frau mit ihrem überschwenglichen Tun an Jesus hinein. Zum „Gedächtnis Jesu" gehören auch die geschichtlichen Menschen, die eine positive Einstellung zu ihm hatten. Auch solch „emotionales" Verhalten gegenüber Jesus hat beispielhafte und damit auch eine missionarisch werbende Kraft. Darüber hinaus steht es in engster Verbindung mit dem zentralen Heilsgeschehen des Kreuzes und der Auferstehung Jesu. Dies verleiht ihm eine einzigartige Bedeutung.

Matthäus (Mt 26, 6–13) hat die Markusversion weitgehend übernommen und gestrafft. Dadurch wirkt die Matthäusfassung im ganzen prägnanter und pointierter, z. B. V. 9: „Wozu diese Verschwendung? Man hätte dies teuer verkaufen und den Armen geben kön-

---

[38] „Die Frau hat Jesus eine Ehre erwiesen, nach der auch die Christen nach Ostern verlangten, eine Jesus zustehende, ihm als dem Sohn Gottes geschuldete Ehre. Es ist, wenn man will, die Begründung einer kultischen Verehrung Jesu, eines Kultes, der dem schmählich getöteten, von Gott aber auferweckten Herrn gilt", *Schnackenburg,* Markus II 231. – Reichlich konstruiert ist dagegen die Interpretation von *Pesch,* Markus II 33: „Das Liebeswerk rangiert vor dem Almosen und Jesus – als der Ärmste – vor den Armen; die Sorge um die Bestattung eines Toten ist das wichtigste Liebeswerk"; oder: „Jesus ist jetzt der Arme." Davon ist jedoch im Text mit keinem Wort die Rede.

nen." Oder V. 11: „Die Armen habt ihr allezeit bei euch, mich aber habt ihr nicht allezeit." Schließlich V. 12: „Indem sie nämlich dieses Salböl auf meinen Leib ausgoß, hat sie es zu meinem Begräbnis getan." Man sieht, die leichten Änderungen des Matthäustextes haben zugleich den Charakter des „ältesten Kommentars" zu Markus. Sie betonen die christologische Pointe sowie den Hinweis auf das Begräbnis Jesu.

Lukas hat die ganze Geschichte weggelassen und bringt statt dessen die Erzählung von der „Sünderin" (Lk 7,36–50), in welcher manche Züge der Salbungsgeschichte wiederkehren. Darüber wird eigens zu reden sein.

Dagegen hat *Johannes* die Erzählung von der Salbung Jesu in Betanien übernommen (Joh 12,1–8), allerdings in einer anderen Version[39]. Die Frage nach der gegenseitigen Beeinflussung und Abhängigkeit der Texte ist schwierig und umstritten. *R. Pesch* meint: „Joh 12,1–8 ist gegenüber Mk sekundär und weiter entwickelt, Lk 7,36–50 von Mk 14,3–9 beeinflußt."[40] Das ist, was das Verhältnis zwischen der Markusfassung und der johanneischen Version betrifft, zweifellos richtig. Darüber hinaus scheinen gewisse Beziehungen zwischen Joh 12,1–8 und Lk 7,36–50 vorzuliegen, besonders in V. 3, wo davon die Rede ist, daß Maria die Füße Jesu salbt und sie mit ihren Haaren abtrocknet (vgl. Lk 7,38), eine Wendung, von der man eher annehmen möchte, daß sie aus der lukanischen Tradition auf Wegen, die man nicht mehr genau rekonstruieren kann, in die johanneische Tradition gelangt ist. Die wichtigste Frage ist jedoch, ob Johannes eine bereits festgeprägte Version der Salbungsgeschichte vorlag, vielleicht sogar in der Form einer schriftlichen Quelle, oder ob die johanneische Version eine selbständige Fassung des Evangelisten oder des johanneischen Kreises ist, die auf eigenständiger, mündlicher Überlieferung beruht. Für die erste Lösung, daß der Evangelist die Salbungsgeschichte aus „seiner Quelle" geschöpft habe, tritt z. B. nachdrücklich *R. Schnackenburg* ein[41]. Ich

---

[39] Zu Joh 12,1–8 vgl. *R. Schnackenburg*, Das Johannesevangelium II. Teil (HThK IV/2) (Freiburg i. Br. 1971) 457–467; *Blank*, Johannes 1 b, 290–291.

[40] *R. Pesch*, Markus II 335.

[41] *Schnackenburg*, Johannes II 466; vgl. 467: „... im ganzen dürfte schon die Quelle die Salbung so erzählt haben, wie sie uns vorliegt". Dort auch die nähere Begründung für diese Auffassung.

kann mich dieser Meinung jedoch nicht anschließen. Vielmehr meine ich, daß man eine gründliche Bearbeitung der Salbungsgeschichte in der johanneischen Tradition annehmen muß. Das wichtigste Moment, bei dem einzusetzen ist, ist die Verbindung der Salbungsgeschichte mit der Erzählung von der „Auferweckung des Lazarus" (Joh 11)[42]. Diese Veränderung kann auf gar keinen Fall ursprünglich sein; sie beruht vielmehr auf bewußter Konstruktion. Von daher kommt es dann auch zur Übernahme der drei Geschwister Lazarus, Maria und Martha, in der Salbungsgeschichte, die eine historische oder traditionsgeschichtliche „Harmonisierung" zwischen der Markus- und der Johannesversion ganz unmöglich macht. Daraus ist m. E. zu schließen: Dem johanneischen Kreis lag in der mündlichen Tradition eine Erzählung der „Salbung in Betanien" vor, die in den Grundzügen mit der Markus- oder auch mit der Matthäusversion der Geschichte übereinstimmte. Diese Geschichte wurde im johanneischen Kreis mit der „Auferweckung des Lazarus" verbunden und dieser angepaßt. Entsprechend wurden in die Darstellung eine Reihe „konkreter" Personen und Züge eingetragen, so vor allem die drei Geschwister Lazarus, Martha und Maria, sowie die Gestalt des Judas Iskariot. Der Zug, daß Maria nicht das Haupt, sondern die Füße Jesu salbt und sie mit ihren Haaren abtrocknet (V. 3), verbindet die johanneische Version mit Lk 7,38.

Ein weiterer interessanter Zug der johanneischen Version lautet: „Das ganze Haus wurde vom Geruch des Öles erfüllt" (V. 3b). Was hat dieser Hinweis, daß der Duft des kostbaren Parfums das ganze Haus erfüllt und alle den Wohlgeruch mitbekommen, zu bedeuten? Da bei Johannes der ausdrückliche Hinweis auf die „Verkündigung des Evangeliums in der ganzen Welt" fehlt, könnte man geneigt sein, dies als johanneischen Ersatz für diese Wendung zu verstehen. Man verweist dazu häufig auf die Stelle 2 Kor 2, 14–16, wo Paulus vom „Wohlgeruch der Erkenntnis Christi" spricht, den er als Verkünder des Evangeliums in der ganzen Welt (ἐν παντὶ τόπῳ) verbreitet. „Denn Christi Wohlgeruch sind wir für Gott bei denen, die gerettet werden, und bei denen, die verlorengehen; diesen ein Geruch vom Tod zum Tode; jenen ein Geruch vom Leben zum Leben." Klar ist, daß Paulus hier an das Evangelium denkt. Kann er zu diesem Ge-

---

[42] vgl. *Blank*, Johannes 1 b, 254 ff; 290 f.

danken durch die Salbungsgeschichte veranlaßt worden sein? Auszuschließen ist das nicht. – Daß sich mit dem „kostbaren Salböl" gerade die Assoziation des „Duftes" besonders stark verbunden hat, zeigt auch die alte Interpretation bei *Ignatius von Antiochien*, Eph 17,1, wo es im Anschluß an die Markus/Matthäus-Fassung heißt: „Deswegen nahm der Herr Salbe auf sein Haupt, damit er der Kirche Unvergänglichkeit zuwehe. Salbt euch nicht mit dem üblen Geruch der Lehre des Fürsten dieser Welt, damit er euch nicht in Gefangenschaft fortführe von dem Leben, das vor euch liegt."

Johanneische Modifikation ist es wohl auch, wenn Judas Iskariot als „Kritiker Jesu" hingestellt wird (V. 4–8). Entsprechend ist auch der Schluß der Geschichte bei Johannes modifiziert. V. 7 lautet die Weisung Jesu: „Laß sie, damit sie es für den Tag meines Begräbnisses aufbewahre." Bei Johannes findet, im Unterschied zu den Synoptikern, eine sorgfältige Einsalbung des Leichnams Jesu vor dem Begräbnis statt (Joh 19,38–42); deshalb die Mahnung, vom Salböl bis dahin noch etwas aufzubewahren. Ist dies vielleicht auch der Grund, warum bei Johannes nicht das Haupt Jesu, sondern nur die Füße gesalbt werden, weil er sich vorstellt, daß dann vom Öl noch etwas zurückbleibt? Schließlich endet die johanneische Version ganz betont mit der Aussage: „Denn die Armen habt ihr allezeit bei euch; mich aber habt ihr nicht allezeit" (V. 8). Dies entspricht der christologischen Pointe der Geschichte bei Johannes. Die Wendung ist aber auch zu sehen in Verbindung mit anderen johanneischen Aussagen, die den zeitlich begrenzten Charakter der „Gegenwart Jesu" und seines Offenbarerwirkens in der Welt betonen (z. B. Joh 7,33f; 9,4f; 11,9f; 12,35).

4. Aus der Matthäusüberlieferung[43]

4.1. Allgemeine Bemerkungen zur Matthäusüberlieferung

Zunächst ist festzustellen, daß Matthäus über die aus der Markusüberlieferung übernommenen Frauengeschichten hinaus (vgl. oben S. 11 f) keine eigenen Erzählungen hat, in welchen von Bewegungen Jesus mit Frauen die Rede ist.

Mt 20,20–23 (par. Mk 10,35–40): Bei der Bitte der Zebedäussöhne um die Ehrenplätze im messianischen Reich sind es nicht, wie bei Markus, die beiden Jünger Johannes und Jakobus, die selber um die Vergabe der „messianischen Ehrenplätze" bitten, sondern deren Mutter. Die Mutter tritt mit ihren beiden Söhnen vor Jesus hin, fällt vor ihm nieder und trägt ihm die Bitte vor (Mt 20,20 f). Dies ist zweifellos eine redaktionelle Änderung des Matthäus und nicht ursprünglich. Sie soll wahrscheinlich die Jünger Jesu entlasten und die inzwischen wohl als „töricht" empfundene Bitte der Mutter zuschreiben, der man so etwas im Interesse ihrer Söhne eher zutrauen mochte. Daß dies kaum als eine Aufwertung der Frau verstanden werden soll, dürfte klar sein.

Hängt dieser Befund vielleicht mit einer vorwiegend männlich geprägten Zusammensetzung der „Matthäusschule" zusammen, wenn man mit der begründeten Annahme rechnen darf, daß sich diese nach dem Vorbild des rabbinischen Schulbetriebes organisiert hatte? Freilich ist es nicht so, daß Frauen in der Gemeinde des Matthäus keinen Platz gehabt hätten. Matthäus übernimmt Mk 3,31–35 (= Mt 12,46–50), wo Jesus gegenüber seinen leiblichen Verwandten eine neue, „geistliche" Verwandtschaft etabliert, die „neue, endzeitliche Gottesfamilie", die in der Vaterschaft Gottes und in der christologisch begründeten Bruderschaft ihre Grundlage hat, wenn es heißt:

„Und er streckte seine Hände über seine Jünger und sprach:
Siehe da, meine Mutter und meine Brüder!
Denn wer den Willen meines Vaters im Himmel tut,
der ist mir Bruder, Schwester und Mutter" (Mt 12,39 f; par. Mk 3,34 f).

---

[43] Zum Folgenden vgl. *E. Klostermann*, Das Matthäusevangelium (HNT 4) (Tübingen ⁴1971); *A. Schlatter*, Der Evangelist Matthäus (Stuttgart ⁶1963); *J. Schmid*, Das Evangelium nach Matthäus (RNT 1) (Regensburg ³1956); *J. Schniewind*, Das Evangelium nach Matthäus (NTD 2) (Göttingen ⁵1950); *E. Schweizer*, Das Evangelium nach Matthäus (NTD 2) (Göttingen ¹³1973); *W. Trilling*, Das Evangelium nach Matthäus, 2 Bde. (Geistliche Schriftlesung 1) (Düsseldorf 1962/65); *J. Jeremias*, Die Gleichnisse Jesu (Göttingen ⁶1962).

Hier sind die redaktionellen Änderungen des Matthäus gegenüber dem Markustext aufschlußreich. Während es bei Markus heißt: „Und er schaute die rings im Kreis um ihn Herumsitzenden an" (καὶ περιβλεψάμενος τοὺς περὶ αὐτὸν κύκλῳ καθημένους Mk 3,34a), wobei man sich diesen Kreis durchaus aus Männern und Frauen gemischt vorstellen kann, heißt es bei Matthäus: „Und er streckte seine Hand aus über seine Jünger" (καὶ ἐκτείνας τὴν χεῖρα αὐτοῦ ἐπὶ τοὺς μαθητὰς αὐτοῦ Mt 12,49), was eher an eine männliche Gruppe denken läßt. Aber vielleicht muß man die von Matthäus immer wieder in Schutz genommenen „Kleinen" in der Gemeinde (vgl. Mt 18,10.14) als einen Kreis verstehen, der neben den schwächeren Gemeindegliedern in jeder Form auch die Frauen eingeschlossen hat.

Auch an das Logion aus Q von der „Scheidung der Geister" (Mt 10,34–36; vgl. Lk 12,51–53) wäre zu erinnern:

„Wähnet nicht, ich sei gekommen, Frieden auf die Erde zu bringen; ich bin nicht gekommen, Frieden zu bringen, sondern das Schwert.
Denn ich bin gekommen zu entzweien
einen Mann gegen seinen Vater,
eine Tochter gegen ihre Mutter,
eine Schwiegertochter gegen ihre Schwiegermutter,
und die Feinde eines Menschen werden seine Hausgenossen sein."

Hier ist wohl das Schriftzitat Micha 7,6 (= Mt 10,35–36) als Illustration zu V. 34 aufgenommen worden, um aufzuzeigen, worin die von Jesus gebrachte Auseinandersetzung, der Konflikt, besteht. Doch wird an dieser Illustration deutlich, daß es sich hier nicht um einen geschlechtsspezifischen Konflikt handelt, sondern um einen Konflikt, der Frauen genauso treffen kann wie den Mann. Ursache für diesen Konflikt ist aber die Botschaft Jesu oder auch die Stellungnahme zu Jesus selbst, was nicht getrennt werden kann. Jeder, der sich für diese Botschaft entscheidet, muß also damit rechnen, daß es zwischen ihm und seinen nächsten Freunden und Hausgenossen zu harten Auseinandersetzungen kommen kann.

Fragt man nach festgeprägten Bezeichnungen für die Christen bei Matthäus, so sind es hauptsächlich zwei, die hier besonders in Frage kommen:

a) Jünger, μαϑητής[44]; die Christen sind die „Schüler", bzw. die Jünger Jesu.

b) Bruder, ἀδελφός[45]; untereinander sind die Christen Brüder, eine Bezeichnung, die letztlich auf dem Glauben an die bleibende Vaterschaft Gottes beruht, worin der Gedanke der „Gottesfamilie" eingeschlossen ist, aber auch der Gedanke, daß die Jünger „Brüder Jesu" sind und in gewisser Hinsicht auch an seiner Gottessohnschaft Anteil haben. Anders als bei Paulus (vgl. 1 Kor 7,15; 9,5; Röm 16,1–15) begegnet bei Matthäus die Bezeichnung „Schwester", ἀδελφή, für eine Mitchristin nicht.

Es bleibt jedenfalls interessant, daß für die Christen bei Matthäus vorwiegend „maskuline" Bezeichnungen verwendet werden, „Jünger" und „Brüder", und daß in diesem Vokabular zumindest das „Dominieren männlicher Rollen" deutlich ist. Es ist wohl, wie schon angedeutet, jüdischer (genauer: judenchristlich vermittelter) Einfluß, der sich hier auswirkt, ohne daß man deshalb schon von einer bewußten „Rejudaisierung" sprechen dürfte. Auch die Aussage:

„Ihr aber laßt euch nicht Rabbi nennen;
denn Einer ist euer Lehrer,
ihr alle aber seid Brüder" (Mt 23,8),

besagt zwar, daß es für den christlichen Schülerkreis nur einen einzigen Lehrer, nämlich Jesus Christus allein, gibt und geben kann und daß in diesem Kreise alle anderen in einem Verhältnis der Brüderschaft zueinander stehen; aber das scheint nicht ohne weiteres zu bedeuten, daß damit auch schon das Modell des rabbinischen Schülerkreises völlig aufgegeben sei. Mit dem Festhalten an diesem „Schul-Modell" war offenbar von selbst ein Zurücktreten des weiblichen Elementes gegeben. Die Beobachtung ist deshalb von Bedeutung, weil gerade das Matthäusevangelium auf das bis heute vorherrschende Verständnis einer männlich fixierten Kirchenstruktur maßgeblich eingewirkt hat.

Frauen kommen bei Matthäus zusätzlich nur in drei Gleichnissen

---

[44] μαϑητής für „Schüler, Jünger" oder auch im weiteren Sinne für „Anhänger" Johannes des Täufers, des Mose, der Pharisäer und schließlich Jesu, vgl. *Aland*, Konkordanz 753 f. – Dazu *J. Blank*, Lernprozesse im Jüngerkreis Jesu, in: ThQ 158 (1978) 163–177 (vgl. auch *ders.*, Der Jesus des Evangeliums [München 1981] 95–116).

[45] ἀδελφός, „Bruder" als Bezeichnung der Christen: Mt 5,22.23.24.47; 7,3.4.5; 12,48.49.50; 18,15.21.35; 23,8; 25,40; 28,10.

vor: a) im Gleichnis vom Sauerteig, das aus der Logienquelle stammt (Mt 13,33 par. Lk 20,21), b) im Gleichnis von den zwei ungleichen Söhnen (Mt 21,28–32) und c) im Gleichnis von den törichten und klugen Jungfrauen (Mt 25,1–13).

4.2. Das Gleichnis vom Sauerteig, Mt 13,33 (par. Lk 20,21)

Das Gleichnis, das nur aus einem einzigen Satz besteht, wird als „Reich-Gottes-Gleichnis" eingeführt; es soll also etwas über Wesen und Wirken der Gottesherrschaft sagen. Nach *J. Jeremias* gehört es zu den „Kontrastgleichnissen": „Ihr Sinn ist: Aus den kümmerlichsten Anfängen, aus einem Nichts für menschliche Augen schafft Gott seine machtvolle Königsherrschaft, die die Völkerwelt umfassen wird."[46] Man darf also nicht den modernen Gedanken einer „Entwicklung" oder gar eines kontinuierlichen „Fortschritts" in diesen Text hineintragen. Das Kommen der Gottesherrschaft ist entscheidend das „Werk Gottes"; doch besteht zwischen der Verkündigung der nahen Gottesherrschaft durch Jesus und ihrer dereinstigen Vollendung ein Wirkungszusammenhang, auf den in diesem Gleichnis hingewiesen werden soll.

Der Vergleich mit dem „Sauerteig" und seiner unausbleiblichen Wirkung ist dem rabbinischen Judentum geläufig. Der Ansatzpunkt für diesen Vergleich dürfte wohl beim Mazzot-Fest liegen, dem „Fest der ungesäuerten Brote", an dem das ganze Haus gereinigt werden muß[47]. „Sauerteig" wird auch zum Bild für negativ ansteckende Wirkungen, die von einem Menschen oder von einer Gruppe ausgehen, so in dem Jesuswort: „Seht zu, hütet euch vor dem Sauerteig der Pharisäer und vor dem Sauerteig der Herodianer!" (so Mk 8,15; par. Mt 16,6: „Seht zu und hütet euch vor dem Sauerteig der Pharisäer und Sadduzäer!"; Lk 12,1: „Hütet euch vor dem Sauerteig, das heißt vor der Heuchelei, der Pharisäer!").

Im Gleichnis vom Sauerteig wendet Jesus das Bild der „dynamischen" und unausbleiblichen Wirkungen des Sauerteiges positiv

---

[46] *Jeremias,* Gleichnisse 148.
[47] Zum Stichwort „Sauerteig", ζύμη vgl. Mt 13,33; 16,6.11.12; Mk 8,15; Lk 12,1; 13,21; 1.Kor 5,6.7.8; Gal 5,9; ἄζυμος Mt 26,17; Mk 14,1.12; Lk 22,1.7; Apg 12,3; 20,6 (an den genannten Stellen handelt es sich jedesmal um das „Fest der ungesäuerten Brote", das Mazzot-Fest); 1 Kor 5,7.8. – *Windisch,* Art. ζύμη, in: ThWNT II 904–908; *Billerbeck* I 669f; 728f; II 812ff.

an[48], wenn er die Gottesherrschaft und ihre Wirkungsweise damit vergleicht. Zugleich zeigt sich in der sprachlichen Gestalt die Transformation einer geläufigen Metapher in eine anschauliche Erzählung: „Eine Frau will Brot backen. Zu der großen Menge Mehl kommt nur ein winziges Stück Sauerteig; die Hausfrau vermengt beides, deckt ein Tuch darüber und läßt es stehen. Nach einiger Zeit ist das Erstaunliche geschehen: Das ganze Mehl ist durchsäuert. Die kleine Menge tat große Wirkung."[49] Durch die Erzählung gewinnt das Bild eine plastische Anschaulichkeit, wie sie für die authentischen Gleichnisse Jesu typisch ist.

4.3 Das Gleichnis von den ungleichen Söhnen, Mt 21,28–32

Dieses Gleichnis gehört zum Sondergut des Matthäus. Wieweit es in der vorliegenden Fassung ursprünglich ist, ist umstritten[50]. Deutlich ist, daß nach V. 31 a eine Zäsur zu machen ist; dann ergibt sich a) die Gleichniserzählung von den zwei Söhnen; b) die Deutung bzw. Anwendung durch Jesus V. 31 b–32. Hier ist die Frage, ob V. 31 b den ursprünglichen Abschluß der Gleichniserzählung bildet und V. 32 einen späteren, „heilsgeschichtlichen" Zusatz[51] oder ob V. 31 b–32 als Ganzes nachträgliche Interpretation ist.

Das Gleichnis, das mit der Aufforderung, selbst zu urteilen, beginnt – „Was meint ihr?" – und sich nach Matthäus an die Gegner Jesu (die „Hohenpriester und Ältesten des Volkes", so nach Mt 21,23) wendet, handelt von zwei Söhnen, die beide vom Vater den Auftrag bekommen: „Geht heute hinaus und arbeitet in meinem Weinberg." Während der erste Sohn ja sagt, aber nicht hinausgeht,

---

[48] „Die Anschauung haftet lediglich an der der Hausfrau, dem Bäcker sehr erwünschten und allgemein bewunderten Fähigkeit der ζύμη, einen ganzen Teig zu durchdringen" (*Windisch*, aaO. 907).

[49] *Trilling*, Matthäus Bd. 2, 38. Vgl. auch Thomas-Evangelium, Nr. 96: „Jesus (sprach): Das Reich des Vaters gleicht einer Frau. Sie nahm ein wenig Sauerteig; sie (verbarg) ihn im Mehl. Sie machte ihn zu großen Broten. Wer Ohren hat, möge hören!"

[50] Vgl. dazu *Jeremias*, Gleichnisse, 78 f; *Schweizer*, Matthäus 267 ff.

[51] *Jeremias*, Gleichnisse 79. Nach ihm gehört das – ursprüngliche – Gleichnis zu den Gleichnissen, in denen vor allem von Gottes Erbarmen mit den Verschuldeten die Rede ist. Diese enthalten „die eigentliche Frohbotschaft", nämlich die Hinwendung Gottes zu den Sündern. Diese „Gleichnisse, die die Heilsbotschaft im engeren Sinne zum Gegenstand haben, sind – wahrscheinlich *ohne Ausnahme*, nicht zu den Armen, sondern zu den Gegnern gesagt" (aaO. 124; ferner 125 f).

sagt der zweite Sohn: „Ich will nicht", ändert aber seinen Entschluß und geht dann doch. Auf die entscheidende Frage Jesu: „Wer von den beiden hat nun den Willen des Vaters getan?", lautet die zutreffende Antwort der Gegner, die damit auch sich selber das Urteil sprechen: „Der Zweite". Daraufhin erfolgt die Anwendung Jesu:

31b Amen, ich sage euch,
   die Zöllner und die Huren kommen vor euch in das Reich Gottes.
32 Denn es kam Johannes zu euch mit dem Weg der Gerechtigkeit,
   und ihr habt ihm nicht geglaubt ...
   Ihr aber habt es gesehen,
   und es tat euch später nicht leid, so daß ihr ihm geglaubt hättet."

Für unser Interesse kommt es auf die Wendung an: „Die Zöllner und die Huren kommen vor euch in das Reich Gottes!" „Das kleine Gleichnis wendet Jesus auf die Gegner mit einem unglaublich scharfen Angriff an. *Zöllner und Huren* werden eher in das Königtum Gottes eingehen als sie."[52] Ob diese Aussage nun auf Jesus selbst zurückgeht – was für V. 31 b möglich sein dürfte, während V. 32 eher nachträgliche Erweiterung zu sein scheint – oder nicht, auf jeden Fall hat sich darin insofern authentische Jesustradition niedergeschlagen, als auf die Wirkung der Bußpredigt, wie sie ursprünglich von Johannes dem Täufer ausgegangen war und in der Heilspredigt Jesu von der nahen Gottesherrschaft fortgesetzt wurde, zurückgeschaut wird. Bei welchen Kreisen vor allem hat diese Predigt gewirkt? Antwort: Nicht bei den Hohepriestern, Ältesten und Schriftgelehrten, sondern bei den Zöllnern und Huren, bei den „Verachteten", den „Unreinen" und „Sündern". Wenn hier in aller Klarheit von den „Huren" die Rede ist[53], daß sie zusammen mit den Zöllnern zuerst in das Reich Gottes kommen, dann ist darin bereits die Annahme dieser Frauen durch Jesus mitgesetzt. Es gibt keine menschliche Situation, keine noch so entehrende Situation, wie es der Status der Dirnen fast zu allen Zeiten war und ist, aus der heraus der Zugang zum Reich Gottes verwehrt wäre. Im Gegenteil, diese „Erniedrigten und Beleidigten" verstehen den Anruf des Evangeliums besser als die etablierten Frommen. Indem Jesus diesen Menschen sich verbündete, gab er ihnen auch eine neue Selbstachtung zurück.

---

52 *Trilling*, Matthäus 2, 203.
53 Vgl. *Hauck – Schulz*, Art. πόρνη, in: ThWNT VI 579–595; *A. Hermann – B. Herter*, Art. Dirne, in: RAC III 1149–1213.

4.4. Das Gleichnis von den klugen und törichten Jungfrauen, Mt 25, 1–13

Das gleichfalls zum matthäischen Sondergut gehörende Gleichnis verweist auf einen anderen Bereich. Die Frage nach seiner Echtheit ist ebenso kontrovers wie die nach seiner ursprünglichen Bedeutung[54]. Nach *J. Jeremias,* der sich am entschiedensten für eine ursprüngliche jesuanische Herkunft eingesetzt und dafür auch die gewichtigsten Argumente beigebracht hat, müßte man bei diesem Gleichnis den „doppelten Sitz im Leben" ganz wesentlich in Rechnung stellen. Das Gleichnis, wie es nach ihm von Jesus erzählt wurde („Sitz in der Verkündigung Jesu"), war ursprünglich keine „Allegorie", „sondern die Schilderung einer wirklichen Hochzeit, mit der Jesus die Menge angesichts der bevorstehenden, eschatologischen Krise aufrütteln wollte"[55]. Um seine Auffassung zu stützen, verweist *Jeremias* auf die bestehenden Hochzeitsbräuche, vor allem auf „die Einholung des Bräutigams mit Lichtern und die gelegentliche Verzögerung seines Kommens"[56]. Es handelt sich nach ihm um ein „Krisis-Gleichnis", bei dem die „Plötzlichkeit" der Ankunft des Bräutigams als Metapher für die unerwartet herandrängende Endkatastrophe fungiert. „So, als aufrüttelnden Weckruf angesichts der bevorstehenden eschatologischen Krisis, wird Jesus das Gleichnis gemeint und wird die Menge es verstanden haben."[57] Erst die Urkirche („zweiter Sitz im Leben" in der urkirchlichen Verkündigung) deutete den Bräutigam, der ursprünglich nur eine Figur in der Gleichniserzählung abgab, auf Jesus, und sein mitternächtliches Kommen auf die Parusie. Dabei blieb die Urkirche zwar innerhalb der ursprünglichen Linie des Gleichnisses, dennoch „bedeutete es eine wesentliche Akzentverschiebung, wenn aus dem Weckruf an die Menge jetzt ein Mahnwort an die Jüngerschar und aus dem

---

[54] Vgl. *Jeremias,* Gleichnisse 48 f.; 171 ff.; *Schweizer,* Matthäus 303 ff; *G. Bornkamm,* Die Verzögerung der Parusie (1951), in: *ders.,* Geschichte und Glaube, Erster Teil (Gesammelte Aufsätze III) (München 1968) 46–55; *E. Gräßer,* Das Problem der Parusieverzögerung in den synoptischen Evangelien und in der Apostelgeschichte (Berlin ³1977) 119–125; *E. Linnemann,* Gleichnisse Jesu (Göttingen ²1962), 130–134; 182–187. Zur gesamten Interpretationsproblematik vgl. *Linnemann,* aaO. 182 ff, Anm. 7.
[55] *Jeremias,* Gleichnisse 171.
[56] Ebd. 172.
[57] Ebd. 50.

Gleichnis eine Allegorie auf den himmlischen Bräutigam Christus und die ihn erwartende Gemeinde wurde"[58]. Dagegen vertritt *E. Linnemann* die Auffassung, daß es sich auch bei der vorliegenden Fassung nicht um eine Allegorie, sondern um eine Parabel handele, bei der sich die verschiedenen Einzelzüge aus ihrer Funktion im Rahmen der Gesamterzählung verstehen lassen; diese Parabel sei allerdings erst in der Gemeinde entstanden[59].

Für nachösterliche Entstehung des Gleichnisses, und zwar im Hinblick auf die Bewältigung der „Parusie-Naherwartung" sind nach *R. Bultmann*[60] vor allem *G. Bornkamm* und *E. Gräßer* eingetreten. Nach *Bornkamm* handelt es sich um eine andere eschatologische Situation als in den vorausgegangenen Gerichtsgleichnissen. „Voraussetzung für das Geschehen unserer Parabel ist das anfängliche Ausbleiben des Bräutigams. Dieser Zug gehört so fest zur Substanz des Gleichnisses, daß sich von ihm her allein die Handlung im einzelnen verstehen läßt. Nichts berechtigt darum zu der in neueren Auslegungen wiederholt geäußerten Meinung, dies sei nur ein unbetonter Zug, der die Verlegenheit der törichten Jungfrauen motivieren wolle. Tatsächlich bestimmt sich von diesem Zug aus allein, warum die einen als klug, die andern als töricht bezeichnet werden können."[61] Von dieser Überlegung her ergibt es sich, daß die Interpretation von V. 5 („Da sich aber das Kommen des Bräutigams verzögerte, nickten alle ein und schliefen") zum Angelpunkt der Diskussion um das Gleichnis wird. Ähnlich meint *E. Gräßer:* „Es kann kein Streit sein, daß das Gleichnis so, wie es jetzt dasteht, eine Allegorie auf die Ankunft des Menschensohnes ist"; dabei hänge die entscheidende Frage an der Beurteilung von V. 5, ob es sich hier um einen „unbetonten Nebenzug" handle oder ob dies nicht vielmehr der Angelpunkt der Erzählung sei[62]. Es sei noch angemerkt, daß die

[58] Ebd.
[59] *Linnemann,* Gleichnisse 132. 184, Anm. 8.
[60] *Bultmann,* Geschichte 125 zu Mt 25,1–13: „Eine völlig von Allegorie überwucherte Gemeindebildung mit stark angedeuteter Beziehung auf die Person Jesu"; auch 190f: „Ob ihr ein ursprüngliches Gleichnis zu Grunde liegt, ist nicht mehr zu entscheiden."
[61] *Bornkamm,* Die Verzögerung der Parusie 49 f.
[62] *Gräßer,* Parusieverzögerung 119. „Eine ältere Gestalt des Gleichnisses herauszuschälen, die nur hat sagen wollen: Seid bereit! Die Krisis steht vor der Tür! Sie wird plötzlich kommen wie der Bräutigam! eine Form also, die ganz ohne Bezug auf die Parusieverzögerung war, mag schwerlich gelingen" (aaO. 125).

Deutung des Gleichnisses auf die Wiederkunft Christi, die christologisch-eschatologische Deutung also, die „klassische" Deutung der alten Kirche und des Mittelalters ist, die auch die mittelalterliche Kunstauffassung weitgehend bestimmte[63].

Dagegen meint *W. Trilling,* daß in den Matthäustexten Mt 24, 45–51; 25, 1–13 und 25, 14–30 nicht das Problem der Parusieverzögerung maßgeblich sei. Vielmehr gewinne man den Eindruck, „daß in der Kirche des Matthäus weder eine hochgespannte Parusieerwartung herrschte noch eine spezielle Problematik um das Ausbleiben der Parusie empfunden wurde, daß gerade deshalb aber die Mahnung zur Bereitschaft, die Warnung vor sorglosem und leichtfertigem Leben, verbunden mit der Drohung vor dem Endgericht, um so dringlicher wurde"[64].

Es fällt zunächst schwer, das Gleichnis von den „klugen und törichten Jungfrauen" als „Krisis-Gleichnis" im Sinne von *J. Jeremias* zu verstehen. Denn es scheint hier weniger um die bevorstehende „eschatologische Krisis" zu gehen als vielmehr um die Erwartung (und Problematik) der Heilsvollendung und um die Bereitschaft für deren Kommen. Das Bild (oder die verschiedenen Bilder) der Hochzeit[65] evozieren ja primär eine positive Einstellung und Erwartung, während Verzögerung und Plötzlichkeit des Kommens des Bräutigams als wesentliche Spannungselemente innerhalb der Geschichte gesehen werden müssen. Auch wenn der „Bräutigam" keine feste Metapher für den „Messias" ist[66], so ist dennoch das Bild der „Hochzeit" als Metapher für die „Heilszeit" geläufig (vgl. Mk 2, 19f par. Mt 9, 15; Lk 5, 35; Joh 2, 1–11; 3, 29f). Man kann also davon ausgehen, daß die Metaphern „Hochzeit" und „Bräutigam" für die Gegenwart des Endheils bekannt waren, und es steht auch nichts im Wege, daß Jesus diese Metaphorik gebraucht hat. In der Urkirche hat man dann diese Metaphorik weiter ausgesponnen (vgl. vor allem Offb 21, 2.9 auch 2 Kor 11, 2); dies zeigt auch die „christologische In-

---

[63] Vgl. dazu *J. Seibert,* Art. Jungfrauen, in: Lexikon christlicher Kunst (Freiburg i. Br. 1980) 169 f.

[64] *W. Trilling,* Das wahre Israel. Studien zur Theologie des Matthäus-Evangeliums (StANT X) (München 1964) 44 f.

[65] Vgl. *Jeremias,* Gleichnisse 171 ff; Billerbeck I 500–518 (zu Mt 9, 15).

[66] *J. Jeremias,* Art. νύμφη, νυμφίος, in: ThWNT IV 1094: Das AT kennt zwar das Bild von der Ehe JHWHs mit Israel. „Nirgendwo erscheint jedoch im AT der Messias als Bräutigam."

terpretation" des „Bräutigams" in Mk 2, 20 (par. Mt 9, 15 b; Lk 5, 35),
wo das Gemeindefasten mit der Abwesenheit des Bräutigams begründet wird. Hier ist also die Gleichsetzung Jesus Christus = der
Bräutigam bereits vollzogen. Man wird auch *E. Linnemann* darin zustimmen müssen, daß es sich hier um eine „Parabel" handelt, deren
Einzelzüge aus der Gesamtintention der Erzählung heraus verständlich sind, und nicht um eine „Allegorie". Bleibt eigentlich nur noch
die Frage, ob die Erzählung in dieser Form im Munde Jesu denkbar
ist oder ob es sich um eine Bildung des Evangelisten Matthäus oder
seiner Schule und/oder Tradition handelt. Wenn Jesus vom Endheil
in Bildern der Hochzeitsmetaphorik gesprochen hat, dann kann er
im Prinzip auch der Autor der Gleichniserzählung sein. Dann wäre
der ursprüngliche Sinn der Geschichte *die Mahnung zur Wachsam-
keit;* näherhin *die Mahnung, in der Erwartung der noch ausständigen
Heilsvollendung nicht zu erlahmen.* Das würde nicht ausschließen,
daß die Geschichte in der mündlichen Überlieferung nach Ostern
eine christologische Bearbeitung und Transformation erfahren
hätte. Dabei wurde vor allem die klare Identifikation von „Bräutigam" und Jesus als dem kommenden Menschensohn vorgenommen.
Es unterliegt keinem Zweifel, daß die letzte, uns bei Mt 25, 1–13 vorliegende Fassung die Parusieerwartung bzw. -verzögerung im Blick
hat. „Jeder Christ weiß, wer dieser Bräutigam ist, der auch auf sich
warten lassen kann, wer die klugen und törichten Mädchen sind,
was das Hochzeitsfest bedeutet und welchen Schrecken vor allem
die geschlossene Tür auslöst (vgl. 22, 1–13)."[67]

Die Gegenüberstellung von „klugen und törichten Menschen",
von „Weisheit und Torheit" samt ihren segensreichen oder fatalen
Folgen für die Menschen ist ein fester Topos der „Weisheitstradi-
tion" (vgl. Spr 8; 9, 1–6.13–18), den Jesus ebenfalls aufgegriffen und
gebraucht hat. In dieser Alternative geht es immer um „Leben oder
Tod, Heil und Unheil" des Menschen, so schon in der alttestamentlichen Weisheit. Damit ließ sich der eschatologische Entscheidungs-
charakter sehr gut verbinden. Im „Gleichnis vom Hausbau" wird
dem klugen Mann, der sein Haus auf Felsen baut, der Tor gegenübergestellt, der sein Haus auf Sand baut (Mt 7, 24–27 par. Lk
6, 47–49). Genau so stehen sich hier die klugen und die törichten

---

[67] *Trilling,* Matthäus 2, 276.

Mädchen gegenüber. Die Matthäusfassung hat dabei einen *paräneti-schen Skopos*. Bekanntlich legt der Evangelist Matthäus größten Wert auf die „guten Werke", auf die christliche Praxis. Das Lippenbekenntnis, das nur „Herr, Herr" sagt, genügt ihm nicht (vgl. die erhellende Entsprechung von Mt 7, 21–23 mit Mt 25, 11!). „Klug sind jene, die die Worte des Evangeliums hören und tun; töricht jene, die die Worte hören, aber nicht danach handeln. Die einen bringen das Öl mit, die anderen nur leere Gefäße. Das Öl ist das im Leben verwirklichte Evangelium."[68] Es geht bei den „klugen und törichten Jungfrauen" letztlich um jene „Weisheit" und „Torheit", deren eigentliches Kriterium das Evangelium ist (vgl. dazu 1 Kor 1, 18–25).

Dieses Kriterium aber ist, das zeigen die Bilder von den „klugen und törichten Jungfrauen", gerade nicht geschlechtsspezifisch; vielmehr herrscht ihm gegenüber „Gleichberechtigung" in vollem Umfang (vgl. das Gegenstück vom „klugen und törichten Mann"). Ein Hinweis auf die „Wirkungsgeschichte" des Gleichnisses sei noch gestattet. Sie hat nicht nur auf das Verständnis der Kirche als der „Braut Christi" eingewirkt, sondern auch auf das eschatologische Verständnis der christlichen Ehelosigkeit, etwa im Hinblick auf die weiblichen Orden[69].

5. Aus der Lukasüberlieferung[70]

Im Sondergut des Lukas begegnen, wie man schon oft bemerkt hat, die meisten Frauengeschichten. *J. Schmid* meint dazu: „Zu den Verachteten und Zurückgesetzten gehörten im Judentum auch *die Frauen*. Jesus hat ihnen erst die ihnen gebührende volle Menschenwürde gegeben. In keinem Evangelium treten sie aber so stark her-

---

[68] Ebd. 275.
[69] Einen guten Überblick über die Auslegungstradition der Kirchenväter und des Mittelalters bietet die „Catena aurea in quatuor Evangelia" des Thomas von Aquin, 2 vol., Marietti-Ausgabe (Turin – Rom 1953) I 363–366.
[70] *Kommentare zu Lukas:* E. Klostermann, Das Lukasevangelium (HNT 5) (Tübingen ⁵1975); *W. Grundmann,* Das Evangelium nach Lukas (Berlin ³1964); *K.-H. Rengstorf,* Das Evangelium nach Lukas (NTD 3) (Göttingen 1949); *J. Schmid,* Das Evangelium nach Lukas (RNT 3) (Regensburg ³1955); *H. Schürmann,* Das Lukasevangelium, I. Teil (HThK III/1) (Freiburg i. Br. ²1982); *J. Ernst,* Das Evangelium nach Lukas (RNT 3) (Regensburg 1977); ferner:

vor wie bei Lukas."[71] Man wird davon ausgehen dürfen, daß nach Lukas auch die Frauen zu den „Menschen des Wohlgefallens" gehören, denen nach Lk 2, 14 das Endheil verheißen wird. *J. Ernst* meint allerdings: „Wahrscheinlich spiegeln sich hier die Erfahrungen der apostolischen Zeit: Frauen als Gastgeberinnen sichern den Heimatlosen einen gewissen Grad an Häuslichkeit (Lukas interessiert sich stark für Unterkunftsprobleme: Apg 16, 14 f; 17, 4), als Reisebegleiterinnen sorgen sie sich um das leibliche Wohl der Missionare (vgl. Lk 8, 2 f; 1 Kor 9, 5)."[72] Dies mag als ein Motiv neben anderen mitspielen. Entscheidend ist jedoch, daß die Zuwendung Jesu zu den Frauen, wovon Lukas berichtet, ganz stark *im Zeichen der Heils-Begegnung und Heils-Zuwendung steht,* und man wird sie auch weitgehend unter diesem Gesichtspunkt betrachten müssen.

5.1. Die Auferweckung des Jünglings von Nain, Lk 7, 11–17

Die erste Erzählung, der wir uns zuwenden, berichtet von der Auferweckung eines toten jungen Mannes, den man gerade beerdigen will. Sie gehört zu den „großen Heilszeichen" der Jesus-Überlieferung, wie auch der Chorschluß ausdrücklich hervorhebt: „Furcht aber ergriff alle und sie verherrlichten Gott und sprachen: Ein großer Prophet ist unter uns auferstanden! und: Heimgesucht hat Gott sein Volk" (V. 16)! Nach *J. Ernst* handelt es sich um „eine ältere, im palästinensischen Raum gewachsene Erzähleinheit, die von Lk redaktionell überarbeitet wurde. Als Vorbild hat ohne Zweifel die dem Propheten Elija zugesprochene Totenerweckung (1 Kön 17, 7–24) gedient."[73] Dazu kommt eine ältere, judenchristliche „Prophet-Christologie", die in Jesus den „endzeitlichen Propheten" (vgl. Dtn

---

H. Conzelmann, Die Mitte der Zeit (Tübingen 1954); *H. Flender,* Heil und Geschichte in der Theologie des Lukas (München 1965); *G. Voß,* Die Christologie der lukanischen Schriften in Grundzügen (Paris – Brügge 1965); *G. Lohfink,* Die Sammlung Israels (StANT XXXIX) (München 1978).
[71] *Schmid,* Lukas 21. – Dagegen *Ernst,* Lukas 17: „Ein charakteristischer Zug der lk Darstellung, hinter dem ‚welthaftes' Denken aufscheint, ist die auffällige Hervorhebung von Frauengestalten im Sondergut …" – Wieso darin „welthaftes" Denken aufscheint, ist unerfindlich; es geht vor allem um die Darstellung der „Heilszuwendung".
[72] *Ernst,* Lukas 18.
[73] Ebd. 251.

18,15 ff) erblickte, möglicherweise auch den „Elija redivivus"[74]. Zu beachten ist auch, daß die Erzählung Lk 7,11–17 im Vergleich mit 1 Kön 17,17–24 mit dem typologischen „Überbietungsmotiv" arbeitet. Sowohl der Rang des Wundertäters ist höher, er ist „der Kyrios"; als auch die Art des Vorgehens, es bedarf keiner vorbereitenden Manipulation, vielmehr genügt das Befehlswort Jesu.

Auf seinen Wanderungen durch Galiläa kommt Jesus auch in eine „Stadt" namens Nain[75]. Er begegnet dabei im Stadttor einem Leichenzug. Man trägt einen jungen Mann zu Grabe, „den einzigen Sohn seiner Mutter, und die war Witwe". Damit ist eine doppelte Notsituation gegeben, nämlich einmal durch den Tod des Jünglings, zweitens durch die besondere Notlage der Witwe (vgl. oben S. 18 ff). Die rettende Hilfe geht in der Erzählung ganz von Jesus aus. Jesus, hier ausdrücklich als ὁ κύριος, „der Herr"[76] bezeichnet, was an dieser Stelle im Sinne des entsprechenden „Hoheitstitels" gemeint ist, wird von Mitleid ergriffen. Er redet zunächst die Frau an: „Weine nicht!", eine Aufforderung, die nicht bloß „tröstlich" gemeint ist, sondern als Evozierung von Vertrauen und Glauben; es geht um die Glaubensbereitschaft der Frau. Wenn Jesus die Totenbahre berührt und dann sein Machtwort spricht: „Jüngling, ich sage dir: Stehe auf!", dann handelt er als der „Herr über Leben und Tod", anders als der Prophet Elija, der sich dreimal auf den toten Sohn legt und Gott um Hilfe bitten muß[77]. Der Jüngling richtet sich auf, beginnt

---

[74] „Fragt man nach dem theologiegeschichtlichen Raum, in dem eine solche Christologie beheimatet war, so stößt man auf die frühe judenchristliche Gemeinde in Palästina, in der sich der Prophetentitel lange halten konnte" (*Ernst,* Lukas 251). – Zum „endzeitlichen Propheten" vgl. *O. Cullmann,* Die Christologie des Neuen Testaments (Tübingen 1957) 11–49.

[75] „Naim lag an der Straße, die vom See Genesareth am Fuße des Tabor vorbei durch die Ebene Estrelon nach Samaria führte. Naim war nur ein kleines Dorf, Lukas spricht von einer Stadt": *Stöger,* Das Evangelium nach Lukas (Geistliche Schriftlesung 3/1.2) (Düsseldorf 1964/66) 1, 199; vgl. ferner *E. W. Saunders,* Art. Nain, in: BHHW II 1283 f.

[76] Zu κύριος als Hoheitstitel vgl. *Foerster,* Art. κύριος, in: ThWNT III 1038–1098; *Cullmann,* Christologie 200–244; *F. Hahn,* Christologische Hoheitstitel (Göttingen 1963) 67–132.

[77] Vgl. dazu 1 Kön 17,17–24. „Hierauf streckte er sich dreimal über den Knaben hin, rief zum Herrn und flehte: Herr mein Gott, laß doch das Leben in diesen Knaben zurückkehren! Der Herr erhörte das Gebet des Elija. Das Leben kehrte in den Knaben zurück, und er lebte wieder auf" (V. 21 f). Man könnte bei dieser Geschichte noch an eine Mund-zu-Mund-Beatmung denken. – Auch darin liegt

wieder zu sprechen und wird von Jesus seiner Mutter zurückgegeben. Wie bei allen Totenerweckungsgeschichten im Neuen Testament, so ist auch hier die Frage nach der Historizität schwer zu beantworten[78]. Hier liegt in der Tat für unsere historisch-kritische Vernunft ein nicht leicht zu überwindender Anstoß, der mit einfachen Glaubensbehauptungen nicht aus der Welt geschafft werden kann. Die Ortsangabe bietet für sich genommen noch keine Gewähr für die „Historizität". Auch die starke Anlehnung an das alttestamentliche Vorbild 1 Kön 17, 17–24 (vgl. auch 2 Kön 4, 8–37 aus dem Elischa-Wunderzyklus) spricht eher gegen die Historizität der Geschichte. Entscheidend sind auf jeden Fall die theologisch-kerygmatischen Motive: Das „Überbietungsmotiv": Jesus als der endzeitliche Prophet und Heilbringer, der das volle Endheil bringt; Jesus als der „Herr über Leben und Tod"; Jesus, der „Heiland", der Mitleid hat mit der Not einer Witwe, der nur Gott bzw. sein „Sohn und Stellvertreter" noch helfen können. Das christologisch-soteriologische Motiv steht hier eindeutig im Vordergrund. In Jesus selbst begegnet der „Helfer der Witwen und Waisen".

5.2. Jesus und die Sünderin, Lk 7, 36–50[79]

Schon der Aufbau läßt eine komplizierte Textstruktur erkennen:

1. Jesus wird von einem zunächst ungenannten Pharisäer zum Essen eingeladen und nimmt die Einladung an, V. 36.
2. Das Auftreten der Sünderin und ihr Verhalten gegenüber Jesus, V. 37–38.
3. Die Reaktion des Pharisäers und die Antwort Jesu, die in einem Gleichnis erfolgt, V. 39–47.
4. Der Zuspruch der Sündenvergebung, V. 48–50.

Nach *R. Bultmann*[80] ist die Analyse „schwierig und unsicher". Nach ihm läge die Pointe der Geschichte in V. 47. „Nun aber ist fraglich, ob man V. 44–47 nach V. 41–43 verstehen darf: Der Liebeserweis ist der Erkenntnis-

---

eine Steigerung der neutestamentlichen Wundergeschichte, daß der Tod schon lange eingetreten ist und man sich schon auf dem Weg zum Grab befindet.
[78] Vgl. dazu *J. Blank*, Die biblischen Wunderberichte als Kerygma und als Glaubensgeschichten, in: *ders.*, Verändert Interpretation den Glauben? (Freiburg i. Br. 1972) 138–159, hier 148 ff.
[79] Vgl. dazu außer den Kommentaren die ausgezeichnete Meditation von *K. Schäfer*, Zu Gast bei Simon. Eine biblische Geschichte langsam gelesen, (Düsseldorf 1973); *Jeremias*, Gleichnisse 126 f.
[80] *R. Bultmann*, Geschichte 19.

grund dafür, daß sie schon früher die Sündenvergebung erhalten hat; oder ob V. 41–43 nachträglich eingefügt sind und V. 44–47 ursprünglich die Liebe der Frau als Realgrund der nunmehr ausgesprochenen Sündenvergebung hinstellen."[81] Nach *Bultmann* wäre die Erzählung eine Kombination einer ursprünglich selbständigen Gleichniserzählung (V. 41–43) und ihrer überarbeiteten Anwendung (V. 44–47) mit der Salbungsgeschichte Mk 14,3 bis 9. V. 48–50 sind nachträglich hinzugefügt[82].

Ob die vorausliegende Traditionsgeschichte aber tatsächlich so ausgesehen hat, darf man bezweifeln[83]. Weithin akzeptiert ist die Auffassung, daß V. 48–50, wo der Frau die Sündenvergebung noch einmal ausdrücklich zugesprochen wird, nachträglich an die Erzählung angehängt wurde, vielleicht in Analogie zu Lk 5,20f (die „Heilung des Gelähmten")[84]. Daß die „Salbung von Betanien" (Mk 14,3–9; vgl. die Analyse oben S. 22ff) auf die literarische Gestaltung von Lk 7,36–50 eingewirkt haben mag, ist nicht ausgeschlossen; bekanntlich hat sie Lukas am Anfang der Passionsgeschichte weggelassen; der Grund dafür lag aber sicher darin, daß er in seinem Sondergut eine ähnliche Erzählung von der „Sünderin" bereits vorfand. Es ist also nicht so, daß Lukas die Geschichte Mk 14,3–9 mit der Gleichniserzählung erst kombiniert hätte.

Interessant ist weiter, daß der Name des Pharisäers „Simon" heißt (vgl. Mk 14,3). *Die Unterschiede* sind aber auch deutlich: In der lukanischen Erzählung handelt es sich um eine Einladung Jesu bei einem Pharisäer. Die Frau, die Jesus salbt, wird ausdrücklich als „Sünderin" bezeichnet. Darüber hinaus sind Erzählung und Gleichnis in der vorliegenden synchronen Fassung genau aufeinander abgestimmt; der Charakter der Gleichniserzählung als eines „Sprechaktes" (Austin) kommt hier ganz deutlich zum Vorschein. Handlungsrahmen und Gleichniserzählung sowie die Applikation des Gleichnisses entsprechen einander und ergeben eine runde Situation. Man wird deshalb gut daran tun, die Geschichte primär auf der „synchronen" Ebene zu interpretieren. Traditionsgeschichtlich spricht meines Erachtens nichts gegen die Annahme einer lukanischen Sonderüberlieferung, in der die Erzählung von der Sünderin in Verbindung mit dem Gleichnis bereits vorgegeben war. Lukas hat dann den einen oder anderen Zug aus der Markuserzählung übernommen. Dafür, daß es für die Salbungsgeschichte noch

---

[81] Ebd.

[82] Ebd. 19f.

[83] Zur komplizierten Vorgeschichte von Lk 7,36–50 vgl. *Schürmann*, Lukas I 441f; *Ernst*, Lukas 255, meint: „Offensichtlich laufen hier zwei unterschiedliche Traditionen (Todessalbung und reuige Sünderin) durcheinander"; das ist vielleicht doch zu grob geurteilt.

[84] *Schürmann*, Lukas I 440: „Mit einiger Sicherheit kann man urteilen, daß die Verse 48ff der Erzählung sekundär zugewachsen sind"; er möchte diesen Vorgang jedoch schon auf der vorlukanischen Ebene festmachen. Mir scheint lukanische Redaktion näher zu liegen.

eine andere Version gegeben haben muß, ist Joh 12,3 ein deutlicher Beleg, der hierin mit Lukas übereinstimmt und von Markus abweicht.

Für das Überlieferungsinteresse und den „Sitz im Leben" scheint mir das Urteil von *H. Schürmann* vertretbar: „Die Erzählung von der Sünderin ist in einer Umgebung tradiert worden, in der die Mahlgemeinschaft mit (bekehrten) Sündern, wohl auch die mit Frauen, verteidigt werden mußte. Wir werden ob des Charakters des Judentums als einer ausgeprägten ‚Männerreligion' an den palästinensischen Raum denken müssen, zumal dort – in pharisäisch bestimmter Umgebung – auch das Problem der Gemeinschaft mit Sündern besonders akut war."[85]

Die Erzählung berichtet davon, daß Jesus von einem zunächst ungenannten Pharisäer zum Essen eingeladen worden war und daß er der Einladung in das Haus des Pharisäers folgte (V. 36). Später erfahren wir, daß der Pharisäer den Namen „Simon" trug (V. 40), was um der direkten Rede willen auch nachgetragen sein kann. Es ist ein typisch lukanischer Zug, wenn hier davon berichtet wird, daß Jesus auch bei Pharisäern gelegentlich zu Gast war (vgl. dazu auch Lk 14,1–24). Solche Kontakte Jesu mit Pharisäern oder auch umgekehrt darf man wohl für die Frühzeit der Wirksamkeit Jesu annehmen; dies wird jedenfalls dem historischen Befund eher entsprechen als die einseitig jesusfeindliche Darstellung der Pharisäer bei Markus, Matthäus und Johannes[86]. Vielleicht wollte der Pharisäer Jesus eine Ehre erweisen oder ihn überhaupt näher kennenlernen. Freilich weiß er nicht, worauf er sich damit eingelassen hat.

In diesen vermutlich nur aus Männern bestehenden Kreis tritt nun völlig unangemeldet eine Frau ein, und damit wird die Sache dramatisch. Die Frau wird als „Sünderin, die in der Stadt lebte", καὶ ἰδοὺ γυνὴ ἥτις ἦν ἐν τῇ πόλει ἁμαρτωλός, bezeichnet. Sie muß schon vorher von Jesus und seiner Predigt angesprochen gewesen sein, wenn sie es von sich aus fertigbringt, die Hemmschwelle der Konvention zu überschreiten und in das Haus des Pharisäers einzutreten. Sie kommt mit einem Alabastergefäß mit Salböl (vgl. Mk 14,3). Sie tritt, völlig in Tränen aufgelöst, von hinten an Jesus heran. Ihre Tränen fallen auf Jesu Füße. Sie trocknet die Füße Jesu mit ihrem Haar, küßt sie und salbt sie mit dem Öl. Die Szene macht in ihrer Überschwenglichkeit einen tiefen Eindruck. Die Frau scheint

---

[85] *Schürmann*, Lukas I 442.

[86] Zur Frage: Wie stand Jesus zu den Pharisäern? vgl. *Blank*, Johannes I b, 91 f.

völlig aufgelöst; die Tränen und das offene Haar machen ihre rück-
haltlose Hingabe deutlich. Dabei spricht sie kein einziges Wort.

Was ist hier mit dem Begriff *Sünderin* gemeint? Zunächst ist
J. Ernst zuzustimmen, wenn er sagt: „Lk hat die aus seinem Sondergut stammende Erzählung von der Sünderin in die Q-Folge einge-
schoben, weil sie ihm als Beleg für den kurz zuvor referierten Vorwurf, Jesus sei ein Freund der Zöllner und Sünder, wichtig ist."[87]
Aber was ist mit dem Begriff „Sünderin" näherhin gemeint? Im allgemeinen wird der Ausdruck „Sünderin", γυνὴ ἁμαρτωλός, so verstanden, daß es sich um eine „stadtbekannte Dirne" handelte. „Die
Frau, die hier erscheint und den Mittelpunkt der ganzen Erzählung
bildet, ist offenbar eine stadtbekannte Dirne, nicht bloß eine Frau,
die in einem schlechten Ruf stand, oder bloß eine Sünderin im Sinne
des pharisäischen Frömmigkeitsideals."[88] Obwohl der Ausdruck
„Sünderin" nicht unbedingt eine Dirne bezeichnen muß, dies geht in
der Tat nicht eindeutig aus dem Ausdruck selbst hervor, wird man
wohl doch eher an eine Frau denken, die sich sexueller Vergehen
schuldig gemacht hatte bzw. als Dirne in einem permanenten Sün-
denzustand lebte[89] (vgl. auch Joh 4; 7, 53 – 8, 11). Ein entscheidender
Punkt ist auch hier neben der moralischen Disqualifikation *die permanente kultische Unreinheit, in der eine „Sünderin" sich befindet.* Es
handelt sich also nicht nur um einen Verstoß gegenüber einer gesellschaftlichen Konvention, wenn diese Frau überraschend das Haus
des Pharisäers betritt; vielmehr dringt mit ihr die Sphäre der kultischen Unreinheit selber in das „reine" Haus des Pharisäers ein. Und

[87] *Ernst*, Lukas 254.
[88] Siehe *Schmid*, Lukas 147; *Schürmann*, Lukas I 431; *Ernst*, Lukas 256; *Grundmann*, Lukas 170: „Als Sünderin kann sie bezeichnet werden, weil sie eine Dirne
ist, eine Prostituierte, aber auch weil sie Frau eines Mannes ist, den die Pharisäer
als Sünder betrachten, weil er das Gesetz nicht achtet und nicht nach seiner Regel
lebt." – Anders meint *K. Herbst,* Was wollte Jesus selbst? Bd. 2 (Düsseldorf 1981)
Nr. 403: „Eine berufsmäßige Dirne hätte das Haus des Pharisäers gar nicht betre-
ten können. Es war also eine Frau, von deren Sünden nur der Gastgeber wußte."
Diese Interpretation ist nicht ganz überzeugend.
[89] Billerbeck II 162 z. St.: γυνὴ ἁμαρτωλός „kann ganz allgemein eine Frau bezeichnen, deren Haltung den pharisäischen Satzungen nicht entsprach ... Wahrscheinlich ist unter γυνὴ ἁμαρτωλός speziell eine Prostituierte zu verstehen;
auch das Verbum *ḥatá* wird in der Bedeutung ‚unzüchtig leben', oder ‚Unzuchtssünden begehen' absolut gebraucht." – Zum Dirnenwesen in der Antike vgl. oben
Anm. 53.

wenn Jesus sich sogar von dieser Frau anfassen läßt, dann scheut er ja den Kontakt mit dieser Welt des „Unreinen" nicht; er läßt sich gleichsam selber davon anstecken. Hier, an dieser Stelle, liegt für den Pharisäer der eigentliche Anstoß.

Dieser Anstoß wird als Gedanke des Pharisäers gegenüber Jesus artikuliert: „Wenn dieser Mann ein Prophet wäre, dann wüßte er wohl genau, was das für ein Weib ist, das ihn da anfaßt, daß sie nämlich eine Sünderin ist." Die Aussage setzt voraus, daß Jesus als „Prophet", vielleicht sogar als der „endzeitliche Prophet" angesehen wurde und daß der Pharisäer diese Rollenidentifikation kannte. Der Prophet verfügt über eine besondere Kenntnis des Innern eines Menschen; ein echter Prophet wird sich also niemals von einem solchen Subjekt anfassen lassen! Jesu Verhalten scheint nun diesen Ruf, ein Prophet zu sein, endgültig zu widerlegen. Wenn der Pharisäer vielleicht Jesus hatte testen wollen, dann ist dieser Test für Jesus ohne Zweifel negativ verlaufen. Jesus kann kein Prophet sein.

Doch nun wird dieses dezidierte Urteil von Jesus selbst unterlaufen. Und zwar zuerst mit einem Gleichnis: „Simon, ich habe dir etwas zu sagen." Es folgt die Geschichte von den „ungleichen Schuldnern" (V. 41 ff). Die Geschichte wird so erzählt, daß der Pharisäer Simon darin einbezogen wird. Er muß selbst sein Urteil abgeben und damit auch über sich selbst urteilen:

„Ein Geldverleiher hatte zwei Schuldner; der eine war ihm fünfhundert Denare schuldig, der andere fünfzig.
Als sie ihre Schulden nicht bezahlen konnten, erließ er sie beiden.
Wer von ihnen wird ihn nun mehr lieben?
Simon antwortete:
Ich nehme an, der, dem er mehr erlassen hat!
Jesus sagt zu ihm: Du hast recht!"

Das Gleichnis stellt *das Geschehen der Sündenvergebung*, die im Hinblick auf die Sünderin als schon erfolgt vorausgesetzt wird, in den Mittelpunkt der Diskussion. In der Predigt Jesu hatte die Frau wohl schon für sich persönlich den Heilszuspruch der Gottesherrschaft erfahren; sie hatte sich schon vom Wort der göttlichen Liebe, der Freudenbotschaft für die Armen, treffen lassen und innerlich den Ruf zur Umkehr schon angenommen. Im Hinblick darauf stellt Jesus nebeneinander: „große Schuld und kleine Schuld – große Dankbarkeit und kleine Dankbarkeit. Nur die, die um große Schuld

wissen, können ermessen, was Güte bedeutet."[90] Das Gleichnis erschließt in unserer Erzählung zunächst die Situation der Frau. Simon hat, was die Geschichte betrifft, richtig verstanden. Jetzt aber
wird er mit Hilfe des Gleichnisses von Jesus aufgefordert, auch zu
verstehen, was es mit dieser Frau auf sich hat. Dabei muß er lernen,
auch sein eigenes Selbstverständnis und seine „Versäumnisse" Jesus
gegenüber einzusehen und zu korrigieren. „Siehst du diese Frau?"
Es geht darum, sie wahrzunehmen und sich mit ihrem überschwenglichen Verhalten auseinanderzusetzen.

„Als ich in dein Haus kam, hast du mir kein Wasser zum Waschen der Füße
   gegeben;
sie aber hat ihre Tränen über meinen Füßen vergossen und sie mit ihren
   Haaren abgetrocknet.
Du hast mir zur Begrüßung keinen Kuß gegeben;
sie aber hat mir, seit ich hier bin, unaufhörlich die Füße geküßt.
Du hast mir nicht das Haar mit Öl gesalbt;
sie aber hat mir mit ihrem wohlriechenden Öl die Füße gesalbt" (V. 44 ff).

Letztlich geht es dabei um das Verhältnis zu Jesus. Wenn Simon vorher über die Frau verächtlich dachte, so muß ihm jetzt deutlich werden, daß nicht diese Frau, sondern er selber in dieser Situation die
schlechte Figur macht, und zwar im Sinne der „geringeren Liebe",
der die „größere Liebe" der Frau gegenübersteht. Daraufhin folgt
nun das eigentliche Schlußwort der Geschichte:

„Deshalb sage ich dir:
Ihr sind viele Sünden vergeben,
   weil sie (mir) soviel Liebe gezeigt hat.
Wem aber weniger vergeben wird,
   der zeigt auch nur wenig Liebe" (V. 47).

Man muß die abschließende Sentenz ganz in Anlehnung an die Geschichte verstehen; es geht nicht allgemein um die Liebe der Frau
überhaupt, sondern um ihr Verhalten gegenüber Jesus und was
darin alles zum Vorschein kommt. Im Verhalten der Frau zeigt sich
die „größere Liebe", während sich im Verhalten des Pharisäers Simon zeigt, daß er, was seine Liebe zu Jesus angeht, hinter der Frau
weit zurücksteht. Die Liebe entspricht dem Maß der erfahrenen Vergebung und umgekehrt. Dabei ist es wohl müßig, zu fragen, ob die

---

[90] *Jeremias,* Gleichnisse 127.

Liebe die Folge oder der Grund der Vergebung sei. Hier herrscht nicht die Logik einer kausalen Abfolge, sondern die Dialogik der Begegnung. Jedenfalls hat Jesus diese Frau angenommen, und er nimmt sie jetzt auch gegenüber den Einwänden des Simon in Schutz. Indem Jesus zu dieser Frau steht, zeigt er zugleich, wie ernst ihm das Wort von Vergebung und Liebe ist. Damit ist die Erzählung eigentlich abgeschlossen.

V. 48–50 unterstreichen noch einmal den Gedanken der Sündenvergebung. Die Verse klingen eher wie eine angehängte These, welche Jesu Vollmacht der Sündenvergebung noch einmal besonders unterstreichen soll. Die Funktion dieser Aussage dürfte ähnlich sein wie in der Erzählung von der „Heilung des Gelähmten" (Mk 2,1–2 par.): Jesu Verhalten bleibt für seine Gemeinde und seine Jünger verbindlich und verpflichtend. Genauso wie Jesus haben auch sie nicht zu verurteilen, sondern zu vergeben, und zwar allen Menschen. Jedem, der Glauben und Liebe hat, muß und wird die Vergebung widerfahren.

Was die Erzählung in dieser Begegnung der Sünderin mit Jesus berichtet, ist wohl dieses, daß Jesus einer in vielerlei Hinsicht kompromittierten Frau durch sein Verhalten Würde und Selbstachtung zurückgab. Als die Frau zu Jesus kam, war sie „eine rechtlose, wertlose, verachtete Außenseiterin, ein Sündenbock. An ihr dürfen die Rechtschaffenen alles das verfolgen und bestrafen, was in ihnen selber drinsteckt, aber nicht gelebt, nicht einmal eingestanden werden darf. Auf diese Rolle ist die Frau festgelegt, aus ihr kommt sie nicht mehr heraus. Man weiß, wer und was sie ist und wie man sie zu behandeln hat: als den letzten Dreck."[91] Nun ist sie Jesus begegnet, und das hat sie verändert. „In dem Licht, das von Jesus auf sie fällt, sieht ihr Leben anders aus; die Frau kennt sich selber nicht mehr wieder. Sie fühlt sich anders in dieser ihrer Haut. Sie bekommt wieder Mut zu ihrem Leben; sie kann vielleicht doch noch jemand anderen aus sich machen – den, den Jesus im Auge hat. Die Frau merkt, daß sie eine Zukunft hat."[92]

---

[91] *Schäfer*, Zu Gast bei Simon 143.
[92] Ebd. 145.

5.3. Die dienenden Frauen, Lk 8,1–3

Der Text Lk 8,1–3 hat den Charakter eines *Sammelberichtes* und bildet zugleich die Überleitung von der Szene der „Sünderin" (Lk 7,36–50) zur lukanischen Gleichnisrede (Lk 8,4–18.19–21). „Luk stellt vor die folgenden Abschnitte in 8,1–3 eine ‚Gesamtaufnahme‘, die Aufschluß gibt über die Situation. (Diese schaut nicht nur auf 8,4–56 voraus, sondern schon auf 9,1–50.) Dabei ist ihm besonders wichtig, daß Jesus die Botschaft vom Reich Gottes nun systematisch in jegliche Ortschaft bringt."[93] In diesem Zusammenhang ist nicht nur von den „Zwölf" die Rede, sondern auch von Frauen, die Jesus begleiten und ihm dienen:

„Und es geschah im folgenden,
daß er Stadt um Stadt und Dorf um Dorf durchwanderte,
indem er predigte und die Freudenbotschaft von Gottes Herrschaft verkündigte,
und die Zwölf mit ihm,
und einige Frauen, die von bösen Geistern und Krankheiten geheilt worden waren,
Maria, genannt Magdalena, von der sieben Dämonen ausgefahren waren,
und Johanna, Frau des Chuzas, eines Verwalters des Herodes,
und Susanna
und viele andere, die ihnen mit ihrem Vermögen dienten".

Die vorliegende Notiz gehört zwar nach ihrer literarischen Bezeugung zum lukanischen Sondergut, ist aber traditions- und redaktionsgeschichtlich nicht ganz so einfach zu bestimmen. *Schürmann* geht davon aus, daß Lukas in 8,1–3 „sowohl die Redenquelle wie seine Sondervorlage benutzt" habe und versteht entsprechend V. 1 als lukanische Redaktion einer Notiz von Q (vgl. Mt 9,35), während Lukas die Verse 2–3 nicht erst aufgrund von Mk 15,40 und 16,1–8 gebildet habe. Nach ihm spricht vieles dafür, „daß auf die beiden Frauenerzählungen 7,11–17.36–50 vormals als generalisierende Abschlußnotiz etwas wie 8,2f. gefolgt ist". „Der ‚Sitz‘ im Gemeindeleben dieser kleinen Komposition wird die Frauenfrage gewesen sein ... Jesus hat einer armen Witwe geholfen, eine Sünderin angenommen und besessene Frauen geheilt; er hat sie in seine Gemeinschaft aufgenommen und sich von ihnen bedienen lassen. Die Gemeinde der Jünger Jesu wird es allen Anfeindungen zum Trotz ähnlich halten."[94] Dagegen erblickt *J. Jeremias* in diesem Ab-

---

[93] *Schürmann*, Lukas I 444.
[94] Vgl. ebd. 447 f; anders *Ernst*, Lukas 260.

schnitt reine lukanische Redaktion. „Einziger Anhaltspunkt für traditionelles Gut: Die Namen waren Lukas vorgegeben."[95]

V. 1 berichtet, daß Jesus seine Tätigkeit als Wanderprediger wieder aufnimmt mit der Verkündigung der Gottesherrschaft, auch nach Lukas das Zentral-Motiv der Verkündigung Jesu[96]. Dabei begleiten ihn die Zwölf („Apostel"), die späteren Zeugen der Jesuszeit (vgl. Apg 1,22).

Ebenso begleiten Jesus „einige Frauen", von denen gesagt wird, daß sie von dämonischer Besessenheit und von Krankheiten geheilt worden waren. Die vermutlich lukanischen Wendungen[97] sind so allgemein gehalten, daß daraus nichts Spezifisches erschlossen werden kann. Am nächsten liegt natürlich die Vermutung, daß Jesus diese Begleiterinnen Jesu bewußt im Anschluß an die Erzählung von der „Sünderin" erwähnt, um die positive Einstellung Jesu gegenüber Frauen noch einmal zu belegen und daß er wohl auch die Vorstellung hatte, die von Jesus geheilten Frauen und die von ihm bekehrte Sünderin hätten sich Jesus sofort angeschlossen. Dies ist auf der Ebene der lukanischen Reflexion möglich.

Außerdem muß man die Bemerkung mit der Notiz von den *Frauen unter dem Kreuz* vergleichen (vgl. Mk 15,40f par. Mt 27,55; Lk 23,49; Joh 19,25). Bei Markus ist zu lesen:

„Es waren aber auch Frauen da, die von ferne zuschauten,
unter ihnen auch Maria Magdalena und Maria – die Mutter von Jakobus
    dem Kleinen und von Joses – und Salome,
die ihm, als er in Galiläa war, folgten und dienten,
und viele andere, die mit ihm hinauf nach Jerusalem gezogen waren" (Mk 15,40f).

Die Frauen unter dem Kreuz waren also nach Markus bereits in Galiläa in der näheren Umgebung Jesu, wo sie ihm „folgten und dienten" (ἠκολούθουν αὐτῷ καὶ διηκόνουν αὐτῷ). Lukas bringt in der entsprechenden Parallelstelle (Lk 23, 49) nur die Bemerkung: „Alle ihm Bekannten aber standen von ferne dabei und sahen dies, auch

[95] *J. Jeremias,* Die Sprache des Lukasevangeliums. Redaktion und Tradition im Nicht-Markusstoff des dritten Evangeliums (Göttingen 1980) 176–178.
[96] Vgl. Lk 4,43; 9,2; 10,11 u.ö. Dazu *Conzelmann,* Mitte 96 ff. „Das Neue, was Jesus (gegenüber dem Täufer) lehrt, ist nicht die Botschaft von der *Nähe* des Reiches, sondern die vom Reich überhaupt" (ebd. 97).
[97] vgl. *Jeremias,* Sprache 176 f.

Frauen, die ihm von Galiläa herauf gefolgt waren." Namen werden keine mehr erwähnt. Es ist demnach nicht zu bezweifeln, daß Lukas an dieser Stelle eine Reminiszenz an 8,2 f nahelegen will und daß er die Namen der Frauen absichtlich vorgezogen hat. Wir haben es also in Lk 8,2–3 nicht mit einer „Vorlage" (gegen *Schürmann*, vgl. oben), sondern mit lukanischer Redaktion zu tun. Lukas will nicht erst nachträglich sagen, daß die Frauen in Galiläa bereits zur Begleitung Jesu gehörten, sondern zeigen, wie dies faktisch zugegangen ist. Die Änderung war freilich möglich, weil schon der Markustext die Bemerkung enthielt, daß die Frauen unter dem Kreuz schon in Galiläa zur festen Begleitung Jesu gehörten. An der Richtigkeit dieser Bemerkung zu zweifeln besteht freilich kein Grund, so daß man die Tatsache als solche als historisch gesichert gelten lassen darf.

Verschieden sind freilich bei Markus und Lukas die Namen der Frauen, bis auf Maria Magdalena. Hier dürfte Lukas die Namen deshalb geändert haben, weil ihm andere Traditionen vorlagen.

Maria Magdalena (Maria aus Magdala) ist der erste und bekannteste Name. „Magdala" ist eine Stadt am Westufer des Sees Gennesaret. Der Name wird abgeleitet von *Migdal Nunaja* und bedeutet „Fischturm", was darauf hindeutet, daß die Bevölkerung damals hauptsächlich vom Fischfang gelebt hat[98]. Maria Magdalena gehört in der Evangelientradition zu den Frauen unter dem Kreuz Jesu sowie zu den Frauen, die am Ostermorgen das „leere Grab" entdecken und zu den ersten Zeugen der Auferstehung Jesu werden[99]. Mehr als dieses wissen wir im Grunde genommen von Maria Magdalena nicht. Nach Lk 8,2 b soll aber Jesus von ihr sieben Dämonen ausgetrieben haben; es würde sich dann um einen besonders schweren Fall von Besessenheit gehandelt haben. Dies mag auch der Anlaß gewesen sein, später die „große Sünderin" von Lk 7,36–50 mit Maria Magdalena zu identifizieren, wofür es freilich im Kontext keinerlei Anhalt gibt[100]. Dies gilt erst recht, wenn der Name hier redaktionell eingetragen wurde.

---

[98] Zu Magdala vgl. Billerbeck I 1046 f; *E. W. Saunders*, Art. Magdala, in: BHHW II 1121; – *Negev – Rehork*, Archäologisches Lexikon zur Bibel (München 1972) 226.

[99] Vgl. Mk 15,40.47; Mt 27,56.61; 28,1; Lk 8,2; 24,10; Joh 19,25; 20,1.11.16.18.

[100] „Aus der Art, wie Lukas diese Frau neu einführt und charakterisiert, nachdem er eben vorher die Begegnung mit der namenlosen Sünderin erzählt hat, muß der

Freilich war es dann gerade dieser lukanische Zusatz, daß Jesus von Maria Magdalena sieben Dämonen ausgetrieben habe, der als „Leerstelle" die Phantasie der späteren Erklärer und Leser intensiv beschäftigte und so aus dieser Frau einerseits das Urbild einer wild ausschweifenden Kurtisane, andererseits das Urbild der „großen Büßerin" gemacht hat, die auch in ihrer Buße noch von hinreißend schöner Attraktivität ist, wie sie uns von vielen Bildern vertraut ist. – Die alte Schriftauslegung hat mit ihrer harmonisierenden Denkweise eine Reihe von Identifikationen vorgenommen. Danach sollte Maria Magdalena identisch sein a) mit der großen Sünderin (Lk 7,37); b) mit Maria, der Schwester der Martha (Lk 10,39.42); c) mit der Schwester des Lazarus (Joh 11,1.2.19.20.28.31.32.45). All diese Identifikationen können natürlich nicht als historisch gesichert gelten, sondern sind das Ergebnis erfindungsreicher Kombinationen.

Darüber hinaus spielt Maria Magdalena in den neutestamentlichen Apokryphen eine beachtliche Rolle, auf die hier nicht näher eingegangen werden kann[101]. Ebenso hat sich die christliche Legende ihrer bemächtigt[102], auf der dann auch die künstlerischen Darstellungen beruhen. Nach der Legende soll ihr Grab in Vézelay (Burgund) sein; ihr Fest wird am 22. Juli gefeiert.

Daneben werden noch zwei andere Frauen genannt, die sonst im Neuen Testament nicht mehr vorkommen: *Johanna,* die Frau eines Beamten des Herodes Antipas (4–39 n. Chr.), des Landesherrn Jesu, mit Namen Chuzas[103]; die Frau wird der Gemeindetradition des Lukas bekannt gewesen sein; hinzu kommt, daß Lukas überhaupt gern „Standespersonen erwähnt, weil er das Christentum in der Welt beheimaten will!"[104]. – Von der anschließend genannten *Susanna* kennen wir nichts außer dem Namen.

Von diesen namentlich Genannten sowie von den „vielen anderen" Ungenannten sagt Lukas noch, daß sie Jesus und seinen Jüngern mit ihrem Vermögen gedient hätten. Ob es sich dabei um „rei-

zwingende Schluß gezogen werden, daß er die beiden Frauen unterschieden hat", so mit Recht *Schmid,* Lukas 156.
[101] Vgl. *Hennecke – Schneemelcher,* Neutestamentliche Apokryphen 2 Bde. (Tübingen ³1959/64) II 649 Register.
[102] Zur christlichen Legende der „Maria Magdalena" vgl. Die Legenda aurea des Jacobus de Voragine, aus dem Lateinischen übersetzt von Richard Benz (Heidelberg o. J.) 470–482.
[103] Die Ableitung des Namens ist unterschiedlich. Nach *Ernst,* Lukas 261, erinnert der Name *Chuza* „vielleicht an die idumäische Gottheit Kos", während Billerbeck III, 164 z. St. auf eine Baraita verweist, wonach *kuzza* = „Krüglein" „eine bildliche Bezeichnung für einen unangesehenen Menschen war im Gegensatz zu *kadda* = „Eimer", einem hochgestellten Mann".
[104] *Schürmann,* Lukas I 446, Anm. 20.

che Frauen" gehandelt hat, ist aus der vagen Angabe nicht zu entnehmen. Allerdings spielen in den Synagogengemeinden der jüdischen Diaspora vornehme „gottesfürchtige Frauen" eine gewisse Rolle (vgl. Apg 13, 50; 16, 14f; 17, 4.12); ähnlich in den paulinischen Missionsgemeinden (vgl. Apg 16, 14f; 18, 1–4; 1 Kor 1, 11). Aus diesen Schichten kamen zu einem Großteil die ersten Anhänger der neuen Christengemeinden.

Die Notiz ist, trotz ihrer Kürze, ein weiterer Hinweis darauf, daß Frauen zur festen Begleitung Jesu gehört hatten und gegenüber Jesus und seinen Jüngern wohl auch die Aufgabe der täglichen Versorgung übernommen hatten. Daß sie auch an der „Nachfolge" beteiligt waren – weniger an der Predigt –, ist anzunehmen; im Hinblick auf die Reich-Gottes-Botschaft darf man auch von „Gleichberechtigung" sprechen. Daß sie schließlich, anders als die Jünger, die die Flucht ergriffen (Mk 14, 50), bis unter das Kreuz Jesu durchhielten, verleiht ihnen schon für die Zeit des irdischen Jesus eine besondere Stellung. Nicht zu Unrecht sagt *A. Stöger:* „Die galiläischen Frauen gehören zum *Grundstock der Kirche.*"[105] Gerade darin tritt auch der große Unterschied gegenüber dem Judentum hervor. So heißt es in den „Sprüchen der Väter":

„Jose ben Jochanan aus Jerusalem sagt:
Dein Haus sei weit offen, und die Armen seien Söhne des Hauses.
Und verweile nicht zu sehr im Gespräch mit der Frau."

Dazu die Glosse:

„(Von der eigenen Frau haben sie das gesagt. Um wieviel mehr gilt es von der Frau seines Nächsten. Von da her sagen die Weisen:
Immer, wenn der Mensch lang im Gespräch mit einer Frau verweilt, zieht er sich Unheil zu; er vernachlässigt die Worte der Tora, und schließlich wird er die Hölle erben.)"[106]

Zusammenfassend darf man wohl mit *Schürmann* sagen: „Daß Jesus Frauen in seiner Gefolgschaft duldet, ist gewiß im palästinensischen Raum ein äußerst anstößiges Verhalten, das eine Initialzündung geben mußte für die gesellschaftliche und religiöse Stellung der Frau in der Kirche und über diese hinaus … Nunmehr gibt es in

---

[105] *Stöger,* Lukas 1, 218.
[106] Zitiert nach *G. Stemberger,* Der Talmud. Einführung, Texte, Erläuterungen (München 1982) 72.

der religiösen Wertung nicht mehr ‚Mann und Frau' (Gal 3,28). Jesus erlöste die Frau durch sein unbekümmertes Verhalten grundsätzlich in eine neue gesellschaftliche Stellung (deren soziologische Realisierung freilich viel Zeit brauchte). Die Frauen sind nun wie selbstverständlich in den Zusammenkünften der Jünger Jesu dabei; sie haben im Gemeindeleben ihre wichtigen Aufgaben."[107]

5.4. Jesus als Gast bei Martha und Maria, Lk 10,38–42

Die kurze Erzählung, wie Jesus auf dem Weg nach Jerusalem bei den Schwestern Martha und Maria einkehrt, gehört gleichfalls zum lukanischen Sondergut. Sie ist leicht als in sich geschlossene Texteinheit zu erkennen. Die Perikope wird von *Bultmann* zu den „biographischen Apophthegmata" gerechnet[108]. Danach haben die zu dieser literarischen Gattung gehörenden Texte „idealen Charakter", und zwar deshalb, „weil sie in einer bildhaften Szene eine Wahrheit zum Ausdruck bringen, die über die Situation übergreift, so daß diese symbolischen Charakter erhält"[109]. Damit ist jedoch ein historischer Kern keineswegs ausgeschlossen; man darf eher annehmen, daß eine vorausliegende Tradition zu einer lehrhaft-typologischen Aussage zurechtstilisiert wurde. Klar ist auch, daß in der Erzählung zwei verschiedene „Typen" oder „Rollen" einander gegenübergestellt werden, so daß die spätere Allegorisierung der Geschichte im Hinblick auf das aktiv-weltliche und beschaulich-klösterliche Leben (vita activa et contemplativa) nicht so abwegig erscheint; sie ist in der Struktur des Textes selber angelegt. Erzähltechnisch ist von Bedeutung, daß hier ein Gegensatz (eine „Opposition") dargestellt wird. Hauptaktant ist natürlich Jesus selbst und sein Wort. An ihm entscheidet sich der Gegensatz in einer Art „Konkurrenzverhalten" der beiden Frauen Maria und Martha. Beide haben je auf ihre Art ein positives Verhältnis zu Jesus; *Martha* im Hinblick auf die leibliche Fürsorge; *Maria* dagegen im unmittelbaren Interesse am Wort Jesu.

Die Geschichte hat ihren Ort im sogenannten „lukanischen Reisebericht" (Lk 9,51 – 18,14): Jesus wandert mit seinen Jüngern von Galiläa nach Jeru-

---

[107] *Schürmann*, Lukas I 446f.
[108] *Bultmann*, Geschichte 58ff.   [109] Ebd. 59.

salem, und zwar durch Samaria hindurch; doch die Samariter nehmen ihn nicht auf (vgl. Lk 9,52 f). Im Gegensatz dazu findet Jesus Aufnahme bei diesen beiden Frauen. Damit wird auch eine „idealtypische Situation" geschildert. Denn man muß zweifellos mit der lukanischen Absicht rechnen, urchristliche Missionspraxis bereits in der Jesuszeit zu verankern, um ihr damit eine jesuanische Begründung zu geben. Die „jesuanische Urzeit" ist für die „Zeit der Kirche" vorbildhaft und verbindlich. Ob damit schon bewußt zu späteren innerkirchlichen Auseinandersetzungen Stellung genommen werden soll, wie *J. Ernst* meint: „Die Aktivisten wollen statt der beschaulichen Zurückgezogenheit die soziale Tat. Was hat den Vorrang: das Hören auf das Wort des Herrn oder die praktische Diakonie im Alltag?"[110], scheint mir doch etwas zu forciert und zu „modern" gedacht. Richtig ist freilich, daß Lukas, was das „Wort (Gottes)" angeht, hier eine klare Linie vertritt im Sinne einer „Priorität des Dienstes am Wort" (vgl. dazu bes. Apg 6,1–2). – Dem Text liegt eine Tradition zugrunde, die von Lukas redaktionell bearbeitet wurde[111].

Bei ihrer Wanderung (die Einführung ἐν δὲ τῷ πορεύεσθαι αὐτούς verweist auf den größeren Zusammenhang der „Wanderung von Galiläa nach Jerusalem") kommen Jesus und die Jünger in ein ungenanntes Dorf und werden dort von einer Frau namens Martha gastfreundlich aufgenommen (V.38). Schon hier sei angemerkt, daß es nicht statthaft ist, das namenlose Dorf mit „Betanien" (vgl. Joh 12,1) gleichzusetzen und auf diese Weise die johanneische Martha-Maria-Maria-Lazarus-Tradition zur harmonisierenden Erklärung heranzuziehen, wie dies oft geschehen ist[112]. Aus der Erzählung geht nicht deutlich hervor, ob das Dorf noch in Samaria oder schon in Judäa liegt. Wollte Lukas den Kontrast zwischen den ungastlichen Samaritern (Lk 9,52 ff) und der gastfeundlichen Frau besonders unterstreichen, dann liegt es näher, an eine samaritanische Ortschaft zu denken. Wichtiger scheint der Gedanke, daß auch auf dieser Wanderung Jesus als „Zeichen des Widerspruchs" erscheint (vgl. Lk 2,34 b). Unfreundliche und freundliche Stellungnahme werden gegenübergestellt.

Die Frau hat eine Schwester namens Maria, die sich, sobald Jesus im Hause ist, sogleich „zu den Füßen des Herrn" setzt, um sein Wort zu hören (V.39). Die Bezeichnung „Herr" ist ohne Zweifel im Sinne des

---

[110] *Ernst*, Lukas 355.
[111] Vgl. dazu *Jeremias*, Sprache 193 ff.
[112] vgl. etwa *Schmid*, Lukas 196; *Stöger*, Lukas 1, 305.

christologischen Kyriostitels gemeint, den Lukas sehr häufig gebraucht. Zum Herr-Sein Jesu gehört aber auch die unüberbietbare Bedeutung und Autorität des „Wortes Jesu". Jesus wirkt durch sein Wort, genauer durch das „Wort vom Reiche Gottes", das als Heilswort verstanden werden muß. Denn das Wort, das Jesus verkündet, ist ja „das Wort Gottes" (vgl. Lk 4,22.32.36; 5,1; 8,11 u.ö.), das als Wort des Heils alle anderen menschlichen Dinge an Bedeutung übertrifft. So gesehen, zeigt Maria, daß sie wirklich verstanden hat, worauf es in der Begegnung mit Jesus ankommt, nämlich auf das Interesse am Wort Jesu. Demgegenüber widmet sich Martha völlig den Geschäften der Gastfreundschaft (περιεσπᾶτο περὶ πολλὴν διακονίαν). Obgleich Lukas solche „diakonía" keineswegs gering achtet, findet hier doch eine deutliche Prioritätensetzung statt; vgl. auch Apg 6,2: „Da riefen die Zwölf die Gesamtheit der Jünger zusammen und sagten: Es geht nicht an, daß wir das Wort Gottes vernachlässigen und den Dienst tun an den Tischen." Der „Dienst des Wortes" hat den Vorrang vor dem „Dienst bei den Tischen", das heißt bei der täglichen Versorgung der Witwen und Armen. Dennoch ist auch dieser Dienst keineswegs gleichgültig, wie die Sorge um seine gute Regelung Apg 6,3 ff zeigt. Auch wird hier Martha keineswegs wegen ihres Dienstes getadelt. Vielmehr geht der Anstoß von ihr aus, wenn sie zu Jesus sagt: „Herr, kümmert es dich nicht, daß meine Schwester mich allein aufwarten läßt! Sag ihr, daß sie mir helfen soll!" (V. 40 b.c). Martha beklagt sich also über die mangelnde Unterstützung von seiten ihrer Schwester; sie betrachtet anscheinend deren Verhalten als offenkundige „Faulheit". Nun aber tritt Jesus ausdrücklich auf die Seite der Maria und rechtfertigt ihr Verhalten mit den Worten:

„Martha, Martha, du sorgst und kümmerst dich um vieles;
aber nur Eines ist notwendig.
Maria hat den guten Teil erwählt,
der wird ihr nicht genommen werden" (V. 41 f)[113].

In der ersten Aussage wird dem „sich Sorgen und Kümmern um vieles" (μεριμνᾷς καὶ θορυβάζῃ περὶ πολλά) das „Eine Notwendige"

---

[113] Zum textkritischen Problem von V. 41–42 vgl. Nestle – Aland ([26]1979) z. St. – *B. M. Metzger*, A Textual Commentary on the Greek New Testament, United Bible Societies, Corrected Edition (London – New York 1975) 153 f.

(ἑνὸς δέ ἐστιν χρεία) gegenübergestellt. Man wird die Aussage wohl im Sinne der großen „Warnung vor dem Sorgen" (Lk 12,22-31; par. Mt 6,25-33) verstehen müssen, wo der „Lebenssorge" um Kleidung und Nahrung die radikale Forderung gegenübergestellt wird: „Doch suchet zuerst sein (des Vaters) Reich, und dieses alles wird euch dazugegeben werden" (Lk 12,31). Das Streben nach der Gottesherrschaft hat gegenüber allen anderen Lebensfragen eine absolute Priorität. Man wird deshalb auch das „unum necessarium" am besten mit der Gottesherrschaft gleichsetzen. – Ähnlich heißt es in der lukanischen Deutung des Sämannsgleichnisses (Lk 8,11-15): „Das unter die Dornen Gefallene sind die, welche (das Wort Gottes, vgl. 8,11) gehört haben, doch unter Sorgen, Reichtum und Lüsten des Lebens gehen sie dahin und bringen die Frucht nicht zur Reife" (Lk 8,14). Das „Sorgen um vieles" kann also für den Menschen gefährlich werden und ihn vom „Wort Gottes" ablenken. Ebenso steht dem „Vielen" das „Eine Notwendige" gegenüber, der Zerstreuung in das Vielerlei der Alltagsgeschäfte die Besinnung und Sammlung auf das, worauf es letztlich ankommt. Darum hat Maria „den guten Teil erwählt", den ihr niemand nehmen kann. Die Aussage erinnert auch an Ps 127,2: „Den Seinen gibt es der Herr im Schlafe." Hier ist anzumerken, daß die „Lehre der Geschichte" sich natürlich an alle Christen wendet, an Männer und Frauen. Es geht hier nicht um die Begründung zweier verschiedener kirchlicher „Stände"; damit hat die Erzählung überhaupt nichts im Sinn. Und gerade hier ist es dann bemerkenswert, wenn eine Frau, Maria, das tut, worauf es für jeden Christen, gerade auch für den Mann, immer wieder ankommt: auf die grundsätzliche Orientierung am Wort Jesu. Vielleicht könnte man im Sinne der vorliegenden Typologie noch sagen, dies hat die Frau besser verstanden!

Ambrosius von Mailand sagt dazu in seinem Lukaskommentar:

„Doch nicht so sehr um einen Tadel für die in guter Dienstleistung sich mühende Martha handelt es sich, sondern um die Bevorzugung der Maria, weil sie den besseren Teil sich erwählte. Jesus verfügt ja über mehr denn genug Güter und reicht deren eine Menge dar. Darum erwählte sie als die Weisere das, was in ihren Augen das Vorzüglichere war. So dünkte ja auch den Aposteln als das Beste nicht ‚vom Gotteswort abzulassen und den Tisch zu besorgen'. Beides freilich ist eine Funktion der Weisheit; auch Stephanus, ein erkorener Diener (Diakon), war ‚voll der Weisheit'. Wer dem Dienste obliegt, soll eben darum dem Lehrer (des Wortes Gottes) gern zu Diensten sein, der

Lehrer den Diener hierzu ermuntern und begeistern; denn es gibt nur *einen* Leib der Kirche, wenn auch verschiedene Glieder. Eines bedarf des anderen."[114]

Die Erzählung macht, so könnte man sagen, die volle Gleichberechtigung der Frau gegenüber dem Wort Jesu, dem Evangelium, deutlich. Das haben die Frauen, wie viele religiöse Frauenbewegungen, gerade im Mittelalter, zeigen, auch verstanden; sie haben sehr viel mehr Interesse an der Heiligen Schrift gehabt, als die Kirchenmänner, die die Frauen und ihre geistlichen Bedürfnisse oft wenig ernst genommen haben.

Auch für die Juden war die Beschäftigung mit der Tora allen anderen Bedürfnissen vorzuziehen:

„Rabbi Meïr sagte:
Gib dir weniger Mühe mit weltlicher Arbeit als mit der Tora …
Bist du nachlässig im Gesetzesstudium,
dann stellen sich viele störende Dinge dir entgegen.
Gibst du dir aber mit dem Gesetzesstudium Mühe,
dann ist Er bereit, dir einen reichen Lohn zu geben."[115]

In der Jüngergemeinde Jesu nimmt das Wort Jesu diejenige Stelle ein, die im Judentum der Tora zukommt. Darüber hinaus, im damaligen Judentum war es nicht nötig und weithin auch nicht üblich, daß Frauen dem Torastudium oblagen. Ausnahmen mag es gegeben haben; sie bestätigen freilich nur die Regel. In der christlichen Gemeinde müssen auch die Frauen ein Minimum an religiöser Information mitbekommen; sie sind, was das Grundwissen im Hinblick auf die Taufe und das christliche Leben anbelangt, den Männern prinzipiell gleichgestellt und auch in gleicher Weise gefordert. Auch die altchristliche Taufkatechese kennt hier keine prinzipiellen Unterschiede.

---

[114] *Ambrosius von Mailand*, Lukaskommentar VII, 86, übersetzt von Dr. Joh. Ev. Niederhuber (BKV) (München 1917) 369 f.
[115] Sprüche der Väter IV, 12; zitiert nach *P. Rießler*, Altjüdisches Schrifttum außerhalb der Bibel (Heidelberg ⁴1979) 1071.

5.4.1. Martha-Maria-Lazarus-Tradition im Johannesevangelium[116]

Es legt sich nahe, die johanneische Tradition über Martha, Maria, Lazarus an dieser Stelle mitzubehandeln. Die Namenverbindung findet sich gleich am Beginn der großen johanneischen Erzählung von der „Auferweckung des Lazarus": „Es war aber einer krank, Lazarus von Betanien, aus dem Dorf der Maria und ihrer Schwester Martha. Maria aber war jene, die den Herrn mit Öl gesalbt und seine Füße mit ihren Haaren getrocknet hat, deren Bruder Lazarus krank war" (Joh 11,1 f)[117]. Im Johannesevangelium sind diese Namen fest mit der „Auferweckung des Lazarus" verbunden; ferner mit der „Salbung in Betanien" (Joh 12,1–8.9–11). Die Erzählungen haben bei Johannes insofern eine wichtige literarische Funktion, als sie den unmittelbaren Anstoß zur Verhaftung und Hinrichtung Jesu geben.

Deutlich sind hier die traditionsgeschichtlichen Querverbindungen zum Sondergut des Lukas (Lk 10,38–42; ferner die Parabel „Vom Reichen und dem Armen", Lk 16,19–31; der „Arme" trägt den Namen „Lazarus"). – Meine Auffassung ist, daß es sich in Joh 11 in der vorliegenden Fassung um eine Bildung des Evangelisten oder seiner „Schule" handelt und daß man die Namen, die aus der Tradition geläufig waren – die Frage, wie die traditionsgeschichtlichen Querverbindungen aussehen oder gelaufen sein mögen, kann hier auf sich beruhen bleiben; ich selbst bin der Meinung, daß es sich nicht um literarisch fixierte Verbindungen handelt, sondern um Verbindungen auf der Ebene der mündlichen Tradition –, für diese neue Geschichte einfach übernommen hat. Für eine historische Urteilsbildung ist diese Geschichte nicht sehr ergiebig. Nur dies könnte man daraus erschließen, daß Jesus Freunde hatte, mit deren Hilfe und Gastfreundschaft er rechnen durfte, und daß es unter diesen Freunden auch Frauen gab.

Wenn die johanneische Tradition solche Geschichten aufnahm und weiterbildete, dann kann daraus ebenfalls entnommen werden,

---

[116] Vgl. zum Folgenden *Blank,* Johannes 1 b, 254–286, dort weitere Lit.; siehe auch oben S. 26 ff.

[117] *Maria:* Joh 11,1.2.19.20.28.31.32.45; 12,3; eine Identifikation dieser Maria mit „Maria Magdalena" (Joh 19,25; 20,11.16.18) findet bei Joh nicht statt. – *Martha:* Joh 11,1.5.19.20.21.24.30.39; 12,2. – *Lazarus:* Joh 11,1.2.5.11.14.43; 12,1.2.9.10.17.

daß in der oder den johanneischen Gemeinden Frauen als gleichberechtigte Mitglieder galten. Jedenfalls lassen sich in den johanneischen Texten keine frauenfeindlichen Tendenzen erkennen.

5.5. Die Heilung einer verkrüppelten Frau am Sabbat, Lk 13, 10–17

Der zum lukanischen Sondergut gehörende Wunderbericht von der „Heilung einer verkrüppelten Frau" ist auch den *„Sabbatkonflikten"*[118] zuzuordnen. Der Aufbau der Geschichte ist durchsichtig: a) V. 10 bringt eine knappe Einleitung; b) V. 11–13 schildert die Krankheit und die Heilung der Frau durch Jesus; c) V. 14–16 bringen ein Streitgespräch wegen der Sabbatverletzung; d) V. 17 bringt die Akklamation (den „Chorschluß"). Nach *Bultmann* wäre die Geschichte eine „weitere Variante des Motivs der Sabbatheilung", die vielleicht aufgrund eines ursprünglich selbständigen Logions komponiert worden wäre; „und zwar ist diese Komposition die ungeschickteste von den drei Sabbatheilungen"[119], weil die Heilung vor der Debatte erfolgt. Aber dies ist kein überzeugendes Gegenargument (vgl. auch Joh 5, 1–16). Damit kommt nur zum Ausdruck, daß die Sabbatheilungen und sonstigen Sabbatkonflikte wohl doch sehr fest mit dem Verhalten des historischen Jesus zusammenhängen; zweitens daß auch im Hinblick auf die eigene Sabbatpraxis die Urgemeinde sich tatsächlich am Verhalten Jesu orientierte und seine „freie" Praxis beibehielt; und schließlich, daß drittens auch die Diskussion um den Sabbat in der Urgemeinde (intern oder mit dem Judentum) weitergeführt wurde. Für Lukas ist die Geschichte auch deshalb wichtig, weil sie *die Heilszuwendung Jesu an ganz Israel* unterstreicht[120].

Daß Jesus am Sabbat in die Synagoge geht und lehrt, gehört zum festen Bestand des lukanischen Jesusbildes (vgl. Lk 4, 16–30). Auch nach Lukas ist das jüdische Volk als die Verkörperung des heilsgeschichtlichen Israel der erste und unmittelbare Adressat der Reichsbotschaft Jesu.

---

[118] Vgl. dazu *E. Lohse*, Art. σάββατον, in: ThWNT VII 1–35; – Billerbeck I 610–630; – *E. Neuhäusler*, Jesu Stellung zum Sabbat, in: BuL 12 (1971) 1–16; *Blank*, Johannes 1b, 16f.
[119] Vgl. *Bultmann*, Geschichte 10.
[120] Zum Anteil der Redaktion vgl. *Jeremias*, Sprache 228–230.

In der Synagoge befindet sich auch eine kranke Frau. Das Krankheitsbild berichtet: die Frau ist schon achtzehn Jahre lang krank und leidet an einer chronischen Verkrümmung der Wirbelsäule; sie kann sich nicht aufrichten[121]. Zwar waren Frauen nicht unbedingt zur regelmäßigen Teilnahme am Synagogengottesdienst verpflichtet; darüber hinaus waren in der Synagoge schon früh die Frauen von den Männern getrennt[122] und konnten am Synagogengottesdienst nicht aktiv mitwirken. Vielleicht hat Lukas die Geschichte deshalb gebracht, weil er an die ihm vertraute Situation der jüdischen Diasporagemeinden denkt mit ihrem relativ hohen weiblichen Anteil (vgl. die entsprechenden Berichte der Apostelgeschichte). Wahrscheinlich geht es ihm auch hier darum, die spätere kirchliche Praxis bereits in der Jesuszeit zu verankern.

Die Beschreibung der Krankheit ist mehr oder weniger stereotyp. Sie zeigt darüber hinaus das typisch lukanische Krankheitsverständnis, wonach jede Krankheit in die Nähe dämonischer Besessenheit rückt (die Frau hatte einen „Siechengeist"). Für Lukas liegen medizinische Krankheit und dämonische Besessenheit nicht so weit auseinander wie für uns. Die Heilung der Frau erfolgt in diesem Fall durch die Auflegung der Hände[123], also durch eine Art Kraftübertragung, in Verbindung mit dem Wort: „Weib, sei frei von deinem Siechtum" (V. 12b). Sie tritt sofort ein; die Frau „richtete sich auf und pries Gott" (V. 13).

Das anschließende Streitgespräch, das sich am „Sabbatkonflikt" entzündet, zeigt zunächst den „jüdischen Anstoß" an der Sabbatverletzung Jesu. Diese liegt nicht primär darin, daß Jesus überhaupt am Sabbat heilte; auch im Judentum brach höchste Not, vor allem Lebensgefahr, das Sabbatgebot[124]. Der Einwand des Synagogenvorste-

---

121 *Grundmann*, Lukas 279 z. St. meint: „Sie hatte eine Verkrümmung, die der Mediziner *Skoliasis hysterica* nennt."
122 Zur synagogalen Praxis vgl. *Schürer*, Geschichte II 527, Anm. 94: „Die Trennung der Geschlechter ist wohl als selbstverständlich vorauszusetzen, wenn sie auch zufällig in keiner der älteren Quellen ausdrücklich erwähnt wird." – *Billerbeck* IV/1, 115–152 (7. Exkurs: Das altjüdische Synagogeninstitut), hier 139; vgl. Tosefta Sukka 4,1 ff; auch II, 807, oben zitiert.
123 Vgl. dazu *G. Theißen*, Urchristliche Wundergeschichten (Gütersloh 1974) 100: „2. Die heilende Berührung … Die Handauflegung ist somit ein therapeutisches Motiv."
124 Billerbeck I 623 oben: „Die eigene Antwort des Pharisäers würde gelautet ha-

hers ist ja an sich nicht unvernünftig, wenn er zum Volk sagt: „Es gibt sechs Tage, an denen gearbeitet werden soll; an ihnen kommt und laßt euch heilen, nicht aber am Sabbattag" (V. 14). Wenn man achtzehn Jahre krank ist, kommt es auf einen Tag mehr oder weniger auch nicht mehr an. Man kommt hier kaum an der Annahme vorbei, daß Jesus durch seine Sabbatheilungen bewußt hat provozieren und demonstrieren wollen. Die Sabbatheilungen gehören zu den „Zeichenhandlungen" Jesu[125]. Was Jesus vor der versammelten Synagogengemeinde demonstrieren will, ist nichts anderes als die Nähe der Gottesherrschaft. Nur in diesem Zusammenhang kann Jesus den Einwand des Synagogenvorstehers als „Heuchelei" bezeichnen und mit einer Gegenfrage abtun (V. 15).

Der eigentliche Skopos steckt freilich in der Aussage: „Diese aber, die ja *eine Tochter Abrahams* ist, die der Satan achtzehn Jahre lang gebunden hatte – seht doch! –, darf sie nicht am Sabbattag von ihrer Fessel erlöst werden?" (V. 16). Dazu ist die Aussage aus der Erzählung vom „Zöllner Zachäus" (Lk 19,1–10) zu vergleichen: „Heute ist diesem Hause Heil widerfahren, weil auch er *ein Sohn Abrahams* ist" (Lk 19,10). In beiden Fällen handelt es sich wohl um lukanische Redaktion[126], die die „heilsgeschichtliche Sicht" des Lukas zum Ausdruck bringt: In der Verkündigung Jesu erfolgt das Heilsangebot an ganz Israel, und davon soll niemand ausgenommen sein, weder diese „gekrümmte Frau" noch der „Oberzöllner" und Römerfreund Zachäus. Man könnte auch an diese Geschichte das Schlußwort Lk 19,10b anfügen: „Denn der Menschensohn ist gekommen, zu suchen und zu retten, was verloren war." Es geht um die demonstrative Zuwendung des Heils an diese Frau, die eben auch als „Tochter Abrahams" zu dem zu rettenden Israel gehört und deren *Gleichberechtigung* durch die volle *Gleichbehandlung durch Jesus* im positiven Sinne herausgestellt wird.

---

ben: Das Heilen am Sabbat ist bei drohender Lebensgefahr erlaubt; aber wo keine Gefahr im Verzuge ist, ist es unbedingt verboten."

[125] vgl. *M. Trautmann*, Zeichenhafte Handlungen Jesu. Ein Beitrag zur Frage nach dem geschichtlichen Jesus (Forschung zur Bibel 37) (Würzburg 1980) 278–318: „Jesus intendierte mit dieser Sabbat-Verletzung sicherlich die Provokation seiner Umgebung, denn sein Tun mußte den Protest der Gesetzestreuen hervorrufen" (315).

[126] Gegen *Jeremias*, Sprache 230 z. St., der hier „Tradition" vermutet.

Die abschließende „Akklamation" oder besser „Reaktion" ist zwiespältig. Die Gegner Jesu müssen sich ob ihrer Engherzigkeit schämen, während das Volk sich über die „herrlichen Taten Jesu" freut (V. 17). Das lukanische Entscheidungsmotiv kommt auch hier wieder zum Vorschein.

Im Hinblick auf unser Thema kann man zusammenfassen: Jesus stellt durch seine Gleichbehandlung der Frau im Sinne der Heilszuwendung auch deren Gleichberechtigung vor Gott und seinem Heilswillen unter Beweis. Die Bezeichnung als „Tochter Abrahams" zeigt, daß auch die Frauen voll zur endzeitlichen Heilsgemeinde gehören sollen.

5.6. Zwei Frauengestalten in lukanischen Gleichnissen:
1) Das Gleichnis von der verlorenen Drachme, Lk 15, 8–10;
2) Das Gleichnis vom bösen Richter und der Witwe, Lk 18, 1–8

Um das lukanische „Frauenbild" abzurunden, dürfen die beiden Gleichnisse nicht übergangen werden. Kommen in ihnen doch zwei Verhaltensweisen zum Vorschein, die als solche vielleicht nicht exklusiv und typisch weiblich sind, die aber den beiden Frauen doch eine besondere Pointe verleihen, nämlich der Erfolg durch unerbittliche Ausdauer, wobei im zweiten Fall noch ein gutes Stück von „impertinenter Penetranz" dazukommt.

5.6.1. Das Gleichnis von der verlorenen Drachme (Lk 15, 8–10) ist das lukanische „weibliche Gegenstück" zum Gleichnis vom „verlorenen Schaf" (Lk 15, 1–7; par. Mt 18, 12–14), mit dem es wohl ein ursprüngliches „Doppelgleichnis" bildet[127]. Für jesuanische Ursprünglichkeit des knappen Gleichnisses spricht vor allem das palästinensische Kolorit der Bildersprache[128]. Es handelt sich um eine „arme Frau", wenn sie an ihrem Kopfschmuck nur zehn Drachmen hatte[129]; und wenn ihr davon eine einzige verlorengegangen war, dann ist auch für sie dieser Verlust entsprechend groß. Man versteht

---

[127] So mit *Jeremias*, Gleichnisse 90.
[128] Zum Verhältnis von „Tradition" und lukanischer Bearbeitung vgl. *Jeremias*, Sprache 248.
[129] *Jeremias*, Gleichnisse 134.

es, wenn sie das ganze Haus oder besser, ihre kleine, fensterlose Hütte durchsucht und ausfegt, bis sie die verlorene Drachme wiedergefunden hat. Entsprechend groß ist dann auch ihre Freude: „Hat sie aber gefunden, ruft sie ihre Freundinnen und Nachbarinnen zusammen und sagt zu ihnen: Freut euch mit mir, denn ich habe meine verlorene Drachme wiedergefunden. Ich sage euch, ebenso wird Freude sein bei den Engeln Gottes über einen einzigen Sünder, der umkehrt" (Lk 15,9–10).

Die Pointe des Gleichnisses ist die Freude über das Wiederfinden des Verlorenen. Nach *J. Jeremias* schließt das Gleichnis „mit einem Satz, der eine Umschreibung des Gottesnamens enthält, weil von Gott Affekte ferngehalten werden sollen"[130]. Dementsprechend wäre Lk 15,10 zu übersetzen: „So sage ich euch, wird sich Gott über einen einzigen Sünder freuen, der umkehrt." Damit aber wäre dieses Gleichnis auch ein Beleg für „weibliche Züge im Gottesbild"[131]. Gerade dieses „weibliche Verhalten" der armen Frau wird zum Vergleich herangezogen für das Verhalten Gottes gegenüber dem umkehrenden Menschen. Dann müßte man das ursprüngliche Doppelgleichnis „Verlorenes Schaf/verlorene Drachme – männliches und weibliches Verhalten" sehr viel deutlicher zusammensehen, wenn man die Frage nach dem Gottesbild des Doppelgleichnisses stellt. Im darauf folgenden Gleichnis vom „Verlorenen Sohn" (Lk 15,11–32) ist dagegen wieder die Bildsprache der männlich-patriarchalischen Verhältnisse vorherrschend.

5.6.2. Bei dem Gleichnis vom bösen Richter und der Witwe (Lk 18,1–8) ist bei der Textanalyse und Interpretation wohl doch stärker als üblich der „dreifache Sitz im Leben" zu berücksichtigen. Deutlich ist einmal die Spannung zwischen der eigentlichen Gleichniserzählung (V. 2–5) und der nachfolgenden Gleichniserklärung oder, richtiger, -anwendung (V. 6–8), die ganz ähnlich wie beim Gleichnis vom „Ungerechten Verwalter" (Lk 16,1–9) in einem doppelten Ansatz erfolgt. Auch was den Gleichnisstoff (das „Sujet") angeht, besteht zwischen diesen beiden Gleichnissen eine gewisse Ähnlichkeit, weil in beiden Fällen „Typen" herangezogen werden, die man kaum als „morali-

---

[130] Ebd. 134f.
[131] Vgl. z. B. *R. Haughton*, Ist Gott ein Mann?, in: Concilium 16 (1980) 264–270.

sche Vorbilder" ansprechen kann. Aber auch die Einleitung V.1 dürfte nicht ursprünglich sein[132]. So ergibt sich als erste Gliederung: a) V.1: die Einleitung; b) V. 2–5: die Gleichnis-Erzählung; c) V. 6 bis 8 a.b die Anwendung.

In V.1 stellt Lukas dem Gleichnis wie auch sonst öfter (vgl. Lk 15,1 f; 18,9) eine Einleitung voran, die zugleich das Vorverständnis auf den eigentlichen Inhalt hinlenken soll: „Er sagte ihnen auch im Gleichnis, daß sie allezeit beten und nicht müde werden sollen." Diese Mahnung zum unablässigen Beten (vgl. 1 Thess 5,17) geht doch wohl insofern am Kern der Erzählung vorbei, als es hier eher um eine permanente Grundeinstellung geht, während es der Erzählung auf die Beharrlichkeit in einem ganz bestimmten, gezielten Anliegen ankommen dürfte.

Die Gleichniserzählung V. 2–5 nimmt ihren „Stoff", ähnlich wie das Gleichnis vom „Ungerechten Verwalter" (Lk 16,1–9), ganz aus dem „vollen Menschenleben", das immer interessante Aspekte bietet, wenn man es recht zu packen weiß[133]. An ihrer jesuanischen Herkunft ist um so weniger zu zweifeln, als sie keine „moralisierenden Absichten" erkennen läßt und der nachfolgenden Applikation eher gewisse Schwierigkeiten gemacht hat[134].

Die Geschichte handelt von einem „ungerechten Richter", „ohne Gottesfurcht und Achtung vor den Menschen", und einer armen Witwe, die in einer Streitsache, wahrscheinlich in einer vermögensrechtlichen Angelegenheit, endlich zu ihrem Recht kommen will. Die Charakteristik des Richters ist für den (alten und modernen)

---

[132] Zum Ganzen vgl. *Jeremias*, Gleichnisse 153–156, der in diesem Fall Lk 16,1–8 als ursprüngliche Einheit versteht; siehe auch *ders.*, Sprache 271; dagegen *Bultmann*, Geschichte 189: „Die Anwendung V. 6–8 ist sicher sekundär (vgl. Jülicher)."

[133] Vgl. dazu die von *Jeremias*, Gleichnisse 154, Anm. 1 mitgeteilte Geschichte von den Praktiken am Gerichtshof von Nisibis (Mesopotamien). – Die bekannteste Neubearbeitung des Stoffes ist das Stück „Der kaukasische Kreidekreis" von *B. Brecht* mit der Figur des „Azdak", vgl. *Brecht*, Werkausgabe (Frankfurt a. M. 1967) 5, 1999–2105.

[134] Gegen *E. Linnemann*, Gleichnisse Jesu (Göttingen ²1962) 127, die annimmt, wir hätten es „mit einem Wort des erhöhten Herrn, einem Prophetenwort also" zu tun, „das im Namen und im Geiste Jesu zur Gemeinde der Glaubenden gesprochen wurde". Dafür gibt es in der Geschichte selbst nicht den geringsten Anhaltspunkt; erst die sekundären Zusätze verweisen darauf, die man freilich nicht zum Angelpunkt der Interpretation machen darf.

Orient nicht ungewöhnlich (vgl. Anm. 133); man rechnet damit, daß Bestechungen sowohl den Gang der Verhandlungen beschleunigen als auch das Urteil günstig beeinflussen können. Nicht von ungefähr haben bereits die alttestamentlichen Propheten die Richter vor Bestechlichkeit gewarnt, vgl. Jes 1,23: „Deine Fürsten sind Abtrünnige und Diebsgenossen. Sie alle lieben Bestechung und jagen Geschenken nach. Der Waise schaffen sie kein Recht, und die Sache der Witwe lassen sie nicht vor sich kommen" (vgl. ferner Am 5,7.10–13; Jes 5,7.23; Jer 5,28; Zef 3,3 u. ö.). „Die hier gezeichnete Gestalt des Richters stellt nicht einen Ausnahmefall, sondern den Normaltyp des orientalischen Richters dar."[135] Auch die Witwe erscheint in der „typischen Rolle" (vgl. oben S. 18 f) der armen, recht- und schutzlosen Frau. Als solche erscheint sie vor dem Richter und bittet um Rechtshilfe: „Schaffe mir Recht gegen meinen Widersacher" (V. 3). Aber zunächst nimmt der Richter die Frau trotz ihres wiederholten Kommens und eindringlichen Bittens einfach nicht zur Kenntnis; wahrscheinlich, weil sie nicht in der Lage ist, mit Geld oder Geschenken auf sich aufmerksam zu machen. Doch mit der Zeit wird sie ihm durch ihre Beharrlichkeit lästig. So überlegt er sich: „Wenn es mir auch im Grunde egal ist, was Gott oder die Menschen über meine Einstellung und mein Verhalten denken, aber diese Frau geht mir doch allmählich auf die Nerven; darum will ich ihr zu ihrem Recht verhelfen, sonst macht sie mir am Ende noch einen Skandal." „Nicht die Furcht vor einem Wutausbruch der Frau, sondern ihre Beharrlichkeit bringt ihn zum Nachgeben. Er sieht die ewige Quengelei und will seine Ruhe haben."[136]

Damit ist die Geschichte zu Ende. Sie hat manche Ähnlichkeit mit der vom „bittenden Freund" (Lk 11,5–8) und stellt wohl das „weibliche Gegenstück" zu dieser dar. Die Witwe hat nichts anderes einzusetzen als ihr Rechtsgefühl und ihre zähe Beharrlichkeit, mit der sie immer wieder vor dem Richter erscheint und ihre Sache vorbringt; dabei mag sie wohl auch immer zudringlicher und ausfälliger geworden sein und mit kräftigen Schimpfwörtern nicht gespart haben. Jedenfalls machte sie Eindruck auf diesen abgebrühten Kerl, so daß er

---

[135] *Schmid*, Lukas 279.
[136] *Jeremias*, Gleichnisse 153 f; dort auch 271 die Anhaltspunkte für unsere Paraphrase.

einen handfesten Krach befürchten mußte. So gab er, keineswegs aus ehrenwerten Gründen, schließlich nach. Er half der Frau zu ihrem Recht. Die Pointe liegt in einem *Schluß a minori ad maius:* Wenn schon ein solcher Mensch sich dem beharrlichen Insistieren einer Witwe nicht versagt, um wieviel mehr wird dann Gott auf das beharrliche Bitten seiner Kinder hören und antworten. Ursprünglich war das Gleichnis also eine Parabel, die zum beharrlichen Bittgebet aufmuntern sollte; man sollte beim Beten gegenüber Gott so aufdringlich unverdrossen sein wie diese Witwe. Wenn schon böse Menschen, wie dieser Richter da, dem letzten Endes nicht mehr widerstehen können, um wieviel weniger Gott, der seine Geschöpfe liebt. Die ursprünglichen Adressaten des Gleichnisses dürften die Jünger Jesu gewesen sein.

In diese Richtung geht dann auch die erste Erklärung V. 6–7, die als ein „Herrenwort" (εἶπεν δὲ ὁ κύριος, vgl. Lk 16,8) eingeführt wird: „Hört, was der ungerechte Richter sagt! Sollte dann Gott nicht erst recht seinen Auserwählten Recht schaffen, die Tag und Nacht zu ihm rufen, und wird er sie vielleicht warten lassen?"[137] Damit ist freilich noch nicht gesagt, daß diese Erklärung auf Jesus selbst zurückgeht. Vielmehr wird man sich die Sache eher so zu denken haben, daß die Erzählung für sich genommen zu Mißverständnissen Anlaß geben konnte, ähnlich wie beim Gleichnis vom „Ungerechten Verwalter". Das „Herrenwort" beseitigt als erste Interpretationshilfe diese Schwierigkeiten und gibt damit der Gemeinde eine vertretbare Interpretation. Die Auslegung hat in diesem Fall den Skopos wohl richtig getroffen.

Dem folgt als zweiter Zusatz die Aussage: „Ich sage euch: Er (Gott) wird ihnen Recht verschaffen in Bälde", V. 8a. Hier geht es nicht mehr um die schnelle Gebetserhörung, sondern um die endgültige Befreiung aus der gegenwärtigen, endzeitlichen Drangsal. Das

---

[137] Der Zusatz καὶ μακροθυμεῖ ἐπ' αὐτοῖς, ist schwierig zu übersetzen. Wörtlich: „Und er hat Geduld mit ihnen", so *Jeremias*, Gleichnisse 154; vgl. die Diskussion daselbst. Unmöglich scheint mir die Übersetzung von *R. Pesch*, Synoptisches Arbeitsbuch 3/Lukas: „und wird großmütig sein gegen sie?" Es scheint nur zwei sinnvolle Möglichkeiten zu geben: a) man faßt das καὶ μακροθυμεῖ als einen Teil der Frage auf, und übersetzt dann: „wird er sie – die Auserwählten – vielleicht warten lassen?", wird er nicht vielmehr sofort helfen?, oder b) man faßt es adversativ auf: „auch wenn er sie warten läßt", auch wenn er seine Hilfe verzögert. Wir entscheiden uns aus Kontextgründen für die Auffassung a).

„Recht schaffen", das in der Parabel zur Bildhälfte gehört, wird jetzt „realistisch" verstanden im Hinblick auf das nahe bevorstehende Endgericht. Hier, auf dieser Ebene, kann man mit *J. Jeremias* die Auffassung vertreten, daß dies „im Blick auf die Notzeit" gesagt ist: „Verjagtwerden, Beleidigungen, Denunziationen, Verhöre, Martyrien, letzte Anfechtungen des Glaubens, wenn Satan sich offenbart[138]". Aber das ist wohl schon die Auslegung der nachösterlichen Gemeinde („Zweiter Sitz im Leben"), jedenfalls nicht der ursprüngliche Sinn des Gleichnisses. Hier geht es um die Bewältigung der „Naherwartung"[139].

Auch die abschließende Sentenz V. 8b: „Aber wird der Menschensohn, wenn er kommt, auf der Erde den Glauben finden?", macht einen alles andere als ursprünglichen Eindruck. Lukas ist am Vorhandensein oder Nichtvorhandensein der πίστις, des Glaubens, offensichtlich interessiert (vgl. Lk 7,9.50; 8,25.48; 17,5.6.19; 18,8.42; 22,32). Ich neige dazu, die abschließende Frage als *lukanische Bildung* aufzufassen; Lukas macht sich, wohl im Hinblick auf Erfahrungen seiner eigenen Zeit, darüber Gedanken, ob der Menschensohn bei seiner Parusie die πίστις in ausreichendem Maße antreffen wird; denn diese ist ja die schlechthinnige Heilsbedingung.

Es scheint kein Zweifel, daß in der ursprünglichen Parabel die arme, hilflose, allein auf sich gestellte Witwe als nachahmenswertes „Vorbild" dargestellt werden soll. So unbeirrbar und beharrlich wie sie soll sich der Beter gegenüber seinem Gott verhalten. Jesus empfiehlt sie als Vorbild allen, auch den Männern.

6. Aus der Johannesüberlieferung

Zu besprechen sind im Folgenden die Erzählungen „Jesus und die Samariterin am Jakobsbrunnen" (Joh 4,1–26.27–42) und „Jesus und die Ehebrecherin" (Joh 7,53 – 8,11). Die johanneische Variante der „Salbung in Betanien" (Joh 12,1–8) wurde schon früher besprochen

---

[138] *Jeremias,* Gleichnisse 156.
[139] Vgl. dazu *E. Gräßer,* Das Problem der Parusieverzögerung in den synoptischen Evangelien und in der Apostelgeschichte (Berlin ³1977) 36f.

(vgl. S. 26 ff), ebenso wurde zur „Auferweckung des Lazarus" schon das wichtigste gesagt. Diese beiden „Frauengeschichten" bleiben also hier außer Betracht. In der heutigen „feministischen" Betrachtungsweise haben diese beiden Texte einen verhältnismäßig hohen Stellenwert, was die Frage nach der neuen Einstellung Jesu zur Frau betrifft. Dies gilt auf jeden Fall für die Geschichte „Jesus und die Ehebrecherin" auch historisch mit vollem Recht, während sich bei der „Samariterin" kaum alle Zweifel beseitigen lassen[140]. Hierbei mag sich zeigen, daß nicht nur die Frage nach der traditionsgeschichtlichen Genese unserer Texte von Bedeutung ist, sondern auch deren Rezeptions- und Wirkungsgeschichte, also die Frage: In welchen Geschichten haben sich bis heute Frauen im Evangelium am besten verstanden gefühlt, womit konnten sie sich am besten identifizieren? In welcher Weise hat die Gestalt Jesu am meisten auf Frauen eingewirkt? Wenn man diese Frage stellt, dann gewinnen neben den lukanischen Frauengeschichten diese zwei aus dem Johannesevangelium einen sehr beachtlichen Stellenwert.

6.1. Jesus und die Samariterin am Jakobsbrunnen, Joh 4, 1–26.(27–42)[141]

Joh 4, 1–42 berichtet ausführlich von einem Aufenthalt Jesu in Samaria, näherhin in einem Ort namens Sychar, nahe bei dem Jakobsbrunnen. Dort trifft Jesus eine samaritanische Frau. Es kommt zu einem Gespräch über so zentrale religiöse Fragen wie die Heilsfrage, symbolisiert in der Vorstellung vom „lebendigen Wasser", die rechte Gottesverehrung und den Messias. Jesus bleibt zwei Tage an dem Ort und findet bei den Samaritern Glauben.

Die Erzählung ist sowohl literarisch wie in ihrer theologischen Gedankenführung hervorragend aufgebaut, aus einem Guß. Sie gliedert sich folgen-

---

[140] Vgl. *Wolff,* Jesus der Mann 94 ff; *L. Swidler,* Jesu Begegnung mit Frauen, in: *Moltmann-Wendel,* Menschenrechte 141 ff.
[141] Dieser Abschnitt ist eine gekürzte Zusammenfassung der Exegese in *Blank,* Johannes 1 a, 280–312; dazu ferner die Kommentare zum Johannesevangelium, *R. Bultmann,* Das Johannesevangelium (KEK) (Göttingen ¹¹1950); *R. Schnakkenburg,* Das Johannesevangelium, 3 Bde. (HThK IV/1–3) (Freiburg – Basel – Wien) I (1965); II (1971); III (1975); *H. Strathmann,* Das Evangelium nach Johannes (NTD 4) (Göttingen 1954); *M. J. Lagrange,* Évangile selon Saint Jean (Paris ⁷1948).

dermaßen: a) Jesus am Jakobsbrunnen, V. 1–6; b) Die Samariterin; das „lebendige Wasser", V. 7–15; c) Der wahre Gottesdienst und der Messias, V. 16–26; d) Jesu Speise; die bevorstehende „Missions"ernte, V. 27–38; e) Der Missionserfolg in Samaria, V. 39–40.

Für unsere Absicht ist vor allem der Abschnitt V. 1–26 von Wichtigkeit; der zweite Teil, V. 27–42, kann weitgehend auf sich beruhen bleiben.

Die Erzählung verarbeitet eine Reihe von geographischen, historischen und religionsgeschichtlichen Problemen, auf die hier im einzelnen nicht näher eingegangen werden kann[142].

Samaria bezeichnet hier die Landschaft Samaria, die weitgehend identisch ist mit dem Kernland des ehemaligen „Nordreiches Israel" (930–721 v. Chr.), zur Jesuszeit charakterisiert durch ihre Lage zwischen Judäa im Süden und Galiläa im Norden. – *Die Stadt Sychar* ist wohl nicht, wie der Kirchenvater Hieronymus gemeint hat, mit dem alten *Sichem* identisch, das von Johannes Hyrkanos 128 v. Chr. endgültig zerstört worden war und in dessen Nähe später Vespasian die Stadt *Flavia Neapolis,* das heutige *Nablus,* errichten ließ (72 n. Chr.), sondern mit dem nicht weit davon entfernten Ort *Askar.* Der „Jakobsbrunnen" liegt davon etwa 1,5 km entfernt. Sychar liegt in dem Paß zwischen dem Berg Ebal und dem Berg Garizim.

Die Samaritaner (die ältere jüdische Bezeichnung ist *Sichemiten*) haben seit der Zerstörung des Nordreiches durch die Assyrer (721 v. Chr.) eine eigenständige Entwicklung genommen. Was *die religiösen Differenzen zwischen Samaritanern und Juden* betrifft, so haben hier verschiedene Gründe und Motive für ihre Entstehung mitgespielt, vor allem in der nachexilischen Entwicklung. Der legitime Kultort der Samaritaner ist, und zwar bis heute, der Berg Garizim. Als Heilige Schrift gilt ihnen nur der Pentateuch; die Propheten und die übrigen Schriften lehnen sie ab.

Die Stellungnahme der jüdischen Rabbinen gegenüber den Samaritanern waren unterschiedlich; doch führte der Synkretismus der Samaritaner und ihre relative Aufgeschlossenheit gegenüber dem Hellenismus bei den orthodoxen Juden deutlich zu einer negativen Einstellung, vgl. Sir 50,25 f:
„Gegen zwei Völker empfindet meine Seele Ekel,
und das dritte ist kein Volk:
Gegen die Bewohner von Seïr und Philistäa
und das törichte (= gottlose) Volk, das in Sichem wohnt."[143]

Über *die Einstellung Jesu zu den Samaritanern*[144] ist nach den vorliegenden neutestamentlichen Zeugnissen eine einheitliche Linie nicht auszumachen. Die Synoptiker wissen nichts von einem längeren Aufenthalt Jesu in Samaria und erst recht nichts von einer Verkündigungstätigkeit daselbst. Dagegen

---

[142] Ausführliche Besprechung mit Belegen bei *Blank,* Johannes 1 a, 280 ff.
[143] Zum Gesamtproblem des Verhältnisses von Juden und Samaritern vgl. Billerbeck I 538–560; ferner *H. G. Kippenberg – G. A. Wewers,* Textbuch zur neutestamentlichen Zeitgeschichte (NTD – Ergänzungsreihe 8) (Göttingen 1979) 89–106.
[144] Vgl. *Blank,* Johannes 1 a, 282.

erfahren wir *in der Apostelgeschichte,* daß es im Zusammenhang mit der ersten Verfolgung der Jerusalemer Urgemeinde, die man wohl richtiger als eine Verfolgung der hellenistischen Gemeindeglieder bezeichnen muß, zu einer Verkündigungstätigkeit in Samaria kam; namentlich erwähnt wird der Hellenist Philippus (vgl. Apg 8,1–25).

Unsere Geschichte muß auf dem geschilderten Hintergrund verstanden werden. An ihrer Historizität in ihrer vorliegenden Fassung sind jedoch Zweifel erlaubt. Selbst wenn man eine johanneische Sonderüberlieferung mit einem „historischen Kern" annehmen mag – was nicht grundsätzlich ausgeschlossen werden kann; auch die Situation im Ganzen könnte durchaus in das überlieferte Bild des historischen Jesus passen –, so hat demgegenüber doch die theologische Gestaltung der Geschichte durch den Evangelisten bei weitem das Übergewicht.

Die Exposition der Geschichte (V. 1–6). Jesus verläßt Judäa und zieht nach Galiläa. Das Fortgehen Jesu wird durch einen möglichen Konflikt zwischen Jesus und den Pharisäern motiviert. Der kürzeste und wohl auch günstigste Weg von Judäa nach Galiläa war der Weg mitten durch Samaria hindurch; als Alternativen standen der Weg durch die Jordansenke oder an der Küste entlang offen, die freilich länger und beschwerlicher waren. Dieser Weg führt auch heute noch an Sichem (Nablus) bzw. Sychar, beide in der Talsohle zwischen dem Ebal und dem Garizim gelegen, vorbei. Auf dieser Wanderung also kommt Jesus nach Sychar. Dort befindet sich auch der „Jakobsbrunnen". Das Alte Testament kennt diese Bezeichnung noch nicht; sie beruht offenbar auf einer Lokaltradition, die bei dem reichen Vorkommen von Quellwasser in dieser Gegend naheliegend war und die Jakobsüberlieferungen auch mit der Landschaft um Sichem verknüpft sind[145]. Die ganze Szene zielt darauf hin, das nachfolgende Gespräch auch stimmungsmäßig gut vorzubereiten.

Die Samariterin. Das lebendige Wasser (V. 7–15). Während Jesus in der Mittagshitze sich am Brunnenrand niedergelassen hat, kommt eine Samariterin, um Wasser zu schöpfen. Dies nimmt Jesus zum Anlaß, um die Frau zu bitten: „Gib mir zu trinken" (V. 7). V. 8 ist eine erläuternde Zwischenbemerkung, um darauf hinzuweisen, daß Jesus mit der Frau allein war. Die Jünger waren inzwischen fortgegangen, um in der Stadt Lebensmittel einzukaufen; sie sind bei dem ganzen Gespräch als abwesend zu denken.

---

[145] „Solche Brunnen, die man gebaut hat, um eine tiefer liegende Quelle zu fassen, sind in Palästina nicht selten" (*Lagrange,* Saint Jean 104).

Die Frau empfindet die Bitte Jesu als ganz und gar außergewöhnlich und überraschend. Fällt es ohnehin schon aus dem Rahmen, daß ein Jude überhaupt einen Samariter um etwas anspricht oder bittet, so erst recht, *wenn ein jüdischer Mann gegenüber einer samaritanischen Frau das tut.* Die Zwischenbemerkung: Juden verkehren normalerweise nicht mit Samaritanern, weist auf diesen Umstand ausdrücklich hin. Der freie Umgang mit einer Frau in der Öffentlichkeit war im allgemeinen verpönt; er war es erst recht bei den jüdischen Rabbinen[146]. Von Rabbi Elieser (um 90 n. Chr.) ist der Spruch überliefert: „Wer das Brot eines Samariters ißt, ist wie einer, der Schweinefleisch ißt"; das heißt, er ist total unrein[147]. Ebenso verstieß das Gespräch zwischen einem Rabbi und einer Frau in der Öffentlichkeit gegen die herrschende Sitte. Auf jeden Fall ist mit der Bitte Jesu das Gespräch in Gang gekommen, und es zeigt sich, daß die Bitte nur der erste Anlaß dazu war und von vornherein in eine andere Richtung zielte.

Jesu Antwort auf die erstaunte Frage der Frau führt nun sehr schnell über den unmittelbaren Anlaß hinaus und enthüllt diesen als Vorwand, wenn Jesus in anspielungsreicher und vieldeutiger Weise sagt: „Wenn du die Gabe Gottes kenntest und wer es ist, der zu dir sagt: Gib mir zu trinken, so hättest du ihn wohl gebeten, und er gäbe dir lebendiges Wasser." Es geht also gar nicht um das Trinkwasser, sondern um die „Gabe Gottes", und damit ist in unserem Zusammenhang die Offenbarung und was sie vermittelt, nämlich das Endheil, das „ewige Leben" gemeint, die für den Menschen ganz und gar den Charakter der „Gabe Gottes" besitzen. Offenbarung und Heil sind im johanneischen Verständnis ihrem ganzen Wesen nach „göttliche Gabe". Damit ist nicht nur gesagt, daß der Mensch sich das Heil nicht selber geben kann, sondern es als Gabe Gottes erbitten und empfangen muß; vielmehr gibt es dieser „Gabe" gegenüber nur das „Empfangen" als die rechte menschliche Haltung.

Zur Gabe gehört freilich unbedingt auch der Geber, auf den in V. 10 ebenfalls angespielt wird. So ergibt sich eine merkwürdig paradoxe Situation. Vordergründig bittet Jesus in brütender Mittagshitze die Samariterin um einen Schluck Wasser (und zeigt damit an, wie

---

146 Vgl. dazu oben S. 53.
147 *Kippenberg – Wevers,* Textbuch 106; Billerbeck I 541 f.

der Mensch sich dem „Geber" gegenüber verhalten sollte), in Wahrheit ist er es aber, der über die Gabe Gottes verfügt und sie dem Menschen mitteilen könnte, wenn dieser ihn darum bäte. Die „Gabe Gottes" aber, die Jesus anzubieten hat, wird näher umschrieben mit dem Ausdruck *„Lebendiges Wasser (Lebenswasser)":* „Er würde dir wohl lebendiges Wasser geben." Damit ist das symbolische Stichwort gefallen, um das sich in den folgenden Versen alles dreht und mit dessen Mehrdeutigkeit im Folgenden nun bewußt gespielt wird.

Lebendiges Wasser[148]. Wasser ist, zumal im Orient und überhaupt in wasserarmen Gegenden, vor allem in der Wüste, das Lebenselement schlechthin; nur dort, wo es gutes und klares Wasser gibt, ist auch Leben möglich für Pflanzen, Tiere und Menschen. So ist es nicht verwunderlich, wenn sich im Bild des Wassers *das Leben* einfachhin symbolisiert und wenn im Durst der Lebens-Durst des Menschen, sein intensivstes Lebensverlangen, aufscheint. Dabei hat man nicht nur an das sinnliche Element H_2O zu denken, sondern an die gesamten belebenden und erquickenden Wirkungen, die vom Wasser auf die menschliche Seele, auf das gesamte Lebensgefühl ausgehen. So verwundert es auch nicht, daß sowohl in der alttestamentlichen Psalmensprache (z. B. Ps 42) das „Wasser" zum Sinnbild für „Heil" wird; ebenso in der religiösen Sprache der Umwelt des Johannesevangeliums.

Jesus hatte zu der Frau vom „lebendigen Wasser" gesprochen, das er zu geben vermag. Das hatte die Frau richtig aus der Aussage Jesu herausgehört. Was sie jedoch nicht begriffen hatte, ist der symbolische Sinn der Rede Jesu. So kommt es zu einem „johanneischen Mißverständnis". Die Frau bezieht den Ausdruck „lebendiges Wasser" unmittelbar auf den Brunnen und meint: „Du hast kein Schöpfgefäß und der Brunnen ist tief; wo willst du lebendiges Wasser hernehmen?" Ohne ein Schöpfgefäß Wasser schöpfen zu wollen, das klingt doch recht mysteriös und wunderbar; so daß die Frau die halb skeptische, halb neugierige Frage stellt – mit der sie im Grunde, ohne das zu ahnen, tatsächlich an die Wahrheit rührt: „Bist du vielleicht größer als unser Vater Jakob, der uns den Brunnen gab? Er selbst hat daraus getrunken und seine Söhne und sein Vieh" (V. 12). Natürlich ist es die Überzeugung des Johannes, daß Jesus als der „endzeitliche Offenbarer" auch „größer" ist als der Stammvater Jakob und seine Söhne, die Väter der „zwölf Stämme Israels", ja grö-

---

[148] Zur Symbolik „Lebendiges Wasser" vgl. *Blank,* Johannes I a, 288 f; *Bultmann,* Johannes 133–136; *Schnackenburg,* Johannes I 462 ff.

ßer als selbst Abraham (vgl. 8, 56–58). Die Jesusoffenbarung geht in der Tat über alle diese Traditionen hinaus.

Das „Mißverständnis" gibt Anlaß, das Symbol des „lebendigen Wassers" noch zu verdeutlichen (V. 13 b–14). Es ist ein in jeder Hinsicht „wunderbares Wasser", das bei dem, der davon trinkt, allen Durst endgültig stillt; er wird überhaupt nicht mehr dürsten. Die Gabe Gottes, um die es hier geht, ist so beschaffen, daß sie dem Menschen eine endgültige Befriedigung verschafft, so daß sein Lebensdurst ein für allemal gestillt ist. Die Aussage wird noch dadurch bekräftigt, daß es heißt: Dieses „Wasser, das ich ihm gebe, wird in ihm zu einer Quelle, deren Wasser fortquillt zum ewigen Leben". Die johanneische Sprache verdeutlicht das Symbol vom „lebendigen Wasser" durch den Hinweis auf das ewige Leben, das heißt auf den endzeitlichen Charakter der Gabe Jesu. Die „Gabe Jesu" ist das ewige Leben, und dieses ist dadurch gekennzeichnet, daß es eine völlig andere, neue „Lebensqualität" besitzt als das dem Tod verfallene irdisch-kosmische Leben. Jesus und die Samariterin denken und sprechen von zwei verschiedenen Ebenen her. Jesus ist als Offenbarer der Repräsentant der „göttlichen Welt" und ihrer Heilsgabe, während die Samariterin „von unten", vom irdisch-menschlichen Erfahrungshorizont her, denkt und redet. Die „Mißverständnisse" zeigen diese Verschiedenheit an. Von der irdisch-menschlichen Erfahrung her gedacht sind die Bilder vom „Lebenswasser", vom „Jungbrunnen", von einem Wasser, das dem Menschen unendlich zur Verfügung steht oder ihm gar ein neues „Lebensgefühl" vermittelt, nichts anderes als Märchen, mythische Wunschbilder, Illusionen, allenfalls Hoffnungsbilder für ein geglücktes Leben. Der Mensch spürt allerdings, daß diese Wunschbilder sich niemals realisieren werden. Demgegenüber sagt das Johannesevangelium, daß allein die Jesusoffenbarung das „ewige Leben" vermittelt, und zwar schon hier und jetzt. Im Glauben kann der Mensch schon jetzt Anteil an der göttlichen Lebensfülle gewinnen. Jesus schenkt dem Menschen das neue Leben; er gibt es ihm wirklich zu eigen, so daß es im Menschen selbst zu einer „Quelle wird, die fortsprudelt ins ewige Leben". Damit soll wohl doch mehr gesagt sein, als daß das neue Leben ewig dauert und keinen Tod mehr zu fürchten braucht. Vielmehr wird hier auch gesagt, daß dieses neue Leben im Menschen zu einer produktiven und dynamischen Kraft wird, die ihr schöpferisches Eigenleben entfaltet, so daß auf diese Weise der Mensch auch zu einer völlig neuen Lebenseinstellung und Lebenspraxis kommt. Das „ewige Leben" erschließt die letzte Sinntiefe des menschlichen Lebens überhaupt.

Wie das Mißverständnis V. 15 anzeigt, hat die Frau diese Dimension der Aussagen Jesu noch keineswegs begriffen. Zwar bittet sie: „Herr, gib mir dieses Wasser", und zeigt darin, daß sie im Innersten durch die seltsamen Worte des fremden Mannes angerührt ist; solch ein Wasser, das alle Menschenmühsal mit einem Schlag beendet, das könnte man brauchen! Dann wäre man auch die lästige Arbeit des täglichen Ganges zum Brunnen, des Wasserschöpfens und Wassertragens endlich los. Was wünschen wir Menschen uns denn nicht sehnlicher als so ein Wundermittel, das uns vor aller Daseinslast befreit?

Der wahre Gottesdienst und der Messias (V. 16–26). Das Gespräch zwischen Jesus und der Samariterin hatte zuletzt wieder zu einem Mißverständnis geführt. Die Frau hatte die Rede vom „lebendigen Wasser", das allen Durst stillt und ewiges Leben vermittelt, noch im Sinne der Illusion eines „Schlaraffenlandes" verstanden, als Beendigung der Mühsal menschlicher Lebensfristung. Sie hatte nicht begriffen, daß es um die neue eschatologische Existenz des Menschen ging, um die radikal neue, von allem Irdischen verschiedene Lebensqualität, *die in dem neuen, durch Jesus eröffneten Gottesverhältnis gründet* und letztlich auch eine neue Form der Gottesverehrung hervorruft. Im Fortgang des Gesprächs geht Jesus auf das Mißverständnis gar nicht näher ein; es wird sich später von selbst auflösen. Vielmehr wendet er sich, scheinbar ganz unmotiviert, mit einer neuen Anrede an die Frau, sie möge ihren Mann holen und herbringen (V. 16). Darauf antwortet die Frau: Ich habe keinen Mann (V. 17), eine Antwort, die, wie sich bald herausstellt, nur teilweise richtig ist. Jesus gibt darauf die enthüllende Antwort: Du hast recht, wenn du sagst, daß du keinen Mann hast. Denn fünf Männer hast du gehabt, und der, den du jetzt hast, ist nicht dein richtiger Mann (V. 18). Das bedeutet zunächst: Jesus weiß, ohne daß ihm jemand etwas gesagt hat, über die Verhältnisse dieser Frau Bescheid. Das gehört nach Johannes zu seinem Wissen als Offenbarer, der weiß, wie es um den Menschen steht, und der kein fremdes Zeugnis nötig hat (vgl. 2,24f).

Die präzise Bedeutung der V. 16–18 ist bei den Exegeten umstritten. Spricht Jesus vom „problematischen Privatleben der Frau", die somit als eine „Frau mit Vergangenheit" erscheint, wobei denn freilich bemerkenswert ist, daß Jesus davon kein Aufhebens macht und darauf auch gar nicht näher eingeht, es vielmehr bei der bloßen Feststellung bewenden läßt, oder haben die Verse einen symbolischen, typologischen Sinn? Während *Bultmann* und *Schnackenburg* mehr für die erste Meinung plädieren[149], optiert *H. Strathmann* in seinem Kommentar für die zweite. Er meint, die Frau sei „überhaupt keine Gestalt aus Fleisch und Blut. Sie ist ein Typus, aber nicht der eines jammervoll verkommenen Weibes, das in einem ‚Maximum von ehelicher Verwirrung und Verirrung' lebt, sondern ein Symbol des Samaritertums, eine Personifikation der samaritanischen Gemeinde"[150].

Geht man davon aus, daß nach jüdischer Auffassung eine Frau sich nur zweimal, höchstens dreimal verheiraten sollte[151] und daß es darüber hinaus für eine Frau äußerst schwierig war, eine Ehe aufzulösen, weil die Scheidung nur vom Manne eingeleitet werden konnte, dann würde hier in der Tat eine auch im jüdischen Sinne höchst fragwürdige Person vorgeführt. Und Jesus, der mit der Frau spricht, erscheint dann als ein Mann, der im Vergleich zu den herrschenden jüdischen Vorurteilen seiner Zeit unglaublich vorurteilsfrei und souverän agiert[152]. Er gibt sich nicht einmal als Sittenprediger und Moralist, sondern zielt auf eine ganz andere Ebene. Hier könnte man im Anschluß an *Bultmann* und *Schnackenburg* sagen: Die eigentliche Problematik liegt für den johanneischen Jesus, der darin durchaus mit dem „historischen Jesus" der Synoptiker übereinstimmt, nicht vordergründig auf der moralischen Ebene. Sie liegt tiefer, nämlich im religiösen Bereich, wo es um Glauben und Unglauben geht. Die entscheidende Heilung des Menschen muß also dort ansetzen, wo „das Ganze" des Menschen ins Spiel kommt. – Andererseits braucht man deshalb der Geschichte eine tiefere symbolische Bedeutung nicht abzusprechen[153], die dann auf der religiös-kultischen Ebene läge.

Es ist nur folgerichtig, wenn eine Frau, von solch wunderbarem

---

[149] *Bultmann,* Johannes 138; *Schnackenburg,* Johannes I 467 ff.
[150] *Strathmann,* Johannes 84.
[151] Billerbeck II 437.
[152] Hier liegt wohl der entscheidende Eindruck, der *H. Wolff,* Jesus der Mann (vgl. 80–101), dazu veranlaßte, Jesus als den „nicht animosen Mann" zu bezeichnen, der „bewußt" gelebt hat.
[153] Vgl. *Blank,* Johannes 1 a, 295.

Wissen Jesu unmittelbar betroffen, in Jesus einen „Propheten" erblickt. Prophet bedeutet in diesem Fall einen Mann, der über eine übernatürliche Erkenntnis verfügt, die ihm Einblick in verborgene Tatbestände ermöglicht, sei es, daß er über die Zukunft Bescheid weiß, sei es, über allerpersönlichste Geheimnisse des Menschen. Zugleich ist mit dem Begriff des „Propheten" eine Richtung angedeutet, in diesem Propheten den „endzeitlichen Propheten wie Mose" zu sehen, den die Samaritaner erwartet haben[154]. Von diesem Propheten heißt es im Samaritanischen Pentateuch zu Ex 20,21 b:

„Einen Propheten wie dich will ich ihnen aus ihren Brüdern erwecken und meine Worte in seinen Mund geben. Und er wird ihnen alles sagen, was ich ihm befehlen werde. Und wer auf seine Worte nicht hören wird, die er in meinem Namen sprechen wird, von dem will ich Rechenschaft fordern."[155]

Von diesem Propheten erwartete man wohl auch die endgültige Regelung kultischer Streitfragen, so daß es nicht verwunderlich ist, wenn die Samariterin auch gleich mit dem zentralen Streitpunkt zwischen Juden und Samaritanern herausrückt. Die Samaritaner beten aufgrund der von den Vätern überkommenen Sitte JHWH-Gott auf dem Berg Garizim an, auch nachdem der frühere Tempel zerstört worden war. Sie haben dort ihren Kultort, während die Juden behaupten, in Jerusalem sei der richtige Kultort; dort „müsse man anbeten", wie es dogmatisch-polemisch formuliert wird. In der Frage nach dem „richtigen Kultort" meldet sich die Frage nach der „wahren Religion" zu Wort (V. 20); und genau auf diese Kernfrage hat Jesus auch eine Antwort parat (V. 21–24).

Jesus verweist V. 21 darauf, daß eine Zeit kommen wird – der Begriff „Stunde" bedeutet in unserem Kontext den neuen Zeitpunkt, der zugleich eine neue Epoche einleiten wird, näherhin die Endzeit –, in der man weder auf dem Garizim noch in Jerusalem den Vater anbeten wird. In dieser Zeit wird also die Frage nach dem richtigen Kultort endgültig überholt sein. Es ist nicht von ungefähr, wenn in diesem Zusammenhang die Bezeichnung „Vater" (dreimal) fällt. Der neue Gottesdienst der Endzeit, wie ihn Jesus verkündet, hängt unmittelbar mit der neuen Gotteserfahrung, die auf Jesus zurück-

---

[154] Zur Endzeiterwartung der Samaritaner vgl. *Kippenberg – Wewers*, Textbuch 97–101.
[155] Ebd. 100.

geht, zusammen, die sich vornehmlich in dem neuen Gottesnamen „Vater – Abba" artikuliert. Wo die Menschen Gott als Vater in vollem Vertrauen anerkennen und ehren, da hört auch aller Streit um die wahre und die falsche Religion, um den richtigen und falschen Gottesdienst auf. Das erscheint an dieser Stelle noch als eine Möglichkeit der Zukunft. – V. 22 bringt eine Zwischenbemerkung, die vielleicht auch darauf hindeutet, daß der Verfasser des Textes selber Jude ist und nicht Samariter, wenn er eine relative Überlegenheit des jüdischen Kultes gegenüber dem samaritanischen betont. „Ihr – die Samariter – verehrt, was ihr nicht kennt, wir – die Juden – verehren was wir kennen." Das ist der jüdische Standpunkt, der den Samaritanern zwar auch einen JHWH-Kult zugesteht, aber einen von minderem Rang. Die Samaritaner haben eben doch nicht ganz die wahre Religion. Sie haben zwar den richtigen Gott JHWH, aber in Wirklichkeit kennen sie diesen Gott nicht. Dazu kommt die Aussage, deren Gewicht nicht unterschätzt werden darf: *Denn das Heil kommt aus den Juden* (V. 22 c). Der johanneische Kreis bekennt sich hier, trotz aller sonstigen Polemik gegen „die Juden" doch zu dem grundlegenden, heilsgeschichtlich bedeutsamen Faktum der Herkunft des „Heils", konkret der Person Jesu, aus dem Judentum.

V. 23 nimmt die Aussage, daß in der Endzeit der gesamte ortsgebundene Tempelkult erledigt sein wird, erneut auf und sagt, daß diese Stunde *jetzt mit Jesus angebrochen sei:* „Vielmehr kommt die Stunde, und jetzt ist sie da." Es handelt sich um das erfüllte Jetzt der endzeitlichen Heilsgegenwart, und zwar diesmal bezogen auf den „neuen Gottesdienst". Wodurch ist der Gottesdienst der neuen Zeit bestimmt? Die Antwort, die Johannes auf diese Frage gibt, lautet: Die Zeit ist jetzt gekommen, wo die wahren Gottesverehrer, die wahren Frommen „den Vater anbeten werden in Geist und Wahrheit". Wie ist diese Anbetung „in Geist und Wahrheit" gemeint? Es geht hier nicht um eine spiritualistisch verstandene „Innerlichkeit", sondern um die mit Jesus selbst gekommene Form der eschatologischen Gottesverehrung. Der „eschatologische Kult" ist aber zugleich der „christologische Kult", der Gottesdienst, dessen Mitte durch Jesus bestimmt ist. Für den johanneischen Kreis ist Jesus Christus an die Stelle des Tempels getreten. Darum braucht es keinen Tempel, kein „Haus Gottes" im materiellen Sinne mehr. Soweit der negative Aspekt der Aussage Jesu.

Danach ist nun positiv zu sagen: „Geist und Wahrheit" bezeichnen in umfassender Weise den Grundcharakter des neuen Gottesdienstes, das neue „christliche" Vorzeichen vor der Klammer, das prinzipiell vor allen Gottesdienstformen steht, mag es sich um persönliches oder um gemeinschaftliches Beten handeln, um Wortgottesdienst und Eucharistiefeier. *Für diesen Gottesdienst ist es viel wichtiger, in welcher Weise er geschieht, als an welchem Ort.* Darin besteht ja die neue Gotteserfahrung der Jesusjünger, daß sie durch Jesus gelernt haben, Gott als den „Vater", als „Abba", wahrzunehmen und sich selbst in neuer Weise als die Familie der Söhne und Töchter Gottes zu verstehen. Der wahre „Ort Gottes" ist also die Gemeinde der Jesusjünger, der Glaubenden. Eben solche Gottesverehrer, die diesen neuen eschatologischen Gottesdienst „im Geist und in der Wahrheit" darbringen, sucht der Vater. Es ist klar, daß an diesem Gottesdienst auch die Frau in voller, gleichberechtigter Weise Anteil hat. Hier mag der entscheidende Skopos liegen, weshalb Johannes diese Offenbarungsrede über das Lebenswasser und den neuen Kult an eine Frau gerichtet sein läßt. Leider wissen wir zu wenig über die Gottesdienstgestaltung in den johanneischen Gemeinden, um abschätzen zu können, welchen Anteil die Frauen in der Gestaltung des Gottesdienstes – etwa in der Verkündigung – hatten. Vermutlich war er größer, als wir uns das heute vorstellen können.

V. 24 sagt abschließend, erst dieser „neue" Gottesdienst entspräche auch dem wahren göttlichen Wesen. Dabei geht es nicht um die „Substanz", sondern um die Freiheit, die Unverfügbarkeit und Lebendigkeit Gottes, um die Art seines Offenbarungshandelns gegenüber der Welt, in dem sich seine Liebe zur Welt bekundet. Das ist hier offenbar gemeint, wenn es heißt: „Gott ist Geist (pneuma)".

Darauf sagt die Frau, die in unserem Text mit ihrem Verständnis immer etwas nachhinkt (aber das tun im Johannesevangelium auch die Jünger): „Ich weiß, wenn der Messias kommt, dann wird er uns alles verkünden" (V. 25). Die Messiaserwartung der Samaritaner (vgl. oben S. 77) gilt dem in Dtn 18,15–18 verheißenen „Propheten wie Mose". Als solcher wurde Jesus in unserem Text eingeführt. Das Mißverständnis wird aus formalen Gründen durchgehalten, damit die Selbstoffenbarung Jesu als abschließender Höhepunkt desto besser herauskommt: „Spricht Jesus zu ihr: ICH BIN's, der mit dir redet." Damit hat Jesus der Frau zunächst bestätigt, daß er der Messias ist; doch darf auch der Anklang an das johanneische ICH BIN an dieser Stelle nicht überhört werden. Wenn der Mensch Jesus begegnet, dann tritt ihm auch, ob Frau oder Mann, die Glaubensforderung gegenüber.

Im zweiten Teil (4, 27–42) wird die Frau nur noch zweimal erwähnt. V. 27–30, ein Zwischenstück von überleitendem Charakter, schildert die Rückkehr der Jünger und ihr Erstaunen, als sie Jesus im Gespräch mit der Samariterin begriffen sehen. Dies entspricht ganz der Außergewöhnlichkeit der Situation im Rahmen damaliger Verhältnisse. Die Frau läßt nach der letzten Antwort Jesu ihren Wasserkrug am Brunnen stehen, so betroffen ist sie von dieser neuen, einzigartigen Begegnung. Sie eilt in die Stadt zurück und sagt zu den Leuten: „Kommt, seht einen Menschen, der mir alles gesagt hat, was ich getan habe; vielleicht ist dieser der Messias" (V. 29). So wird sie, aus ihrer persönlichen Erfahrung heraus, auch zur ersten „Missionarin". Es gelingt ihr, die Leute von Sychar für Jesus zu interessieren, so daß Jesus zwei Tage in der Stadt bleibt (V. 39–42). Daraufhin glauben jetzt viele an Jesus „um seines Wortes willen" und kommen aus eigener Überzeugung zu dem Bekenntnis: „Dieser ist in Wahrheit der *Retter der Welt.*"

Freilich steht in der Erzählung „Jesus und die Samariterin am Jakobsbrunnen" Jesus als der Offenbarer Gottes, als der endzeitliche Lebensspender, Prophet, Messias und Retter der Welt im Zentrum der Geschichte; „und auf der Frau ruht in Wahrheit gar kein selbständiges Interesse"[156]. Gleichwohl darf man die Geschichte auch nicht unterbewerten, vor allem dann nicht, wenn man sie auf der synchronen Ebene zu verstehen sucht. Denn sie verweist auf mancherlei wichtige Zusammenhänge. Daß *die Heilsfrage des Menschen* in Verbindung mit dem Symbol des „Lebenswassers" und dem implizit damit vorausgesetzten „Lebensdurst" des Menschen erörtert wird, ist zweifellos erhellend und bedeutsam. Man wird hier an den „Karamasoffschen Lebensdurst" bei Dostojewski erinnert. Dort sagt Iwan Karamasoff:

„Nehmen wir an, ich hörte auf, an das Leben zu glauben, an das Weib, das mir teuer war, an die höhere Ordnung der Dinge, nehmen wir an, ich überzeugte mich sogar, daß alles ein gesetzliches, verfluchtes und vielleicht vom

---

[156] K. *Thraede,* Art. Frau, in: RAC VIII 197–269, hier 227.

Teufel beherrschtes Chaos ist und daß mich alle Schrecken der menschlichen Verzweiflung überfallen – so würde ich doch leben wollen, leben! Und da meine Lippen einmal diesen Becher berührt haben, so – das weiß ich! – werde ich mich nicht früher von ihm losreißen, als bis ich ihn ganz, bis auf die Neige geleert habe! Übrigens werde ich den Becher so gegen mein dreißigstes Lebensjahr bestimmt wegwerfen, selbst wenn ich ihn nicht bis zur Neige geleert haben sollte, und fortgehen ... wohin, weiß ich nicht. Bis zu meinem dreißigsten Jahre aber, das weiß ich mit Sicherheit, wird meine Jugend alles besiegen – jede Enttäuschung, jede Verzweiflung, jeden Ekel vor dem Leben. Ich habe mich schon oft gefragt: Gibt es wohl in der Welt eine Verzweiflung, die diesen rasenden, wütenden und vielleicht unanständigen Lebensdurst in mir besiegen könnte? Und ich bin zu der Überzeugung gelangt, daß es wahrscheinlich keine solche Verzweiflung gibt – das heißt wiederum nur bis zu meinem dreißigsten Jahr, danach werde ich selbst nicht mehr wollen ..., so scheint mir wenigstens. Dieser Lebensdurst, dieses Lechzen nach Leben wird von manchen schwindsüchtigen Geifermoralisten häufig gemein genannt, besonders von Dichtern. Es ist allerdings ein zum Teil Karamasoffscher Zug, das ist wahr, und auch in dir steckt unbedingt dieser Lebensdurst, aber warum soll er denn etwas Gemeines sein? Es gibt noch so ungeheuer viel Zentripetalkraft auf unserem Planeten. Leben will man, Aljoscha, und ich lebe, wenn auch wider die Logik."[157]

Hier geht es darum, *das Leben* in seiner ganzen, unverkürzten Fülle auszukosten. „Damit ich ungebunden frei / erfahre, was das Leben sei", heißt es im „Faust". Auch dies ist eine oft bestätigte Erfahrung, daß dieser „Lebensdurst" bei Männern wie bei Frauen in einer sexuellen Ausschweifung seine letzte Erfüllung sucht und darin immer wieder enttäuscht wird. In diesem Sinne könnten die „sechs Männer" der Samariterin als Hinweis bedeutsam sein, und zwar für beide Seiten. Männer gebrauchen die Frau, sie sind dem Weibe verfallen und suchen es als „Lust- und Erfüllungsobjekt" bis hin zum romantischen Erlösungsgefühl, welches das Weib vermitteln soll (vgl. *Richard Wagner*). Umgekehrt sucht die Frau nach dem Mann, der sie als Mensch (auch geistig!) ernst nimmt und anerkennt. Daß Sexualität (sexuelle Liebeserfahrung und Liebessehnsucht) und Religion sehr viel miteinander zu tun haben, ist bekannt[158]; ebenso, daß im Zusammenhang der beiden Dimensionen gefährliche und selbstzerstörende Verwechslungen stattfinden können. In diesem Sinne ist es meines Erachtens anthropologisch höchst bedeutsam, daß Jesus

---

[157] Vgl. *F. M. Dostojewski*, Die Brüder Karamasoff (Darmstadt 1979) 372 f.
[158] *W. Schubart*, Religion und Eros, hrsg. von F. Seifert (München 1978).

in diesem Gespräch mit der Samariterin die beiden Dimensionen entwirrt, und zwar dadurch, daß die „moralische Seite" zunächst völlig übergangen wird. Der entscheidende Punkt ist die „religiöse Frage". Jesus sucht und sieht hinter der „moralischen, sexuellen Notlage" die tiefere menschliche Lebensfrage, nämlich die existentielle, religiöse Not des Menschen, sein tiefstes Verlangen nach dem „wahren, ewigen Leben". Dieses gewinnt der Mensch nach der Botschaft unseres Textes erst und allein durch den Glauben an Jesus. Erst von dorther kann der Mensch auch seine anderen Lebensnöte richtig bestehen. Eben dieses wird am Beispiel der Samaritanerin gezeigt. Vielleicht deshalb, weil sie als Frau die religiös ansprechbarere ist im Vergleich zum Mann? Das könnte sein. Aber richtiger scheint mir, *daß es hier um die Erschließung der religiösen Dimension des Menschen überhaupt geht.* Und in dieser Hinsicht bleibt für uns aus der Geschichte von der Samariterin noch immer vieles zu lernen.

6.2. Der „synoptische" erratische Block im Johannesevangelium: Jesus und die Ehebrecherin, Joh 7,53 – 8,11

Die letzte Perikope, die unter dem leitenden Gesichtspunkt „Frauen in der Jesusüberlieferung" zu behandeln ist, ist die Erzählung von der auf frischer Tat ertappten Ehebrecherin[159]. Sie gehört ursprünglich nicht zum Johannesevangelium und hat literarisch, traditions- und formgeschichtlich, ebenso theologisch, mit diesem nichts zu tun. Sie stellt nach *Schnackenburg* „einen Fremdkörper dar, der auch den Zusammenhang von Kap. 7–8 störend unterbricht"[160]. Aus diesem Grund wird die Geschichte auch von manchen Exegeten weggelassen oder erst am Schluß des Johannesevangeliums behandelt. Unter den „Frauengeschichten" der Jesustradition nimmt sie gleichwohl einen hervorragenden Platz ein. Denn nicht nur muß man ihr, trotz der eigenartigen Überlieferungsgeschichte, einen hohen Grad an jesuanischer Authentizität bescheinigen, sondern in ihr kommt auch das neue Verhältnis zur Frau am schönsten und über-

---

[159] Zur gesamten Perikope vgl. *Blank,* Johannes 1 b, 113–126; – *U. Becker,* Jesus und die Ehebrecherin. Untersuchungen zur Text- und Überlieferungsgeschichte von Joh 7,53 – 8,11 (BZNW 28) (Berlin 1963); ferner die unter Anm. 141 angeführten Johanneskommentare.

[160] *Schnackenburg,* Johannes II 236.

zeugendsten zum Ausdruck. Ohne diese Geschichte würde uns etwas Wesentliches am überlieferten Jesusbild fehlen.

Der Text der Geschichte lautet:

Und sie gingen weg, ein jeder in sein Haus. Jesus aber ging zum Ölberg. Am Morgen ging er wieder zum Tempel und das ganze Volk kam zu ihm, und er setzte sich hin und lehrte sie. Da bringen die Schriftgelehrten und Pharisäer eine Frau, die beim Ehebruch ertappt worden war, stellten sie in die Mitte und sagen zu ihm: Meister, diese Frau wurde auf frischer Tat beim Ehebruch ertappt. Im Gesetz aber hat Mose uns geboten, solche Frauen zu steinigen; was sagst du dazu? Dies sagten sie freilich, um ihn auf die Probe zu stellen, um eine Anklage gegen ihn zu erhalten. Jesus aber bückte sich und schrieb mit dem Finger auf den Boden. Als sie ihn aber hartnäckig weiter fragten, richtete er sich auf und sprach zu ihnen: Wer von euch ohne Sünde ist, der werfe den ersten Stein auf sie! Und wieder bückte er sich und schrieb auf den Boden. Als sie dies gehört hatten, gingen sie, einer nach dem andern, fort, angefangen bei den Ältesten, und er blieb allein zurück und die Frau, die in der Mitte stand. Da richtete sich Jesus auf und sprach zu ihr: Frau, wo sind sie denn? Hat keiner dich verurteilt? Sie sagte: Keiner, Herr. Da sprach Jesus: Auch ich verurteile dich nicht; gehe hin und sündige von jetzt an nicht mehr (Joh 7,53 – 8,11).

Zur Textgeschichte: „Die ältesten und wichtigsten griechischen, syrischen, armenischen, georgischen, koptischen und lateinischen Zeugen für den neutestamentlichen Text kennen übereinstimmend die Ehebrecherinperikope nicht. Es legt sich der Schluß nahe, daß die Perikope erst zu einem späteren, noch näher zu bestimmenden Zeitpunkt in Joh zwischen Kapitel 7 und 8, oder an anderer Stelle des neutestamentlichen Kanons, Aufnahme gefunden hat. Dazu stimmt die weitere spätere Überlieferung …, die zwar größtenteils für die Existenz der Geschichte von der Ehebrecherin eintritt, die aber noch deutlich zeigt, daß der Abschnitt nur sehr langsam, im Westen schneller als im Osten, als kanonische Erzählung anerkannt wurde."[161] Wir haben es mit einer sogenannten „Wanderperikope" zu tun, mit einem Text, der als selbständige mündliche Überlieferung in den christlichen Gemeinden im Schwange war, der aber lange Zeit hindurch in keinem der kanonischen Evangelien einen Platz fand. Die großen ägyptischen Handschriften kennen die Perikope nicht, dagegen fand sie Aufnahme in den Kirchenordnungen der syrischen Didaskalia und der Apostolischen Konstitutionen. Die altlateinische (westliche) Textüberlieferung bringt die Perikope relativ früh. Vor allem Hieronymus und Augustinus sind wichtige Zeugen für die westliche Tradition; beide halten den Text für kanonisch[162].

---

[161] *Becker*, Ehebrecherin 25.
[162] Zur Textkritik vgl. *Metzger*, Textual Commentary 219–223; dazu den Apparat von Nestle – Aland (²⁶1979) z. St.

Dieser eigenartige Tatbestand hängt offenkundig mit dem Inhalt dieser Erzählung zusammen. Er spiegelt die Spannung zwischen Treue zur Jesusüberlieferung und den Interessen der Kirchendisziplin. Da die werdende Kirche in der Behandlung von Ehescheidung, Ehebruch und Unzuchtssünden mehr zu einer gewissen Strenge geneigt war, war ihr die Milde, mit der Jesus diese Frau behandelt, unangenehm. Andererseits war die Perikope als Jesusüberlieferung vorgegeben, und man konnte sich dieser Autorität nicht einfach entziehen. Wenn sie dann trotzdem ins Johannesevangelium aufgenommen wurde, ist dies als ein Sieg der Jesustradition gegenüber den Interessen einer strengen Kirchenordnung zu betrachten. Das ist auch ein gewichtiges Argument dafür, daß es sich hier um alte, authentische Jesustradition handelt.

Zur literarischen Gattung: Sie ist nicht leicht zu bestimmen. *Bultmann*[163] bezeichnet die Geschichte als „apokryphes Apophthegma": Jesu Urteil wird gefordert, und Jesus antwortet mit einem Wort, das einheitlich mit der Situation verknüpft ist. Doch kommen in der Erzählung novellistische Züge dazu, Jesu Schweigen und das Gespräch mit der Frau. Nach *Becker* wäre die Geschichte den synoptischen Streitgesprächen zuzuordnen. „Sie stellt eine geschlossene Perikope dar, in der in ganz stilgemäß einer knappen Exposition mit der Einführung der Gegner und Vorbereitung der Frage das eigentliche Gespräch folgt, veranlaßt durch eine direkte, präzis gestellte Frage der Gegenpartei und abgeschlossen durch ein einziges Wort Jesu, das knapp und pointiert den Interpellanten antwortet. Auf diesem Wort liegt der Nachdruck der Erzählung."[164] Dagegen betont *Schnackenburg* das Schweigen Jesu und die „Zeichenhandlung" des Schreibens. „Nicht ein Streitgespräch steht im Mittelpunkt, sondern das Verhalten Jesu zu einer Sünderin und den Menschen, die sie anklagen."[165] Verschiedene Motive kommen vor, denen man auch anderwärts in den Evangelien begegnet, so daß die Gegner Jesus auf die Probe stellen wollen, ihn „versuchen" (vgl. Mk 12,13–17 par.), indem sie ihm eine Falle stellen. Das Motiv „Jesus und die Sünderin" verweist auf die Erzählung Lk 7,36–50, was wohl dazu geführt hat, die Geschichte hinter Lk 21,38 zu postieren. Ein drittes Motiv, daß Jesus auf den Boden, „in den Sand", schreibt, ist ein Vorgang, der wohl als Zeichenhandlung verstanden werden darf. Schließlich der Schluß der Geschichte, der Freispruch der Frau. Man sieht, die gattungsgeschichtliche Zuordnung will kaum eindeutig gelingen. Doch sollte man sich dessen bewußt bleiben, daß die Erzählung, so wie sie inhaltlich den Rahmen des „Üblichen" sprengt, sich auch nicht völlig eindeutig einer bestimmten Gattung zuordnen läßt.

Das historische Problem. Becker nennt in seiner Arbeit vor allem drei Gesichtspunkte, die dafür sprechen, daß der historische Ort der Geschichte im Leben Jesu zu suchen ist: 1) die Frage, um die es im Streitgespräch vorder-

---

[163] *Bultmann,* Geschichte 67.
[164] *Becker,* Ehebrecherin 83.
[165] *Schnackenburg,* Johannes II 233.

gründig geht, ist im Judentum zur Zeit Jesu lebhaft diskutiert worden; 2) Jesus entscheidet in diesem Fall eindeutig gegen die Tora und ihre Vertreter; 3) er vergibt in eigener Vollmacht, bedingungslos[166].

Die Bemerkung, „daß jeder nach Hause ging" (V. 53), gehört schon zum Anfang der Geschichte von der Ehebrecherin und verweist wohl in Verbindung mit der nachfolgenden Aussage darauf, daß vorher ein anderes Streitgespräch zwischen Jesus und seinen Gegnern stattgefunden hatte. Hier bietet sich der Vers nicht ungeschickt für die Überleitung zu der neuen Geschichte an.

Jesus dagegen geht auf den Ölberg, der östlich vom Tempel auf der anderen Seite des Kidrontales liegt und den schönsten Blick auf den Tempelplatz bietet. Der Text hat offenbar eine ähnliche Situation im Auge wie sie uns in Lk 21,37f berichtet wird. Danach lehrt Jesus tagsüber im Tempel, während er abends die Stadt verläßt und die Nacht auf dem Ölberg verbringt. Am nächsten Morgen geht er wieder in den Tempel, um zu lehren. So soll es nach Lukas Jesus während der letzten Woche nach dem Palmsonntag gehalten haben. Durch diese Zeitangabe wäre dann die Geschichte dem Zyklus der Streitgespräche in Jerusalem zuzuordnen. Die Einleitung lehnt sich stark an diese allgemeine Schilderung von Lk 21,37f an (8,1–2).

V. 3 bringt den eigentlichen Beginn der Geschichte. Schriftgelehrte und Pharisäer – eine Gruppierung der Gegner Jesu, die das Johannesevangelium nicht kennt, die aber bei den Synoptikern häufiger vorkommt, bringen eine Frau, die beim Ehebruch auf frischer Tat ertappt worden war. Sie stellen diese „in die Mitte"; so wird sie zum Zentrum des ganzen Geschehens. In unmittelbarer Verbindung damit legen sie Jesus eine Frage vor. Sie berichten zuerst den Tatbestand, diese Frau ist in flagranti ertappt worden. Danach kommt die Streitfrage: Mose hat in der Tora geboten, daß man eine solche Frau steinigen soll. Welche Meinung vertrittst du in dieser Sache? V. 6 stellt fest, daß es sich um eine „Fangfrage" handelt. Man erwartet, daß Jesus sich in dieser heiklen Gesetzesmaterie verfängt und eine Antwort gibt, die ihn vor den jüdischen Toragelehrten in jedem Fall kompromittieren würde. Entweder ist er zu streng, dann ist seine angebliche Güte und Menschenfreundlichkeit nur ein äußerlicher Schein; oder er ist zu lax und liberal, dann hapert es mit seiner

---

[166] *Becker*, Ehebrecherin 174.

Frömmigkeit. Die Fangfrage ist ähnlich angelegt wie in der Erzählung von der Steuermünze (Mk 12,13–17 par.). Die Fragesteller rechnen damit, daß jede Antwort Jesu für ihn selber zur Falle wird. Und Jesus reagiert auch hier mit der gleichen überlegenen Souveränität.

Ehebruch[167] wird durch den Dekalog ausdrücklich verurteilt (Ex 20,14) und nach verschiedenen Geboten der Tora streng bestraft. Doch liegt der Tatbestand des Ehebruches nur vor, wenn ein verheirateter Mann mit einer verheirateten Frau oder einer Verlobten (die Verlobung stand in dieser Hinsicht der Ehe gleich) geschlechtlichen Umgang hatte. Der Mann kann nur die Ehe eines anderen Mannes, dagegen nicht die eigene Ehe brechen. Unbedingte eheliche Treue obliegt nur der Frau, die durch die Eheschließung Eigentum des Mannes geworden ist. Es geht also vor allem um den Schutz des Rechtes des Ehegatten auf den exklusiven Besitz der Frau. Auf Ehebruch stand die Todesstrafe (vgl. Lev 20,20; Dtn 22,22). War die Todesart nicht näher angegeben, dann erfolgte die Hinrichtung durch Erdrosselung. Dagegen gebietet Dtn 22,23 f für den Beischlaf mit einer Verlobten den Tod durch Steinigung. Viele Autoren schließen daraus, daß die Frau gesteinigt werden soll, daß es sich um eine Verlobte gehandelt hätte; andere wenden dagegen ein, daß die Frau verheiratet gewesen sei, und verweisen darauf, daß das Strafrecht der Mischna zur Zeit Jesu noch nicht in vollem Umfange in Kraft stand[168]. Die Frage ist, da es sich in beiden Fällen um die Todesstrafe für Ehebruch handelt, nicht so wichtig. Dagegen ist mehr bedeutsam, daß es bei den Pharisäern schon damals Bestrebungen gab, mit Hilfe der Kasuistik dafür zu sorgen, daß die Todesstrafe möglichst selten vollstreckt wurde.

Die Aussage: „damit sie einen Grund zur Anklage gegen ihn hätten" (V. 6 b), ordnet das Streitgespräch in das Vorgehen gegen Jesus ein. Man sammelt schon Anklagen gegen Jesus, um ihm den Prozeß machen zu können. Auch dies mag ein Grund gewesen sein, die Geschichte an dieser Stelle im Johannesevangelium unterzubringen. V. 6 c schildert die erste Reaktion Jesu auf die Frage. Er gibt zuerst überhaupt keine Antwort, sondern läßt die Fragesteller mit der Frau stehen, bückt sich und schreibt mit dem Finger auf dem Boden. Die

---

[167] Zum Gesamtproblem vgl. *R. De Vaux*, Das Alte Testament und seine Lebensordnungen I (Freiburg – Basel – Wien 1960) 71 f; – Billerbeck II 519 f; *Hauck*, Art. μοιχεύω, in: ThWNT IV 737–745; – *K. Berger*, Die Gesetzesauslegung Jesu (Neukirchen 1972) 307–326; – Art. Adultery, in: Encyclopaedia Judaica 2 (Jerusalem 1971) 313–316.
[168] Nach *Schnackenburg*, Johannes II 227 soll es sich um eine Ehefrau gehandelt haben.

Deutung dieser Geste ist nicht einfach. Sie kann ein Desinteresse an der ganzen Sache überhaupt bedeuten. Sie kann aber auch einen symbolischen Sinn haben[169]. Manche Ausleger denken an Jer 17,13 f: „Du Hoffnung Israels, Herr! Alle, die dich verlassen, werden zuschanden; die sich von dir abwenden, *werden auf die Erde geschrieben;* denn sie haben den Herrn verlassen, die Quelle lebendigen Wassers" (nach dem griechischen Text). Diese Interpretation hat große Wahrscheinlichkeit für sich. Es geht also um eine Zeichenhandlung. Gott müßte eigentlich alle Menschen in den Staub schreiben. „Es ist eine Nichtigkeitserklärung, wie auch ein rabbinischer Text nahelegt, ein Strafurteil über die Schuldigen und um ihre Schuld Wissenden."[170]

Die Ankläger aber geben nicht nach und beharren auf ihrer Frage (V. 7 a). Da richtet Jesus sich auf und spricht die Worte, die zweifellos zu den bedeutsamsten Worten der Jesusüberlieferung gehören und die mit Recht in den Rang einer nicht zu überbietenden Sentenz gelangt sind: „Wer von euch ohne Sünde ist, der werfe den ersten Stein auf sie" (V. 7 b). Im Hintergrund steht der Brauch, daß im Falle der Vollstreckung eines Todesurteils auf Steinigung die ersten Zeugen auch den ersten Stein zu werfen hatten (vgl. Lev 24,10–16; Dtn 17,2–7; auch die Steinigung des Stephanus Apg 7,54–60)[171]. Sie übernahmen damit die volle Verantwortung für die Hinrichtung. Die Aussage bedeutet, daß nur der solche Verantwortung übernehmen könne, der sich selber von jeder Sünde und von jeder Verfehlung frei weiß. Nur ein ganz und gar Unschuldiger hätte das Recht, den anderen schuldig zu sprechen und hinzurichten. Aber wer ist ganz und gar unschuldig? Niemand! (Vgl. auch das Jesuswort der Bergpredigt: „Richtet nicht, damit ihr nicht gerichtet werdet" [Mt 7,1].) An dieser Stelle berührt sich die synoptische Jesustradition auch mit Paulus, wenn er sagt: „Denn alle haben gesündigt und ermangeln der Anerkennung durch Gott" (Röm 3,23). Es gibt kein Jesuswort, das mit solcher Entschiedenheit die Korruptheit aller Menschen durch das Böse ausspricht. Dieses Wort steht lapidar im Raum mit der klaren Schärfe einer bis ins Letzte durchdringenden

---

[169] Vgl. *Schnackenburg*, Johannes II 228 f.
[170] Ebd. 229.
[171] *O. Michel*, Art. Steinigung, in: BHHW III 1861 f.

Wahrheit. Jesus läßt es ohne jeden weiteren Kommentar stehen und bückt sich wieder, um weiter auf den Boden zu schreiben. Und dieses Wort wirkt. Es hat alle bis ins Innerste getroffen (V. 9). Die Wirkung zeigt sich darin, daß von den Anklägern einer um den andern verschwindet. Die Älteren, jene mit der meisten Lebenserfahrung, gehen zuerst. Sie haben dem Wort Jesu nichts entgegenzusetzen; und auch die Jüngeren, die das Leben und damit auch sich selbst noch nicht so gut kennen, werden unsicher und gehen fort. Nur die im Mittelpunkt stehende Frau und Jesus bleiben zurück. „Relicti sunt duo, misera et misericordia – Übrig bleiben die zwei, die Erbarmenswerte und die Barmherzigkeit."[172]

Jetzt kommt es zur Begegnung Jesu mit dieser Frau (V. 10). Jesus blickt auf und fragt: „Hat dich keiner verurteilt?" Die Frau war dem allgemeinen Verdikt ihrer Richter entkommen. Nun steht sie Jesus in ihrer einfachen Menschlichkeit gegenüber, in ihrer Scham und in ihrer Schuld. Aber Jesus nimmt sie aus der Verlegenheit und Unsicherheit heraus, indem er die Schuldfrage gar nicht stellt und auch über die Anklage gegen die Frau kein einziges Wort verliert, sondern nur noch auf das Verhalten der Ankläger reflektiert. Man spürt förmlich die Erleichterung der Frau, ihre Befreiung in der Antwort: „Keiner, Herr". Darauf die Antwort Jesu, die die ganze problematische Situation der Frau im positiven Sinne entscheidet: „Auch ich verurteile dich nicht; gehe hin und sündige fortan nicht mehr." Dies ist in der Tat ein vollmächtiges Wort der Sündenvergebung. Jesus will nicht verurteilen, sondern befreien. Er gewährt mit dieser Entscheidung der Frau das Leben. Er gibt ihr damit zugleich einen neuen Lebensmut, eine neue Chance. Freilich, Jesus heißt das, was die Frau getan hat, nicht gut. Aber das braucht nicht eigens gesagt zu werden; entscheidend ist der neue Anfang für diese Frau. Mit Recht gehört diese Geschichte zu den Höhepunkten des Evangeliums, weil darin die ganze Bedeutung dessen, was Jesus gebracht hat, sichtbar wird. Dagegen macht uns die frühe Überlieferungsgeschichte[173] dieser Perikope klar, welche Schwierigkeiten es von Anfang an gab, die Sache Jesu in dieser Welt und ihren Strukturen zur Geltung zu bringen.

---

[172] *Augustinus*, Johannestraktate 33,5.
[173] Zur Überlieferungs- und Wirkungsgeschichte der Ehebrecherin-Perikope vgl. *Blank*, Johannes 1 b, 120–126.

7. Schlußbetrachtung

Abschließend sei versucht, ein Ergebnis unserer Untersuchung der Frauen-Perikopen in den Jesusüberlieferungen der Evangelien zu formulieren.

Da wäre als erstes festzustellen, daß die Evangelientexte, die von Frauen handeln, zahlreicher und ergiebiger sind, als man auf Anhieb erwarten mochte. Zwar sind es vor allem Frauen aus der sozialen Unterschicht, arme Frauen, zahlreiche Witwen, die in diesen Texten vorkommen. Doch wird darüber hinaus, zumal in Gleichnissen, noch ein weiterer Hintergrund sichtbar; auch im lukanischen und johanneischen Sondergut.

Auch hat sich der Eindruck bestätigt, daß Jesus von Nazaret eine neue, andere Umgangsweise mit den Frauen praktiziert hat, als sie im damaligen Judentum weitgehend üblich war. Er hat damit Aufsehen und Anstoß erregt. Das entscheidende Motiv für diese „neue Umgangsform" wird man wohl in Jesu Grundverständnis der Botschaft von Gottes Herrschaft und Reich, in seiner Heilsverkündigung und seinem Heilswirken sehen müssen. Die Frauen, von denen die Rede ist, gehören offensichtlich zu den „Armen" oder „Bedrängten", denen zuerst das Evangelium gepredigt werden soll und die wohl auch am meisten für die Heilsbotschaft aufgeschlossen waren. Sie haben die ihnen dargebotene Chance am ersten begriffen und ergriffen. Weil Jesus für die Armen, die Schwachen, die Unterdrückten und Außenseiter, für die Zöllner und Sünder eintrat, darum trat er auch auf die Seite der Frauen, von denen ein Großteil zu diesen Gruppen gehört haben dürfte, um ihnen zu ihrem „Recht" zu verhelfen.

Natürlich war für dieses Verhalten – wie sollte es anders sein? – der religiöse Gesichtspunkt entscheidend, nicht ein sozialer Reformwille. Die Gleichbehandlung der Frau durch Jesus beruht letztlich darauf, daß für Jesus die Frau in der Liebe Gottes dem Manne völlig gleichgestellt und gleichberechtigt ist und weil recht eigentlich in dieser unbedingten Liebe die wahre Menschenwürde von Mann und Frau beruht, nicht in äußerlichen sozialen oder psychologischen Tatbeständen. Gott will das Heil eines jeden Menschen; darum wirkt Jesus die Zeichen des Heils auch gegenüber den Frauen. Frauen schließen sich dem Jüngerkreis an, wandern mit und übernehmen die tägliche Fürsorge für Jesus und die Jünger. Frauen zeigen sich für das Wort Jesu besonders aufgeschlossen und fühlen sich in ihrem tiefsten, religiös-menschlichen Empfinden angesprochen, anerkannt und wohl auch verstanden. Da ist ein Mann, in dessen Nähe sie verweilen können, wo sie sich frei fühlen, vor allem frei von Angst. Alle diese Frauen gehören wirklich zum „Grundstock der Kirche" und haben von Anfang an entscheidend dazu beigetragen, daß das Christentum sich nicht als eine reine „Männerreligion" etablierte. Die Stellung der Frau in der Urgemeinde ist sicher durch die praktische Einstellung Jesu zu Frauen grundgelegt und entscheidend mitbestimmt worden; es ist ein besonderer Zug, der die Urgemeinde von anderen Gruppierungen des Judentums (Pharisäer, Qumran) deutlich unterscheidet.

Wenn in der späteren Entwicklung des Urchristentums zur „Großkirche" dann doch das weibliche Element wieder in den Hintergrund gedrängt wurde und das männliche Element dominierte, zumal was die Kirchenordnung angeht, so hängt dies mit dem abendländisch-römischen Patriarchalismus zusammen, der die Frauen an der vollen, unverkürzten Teilnahme und Entfaltung ihrer Möglichkeiten in der Ausgestaltung des Christlichen weitgehend hinderte.

Allerdings waren auch zu allen Zeiten Frauen gute Hörer und Leser der Evangelien, und so blieb es ihnen nicht verborgen, wie Jesus zu den Frauen gestanden hatte und mit ihnen umgegangen war; als Beispiel sei der Gedichtzyklus „Das Geistliche Jahr" der Annette von Droste-Hülshoff genannt. Aus den Evangelien haben die Frauen auch immer wieder ihre Selbstachtung und den Anruf zur vollen Selbstverwirklichung ihrer christlichen Persönlichkeit gewonnen. Von den vielen großen Frauengestalten sei hier nur die kleine Therese von Lisieux erwähnt, die inmitten eines tief verängstigten und verklemmten Katholizismus im 19. Jahrhundert mit unglaublicher innerer Freiheit und Kühnheit den synoptischen, den historischen, den menschlichen Jesus ganz neu für sich entdeckte. Wo man diesem Jesus begegnet, da brechen offenbar immer wieder befreiende Kräfte auf, da gewinnt man den Mut zur eigenen Phantasie und zu neuen Wegen, zu neuen Erfahrungen, die Frauen und Männer machen können, im Hinblick auf ihre wahre Menschwerdung aber auch machen müssen. Da geht es mit dem Christentum und mit dem Menschen weiter. Im Christentum heißt der eigentliche befreiende und emanzipatorische Anstoß eben doch: Jesus von Nazaret. Und man darf auch überzeugt sein, daß eine Frauenbewegung, die sich von dort inspirieren läßt, manches in Bewegung bringen wird, auch in der römisch-katholischen Kirche.

II

Die Mutter Jesu im Neuen Testament

Von Robert Mahoney, Saarbrücken

Im Laufe der Geschichte hat das Bild keiner anderen einzelnen Frau einen so großen Einfluß auf das Denken von Männern über Frauen und von Frauen über sich selbst gehabt, wie das Bild der Christen von Maria, der Mutter Jesu. Dieses Bild stammt zu einem Teil aus der Theologie, wo ein eigener dogmatischer Traktat Maria, der jungfräulichen Mutter Gottes, gewidmet ist. Zu einem noch größeren Teil stammt es aus einem Zusammenspiel zwischen Liturgie, Kunst und Volksfrömmigkeit. Nun hat nicht nur Maria das Bild der Frau in allen Epochen entscheidend mitgeprägt; das in fast jeder Gesellschaft verschiedene, aber nicht minder selbstverständlich gültige Bild der Frau hat seinerseits die stetig wachsende Kunst, Liturgie und Volksfrömmigkeit in bezug auf Maria wiederum selbst stark beeinflußt: eine gegenseitig sich stärkende Wechselwirkung. In unseren Tagen wird nunmehr das in unserer Gesellschaft gültige Bild der Frau einer überfälligen Revision unterzogen. Es bietet sich an, aus dem sich neu ergebenden Blickwinkel auf das am frühesten greifbare Bild Mariens, nämlich das des Neuen Testaments, zurückzuschauen, um erneut den Anfang der langen Wechselwirkung zu konstatieren und, wenn möglich, um die besondere Frage nach der Rolle Mariens als Frau zu stellen.

1. Die Mutter Jesu bei Paulus

In den ältesten Schriften des Neuen Testaments, den Briefen des Apostels Paulus, wird Maria nicht namentlich genannt, nur einmal indirekt erwähnt. Die Stelle ist Gal 4,4, wonach Gott seinen Sohn sandte, „geboren von einer Frau und dem Gesetz unterstellt"[1]. Wäh-

---

[1] Biblische Texte werden nach der neuen Einheitsübersetzung der Heiligen Schrift zitiert.

rend hierin manche früheren Ausleger eine Anspielung auf die Jungfrauengeburt gesehen haben, versteht man heute den Ausdruck „geboren von einer Frau" als Unterstreichung des echten Menschseins Jesu[2]. An anderen Stellen bei Paulus ist von Jesu Geburt die Rede, aber nicht von seiner Mutter[3]. Es ist nicht ausgeschlossen, daß Paulus etwas mehr über Maria wußte; sie hat jedoch keine Rolle in der von ihm hinterlassenen Theologie gespielt. Auf längere Sicht werden allerdings seine Ansichten über den Umgang mit Frauen und über Sexualität[4] spätere Auswirkungen auf christliche Auffassungen von Maria gehabt haben: welche Tugenden ihr zugeschrieben und welche Eigenschaften ihr unbedingt abgesprochen werden mußten[5].

2. Maria im Markusevangelium

2.1. Mk 3,20f.31–35

In dem ältesten der vier Evangelien spielt die Mutter Jesu kaum eine größere Rolle als bei Paulus. Nach Mk 3,31 kamen sie und Jesu Brüder[6], als Jesus, von vielen Menschen umgeben, in einem Haus war. Sie ließen ihn herausrufen, aber er erwiderte:

Wer ist meine Mutter, und wer sind meine Brüder? Und er blickte auf die Menschen, die im Kreis um ihn herumsaßen, und sagte: Das hier sind meine Mutter und meine Brüder. Wer den Willen Gottes erfüllt, der ist für mich Bruder und Schwester und Mutter (Mk 3,33–35).

---

[2] Siehe *F. Mußner*, Der Galaterbrief (HThK IX) (Freiburg – Basel – Wien 1974) 268 f, mit weiterer Literatur. Besonders eindeutig: *„der Sohn wurde Mensch und Jude:* das allein will hier der Apostel betonen" (aaO. 270 A.120).

[3] Vgl. Röm 1,3 f; Phil 2,6 f.

[4] Siehe in diesem Band hierzu die Aufsätze von G. Dautzenberg und H. Merklein.

[5] Siehe die historische Übersicht (ohne daß dabei besonders auf Paulus eingegangen wird) von *M. Schmaus*, Art. Maria, in: Sacramentum Mundi III, 334–349.

[6] In Vers 32 wird nach einigen Handschriften „und deine Schwestern" hinzugefügt; wohl zu Unrecht. *J. Blinzler*, Die Brüder und Schwestern Jesu (SBS 21) (Stuttgart 1967) 66 f schreibt: „Eine so freimütige, ja bevormundende Haltung, wie sie die Herrenbrüder in den Szenen Mk 3,21.31–35 Par. und Joh 7,2–5 Jesus gegenüber bekunden, ist nun aber im Orient von seiten jüngerer Brüder dem Erstgeborenen gegenüber undenkbar…. Die Herrenbrüder von Mk 3 und Joh 7 müssen also älter gewesen sein als Jesus, zum mindesten der Wortführer unter ihnen." Blinzler schließt für Markus aus Mt 1 und Lk 1: „Dann aber ist es ausgeschlossen, daß sie Söhne Marias waren" (aaO.). Zur Frage Jesu leiblicher Geschwister s. u. zu Mk 6,1–6a (bes. Anm. 16).

Gleich, ob diese Perikope in V. 34 oder in V. 35 gipfelt[7], ist klar, daß es gerade nicht um Maria (hier ohne Namen) geht, sondern um die verwandtschaftsartige Nähe der (den Willen Gottes erfüllenden) Jünger zu Jesus[8].

Im größeren Rahmen jedoch ist schon Mk 3,20 f, der sonst etwas verloren wirkt, als der eigentliche Anfang der übergreifenden, zusammenhängenden Perikope 3,20–35 anzusehen[9]. In diesem Licht ergibt sich ein größeres Problem mit der Person Jesu Mutter. Mk 3,20 f lautet:

Jesus ging in ein Haus, und wieder kamen so viele Menschen zusammen, daß er und die Jünger nicht einmal mehr essen konnten. Als seine Angehörigen davon hörten, machten sie sich auf den Weg, um ihn mit Gewalt zurückzuholen; denn sie sagten: Er ist von Sinnen.

Das Haus in V. 20 bildet die Szene für alles weitere bis V. 35. Die Angehörigen, die sich in V. 21 auf den Weg machen, haben Zeit bis zu ihrer Ankunft in V. 31; es entsteht eine typisch markinische Erzählkonstruktion A–B–A[10]. Ein Kontrast ergibt sich aus den Angehörigen und Schriftgelehrten auf der einen Seite und Jesu näheren

---

[7] *M. Dibelius,* Die Formgeschichte des Evangeliums (Tübingen ²1933) 60, und *R. Bultmann,* Die Geschichte der synoptischen Tradition (Göttingen ²1931; ⁷1967) 29, sind darin einig, daß eine Spannung zwischen den beiden Versen herrscht: Dibelius sieht in V. 34 den ursprünglichen Schluß und in V. 35 eine sekundär verallgemeinernde, moralisierende Bildung; Bultmann sieht in V. 35 den Ursprung für ein biographisches Apophthegma.

[8] So die heutigen Exegeten allgemein; siehe *R. Pesch,* Das Markusevangelium I. Teil (HThK II/1) (Freiburg – Basel – Wien ²1977) 221–225, und *J. Gnilka,* Das Evangelium nach Markus (EKK II/1) (Zürich – Einsiedeln – Köln und Neukirchen-Vluyn 1978) 147.152 f. Verschiedentlich wird eine gegen die in der späteren Kirche aktiven Brüder Jesu gerichtete Nebenspitze gesehen; vgl. *R. Pesch,* aaO. 224; zurückhaltend *J. Gnilka,* aaO. 153.

[9] *R. Bultmann,* aaO. 28 f (biographisches Apophthegma, aber zusammengehörig; „V. 21 ... beruht offenbar auf guter alter Tradition"), und *E. Haenchen,* Der Weg Jesu (Berlin ²1968) 139–150, bes. 139 f, sehen Mk 3,21 und 3,31 ff als ursprünglich miteinander verbunden. Die meisten Exegeten sehen darin eine redaktionelle Verknüpfung von Markus; so *R. Pesch,* aaO. 212.222; *J. Gnilka,* aaO. 144–148.

[10] In ähnlicher Weise verschafft Markus für Jairus Zeit zwischen dem Weggang mit Jesus in 5,24 einerseits und der Begegnung mit den Leuten des Synagogenvorstehers in 5,35 andererseits durch den Einschub der Episode der kranken Frau, 5,24 b–34; vgl. auch Mk 14,1 f. 10 f mit der Salbung 14,2–9 (aber s. hierzu *R. Pesch,* Das Markusevangelium II. Teil (HThK II/2) (Freiburg – Basel – Wien 1977) 328 f, der für vormarkinische Zusammengehörigkeit von 14,1–11 argumentiert).

94

Verwandten auf der anderen: vor allem bringen dies die Schlußverse zum Ausdruck mit der Gegenüberstellung zwischen denen „draußen" und denen, die „im Kreis um" Jesus sind[11].

Nun wird in V. 21 die Mutter Jesu nicht ausdrücklich zu den Angehörigen gezählt, die Jesus mit Gewalt holen wollten, weil sie meinten, er sei von Sinnen[12]. Aber nach obiger Strukturanalyse muß Maria zumindest von Markus – eventuell auch von der vormarkinischen Tradition – zu denen, die Jesus während seiner Mission kritisch gegenüberstanden, gezählt worden sein[13]. Diese Schlußfolgerung im Bereich der urchristlichen Überlieferung muß nicht automatisch auf die historische Maria übertragen werden[14], aber sie schließt mindestens für weite Teile des Urchristentums eine etwaige Gegentradition aus, wonach Maria zu Jesu Lebzeiten zu seinen Unterstützern gezählt worden wäre. Dieses Ergebnis ist zwar im späteren christlichen Sinne nicht sehr positiv für Maria, aber historisch nicht sehr negativ. Auf alle Fälle erscheint die Mutter Jesu in Mk 3, nicht weil der Evangelist an ihrer Person interessiert wäre, sondern um im Sinne des Dramas den Hintergrund für die Aussprüche Jesu in Mk 3, 33–35 zu liefern.

---

[11] Der in mehreren Einzelheiten sich zeigende Kontrast in Mk 3, 20–35 wird in *R. E. Brown – K. P. Donfried – J. A. Fitzmyer – J. Reumann* (Hrsg.), Mary in the New Testament (Philadelphia und New York 1978) 54–59, detailliert ausgearbeitet. Der doppelte Vorwurf in Vers 21 („Er ist von Sinnen") und in Vers 22 („Er ist von Beelzebul besessen") erweise eine harte Opposition; und wie Jesus auf den Vorwurf von Vers 22 mit seinen Worten in Versen 23–29 antwortet, so seien seine Worte in den Versen 33–35 möglicherweise auch als implizite Antwort auf den Vorwurf von Vers 21 zu verstehen (aaO. 57 f).

[12] Mk 3, 21 f gehört zu den ganz wenigen Markustexten, die weder von Matthäus noch von Lukas übernommen wurden. Der Grund liegt wohl in der schon vor dem Ende des ersten Jahrhunderts empfundenen Anstößigkeit des Textes. Schon zu Markus' Zeit *könnte* eine ähnliche Motivation zu der Streichung des möglicherweise vorhandenen Namens von Jesu Mutter aus dem vormarkinischen Vers 21 geführt haben.

[13] Zum Ausdruck οἱ παρ' αὐτοῦ (Mk 3, 21 als „seine Angehörigen" übersetzt) s. *R. Pesch,* Markusevangelium I 212, bes. Anm. 4: „Der Evangelist hat οἱ παρ' αὐτοῦ als die Familie Jesu dadurch identifiziert, daß er 3, 31–35 eine Überlieferung vom Kommen der Mutter und der Brüder Jesu anfügte." Wir dürfen hinzufügen, daß Markus' relative Unempfindlichkeit von einigen alten Handschriften nicht geteilt wurde, die „seine Angehörigen" in 3, 21 in „die Schriftgelehrten und die Anderen" abänderten.

[14] Für eine differenzierte Diskussion s. *R. E. Brown u. a.,* Mary 283–285. *G. Stählin,* Art. Maria im NT, in: RGG³ IV, 747 f, urteilt härter und mit ungerechtfertigter Sicherheit.

2.2. Mk 6,1–6a

In Mk 6,1–6a erfährt Jesus eine Ablehnung in seiner eigenen Heimat. Viele Zuhörer staunen über ihn und sagen in V. 3:

Ist das nicht der Zimmermann, der Sohn der Maria und der Bruder von Jakobus, Joses, Judas und Simon? Leben nicht seine Schwestern hier unter uns?

Weil es ihm um etwas anderes geht, kümmert es den Evangelisten nicht, wenn *wir* daraufhin nach der unterbliebenen Erwähnung des Vaters Jesu fragen[15]; ebensowenig sollten wir daran Anstoß nehmen, daß offensichtlich Jesu leibliche Geschwister aufgezählt werden[16]. Die Jungfräulichkeit Mariens ist für Markus hier nicht das Thema, und so kann er die hinter 6,3 stehende Tradition ohne Bedenken übernehmen[17].

Wichtig dagegen ist der gleich darauf folgende Spruch Jesu:

Nirgends hat ein Prophet so wenig Ansehen wie in seiner Heimat, bei seinen Verwandten und in seiner Familie (Mk 6,4).

---

[15] Einige Handschriften ergänzen ihn, aber sicherlich zu Unrecht. Die wahrscheinlichste Erklärung für die Nichterwähnung Josefs liegt in der vermutlich ursprünglichen, einfachen Absicht, Jesus näher zu identifizieren, auf ihn hinzuweisen, nachdem sein Vater wohl vor längerer Zeit verstorben war: s. *R. Pesch,* Markusevangelium I 319. Die Deutung, die hierin Jesu illegitime Geburt belegt findet, ruht auf erst für später nachgewiesenen Vorwürfen und entbehrt jeder Grundlage im Text. Aber auch eindeutig ohne Grundlage im markinischen Text bleibt die Vermutung u. a. von *J. Gnilka,* Markus I 231f, daß in Mk 6,3 auf die Jungfrauengeburt Bezug genommen werde.

[16] Grundlegend für die Diskussion sind *J. Blinzler,* Die Brüder und Schwestern Jesu (s. o. Anm. 6), und *L. Oberlinner,* Historische Überlieferung und christologische Aussage. Zur Frage der „Brüder Jesu" in der Synagoge (FzB 19) (Stuttgart 1975). Vgl. nun den umstrittenen „Exkurs: Zur Frage der Brüder und Schwestern Jesu" in: *R. Pesch,* Markusevangelium I 322–324; hieß es noch in der 1. Auflage (1976) auf S. 324: „Unvoreingenommene Exegese erlaubt nur die Feststellung, daß Mk 6,3 die Namen von 4 leiblichen Brüdern Jesu und die Existenz von leiblichen Schwestern historisch bezeugt sind", wurden diese Worte in der derentwegen notwendigen 2. Auflage (1977) gestrichen und der Gewißheitsgrad des Arguments insgesamt etwas zurückgeschraubt, aber Pesch hat seine grundsätzliche Position nicht geändert.

[17] Natürlich wird ein Verständnis der „Brüdern und Schwestern" etwa als „Vettern und Basen" nicht eindeutig ausgeschlossen; doch im *Markusevangelium* gibt es keinen Grund, ein solch ungewöhnliches Verständnis in 6,3 anzunehmen. Zu dem mit Mk 6,3 übereinstimmenden Namen in Mk 15,40f. 47; 16,1 s. *R. Mahoney,* Two Disciples at the Tomb. The Background and Message of John 20,1–10 (Theologie und Wirklichkeit 6) (Bern und Frankfurt 1974) 105–109. – Zur Unterscheidung Jungfräulichkeit *ante* bzw. *post partum* s. u. Anm. 41.

Für Markus steht fest, daß Jesu Familie – und seine soeben namentlich erwähnte Mutter bildet darin keine Ausnahme – zumindest zur Zeit der Mission Jesu eher seinen Gegnern zuzurechnen sei[18]. Dasselbe wird für die vormarkinische Tradition gegolten haben, die in diesem Fall wohl nicht auf ein kaum erklärbares nachösterliches Theologumenon, sondern eher auf historische Erinnerung zurückzuführen ist[19].

2.3. Zusammenfassung

Wenn wir nach den Implikationen der markinischen Darstellung für Marias Status als Frau fragen, ist zunächst klar, daß die Basis für ein Urteil sehr schmal ist. Daß Maria in der vormarkinischen Tradition und im Evangelium so wenig vorkommt, hat an sich nichts mit ihrem Frausein zu tun. Daß sie als Mutter von mindestens sieben Kindern hingestellt wird, ist keineswegs diskriminierend gedacht, sondern wäre vielmehr – hätte man danach gefragt – als Segenszeichen zu werten gewesen. Daß sie eher zu Jesu Gegnern gezählt wird, ist ein Schicksal, das sie mit seinen übrigen männlichen und weiblichen Verwandten teilt. Paradoxerweise könnte man ihren (zunächst) unabhängigen und kritischen Stand gegenüber der starken Persönlichkeit Jesu als ein Zeichen persönlicher Charakterstärke ansehen, ein Eindruck, der durch ihren nach dem Tode Jesu möglicherweise historisch erfolgten Eintritt in den Jüngerkreis nur bekräftigt werden kann[20].

3. Maria im Matthäusevangelium

3.1. Mt 1, 1–17

Daß die jeweils ersten zwei Kapitel der Evangelien nach Matthäus und nach Lukas, worin die sogenannte „Kindheitsgeschichte" Jesu erzählt wird, von einer anderen literarischen Art als der Rest der Evangelien sind, darf hier als bekannt vorausgesetzt werden[21]. Wenn

[18] Siehe *R. Pesch*, Markusevangelium I 320–322; *J. Gnilka*, Markus I 232 f.
[19] Siehe *R. Pesch*, aaO. 322.
[20] Zu Apg 1 s. u. 4.5.
[21] Siehe *A. Vögtle*, Die Genealogie Mt 1, 2–16 und die matthäische Kindheitsge-

im übrigen Evangelium schon gilt, daß die historische Genauigkeit der einzelnen Aussagen nicht ohne weiteres angenommen werden darf[22], gilt dies *a fortiori* für die Kindheitserzählungen[23].

Der Stammbaum Jesu, womit Matthäus sein Evangelium eröffnet, ist so konstruiert, daß er von Abraham via David über dreimal vierzehn Generationen bis zu Josef, dem Mann Marias, reicht (Mt 1, 1–17)[24]. Viermal wird die formelhafte Aufzählung der Väter durch die Nennung einer außergewöhnlichen Mutter ergänzt. Welchen Grund Matthäus hatte, ist nicht eindeutig, aber wahrscheinlich will er damit ein besonderes Vorhaben Gottes mit Maria, der Mutter Jesu, schon signalisieren[25]. Am Ende des Stammbaums ändert sich dann auch die Formel:

Jakob war der Vater von Josef, dem Mann Marias; von ihr wurde Jesus geboren, der der Christus (der Messias) genannt wird (Mt 1, 16)[26].

Diese Formulierung ebnet den Weg für die nachfolgende Erzählung über Jesu Geburt von Maria als Jungfrau.

---

schichte, in: BZ NF 8 (1964) 49–58. 239–262; 9 (1965) 32–49; *ders.*, Offene Fragen zur lukanischen Geburts- und Kindheitsgeschichte, in: Bibel und Leben 11 (1970) 51–67 (beide Aufsätze sind abgedruckt in *ders.*, Das Evangelium und die Evangelien. Beiträge zur Evangelienforschung [Düsseldorf 1971] 57–136 und 43–56, wonach hier zitiert wird); *ders.*, Messias und Gottessohn. Herkunft und Sinn der matthäischen Geburts- und Kindheitsgeschichte (Düsseldorf 1971); *R. E. Brown*, The Birth of the Messiah. A commentary on the infancy narratives in Matthew and Luke (London 1977), bes. 25–38.

[22] Dies wird auch nicht (mehr) als Widerspruch in den kirchlichen Dokumenten über die Historizität der Evangelien gesehen. – Für eine grundlegende und zugleich praktische Diskussion eines exegetischen Konzeptes zur Natur der Tradition s. die Rezension von R. Pesch' Markuskommentar von *J. Blank*, in: BZ NF 23 (1979) 129–135.

[23] Es ist nicht ausgeschlossen, daß einige Details historisch zutreffen. Es bliebe jedoch eine „false supposition [,] that historicity is to be presupposed unless disproved. Such a presupposition is invalid in writings that do not have history as their primary goal"; so *R. E. Brown* u.a., Mary 27 f (s. Anm 11).

[24] Dies ist Matthäus' erklärte Absicht in Vers 17 (vgl. 1, 1), aber die Zahlen stimmen nicht (s. *A. Vögtle*, Genealogie 87–92. 95–99; *R. E. Brown*, Birth 69 f. 74–84).

[25] Siehe *E. Lohmeyer (– W. Schmauch)*, Das Evangelium nach Matthäus (KEK, Sonderband) (Göttingen ³1962) 5: „Gottes Weg ist oft der Umweg". Es wird viel um die vier Frauen gerätselt; s. *A. Vögtle*, aaO. 92–95; *R. E. Brown* u.a., Mary 77–83.

[26] Es muß erwähnt werden, daß es zu Vers 16 variierende Lesarten gibt; doch darf der Wortlaut oben als verhältnismäßig gesichert gelten. Siehe *B. M. Metzger*, A Textual Commentary on the Greek New Testament. A Companion Volume to the United Bible Societies' Greek New Testament (third edition) (London – New York 1971) 2–7.

Merkwürdig bleibt dabei die Aufführung des Stammbaumes *Josefs*, der letzten Endes Jesus nicht gezeugt haben soll. Aber Josef ist es doch, der in der folgenden Erzählung die führende Rolle überhaupt übernehmen und Jesus als seinen Sohn und damit als Davids Sohn anerkennen wird. Daß bei der Zeugung die Frau die Hälfte des Erbgutes beiträgt und daß der Mann nicht allein das Wesen des Kindes bestimmt, war damals noch nicht bekannt, und ein etwaiger Stammbaum über Maria wäre kaum zu erdenken gewesen[27]. Schon durch die Genealogie also wird Jesus als davidischer Messias ausgewiesen.

3.2. Mt 1, 18–25

In Mt 1, 18 wird Maria, mit Josef zwar verlobt, aber noch nicht mit ihm zusammen, durch das Wirken des Heiligen Geistes schwanger[28]. Josef, der meint, sich von ihr trennen zu müssen, hätte dies auch im Verborgenen, ohne Skandal, tun können[29]. Aber ein Engel Gottes erscheint ihm im Traum und eröffnet ihm (und dem Leser des Evangelium) Gottes Plan: er, Josef, Davids Sohn (hier so angesprochen), soll Maria und ihr werdendes Kind annehmen, denn das Letztere ist vom Heiligen Geist; ferner, er, Josef, wird das Kind „Jesus", Retter des Volkes Israel, nennen[30]. Zur Begründung dieser Ereignisfolge führt dann Matthäus in 1,23 den Spruch aus Jes 7,14 an, worin Gott mit der Stimme des Propheten dem Haus David ein Zeichen ankündigte[31]:

---

[27] Die Ansicht, daß die von der des Matthäus abweichende Genealogie des Lukas (Lk 3,23–38) den Stammbaum Mariens wiedergeben könnte, wie die des Matthäus den des Josef (oder eben umgekehrt), kann heute nicht ernsthaft aufrechterhalten werden; siehe *H. Schürmann*, Das Lukasevangelium I. Teil (HThK III/1) (Freiburg – Basel – Wien 1969) 198–204.

[28] „Schwanger durch das Wirken des" ist im griechischen Text einfach „ἐν γαστρὶ ἔχουσα ἐκ", buchstäblich „im Bauch habend von": noch undeutlicher als das ohnehin unbestimmte Lk 1,35 (s. u.).

[29] Dies scheint der wichtigste Inhalt von 1,19 zu sein. Zur Logik des Verses (besonders zum Wort „gerecht" als Attribut des Josef und zu den Gesetzesbestimmungen) s. *R. E. Brown*, Birth 125–128; *R. E. Brown u. a.*, Mary 83–85, bes. Anm. 174.

[30] Wichtig ist, daß der Davidide *Josef* ihn benennt, und damit als Sohn und Davidide anerkennt, und auch daß Josef ihn *benennt*, und damit in Gottes Auftrag sein Wesen mitbestimmt. Siehe *E. Lohmeyer*, Matthäus 13–16.

[31] Das Zitat stimmt wörtlich mit der ältesten griechischen Übersetzung des Alten

„Seht, die Jungfrau wird ein Kind empfangen,
einen Sohn wird sie gebären,
und man wird ihm den Namen Immanuel geben",
das heißt übersetzt: Gott ist mit uns.

Nun ist es ein Leitmotiv des Matthäusevangeliums, daß die Ereignisse im Zusammenhang mit Christus die Worte der Schrift erfüllen[32]. Wenn er eine Entsprechung zwischen der Schrift und der ihm überkommenen Jesustradition erkennt, baut er sie aus und fühlt sich frei, eventuell Fehlendes in der Jesustradition aus seiner Kenntnis der Schrift zu ergänzen, denn er weiß, daß die eine die genaue und unfehlbare Vorhersage der anderen ist[33]. Dabei ist es dem Leser nicht immer klar, welchen Anteil seiner Angaben Matthäus gerade aus der Tradition schöpft und welchen aus der Schrift. Unser Interesse gilt besonders dem Wort „Jungfrau", bekanntlich eine ungenaue Übersetzung der griechischen Septuaginta; im hebräischen Urtext steht 'almāh, „junge Frau"[34].

Eines ist jedenfalls klar: unabhängig davon, ob das Element der Jungfräulichkeit Marias schon in der dem Matthäus zukommenden Jesustradition enthalten war oder nicht, ist dessen Vorkommen an dieser Stelle für ihn von pointiertem christologischem Interesse, und zwar gerade als präzise Erfüllung einer genauen Vorhersage. Über

Testaments, der Septuaginta, überein, mit der kuriosen Ausnahme, daß es „καλέσουσιν" (sie werden ihn nennen) anstatt „καλέσεις" (du wirst ihn nennen) liest. In Mt 1,21 hatte Matthäus selbst auch „καλέσεις". Aber der hebräische Text von Jes 7,14 ist in diesem Punkt problematisch; s. *H. Wildberger,* Jesaja. I. Teilband Jesaja 1–12 (BK X/1) (Neukirchen 1972) 267. Zu Jes 7,14 siehe weiter *R. E. Brown,* Birth 143–155.

[32] Siehe *W. Trilling,* Das wahre Israel. Studien zur Theologie des Matthäusevangeliums (StANT X) (München 1964) 174–179; *R. E. Brown,* Birth 96–104.

[33] Von seiner Lektüre von Sach 9,9 (vgl. Mt 21,5) fühlt sich Matthäus berechtigt, aus dem jungen Esel in Mk 11,1–11 zwei Tiere zu machen (Mt 21,1–11), mit dem Ergebnis, daß Jesus nun anscheinend auf den Rücken aller beiden in Jerusalem einzieht.

[34] Die griechischen Übersetzungen von Aquila, Theodotion und Symmachus bringen alle anstatt ἡ παρθένος das an sich bessere ἡ νεᾶνις, wenn auch vermutlich als Reaktion auf den christlichen Gebrauch dieser Stelle. „Jungfrau" in Jes 7,14 wäre an sich nicht verwunderlich, weil nicht gesagt ist, daß sie auch *nach* der Empfängnis Jungfrau sei. Trotzdem ist die Entscheidung der Bischofskommission für die neue Einheitsübersetzung zu bedauern, bei ihrer endgültigen Fassung „Jungfrau" aus der Anmerkung der vorläufigen Ausgabe wieder in den Text von Jes 7,14 zu setzen. Die neue Anmerkung dazu: „Jungfrau: nach G und Mt 1,23; das hebräische Wort almáh wird auch als ‚junge Frau' gedeutet" stellt die Semantik auf den Kopf. Weiter s. unten, Anm. 45.

weitere mögliche Aspekte der Jungfräulichkeit wird nicht reflektiert: ob sie für die Mutter Jesu passend oder wünschenswert oder überhaupt ziemlich sei, das ist hier irrelevant. So fährt Matthäus auch fort: Josef wacht auf, nimmt seine Frau zu sich, verkehrt nicht mit ihr, bis sie einen Sohn gebiert, und er nennt den Sohn Jesus [35].

3.3. Mt 2,1–12.13–15.19–23

In 2,11 sind die Sterndeuter am Ziel: sie „sahen das Kind und Maria, seine Mutter" zu Hause in Bethlehem. Warum Maria hier namentlich hervorgehoben wird, ist nicht klar. Es kann sein, der Evangelist wollte an diesem Punkt die Zusammenführung zweier Stränge signalisieren: die präzise Erfüllung von Jes 7,14 nach Mt 1 und den auch vom Alten Testament vorausgezeichneten Weg der Sterndeuter[36]. Auf jeden Fall zentral in 2,1–12 ist das Epiphaniegeschehen, nicht etwa die Geburt, die nur indirekt in 2,1a erwähnt wird.

Im nächsten Abschnitt ergreift Josef aufgrund weiterer Engelserscheinungen im Traum wieder die Initiative und führt „das Kind und seine Mutter" (viermal, ohne Namensnennung) zum Schutz vor Herodes nach Ägypten und später zur Übersiedlung nach Nazaret zurück. Maria ist passiv wie durchweg in Mt 1 und 2; an ihrer Person zeigt der Evangelist kein Interesse[37].

3.4. Mt 12,46–50; 13,53–58

Die weiteren Stellen im Matthäusevangelium, wo Maria erwähnt wird, sind aus dem Markusevangelium übernommen. Mk 3,20f fehlt dabei ganz; die Entsprechung zu Mk 3,31–35 in Mt 12,46–50 zeigt,

---

[35] Siehe *E. Lohmeyer*, Matthäus 17: „Joseph handelt, wie die Erzväter auf Weisungen Gottes handelten, in stillem willigem Gehorsam; er tut nicht nur das Gesagte, sondern auch das darin oder darüber hinaus Gemeinte: ‚Und er erkannte sie nicht'." Das „Gemeinte" ist natürlich im matthäischen, aber nicht im jesajanischen Sinne zu verstehen. Siehe auch unten, Anm. 41.

[36] Möglich ist auch, daß „Maria" an dieser Stelle in vormatthäischer Tradition stand, ursprünglich unverbunden mit einer Vorlage für Mt 1, um die historische Information über ihren Namen weiterzugeben; s. *A. Vögtle*, Messias (s. Anm. 21) 22.

[37] Matthäus will zeigen, wie die Ereignisse im Zusammenhang von Jesu Geburt die Worte und Geschehnisse des Alten Testaments wieder aufnehmen, bzw. wie das Alte Testament als Vorbereitung für den Weg Jesu Christi zu lesen ist. Vgl. *A. Vögtle*, Messias 32–54.

von heute aus gesehen, Jesu Mutter und seine Brüder in einem etwas günstigeren Licht[38]. In der Entsprechung zu Mk 6,1–6a, Mt 13,53–58, wird anscheinend auf Jesu Verwandte Rücksicht genommen[39]. Überraschen mag die Unbekümmertheit, mit der auch Matthäus an diesen Stellen von Jesu Brüdern und Schwestern spricht und die Brüder in 13,55 sogar aufzählt[40]: wenn der Leser innerhalb des Kontextes des gesamten Matthäusevangeliums bleibt, muß er annehmen, daß die Eltern Jesu nach seiner Geburt weitere Kinder zeugten – eine Annahme, die dem von Jesaja vorausgesagten Zeichen keineswegs rückwirkend zuwiderläuft[41].

3.5. Zusammenfassung

Nur in Kapitel 1 und 2 bringt Matthäus etwas mehr über Maria als Markus. Wegen ihrer besonderen Rolle in Gottes Plan behandelt er sie an den von Markus übernommenen Stellen ein wenig schonen-

---

[38] Weil bei Matthäus kein solcher Kontrast wie in Mk 3,20–35 entsteht, wird Jesu leibliche Familie nicht durch die Jünger ersetzt, sondern sie dient als Auslöser für Jesu Wort über die wahre, eschatologische Familie; s. *R. E. Brown u.a.*, Mary 98f.

[39] Lautete Mk 6,4, daß ein Prophet nirgendwo „so wenig Ansehen wie in seiner Heimat, bei seinen Verwandten und in seiner Familie" habe, wird „bei seinen Verwandten" in Mt 13,57 gestrichen. Doch mag die Änderung stilistisch motiviert gewesen sein (vgl. – mit anderem Ansatz – *E. Lohmeyer*, Matthäus 231: „bei Mt sichtlich in ursprünglicherer Form").

[40] Statt des Bruders „Joses" Mk 6,3 steht „Josef" Mt 13,55.

[41] Daß Mt 13,55 „Sohn des Zimmermanns" (auch anders als Mk 6,3) lautet, widerspricht nicht Mt 1: erstens wird hier die öffentliche Ansicht ausgesprochen, zweitens hat Josef nach Mt 1 Jesus als seinen Sohn angenommen. Aber auch die Nennung weiterer Kinder steht nicht dazu in Widerspruch: hat die Septuaginta mit „Jungfrau" in Jes 7,14 die Geburt eines *Erst*geborenen (wenn auch mit männlicher Mitwirkung) angekündigt, wollte Mt 1 damit Jesu Empfängnis durch eine Jungfrau *ohne Mitwirkung eines Mannes* anzeigen; doch wurde in Mt 1 weder angedeutet noch negiert, daß nach der Geburt des Erstgeborenen Jesus andere Kinder in natürlicher Weise folgen würden: dies liegt außerhalb des Horizonts der Erzählung. Weil die Entsprechung zu Mk 3,20f bei Mt fehlt, versuchen Jesu Brüder ihn hier nicht zu bevormunden und brauchen deswegen nicht älter als er zu sein; vgl. die Logik *J. Blinzlers* oben in Anm. 6. – In den ersten Jahrhunderten erwachte das Interesse langsam; Kirchenväter und Theologen entwickelten verschiedene Vorstellungen. „Seit dem 4. Jh. wird ausdrücklich von der immerwährenden Jungfrau gesprochen. Seit dem 7. Jh. (Lateransynode 649) begegnet der Sprachgebrauch, daß M. vor, in und nach der Geburt Jungfrau gewesen sei"; so *M. Schmaus*, Art. Maria, in: Sacramentum Mundi Bd. III (1969) 334–349, hier 339. Siehe *R. E. Brown u.a.*, Mary 267–278.

der, wenngleich er ihre Rolle, als Jungfrau den Messias durch den Heiligen Geist zu empfangen und ihn zu gebären, am Anfang als eine passive schildert, durchweg unter der Führung ihres davidischen Mannes Josef, der Jesu Adoptivvater wurde.

4. Maria im Lukasevangelium und in der Apostelgeschichte

4.1. Lk 1,26–38

Die Geburts- und Kindheitsgeschichte bei Lukas weist eine ganze Reihe von Differenzen zu der des Matthäus auf[42]; hier von Interesse ist seine abweichende Behandlung von Maria. Sie spielt in Lk 1 u. 2 eine aktive, führende Rolle. In der Erzählung über die Ankündigung der Geburt Jesu, Lk 1,26–38, ist es Maria, die nicht irgendeinen Engel im Traum, sondern den Engel Gabriel[43] sozusagen leibhaft empfängt; er grüßt sie dann auch mit größtem Respekt[44]. Marias innere Reaktion, sogar ihre Gedanken sind dem Evangelisten erzählenswert, bevor er den Engel die eigentliche Ankündigung aussprechen läßt. Die Ankündigung in V. 31 erinnert an Gen 16,11 und Ri 13,35, aber wegen des Kontexts – Maria wurde schon in V. 27 als Jungfrau eingeführt – ist die Beziehung zu Jes 7,14 am engsten[45]. Im Gegensatz zum Matthäusevangelium ist hier die äußere Entsprechung auf der terminologischen Ebene – hier Jungfrau, dort Jungfrau – nicht selbst eine Hauptsache, sondern zunächst untergeordnet und einleitend: denn die Ankündigung ist mit V. 31 nicht erschöpft, sondern gipfelt erst in V. 32 f:

Er wird groß sein und Sohn des Höchsten genannt werden. Gott, der Herr,

---

[42] Zu den Differenzen s. *R. E. Brown*, Birth 33–36. Zur Traditionsgeschichte von Luk 1–2 s. *H. Schürmann*, Lukasevangelium (s. Anm. 27) 140–145.

[43] Vgl. Dan 8,15–26; 9,20–27; Lk 1,11–20; s. *H. Schürmann*, aaO. 37.41–43.

[44] Siehe *H. Schürmann*, aaO. 43 f.

[45] Die Beziehungen sind zur Septuagintafassung am deutlichsten; s. *H. Schürmann*, aaO. 46 f. Zu Jes 7,14 s. weiter *H. Haag*, Is 7,14 als alttestamentliche Grundstelle der Lehre von der Virginitas Mariae, in: Jungfrauengeburt gestern und heute, hrsg. von *H. J. Brosch* (Mariologische Studien 4) (Essen 1969) 137–144, nachgedruckt in: *H. Haag*, Das Buch des Bundes. Aufsätze zur Bibel und zu ihrer Welt, hrsg. von B. Lang (Düsseldorf 1980) 180–186; *A. Vögtle*, Offene Fragen (Anm. 21) 45 f.

wird ihm *den Thron* seines Vaters *David* geben. Er wird über das Haus Jakob *in Ewigkeit* herrschen, und seine *Herrschaft* wird kein Ende haben.

Damit kündigt der Engel Gabriel nichts Geringeres an als die Erfüllung der Hoffnungen Israels, das Erscheinen des Messias[46]. Wir dürfen nicht vergessen, daß auch hier die wesentliche Botschaft nicht mariologisch ist, sondern christologisch.

Marias Antwort in V. 34 wirft Probleme auf: „Wie soll das geschehen, da ich keinen Mann erkenne?" Daß sie an dieser Stelle etwas fragt, ist (besonders literarisch) verständlich[47]; aber was sie fragt, genauer: ihre Begründung, ist es nicht. Denn der Engel sagte nicht „du hast", sondern „du wirst empfangen", und das zu einer immerhin verlobten Jungfrau[48]. Zweitens ist nicht ersichtlich, warum Zacharias wegen einer ähnlich gearteten Frage in Lk 1,18 von Gabriel mit Stummheit bestraft werden sollte, während Maria nichts Nachteiliges widerfährt[49]. Die Lösung scheint allein in der Erzählstruktur zu liegen, die einen Einwand des Empfängers der Verkündigung erfordert, damit daraufhin als letztes Element ein göttliches Zeichen genannt werden kann[50]. Es ist zwar angezweifelt worden, daß Lukas hier überhaupt von einer Jungfrauengeburt sprechen wollte[51]. Aber erstens kann man gerade nur dann das Fehlen der Logik in V. 34 (dessen Echtheit nicht zuletzt aus strukturtechnischen Gründen als sicher gelten kann) übersehen, wenn man den Text schon mit der Jungfrauengeburt im Hinterkopf liest; d.h., nur dann ist er potentiell sinnvoll. Und zweitens erscheint es bei Lukas in der von ihm konstruierten fortlaufenden Parallele zwischen Jesus und Johannes

[46] Siehe *H. Schürmann*, aaO. 47–49.
[47] Zum Ankündigungsmuster (Struktur vergleichbarer Stellen) s. besonders *R. E. Brown* u. a., Mary 112–115, davon 114f zu Lk 1,34.
[48] „Da ich keinen Mann erkenne" bedeutet „da ich keinen geschlechtlichen Umgang mit einem Mann habe". Nebenbei wird der eventuelle Vorwurf einer illegitimen Geburt ausgeschlossen.
[49] Eine differenzierende Begründung zum Fall Zacharias gibt *H. Schürmann*, aaO. 37.
[50] Vgl. Gen 17,17f; Ex 3,11; Ri 6,15; 13,16f; s. Anm. 44, und auch *H. Schürmann*, aaO. 49f.
[51] Diskutiert in *R. E. Brown u. a.*, Mary 120f. Häufig hat es sich die ältere Exegese mit einer historisierenden und psychologisierenden Auslegung von Vers 34 schwer gemacht; doch muß eine solche Ausdeutung versagen: der Vers „muß in seiner literarischen Funktion... im Sinne des Schriftstellers Lukas verstanden werden"; so *H. Schürmann*, aaO. 51.

dem Täufer erforderlich, daß die Ereignisse im Zusammenhang mit Jesu Geburt die Umstände bei der Geburt des Johannes (hier als Zeichen für Maria in 1,36 f kurz wiederholt) übertreffen.

Nun ist auch V. 35 problematisch, unter anderem, weil er V. 31–33 zum Teil wiederholt[52]; nicht angezweifelt werden sollte, daß Lukas durch V. 35 unter anderem auch sagen wollte, daß Jesus ohne Mitwirkung eines Mannes empfangen wurde. Am wahrscheinlichsten ist es, daß das Traditionselement „Jungfrauengeburt" Lukas vorgegeben war[53]. Jedenfalls präsentiert er die Jungfräulichkeit Marias nicht als Auszeichnung ihrer Person, sondern als sich eröffnende Möglichkeit für den Heiligen Geist, ein mächtiges Werk in der Person Jesu Christi einzuleiten[54]. „Denn *für Gott ist nichts unmöglich*" (1,37). Die wahre Auszeichnung für Maria stellt ihre abschließende Antwort an den Engel in 1,38 dar: „Ich bin die Magd des Herrn: mir geschehe, wie du es gesagt hast." Trotz des Ausdrucks „mir geschehe" ist klar, daß Maria nicht passiv, sondern aktiv und mitwirkend ist.

4.2. Lk 1,39–56

Dementsprechend bricht Maria gleich auf, und eilt von Nazaret in Galiläa zu einer Stadt im Bergland von Judäa, um ihre Verwandte Elisabet zu besuchen[55]. Elisabet, angeregt durch das Hüpfen des Kindes in ihrem Leib, empfängt sie mit zutreffendem Lob:

---

[52] Siehe *R. E. Brown*, Birth 311–316; er spricht (aaO. 312) von einer „conglomeration of ideas in 1:35" und „early Christian formulations of Christology", zieht einen aufschlußreichen Vergleich mit Röm 1,3 f und schreibt zum Schluß (aaO. 316): „By moving the christological moment from the resurrection to the conception, Luke tells us that there never was a moment on this earth when Jesus was not the Son of God."

[53] Siehe *H. Schürmann*, aaO. 56: „die Annahme, in einer früheren und nicht mehr zu rekonstruierenden Form habe die Aussage von der Jungfrauengeburt gefehlt, wagt sich in unkontrollierbare Gefilde." Siehe auch *A. Vögtle*, Offene Fragen 44.

[54] Wenn *H. Schürmann* (aaO. 56) zu Vers 35 abschließend schreibt, daß „die Gesamttendenz der Perikope ... gerade in der Aussage von der jungfräulichen Empfängnis gipfelt", verwischt er damit leicht seine eigene soeben vollzogene (aaO. 52–56) eindeutige Analyse des klaren christologischen Inhalts dieses Verses.

[55] Nach Lk 1,36 sind Elisabet und Maria verwandt; *H. Schürmann* (aaO. 56 Anm. 113) leitet daraus in Verbindung mit Lk 1,5 „die Vermutung priesterlicher Abstammung" für Maria ab. Doch weder der sonstige Wortlaut der Evangelien

Gesegnet bist du mehr als alle anderen Frauen, und gesegnet ist die Frucht deines Leibes. Wer bin ich, daß die Mutter meines Herrn zu mir kommt? ... Selig ist die, die geglaubt hat, daß sich erfüllt, was der Herr ihr sagen ließ (Lk 1,42 f.45)[56].

Vor allem der letzte Vers wird es sein, der die besondere Botschaft des Evangelisten trägt und den Grund angibt, warum für ihn Maria in diesem Teil des Evangeliums die Hauptrolle spielt.

Sogleich erreicht Marias Rolle ihren vorläufigen Höhepunkt mit dem Lobgesang des „Magnifikat" (Lk 1,46–55)[57]. Wiewohl das Gedicht mit seinen mannigfachen Anspielungen und kleineren Zitaten aus der Schrift, mit seinem Lobpreis der schon vollzogenen Rettung eher eine nachösterliche Theologie widerspiegelt, paßt es hier als eine Vorausverkündigung des Evangeliums mit starkem lukanischem Akzent[58]. Wichtig für uns ist, daß Maria, die Frau, diese Vorauskündigung spricht und daß sie sich selbst als die erste, an der das Evangelium seine Wirkung hat entfalten können, vorstellen kann. Weit davon entfernt, daß Maria hier wegen ihres Status als Frau Nachteile erfahren muß, besingt sie den Umsturz der bisherigen ungerechten Ordnung, unter der sie und viele andere diskriminiert und ausgebeutet wurden, als schon vollzogen. Nun ist sie selber das lebendige Beispiel für die neue Ordnung, die durch Gottes mächtige und erbarmungsvolle Taten errichtet wird[59]. Wie einst Hanna, die Mutter Samuels, deren Danklied in 1 Sam 2,1–10 Modell für das Magnifikat gestanden hat, und wie die Sänger von Ps 113 lobpreist sie Gott, der auf das Äußere der Person nicht achtet, der nicht an menschliche Vorleistung gebunden ist, der menschliche Verhältnisse radikal ändern kann und radikal ändert. Sie besingt eine neue, mit

---

noch die heutige historische Kritik sind mit einer (engeren) Blutsverwandtschaft zwischen Jesus und Johannes dem Täufer leicht vereinbar; vgl. *R. E. Brown*. Birth 285.

[56] Lk 1,28 und 1,42 sind die Quelle für den ersten Teil des christlichen Gebetes *Ave Maria*. Der Kontext des Gebets (vgl. den viel späteren zweiten Teil) gibt denselben Worten eine deutlich andere – selbstverständlich nicht illegitime – Richtung als der christologisch-eschatologische Kontext im Lukasevangelium.

[57] Nicht alle alten Handschriften nennen in 1,46 Maria als Sprecherin des Magnifikat; einige wenige nennen Elisabet. Vgl. dazu *B. M. Metzger*, Textual Commentary 130f (s. Anm. 26).

[58] Die Kritik ist über die Herkunft des Liedes uneinig; s. *H. Schürmann*, aaO. 78f.

[59] Siehe *H. Schürmann*, aaO. 70–80.

der bevorstehenden Geburt des Messias vollzogene Gottesordnung, die nicht auf gegenseitig abverlangtem Ehrerbieten beruht, sondern auf Gottes Zuwendung und Anerkennung. Die Anerkennung Gottes macht den Menschen zum Menschen.

4.3. Lk 2, 1–52

Bei der Geburt Jesu in Lk 2 bleibt Maria weiterhin, besonders im Vergleich zum Matthäusevangelium, die Aktive. Im Gegensatz zu Matthäus ist hier die Geburt selbst wichtig, vielleicht als Antwort auf römisch-hellenistisches Interesse, Kaiserkult und sogar Vergil[60]. Bei der rituellen Reinigung ist es Maria, an die sich Simeon mit seiner Prophetie über Jesus in besonderer Weise wendet; zu ihr sagt er auch: „Dir selbst aber wird ein Schwert durch die Seele dringen" (Lk 2,35). Im griechischen Text ist dieser Satz ein *à-propos* zum Wort „widersprochen" am Ende von V. 34; nach dem längeren, glorreichen Teil der Prophetie zeigt er, wie tiefreichend der Widerspruch sein wird. Das kann bedeuten, daß auch Maria aufgrund ihrer zukünftigen Reaktion zu Jesus wird beurteilt werden müssen[61]. Der präzise Sinn des Satzes bleibt jedoch unklar; er belegt jedoch zumindest auf der dramatischen Ebene ein unübersehbares Interesse an der Person Marias.

Beim Auffinden des zwölfjährigen Jesus im Tempel ist es Maria, die für sich und Josef spricht (2,48). Nach seiner Rückkehr wird in 2,51, ähnlich wie beim Besuch der Hirten in 2,19, bemerkt, daß Maria lang über die Ereignisse nachdachte:

Maria aber bewahrte alles, was geschehen war, in ihrem Herzen und dachte darüber nach (2,19).
Seine Mutter bewahrte alles, was geschehen war, in ihrem Herzen (2,51).

Hier ist kein versteckter Hinweis darauf, als sei Maria die Quelle für Kap. 1 u. 2 des Lukasevangeliums; vielmehr wird Maria wie in Kap. 1 von Lukas als Beispiel hingestellt, indem sie das Wort aufnimmt und in sich wirken läßt: sie ist der ideale Jünger[62].

---

[60] Zu Vergil s. *R. E. Brown*, Birth 564–570, mit Literatur.
[61] Einen kurzen Überblick über die Meinung bietet *H. Schürmann*, aaO. 129f; aber seine eigene Lösung bleibt ebenso fraglich. Vgl. *R. E. Brown u. a.*, Mary 154–157, die mit der obigen, plausibel argumentierten Meinung schließen.
[62] Siehe *R. E. Brown u. a.*, Mary 147–152.161f.

Nach Kap. 2 hat Lukas aus seiner Tradition andere Personen als Beispiele und Träger seines Dramas. Maria wird später im Evangelium nicht mehr namentlich genannt[63], wenn auch dreimal von ihr die Rede ist. Zweimal wird sie an den gleichen Stellen, die auch Matthäus von Markus übernommen hatte, erwähnt: in Bezug auf Jesu Mutter und die übrige Familie gibt es dabei nur leichte Veränderungen, insgesamt eindeutig in Richtung einer noch schonenderen Behandlung[64].

Die dritte Erwähnung ist in einem vieldiskutierten Stück aus dem lukanischen Sondergut:

Als er das sagte, rief eine Frau aus der Menge ihm zu: Selig die Frau, deren Leib dich getragen und deren Brust dich genährt hat. Er aber erwiderte: Selig sind vielmehr die, die das Wort Gottes hören und es befolgen (Lk 11,27f).

Obwohl die erste Seligpreisung äußerlich Maria betrifft, ist sie in Wirklichkeit als Kompliment für Jesus gemeint; an die Person der Mutter Jesu wird man in erster Linie nicht wirklich gedacht haben[65]. Jesu Antwort fällt dementsprechend nicht zu Lasten Marias aus; er greift die angebotene Form der Seligpreisung auf und nimmt die Gelegenheit wahr, den wahren Grund des Seligseins zu verkünden. Freilich ist es gerade Maria, die in Lk 1 u. 2 als Beispiel solchen Seligseins gedient hatte. Es könnte sein, daß der Evangelist auch jetzt an sie denkt, aber es ist eher unwahrscheinlich; seit Kap. 3 hat er Maria praktisch unberücksichtigt gelassen, während die Themen

---

[63] Interessant ist die Formulierung am Anfang der lukanischen Genealogie Jesu in 3,23–38: „Man hielt ihn für den Sohn Josefs." Maria wird zwar nicht erwähnt, aber hierin liegt die einzige deutliche Anspielung in den Evangelien außerhalb von Mt 1 und Lk 1 auf die Jungfrauengeburt.

[64] Lk 4,22 (par Mk 6,3; Mt 13,55) erwähnt weder Mutter noch Geschwister; gefragt wird: „Ist das nicht der Sohn Josefs?" Lk 4,24 (par Mk 6,4; Mt 13,57) nennt weder Verwandte noch Familie; gesagt wird: „Kein Prophet wird in seiner Heimat anerkannt". Wie bei Matthäus fehlt Mk 3,21. Lk 8,19–21 (par Mk 3,31–35; Mt 12,46–50) baut keinen Kontrast auf zwischen Mutter und Brüdern einerseits und denen, die das Wort hören und tun, andererseits; vielmehr scheinen die Gruppen zusammengezogen zu werden.

[65] Zu Vergleichen aus der jüdischen Literatur s. (H. L. Strack –) P. Billerbeck, Kommentar zum Neuen Testament aus Talmud und Midrasch Bd. II (München ⁴1965) 187f. Zur Diskussion s. R. E. Brown u.a., Mary 170–172.

„das Wort Gottes hören und es befolgen" grundlegende Motive der Evangelien sind[66].

4.5. Apg 1, 13 f

Lukas erwähnt Jesu Mutter ein letztes Mal am Anfang des zweiten Teiles seines Doppelwerkes, der Apostelgeschichte. Nachdem die elf Jünger im Obergemach aufgezählt werden, heißt es weiter:

Sie alle verharrten dort einmütig im Gebet, zusammen mit den Frauen und mit Maria, der Mutter Jesu, und mit seinen Brüdern (Apg 1, 14).

Der Vers wirkt wie eine Momentaufnahme oder eher wie ein Gemälde. Er ist Teil der ersten der lukanischen Summarien in der Apostelgeschichte, und sein präziser historischer Wert ist zweifelhaft[67]. Daß der Herrenbruder Jakobus zur späteren christlichen Gemeinde gehörte, ist sicher[68]; es ist auch nicht unwahrscheinlich, daß – sollte sie noch gelebt haben – Maria sich spätestens zur selben Zeit der Gemeinde angeschlossen hätte[69]. Historisch gesehen wird es dann am Anfang verschiedene Gruppen von Jesusjüngern gegeben haben: Apostel, Familie, Galiläer, Judäer, strenggläubige Juden, Sektierer, vielleicht andere mehr[70]. Für Lukas ist Maria hier Garant und Symbol der Einheit und Echtheit in seinem Idealbild der ersten Jerusalemer Gemeinde. Ihr Erscheinen an dieser Stelle schlägt weiter einen

---

[66] Die Themen fallen zusammen auch in Lk 8, 15.21; vgl. *H. Conzelmann*, Die Mitte der Zeit, Studien zur Theologie des Lukas (BHTh 17) (Tübingen ⁵1964) 217. Immerhin ist Lk 8, 21 auch eine „Marienstelle"; möglich ist, daß gerade das Vorkommen der Mutter Jesu Lukas besonders an die Verknüpfung Wort/Tun denken ließ: vgl. Lk 1, 38.

[67] Siehe besonders *E. Haenchen*, Die Apostelgeschichte (KEK III) (Göttingen ⁵1965) 121 f; s. auch *H. Conzelmann*, Die Apostelgeschichte (HNT 7) (Tübingen 1963) 23; *G. Lohfink*, Die Himmelfahrt Jesu. Untersuchungen zu den Himmelfahrts- und Erhöhungstexten bei Lukas (StANT 26) (München 1971) 152; *W. Pesch*, Maria in biblischen Texten. Meditationen – Bilder (Würzburg 1979) 50.53.

[68] Siehe Apg 12, 17; 15, 13; 21, 18; 1 Kor 15, 7; Gal 1, 19; 2, 9.12; *F. Josephus*, Antiquitates Iudaeorum XX 200. Jakobus avancierte zum Leiter der Gemeinde in Jerusalem.

[69] *E. Haenchen* (aaO. 122) vermutet, daß aufgrund der in 1 Kor 15, 7 für Jakobus berichteten Erscheinung auch Jesu Mutter und Brüder sich der Gemeinde anschlossen.

[70] Siehe *W. Pesch*, aaO. 50; *H. Conzelmann*, Geschichte des Urchristentums (NTD – Ergänzungsreihe Nr. 5) (Göttingen ²1971) 41–45.

Bogen zum Anfang des Lukasevangeliums, wo sie als Beispiel des ersten Jüngers fungierte; ihre Gegenwart an Bord der gerade vom Stapel laufenden Kirche ist ein stabilisierender Faktor der Kontinuität in der Gesamtwirksamkeit des Heiligen Geistes.

4.6. Zusammenfassung

Maria genießt eine ganz andere Stellung bei Lukas als bei Markus oder Matthäus. Sollte ein Grund dafür in der Lukas zukommenden Jesustradition liegen, ist dieser Grund jedenfalls nicht in Lk 3–24 ersichtlich. Ausschlaggebend dürfte Lukas' eigenes Konzept für den Aufbau seiner ersten zwei Kapitel gewesen sein. Hinzu kommt sein prinzipielles Anliegen, Frauen, wie überhaupt den gesellschaftlich Benachteiligten, eine positive Rolle zukommen zu lassen. Marias Rolle bei Lukas ist eine nicht nur für Frauen äußerst positive. Hierin ist auch ein Hauptpfeiler der späteren mariologischen Entwicklung zu sehen.

5. Die Mutter Jesu im Johannesevangelium

5.1. Joh 2, 1–12

Jesu Mutter wird im Johannesevangelium nicht namentlich genannt; sie erscheint nur zweimal, am Anfang und am Ende Jesu öffentlicher Tätigkeit[71]. Bei der Hochzeit zu Kana ist sie in 2,1 schon „dabei", wenn in 2,2 gesagt wird, „auch Jesus und seine Jünger waren ... eingeladen." Ihre Rolle in dieser ersten der johanneischen Wundergeschichten oder Zeichen ist auf jeden Fall dem christologischen Thema untergeordnet: der ersten Epiphanie, die zum Glauben an Jesus führt[72]. Warum es gerade Maria ist, die die Notsitua-

---

[71] Daß Joh 6,42 eine Parallele zu Mk 6,3 und Joh 4,44 eine Parallele zu Mk 6,4 bieten (s. oben), sei hier nur erwähnt.

[72] Zu den johanneischen Zeichen s. *R. Schnackenburg*, Das Johannesevangelium I. Teil (HThK IV/1) (Freiburg – Basel – Wien ²1967) 344–356; zur Deutung dieser Geschichte s. besonders *ders.*, aaO. 341: „Das Wichtigste ist ihm [dem Evangelisten] die Herrlichkeitsoffenbarung Jesu (V 11), und jede Deutung, die sich von dieser *christologischen* Sicht entfernt, führt vom Zentrum ab."

tion Jesus bekanntgibt, ist nicht sicher; vielleicht, weil sie als Mutter noch vor seinem ersten großen Zeichen in der Lage ist, den Weg mit ihrer Forderung nach Gehorsam und Zuversicht zu ebnen: „Was er euch sagt, das tut!" (2, 5). Jesu Zurückweisung in V. 4 war nicht übermäßig schroff, garantiert jedoch die „christologische Distanz" und erinnert uns an das den Synoptikern sowie Johannes gemeinsame Thema, daß leibliche Verwandtschaft allein noch kein Kriterium wahrer Nähe zu Jesus darstellt[73]. Jesu Mutter ist überdies ein lebendiger Hinweis auf seinen irdischen Ursprung: wenn in Joh 1–4 die Ersetzung der alten Ordnung durch die neue ein Thema ist[74], so ist Maria die Erinnerung an Jesu jüdische Herkunft; wenn der göttliche Mensch seine Herrlichkeit von jetzt an enthüllt[75], ist sie die Person, von der er seinen undoketischen Ursprung im Fleisch genommen hat. Wahrscheinlich stammt ihre Rolle in dieser Geschichte schon aus der vorjohanneischen Quelle[76]; ihre Anwesenheit wäre für den vierten Evangelisten ausreichender Grund gewesen, dieses Zeichen an den Anfang seiner Darstellung zu setzen[77].

---

[73] Siehe R. *Schnackenburg*, aaO. 333; A. *Dauer*, Die Passionsgeschichte im Johannesevangelium. Eine traditionsgeschichtliche und theologische Untersuchung zu Joh 18,1 – 19,3 (StANT 30) (München 1972) 323.

[74] Siehe C. H. *Dodd*, The Interpretation of the Fourth Gospel (Cambridge 1953) 297–317; R. E. *Brown*, The Gospel According to John (i–xii) (Anchor Bible 29) (New York 1966) cxliii–cxliv.

[75] Siehe die kritische Diskussion des Begriffs des „göttlichen Menschen" (mit weiterer Literatur) in R. *Fuller*, The Foundations of New Testament Christology (New York 1965) 68–72.97f.

[76] Besonders interessant sind die Überlegungen von B. *Lindars*, The Gospel of John (New Century Bible) (London 1972) 127: „... the resulting pre-Johannine story belongs to a special class of folk-legend. It is a story of the early life of Jesus, when he is still with his mother and brothers (cf. verse 12), and it probably did not include mention of the disciples. Stories of this kind abound in the apocryphal infancy gospels, and we have one very beautiful example in Lk 2.41–52." Vgl. R. E. *Brown u.a.*, Mary 185f.

[77] Im (vorjohanneischen?) Übergangsvers 2,12 zieht Jesus „mit seiner Mutter, seinen Brüdern [erstmals erwähnt] und seinen Jüngern nach Kafarnaum hinab." Seine Brüder erscheinen wieder in 7,1–10, wo ausdrücklich gesagt wird, sie glaubten nicht an ihn (Vers 5). Damit wird die markinische Tradition von der Opposition zu Jesus innerhalb seiner Familie bestätigt. Weiter bemerkenswert ist die Unbedenklichkeit, mit der in diesem Evangelium, das die Präexistenz Jesu kennt, von seinen Brüdern gesprochen wird. – R. *Schnackenburg*, Das Johannesevangelium II. Teil (HThK IV/2) (Freiburg – Basel – Wien 1971) 195.198, bestreitet die oft gesehene Parallelität zwischen Joh 2,1–11 und 7,1–10.

5.2. Joh 19,25–27

Zwischen der Kreuzigung Jesu in Joh 19,18 und seinem Tod 19,30b gibt es vier Kurzszenen, die alle christologisch bedeutsam sind. Die dritte erzählt von Jesu letzter Anweisung, wonach seine Mutter den Jünger, den Jesus liebte, als Sohn annimmt und der Jünger Jesu Mutter als seine eigene nimmt. Zu dieser Episode wie auch zu der Person des Jüngers, den Jesus liebte, gibt es unzählige Interpretationen; noch hat keine sämtliche Fragen beantworten noch alle Exegeten befriedigen können[78]. Vielfach steht bei der Interpretation das Bedürfnis Pate, ein „tieferes theologisches Verständnis" zu entdekken. Nicht irrelevant mag hier die Pietät des Sohnes sein, ein letztes Beispiel für die in Joh 13,1 angegebene Überschrift über die zweite Hälfte des Evangeliums zu geben: „Da er die Seinen, die in der Welt waren, liebte, erwies er ihnen seine Liebe bis zur Vollendung."[79] Mag, zweitens, die Anwesenheit von Jesu Mutter hier und am Anfang seiner öffentlichen Tätigkeit eine stilistische „inclusio" darstellen oder nicht, jedenfalls ist sie wieder ein antidoketischer Hinweis, diesmal, daß der Jesus, der im Begriff ist, am Kreuz zu sterben, ein Jesus des Fleisches ist[80]. Schließlich zeigen Jesu Worte an sie und an den anonymen Jünger, daß Jesus wirklich sterben wird und weiß, daß er sterben wird. Obwohl Auferstehung und Verherrlichung sozusagen „in der Luft" liegen, bedeutet sein Tod einen definitiven Bruch. Mit Joh 19,27 wissen wir, daß Jesus nicht in ein solches irdi-

---

[78] Siehe u. a. *R. Mahoney,* Two Disciples (s. Anm. 17). Heute gibt es zumindest weitgehende Einigkeit, daß dieser Jünger nicht etwa Johannes, Sohn des Zebedäus, sein soll; weiter, daß sein Erscheinen an den drei sicheren Stellen in der ersten Auflage des Evangeliums (13,21–30; 19,25–27; 20,1–10) mit schweren historischen Problemen behaftet bleibt. Im Anhangskapitel 21 wird ganz am Ende (21,24) dieser Jünger als Zeuge und Schreiber des Evangeliums angegeben.

[79] In Joh 19,30 wird Jesus als letztes Wort sagen: „Es ist vollbracht!" – zum Ende gebracht, vollendet.

[80] Joh 19,34 wird oft antidoketisch gedeutet. Zum Antidoketismus im vierten Evangelium s. weiter: *R. Schnackenburg,* Johannesevangelium I 150–153; *R. E. Brown,* John (s. Anm. 74) lxxvi–lxxvii (beide zurückhaltend). Auf alle Fälle wird das Evangelium in den ersten Jahrhunderten antidoketisch gebraucht; s. *J. N. D. Kelly,* Early Christian Doctrines (London ⁵1977) 141 f. 147.197 f. 280. Schon Ignatius von Antiochien, fast ein Zeitgenosse des vierten Evangelisten, hat Maria als antidoketischen Garanten genommen; s. *J. N. D. Kelly,* aaO. 492; *J. Quasten,* Patrology I. The Beginning of Patristic Literature (Utrecht – Antwerp ⁵1975) 65. Vgl. auch oben Teil 1 (zu Paulus) mit Anm. 2.

sches Verhältnis zurückkehren wird, das mit Worten wie „seine Mutter" umschrieben werden kann. Ab dieser Stunde, der Stunde seines Todes, werden die natürlichen Verpflichtungen, die er hatte, von einem anderen übernommen und ausgeübt. Jesus bleibt in majestätischer Weise Herr der Situation: wie er in Joh 13,27 selbst die ihm feindlichen Mächte in Aktion setzte, scheidet er jetzt, nachdem alles geordnet ist, in königlicher Würde aus dem diesseitigen Leben[81].

5.3. Zusammenfassung

Mit beiden johanneischen Szenen, wo die Mutter Jesu erscheint, gibt es historische Probleme; dies gilt besonders für die Szene unter dem Kreuz[82]. Nichtsdestoweniger hat gerade diese Szene, mit lukanischer Brille gelesen, der fortgeschrittenen Mariologie mächtige Impulse gegeben: Maria als neue Eva, Mutter aller Gläubigen bzw. der Kirche, Mediatrix aller Gnade, Co-Redemptrix[83]. Als Ausleger des vierten Evangeliums müssen wir aber besonders bei diesen Sze-

[81] *H. Schürmann,* Jesu letzte Weisung. Jo 19,26–27 a, in: *ders.,* Ursprung und Gestalt. Erörterungen und Besinnungen zum Neuen Testament (Düsseldorf 1970) 13–28, sieht in diesem Text einen tieferen Sinn: „Der ‚Jünger, den Jesus liebte‘, steht unter dem Kreuz als Traditionszeuge (Autor) des Johannesevangeliums. In Maria werden alle, die vom Erhöhten das Heil erwarten, die sein Wort annehmen wollen, diesem Zeugen und damit seinem Evangelium anvertraut. Jesus selbst erklärt vom Kreuz her dieses Evangelium gewissermaßen als ‚kanonisch‘ und für die Kirche verbindlich. In solcher Weise stiftet der ‚Erhöhte‘ vom Kreuze her für alle Zeiten die Einheit der Glaubenden…" (aaO. 25). Mit kritischer Nuancierung wird Schürmanns Ergebnis verschiedentlich übernommen von: *A. Dauer,* Passionsgeschichte (s. Anm. 73) 318–333 (hier: 326 Anm. 85. 329–333); *R. Schnackenburg,* Das Johannesevangelium III. Teil (HThK II/3) (Freiburg – Basel – Wien 1975) 319–325; *J. Blank,* Das Evangelium nach Johannes 3. Teil (Geistliche Schriftlesung 4/3) (Düsseldorf 1977) 120–125. Doch bleibt das Ergebnis m. E. fraglich; vgl. *R. Mahoney,* aaO. 95–103. – Zur Würde s. *J. Blank,* aaO. 119f.
[82] *A. Dauer,* aaO. 198–200, faßt die Gründe zusammen, warum Joh 19,26 f nicht historisch getreues Überlieferungsgut darstellen kann; er selbst meint, Jesu Verfügung (seine Mutter und den Jünger, den er liebte, betreffend) sei zu einer früheren Zeit und an anderem Ort erfolgt und dann vom Evangelisten in die Kreuzigungsszene versetzt (aaO. 200). Dies bleibt letztlich nur eine Vermutung, worauf eine Interpretation kaum aufgebaut werden kann; vgl. *J. Blank,* aaO. 120f.
[83] Mariologische, typologische und symbolische Deutungen besprechen und kritisieren *A. Dauer,* aaO. 327–331; *R. Schnackenburg,* aaO. 326–328; *R. E. Brown u. a.,* Mary 214–218, jeweils mit Literaturangaben. Siehe auch die kritischen Bemerkungen von *E. Haenchen,* Das Johannesevangelium. Ein Kommentar (Tübingen 1980) 552.

nen auf die alles überragende christologische Ausrichtung des gesamten Evangeliums insistieren. Implikationen für die Person Marias sind höchstens spekulativ und unsicher; sie werden nicht zuletzt durch die Beobachtung unwahrscheinlich gemacht, daß Jesu Mutter – wie auch der Jünger, den Jesus liebhatte – in diesem Evangelium anonym bleibt, ein Hinweis, daß es bei beiden mehr auf ihre Rollen im Gesamtdrama des Evangeliums ankommt als auf die Kenntnis historischer Einzelheiten ihrer Person[84].

6. Ergebnisse

Im Neuen Testament gibt es nicht nur ein Bild von Maria, sondern mindestens deren vier: jeder Evangelist läßt die Mutter Jesu so auftreten, wie er sie für die Gestaltung seiner christologischen Botschaft braucht. Kein Evangelist, außer Lukas in seinen ersten zwei Kapiteln, zeigt ein besonderes Interesse an ihrer Person[85]. Markus, der historischen Situation am nächsten, schildert sie als Mutter von sieben Kindern[86], die mindestens zu Anfang der missionarischen Tätigkeit ihres Sohnes ihm kritisch gegenüberstand. Trotzdem ist Markus' Schilderung keineswegs für Maria als Frau diskriminierend. Eher könnte ein solcher Vorwurf Matthäus treffen: von der Struktur seines Konzepts für die ersten zwei Kapitel her trägt Maria eine Schlüsselstellung, aber in der erzählerischen Ausführung wird sie ständig ihrem davidischen Mann Josef eindeutig untergeordnet. Hätte es ein dem Magnifikat ähnliches Lied im Matthäusevangelium gegeben, wäre die Ehre, das Lied auszusprechen, vermutlich Josef zugefallen. Natürlich hat Matthäus sie nicht bewußt diskriminiert; er blieb im Rahmen der sozialen Anschauungen des ersten Jahrhunderts[87]. Sig-

---

[84] Siehe *J. Blank*, aaO. 121.

[85] Eine mögliche Ausnahme ist Joh 19,26f; doch bleibt das Hauptinteresse christologisch, vielleicht auch ekklesiologisch. Das übrige Neue Testament (nach Apg 1,14) erwähnt Maria nicht.

[86] Ob der Markustext als historisch ausschlaggebend angesehen werden kann, hängt u. a. vom Verständnis ab, das man von späteren kirchlichen Aussagen gewinnt; vgl. den vernünftigen Vorbehalt bei *R. E. Brown u. a.*, Mary 72.291 f.

[87] Vgl. *V. Klein*, Art. Status of Women, in: Encyclopaedia Britannica Vol. 19 (Chicago etc. 1977) 906–916; hier 907: „... to the members of a stable society the various facets of a role form an integrated whole that is not only coherent in itself

nifikant ist, wo dieser Rahmen gesprengt wurde: in Lk 1 u. 2. Gerade weil eine Frau, die Frau Maria, darin die führende menschliche Rolle hat, haben diese Kapitel ihr besonderes Gewicht: die alte, ungerechte Ordnung wird umgestürzt, die bisher Erniedrigten – allen voran die Frau Maria – werden erhöht; die bisherigen Machthaber gehen leer aus, die Hungernden erfahren die Güte Gottes. Maria als aktiv Mitwirkende ist Gottes erwähltes Instrument bei der Einführung dieses unsagbaren Heils. Die Rolle der Mutter Jesu im Johannesevangelium fällt eindeutig hinter diese Höhe zurück. Nicht nur, daß der vierte Evangelist nichts über eine jungfräuliche Empfängnis bringen konnte oder wollte[88]; sein Gesamtkonzept ließ neben dem göttlichen Jesus keinen Platz für andere mächtige Gestalten.

Wie die drei großen Evangelien als Ausgangspunkt für mariologische Entwicklung dienten, ist hinlänglich bekannt. Im Zuge der sich artikulierenden und entwickelnden Christologie der ersten Jahrhunderte gedieh auch die Mariologie, die Christologie begleitend, ihr dienend und sie stützend. Mit Hilfe der jungfräulichen Mutter Gottes konnte sowohl die Göttlichkeit als auch die Menschlichkeit Jesu Christi zugleich einleuchtender und überzeugender festgehalten werden[89]. Die mariologischen Dogmen stehen in Verbindung mit den christologischen Dogmen. In diesem Bewußtsein ist man auch bemüht, in letzter Zeit gelegentlich auftretende Auswüchse einer unkontrollierten Mariologie in christologische Bahnen zurückzulenken[90].

---

but also closely entwined with complementary roles and supported by a network of social norms that the individual contravenes at his peril. Moreover, they appear to be inevitable and the natural order of things..."

[88] Sie hätte den Gedanken der Präexistenz Jesu untermauert, ohne für den Gedanken des Fleischwerdens nachteilig zu sein.

[89] Siehe Anm. 80; weiter *J. J. Pelikan*, Art. Mary, in: Encyclopaedia Britannica Vol. 11 (Chicago etc. 1977) 560–563; hier 561: „Some scholars have even maintained that the primary connotation of the phrase ‚born of the Virgin Mary' in the Apostles' Creed was this same insistence by the church upon the authentic manhood of Jesus."

[90] Vor dem Zweiten Vatikanischen Konzil versuchte eine Bewegung, die Verkündung neuer mariologischer Dogmen durch das Konzil zu erreichen, aber vergebens. Die mariologischen Impulse des gegenwärtigen Papstes Johannes Paul II. sind letztlich christologisch ausgerichtet: nicht etwa, weil Christologie männlich und Mariologie weiblich wären, sondern weil oberhalb aller Mann-Frau-Differenzen Christus unser Mittler zu Gott ist. Die Notwendigkeit eines Mittlers (Maria) für den Mittler (Christus) wurde empfunden, nachdem während des Mittelal-

Das Marienbild der vier Evangelien kann heute einige Impulse für die Neuwertung der Frau liefern. Es dürfte befreiend wirken, wenn die historische Maria als Mensch und Mutter gesehen werden kann, die im Leben auch ihre Schwierigkeiten hatte. Wenn die Kirche heute bei der Gewährleistung gleicher Rechte für Frauen und Männer nicht in vorderster Linie steht, mag der Aufruf des „Magnifikat" als ebenso unverdächtiger wie unmißverständlicher Anstoß zur Neuorientierung dienen. Wenn eine Frau sich heute fragen muß, ob es in der christlichen Religion für sie einen gleichwertig ehrenhaften Platz ohne Diskriminierung geben kann, kann sie in Lk 1 u. 2 zwar nicht ein jederzeit wiederholbares Beispiel, aber hinter diesem Beispiel doch die vorbildliche Einstellung des Evangelisten und wohl seiner Gemeinde sehen: wie selbstverständlich war diese Frau Maria fähig, das Wort Gottes zu hören, in sich aufzunehmen und bei der Einführung des alles umstürzenden Heils aktiv mitzuwirken. Abgesehen von Jesus selbst hat kein Mann im Lukasevangelium eine größere, wichtigere Rolle.

---

ters Christus zunehmend entmenschlicht und entrückt wurde. In moderner Zeit ist mancherorts die Entrückung Marias so weit gediehen, daß ein Mittler für sie notwendig wurde: „Ad Mariam per Josephum".

III

Die Frauen und die Osterbotschaft

Synopse der Grabesgeschichten
(Mk 16,1–8; Mt 27,62 – 28,15; Lk 24,1–12; Joh 20,1–18)

Von Hubert Ritt, Wuppertal

Mit der Osterbotschaft von der *Auferweckung des Gekreuzigten* steht und fällt der christliche Glaube. Paulus hat dies mit einer Prägnanz zum Ausdruck gebracht, welche bis heute nicht die geringste Aktualität verloren hat: „Ist aber Christus nicht auferweckt worden, dann ist unsere Verkündigung leer und euer Glaube sinnlos" (1 Kor 15,14). Die Ohnmacht des Menschen vor der Übermacht des Todes wird besonders in unseren Tagen immer schrecklicher erfahren; die rasende Entwicklung einer gigantischen Kriegstechnik zwingt uns ständig mehr, das Sterben zu lernen („ars moriendi"). Der Christ wird sich täglich bewußter, daß die „Schicksalsfrage" seines Glaubens an Ostern gebunden ist: „Wenn du mit deinem Munde bekennst: ‚Herr ist Jesus' und in deinem Herzen glaubst: ‚Gott hat ihn von den Toten auferweckt' (ὁ θεὸς αὐτὸν ἤγειρεν ἐκ νεκρῶν), so wirst du gerettet werden" (Röm 10,9). Der vieldiskutierte Themenbereich, wie es zum *Osterglauben* kam, füllt mittlerweile eine ganze wissenschaftliche Bibliothek[1]. Dennoch bestehen auch gegenwärtig noch die peinlichsten Unklarheiten über das Verhältnis zwischen den rhetorisch-argumentativen Texten (z. B. 1 Kor 15) und den lite-

---

[1] Immer noch bietet der Sammelband des internationalen Symposiums von Rom mit seinen 1510 Titeln einen guten Einblick in die Diskussion bis 1970: *E. Dhanis* (Hrsg.), Resurrexit. Actes du Symposium International sur la Résurrection de Jésus (Rom 1974); zur heutigen weitaus differenzierteren Fragestellung empfiehlt sich der informative Überblick bei *P. Hoffmann*, Art. Auferstehung II/1, in: TRE IV, 478–513 (Literatur: 509–513); zum status quaestionis: *A. Vögtle – R. Pesch*, Wie kam es zum Osterglauben? (Düsseldorf 1975); *J. Kremer*, Entstehung und Inhalt des Osterglaubens. Zur neuesten Diskussion, in: ThRv 72 (1976) 1–14; *E. Schillebeeckx*, Die Auferstehung Jesu als Grund der Erlösung. Zwischenbericht über die Prolegomena zu einer Christologie (Quaestiones disputatae, Bd. 78) (Freiburg i. Br. – Basel – Wien 1979).

rarisch-narrativen Textsorten (Ostergeschichten der Evangelien). Auf dieses Problem gehen wir hier nur nebenbei ein, da die formelartigen Wendungen, Bekenntnisse und Hymnen der Urkirche insgesamt den Bezug auf das leere Grab vermissen lassen[2]. Unsere Aufgabe wird es aber sein, nach einer möglichst genauen *Synopse der Grabesgeschichten* (1. Teil) jene Frage zu beantworten, welche leider zu sehr vernachlässigt wurde: Warum wird in der Überlieferung der Evangelien *die Verkündigung der Osterbotschaft ursprünglich und erstrangig an Frauen* gerichtet (2. Teil)? Was läßt sich über die geschichtliche Stellung der Frauen sagen? Warum wird die Zentralaussage der synoptischen „Grabesgeschichten", ἠγέρθη, „er ist auferweckt worden" (Mk 16,6; Mt 28,6; Lk 24,6) nicht primär den Männern aus dem Jünger- und Apostelkreis anvertraut? Wie ist es also möglich, daß zwar die frühesten literarischen Angaben ausschließlich Männer als authentische Zeugen der „Erscheinungen" des Auferstandenen ausweisen (vgl. 1 Kor 15,5–8), wogegen in späteren Texten auch Frauen genannt werden (Mt 28,9–10; Joh 20,11–18)? Warum kommt im Erzählablauf des Johannesevangeliums Maria von Magdala wohl zuerst zum „geöffneten" Grab (Joh 20,1), aber erst Petrus und der „geliebte Jünger" entdecken danach das „leere" Grab? Wie soll der Stellenwert ermessen werden, den die „Grabesgeschichten" einnehmen, wenn es um die Frage geht, „wie die Auferweckung Jesu als die Wirklichkeit erkannt werden kann, die für das gesamte Glaubensleben der nachösterlichen Christen bestimmend ist?"[3] Angesichts dieser bedeutungsvollen Fragestellung müssen unsere Texte mit größter Aufmerksamkeit gelesen werden;

---

[2] Es darf aber auf keinen Fall vergessen werden, daß auch im katechismusartig stilisierten „Urcredo" 1 Kor 15,3b–5 die einzelnen aufeinanderfolgenden Etappen des Geschehens „enumerativ" angegeben sind: ὅτι Χριστὸς ἀπέθανεν... καὶ ὅτι ἐτάφη καὶ ὅτι ἐγήγερται... καὶ ὅτι ὤφθη... So steht die Grablegung gleichrangig zwischen den Aussagen über den Tod und die Auferweckung Jesu. Insofern nun alle Oster*geschichten* die Oster*botschaft* „auslegen" (erklären, entfalten...), ist die Reflexion über das „leere" Grab eine konsequente Entwicklung der neutestamentlichen Textproduktion. Vgl. *F. Mussner,* Zur stilistischen und semantischen Struktur der Formel von 1 Kor 15,3–5, in: *R. Schnackenburg – J. Ernst – J. Wanke* (Hrsg.), Die Kirche des Anfangs (FS H. Schürmann) (Freiburg i. Br. – Basel – Wien 1978) 405–416.
[3] *W. Thüsing,* Die neutestamentlichen Theologien und Jesus Christus I. Kriterien aufgrund der Rückfrage nach Jesus und des Glaubens an seine Auferweckung (Düsseldorf 1981) 115.

nur eine methodisch gesicherte und traditionsgeschichtlich orientierte Erklärung der erzählenden Ostertexte aller kanonischen Evangelien kann uns helfen, eine Antwort auf die konkrete Frage zu finden: *Welche Bedeutung haben die Frauen für die Verkündigung der Osterbotschaft?*

1. Synopse der Grabesgeschichten

1.1. Hinführung zum Text

Eine kontinuierliche Lektüre des *Markusevangeliums*[4] läßt zwar eine relativ geringe Zahl von Frauengestalten erkennen, welche für den Handlungsablauf eine Rolle spielen; und dennoch sind einige Beobachtungen interessant: Von den 17 im ältesten Evangelium berichteten Wundergeschichten wird bereits der Beginn des Heilwirkens Jesu am Beispiel der Schwiegermutter des Petrus (Mk 1,29–31) mit dem zum Heilgestus gehörenden ἤγειρεν αὐτήν (er richtet sie auf, V.30) gekennzeichnet[5]. Folgerichtig wird dann in dem kompositio-

---

[4] Die literarkritischen Vorentscheidungen und das gattungsgeschichtlich beigebrachte Vergleichsmaterial üben auch in den neuesten Kommentarwerken (z. B. von R. Pesch, J. Gnilka, W. Schmithals) einen erheblichen Einfluß auf die Kommentierungsresultate der Ostergeschichten aus. Gerade für solche Texte, die dem heutigen Leser große Verständnisschwierigkeiten bereiten, sind sehr divergierende Forschungspositionen eher verwirrend; zusätzlich ist zu bedenken: „Wie wenige andere neutestamentliche Themen ist die Auferstehung Jesu in Gefahr, in den Bannkreis weltanschaulicher Vorentscheidungen zu geraten, die das theologische Verständnis präjudizieren"; dieses Zitat stammt aus: *J. Roloff,* Neues Testament (Neukirchen-Vluyn 1977) 196. Teilweise müßte für das Verständnis eines Kommentars noch – nolens volens – die Vorgeschichte des Kommentarwerkes (!) gelesen werden, wie z. B.: *R. Pesch,* Der Schluß der vormarkinischen Passionsgeschichte und das Markusevangelium: Mk 15,42 – 16,8, in: *M. Sabbe* (Hrsg.), L'Évangile selon Marc. Tradition et rédaction (Bibliotheca Ephemeridum Theologicarum Lovaniensium, Bd. 34) (Gembloux 1974) 365–409; umso erfreulicher sind Arbeiten, welche den Mut haben, klar verständliche Aussagen zu machen: *A. Lindemann,* Die Osterbotschaft des Markus. Zur theologischen Interpretation von Mark 16,1–8, in: NTS 26 (1980) 298–317; *G. Lohfink,* Der Ablauf der Osterereignisse und die Anfänge der Urgemeinde, in: ThQ 160 (1980) 162–176; *E. Schweizer,* Auferstehung – Wirklichkeit oder Illusion?, in: EvTh 41 (1981) 2–19.
[5] Zuerst wird an einem *Mann* in der Öffentlichkeit der Synagoge eine Dämonenbannung durchgeführt (Mk 1,21–28), dann schließt sich das Heilungswunder an einer *Frau* an (Mk 1,29–31), welche im familiären Bereich des Hauses lebt. Die

nell geschickt erzählten Doppelbericht von der Heilung der blutflüssigen Frau und Erweckung der Tochter des Jairus (Mk 5, 21–43) das Machtwort der Totenerweckung des Mädchens ausgedrückt durch: Σοὶ λέγω, ἔγειρε (ich sage dir, steh auf!, V. 41). Sollte dies ein reiner Zufall sein, daß hier immer das Lexem ἐγείρειν verwendet wird, das insgesamt im Neuen Testament 52mal für die Auferstehung bzw. Auferweckung Jesu verwendet wird? Um so merkwürdiger ist, daß die Ansage der Auferstehung Jesu in den Leidensankündigungen (Mk 8, 31; 9, 31; 10, 33 f) ausnahmslos mit dem Synonym ἀναστῆναι ausgedrückt wird, wobei der Nachklang der ältesten Formulierung (Mk 8, 31) im redaktionellen Schweigegebot (Mk 9, 9) erkennbar ist. Die gesamte vorwiegend kerygmatisch gestaltete Perspektive des Markusevangeliums ist zweifellos auf die Passions- und Auferstehungsdarstellung hin ausgerichtet; somit müssen die Hinweise auf das Leiden und den Tod (Mk 2, 20; 3, 6; 9, 12; 10, 45; 11, 18.27–33; 12, 1–9.10–12; 14, 8) einerseits und die „geheimen Epiphanien" des Auferstandenen (= „Christophanien") andererseits bei der Frage nach der Textkomposition mitbeachtet werden. Zu diesen letzteren, den literarisch als „Epiphaniegeschichten" gestalteten Texten gehören der Seewandel[6] (Mk 6, 45–52) und die Verklärung Jesu (Mk 9, 2–8). Der Bezug unserer Perikope vom Grabbesuch der Frauen zur Geschichte von der Salbung Jesu zum Begräbnis (Mk 14, 3–9; ausdrücklich in V. 8) muß später in seiner Tragweite für die gesamte Textkonstituierung der Passionserzählung erfaßt werden.

Selbstverständlich müssen wir unseren Beitrag begrenzen und können als Voraussetzung für das Verständnis der folgenden Darlegung auf die Ausführungen von J. Blank in diesem Buch hinweisen[7]. Dennoch möchten wir auch an dieser Stelle an das *Lukasevangelium*[8] erinnern, dessen Summarium Lk 8, 1–3 die hervorragende Be-

---

Literatur zum Verbum ἐγείρειν und die Stellenübersicht bietet *J. Kremer*, Art. ἐγείρω, in: Exegetisches Wörterbuch zum Neuen Testament I, 899–910.

[6] Vgl. *H. Ritt*, Der „Seewandel Jesu" (Mk 6, 45–52 par). Literarische und theologische Aspekte, in: BZ 23 (1979) 71–84.

[7] *J. Blank*, Frauen in den Jesusüberlieferungen (in diesem Band).

[8] Vgl. *M. Hengel*, Maria Magdalena und die Frauen als Zeugen, in: *O. Betz* – *M. Hengel* – *P. Schmidt* (Hrsg.), Abraham unser Vater. Juden und Christen im Gespräch über die Bibel (FS O. Michel) (Leiden – Köln 1963) 243–256; *F. Neirynck*, Le récit du tombeau vide dans l'évangile de Luc (Lc 24, 1–12), in: Orientalia Lovaniensia periodica 6/7 (1975/76) 427–441.

deutung der Frauen in ihrer Parallelität zum Jüngerkreis erkennen läßt. Die Reihenfolge von genannten Personen erlaubt in biblischen Personenlisten vielfach einen Rückschluß auf die Rangstellung, so daß es nicht verwunderlich ist, wenn Maria von Magdala und Johanna, die Frau des Chuzas, in der Frauenliste Lk 24, 10 wiederkehren.

1.2. Textanalyse von Mk 16, 1–8; Mt 27, 62 – 28, 15; Lk 24, 1–12

Obwohl die exegetischen Arbeiten in der literarkritischen und traditionsgeschichtlichen Beurteilung der Grabesgeschichten viele Divergenzen aufweisen, beabsichtigen wir hier keinesfalls eine Detailanalyse, welche sich den monographischen Werken nur in bescheidenstem Ausmaß hinzufügen ließe[9]. Wir müssen vielmehr auf der Grundlage des aktuellen Forschungsstandes genau dort eine präzise Auskunft der Texte erwarten, wo die *Funktion der Frauen für die kerygmatisch, historisch und apologetisch vermittelte Erfahrung* bestimmt werden soll: *Jesus ist von den Toten auferstanden;* hier geht es um den zentralen Inhalt des christlichen Glaubens.

1.2.1. Zu Mk 16, 1–8

Die Grabesgeschichten, wie sie uns in der heute vorliegenden Textgestalt begegnen, sind durch zahlreiche Verweise kontextorientiert und dadurch eng mit der Grablegungsgeschichte verbunden[10]. Eine

---

[9] Trotz aller Unterschiede in den Einzelergebnissen liegen verschiedenste Versuche von übersichtlichen Exegesen vor, welche die Ostergeschichten erklären, z. B. *H. v. Campenhausen,* Der Ablauf der Osterereignisse und das leere Grab (Heidelberg ³1966); *U. Wilckens,* Auferstehung. Das biblische Auferstehungszeugnis historisch untersucht und erklärt (Themen der Theologie, Bd. 4) (Stuttgart – Berlin 1970); *J. Kremer,* Die Osterevangelien – Geschichten um Geschichte (Stuttgart – Klosterneuburg 1977).

[10] Vgl. *R. Pesch,* Das Markusevangelium II (Freiburg i. Br. – Basel – Wien 1977) 519 f; hier stellt Pesch beinahe endlos alle Textbezüge zwischen der vorangehenden Perikope vom Begräbnis Jesu (Mk 15, 42–47) und dem Textstück vom Grabbesuch der Frauen zusammen. Viel wichtiger ist aber der *Unterschied* zwischen solchen *„Berichten"* (Mk 15, 42–47), die den Anschein einer chronikartigen Faktenaufzählung erwecken, auf der einen Seite und – formal (weil dialogisch konstruiert) sowie inhaltlich völlig unterschiedlich – der *„Bekenntniserzählung"* (Mk 16, 1–8) auf der anderen Seite; denn in einer „Bekenntniserzählung" liegt der

literarkritische Analyse als formal-synchronischer Arbeitsprozeß beobachtet erst innerhalb der zu Mk 16,5a („und sie gingen in das Grab *hinein*") und zu Mk 16,8a („und sie kamen *heraus*") parallelen synoptischen Tradition – szenisch klar umklammert – eine *stilechte Angelophanie* mit ihren typischen Elementen: Optische Wahrnehmung des (Mk/Mt) oder der beiden (Lk) göttlichen Boten, die Furchtreaktion, die korrespondierenden Trostformeln und – als eindeutiger Höhepunkt – die akustisch vernehmbare und konzentrisch angelegte *Offenbarungsbotschaft:*

a   Ἰησοῦν ζητεῖτε τὸν Ναζαρηνὸν τὸν ἐσταυρωμένον·
       Ihr sucht Jesus, den Nazarener, den Gekreuzigten;

b   ἠγέρθη, οὐκ ἔστιν ὧδε·
     er ist auferweckt worden, er ist nicht hier;

a'   ἴδε ὁ τόπος ὅπου ἔθηκαν αὐτόν.
       siehe, hier ist der Ort, wohin sie ihn gelegt hatten.

Nachdem die *Identität* Jesu von Nazaret, des *Gekreuzigten,* festgestellt ist, wird im effektiven Aorist die Mitteilung des geschichtlichen Handelns Gottes in voller *Realität* zum Ausdruck gebracht: *„Er ist auferweckt worden."* Der Interpret des Geschehens spricht das Offenbarungswort genau an der Stelle, wo der Hörer (Leser) in den vorangegangenen Epiphaniegeschichten des Markusevangeliums die Himmelsstimme vernahm (Mk 1,11par; 9,7par). Die bekenntnisartige Wendung ἠγέρθη „bedeutet" – so urteilt mit Recht A. Lindemann[11] – „zweierlei: Einerseits ist das Bekenntnis als Offenbarung dargestellt, d. h. es verdankt sich nicht selbst oder der religiösen Eingebung der Frauen am Grab, sondern einer von außen kommenden Mitteilung; andererseits aber ist eben diese Mitteilung so formuliert, daß sie für den Leser keine übernatürlichen Züge enthält: Das, was der νεανίσκος (= Jüngling; Anm. d. Verf.) hier als erster ausspricht, ist dasselbe, was die Christen zu allen Zeiten aussprechen: ‚Jesus, der Gekreuzigte, ist auferweckt.'" Daß nun das „leere Grab" nur mehr zur selbstverständlichen Konsequenz und nicht zur Voraussetzung dieser Osterbotschaft geworden ist, läßt der

---

Schwerpunkt in der Deutung (im Sinnbezug zum Hörer/Leser) des erzählten Geschehens.
[11] *A. Lindemann,* Die Osterbotschaft (s. Anm.4) 304f.

Text in seiner weiteren Folge eindeutig erkennen: „Siehe, hier ist der Ort, wohin sie ihn gelegt hatten" (Mk 16,6; vgl. Mt 28,6).

Die Osterbotschaft der Angelophanie ist aber noch keinesfalls zu Ende. Das eigentliche Problem beginnt erst mit der rätselvollen Spannung, welche den Erzählzusammenhang in V. 7 u. 8 erfüllt: Der Auftrag an die Frauen im *gegenwärtigen* Moment der Rede blickt *prospektiv* in die Zukunft: Die Frauen müssen „seinen Jüngern und dem Petrus berichten", daß ihnen der Auferstandene „nach Galiläa vorangeht und sie ihn dort sehen werden". Hier wird deutlich, daß das sukzessive Geschehen des Osterereignisses aus der (zwar nur „Etappen" aufzählenden) Bekenntnistradition für die Ostergeschichten strukturbildend wirkte (vgl. 1 Kor 15,4f: ...ἐγήγερται... ... ὤφθη Κηφᾷ... = er wurde auferweckt... er erschien ...). Ein Auftrag wird topisch zur Ereignissequenz der Angelophanie gehören[12]; dies läßt sich wohl nicht mit letzter Sicherheit behaupten, ist aber sehr wahrscheinlich. Anders verhält es sich mit dem *retrospektiven* Galiläahinweis (Mk 14,28): Dort wurde der Tod des Hirten – durch die Schriftreflexion mit Sach 13,7 – nicht allein als Flucht und Zerstreuung der Herde gedeutet, sondern – theologisch – bereits mit der Heilszusage (Sammlung der Herde in Galiläa!) verbunden. Jetzt – zur Zeit der Evangelienkomposition – bestätigt sich Galiläa als unverwechselbare Stätte der „Offenbarung", nicht nur als kerygmatisch stilisierter Schauplatz der ehemaligen Verkündigung des irdisch-geschichtlichen Jesus, sondern auch als historisches Kernland der nachösterlichen Jesusbewegung. Mit der zum Stil der Epiphaniegeschichte gehörenden Flucht nach einem ekstatischen Erlebnis (Mk 16,8bd) schließt die Perikope. Offen bleibt zunächst die Bedeutung der markinischen Notiz: „Und sie sagten niemandem etwas" (V. 8c); darauf werden wir erst später zurückkommen können. Die

---

[12] Mit Willkür und Phantasie werden Parallelen gesammelt (vgl. *R. Pesch,* aaO. 534), z.B. die Entlassungsformel einer Heilungsgeschichte (Mk 1,44), die Sendungsformel einer Prophetenberufung (Jes 6,9), anstatt die wenigen topisch interessanten Stellen von Aufträgen innerhalb von Angelophanien anzuführen: Num 22,35 („Der Engel des Herrn antwortete Bileam: συμπορεύθητι μετὰ τῶν ἀνθρώπων. πλὴν τὸ ῥῆμα, ὃ ἐὰν εἴπω πρὸς σέ); Aufträge im Zusammenhang mit der Ankündigung der Geburt (Ri 13: Simson) oder der Bereitung eines Opfers (Ri 6,20: Gideon); das beglaubigende Zeichen (Bestätigungsvision in Mk 16,7: ἐκεῖ αὐτὸ ὄψεσθε), das zwingend zu Verkündigungsschemen (vgl. Lk 1,5–25.26–38) gehört, ist eher typisch als ein Auftrag.

Spannung, die sich aus diesem Schweigen (V. 8) zu dem vorhin beschriebenen Auftrag (V. 7) ergibt, muß zur theologischen Absicht des Markusevangeliums gehören, welches mit diesem Vers ursprünglich endete.

1.2.2. Zu Mt 27,62 – 28,15

Wie sich sekundär an Einzelzüge der Epiphaniegeschichte apologetisch motivierte Legenden anschließen, zeigt Mt 28,11–15, welcher Text selbst wiederum eine Fortsetzung der Tradition von Mt 27,62–66 darstellt: Die massive Gegenpropaganda gegen die christliche Osterbotschaft verbreitet die boshafte These vom Leichenraub und unterschiebt den Jüngern einen raffinierten Betrug. Um so mehr erscheinen nun die Frauen in der erzählerischen Tendenz des Matthäusevangeliums[13] als besonders privilegierte Adressaten der Osterbotschaft. Die Inclusio (Mt 27,62–66 und Mt 28,11–15) betont als literarische Umklammerung der „Grabesgeschichte" – verstärkt durch das Geldmotiv (Mt 28,12.15) im Zusammenhang mit der Darstellung des Judasverrats (Mt 26,15; 27,3–9) – den Gegensatz aller beteiligten Personen in dieser „Ostergeschichte" zu den *Frauen*, die allein Handlungsträger des Geschehens sind. Ihre Bedeutung wird in dreifacher Weise verstärkt: a) In der äußeren narrativ „bis auf den heutigen Tag" (Mt 28,15) geltend gemachten Lügengeschichte vom Diebstahl der Leiche Jesu durch die Jünger (Mt 27,64; 28,13) treten die Jünger in den dunklen Hintergrund (vgl. Mt 26,56); die Kontrapointe der jüdischen Erzählgemeinschaft weist den Jüngern eine Zwielicht-Stellung zu, so daß die Pointe der christlichen Botschaft ἠγέρθη (= er ist auferweckt worden) an die Frauen in um so schärferen Kontrast hervortritt. b) Weiter wird eine viel massivere Ausgestaltung der Ostergeschichte durch „Epiphaniemotive" ein ganz bestimmtes Ziel im Auge haben: das Erdbeben (V. 2 a) (vgl. Ex 19,18; Ps 114,7), der „Engel des Herrn" (V. 2 b) (vgl. Mt 1,20.24;

---

[13] Vgl. *Th. R. W. Longstaff*, The women at the tomb: Matthew 28:1 re-examined, in: NTS 27 (1981) 277–282; *R. Kratz*, Auferweckung als Befreiung. Eine Studie zur Passions- und Auferstehungstheologie des Matthäus (Stuttgart 1973); eine erzähltextanalytisch sehr instruktive Arbeit: *A. Stock*, Die matthäische Ostergeschichte, in: *A. Stock – M. Wichelhaus*, Ostern in Bildern, Reden, Riten, Geschichten und Gesängen (Zürich – Einsiedeln – Köln 1979).

2,13; Gen 16,7–11; 22,11; Ex 3,2), sein Herabsteigen und triumphales Sitzen (V.2b–d), sein Aussehen (V.3) (vgl. Dan 7,9f; 10,6), der extreme Kontrast des Geschehens zu den „wie Tote" schlafenden Wächtern (V.4), die Appelle καί ίδού (und siehe, V.2a.7a), welche die eigentliche Grabesgeschichte umklammern, alle diese vielfältigen Epiphanie-Motive bekräftigen die Aussage: Die Osterbotschaft stammt unmittelbar *von Gott* und sie ist primär an die Frauen adressiert, welche nun das Grab „mit Furcht und *großer Freude*" (V.8b) verließen. c) Schließlich wird im Matthäusevangelium durch das besondere Galiläainteresse des Evangelisten der Auftrag an die Frauen (V.7) in Mt 28,9–10 legendär ausgestaltet, so daß die Frauen auch zu *Zeugen des erscheinenden Auferstandenen* werden. Hier handelt es sich kaum um eine apologetische Tendenz, die Leichenraubhypothese ad absurdum zu führen, sondern um eine literarisch-fiktive Brücke der matthäischen Redaktion, den Erzählkomplex von der „Stelle, wo er (= der Gekreuzigte) lag" (V.6), dorthin zu führen, wohin der Auferstandene „vorausgeht: nach Galiläa" (V.7).

1.2.3. Zu Lk 24,1–10

Die vielen redaktionellen Abänderungen des Lukastextes spiegeln die auffallende Eigenkonzeption des Theologen Lukas, wobei aber zweifellos die Abhängigkeit von Mk 16,1–8 festzustellen ist. Die „Grabesgeschichte" wird szenisch anders motiviert, indem die Aporie eingeführt wird, daß die Frauen den „Leib" (σῶμα) des Kyrios Jesus nicht finden (V.3–4a) und die beiden (!) Engel – im Aussehen vergleichbar mit Mt 28,3 – ihr Antlitz bis zur Erde neigen. In Korrespondenz dazu, daß sie Jesu Leib nicht *finden*[14], wird sprichwörtlich gesagt: „Was *sucht* ihr den Lebenden unter den Toten?" Nicht nur diese für die lukanischen Entrückungsgeschichten typischen Merkmale (Nichtauffinden einer gesuchten Person), sondern vor allem die Veränderung im weiteren Text zeigen die für Lukas charakteristi-

---

[14] Der Einfluß von Gattungsmotiven z. B. von Erzählungen, welche die Suche und Nichtauffindbarkeit von entrückten bzw. auferweckten Personen auf die „Bekenntniserzählung" Lk 24,1–12 ausübte (so etwa 2 Kön 2,16–18), muß beachtet werden; man darf sie aber keinesfalls überbewerten, wie dies *R. Pesch,* aaO. 522–527 sogar für Mk 16,1–8 tut. Die zentrale Aussage bleibt in der synoptischen „Bekenntniserzählung" das ήγέρθη.

sche Darstellung: Es wird bei ihm einfach die bei Mk 16,7 auf Galiläa ausgerichtete Erscheinungsverheißung in eine „Erinnerung" an eine in Galiläa geäußerte Leidens- und Auferstehungsansage Jesu umgewandelt (V. 6 c.7). So wird entsprechend der lukanischen Jerusalemkonzeption das stringente „Muß" im Heilsweg Jesu ebenfalls zum Inhalt der den Frauen geoffenbarten Osterbotschaft.

Die völlige Disparatheit der Verse 9–12 fällt ganz besonders auf, so daß der Umgang des Evangelisten mit einzelnen ihm vorliegenden Traditionssplittern zu einer „umfassenden Neugestaltung der Markus-Vorlage" wird[15]. Die Frauen „verkündigten" (ἀπήγγειλαν, V. 9) die Osterbotschaft den Elf und „allen übrigen (Jüngern)". Dann wird die Frauenliste angefügt und wiederholt (V. 10): „Sie erzählten es (ἔλεγον) den Aposteln", jedoch – welche Reaktion – „die Apostel hielten das alles für Geschwätz (ὡσεὶ λῆρος) und glaubten den Frauen nicht" (V. 11). Der Augenzeuge Petrus, der selbst das leere Grab inspizierte, geriet nur „in Verwunderung über das, was geschehen war" (V. 12).

1.3. Joh 20, 1–18

„Nur wer sich, kritisch und liebend zugleich, in den Text des Johannesevangeliums versenkt, kann die ursprünglichen Umrisse und Farben dieses Gemäldes noch sehen"; dieses Urteil von E. Haenchen[16] trifft uneingeschränkt auf die johanneische Darstellung zu. Wir können hier nicht allen Spannungen der Texteinheit Joh 20,1–18 in einer literarkritischen Analyse nachgehen[17], jedoch halten wir folgende Textentwicklung für sehr wahrscheinlich:

1.3.1. Ausgehend von V. 18 a („Maria von Magdala ging und verkündete den Jüngern") läßt sich ein Rest eines alten Traditionssplitters erkennen, der von einem Grabbesuch dieser auch in V. 1 ge-

---

[15] *G. Schneider*, Die Passion Jesu nach den drei älteren Evangelien (Biblische Handbibliothek, Bd. 11) (München 1973) 151.

[16] *E. Haenchen*, Das Johannesevangelium. Ein Kommentar, hrsg. von U. Busse (Tübingen 1980) 580.

[17] Vgl. *R. Schnackenburg*, Das Johannesevangelium III (Freiburg i. Br. – Basel – Wien 1975) 355–361; *J. Blank*, Das Evangelium nach Johannes III (Düsseldorf 1977) 160 f; *J. Becker*, Das Evangelium nach Johannes II (Gütersloh – Würzburg 1981) 605–612; *R. P. Mahoney*, Two Disciples at the Tomb. The Background and Message of John 20,1–10 (Frankfurt a. M. 1974) 194–227.

nannten Maria von Magdala und anderer Frauen (Plural in V. 2!) weiß. Diese Begebenheit „am ersten Tag der Woche... frühmorgens" wird gattungsgeschichtlich als Angelophanie vorgelegen sein, wovon nur mehr der erste Dialogteil (V. 12–13 a) erhalten ist.

1.3.2. Bereits die vorjohanneische Überlieferung verband nun diese Epiphaniegeschichte a) mit dem Motiv vom Leichenraub (V. 2 b. 13 b. 15 c), das wir bereits aus Mt 28, 13–15 kennen; b) weiter integrierte man auf dieser Traditionsstufe einen Bericht von einer Grabinspektion des Petrus, welche – aus Lk 24, 12 bekannt – den Grundbestand der Verse 3–10 ausmacht und vielleicht (vgl. Lk 24, 24) noch andere Jünger in der Begleitung des Petrus wußte. Diese Geschehensabfolge wäre uns von Lk 24, 22–24 verbürgt. c) Nun kennen wir aber von Mt 28, 9 f her eine weitere Textentwicklung: Die ursprüngliche Angelophanie wird zu einer Christophanie ausgebaut, welche wir nach dem „verbindenden" V. 14 im Teilbestand der Verse 15 ab. 16 vor uns haben, so daß V. 18 b zum Wortlaut einer Osterbotschaft wurde, die nun nicht mehr ein für Angelophanien zentrales ἠγέρϑη (= er ist auferweckt worden) zum Inhalt hat. Es wird folgerichtig der „Auftrag" mit der Ankündigung einer Bestätigungsvision, (in Galiläa) „den Herrn zu sehen" zu einem kurzen bekenntnisartigen Bericht stilisiert und zitiert (ὅτι):

„Ich habe den Herrn gesehen (ἑώρακα τὸν κύριον)."

1.3.3. Daß V. 18 c noch fortsetzt „und er habe ihr dies gesagt", verweist auf die – auch von Mt 28, 9 f bekannte – Szene der Berührung Jesu durch Maria von Magdala, welche in einem typisch dem Evangelisten zuzuschreibenden offenbarenden Wort (V. 17) vom „Aufstieg Jesu" die johanneische Interpretation des Geschehens anfügt und als Auftrag der Christophanie formuliert. „Jetzt ist die Stunde des Aufstiegs Jesu zum Vater, und das bedeutet für seine ‚Brüder', daß er auch ihnen einen Platz beim Vater bereitet, daß er ihnen jene Gemeinschaft mit Gott vermittelt, die er ihnen als Frucht seines Weggangs vorhergesagt hatte (vgl. 14, 21.23.28)."[18]

1.3.4. Die Einführung des „geliebten Jüngers" in das Textstück vom Grabbesuch des Petrus (V. 3–10) geht selbstverständlich auf die Redaktion des vierten Evangeliums zurück, die den autoritativen Traditionsträger, den „geliebten Jünger" nun in Joh 20, 8 zum „Ur-

---

[18] R. Schnackenburg, aaO. 377.

bild des Glaubens" machte, ja ihn sogar mit theologischer Absicht Petrus „im Wettlauf" gegenüberstellt.

Deutlich wird hier vor allem, daß die vorausgesetzte Angelophanie (V. 12) nur mehr den *Ort* angibt; *wo* das Haupt und *wo* die Füße des Leichnams Jesu lagen; es wird gleichsam der „Indizienbeweis" suggeriert, der sich aus der Grabinspektion der beiden Jünger (V. 3–10) ergibt. Trotz der traditionsgeschichtlichen Zusammenhänge mit den synoptischen Grabeserzählungen (vgl. V. 13) wird aber die Botschaft der Ostergeschichte, das *Daß* des Auferwecktseins Jesu in die folgende Wiedererkennungsszene (ab V. 14) gestellt.

2. Die Bedeutung der Frauen für die Verkündigung der Osterbotschaft

Es müßte uns in den bisherigen Ausführungen gelungen sein, „die *Grundhaltung der Rezeptivität*" eingeübt zu haben. Diese Forderung betont mit Recht Kl. Haacker[19], um die Intention unserer biblischen Verfasser für unsere Fragestellung verstehen zu können.

Wir hatten vorhin in der komplex verflochtenen johanneischen Ostergeschichte einen Traditionssplitter erkannt, der von einem einfachen „Grabbesuch der Frauen am Morgen des ersten Wochentages" (= Sonntags) berichtet (Joh 20, 1 f). Genau diese Überlieferung begegnet uns auch innerhalb der Emmausgeschichte (Lk 24, 22 c.23 a): „(Einige Frauen)… waren in der Frühe beim Grab, fanden aber seinen Leichnam nicht", wobei auch hier ein Hinweis auf eine Angelophanie erfolgt (Lk 24, 23 b). Es ist daher sehr wahrscheinlich, daß auch bereits im vormarkinischen Traditionsprozeß eine Notiz vom „Grabbesuch der Maria von Magdala und anderer Frauen" mit der eigentlichen Ostergeschichte (Angelophanie) (Mk 16, 5–8) kombiniert wurde, so daß in der Exposition (Mk 16, 1–4) vier Zeitangaben miteinander verschränkt wurden (ursprünglich dürfte καὶ διαγενομένου τοῦ σαββάτου [= als der Sabbat vorüber war] auf alle Fälle zum „Grabbesuch" gehört haben, wogegen die „Ostergeschichte" wahrscheinlich mit τῇ μιᾷ τῶν σαββάτων [= am

---

[19] *Kl. Haacker*, Neutestamentliche Wissenschaft. Eine Einführung in Fragestellungen und Methoden (Wuppertal 1981) 15.

ersten Tag der Woche] eingeleitet wurde; da beide Bezeichnungen der Morgenstunde zu möglichen Epiphaniemotiven gehören können, ist die Entscheidung für λίαν πρωΐ [= sehr früh] und ἀνατείλαντος τοῦ ἡλίου [= als die Sonne aufging] kaum eindeutig möglich). Eine Folgerung darf aber bereits gezogen werden:

2.1 Es wäre besser, wenn wir die „Grabesgeschichten" etwas differenzierter sehen würden und daher auch den Frauen in der Aussage dieser Texte unterschiedliche Positionen zuweisen könnten:

2.1.1. In den kurzen *„chronikartigen Berichten vom Grabbesuch"* haben die Frauen eine Bedeutung, welche das *historische* Faktum solcher Besuche beim Grab in Jerusalem verbürgt. Erst daraus abgeleitet – zur Sicherung der Zeugenschaft für Petrus (Joh 20,3; Lk 24,12) und andere Jünger (Lk 24,24; Joh 20,10) – wird die Tradition gestaltet und erweitert[20].

2.1.2. In den nach dem Vorbild von Epiphaniegeschichten sehr vielfältig gestalteten *„Bekenntniserzählungen"* sind die Frauen die ersten Adressaten der Osterbotschaft ἠγέρθη (= er ist auferweckt worden). Im Stilmittel der Angelophanie kommt den Frauen eine *kerygmatische* Bedeutung zu, welche *das* Hauptproblem der Passions- und Auferstehungs*verkündigung* der Evangelien narrativ (als Geschichten) und zugleich bekenntnisartig (als Konstatierung einer geschichtlichen Tat Gottes) entschlüsselt: Der gekreuzigte Jesus von Nazaret ist von Gott von den Toten auferweckt worden! Diese *ke-*

---

[20] Es ist daher sehr fragwürdig, in welchem Maß unsere Berichte aus dem Kontakt mit Gattungsmotiven von Erzählungen über die Nichtauffindbarkeit von entrückten oder auferweckten Personen mitgestaltet wurden. Wir teilen aber *auf keinen Fall* die Meinung von *Kl. Berger,* Die Auferstehung des Propheten und die Erhöhung des Menschensohnes. Traditionsgeschichtliche Untersuchungen zur Deutung des Geschickes Jesu in frühchristlichen Texten (Göttingen 1976) 117: „Die Berichte der Evangelien ‚über das leere Grab' wären zutreffender als ‚vergebliche Suche nach dem Leichnam' zu bezeichnen". Berger nennt vor allem Test Hiob 39–40. P. Hoffmann, Art. Auferstehung (s. Anm. 1) 499: „Die Erzählung vom leeren Grab läßt sich… als Veranschaulichung der Auferweckungsbotschaft im Kontext antiker Entrückungslegenden begreifen"; einzelne Gattungsmotive sollten aber nicht für die gesamte Textproduktion überbewertet (verabsolutiert) werden. Zu den gestaltenden Motiven der Texte vgl. *J. Jeremias,* Die älteste Schicht der Osterüberlieferungen, in: *E. Dhanis* (Hrsg.), Resurrexit (s. Anm. 1) 185–196; *A. Schmitt,* Entrückung – Aufnahme – Himmelfahrt. Untersuchungen zu einem Vorstellungsbereich im Alten Testament (Stuttgart 1973).

rygmatische Proklamation wird aber zu keinem „Relikt der Historie" und soll als stolze „Siegestrophäe" über den Tod, nämlich im „leeren Grab", bewundert werden, sondern jetzt erst erlangt die – vorwiegend in Galiläa verkündete[21] – Botschaft Jesu von Nazaret, der Ruf vom Anbruch der „Gottesherrschaft" seine unüberholbare Bedeutung für die gesamte künftige Geschichte. Frauen wird *diese* Osterbotschaft verkündet: Sie bildet einerseits die *Kontinuität* mit Jesus von Nazaret, dem Gekreuzigten, andererseits schafft sie das völlig Neue: Jesus, der gelitten hat, gestorben ist und begraben wurde[22], ist von Gott auferweckt und endgültig von Gott angenommen worden.

2.2. Um diese Kontinuität zu sichern, werden die *Frauenlisten* mit dem *Tod Jesu* (Mk 15,40f; Mt 27,55b.56; Lk 23,49: wegen Lk 8,2f nur allgemeine Nennung) verbunden, sie werden weiter mit dem *Begräbnis Jesu* genannt (Mk 15,47; Mt 27,61; Lk 23,55: wiederum nur Angabe „die Frauen, die ihn von Galiläa her begleitet hatten"), und schließlich werden Frauen nicht mehr nur als „Zeugen" des Geschehens angeführt, sondern als Träger der Handlung beim *Grabbesuch* (Mk 16,1; Mt 28,1; Lk 24,10), der – wie wir oben erwähnt haben und wie durch die lukanische Nachstellung bestätigt wird – mit der *Osterbotschaft von der Auferweckung Jesu* literarisch zur Einheit zusammengefügt wurde. Die übereinstimmend höchste Bedeutung kommt *Maria von Magdala* zu[23], die in der johanneischen Frauenliste (Joh 19,25) ebenfalls als „Zeugin des Todes Jesu" genannt ist und als einzige Person den Geschehenszusammenhang von Joh 20,1–18 erzählerisch gewährleistet. Es mag eine traditionsgeschicht-

---

[21] Daß Galiläa neben seiner theologischen Bedeutung auch topographisch das Fluchtziel der Jünger während des Prozesses Jesu war, bleibt gewiß. Vgl. *Th. Lorenzen*, Ist der Auferstandene in Galiläa erschienen?, in: ZNW 64 (1973) 209–221.

[22] Bis zu diesem Moment wird auf der Ebene der historischen Faktizität argumentiert; typisch dafür ist Lk 23,55: „Die Frauen, die mit Jesus aus Galiläa gekommen waren, gaben ihm das Geleit und sahen zu, wie der Leichnam in die Grabstätte gelegt wurde". Die Vorbereitung der Salbung dieses Leichnams (V. 56) würde nun auf dieser Ebene verbleiben und wirkt – literarisch – als motivierender Anlaß für den Grabbesuch (Lk 24,1).

[23] Vgl. *P. Benoit*, Marie-Madeleine et les disciples au tombeau selon Jn 20,1–18, in: *W. Eltester* (Hrsg.), Judentum, Urchristentum, Kirche (FS J. Jeremias) (Berlin 1960) 141–162.

lich selbständige Erscheinungsgeschichte Jesu vor Maria von Magdala gegeben haben – dafür spricht Joh 20,15–16 und Mt 28,9f –, aber die Erklärung dieser Textentwicklung dürfte sich folgendermaßen ergeben: Strukturell läßt sich das Initialgeschehen der Passions- und Osterüberlieferung in der Bekenntnistradition eindeutig aus der kombinierten Formel 1 Kor 15,3b–5 ablesen[24]. Diese argumentativ aufgereihten Etappen des Geschehens – Χριστὸς ἀπέθανεν... ἐτάφη... ἐγήγερται... ὤφθη (Christus starb... wurde begraben... wurde auferweckt... erschien) – konnten die *Frauen* in den narrativen Textsorten als „Zeugen" (in der Todesstunde und an der Begräbnisstätte Jesu) anführen.

Das historische Faktum vom Grabbesuch der Maria von Magdala und anderer Frauen am Ostermorgen bewirkt innerhalb des Erzählablaufs eine Änderung der Handlungsperspektive: Die Frauen werden zu den „Handlungsträgern"; dies ist wiederum der Anlaß, daß sie auch zu den „Adressaten" der Osterbotschaft werden: Der chronikartige Bericht vom Grabbesuch und die „Bekenntniserzählung" (Angelophanie) von der Auferweckung Jesu verschmelzen zu einer literarischen Einheit. In dieser traditionsgeschichtlichen Textentwicklung läßt sich hinreichend erkennen, daß die *geschichtliche Bedeutung der Frauen* in den Osterüberlieferungen erfaßt werden muß: *Weil* der historische Haftpunkt[25] des Grabbesuchs von Frauen (oder zumindest von Maria von Magdala) zum pragmatischen Ausgangspunkt für eine Erzählung des Osterbekenntnisses gemacht wird, wird *zuerst* diesen Frauen klar: Der Osterglaube ruht auf einer offenbarenden Tat Gottes; in der Auferweckung Jesu realisiert sich Gottes eschatologisch-machtvolles Wirken.

Dieses Osterevangelium bleibt immer mit der historischen Remi-

---

[24] Das wichtigste Werk zu dieser „Pistisformel" bleibt immer noch *W. Kramer*, Christos Kyrios Gottessohn. Untersuchungen zu Gebrauch und Bedeutung der christologischen Bezeichnungen bei Paulus und den vorpaulinischen Gemeinden (Zürich – Stuttgart 1963). Für die heutige Forschung ist mit Nachdruck darauf aufmerksam zu machen, daß wir *kein* „Entwicklungsgesetz" annehmen dürfen, welches als Prinzip der urchristlichen Verkündigung gegolten hätte: Am Anfang würde immer das „Einfache" (Primitive) stehen. Es ist für die Textproduktion durchaus möglich, daß auch komplexere Formen älter sind und einfache Formeln jüngeren Datums sein können.

[25] Vgl. *K. Schubert*, „Auferstehung Jesu" im Lichte der Religionsgeschichte des Judentums, in: *E. Dhanis* (Hrsg.), Resurrexit (s. Anm. 1) 207–229.

niszenz an den Grabbesuch der Frauen verbunden und dennoch übersteigt der Inhalt dieser Osterbotschaft alle Kategorien der historischen Faktizität: Jesus lebt totaliter aliter! Um dieses Bekenntnis sprachlich zum Ausdruck bringen zu können, bedarf es folgerichtig eines sachgerechten biblischen Texttyps, d. h. die vorliegende Epiphaniegeschichte ist dafür am geeignetsten. Um einen literarischen Bezug zu den ebenfalls vorgegebenen Traditionen von einer Grabinspektion des Petrus zu erreichen (vgl. Lk 24,12; Joh 20,3–10) wird der Bericht der Frauen als „leeres Geschwätz" (λῆρος ist Hapaxlegomenon!) (Lk 24,11) bezeichnet. Diese Bemerkung gehört zu den massivsten redaktionellen Stilmitteln, um zu zeigen: Die Garanten der Osterbotschaft sind die „Apostel" (Lk 24,10.11), identisch mit den Zwölf, jene Jüngergemeinde, die so zum Kern des wahren Israels und zur Präformation der künftigen Kirche wird.

Die Notiz vom „Geschwätz" der Frauen ist keinesfalls eine Herabsetzung des Zeugniswertes von Frauen, sondern ein Kompositionsmittel, um die kurzen Traditionsstücke der Grabbesuche zu verbinden. Dieselbe Aufgabe hat auch im Johannesevangelium der Hinweis, daß Maria von Magdala zu Simon Petrus und zum geliebten Jünger läuft, um sie vom „offenen Grab" zu informieren (vgl. Joh 20,2). Das neutrale Konstatieren solcher Grabesvisiten wird gleichrangig von Maria von Magdala (und weiteren Frauen) sowie von Petrus (und dem geliebten Jünger) als Rahmen der „Bekenntniserzählungen" festgehalten: „Jesus, der Gekreuzigte, ist auferweckt." Die Texte zeigen nicht die geringste Scheu, dieses „Bekenntnis" im Kontext der Grabbesuche der Frauen als Deutung des gesamten Osterglaubens auszusprechen. Das „eigentliche" Geschehen der Offenbarung, daß Gott nicht ein Gott der Toten, sondern der Lebenden ist, diese Innendimension des christlichen Glaubens kommt darin zum Ausdruck.

Die *geschichtliche Bedeutung der Frauen* liegt a) zunächst in der Tatsache, daß sie am Ostermorgen zum Grab Jesu kommen (*historischer Haftpunkt;* Ebene des vordergründigen Geschehens); weitaus wichtiger wird aber b) die damit folgerichtig verbundene Bekenntniserzählung: Frauen sind die ersten Adressaten der „von Gott her" (als Angelophanie) geoffenbarten Osterbotschaft: „Jesus, der Gekreuzigte, ist auferweckt" (*Bekenntnis;* Ebene der tiefgründigen Bedeutung des Osterglaubens). Daß in Jesus von Nazaret Gottes eschatologisch-machtvolles Wirken zur höchsten Wirklichkeit geworden ist (Priorität der Oster*botschaft*), wird beim Grabbesuch der Frauen (Faktum des Oster*berichtes*) geoffenbart.

2.3. Wenn die vorhin untersuchten „Bekenntniserzählungen" (synoptisch) die „Auferweckung Jesu" als *theo-logische* Aussage zum Ausdruck bringen, dann begreifen wir auch weitaus eher die rätselvollen sprachlichen Signale, die uns das Markusevangelium mitteilt: Einerseits – von der Topik der Angelophanie her gesehen – kann die überwältigende Botschaft ἠγέρθη (= er ist auferweckt worden) im begrenzten Adressaten dieser Offenbarung, in den Frauen, nur Angst, Schrecken, Zittern und fluchtartige Eile auslösen (Mk 16,8); diesbezüglich schließt der Text (vormarkinisch) bereits gattungsspezifisch: Das Geheimnis Gottes ist ein „mysterium tremendum". Andererseits schließt der Text (markinisch) mit der Bemerkung: „Und sie erzählten niemand etwas." Daß der *Gekreuzigte von den Toten auferweckt wurde* darf *jetzt* offenbar werden (vgl. Mk 9,9): Es ist die Stunde, in der die Osterbotschaft dem glaubenden Christen von Gott immer dann geoffenbart wird, wenn das „Evangelium von Jesus Christus, dem Sohn Gottes" (Mk 1,1) im Glauben angenommen wird. Auch der Besuch der Frauen beim Grab Jesu gehört noch in den Bereich des *(vordergründig)* Rätselhaften und Geheimnisvollen, aber – und darin liegt letztlich wiederum die geschichtliche Bedeutung dieses Ostermorgens – den Frauen konnte nun erstmals (*hintergründig*, weil *nach* Jesu Auferweckung; vgl. Mk 9,9) erstmals offenbar werden: Der irdisch-geschichtliche Jesus und der nachösterliche Christus sind voneinander nicht zu trennen.

IV

Die Stellung der geschiedenen Frau in der Umwelt des Neuen Testamentes

Von Ruthild Geiger, München

1. Scheidung als Realität

Die Rede von der „geschiedenen Frau" setzt zwei Fakten voraus: die Möglichkeit der Ehescheidung und damit implizit das Verständnis der Ehe weniger als einer individualistischen Partnerschaft, die nur auf dem jederzeit widerrufbaren Konsens der Partner beruht, sondern als einer gesellschaftlichen Institution, die vor allem rechtliche, wirtschaftliche und soziale Verpflichtungen mit sich bringt. In diesem Fall muß die Gesellschaft auch für die Beendigung einer so verstandenen Partnerschaft Lösungen bereitstellen.

Relativ einfach erscheint das, wenn die eheliche Gemeinschaft durch den Tod eines Partners beendet wird; hier kann damit gerechnet werden, daß die Familie für die etwa hinterlassene Frau und die noch unselbständigen Kinder sorgt[1].

Die Lebensgemeinschaft kann aber auch schon zu Lebzeiten der Partner beendet werden, auf Wunsch eines oder beider Partner. Mit der Möglichkeit des Scheiterns muß überall gerechnet werden, wo Ehen geschlossen werden, da die Spannung zwischen den gesellschaftlichen Ansprüchen und den persönlichen Schicksalen nicht immer zum Ausgleich kommt. In einer Gesellschaft, die die Mehrehe als Standardform der Ehe kennt, sowie da, wo die Wirtschaft noch ganz auf die Familie bezogen ist, die Ehe also vor allem Produktionsgemeinschaft zur Sicherung des Lebensunterhaltes mit

---

[1] Vgl. schon Codex Hammurabi § 171 (*H. Greßmann,* AOT [Berlin 1926] 398) „... die Gattin wird ihre Mitgift und das Geschenk, das ihr Mann ihr gegeben ... hat, nehmen und am Wohnort ihres Gatten wohnen, so lange sie lebt, wird sie die Nutznießung davon haben." Oder: Altassyrische Gesetze § 46 (aaO. 420) „... so kann sie im Haus ihrer Kinder, wo es ihr gefällt, wohnen. Die Kinder ihres Gatten werden sie beköstigen ..."

meist genau festgelegter Arbeitsteilung ist, spielt der heute in unserer Gesellschaft vorherrschende Abnutzungseffekt in der Zweierbeziehung sicher nur eine untergeordnete Rolle. Unbekannt ist jedoch das Problem der Scheidung auch in diesem Rahmen nicht.

Nun ist zwar für viele antike Autoren die Tatsache, daß Ehen auseinanderbrechen und dies auch öffentlich geduldet und sogar bestätigt wird, ein Zeichen für die Depravation und Entartung der Gegenwart – diese Argumentationsweise ist also durchaus keine neuzeitliche Erfindung –, doch dürfte sich in einem solchen Urteil eher eine plötzliche persönliche Betroffenheit des Sprechers als eine echte Veränderung der gesellschaftlichen Realität spiegeln. Denn selbst wenn die Gesetzgebung ein Verbot der Scheidung ausspricht, setzt sie die Möglichkeit des Scheiterns einer Ehe voraus. Mehr noch: das Problem ist, wenn es zu einer solchen Reglementierung kommt, nicht nur existent, sondern als Problem erkannt und besteht auch schon so lange und in solchem Umfang, daß der Gesetzgeber normierend eingreifen muß. Das Gesetz macht ja nur das eigenmächtige Vorgehen des Scheidungswilligen überflüssig: er ist nicht mehr auf Flucht[2] oder Mord[3] angewiesen, um dem Partner und den damit verbundenen Pflichten zu entgehen. Mehr noch, es gibt beiden Partnern die Möglichkeit, eine neue Bindung einzugehen, ohne dem Vorwurf des Ehebruches ausgesetzt zu sein. Das ist da, wo dem Mann die Polygamie erlaubt ist, vor allem für die Frau von großer Bedeutung. Aber auch für den Mann gibt es hauptsächlich einen wichtigen Aspekt, nicht auf eine Nebenfrau, sondern auf Scheidung und erneute Heirat zuzusteuern: nur in diesem Fall sind die Kinder aus der zweiten Verbindung denen aus der ersten gleichberechtigt, was die gesellschaftliche Stellung und die spätere Aufteilung des Familienvermögens betrifft[4].

[2] Flucht: Codex Hammurabi § 136 (aaO. 394) „Gesetzt ein Mann hat seine Stadt aufgegeben und ist geflohen, nachher ist seine Gattin in ein anderes Haus eingetreten … so wird die Gattin … zu ihrem Gatten nicht zurückkehren."
[3] Mord: Livius (8, 18) berichtet, daß im Jahr 425 a. u. c. = 329 a. Chr. n. 170 römische Matronen, also Angehörige der Oberschicht, ihre Männer ermordet hätten. Auch wenn Livius dieses Motiv nur zur Auffüllung eines ansonsten ereignislosen Jahres bringt, zeigt der Text doch an, auf welche Weise ein Eheproblem gelöst werden konnte und sicher auch gelöst wurde, wenn der Ausweg des Auseinandergehens nicht gangbar war.
[4] *Cicero*, De or. I 183 tadelt einen Mann, der an seinem spanischen Wohnsitz seine schwangere Frau verlassen und in Rom erneut geheiratet hat. Nicht das

Für die Antike ist bei diesen allgemeinen und den folgenden speziellen Ausführungen immer zu bedenken, daß unsere Kenntnis der Lebensverhältnisse jener Zeit sich nur auf die Oberschicht beziehen; auch wenn man annehmen kann, daß die Unterschicht sich einen weithin analogen Rahmen gesetzt hat, so dürften gerade auf diesem Gebiet, wo es bei der normgebenden Schicht zum nicht geringen Teil um Transaktionen von unter Umständen beträchtlichen Vermögenswerten ging, bei der ärmeren Bevölkerung die Verhältnisse für den schwächeren Teil, die Frau, wesentlich schwieriger gewesen sein. Der Rechtsschutz im Fall einer Scheidung war für die Patriziertochter sicher selbstverständlich, für die Handwerkersfrau aber kaum zu erreichen.

2. Rechtliche Regelungen bei einer Scheidung

2.1. Allgemein

In dem sehr enggefaßten Rahmen dieses Beitrages kann die rechtliche Stellung der Frau in der römischen, hellenistischen und jüdischen Umwelt des Neuen Testamentes nicht im Ganzen untersucht werden. Will man jedoch Aufschlüsse über die geschiedene Frau erlangen, muß man sich, was den rechtlichen Teil dieser Frage anbelangt, unter anderem mit dem Eherecht befassen, da dieses nicht nur den Status der verheirateten Frau beschreibt, sondern auch die Modalitäten der Eheauflösung regelt, indirekt also etwas über die Stellung der geschiedenen Frau aussagt.

Im Umkreis des Neuen Testamentes ist als ins Auge fallende Voraussetzung festzustellen, daß das Zusammenleben überall von patriarchalischen Strukturen geprägt war; die Frau verläßt mit der Eheschließung ihre väterliche Familie und gehört fortan der des Ehemannes mehr oder minder fest an. Von zu vermutenden matriarchalischen Strukturen der Vorzeit, die ihren Ausdruck etwa in einer „Besuchsehe"[5] gefunden hätten, ist in den uns vorliegenden Texten

---

Verlassen der Ehefrau ist aber der Grund des Tadels, sondern die Rechtsunsicherheit, welche Kinder jetzt legitim sind, die durch diesen Akt entstanden ist.
[5] Zur Besuchsehe vergleiche aber: Gen 31,43; Laban beansprucht die gesamte Familie Jakobs als seine Familie.

aus hellenistisch-römischer Zeit kaum etwas festzustellen. Vielmehr sind auch die Gesetze, die die Frau vor der Willkür des Ehemannes schützen, eher dem Interesse der Blutsverwandten der Frau an deren Nachkommen, die ja in einem weiteren Sinn Familienangehörige des großväterlichen Hauses und unter Umständen sogar erbberechtigt sind, zu verdanken. Die Wahrnehmung dieser Rechte stand aber nicht der betroffenen Frau selbst zu, sondern sie wurde dabei von einem männlichen Angehörigen vertreten. Die Kinder verblieben im Regelfall in der Familie des Vaters, die Frau kehrte in die Familie ihres Vaters zurück; ihr stand für ihren Unterhalt nach der Scheidung ein den wirtschaftlichen Verhältnissen angemessenes Vermögen zu, das schon bei der Eheschließung festgelegt wurde und während der Dauer der Ehe dem Ehemann „in Hinblick auf" seine Frau zur Verfügung stand.

Entspricht so das Gesamtbild dem vorherrschenden Patriarchat, so gibt es daneben doch noch Einzelfragen, die in Rom, in Griechenland und im Judentum verschieden gelöst wurden:

- Wer stellte den Betrag, der den Unterhalt der geschiedenen Frau sicherte?
- Wer konnte die Scheidung verlangen?
- Welche Gründe werden bei einem solchen Verlangen akzeptiert?

2.2. Rom

In Rom stand die Frau bis in die frühe Kaiserzeit in der Gewalt („manus") des Familienoberhauptes; das konnte ihr Vater sein, aber auch ihr Großvater, wenn er noch lebte und seine Söhne nicht aus ihrem Abhängigkeitsverhältnis entlassen hatte, sie „emanzipiert" hatte. Die Frau wurde zwar durch die Heirat von der manus des Oberhauptes ihrer Familie frei, aber nur, um in die manus ihres Ehemannes bzw. dessen Gewalthabers überzugehen.

Ihre eigene Familie stellte ihr die Mitgift (dos) zur Verfügung, die dem Inhaber der manus als treuhänderisches Eigentum übertragen wurde. Diese Mitgift mußte der Mann im Fall einer Scheidung grundsätzlich wieder herausgeben, aber er konnte für jedes eheliche Kind ein Sechstel einbehalten, jedoch nicht mehr als die Hälfte des Betrages. Weitere Verluste erlitt die Frau, wenn das Verschulden am Zerbrechen der Ehe ihr zugeschoben wurde. Persönliches Eigentum der Frau, mit dem sie durchaus selbständig wirtschaften konnte, mußte schon in der späten Republik der Mitgift nicht mehr unbedingt einverleibt werden[6].

Beide Partner, Mann wie Frau, konnten die Scheidung verlangen; bis zur Zeit Kaiser Konstantins kann die Scheidung – wie auch die Eheschließung – ganz formlos durch einfachen Konsens geschehen, sofern es sich nicht um eine konfarreierte, d. h. feierlich im kultischen Rahmen geschlossene, Ehe handelte; in diesem Falle mußte die Trennung dann in einem analogen Verfahren als diffarreatio vollzogen werden[7].

Die Gründe, die Aussicht auf Anerkennung haben, sind in der frühen Republik bei Mann und Frau höchst asymmetrisch, nähern sich dann aber einander an. In der Frühzeit genügte schon Weingenuß der Ehefrau als Scheidungsgrund, während Trunksucht des Ehemannes kein ausreichender Grund war, die Partnerschaft aufzukündigen.

Eine bedeutsame Verschiebung in diesem ganzen System zeichnet sich zu Beginn der Kaiserzeit ab: Der Senat entläßt auf Geheiß des Kaisers dessen Frau Livia und dessen Schwester Octavia ersatzlos aus dem bestehenden mancipium, „emanzipiert" die beiden Frauen, die dem Augustus am nächsten standen: der Präzedenzfall der gewaltfreien Frau war gegeben.

2.3. Griechenland

In Griechenland ist es zu einer einheitlichen Rechtsentwicklung nicht gekommen, zu sehr bestand die einzelne Polis auf ihrem Sonderrecht. Doch lassen sich einige charakteristische Züge aufzeigen: Mit Rom gemeinsam findet man im griechischen Bereich den Usus, die Frau durch eine Mitgift, die von ihrer väterlichen Familie gestellt wird, materiell zu sichern. Anders als in Rom scheidet die Frau aber aus dieser ihrer Familie auch für die Dauer ihrer Ehe nicht vollständig aus, sondern wird von ihrem κύριος, dem, der über sie be-

---

[6] Zum römischen Eherecht: *N. Liebs,* Römisches Recht (UTB 465) (Göttingen 1975) 119–130.

[7] Zur konfarreierten Ehe: *R. Sohm – Mitteis – Wenger,* Institutionen, Geschichte und System des römischen Privatrechtes § 86 (München – Leipzig) [17]1924.

stimmen konnte, also meist ihrem Vater, an eine andere Familie mehr oder weniger ausgeliehen, um die Erhaltung und Weiterexistenz dieser Familie zu ermöglichen. Die Frau mußte es hinnehmen, wenn ihr Kyrios sie gegen ihren und ihres Partners Willen aus einer bestehenden Ehe herausnahm und anderweitig verheiratete, wenn dies im Interesse der Familie liegen sollte. An diesen Kyrios fiel auch die Mitgift (προίξ) im Fall des Todes der Ehefrau, sofern die Ehe kinderlos geblieben war, oder der Auflösung der Ehe zurück. Bei Verschulden der Frau bleibt die προίξ beim Ehemann. In der Zeit des Hellenismus war jedoch das Kyriat kaum mehr von realer Bedeutung, die Einrichtung der προίξ wird immer mehr verdrängt durch φέρνη (meist persönliche Ausstattung und Geld) und προσφορά (meist Geld und Immobilien), d. h. Vermögenswerte, die während und nach einer Ehe der Frau direkt zur persönlichen Verfügung stehen[8]. Für die Dauer der Ehe mag das ohne große Bedeutung sein, für die verwitwete oder geschiedene Frau brachte es ganz andere Aktionsmöglichkeiten.

Wie sehr sich in hellenistischer Zeit die Rechtslage zugunsten der Frau verschob, zeigen besonders deutlich die zahlreichen Papyri mit Eheverträgen griechischer Kolonisten, die in Ägypten gefunden wurden: Die Mitgift spielt, soweit sie überhaupt noch auftaucht, keine wirtschaftlich bedeutsame Rolle mehr, während die eigentlichen Vermögenswerte in φέρνη und προσφορά übertragen werden, die auch von der Frau selbst gestellt werden konnten – dafür ist die Geschäftsfähigkeit der Frau unabdingbare Voraussetzung[9].

Es ist nun zwar sehr wahrscheinlich, daß diese extremen Veränderungen in der griechischen Handhabung des Ehegüterrechtes nur auf ägyptischem Boden möglich waren; die dortige Fallachenkultur hat ja von Anfang an der Frau eine wesentlich stärkere Rechtsposition zugestanden. Doch daß sich durch den Zusammenstoß der so unterschiedlichen Kulturen eine Veränderung der Stellung der griechischen Frau zu ihren Gunsten ergab, dürfte für die Gesamtsituation bezeichnend sein.

---

[8] *H. J. Wolff,* Die Grundlagen des griechischen Eherechtes, in: *Berneker,* Zur griechischen Rechtsgeschichte (Darmstadt 1968). *K. Thraede,* Ärger mit der Freiheit, in: *G. Scharffenorth – K. Thraede,* Freunde in Christus werden. Die Beziehung von Mann und Frau als Frage an Theologie und Kirche (Gelnhausen – Berlin 1977) 46.
[9] *G. Häge,* Ehegüterrechtliche Verhältnisse in den griechischen Papyri Ägyptens bis Diokletian (Gräzistische Abhandlungen 3) (Köln – Graz 1968).

Da im hellenistischen Bereich schon durch eine bestehende Lebensgemeinschaft eine gültige Ehe gegeben ist, genügt zur Scheidung die
einfache Aufhebung dieser Lebensgemeinschaft. Die Scheidungs-
verträge regeln nur die sich aus den Ereignissen ergebenden vermögensrechtlichen Probleme: Handelte es sich um eine ἀποπομπή,
d. h. die Initiative ging vom Mann aus, er schickte die Frau weg,
mußte er die φέρνη sofort zurückgeben; verließ die Frau von sich
aus die gemeinsame Wohnung und war dies als ἑκουσία ἀπαλλαγή
einzustufen, so wurde dem Mann eine gewisse Rückzahlungsfrist
eingeräumt.

2.4. Judentum

Von den geschilderten eherechtlichen Typen unterscheidet sich die
Ehe im semitischen Bereich grundsätzlich dadurch, daß es sich hier
eher um den Typ der „Kaufehe" handelt, der Unterhalt der Witwe
oder der geschiedenen Frau demnach vom Ehemann bereitzustellen
war. Dies geschah bei der jüdischen Bevölkerung mittels der Ke-
tuba, einer im Ehevertrag festzulegenden Summe, ohne die der
ganze Vertrag nichtig war.

Die hebräischen Termini ba'al (Herr, Besitzer) und bᵉula (Beherrschte, Besitz) für Ehemann und Ehefrau kennzeichnen die Art
der Lösung partnerschaftlicher Probleme wohl hinreichend, ebenso
die Tatsache, daß die Ehefrau im Dekalog unter der Habe des Mannes aufgeführt wird (Ex 20,17). Die Einehe dürfte aus wirtschaftlichen Gründen vorgeherrscht haben, ohne daß der Harem eines
Mächtigen anstößig gewesen wäre.

Die Ehen wurden von den Eltern arrangiert (Gen 21,21; 24,3;
28,1; 34,4 u. ö.), aufgelöst werden konnten sie nur durch einen Akt,
den der Ehemann und nur er setzen mußte. Dabei ist auch im jüdischen Bereich eine gewisse Entwicklung festzustellen: Vor ca. 650
konnte der Mann die Frau ohne Formalitäten entlassen, wie es z. B.
der Text von Gen 21,10 voraussetzt. In der letzten Phase der natio-
nalen Selbständigkeit erscheint dann die Einrichtung des Scheide-
briefes (geṭ); die Ehe wird damit vor einer unüberlegten, überstürz-
ten Auflösung geschützt, allerdings ohne daß die Gründe, die den
Mann zur Ausstellung des geṭ führten, sachlich überprüft werden
mußten. In einer weiteren Stufe werden dann auch die möglichen

Scheidungsgründe festgelegt, die allerdings die Frau immer noch voll der Willkür des Mannes aussetzen[10].

Der Frau stand kein entsprechendes Rechtsmittel zur Verfügung. Zur Zeit des Neuen Testamentes konnte sie bei Vorliegen bestimmter Gründe die Scheidung verlangen, das Rabbinat als registrierende und beglaubigende „Behörde" war auch gehalten, ihr in diesem Fall zur Freiheit zu verhelfen, unter Umständen sogar, indem es gegen den scheidungsunwilligen Ehemann Zwangsmittel einsetzte. Wenn sich der Mann aber trotz allem weigerte, den Scheidebrief auszustellen, war sie dieser Willkür insoweit ausgesetzt, daß sie zwar nicht zum Zusammenleben gezwungen werden konnte, eine neue Heirat ihr aber auch verwehrt war. Eine geschiedene Frau kehrte in die väterliche Familie zurück und konnte dort alle Rechte wahrnehmen, die ihr vor der Ehe zugestanden hatten[11].

Von dieser allgemein gültigen Rechtslage, die in Israel bis heute die Gerichte beschäftigt, finden wir zwei bemerkenswerte Abweichungen:

In Elephantine, der jüdischen Militärkolonie in Oberägypten, fand man jüdische Eheverträge, die Mann und Frau völlig gleiche Rechte einräumten: „If tomorrow or any later day Miphtahya shall stand up in the congregation and say: ‚I divorce As Hor, my husband,‘ the price of divorce shall be on her head... If tomorrow or any later time As Hor shall stand up in the congregation and say... her marriage settlement shall be forfeited."

Die Scheidung konnte hier also ebenso auf den Wunsch der Frau wie auf den des Mannes hin vollzogen werden, eine Formpflicht über die öffentliche Willenserklärung hinaus war nicht vorgesehen, ebensowenig weiterreichende Sanktionen.

Das andere Beispiel: Josephus erzählt in ant 15,7,10 (259), daß Salome ihrem Gatten Kostobar den Scheidebrief geschickt habe. Er tut dies aber nicht, ohne ausdrücklich und betont darauf hinzuweisen, daß dies eine Handlungsweise sei, die bei den Juden nur dem Mann als Privileg zuständе (ἀνδρὶ μὲν γὰρ ἔξεστιν παρ' ἡμῖν τοῦτο ποιεῖν), die Frau aber keinesfalls so handeln dürfe. Auch bei anderen parallel gelagerten Fällen versäumt er den Hinweis auf die entgegengesetzte Rechtslage nicht[12].

---

[10] „Etwas Häßliches", das nach Dtn 24,1 als Scheidungsgrund ausreicht, ist ein überaus dehnbarer Begriff. Vgl. (Strack-)Billerbeck zu Mt 5,31 (I, 303–321, bes. 319 f).

[11] Lev 22,13: Die zurückgekehrte Priestertochter darf wieder vom Opferfleisch essen.

[12] ant 18,5: Herodias trennt sich von Herodes „den väterlichen Gesetzen zum Trotz".

Der Kontakt mit der liberalen Haltung der Nichtjuden bringt also auch hier eine Verbesserung der Situation der Frau, allerdings nur in besonders gelagerten Fällen: Für die Familie des Herodes war das Gesetz auch sonst nicht die absolute Norm, die Militärkolonie Elephantine lag weit ab vom Mutterland und hatte sich auch in anderen Fragen von der jüdischen Tradition entfernt. Bei der Bevölkerung Palästinas der damaligen Zeit sind keine derartigen Veränderungen festzustellen.

Übersehen sollte man diese neue Praxis jedoch keinesfalls, wenn die Stellung der geschiedenen Frau zur Zeit der Urkirche beschrieben werden soll; denn sie zeigt doch deutlich, daß gerade in der Umwelt des Neuen Testamentes ein grundlegender Wandel vor sich ging: die Frau beansprucht mehr Rechte als ihr bisher zugestanden waren, und sie war auch fähig, dies durchzusetzen. Sie kann schrittweise aus der totalen Abhängigkeit heraustreten und ihre Interessen selbst wahrnehmen. Dabei ist die Möglichkeit, von sich aus den Scheidungsakt zu setzen, für die Jüdin in der ägyptischen Kolonie genauso wichtig wie die „Emanzipation" für die Römerin.

3. Die gesellschaftliche Stellung der geschiedenen Frau

Die oben aufgeführten Regelungen für den Fall einer Scheidung geben einen Teilaspekt der Wirklichkeit wieder; entsprechend der grundsätzlich konservativen Haltung der gesetzgebenden Institutionen spiegelt sich darin der eher konservative Teil der Gesellschaft mehr als der liberale. Schon für diesen Teil konnte aber das Urteil des Tacitus (ann 3,34,2) gelten: multa duritia veterum in melius et laetius mutata.

Vielmehr gilt dies aber für die alltäglichen gesellschaftlichen Abläufe. Es ist ja längst klargestellt, daß das zurückgezogene Leben der Frau, ihre Beschränkung auf den häuslichen Bereich eher in Projektionen bestimmter neuzeitlicher Kreise als in der antiken Realität vorhanden waren[13]. Gerade die Betonung solcher hausfraulicher

---

[13] *Ch. Seltmann,* Die Geliebte der Götter (1958) 134, versucht in seinem sehr anregenden Buch, diese Darstellung der abgeschiedenen, in ihrem Heim aufgehenden Frau aus den Bedürfnissen und dem „retrospektiven Wunschdenken" der Gelehrten des 19. Jh. und ihrer Epigonen zu erklären.

Tugenden weist ja auf die andersartigen tatsächlichen Konstellationen hin: die Frauen jener Zeit stehen wichtigen Ämtern vor. So baut in Priene eine Phile einen Aquädukt und das zugehörige Wasserreservoir; die Frauen sind voll geschäftsfähig, bewirtschaften Landgüter, besitzen Rennställe oder Ziegeleien, sie werden dementsprechend auch selbständig besteuert[14], sie können in eigener wie in fremder Sache vor Gericht auftreten[15]. Auch Ausbildungswege stehen ihnen offen: es gibt Berufssportlerinnen, Handwerkerinnen, Ärztinnen. Die Frau – und das gilt sicher auch und gerade für die geschiedene Frau – konnte ein selbständiges Leben führen, Geld und Vermögenswerte nach eigener Entscheidung bewegen, es mußte durchaus nicht immer ein Vater oder Ehemann seine schützende Hand über sie halten. Noch mehr als bei den juristisch festgelegten Fakten gilt hier, daß der persönliche Kontext des Aktionsradius der Frau mehr bestimmte als allgemeingültige Rechtssätze[16].

Trotzdem stellt sich der frühchristliche Rigorismus, der im Neuen Testament und bei den apostolischen Vätern von den Frauen vor allem Unterordnung erwartet, nicht ganz gegen die Mentalität der Zeit. Auch wenn Augustus die Frauen seiner nächsten Umgebung vom mancipium befreite, pries er doch ansonsten allerorten die häusliche Frau, die sich auf die Leitung des jetzt wieder weitgehend autarken Haushaltes konzentrierte, darin aufging und sonst nicht in Erscheinung trat. Seine Schwester Octavia, die nach der Trennung von Marcus Antonius und nach dessen Tod sich ganz der Erziehung der Kinder des Antonius, seien sie nun von ihr oder von ihrer Vorgängerin Fulvia, widmete, wird dementsprechend anerkannt. Für ihre Stellung und ihre Wirkungsmöglichkeiten wichtiger dürfte allerdings die Befreiung vom mancipium gewesen sein.

Andererseits ist der Vorwurf mangelnder Zurückhaltung für Augustus der bequemste Weg, unbequeme Frauen loszuwerden: Seiner Frau Scribonia unterstellt er „perversitatem morum"[17] und trennt sich deshalb von ihr, obwohl wahrscheinlich eher die Leidenschaft

---

[14] Die achäische Kriegssteuer von 146 v. Chr. trifft vor allem Frauen (Polyb. 9, 8, 6).

[15] Val. Max. 8, 3, 1 – Dig. 3, 1, 5.

[16] Zum Leben der Frau im frühen Kaiserreich: *K. Thraede*, Ärger mit der Freiheit (s. Anm. 8).

[17] *Sueton*, Augustus 62.

zu Livia ihn unwiderstehlich ergriffen hatte[18]. Und als Scribonia nach Jahrzehnten, in denen man nichts von ihr gehört hatte, sie also doch wohl häuslich, zurückgezogen und bescheiden gelebt hatte, wieder auftaucht, um ihre und des Augustus Tochter Julia in die Verbannung zu begleiten, in die sie wegen angeblicher moralischer Verfehlungen geschickt wurde, wird über ihr Leben als geschiedene Frau kein Wort verloren.

Zweifellos versuchte die Ideologie des beginnenden Kaiserreiches, die altrömischen Verhältnisse zu beschwören[19] und engte dabei den Spielraum der Frau nach Möglichkeit ein. Daß dabei vor allem die Frauen, die schon an eine gewisse Selbständigkeit gewöhnt waren, betroffen waren, ist anzunehmen. Angesichts der im Altertum überall vorherrschenden Praxis der Frühehe sind das demnach hauptsächlich die geschiedenen Frauen.

Zu diesem restaurativem Gesellschaftsmodell trägt die frühe Kirche noch eine „exegetische" Begründung mit dem Hinweis auf den Sündenfall und seine Folgen bei. Sie stellt sich also nicht einfach gegen die allgemeine Zeitströmung des Libertinismus und paßt sich auch nicht einer allgemein akzeptierten Tendenz zu einer rigiden Moral an, sondern sie sieht sich zwischen den beiden gegenläufigen Tendenzen vor die Wahl gestellt und findet, daß ihre Interessen eher im Modell der augusteischen Restauration verwirklicht werden können.

4. Die geschiedene Frau – kein Thema der Literatur

Wie Scribonia die vielen Jahre verbracht hat, davon berichten die Quellen nichts. Auch sonst ist über das Leben von geschiedenen Frauen kaum etwas in Erfahrung zu bringen. Die Gesetzgebung hat mit vollzogener Scheidung und der Regelung der Folgen ihre Aufgaben erfüllt, ihr Ziel erreicht; die Literatur verliert die Frauen an dieser Stelle aus den Augen. Sie taucht als Typ ebensowenig wie die alte Jungfer auf, obwohl sie sich doch gut zur Charakterisierung und zur

---

[18] Vict. epit. I, 26: amore alienae coniugis obsessus.
[19] *Cicero*, De republ. 6, 28: firmiter maiores nostri stabilita matrimonia esse voluerunt.

Karikierung eignen würde: im Bereich der Literatur sind nur junge Mädchen, Matronen und Witwen vorgesehen. Für das „Leben danach" sind wir auf Analogieschlüsse angewiesen, die sich aus Nachrichten über das Leben der Frau im allgemeinen ableiten lassen. Doch auch wenn den Frauen des frühen römischen Kaiserreiches mehr Möglichkeiten offenstanden, ihr Leben auch nach einer Scheidung zu bewältigen und zu gestalten, als das gewöhnlich im Bewußtsein ist, so sollte das Schweigen der Quellen über die doch gewiß zahlreichen geschiedenen Frauen nicht übersehen werden. Der Problemkreis Scheidung ist für die antike Literatur interessant, weil sich dadurch die Lebensumstände eines Mannes ändern: er verließ seine Frau oder er wurde von ihr verlassen. Der Mann bleibt nicht nur syntaktisch das alleinige Subjekt; die betroffene Frau ist Objekt oder eher begleitender Umstand der Handlung. Für den Mann ist die ehelose Zeitspanne zwischen Scheidung und Wiederheirat eine Übergangsphase, für die Frau wohl oft Dauerzustand ohne absehbares Ende, da die Rechte zu ungleich verteilt waren.

Dafür, daß es den betroffenen Frauen nicht immer unbedingt leicht fiel, das zu akzeptieren, seien zwei weit auseinanderliegende Belege angeführt: Medea, die von Jason verlassen worden war, weil er sich Kreusa zugewandt hatte, schickt dieser ein todbringendes Brautgewand zu – diese Lösung des Problems war wohl nur im Mythos möglich. Kaiser Konstantin beweist da mehr Realitätssinn, als er der ohne hinreichenden Grund verlassenen Frau erlaubt, ins Haus ihres ehemaligen Ehepartners einzudringen und die Mitgift seiner jetzigen Frau an sich zu nehmen.

Die Frage nach der „geschiedenen Frau", der Frau also, die sich nach einer kürzeren oder längeren Ehe auf ein Leben ohne Partner einzustellen hat, weil der Partner sich anders verpflichtet hat, ist in der Antike nicht gestellt.

5. Die synoptischen Texte zur Scheidungsfrage

Die christliche Gemeinde wuchs, wie dem vorher Gesagten zu entnehmen ist, in eine Welt hinein, für die die gesetzlich abgesicherte Möglichkeit zur Trennung einer unbefriedigenden Partnerschaft eine Selbstverständlichkeit war und die diese Möglichkeiten auch in zunehmendem Maß ausnützte. Die Tendenz zur Liberalisierung war eindeutig, auch wenn sie allerorten begleitet wurde von einem ebenfalls nicht zu übersehenden Zug zur Eindämmung des allzu leichtfertigen Rückgriffs auf diese Lösung, zur Rückbesinnung auf die alten überkommenen Werte und schließlich zur Verinnerlichung der moralischen Gesetze.

Zum Abschluß dieser Erörterung sollen nun die synoptischen Texte befragt werden, die Stellungnahmen Jesu zum angeschnittenen Problem bringen. Es geht dabei auch hier nicht primär um den Problemkreis Ehebruch, gesetzwidrige Beziehungen und als Folge davon Scheidung, sondern speziell um das Problem Scheidung. Da dieses Thema ja nur in ehelosen Gemeinschaften bedeutungslos werden kann, ist es im Laufe der Geschichte ständig diskutiert worden; die Literatur zum Thema ist entsprechend umfangreich. Schon deshalb soll hier keine neue exegetische Konzeption vorgelegt, sondern versucht werden, ein überschaubares Bild von der Situation in den synoptischen Evangelien anzubieten, das sich auf die neueren Untersuchungen stützt[20].

Das Wortfeld, das den anvisierten Bereich anzeigt, wird im Neuen Testament durch die Verben (ἀπο)λύω, ἀφίημι und χωρίζω abgedeckt; dabei stellen die beiden erstgenannten den unter Umständen einseitigen Entschluß zur Auflösung einer gesetzlichen Verbindung in den Vordergrund, bezeichnen also den institutionalisierten Endpunkt einer Entwicklung, während χωρίζω den Vorgang des Trennens, den Bruch selbst markiert, der ja wohl meist lange vor dem tatsächlichen Auseinandergehen liegt. Beide Wortgruppen finden sich, wie das Gesamtthema „Scheidung" ja auch, in der paulinischen Paränese von 1 Kor 7 und – als Aussage Jesu – in den drei ersten Evangelien. Auf letztere soll im folgenden etwas näher eingegangen werden.

---

[20] Außer den Kommentaren zu den besprochenen Texten sind die folgenden neueren Monographien besonders herangezogen worden, in denen auch Hinweise auf Aufsätze und ältere Monographien zu finden sind: *H. Baltensweiler*, Die Ehe im Neuen Testament (AThANT 52) (Zürich 1967); *K. Berger*, Die Gesetzesauslegung Jesu (WMANT 40) (Neukirchen 1972); *P. Hoffmann – V. Eid*, Jesus von Nazareth und eine christliche Moral (QD 66) (Freiburg 1975); *H. Merklein*, Die Gottesherrschaft als Handlungsprinzip (FzB) (Würzburg 1978); *K. Niederwimmer*, Askese und Mysterium (FRLANT 113) (Göttingen 1975).

Der Textbefund ist auf den ersten Blick etwas verwirrend. An vier Stellen, Mt 5,31 f; 19,9; Mk 10,11 f; Lk 16,18, ist in verschiedener Weise von Scheidung die Rede, jeweils bezeichnet mit einer Form des Verbums ἀπολύω, das sich zusammen mit einer Form von γαμέω im konditionalen Vordersatz relativischer oder partizipialer Konstruktion befindet, mit dem im Hauptsatz jeweils eine Verbform vom Stamm μοιχ (μοιχάομαι bzw. μοιχεύω) korrespondiert. Scheidung und erneute Heirat bedeutet Ehebruch, auf diesen Nenner läßt sich der Text scheinbar überall bringen; aber die Übereinstimmung ist doch nicht so perfekt, wie es zunächst scheint.

Was bedeutet es, wenn Mt 5,32 die Einschränkung παρεκτὸς λόγου πορνείας bringt, die er in 19,9 mit dem μὴ ἐπὶ πορνείᾳ wieder aufgreift? Wird dem Mann da doch noch ein Scheidungsgrund angeboten, der das radikale Verbot aushöhlt? Oder: auch von der betroffenen Frau ist die Rede – aber was wird eigentlich von ihr gesagt? Bricht sie ihre Ehe (Mk 10,12), wird sie zum Ehebruch veranlaßt (Mt 5,32 a), oder ist ihre Verstoßung Anlaß zum Ehebruch: für den ersten Ehemann, der die Scheidung ausspricht, weil er sich anderweitig binden will (Mt 19,9; Mk 10,11; Lk 16,18 a), oder für den zweiten Ehemann, der sie, die doch schon gebunden ist, heiraten will (Lk 16,18 b)?

Auch der Rahmen des Logions ist recht unterschiedlich: In Mt 5 ist die Bergpredigt der äußere Rahmen, geographisch ist hier also Galiläa als Ort des Geschehens anzunehmen; in Mt 19 wie in Mk 10 ist schon der weitere Einzugsbereich von Jerusalem im judäischen Gebirge anvisiert. Lk 16 dagegen erlaubt keine genauere topographische Fixierung innerhalb des großen Reiseberichtes. Aber auch literarisch im engeren Sinn ist die Zuordnung nicht eindeutig. Zweimal ist das Logion Abschluß eines Streitgespräches mit den Pharisäern, einmal steht es im Rahmen einer radikalisierten Gesetzesauslegung und zuletzt bei Lukas in der Assoziationskette des 16. Kapitels.

5.1. Die Logienquelle Mt 5,32 par. Lk 16,18

Diese letzte Beobachtung bietet nun aber schon den ersten geeigneten Ansatzpunkt für eine Differenzierung an: Mt 5,32 findet seine Parallele in Lk 16,18, da bei beiden Texten die Frage nach der jetzt, nach Jesu Predigt vom Gottesreich, angemessenen Realisierung des

Gesetzes thematisch behandelt wird (Lk 16,17; Mt 5,17–20). Bei der syntaktischen Form steht das Partizip als Ausdrucksmittel der Conditio im Vordergrund. Die günstigste Arbeitshypothese dürfte demnach sein, diesen Text der Logienquelle zuzuweisen. Eine Situation oder eine konkrete Anfrage wird nicht überliefert, das Logion steht isoliert in einem inhaltlich passenden Zusammenhang. Beide Evangelisten halten aber am Leitthema „Gesetz" fest und akzentuieren das Logion nach den Gegebenheiten der anzusprechenden Gemeinde.

Matthäus zeigt deutlich die palästinische Umwelt: Für den Mann wird ganz selbstverständlich die Möglichkeit, mehrere rechtmäßige Frauen zu besitzen, vorausgesetzt, erst die Trennung von der Ehefrau bedeutet Ehebruch, weil er, der die Verantwortung für seinen Besitz aufgegeben hat, verursacht, daß ihn ein anderer sich aneignet und so, durch die Ehe mit der doch eigentlich unabänderlich ihrem ersten Mann verbundenen Frau, mit dieser die Ehe bricht. Die Warnung, eine geschiedene Frau zu heiraten, zieht diese Linie nur weiter aus. Die Klausel παρεκτὸς λόγου πορνείας kann in diesem Zusammenhang als notwendiges Zugeständnis der matthäischen Gemeinde verstanden werden, die Männern, deren Frauen beim Ehebruch ertappt wurden, eine Fortsetzung der so in Frage gestellten Ehe doch nicht mehr zumuten wollte oder konnte[21]; doch bleibt auch der Vorschlag erwägenswert, der hier eine Möglichkeit für Proselyten sehen will, unter πορνεία Verwandtenehen zu verstehen, die in der heidnischen Gesellschaft vielleicht für ganz unbedenklich gehalten wurden, nach dem mosaischen Gesetz aber illegitim waren. Die Klausel gäbe dann die Möglichkeit, solche Ehen zu lösen[22].

Vergleicht man hiermit die *lukanische* Fassung, so stellt man zunächst fest, daß die Abweichungen im Wortlaut begrenzt sind. Und doch ist der Text in seinem Zentrum verändert: nicht nur die geschiedene Frau und der, der sie dann heiratet (V. 18b), begehen Ehebruch, während den ersten Mann „nur" die Schuld des Verursachers trifft, sondern auch der, der in sukzessiver Polygamie lebt, ist des Ehebruches schuldig.

---

[21] So die Mehrzahl der Exegeten.
[22] So zuletzt mit Nachdruck: *Baltensweiler,* aaO. 87–102.

5.2. Mk 10,1–12 par. Mt 19,3–9

In Mk 10,1–12 ist die Vorlage für Mt 19,3–9 zu sehen; hier ist das Logion in den Rahmen einer bei beiden Evangelisten weithin übereinstimmenden Diskussion über das geltende jüdische Scheidungsrecht gefaßt, die nach dem bei Markus üblichen Schema solcher Streitgespräche aufgebaut ist. Die besondere Jüngerbelehrung, auf die das ganze Geschehen hinzielen soll, damit es von da aus nochmals eine Interpretation erfahre, bringt das Logion von der Ehescheidung in veränderter syntaktischer Gestalt und verändertem Inhalt: der konditionale Vordersatz betont durch die relativische Einleitung, die Partikel ἄν und den Konjunktiv des Verbums die Möglichkeit eines solchen Falles, daß nämlich jemand nach erfolgter Scheidung eine Wiederheirat anstreben könnte; die Verwirklichung dieses Vorhabens ist aber als Ehebruch anzusehen. Matthäus spiegelt auch hier den palästinisch-semitischen Hintergrund, wenn er nur vom Mann als möglichem Träger der Handlung spricht. Anders Markus: bei ihm sind Mann und Frau gleichgestellt, beide sind Subjekte der Handlung sowohl für das ἀπολύσῃ und das γαμήσῃ des Bedingungssatzes als auch für das μοιχᾶται des Hauptsatzes. Vielleicht ist die Folgerung erlaubt, daß die Verhältnisse im herodianischen Königshaus, unter Umständen als Indikatoren einer die ganze Gesellschaft bedrohenden Entwicklung, gerade hier bei Markus schon ihren Niederschlag gefunden haben. Gerade bei Markus: er hatte ja auch am ausführlichsten von den Umständen beim Tod des Täufers berichtet. Daß Matthäus diese Nivellierung der Geschlechterrollen nicht übernehmen kann, ist klar, und so spricht die Lücke, die seine Version an dieser Stelle gegenüber dem Markustext aufweist, nicht unbedingt für eine spätere Auffüllung durch Markus.

Eine ipsissima vox Jesu aus den vier Varianten des Logions herauszuschälen dürfte angesichts der geschilderten Tatsachen recht aussichtslos sein; die in der reichhaltigen Literatur angebotenen Rekonstruktionen überzeugen denn auch nur als mögliche Ausgangstexte, nicht aber so, daß sie andere Lösungen unmöglich machen würden. Der viel wichtigere Gesichtspunkt dürfte jedoch die Übereinstimmung im radikalen Anspruch sein, der sich in den abrupt kurzen indikativischen Hauptsätzen zeigt: μοιχᾶται, ποιεῖ μοιχευθῆναι, μοιχεύει. Gegen die Gesetzgebung und die Praxis der jü-

dischen wie der heidnischen Umwelt wird hier auf der Unbedingt-
heit der ehelichen Partnerschaft bestanden, deren Dauer nicht davon abhängt, wielange sich keiner der Partner anderweitig orientiert.
Diese Radikalität weist deutlich über eine überall und allgemein
realisierbare Lebensordnung hinaus; ihre uneingeschränkte Forderung ist an der gänzlich gewandelten Welt, am Eschaton, orientiert[23]
und wirkt, gerade weil der Sprecher die äußere Form eines kasuistischen Rechtssatzes übernimmt und dabei das gesetzte Recht weit
transzendiert, so provozierend, daß sich seither wohl jede Generation daran gerieben hat.

5.2.1. Der markinische Rahmen

Markus und in seinem Gefolge Matthäus bringen das Logion als Abschluß eines Streitgespräches zwischen einer Gruppe von Pharisäern und Jesus. Die Spannung, die zwischen dem Verlauf der Diskussion und dem abschließenden Jesuswort besteht, weist darauf
hin, daß der hier hergestellte Rahmen künstlich ist und zwei ausein-
anderstrebende Inhalte zusammenklammern soll: eine Überlegung
zum Thema Ehe und ein Bescheid zum Thema Scheidung. Im Gespräch argumentiert Jesus auf einer ganz anderen Ebene als im
Schlußlogion, so daß ein neues Bild mit starker Tiefenwirkung entsteht:

Zunächst wird die Aufmerksamkeit des Lesers durch die Frage
der Pharisäer geweckt, ob die jüdische Praxis der Ehescheidung legitim sei. Diese Frage wird letztlich eindeutig negativ beantwortet – allerdings erst „im Haus" und nicht für die pharisäischen Gesprächspartner, denen durch das πειράζοντες αὐτόν in V. 2 ein echtes Interesse an der Sachfrage von vornherein abgesprochen wird.

5.2.2. Die versucherische Frage

Diese Frage wurde in rabbinischen und anderen jüdischen Kreisen
heftig diskutiert, die Vertreter der strengeren und der laxeren Rich-
tungen hatten einen Konsens über die wirklich gültigen Scheidungs-

---

[23] Vgl. schon *M. Dibelius*, Die Formgeschichte des Evangeliums (Tübingen
⁶1971).

gründe noch nicht gefunden[24], und weit darüber hinausgehend hatte die qumrannahe Damaskusschrift[25] eine Zweitehe zu Lebzeiten des ersten Partners als „Netz Belials" bezeichnet: verführt von Belial hält Israel Verhaltensweisen, die als schreiendes Unrecht angesehen werden müssen, für Recht. Und das erste Netz Belials ist eben die sukzessive Polygamie.

Auch im Alten Testament waren schon solche Töne angeklungen, wenn in Mal 2,14ff zu lesen ist: „... keiner breche der Frau seiner Jugend die Treue, denn ich hasse die Scheidung, spricht der Herr ..." Auch wenn dieser Text ursprünglich auf die sehr vielschichtige Mischehenproblematik bezogen war, die durch die Deportation und die Rückkehr mit allen wirtschaftlichen, sozialen, ethnischen und religiösen Konsequenzen entstanden war, geht seine Aussage doch über diesen zeitbedingten Anlaß hinaus.

Vielleicht ist in diesen Äußerungen Maleachis und der Damaskusschrift der Niederschlag grundsätzlicher Diskussionen über das mosaische Gesetz, wie sie offen in Ez 20,25 zu erkennen sind[26], zu sehen; aber auch wenn das zu hoch gegriffen und die heilbringende Funktion des Gesetzes noch ganz unbestritten sein sollte, so läßt sich doch sagen: An der jüdischen Praxis der mindestens für den männlichen Partner reibungslosen Ehescheidung mit bedenkenlos folgender Wiederheirat haben sich jüdische Kreise schon vor der Zeit der christlichen Gemeinde gestoßen. Gegen die allzu leichtfertige Berufung auf das Gesetz, das solches Vorgehen erlaubte, wurde nicht nur legalistisch – durch Einschränkung der akzeptablen Scheidungsgründe – argumentiert, sondern auch auf ganz anderer Ebene: im Gewand der Begründung eines prophetischen Urteils wie bei Maleachis „denn ich hasse die Scheidung, spricht der Herr" oder vom Schöpfungs- und Bundesdenken her: „Als Mann und Frau hat er sie geschaffen; zu zweit gingen sie in die Arche" (Gen 1,27; 7,9) wie die Damaskusschrift.

Es ist demnach durchaus möglich, wenn nicht sogar wahrschein-

---

[24] *(Strack-)Billerbeck*, Kommentar zum Neuen Testament aus Talmud und Midrasch, I 303–321; 801–805.
[25] CD IV 15–21.
[26] Ez 20,25: (... weil sie meine Gebote nicht hielten ...), so habe denn auch ich ihnen Satzungen gegeben, die nicht gut waren, und Gebote, durch die sie nicht am Leben bleiben konnten. (Ich ließ sie unrein werden durch ihre Opfergaben ...)

lich, daß auch Jesus zu diesem Thema befragt worden ist. Das Versucherische an dieser Frage liegt nicht darin, daß es hier keine Diskussion über das Ergebnis geben durfte, und wohl auch nicht darin, daß von vorneherein bekannt war, daß Jesu Antwort dem Gesetz widersprechen würde, sondern gerade in der unentschiedenen Ausgangslage: Welche Antwort die Frager aus dem Befragten auch hervorlockten, sie konnte mittels unbestrittener Autoritäten als gesetzwidrig aufgedeckt und als Zeugnis[27] gegen ihn verwandt werden.

5.2.3. Die Antwort Jesu

Auch der Befragte erfaßt die Situation und reagiert geschickt auf die Provokation, indem er nicht mit ja oder nein antwortet, sondern sie grundsätzlich angeht, grundsätzlicher jedenfalls, als es in der Absicht der Frager gelegen haben kann. Ihr „εἰ ἔξεστιν" = „ist es erlaubt", das die kurze Antwort so nahe gelegt hatte, wird zunächst überhört, dafür als Gegenfrage die nach dem Wortlaut des Gebotes gestellt. Das Gebot aber, auf das sich die Anhänger der einfachen Ehescheidung berufen, steht in Dtn 24, 1–4 und ist als eine syntaktische Einheit aufzufassen; die eigentliche gesetzliche Bestimmung, um derentwillen der ganze Passus abgefaßt ist, ist V. 4, der die Rückkehr einer geschiedenen und dann wiederverheiratet gewesenen Frau zu ihrem ersten Mann verbietet. V. 1–3 enthält die Ober- und Unterbedingungen für die zur Entscheidung anstehende juristische Streitfrage, als solche gekennzeichnet durch כי und אם [28]. Gerade diese Struktur macht deutlich, daß die Realität der leichten Scheidung in Dtn 24, 1–4 gar nicht zur Diskussion steht, sondern nur die Konsequenzen solchen Verhaltens aufgezeigt werden. Die bestehende Institution der Scheidung soll jedenfalls nicht die Perspektive eröffnen, daß der Mann aus späteren Ehen seiner Frau materielle Vorteile erwarten kann. Damit gibt das Gebot aber den Weg zur Scheidung nicht frei – auch durch die Festsetzung der strafrechtlichen Konsequenzen von Mord oder Diebstahl wird ja Mord oder Diebstahl nicht erlaubt, sondern im Gegenteil zu verhindern gesucht.

---

[27] Vgl. Mk 15, 55–58.
[28] *R. Meyer,* Hebräische Grammatik III § 128 e.

Die Pharisäer zitieren jedoch nicht den genauen Wortlaut des Gesetzes, sondern lassen die Verben des Bedingungssatzes γράψει, δώσει als von ἐπέτρεψεν (Mk) bzw. ἐνετείλατο (Mt) abhängige Infinitive γράψαι, ἀπολῦσαι (Mk) bzw. δοῦναι (Mt) erscheinen. Dadurch ist die Satzstruktur des Deuteronomiumtextes aufgelöst zugunsten eines Finalsatzes; die ursprüngliche Oberbedingung ist zum direkten Auslöser des Geschehens geworden, die Unterbedingung wird jetzt als Auftrag oder wenigstens Verfahrensvorschrift für eine juristisch einwandfreie Scheidung verstanden, die ursprüngliche zentrale Aussage – das Verbot der Rückkehr – fällt ganz unter den Tisch. Bis es dazu kommen konnte, daß die Zeitgenossen Jesu auf diese Weise ihre Scheidungspraxis legitimierten, mußten drei Schritte bewältigt werden: die tatsächlich vorkommenden Auflösungen von Partnerschaften mußten – wenn auch als Ärgernis – akzeptiert werden; es mußte der Versuch unternommen werden, die sich daraus ergebenden Folgen zu regeln, und schließlich mußte eben dieser Versuch umgedeutet werden als Anerkennung des Rechtes auf Scheidung. Eine Kritik am leichtfertigen Rückgriff auf diese Auslegung des Gesetzes konnte kaum am Gesetz selbst ansetzen, denn es dürfte fast unmöglich sein, daß eine Gemeinschaft einen einmal zurückgelegten Weg rückwärts geht, wenn die umgekehrte Richtung die – hier männlichen – Partner, die sich schon vorher in der stärkeren Rechtsposition befunden hatten, mit solchen Privilegien ausstattet.

Und so setzt die eigentliche Antwort Jesu an die Pharisäer auf ganz anderer Ebene an: Die σκληροκαρδία der Juden, die Härte ihrer Herzen, hat dieses Gebot erzwungen; die im Deuteronomium gegebene Weisung beweist ja nur, daß das primäre apodiktische Gebot: „Du sollst nicht ehebrechen!", eben nicht befolgt wird, denn es gibt ja tatsächlich verstoßene Frauen; deshalb werden sekundäre kasuistische Regelungen notwendig.

Von der Schöpfung – und hier ist der Kern der positiven Aussage des Textes zu sehen – ist das nicht so angelegt. Die Schöpfungsberichte, die in kurzen Zitaten als Zeugen angeführt werden, sprechen nur von der Bezogenheit von Mann und Frau aufeinander, die von Gott mit der Schöpfung gegeben ist. Diese Partnerschaft kann nicht einfach mit der als gesellschaftlicher Institution verstandenen Ehe gleichgesetzt werden, die als Gebilde von Menschen ja dann auch zur Auflösung dem menschlichen Zugriff ausgesetzt wäre. Jesus unterstreicht in der bei Markus referierten Fassung des Textes durch einen zunächst ganz unscheinbaren Eingriff in den Wortlaut des Zitates aus Gen 2,24 die neue Einheit, die durch die von der Schöpfung gegebene Partnerschaft entsteht: er übergeht das „er wird seiner Frau anhängen", das in der Vorlage zusammen mit „ein Mensch wird seinen Vater und seine Mutter verlassen" die Aktivitäten des Mannes zur Eheschließung beschrieben hatte. Jetzt bilden Gen 1,27 und 2,24 eine Einheit, die durch den Begriff der „zwei" zusammengehalten wird: „Als Mann und Frau schuf er sie, deshalb wird der Mensch seinen Vater und Mutter verlassen und die beiden werden zu einem Leib". Durch die doch wohl bewußte Lücke ist der Bezug des im Zitat zentralen Satzes auf den Mann aufgegeben, das ἄνθρωπος – ein Mensch – ist jetzt nicht mehr notwendig als Synonym für ἀνήρ – Mann – zu interpretieren, sondern es ist für eine generalisierende Deutung auf Mann und Frau offen: beide verlassen ihren bisherigen Familienverband und setzen gemeinsam einen neuen Anfang. Ein Zurück zum vorherigen Zustand kann es da von der Sache, von Gottes Schöpfungsgedanken her, nicht geben. Das kurze Wort Jesu, das das öffentliche Gespräch abschließt, zieht für die Fragesteller den Schluß aus dem, was sich aus dem Nachdenken über die Schöpfung ergibt: „Was Gott zusammengefügt hat, soll der Mensch nicht trennen."

Es ist sicher kein Zufall, daß hier die Termini Ehe, Verlassen und Verstoßen nicht begegnen, sondern vom Zusammenfügen und Trennen gesprochen wird: die menschliche Institutionalisierung der Schöpfungsgabe steht hier ganz im Hintergrund.

Trotzdem läuft das Streitgespräch mit den Pharisäern inhaltlich genau auf das Ziel hin, das auch das Schlußlogion aufgezeigt hatte, das die Ehescheidung direkt anspricht; nur wird hier eine grundsätzlich andere Gattung als Träger der Information verwendet. Die kurze Behauptung, daß jeder, der seine Ehe löst, des Ehebruchs schuldig wird, war in die Form eines kasuistischen Rechtssatzes gekleidet, der im konditionalen Vordersatz sogar an die alttestamentliche Vorlage von Dtn 24,1 anzuklingen schien, inhaltlich aber das geltende Recht weit überstieg. Die juristischen Normen können angesichts dieser absoluten Aussage nicht mehr angesetzt werden, in diesem radikalen Anspruchsgefüge greifen sie nicht mehr, der Zuhö-

V

Die Rolle der Frau in der urchristlichen Mission

Von Alfons Weiser SAC, Vallendar

Die Frauen haben für die Ausbreitung des Evangeliums in urchristlicher Zeit eine sehr große Bedeutung. Dies ist eine in der neutestamentlichen Forschung allgemein anerkannte Tatsache[1]. Nicht in gleicher Weise besteht Einmütigkeit darüber, welche Rollen im einzelnen die Frauen bei der Missionierung gespielt und welche Funktionen sie ausgeübt haben[2]. Eine sachgerechte Beurteilung wird erschwert durch die Quellenlage und durch eigene Vorurteile. Durch

[1] Vgl. z. B. *L. Zscharnack*, Der Dienst der Frau in den ersten Jahrhunderten der christlichen Kirche (Göttingen 1902) 19; *A. v. Harnack*, Die Mission und Ausbreitung des Christentums in den ersten drei Jahrhunderten, 2 Bde. (Leipzig 1924) hier II 589; *E. Käsemann*, An die Römer (HNT 8 a) (Tübingen ³1974) 397; *Thraede*, Art. Frau, in: RAC VIII (1972), 197–269, hier 229–231; *ders.*, Ärger mit der Freiheit. Die Bedeutung von Frauen in Theorie und Praxis der alten Kirche, in: *G. Scharffenorth – K. Thraede* (Hrsg.), „Freunde in Christus werden ...". Die Beziehung von Mann und Frau als Frage an Theologie und Kirche, Kennzeichen Bd. 1 (Gelnhausen 1977) 31–182, hier 99–102; *W.-H. Ollrog*, Paulus und seine Mitarbeiter. Untersuchungen zu Theorie und Praxis der paulinischen Mission (WMANT 50) (Neukirchen-Vluyn 1979) 25; *E. Schüssler Fiorenza*, Die Rolle der Frau in der urchristlichen Bewegung, in: Concilium 12 (1976) 3–9, hier 5. – Literaturüberblick bei *O. Ganghofer*, The Woman in the Church. International Bibliography 1973 – june 1975 indexed by computer, in: RIC. S 21 (1975) 1–45; *E. Patrick*, Women and Religion: A Survey of Significant Literature, 1965–1974, in: TS 36 (1975) 737–765; *R. W. Graham*, Women in the Pauline Churches: A Review Article, in: LexTQ 11 (1976) 25–34.
[2] Vgl. etwa folgende unterschiedliche Stellungnahmen: Frauen spielten zwar eine aktive Rolle im Gemeindeleben, „ohne jedoch eine missionarische oder lehrhafte Verkündigung ausgeübt zu haben." So *G. G. Blum*, Das Amt der Frau im Neuen Testament, in: NT 7 (1964) 142–161, hier 148; 159 f; ähnlich *G. Philips*, La femme dans l'Église, in: EThL 37 (1961) 597–603, hier 598; *B. Gärtner*, Das Amt, Mann und die Frau im Neuen Testament (Ergersheim 1963) 18–24. Dagegen *Thraede*, Ärger (Anm. 1) 102. „Wenn der Apostel Frauen in Mission, Liturgie und kirchlichen Diensten gewähren läßt und mit Anerkennung nicht geizt, so akzeptiert er ‚bestehende Ordnung' der hellenistischen Gemeinden, denen eine verantwortliche Mitarbeit von Frauen im Leben ihrer Städte vertraut war." (Vgl. auch 101.)

rer muß unmittelbar Stellung beziehen: er kann annehmen oder ablehnen, es wird nicht erwartet, daß eigenes Nachdenken des Betroffenen zum selben Ergebnis führen würde. Die Souveränität, mit der der Sprecher hier sein Wort gegen die religiösen Traditionen setzt, läßt prophetisches Selbstbewußtsein erkennen.

Das Gespräch dagegen, das auf das „Was Gott zusammengefügt hat, soll der Mensch nicht trennen" hin angelegt ist, argumentiert in umgekehrter Richtung: Induktiv wird der Hörer von der gemeinsam akzeptierten Basis des Schöpfungsberichtes zu der Erkenntnis geführt, die er begreifen und verstehen soll: die gegenwärtige Scheidungspraxis verstößt gegen die Schöpfungsordnung. Es wäre aber wohl zu kurzatmig geschlossen, sähe man hier nur den anderen pädagogischen Ansatz, den Weisheitslehrer gegenüber dem Propheten. Vielmehr lenkt die entschlossene Wendung zur Schöpfung, zur Urzeit, den Blick gleichzeitig auf die Endzeit, das Eschaton, dessen Gestalt ja nur von der Urzeit her erschlossen werden kann. Wer auf die Endzeit zugeht, hat sein Verhalten nach der Erkenntnis zu richten, daß in der Schöpfung nicht an eine willkürliche Auflösung der Partnerschaft von Mann und Frau gedacht war. Auch hier ist somit der zunächst so festgefügte Rahmen der Weisheitslehre gesprengt – beide Äußerungen Jesu zum Thema Ehescheidung weisen über die gerade zur Diskussion stehende Rechtsstreitigkeit hinaus, sollten also nicht ohne ausführliche Vorüberlegung zur Regelung ebensolcher Streitfälle herangezogen werden.

5.2.4. Die Verknüpfung der beiden Begründungen des Verbotes der Ehescheidung

Das im Kern übereinstimmende Ergebnis, daß Ehescheidung dem erklärten Willen Gottes widerspricht, wird von Mk 10, 1–12 par. Mt 19, 3–9 auf zwei verschiedenen Wegen erzielt. Welches Bild entsteht nun, wenn die beiden Texte miteinander verknüpft werden? Wird der Anspruch des Verbotes, das ja aus beiden Texten abzuleiten ist, noch gesteigert? Die Jüngerbelehrung „im Hause" ist, wie oben erwähnt, kaum ursprünglich mit dem Streitgespräch verbunden gewesen. Der Tradent aber, der die beiden Texte zusammengestellt hat, Markus oder schon ein Vorgänger, zeigt seine Gemeindesituation an: Die jüdischen Gegner stellen zwar die auslösende Frage, erhalten aber als Antwort nicht das erwartete Ja oder Nein, sondern sie werden mit ihrer σκληροκαρδία konfrontiert, die sie den Schöpfungsgedanken so total verkennen läßt. Hätte die Perikope hier ihr Ende, so wäre die Überlegung zu Gen 1; 2 mit dem Verbot der Trennung schon als endgültiger Bescheid aufzufassen, die Tatsache, daß die Frager ausdrücklich als Pharisäer qualifiziert sind, nicht viel mehr als ein Hinweis auf den theologischen und kulturellen Kontext der Diskussion. Dadurch aber, daß Mk 10,11 f den als Rechtssatz geformten Spruch Jesu bringt, läßt sich noch mehr erkennen. Mit den Pharisäern gibt es zwar Auseinandersetzungen um die Grundprinzipien der alttestamentlichen Tradition, in denen man versucht, die jüdische Gegenseite der σκληροκαρδία zu überführen: Ein für Gottes Weisung fühllos gewordenes Herz kann keine ethische Entscheidung treffen, bevor es sich nicht die grundlegenden Gedanken der Schöpfung zu eigen gemacht hat. Gerade am konkreten Beispiel von Ehe und Ehescheidung wird klar, wie unangemessen die Gesetzesauslegung der Juden ist: die willkürliche Aufhebung der Partnerschaft ist nicht freigestellt, gar vielleicht als Privileg Israels, wie dies hier und dort in jüdischen Kreisen angenommen wurde[29], sondern steht im Widerspruch zum Sinn der Ehe und zum apodiktischen Gebot des Dekalogs: Du sollst nicht ehebrechen.

Aber gerade dadurch, daß durch die Einführung einer Jüngerbelehrung im engeren Sinn der „weisheitlichen" Gedankenführung der Charakter einer gewissen Vorläufigkeit zugewiesen wird, verändert sich auch der Inhalt des Schlußlogions. Es wird zur zweiten Stufe und hat jetzt vor allem die Funktion, tatsächlich vorkommende Scheidungen zu beurteilen und die jeweils angemessene Sanktion finden zu helfen. Es ist damit, wohl ziemlich deutlich gegen seine ursprüngliche Absicht, doch wieder in die Nähe der kasuistischen Rechtssätze gelangt, die ihm eigene Radikalität angesichts des Eschaton ist in den Hintergrund getreten – ein Prozeß, der ja auch in der spezifischen Ausformung des Logions bei den einzelnen Evangelisten schon sichtbar geworden war.

Durch formal ganz unbedeutend erscheinende Eingriffe läßt Matthäus die jüdischen Kontrahenten um einiges unfreundlicher erscheinen: durch das eingeschobene κατὰ πᾶσαν αἰτίαν wird eindeu-

---

[29] (Strack-)Billerbeck I 312.

tig die laxe Auslegung Hillels angesprochen; und dadur[ch] die Belehrung über das eigentliche Wesen der Ehe direkt a[n die E]leitungsfrage anschließt, bekommt die nachfolgende Ber[ufung der] Pharisäer auf das Gesetz einen nicht zu übersehenden [Charakter] von gewollter Uneinsichtigkeit und Impertinenz, auf die [auch] das kompromißlose Schlußlogion „… er bricht die Ehe" [eine Ant-] wort ist; bezeichnenderweise ist hier auch die Fiktion von [einer beson-] deren Jüngerbelehrung für diesen Teil aufgehoben und fü[r die Frage] nach der Ehelosigkeit (19,10 ff) aufgespart.

Auch dieser Weg des Scheidungsverbotes, den wir inn[erhalb des] Neuen Testamentes verfolgen können, sollte davor warr[nen,] unmittelbar verwendbare Rechtssätze abzuleiten. Das [heißt aller-] dings nicht, daß das Neue Testament einen ähnlich leicht[en] Lösung einer Ehe freigäbe, wie das in der Umwelt des N[euen Testa-] mentes und in der heutigen Gesellschaft zu beobachten [ist; im Ge-] genteil: auch eine rigide Gesetzgebung hält für jeweils g[ewis-] sene Fälle Auswege bereit, die der ehemüde Partner [nutzen] kann, ohne sich an der Gemeinschaft zu vergehen, oh[ne eines] und damit Rechtsbruchs beschuldigt zu werden. Das W[ort Jesu ver-] sperrt diese Art von legal scheinendem Ausweg und s[oll den] schwächeren Teil, dessen Existenz davon abhängen ka[nn, daß nicht] der nächstbeste Anlaß zum Vorwand genommen wird, [„wegzu-] schicken". Auch wenn die reale Konstitution des Mens[chen ange-] gesichts dieses Postulats aus den verschiedensten Grün[den brechen] kann und wird, ernst genommen wird, wie dies ja d[as Wort] „wenn einer das tut" anzeigt, so ist doch die billige Sel[bstentschul-] digung mit dem Hinweis auf das einwandfreie Verfahr[en unmöglich] geworden. Und damit hat die am Anspruch des Escha[ton orientierte] Paränese nichts von ihrer Aktualität verloren.

die Quellenlage: Nur wie kleine Durchblicke in ein weites, aber in der Ferne nur undeutlich erkennbares Gelände erscheinen die sporadischen Aussagen der Apostelgeschichte und der neutestamentlichen Briefliteratur über den Anteil der Frauen an der Verbreitung des Evangeliums. Durch Vorurteile: Bei der Erforschung dessen, was dem Sichtbaren „zu Grunde" liegt, wirkt sich das Vorurteil aus, ob man auch in der gegenwärtigen Kirche eine stärkere oder eine geringere Beteiligung der Frauen sehen möchte. Der Verfasser der folgenden Ausführungen weiß sich von dem erstgenannten Vorurteil geleitet. Für die Darstellung empfiehlt es sich, zunächst die „passive" und sodann die „aktive" Rolle der Frau bei der Verbreitung des Evangeliums zu betrachten[3].

1. Die Verbreitung des Evangeliums unter den Frauen

Die Einblicke, die das Neue Testament in die Geschichte der urchristlichen Mission gewährt, zeigen, daß das Evangelium besonders unter den Frauen große Verbreitung fand und von ihnen besonders bereitwillig angenommen wurde.

1.1. Der Textbefund

Die Texte lassen in vielfältiger Weise erkennen, daß Frauen von Anfang an als vollwertige Glieder zu den urchristlichen Gemeinden gehörten. Die Apostelgeschichte bezeugt, daß sie in der Urgemeinde Jerusalems im einmütigen Gebet mit den Aposteln versammelt waren (1,14), daß sich immer mehr „Männer und Frauen" der Gemeinde anschlossen (5,14), daß Saulus in die Häuser eindrang, „Männer und Frauen" festnahm (8,3; 22,4) und daß er dies sogar betrieb bis hin nach Damaskus (9,2). Auch die Erwähnung des Fürsorgeproblems der Witwen griechischsprechender Judenchristen (6,1) zeigt deutlich die selbstverständliche Zugehörigkeit von Frauen zur Urgemeinde. Namentlich sind als Glieder der Jerusalemer Gemeinde genannt: Maria, die Mutter Jesu (1,14), Saphira, die

---

[3] Gute methodische Hinweise enthält der Beitrag von *A. Funk*, Mann und Frau in den Briefen des hl. Paulus, in: US 32 (1977) 280–285.

Frau des Hananias (5,1–11), Maria, die Mutter des Johannes Markus (12,12) und ihre Sklavin Rhode (12,13).

Der Sammelbericht über den Missionserfolg in Samaria hebt ausdrücklich die Taufe von „Männern und Frauen" hervor (8,12). Zur Gemeinde von Joppe gehörte eine „Jüngerin namens Tabita" (9,36). Sie stand wegen ihrer Wohltätigkeit in hohem Ansehen. Ihre Sorge galt besonders den Witwen, denn deren Klage bei Tabitas Tod wird eigens erwähnt (9,39). Sie sind wohl wegen ihres engen Kontaktes mit Tabita ebenfalls als Christinnen zu denken.

Nach einer in Apg 16,1 und 2 Tim 1,5 aufgenommenen Überlieferung gehörte zur Gemeinde in Lystra die judenchristliche Mutter des Timotheus. Sie soll Eunike geheißen haben und mit einem Griechen verheiratet gewesen sein. Die Zugehörigkeit von Frauen zu den kleinasiatischen Missionsgemeinden in Ephesus, Kolossä und Laodizäa wird vorausgesetzt in den „Haustafeln" Eph 5,22 – 6,9; Kol 3,18 – 4,1; 1 Tim 2,8–15; (1 Petr 2,18 – 3,7) und für Kreta durch Tit 2,1–10. Außerdem werden inmitten der Ermahnungen für die Diakone (von Ephesus) unvermittelt auch Frauen genannt: Sie sollen „ehrbar sein, nicht verleumderisch, sondern nüchtern und in allem zuverlässig" (1 Tim 3,11). Auffallend breiten Raum nehmen 1 Tim 5,3–16 die Darlegungen über die Witwen der Gemeinde ein. Zu einer Hausgemeinde in oder um Kolossä gehört die im Präskript des Philemonbriefes von Paulus mitangeredete „Schwester Apphia" (Phlm 2). Einzeln erwähnt von der Gemeinde in Laodizäa wird Nympha[4]. Sie wird zusammen mit ihrer Hausgemeinde gegrüßt (Kol 4,15). Getadelt wird die Gemeinde der kleinasiatischen Stadt Thyatira, weil sie in ihrer Mitte die Pseudoprophetin Isebel gewähren läßt (Apk 2,20–25).

Auf europäischem Boden war es die Purpurhändlerin Lydia in Philippi, die als erste den christlichen Glauben annahm, mit „ihrem Haus" von Paulus getauft wurde, die Missionare in ihr Haus einlud

---

[4] Die Textbezeugung läßt nicht sicher erkennen, ob es sich um einen Mann oder eine Frau handelt. „Vielleicht ist ‚ihre' nachträglich in ‚seine' geändert worden, weil man sich später eine Frau nicht mehr als für eine ganze Hausgemeinde verantwortlich denken konnte" (E. Schweizer, Der Brief an die Kolosser [EKK 12] [Zürich – Neukirchen-Vluyn 1976] 178). J. Ernst, Die Briefe an die Philipper, an Philemon, an die Kolosser, an die Epheser (RNT 11) (Regensburg 1974) 244, läßt die Beurteilung der Frage offen.

und allmählich eine Hausgemeinde um sich scharte (Apg 16,12–15.40). Im Philipperbrief wird Lydia zwar nicht erwähnt, Paulus nennt aber ebenfalls Frauen, die sich um die Gemeindegründung verdient gemacht und mit ihm „für das Evangelium gekämpft" haben: Euodia und Syntyche (Phil 4,2 f). Über den Missionserfolg in Thessalonich sagt Lukas: Einige Juden schlossen sich Paulus und Silas an, „außerdem eine große Menge gottesfürchtiger Griechen und nicht wenige vornehme Frauen" (Apg 17,4). Ähnliches berichtet er über Beröa: Viele Juden wurden gläubig „und nicht wenige der angesehenen griechischen Frauen und Männer" (17,12). Die Wirkung der Areopagrede des Paulus bestand darin, daß einige Männer gläubig wurden, „unter ihnen Dionysius der Areopagit, außerdem eine Frau namens Damaris und noch andere mit ihnen" (17,34).

In Korinth traf Paulus mit dem aus Rom vertriebenen judenchristlichen Ehepaar Priska und Aquila zusammen (18,2 f). Paulus wohnte und arbeitete ungefähr eineinhalb Jahre bei ihnen. Dann fuhr er mit ihnen nach Ephesus. Das Ehepaar blieb dort, er selbst aber reiste weiter nach Cäsarea (18,18–22). Als der redegewandte christliche Missionar Apollos in Ephesus auftrat, sollen ihn Priska und Aquila genauer in der Lehre Jesu unterwiesen haben (18,26). Wie aus 1 Kor 16,19 hervorgeht, hat Paulus das Ehepaar nochmals bei seinem zweieinhalbjährigen Aufenthalt in Ephesus angetroffen, denn er schreibt von dort aus: „Aquila und Priska mit ihrer Hausgemeinde senden euch viele Grüße im Herrn." An ihre Zugehörigkeit zur Gemeinde in Ephesus erinnern auch die Grüße, die später der Verfasser des 2. Timotheusbriefes an Priska und Aquila ausrichten läßt (2 Tim 4,19; vgl. 1 Tim 1,3). Die rühmliche Erwähnung Röm 16,3–5 setzt voraus, daß das Ehepaar in der Zeit zwischen der Abfassung des 1. Korintherbriefes und des Römerbriefes wieder nach Rom zurückgekehrt war und auch dort wieder eine Hausgemeinde um sich geschart hatte[5]. Die Zugehörigkeit Priskas zu einer christlichen Gemeinde ist also für Rom, Korinth und Ephesus bezeugt.

---

[5] Röm 16 wird als nach Rom gerichtet angesehen u. a. von *W. G. Kümmel*, Einleitung in das Neue Testament (Heidelberg [18]1976) 297; *A. Wikenhauser* – *J. Schmid*, Einleitung in das Neue Testament (Freiburg – Basel – Wien [6]1973) 458–462; *H. Schlier*, Der Römerbrief (HThK 6) (Freiburg – Basel – Wien 1977) 10–12. – Als Fragment eines Briefes nach Ephesus wird das Kapitel erachtet u. a. von *W. Marxsen*, Einleitung in das Neue Testament (Gütersloh [3]1964) 100;

Daß die korinthische Gemeinde von Anfang an aus Frauen und Männern bestand, daß Frauen den Gemeindegottesdienst mitfeierten und daß sie dabei Gebete und Prophetien sprachen, geht aus 1 Kor 11,2–16 hervor[6]. Zu den Christinnen der Gemeinde in Kenchreä bei Korinth gehört Phöbe (Röm 16,1 f).

Als Paulus nach der Darstellung der Apostelgeschichte von seiner dritten Missionsreise zurückkehrte und sich in Tyrus verabschiedete, wurde er und seine Gefährten von den Christen, auch von „Frauen und Kindern", bis vor die Stadt begleitet (Apg 21,5). In Cäsarea hielten Paulus und seine Gefährten sich im Haus des Evangelisten Philippus auf, „der vier Töchter hatte, prophetisch begabte Jungfrauen" (21,9).

Für die Gemeinde in Rom werden von Paulus folgende Frauen als bekannt vorausgesetzt: Priska (Röm 16,3–5); Maria, Tryphäna, Tryphosa und Persis, „die sich sehr abgemüht haben" um die Gemeinde (Röm 16,6.12); die Mutter des Rufus, die für Paulus selbst zu einer „Mutter" geworden ist (Röm 16,13); Julia, wohl die Ehefrau des Philologus, und außerdem die Schwester des Nereus (Röm 16,15).

Außer diesen *direkten* Textaussagen bezeugen auch *indirekte Angaben,* daß viele Frauen das Evangelium gläubig annahmen und zu den urchristlichen Gemeinden gehörten. Dafür seien einige Beispiele genannt. Im Bericht über die Samariamission heißt es: „Die Menge achtete einmütig auf die Worte des Philippus" (Apg 8,6).

G. Bornkamm, Paulus (Stuttgart ²1969) 249; *Käsemann,* Römer (Anm. 1) 396–400.

[6] Die gegenteilige Anweisung, daß die Frauen im Gemeindegottesdienst schweigen sollen (1 Kor 14,34 f) ist mit überzeugenden Argumenten als Interpolation späterer Zeit aus 1 Tim 2,11 f erwiesen. Diese Auffassung vertreten u. a. *G. Fitzer,* Das Weib schweige in der Gemeinde. Über den unpaulinischen Charakter der mulier-taceat-Verse in 1. Korinther 14 (TEH NF 110) (München 1963); *H. Conzelmann,* Der erste Brief an die Korinther (KEK V) (Göttingen 1969) 289 f; *W. O. Walker,* 1 Corinthians 11:2–16 and Paul's Views Regarding Women, in: JBL 94 (1975) 94–110, hier 95; *G. Dautzenberg,* Urchristliche Prophetie. Ihre Erforschung, ihre Voraussetzungen im Judentum und ihre Struktur im ersten Korintherbrief (BWANT 104) (Stuttgart 1975) 257–273; *Thraede,* Ärger (Anm. 1) 111 f. – Um einen, allerdings wenig überzeugenden Ausgleich beider Stellen bemühen sich u. a. *E. Kähler,* Die Frau in den paulinischen Briefen (Zürich 1960) 70–87; *Blum,* Amt (Anm. 2) 142–161, hier 149 f; *A. Feuillet,* La dignité et le rôle de la femme d'après quelques textes Pauliniens, in: NTS 21 (1975) 157–191, hier 162–170.

Daß es sich dabei um Männer und Frauen handelte, geht deutlich aus Apg 8,12 hervor, wo ausdrücklich von der Taufe auch der Frauen die Rede ist. – Nach Apg 26,10 verfolgte Saulus „viele der Heiligen". Die Paralleldarstellungen sprechen von Männern und Frauen (Apg 9,2; 22,4). – In der Aussage, daß sich „alle Bewohner von Lydda und der Scharon-Ebene" bekehrten (Apg 9,35) sind Frauen mitgemeint. Ist dies schon durch den hyperbolischen Ausdruck „alle Bewohner" zu vermuten, so wird es überdies durch die Erwähnung der „Jüngerin" Tabita (9,36) und der Prophetinnen, die in Cäsarea leben (21,9), belegt. – Die oft in der Apostelgeschichte begegnende Anrede „Brüder" in den Reden setzt als Hörerschaft nicht nur Männer voraus und läßt die Reden nicht nur an sie gerichtet sein, sondern auch an Frauen. Das ergeben der übertragene Sprachgebrauch des Ausdrucks „Brüder" und der jeweilige Kontext. So sind z. B. unter den etwa 120 „Brüdern", die nach Apg 1,15 zur Wahl des Ersatzapostels versammelt sind, sicher im Sinn des Lukas auch die unmittelbar vorher erwähnten Frauen inbegriffen, und die Anrede „Brüder" dürfte auch sie einschließen. Ebenso verhält es sich wohl mit der Pfingstrede des Petrus. Er spricht die Zuhörer an mit „Ihr Juden (ἄνδρες Ἰουδαῖοι) und alle Bewohner von Jerusalem" (Apg 2,14), „Israeliten" (ἄνδρες Ἰσραηλῖται, 2,22), „Brüder" (ἄνδρες ἀδελφοί, 2,29); aber unter den Zuhörern sind sicher sowohl die bereits zur Gemeinde gehörenden Frauen mitgemeint als auch manche von den Frauen, die später in der Apostelgeschichte als Gemeindeglieder genannt sind (z. B. 5,1; 6,1; 8,3; 12,12 f).

Wenn in der Apostelgeschichte mitgeteilt wird, daß „die Zahl der Jünger wuchs" (6,1), so ist dabei auch an den Zuwachs von Frauen gedacht, wie u. a. 5,14 zeigt. Ähnlich verhält es sich mit dem Bedeutungsgehalt des Wortes „Jünger" an manchen anderen Stellen. Daß die Verwendung des männlichen Substantivs auch Frauen umfaßt, wird Apg 21,4f deutlich: Die Missionare kehren in Tyrus bei den „Jüngern" ein, werden aber „von allen mit Frauen und Kindern" verabschiedet. Mitgemeint und mitangesprochen sind auch die Frauen in den Briefpräskripten, selbst wenn nur männliche Anredeformen begegnen. Paulus richtet z. B. seinen Brief nach Rom an „alle ... berufenen Heiligen" (1,7). Der große Anteil der mitangeredeten Frauen geht u. a. deutlich aus den Grüßen des Schlußkapitels hervor (Röm 16), wo unter den 29 Einzelpersonen 9 Frauen genannt sind.

1.2. Deutung des Textbefundes

Der große Anteil der Frauen an den urchristlichen Gemeinden hat mehrere Ursachen. Zu ihnen gehören:

1.2.1. Das Verhalten Jesu gegenüber den Frauen

Jesus selbst wandte sich mit seiner Botschaft von der Herrschaft Gottes in gleicher Weise an Männer und Frauen. Er ließ sie unterschiedslos den Anbruch des Reiches Gottes durch Heilungen (z. B. Mk 5,25–34; Lk 13,10–17), Dämonenbannungen (z. B. Mk 7,24–30) und die Vergebung der Sünden (z. B. Lk 7,36–50) erfahren. Durch seine Weisungen über die Ehe und seine Ablehnung der ungerechten und für die Frau nachteiligen Scheidungspraxis stellte er die Personwürde der Frau auf die gleiche Stufe wie die des Mannes (z. B. Mk 10,2–12 par Mt; Mt 5,31 f par Lk 16,18). Er widmete sich auch in einer für seine Umgebung ungewöhnlichen Weise in persönlichem Gespräch den Frauen (z. B. Mk 7,26–29; Lk 10,38–42; Joh 4,7–27), ließ sich von ihnen begleiten (Lk 8,1–3; 23,27; Mk 15,40 par Mt/Lk)[7] und durch ihr Vermögen unterstützen (Lk 8,3).

1.2.2. Die urchristliche Reflexion über das Heilswerk Christi

Paulus schreibt den Christen der Gemeinden Galatiens, daß sie alle durch den Glauben und die Taufe Söhne Gottes geworden und geeint in Jesus Christus sind, so daß es „nicht mehr Juden und Griechen, Sklaven und Freie, Mann und Frau" gibt (Gal 3,26–28). Die äußerlich weiterbestehenden Unterschiede wirken sich nicht mehr nachteilig aus für die Teilhabe an dem von Christus vermittelten Heil[8]. Diese urchristliche Einsicht ist ein weiterer Grund für die

---

[7] Daß Lukas die Frauen in der Gefolgschaft Jesu auf die „gleiche Stufe mit den Aposteln" stellt, wie *R. Laurentin*, Jesus und die Frauen: Eine verkannte Revolution?, in: Concilium 16 (1980) 275–283, hier 278, meint, wird man angesichts des spezifisch lukanischen Apostelbegriffs (Apg 1,21 f!) nicht sagen können. Ähnliches gilt in bezug auf das Urteil von *M. Brennan*, Frauen und Männer im kirchlichen Dienst, in: Concilium 16 (1980) 288–292, „daß auch auf Frauen die Qualifikationen zutreffen, die Lukas und Paulus zufolge den Apostel ausmachen" (289).

[8] Vgl. *F. Mußner*, Der Galaterbrief (HThK 9) (Freiburg – Basel – Wien 1974) 264. – Wieweit sich aus Gal 3,28 soziologische Konsequenzen zur „Frauenfrage" ziehen lassen, ist kontrovers. Vgl. verschiedene Stellungnahmen bei *Thraede*, Ärger (Anm. 1) 102 f.

Selbstverständlichkeit, mit der Frauen von Anfang an zu den christlichen Gemeinden gehörten.

1.2.3. Das Bewußtsein, zum endzeitlichen Gottesvolk zu gehören, in dem Gott seinen Heiligen Geist unterschiedslos Männern und Frauen schenkt

Lukas läßt Petrus in der Pfingstpredigt aussprechen, daß nun in Erfüllung gegangen ist, was Gott durch den Propheten Joel verheißen hat: „... Ich werde von meinem Geist ausgießen über alles Fleisch. Eure Söhne und Töchter werden prophezeien ... Auch über meine Knechte und Mägde werde ich von meinem Geist ausgießen in jenen Tagen, und sie werden prophezeien" (Apg 2,17f)[9].

1.2.4. Der Verlauf der urchristlichen Mission in den vom Judentum vorgeprägten Bahnen

Die urchristliche Missionsarbeit begann bei den Juden und gelangte über die „Gottesfürchtigen" zu den Heiden[10]. Dabei spielten die jüdischen Synagogen sowohl innerhalb wie außerhalb Palästinas eine große Rolle[11]. Sie waren nicht nur der Versammlungs- und Gebetsraum der jüdischen Gemeinden, sondern auch der zu ihnen gehörenden Proselyten[12] und „Gottesfürchtigen"[13]. Da es gerade unter ihnen

---

[9] *K. H. Schelkle*, Der Geist und die Braut. Frauen in der Bibel (Düsseldorf 1977) 153 sagt dazu: „Männer und Frauen werden in gleicher Weise vom Geist erfüllt ... und zu prophetischer Verkündigung in der Kirche berufen."

[10] Vgl. *W. Schrage*, Art. συναγωγή-κτλ, in: ThWNT VII, 798–850, hier 833f; *K. G. Kuhn*, Art. προσήλυτος, in: ThWNT VI, 727–747, hier 744.

[11] Nach Apg 9,20; 13,5.14; 14,1; 17,10.17; 18,4; 19,8 u.ö. beginnt Paulus seine Missionswirksamkeit jeweils in der Synagoge. Diese schematische Darstellungsweise entspricht zwar ganz der lukanischen Konzeption, und nicht jede Einzelangabe verbürgt historische Zuverlässigkeit; aber aufs Ganze gesehen, hat diese Sicht genügend Anhalt in der geschichtlichen Wirklichkeit, wie z.B. Röm 1,16; 10,14–20; 1 Kor 9,20f; 2 Kor 11,24f zeigen.

[12] D.h. zum Judentum übergetretene Heiden; z.B. Apg 2,11; 6,5; 13,43.

[13] Φοβούμενοι τὸν Θεόν („Gottesfürchtige" Apg 10,2.35; 13,16.26) und σεβόμενοι τὸν Θεόν („Gottesverehrer" Apg 13,50; 16,14; 17,4.17; 18,7) sind Heiden, die zwar den jüdischen Gottesglauben teilen und den Synagogengottesdienst besuchen, aber nicht durch die Beschneidung und Übernahme des ganzen Gesetzes Juden, d.h. Proselyten geworden sind.

sehr viele Frauen gab[14], ist es verständlich, daß dieser große Frauen-
anteil auch der christlichen Mission zugute kam.

1.2.5. Sozialgeschichtliche Faktoren

Der Weg der urchristlichen Mission ging vorwiegend über die
Städte. Die soziale Schichtung der hellenistisch-kaiserzeitlichen
Stadtbevölkerung, in der die Frauen wirtschaftlich, gesellschaftlich
und religiös zum Teil eine beachtliche Selbständigkeit besaßen[15], hat
auch Einfluß auf die soziale Zusammensetzung der christlichen Gemeinden ausgeübt. Der große Anteil der Frauen in ihnen[16] erklärt
sich zum Teil auch von daher.

Ein weiterer religions- und sozialgeschichtlicher Grund dafür
liegt in der Bedeutung, die die Hausgemeinden[17] für die Ausbreitung
des frühen Christentums hatten. Spielten schon im Heidentum häusliche Kultfeiern der Familien und Mysterienvereine eine große

---

[14] Z. B. für Damaskus belegt durch Josephus Bell II 20,2: Die Frauen der Da-
maskener waren „mit wenigen Ausnahmen der jüdischen Gottesverehrung ergeben." – In Rom gehörten u. a. die vornehmen Frauen Beturia Paulina (CIL VI
29756), Flavia Antonina (CIG 9903), Fulvia (Josephus Ant XVIII 3,5) und die
Gattin Neros, Poppaea, (Josephus Ant XX 8,11; Vita 3) zu ihnen. Vgl. *Thraede,*
Ärger (Anm. 1) 94; *Zscharnack,* Dienst (Anm. 1) 20. – Über das Verhältnis der
Frauen zum Religiösen allgemein sagt bereits Strabo I 7 p. 297: ἅπαντες γάρ τῆς
δεισιδαιμονίας ἀρχηγούς οἴονται τὰς γυναῖκας.
[15] Vgl. *Thraede,* Frau (Anm. 1) 229 f; *ders.,* Ärger (Anm. 1) 35–98.
[16] Zu den wirtschaftlich wohlhabenden und sozial höher stehenden Frauen werden zu rechnen sein Tabita (Apg 9,36.41), Maria (Apg 12,12f), Lydia (Apg
16,14f), Priska (Apg 18,2.18 f.26; Röm 16,3–5; 1 Kor 16,19), Phöbe (Röm 16,1f),
Chloe (?) (1 Kor 1,11), Nympha (?) (Kol 4,15) und die summarisch Apg 13,50;
17,4 Genannten. Dem Sklavenstand gehören Rhode (Apg 12,13) und vielleicht
Persis (Röm 16,12) an. „Das hellenistische Urchristentum ist weder eine proleta-
rische Bewegung unterer Schichten gewesen, noch eine Angelegenheit gehobener
Schichten. Charakteristisch für seine soziale Struktur ist vielmehr, daß es verschiedene Schichten umfaßte" (*G. Theißen,* Soziale Schichtung in der korinthischen Gemeinde. Ein Beitrag zur Soziologie des hellenistischen Urchristentums,
in: *ders.,* Studien zur Soziologie des Urchristentums [WUNT 19] [Tübingen 1979]
231–271, hier 267). Ähnlich urteilt *H. Cancik,* Die neutestamentlichen Aussagen
über Geschlecht, Ehe, Frau, in: *ders.,* u. a. (Hrsg.), Zum Thema Frau in Kirche
und Gesellschaft (Stuttgart 1972) 9–45, hier 25 („untere Mittelklasse mit
Aufstiegstendenz") und 33 („mittleres und unteres Bürgertum").
[17] Vgl. *P. Stuhlmacher,* Der Brief an Philemon (EKK 18) (Zürich – Neukirchen-
Vluyn 1975) 70–74 (mit Lit.); *H.-J. Klauck,* Hausgemeinde und Hauskirche im
frühen Christentum (SBS 103) (Stuttgart 1981).

Rolle, so erweisen sich „die jüdischen Haussynagogen (als) das eigentliche Vorbild für die neu entstehenden christlichen Hausgemeinden"[18]. Die soziale Zusammensetzung konnte sehr verschieden sein, aber sie war offen für Männer und Frauen, für Christen jeden Standes, jeder Bildungsschicht und Herkunft. Neben der Großgemeinde waren die Hausgemeinden für Paulus der Ort, „wo die in der Antike besonders gravierenden soziologischen und ethnisch-religiösen Barrieren zwischen Juden und Heiden, Freien und Unfreien, Männern und Frauen, Hoch und Niedrig, Gebildet und Ungebildet zerbrochen und vergleichgültigt wurden zugunsten und von der einen neuen Bindung aller an Christus als den Herrn"[19].

1.2.6. Die Taufe als Zeichen der Initiation

Von Anfang an bestand nie ein Zweifel darüber, daß die Taufe als Zeichen der Zugehörigkeit zu Christus und der Gemeinschaft der Kirche Männern und Frauen in gleicher Weise zu spenden sei. Darin drückt sich die Überzeugung aus, daß ein jeder Mann und eine jede Frau unterschiedslos, vollwertig und unmittelbar Anteil am eschatologischen Gottesvolk erhalten. Im Unterschied zur jüdischen Auffassung über das Bundeszeichen der Beschneidung bedeutete dies eine erhebliche Aufwertung der Frau[20]; denn im Judentum gehörte die Frau nicht unmittelbar und nicht vollberechtigt zum priesterlichen Gottesvolk, sondern nur mittels des Mannes, an dem allein die Beschneidung vollzogen wurde.

2. Die Mitarbeit der Frauen bei der Verbreitung des Evangeliums

Das Neue Testament bezeugt nicht nur die Zugehörigkeit vieler Frauen zu den urchristlichen Gemeinden, sondern auch ihre aktive Beteiligung an der urchristlichen Missionsarbeit.

---

[18] *Stuhlmacher*, Philemon 73.
[19] Ebd. 74.
[20] Dies heben besonders hervor *W. D. Thomas*, The Place of Women in the Church at Philippi, in: ExpT 83 (1971/72) 117–120, hier 117f; *Laurentin*, Jesus (Anm. 7) 275f.

2.1. Der Dienst des Gebetes

Aus der vollwertigen Zugehörigkeit der Frauen zu den urchristlichen Gemeinden ergibt sich, daß sie selbstverständlich auch an allen Lebensvollzügen der christlichen Gemeinden Anteil hatten, nämlich daß sie „festhielten an der Lehre der Apostel, an der Gemeinschaft, am Brotbrechen und an den Gebeten" (Apg 2,42). An manchen Stellen des Neuen Testamentes bezieht sich das in Dank und Bitte sich äußernde Gebet, an dem auch Frauen teilhaben, ausdrücklich auf die Ausbreitung des Evangeliums: Nach der Freilassung des Petrus und Johannes und ihrer Rückkehr „zu den Ihren" (Apg 4,23) beten diese mit ihnen: „Herr, ... gib deinen Knechten die Kraft, mit allem Freimut dein Wort zu verkünden" (4,29). Als Petrus wiederum im Gefängnis festgehalten wird, versammelt sich ein Teil der Jerusalemer Gemeinde im Haus der Maria und ihrer Sklavin Rhode zum Gebet (Apg 12,12). Nach Apg 14,26 f kehren Paulus und Barnabas von der ersten Missionsreise zurück und berichten der Gemeinde in Antiochien, was Gott durch sie gewirkt hat. In diesem Zusammenhang heißt es, daß man ihre Missionsreise betend „der Gnade Gottes empfohlen hatte". Mit den für das Missionswerk Betenden sind sicher nicht nur die 13,1–3 ausdrücklich erwähnten Propheten und Lehrer gemeint, sondern entsprechend dem Kontext die ganze Gemeinde und somit auch die Frauen. Der Dank und Lobpreis für den Durchbruch des Evangeliums zu den Heiden äußert sich unterschiedslos bei Männern und Frauen, wenn Apg 13,48 gesagt wird, daß „die Heiden sich freuten und das Wort des Herrn priesen". Auch Paulus berichtet vom Dankgebet der Gemeinden im Hinblick auf das, was Gott an ihm und durch ihn gewirkt habe. Er teilt mit, daß „die Gemeinden Judäas gehört hatten: Der uns einst verfolgte, verkündet jetzt den Glauben, den er einst zu vernichten suchte, und sie priesen Gott meinetwegen" (Gal 1,23 f). Legt schon der Zusammenhang die selbstverständliche Annahme nahe, daß Männer wie Frauen hier als betende Glieder der Gemeinden gedacht sind, so wird dies noch deutlicher durch Apg 8,3; 9,2; 22,4, wo die von Paulus einst Verfolgten ausdrücklich als Männer und Frauen bezeichnet werden. – In 1 Tim 5,3–16 ist in ausführlicher Weise vom Stand der Witwen innerhalb der Gemeinden die Rede. Trotz vieler offener Fragen zum Verständnis dieses Textes und des urchristlichen Witweninstituts[21] ist eines deutlich: Im Gebet (V. 5) ist „die einzige sichere, quasi-amtliche Funktion der Gemeindewitwen zu erkennen ... Das unablässige Gebet war ... der spezifische Auftrag der Kirche an den Stand der Witwen."[22] Für das Gebet der Witwen werden zwar keine einzelnen Gebetsinhalte genannt, man wird aber annehmen dürfen, daß Dank und Bitte für die Ausbreitung des Evangeliums dazugehörten.

2.2. Der karitative Dienst

Man kann voraussetzen, daß Männer und Frauen der urchristlichen Gemeinden durch das Beispiel und die Weisungen Jesu motiviert waren, Notleidenden zu helfen und dies auch nach Kräften taten[23]. Ein Beispiel derartig tatkräftiger Nächstenliebe ist Tabita. Ihre Gestalt begegnet in einer „missionstheologischen"[24] Erweckungserzählung (Apg 9,36–42)[25]. An der Frau, die von Petrus erweckt wird, haf-

---

[21] *A. Oepke,* Der Dienst der Frau in der urchristlichen Gemeinde, in: NAMZ 16 (1939) 39–53.81–86, sieht m. E. zu Recht in den Witwen „nicht Amtsträgerinnen, sondern Unterstützungsempfängerinnen" (47), die für ihre empfangene Hilfe nach Kräften noch karitative Dienste leisteten; ebenso *ders.,* Art. γυνή, in: ThWNT I, 776–790, hier 788 f; ähnlich *N. Brox,* Die Pastoralbriefe (RNT 7) (Regensburg ⁴1969) 185–189. – Im Unterschied dazu sehen andere den Stand der Gemeindewitwen an als eine Einrichtung mit Amtscharakter und bestimmten Dienstfunktionen. So z. B. *H. Greeven,* Art. Frau III A; in: RGG II, 1069–1070; *S. Solle,* Art. χήρα, in: ThBNT I, 358–360; *H. Vorländer,* Art. γυνή, in: ThBNT I, 354 f; *Schelkle,* Geist (Anm. 9) 128.169.

[22] *Brox,* Pastoralbriefe (Anm. 21) 189.

[23] Man denke etwa an die in der Urgemeinde geübte Nächstenliebe Apg 2,42–46; 4,32–37; 6,1–6, die als Grundhaltung der Christen trotz lukanischer Gestaltung der Summarien nicht zu bezweifeln ist; an die Kollekte für Jerusalem Apg 11,27–30; Röm 15,25–28; 1 Kor 16,1–4; 2 Kor 8,6–15; an die vielfältigen, z. T. auch karitativen Dienste in Korinth (1 Kor 12) und Rom (Röm 12).

[24] Vgl. Apg 9,42.

[25] Die Erzählung wird im *hellenistischen* Judenchristentum in oder um Joppe geformt worden sein. Daß es sich von Anfang an um eine *christliche* Erzählung handelt, geht aus der Charakterisierung der Toten als „Jüngerin" (V. 36) hervor sowie aus der zwar nicht ausgesprochenen, aber doch deutlich erkennbaren Bezugnahme auf Totenerweckungen durch Jesus (vgl. bes. V. 40 a mit Mk 5,40). Die *juden-*christliche Herkunft ist am Namen Tabita und am Einfluß der atl. Erweckungserzählungen 1 Kön 17 und 2 Kön 4 zu erkennen. Daß die Formung im *hellenistischen* Judenchristentum vorgenommen wurde, ergibt sich 1. aus der Übersetzung des Namens Tabita ins Griechische (V. 36) und 2. daraus, daß die Erzählung nicht nur formal, sondern auch in einzelnen sprachlichen Wendungen mit

tet ein verhältnismäßig großes Interesse der Erzählung: Es wird ihr *Name* mitgeteilt, der sowohl im Aramäischen wie Griechischen „Gazelle" bedeutet und auch sonst belegt ist[26]. Sie wird als *Jüngerin* charakterisiert. Diese Bezeichnung (μαθήτρια) kommt nur dieses eine Mal im Neuen Testament vor. Es wird sodann hingewiesen auf ihre *guten Werke* (V. 36), womit wohl das Anfertigen der Kleidung und Wäsche für hilfsbedürftige Witwen (V. 39) gemeint ist, und auf die Unterstützung Armer durch *Almosen.*

Als Petrus im Haus der gestorbenen Tabita angekommen ist, umringen ihn die weinenden Witwen. Sie werden im Sinn des Lukas weder als „Klageweiber" noch als „Witwenstand" zu verstehen sein, sondern ihre Trauer und der Hinweis auf das, was ihnen Tabita bedeutete (V. 39), soll die folgende Erweckung motivieren und überdies Petrus nicht nur als Wundertäter, sondern auch als den darstellen, der aus Mitleid mit den Armen hilft. Dasselbe Motiv setzt Lukas im Blick auf den Wundertäter Jesus Lk 7,11–17 ein[27]. Die Charakterisierung Tabitas als „voll guter Werke und Almosen" (V. 36 b) und das Vorweisen der Kleidungsstücke, die sie für andere gefertigt hat (V. 39 c), werden auf lukanische Bearbeitung der Erzählung zurückgehen; denn beide novellistischen Erzählzüge beabsichtigen, Tabita als des Wunders „würdig" und den helfenden Eingriff des Wundertäters als „dringlich" zu erweisen. Ähnliche Akzentuierungen hat Lukas redaktionell auch Lk 7,2–5; 7,12; Apg 10,2.4 vorgenommen, Sie können aber durchaus ihren Anhalt im konkreten Verhalten der betreffenden Personen haben; denn immerhin würde bei Tabita auf diese Weise gut verständlich, weshalb ihre Person und ihr Name so bekannt waren, wie die Überlieferung es voraussetzt. Daß die karitativ dienende Nächstenliebe wie Tabita sie übte, auch werbend für das Christentum gewirkt hat, geht u. a. aus Apg 2,46; 5,13 hervor, wo von der Hochschätzung dieser christlichen Grundhaltung durch Außenstehende die Rede ist.

---

dem LXX-Text der atl. Erzählungen übereinstimmt. Die Bezugnahme auf die atl. Texte wird aber schon vorlukanisch geschehen sein, da sich ja ein ähnlicher Einfluß vorlukanisch auch in Lk 7,11–17 nachweisen läßt.
[26] Vgl. Josephus Bell IV 3,5.
[27] Vgl. *U. Busse*, Die Wunder des Propheten Jesus. Die Rezeption, Komposition und Interpretation der Wundertradition im Evangelium des Lukas (FzB 24) (Stuttgart ²1979) 165–175.

2.3. Der Dienst persönlicher Fürsorge für die Missionare

Ähnlich wie Frauen schon Jesus und sein Wirken durch materielle und persönliche Hilfe unterstützt haben (Lk 8, 1–3), taten dies auch Frauen gegenüber urchristlichen Missionaren. Lydia „drängte" geradezu Paulus und seine Begleiter zu einem Aufenthalt in ihrem Haus (Apg 16, 15)[28]. Die Gemeinde von Philippi blieb Paulus auch weiterhin durch materielle Unterstützung und persönliche Kontakte besonders verbunden (Phil 4, 10–19). Paulus erwähnt zwar in seinem Dank an die Gemeinde weder Lydia noch andere Frauen eigens, aber es ist anzunehmen, daß gerade Frauen es waren, die in besonderer Weise für ihn Sorge trugen. Im Brief an die Gemeinde nach Rom schreibt er, daß die Mutter des Rufus[29] auch für ihn selbst „zur Mutter geworden ist" (Röm 16, 13). Paulus hat „ihre Mütterlichkeit erfahren"[30]. – Priska und Aquila haben „ihr eigenes Leben für ihn aufs Spiel gesetzt" (Röm 16, 4), d.h., sie retteten ihm in einer auch für sie äußerst gefährlichen Lage das Leben. Es ist ungewiß, welche Situation Paulus im Blick hat. Zu denken wäre wohl an Gefährdungen in Korinth oder Ephesus[31]. – Der Gemeinde in Rom empfiehlt er Phöbe an. Man soll ihr helfend beistehen (παραστῆτε), „denn auch sie ist für viele ein Beistand (προστάτις) geworden, auch mir persönlich" (Röm 16, 2). Die Hilfe, die Paulus selbst von Phöbe erfahren hat und die er hier ausdrücklich erwähnt, meint sicher „Fürsorge im persönlichen Bereich"[32] und nicht, daß Phöbe „auch für Paulus eine

---

[28] Die Missionserzählung Apg 16, 12–15 basiert auf sehr alter Lokaltradition. Dies ergibt sich aus einigen Erzähldetails, die kulturgeschichtlich und archäologisch erstaunlich zutreffend bestätigt wurden. Vgl. dazu *P. Collart*, Philippes. Ville de Macédonie, depuis ses origines jusqu'à la fin de l'époque romaine (Paris 1937) 318–323; 456–459; *W. Elliger*, Paulus in Griechenland. Philippi, Thessaloniki, Athen, Korinth (SBS 92/93) (Stuttgart 1978) 47–50; *A. Suhl*, Paulus und seine Briefe. Ein Beitrag zur paulinischen Chronologie (StNT 11) (Gütersloh 1975) 187. Die kritische Analyse von *Ollrog*, Paulus (Anm. 1) 29, berücksichtigt dies nicht genügend. *G. Schille*, Anfänge der Kirche. Erwägungen zur apostolischen Frühgeschichte (BEvTh 43) (München 1966) 50–53, nimmt an, es handle sich ursprünglich um die Gründungslegende der Gemeinde von Thyatira und erst Lukas habe sie zu einer Philippi-Erzählung umgeformt. Für diese Hypothese bietet der Text keinen hinreichenden Anhalt.

[29] Eine Identität mit dem Mk 15, 21 genannten ist wegen der Häufigkeit des Namens nicht anzunehmen. Vgl. *Schlier*, Röm (Anm. 5) 445.

[30] Ebd. 445.

[31] Vgl. Apg 18, 12; 19, 23; 1 Kor 15, 32; 2 Kor 1, 8; 6, 4f; 11, 23–27.

[32] *Käsemann*, Röm (Anm. 1) 396; ebenso *Schlier*, Röm (Anm. 5) 442.

Autoritätsperson" war im Sinne eines Leitungsdienstes oder Leitungsamtes[33]. Die hier vorgezogene Verständnisweise ergibt sich aus zwei Gründen: 1. Die vorherrschende Bedeutung von προστάτις ist „Beschützerin", „Patronin"[34]. 2. Daß Phöbe eine προστάτις für viele und auch für Paulus geworden ist, wird ausgesprochen als Begründung für den Imperativ, daß man nun auch ihr beistehen solle[35]. Da sich diese Hilfe aber nicht ausdrücklich auf Durchführung von Gemeindediensten Phöbes, sondern auf ihre persönlichen Angelegenheiten bezieht, wird auch ihr eigenes προστάτις-Sein gegenüber Paulus diesen Sinn haben.

2.4. Der Dienst in den Hausgemeinden

Es wurde schon erwähnt[36], welch große Bedeutung die Hausgemeinden für die urchristliche Mission und den Anfang der Gemeindebildungen hatten. Das Neue Testament nennt ohne Unterschied Männer und Frauen, die je nach Vermögen in der Lage und dazu bereit

---

[33] So *Schüssler Fiorenza*, Rolle (Anm. 1), 7. Sie begründet ihre Auslegung mit folgenden Argumenten: 1. Die Exegeten schwächen die Bedeutung der Titel διάκονος (V. 1) und προστάτις (V. 2) ab, „weil sie auf Frauen angewandt werden." 2. Προστάτις wird gewöhnlich mit „Helferin" oder „Beschützerin" wiedergegeben. Das Wort hat aber in der jüdischen Literatur den Beisinn von „Anführer", „Vorsteher", „Statthalter", „Protektor" oder „Verwalter". 3. Paulus verwendet das Verbum προΐσταμαι für den Leitungsdienst in der Gemeinde (1 Thess 5,12), und 1 Tim 3,4f; 5,17 bezeichnet es „den Bischofs-, Diakons- oder Ältestendienst. Darum ist anzunehmen, daß Phöbe ... ein solches Amt innehatte. Sie war für viele und auch für Paulus eine Autoritätsperson." – Trotz aller Berechtigung, die Bedeutung Phöbes für das urchristliche Gemeindeleben hoch einzuschätzen (siehe unten 2.5.1.), legt Röm 16,2 nicht nahe, die von *Schüssler Fiorenza* postulierte Nebenbedeutung von προστάτις zur Auslegung heranzuziehen. Außerdem ist zu beachten, wie sehr auch 1 Thess 5,12; Röm 12,8 bei der Verwendung des Verbums προΐσταμαι für den Leitungsdienst das Element des Fürsorgens mitschwingt. Vgl. *J. Hainz*, Ekklesia. Strukturen paulinischer Gemeinde – Theologie und Gemeinde-Ordnung (BU 9) (Regensburg 1972) 44–46; 194.
[34] Vgl. *W. Bauer*, Wörterbuch zum Neuen Testament (Berlin [5]1963) (Nachdruck) 1425; *B. Reicke*, Art. προΐστημι, in: ThWNT VI 700–703, hier 703. – Allerdings kommt nicht der rechtlich-juridische, sondern nur der übertragene Sinn in Betracht.
[35] Zwischen παραστῆτε und προστάτις besteht also eine sehr enge inhaltliche Verbindung, die ihren grammatikalischen Ausdruck durch καὶ γάρ findet: Παραστῆτε αὐτῇ ..., καὶ γὰρ αὐτή προστάτις ... ἐγενήθη. Vgl. auch *O. Michel*, Der Brief an die Römer (KEK IV) (Göttingen [12]1963) 377f.

waren, ihr Haus für die Zusammenkünfte der ganzen Gemeinde oder einzelner Teilgruppen zur Verfügung zu stellen. In Jerusalem war es Maria, die Mutter des Johannes Markus, in deren Haus[37] sich Christen versammelten (Apg 12,12 f). In Philippi ließ sich Lydia „mit ihrem Haus" taufen (Apg 16,15). Begründete dieses Geschehen selbst schon eine Hausgemeinde, so stellt sich dieselbe überdies als ein gewisses Zentrum der Missionsgemeinde in Philippi dar, wenn es heißt, daß Paulus und Silas später bei ihrem Abschied im Hause Lydias „die Brüder sahen, sie ermahnten und dann fortgingen" (16,40). Die Hausgemeinde des Ehepaares Priska und Aquila ist für die Zeit ihres Aufenthalts in Ephesus (1 Kor 16,19; 2 Tim 4,19) und Rom (Röm 16,5) bezeugt. Ebenfalls in Rom ist um Philologus und Julia[38], Nereus mit seiner Schwester und Olympas eine Hausgemeinde geschart; denn sie werden von Paulus gegrüßt mit „allen Heiligen, die bei ihnen sind" (Röm 16,15). In Laodizäa ist es Nympha, die mit der „Gemeinde in ihrem Haus" Grüße erhält (Kol 4,15). Philemon und seine Frau[39] Apphia stehen einer Hausgemeinde in oder um Kolossä vor (Phlm 1 f). An sie richtet Paulus den Philemonbrief. Ungewiß ist, ob auch Chloe Christin war[40] und ob „die Leute der Chloe", die Paulus Nachrichten aus Korinth übermittelten (1 Kor 1,11), zu ihrer Hausgemeinde gehörten. Manche der erwähnten Frauen waren selbständig, wie etwa Maria, Lydia und Nympha; andere werden zusammen mit ihrem Ehemann genannt, so Priska, Julia und Apphia. Da Priska im Verhältnis zu Aquila mehrmals an erster Stelle genannt wird (Apg 18,18.26; Röm 16,3; 2 Tim 4,19), ist anzunehmen, daß sie auch in den Hausgemeinden die bedeutendere Rolle spielte[41]. Die den Hausgemeinden vorstehenden Frauen und

---

[36] Siehe oben 1.2.5.

[37] Die Erwähnung des Torgebäudes (πυλών) und der Sklavin Rhode weist auf ein stattliches Anwesen hin und auf einen gewissen Wohlstand. Diese Angaben gehören wegen ihres Lokalkolorits vermutlich zum ältesten Bestand der Erzählung und dürften historisch zutreffend sein.

[38] *Harnack*, Mission (Anm. 1) II 592 und *Schlier*, Röm (Anm. 5) 446 vermuten, Julia ist die Frau des Philologus.

[39] So vermutet u. a. von *Harnack*, Mission (Anm. 1) II 592 Anm. 3; *Stuhlmacher*, Phlm (Anm. 17) 30; zurückhaltender *Ollrog*, Paulus (Anm. 1) 43.

[40] Angenommen von *Schelkle*, Geist (Anm. 9) 162 f; zurückhaltender *Thraede*, Ärger (Anm. 1) 97; *Conzelmann*, 1 Kor (Anm. 6) 46.

[41] Zur Vorrangstellung Priskas vgl. *Zscharnack*, Dienst (Anm. 1) 49; *Oepke*, Dienst (Anm. 21) 52; *Harnack*, Mission (Anm. 1) II, 591; *Blum*, Amt (Anm. 2)

Männer stellten sicher nicht nur die Räumlichkeiten zur Verfügung und schufen sicher nicht nur die für die Zusammenkünfte und Gottesdienste nötigen äußeren Bedingungen. Sie werden wohl auch ganz selbstverständlich die Gottesdienste geleitet haben durch Gebet, Verkündigung, Prophetie und weitere Funktionen der liturgischen Feier. Im Blick auf die Hausgemeinden wird nirgendwo im Neuen Testament ein Unterschied zwischen den Rollen der Frauen und Männer artikuliert[42], und im Blick auf umfassendere Gemeindegottesdienste kommt er erst in später Zeit aus antignostischer Tendenz und unter jüdischem Einfluß 1 Tim 2,11 f[43] und in der davon abhängigen Interpolation[44] 1 Kor 14,34 f zum Ausdruck.

Daß Priska zusammen mit Aquila christliche Unterweisung in ihrem Haus in Ephesus erteilt hat, wird Apg 18,26 berichtet. Dort heißt es, daß Priska und Aquila den redegewandten, geistbegabten christlichen Missionar Apollos „zu sich nahmen und ihm den Weg Gottes noch genauer darlegten". Er kannte angeblich nur die Taufe des Johannes, obwohl er die Lehre Jesu genau vortrug (V. 25). Der Bericht des Lukas unterliegt berechtigten historischen Bedenken[45]; denn es ist schwer vorstellbar, daß ein christlicher Missionar mit den von Lukas genannten Qualitäten nichts von der Taufe auf den Namen Jesu wußte und des Nachhilfeunterrichtes in der angegebenen Weise bedurfte, ganz abgesehen davon, daß ja von der Taufe her-

---

146; *Ollrog,* Paulus (Anm. 1) 25; *Schüssler Fiorenza,* Rolle (Anm. 1) 7; *Schlier,* Röm (Anm. 5) 443; *R. Radford Ruether,* Frauen für eine neue Gesellschaft. Frauenbewegung und menschliche Befreiung (München 1979) 81.

[42] Ob er stillschweigend vorausgesetzt wird, wenn es etwa Apg 2,46 heißt, „sie brachen in den Häusern das Brot", insofern damit der im Judentum üblicherweise durch den Hausvater vorgenommene mahleröffnende Ritus des Brotbrechens gemeint ist, der dann zur Bezeichnung des ganzen eucharistischen Mahles wurde? Aber selbst wenn dies der Fall wäre, so müßte dies nicht in gleicher Weise für heidenchristliche Gemeinden gelten.

[43] Vgl. *Brox,* Pastoralbriefe (Anm. 21) 133 f. – Für das Lehrverbot gegenüber den Frauen dürfte auch das spezifische Amts- und „Sukzessions"-Verständnis der Pastoralbriefe von Bedeutung sein.

[44] Vgl. oben Anm. 6.

[45] Sie werden in je verschiedener Weise formuliert von *E. Käsemann,* Die Johannesjünger in Ephesus, in: *ders.,* Exegetische Versuche und Besinnungen I (Göttingen 1964) 158–168 und *E. Schweizer,* Die Bekehrung des Apollos. Apg 18,24–26, in: *ders.,* Beiträge zur Theologie des Neuen Testaments. Neutestamentliche Aufsätze (1955–1970) (Zürich 1970) 71–79. Von den beiden Lösungsversuchen erscheint mir der von *Käsemann* der überzeugendere.

nach nicht mehr die Rede ist. Apollos war ein tüchtiger, selbständiger Missionar, als den ihn auch Paulus schildert (1 Kor 1–4). Läßt sich zwar die Unterweisung des Apollos durch Priska und Aquila historisch nicht erweisen, so ist doch bemerkenswert, daß Lukas keine Schwierigkeiten darin sah, auch die Frau ganz selbstverständlich in der Ausübung christlicher Lehrtätigkeit zu schildern[46].

2.5. Der umfassende missionarische Dienst

Zeigen schon die Hausgemeinden, daß der Dienst der Frauen nicht nur in stillem Gebet, karitativer Hilfe für die Gemeinden und persönlicher Fürsorge für die Missionare bestand, so wird dies erst recht deutlich, wenn man bestimmte Ausdrucksweisen, Substantive und Verben beachtet, mit denen die Bedeutung der Frauen für die urchristliche Mission umschrieben wird.

2.5.1. Phöbe als „Diakonin"

Paulus empfiehlt der Gemeinde in Rom die christliche Schwester Phöbe an, „Diakonin der Gemeinde in Kenchreä" (Röm 16,1)[47]. Das Partizip οὖσαν, die Genitivergänzung „der Gemeinde ..." und die Verwendung des Titels διάκονος, wie er zur Bezeichnung eines an der Gemeindeleitung in Philippi beteiligten Dienstamtes vorkommt (Phil 1,1), lassen annehmen, daß auch Phöbe einen solch

---

[46] Das besondere Interesse des Lukas an der Bedeutung Priskillas zeigt sich auch Apg 18,2. Die Aussage „καὶ Πρίσκιλλαν γυναῖκα αὐτοῦ" ist vermutlich lukanisch redaktioneller Zusatz. So mit guten Gründen *E. Haenchen,* Die Apostelgeschichte (KEK III) (Göttingen ⁷1977) 512. – Der Inhalt sowohl der vorlukanischen Nachricht als auch der lukanischen Zufügung ist aber historisch zuverlässig. Dies ergibt sich aus dem Judenedikt des Claudius (Sueton, Claudius 25; Orosius, Hist Contra Pag VII 6,15 f [CSEL 5,451]) und aus dem auch von Paulus bezeugten Zusammenwirken mit dem Ehepaar. – Die Hervorhebung Priskillas neben Aquila entspricht der „frauenfreundlichen" Tendenz des Lukas. Gegen das Vorhandensein dieser Tendenz spricht nicht etwa die Tatsache, daß Lukas von dem Ehepaar und seiner Bedeutung für die urchristliche Mission weniger berichtet, als er wußte und daß er das Ehepaar hinter Paulus zurücktreten läßt (z. B. Apg 18,18–22); denn diese Nach- und Unterordnung bezieht sich ja nicht allein auf die Frau Priskilla, sondern ebenso auf ihren Mann Aquila und andere Missionare. Sie hängt mit der Einlinigkeit der Darstellung zugunsten des Paulus und der „apostolischen" Tradition zusammen.

[47] „οὖσαν [καὶ] διάκονον τῆς ἐκκλησίας τῆς ἐν Κενχρεαῖς".

ständigen, anerkannten Fürsorge-, Verkündigungs- und Leitungsdienst in der Gemeinde ausübte. Entsprechend der paulinischen Auffassung, daß jeder am Aufbau der Gemeinde beteiligte Dienst und ebenso die in Ansätzen vorhandenen Dienstämter als geistgewirkt gelten (Röm 12; 1 Kor 12), ist auch der Dienst Phöbes zu verstehen: aus den Anregungen des Heiligen Geistes, von denen sie sich führen ließ, und aus ihrem bewährten und anerkannten Einsatz entstand so etwas wie die „Vorstufe zum späteren kirchlichen Amt"[48]. Welcher Art die Dienste im einzelnen waren, die Phöbe als διάκονος und προστάτις (V. 2)[49] in der Gemeinde ausübte, ist nicht mit Sicherheit festzustellen. Anhaltspunkte ergeben sich aber aus der umfassenden Weise, in der Paulus auch sonst Männer wie Frauen als Mitarbeiter in seine Missionsarbeit einbezog und aus der Analogie zu Phil 1, 1. Die dort angeredeten διάκονοι werden sowohl karitative Aufgaben wie auch den Verkündigungsdienst wahrgenommen haben[50] und zusammen mit den ἐπίσκοποι am Leitungsdienst beteiligt gewesen sein. Röm 16, 1 f erlaubt nicht, den Dienst Phöbes auf die Tätigkeit oder das spätere Amt einer Diakonissin im Sinne karitativer Hilfe und Krankenpflege einzuengen[51].

---

[48] *Käsemann*, Römer (Anm. 1) 395; ähnlich *C. K. Barret*, A Commentary on the Epistle to the Romans (London 1957) 282: „on the way to the technical use"; *Ollrog*, Paulus (Anm. 1) 31: „eine feste Funktion"; *Schlier*, Röm (Anm. 5) 441: „so etwas wie ein Amtstitel"; ähnlich *G. Lohfink*, Weibliche Diakone im Neuen Testament (in diesem Band). – Zurückhaltender *P. Hünermann*, Conclusions regarding the Female Diaconate TS 36 (1975) 325–333, hier 325 f.

[49] Siehe oben Anm. 33.

[50] So *J. Gnilka*, Der Philipperbrief (HThK X/3) (Freiburg – Basel – Wien 1968) 35; 39. – Vor allem weist der paulinische Sprachgebrauch von διάκονος, -ία, -εῖν in diese Richtung. Karitativer Dienst ist z. B. Röm 12,7; die Kollekte für Jerusalem Röm 15,25.31; 2 Kor 8,4.19 f; 9,1.12 f; der missionarische Verkündigungsdienst Röm 11,13; 1 Kor 3,5; 2 Kor 3,3.6.9; 4,1; 5,18; 6,3 f; 11,8 gemeint. So auch *Ollrog*, Paulus (Anm. 1) 73 f.

[51] Das geschieht heute nur noch selten, z. B. bei *Michel*, Röm (Anm. 35) 377; *Blum*, Amt (Anm. 2) 145 f: die Stelle belegt „die Existenz eines Diakonissenamtes im apostolischen Zeitalter". – Dagegen zu Recht *Thraede*, Ärger (Anm. 1) 99; *Hainz*, Ekklesia (Anm. 33) 194; *Schelkle*, Geist (Anm. 9) 159 f; *Ollrog*, Paulus (Anm. 1) 31; *Schüssler Fiorenza*, Rolle (Anm. 1) 7. – Überinterpretiert scheint mir der Text, wenn *Radford Ruether*, Frauen (Anm. 41) 82, ihm entnimmt, daß „Frauen offensichtlich als Wanderpredigerinnen ausgedehnte Reisen zwischen den einzelnen Gemeinden" unternahmen; denn der Reise-Anlaß ist Röm 16,1 f nicht genannt und kann durchaus ein rein persönlicher gewesen sein.

Falls sich 1 Tim 3,11 auf weibliche Diakone[52] und nicht nur auf die Ehefrauen der Diakone[53] bezieht, liegt hier eine neutestamentliche Bezeugung des zu einer festen Einrichtung weiterentwickelten Gemeindeamtes der Diakonin vor. Sie wird dieselben Aufgaben wahrgenommen haben wie die männlichen Diakone.

2.5.2. Die Frau als „Mitarbeiterin" im Missionswerk

Priska und Aquila werden zusammen von Paulus gegrüßt als „meine Mitarbeiter ⟨συνεργοί⟩ in Christus Jesus" (Röm 16,3). Sie haben sogar ihr Leben für ihn eingesetzt. Ihnen dankt aber nicht nur Paulus, sondern es danken ihnen „auch alle heidenchristlichen Gemeinden" (V. 4). Bemerkenswert ist, daß unterschiedslos auch die Frau, ja sie zuerst, als „Mitarbeiterin" bezeichnet wird und daß auch ihr der Dank vieler Gemeinden gilt. Aus anderen Stellen der Paulusbriefe geht hervor[54], daß der für ihn ein συνεργός ist, der mit ihm „zusammen als Beauftragter Gottes am gemeinsamen ‚Werk' der Missionsverkündigung arbeitet"[55]. Paulus selbst versteht sich dabei nicht als der Dienstherr, sondern weiß sich zusammen mit seinen Mitarbeitern im Dienst Gottes bzw. Christi. Der missionarische Einsatz Priskas und Aquilas bestand nicht nur in Hilfeleistungen gegenüber Paulus, sondern sie waren ein selbständig missionierendes Ehepaar, bei dem Paulus gelegentlich wohnte, seine Berufsarbeit ausübte und das zeitweise auch mit ihm missionarisch zusammen wirkte[56]. Gut

---

[52] So *A. Oepke*, Art. γυνή, in: ThWNT I 776–790, hier 788; *Brox*, Pastoralbriefe (Anm. 21) 154 (vorzuziehen, aber „nicht zwingend"); *Vorländer*, γυνή (Anm. 21) 355. – Ungenau ist die Äußerung von *Radford Ruether*, Frau (Anm. 41) 85 „Doch auch diese patriarchalische Kirche … ließ weiter die Ordination von Frauen als Diakonissinnen zu (1 Tim 3,11)"; denn an dieser Stelle ist weder von Ordination noch von Diakonissinnen die Rede.

[53] So *Blum*, Amt (Anm. 2) 146 Anm. 1.

[54] 1 Thess 3,2; 1 Kor 3,9; Phil 2,25; 4,3; Phlm 1.24.

[55] *Ollrog*, Paulus (Anm. 1) 67; ähnlich *Hainz*, Ekklesia (Anm. 33) 34–37; 48–51; 295–310.

[56] Die stark auf die paulinische Evangeliumsverkündigung hin gestraffte Darstellung der Apostelgeschichte läßt die große Bedeutung der Missionare und Missionarinnen vor und neben Paulus nicht deutlich hervortreten. Lukas schreibt z. B. Apg 18,19 Paulus die Gemeindegründung in Ephesus zu und läßt das Ehepaar ganz in den Hintergrund treten, nicht ohne erhebliche Spannungen in der Textgestalt. Vermutlich hatte aber das Ehepaar einen beträchtlichen Anteil an der Missionsarbeit in Ephesus. So auch Haenchen, Apg (Anm. 46) 521; 525;

denkbar ist überdies, daß eine Frau wie Priska in besonderer Weise das Evangelium unter den Frauen verbreitete[57].

2.5.3. Die Frau als „sich abmühende" im Missionswerk

Die griechischen Worte κόπος („Mühe", „anstrengende Arbeit") und κοπιᾶν („sich abmühen") beziehen sich im Neuen Testament an vielen Stellen auf die „christliche Arbeit an der Gemeinde und für die Gemeinde"[58]. Näherhin sind die Worte des κοπ-Stammes besonders dem Bereich der Missionsarbeit zugeordnet und kennzeichnen sie als eine „schwere, die ganze Existenz beanspruchende Arbeit"[59]. Dieser Bedeutungsgehalt ist dem Neuen Testament eigen[60]. Paulus wendet diese, für seine eigene Missionsarbeit charakteristische Ausdrucksweise auch auf seine Mitarbeiter an, wie z. B. auf Stephanas in Korinth und auf solche, die wie er „mitarbeiten und sich abmühen" (παντὶ τῷ συνεργοῦντι καὶ κοπιῶντι; 1 Kor 16,16). Zu solchen sich im Missionswerk Abmühenden gehören in Rom die Frauen Maria (Röm 16,6), Tryphäna und Tryphosa sowie Persis (Röm 16,12). An sie sendet Paulus ausdrücklich Grüße. Läßt der Text auch nicht im einzelnen erkennen, durch welche Art des Einsatzes diese Frauen sich um die Gemeinde verdient gemacht hatten[61], so legt doch die

---

H. Conzelmann, Die Apostelgeschichte (HNT 7) (Tübingen 1963) 108; *Ollrog*, Paulus (Anm. 1) 38 Anm. 164. – *Käsemann*, Röm (Anm. 1) sagt: Beide gehören „zu den bedeutendsten urchristlichen Missionaren im Diasporagebiet ..., die ihre Arbeit unabhängig von Paulus begonnen, jedoch in Verbindung mit ihm weitergeführt haben" (397).

[57] Clemens von Alexandrien spricht davon, daß das Evangelium durch die Frauen in die Frauengemächer hineingelangte und auf diese Weise Ärgernis vermieden wurde: διὰ τῶν γυναικῶν καὶ εἰς τὴν γυναικωνῖτιν ἀδιαβλήτως παρεισεδύατο ἡ τοῦ κυρίου διδασκαλία (Strom. III 6,53).

[58] *F. Hauck*, Art. κόπος κτλ., in: ThWNT III, 827–829, hier 828.

[59] *Ollrog*, Paulus (Anm. 1) 75. Ebenso *A. v. Harnack*, κόπος (κοπιᾶν, οἱ κοπιῶντες) im frühchristlichen Sprachgebrauch, in: ZNW 27 (1928) 1–10.

[60] Er bezeichnet die Missionsarbeit der Jünger Jesu Joh 4,38; des Paulus Apg 20,35; 1 Kor 3,8; 15,10; 2 Kor 11,23.27; Gal 4,11; Phil 2,16; 1 Thess 3,5; Kol 1,29 (in Verbindung mit seiner Handarbeit 1 Kor 4,12; 2 Kor 6,5; 1 Thess 2,9; 2 Thess 3,7); seiner Mitarbeiter Röm 16,6 (Maria). 12 (Tryphäna, Tryphosa, Persis); 1 Kor 16,16 (Helfer des Stephanas). – 1 Thess 5,12 und 1 Tim 5,17 sind mit κοπιῶντες Gemeindeleiter gemeint, wobei 1 Tim 5,17 ausdrücklich Wortverkündigung und Lehrtätigkeit hervorgehoben werden (κοπιῶντες ἐν λόγῳ, καὶ διδασκαλίᾳ).

[61] So auch *Thraede*, Frau (Anm. 1) 231.

paulinische Ausdrucksweise nahe, hier an einen verschiedene Dienstarten umfassenden aktiven missionarischen Einsatz zu denken[62], ähnlich wie Paulus selbst ihn ausübte[63].

2.5.4. Die Frau als „Mitkämpferin" im Missionswerk

Im Brief an die Gemeinde in Philippi ermahnt Paulus „Euodia und Syntyche, eines Sinnes zu sein im Herrn" (4,2). Sie haben zusammen mit ihm, „mit Klemens und den anderen Mitarbeitern ⟨συνεργοί⟩ für das Evangelium gekämpft" (συνήθλησαν 4,3). Gegenüber dem „Mitarbeiten" bedeutet das „Mitkämpfen" eine Steigerung[64]. Die Ausdrücke „mitkämpfen" und „Mitstreiter" haben bildhaften Sinn und vergleichen den Einsatz für das Evangelium mit einem Kampf[65]. Aus Phil 1,27 f geht hervor, daß es sich dabei auch um die geistige und mit Worten geführte Auseinandersetzung mit nicht-christlichen Gegnern handelt. Euodia und Syntyche haben zusammen mit Paulus, Klemens und anderen schon in der Gründungszeit der Gemeinde diesen Kampf mitgeführt und waren durch ihre aktive Missionsarbeit, d.h. auch durch die Wortverkündigung und die damit gegebene Auseinandersetzung daran beteiligt[66].

---

[62] So auch *Schüssler Fiorenza*, Rolle (Anm. 1) 6f.

[63] Daß hier „aktive Teilnahme an der missionarischen Wortverkündigung" ausgeschlossen sei, wie *Blum*, Amt (Anm. 2) 147, meint, ist m.E. nicht zu erweisen. – Daß allerdings „nicht jeder κοπιῶν gleich ein Gemeindevorsteher sein" muß, wie *H. Merklein*, Das kirchliche Amt nach dem Epheserbrief (StANT 33) (München 1973) 325, zu bedenken gibt, trifft sicher zu.

[64] Sie ist auch Phil 2,25 zu erkennen, wo Paulus den von der Gemeinde abgesandten Vertreter Epaphroditos als „Bruder, Mitarbeiter und Mitstreiter" (ἀδελφός συνεργός, συστρατιώτης) bezeichnet.

[65] Phil 1,27; 2,25; 4,3; Phlm 2. – Vgl. Gnilka, Phil (Anm. 50) 162.

[66] Die missionarisch-aktive Mitbeteiligung beider Frauen an der Gemeindegründung wird allgemein anerkannt, so z.B. von *Zscharnack*, Dienst (Anm. 1) 47 („Predigt des Evangeliums"); *Harnack*, Mission (Anm. 1) II 592; *Hainz*, Ekklesia (Anm. 33) 202f (gehörten aber deshalb nicht schon zu „den Führern der Gemeinde von Philippi"); *Schelkle*, Geist (Anm. 9) 162; *Ollrog*, Paulus (Anm. 1) 28; *Schüssler Fiorenza*, Rolle (Anm. 1) 7 (das Verbum ist zu stark für eine nur materielle Unterstützung); *V. C. Pfitzner*, Paul and the Agon Motif. Traditional Athletic Imagery in the Pauline Literature, in: NTS 16, Leiden 1967, 161: „They ... are those who have taken a leading part in assisting the Apostle in his missionary labours."

3. Zusammenfassendes Ergebnis

3.1. Das Neue Testament bezeugt, daß das Evangelium besonders unter den Frauen große Verbreitung fand und von ihnen besonders bereitwillig aufgenommen wurde.

3.1.1. Das geht aus direkten und indirekten Aussagen hervor.

3.1.2. Zu den Ursachen der starken Verbreitung unter den Frauen gehören:

- das positive Verhalten Jesu den Frauen gegenüber;
- das urchristliche Bewußtsein, daß durch das Heilswerk Christi trennende Unterschiede aufgehoben wurden;
- die Überzeugung, dem endzeitlichen Gottesvolk anzugehören in dem Gottes Geist unterschiedslos Männern und Frauen geschenkt ist;
- der Weg der Mission über die Synagogen und das Diasporajudentum hin zu den Heiden, wodurch gerade die vielen, dem Judentum nahestehenden Frauen erfaßt wurden;
- der Weg der Mission über die Städte, denn dadurch wurden alle städtischen sozialen Schichten, insbesondere auch hoch- und niedergestellte Frauen, miteinbezogen;
- die große Bedeutung der Hausgemeinden für die Gemeindegründungen, denn zu ihnen gehörten Frauen und Männer;
- die Taufe als Initiationsritus, durch den Frauen und Männer in gleicher Weise Anteil an Christus und der Kirche erhielten.

3.2. Das Neue Testament bezeugt vor allem auch die aktive Beteiligung von Frauen an der urchristlichen Missionsarbeit. Diese Beteiligung geschah auf die folgenden Weisen:

3.2.1. durch das Gebet;

3.2.2. durch den karitativen Dienst;

3.2.3. durch persönliche Fürsorge für die Missionare;

3.2.4. durch vielfältige Dienste in den Hausgemeinden, wozu sowohl die äußere Organisation als auch die geistliche Leitung in der Form von Gebet, Verkündigung und weiteren liturgischen Funktionen gehören konnten;

3.2.5. durch den Dienst der Fürsorge, Verkündigung und vielleicht „Gemeindeleitung" in der Form des weiblichen Diakonates;

3.2.6. durch verschiedene Formen vollwertigen missionarischen Einsatzes, für den Paulus nicht zögert, die Bezeichnungen „Mitarbeit", „sich abmühen", „mitkämpfen" in der gleichen Weise anzuwenden wie für seinen eigenen missionarischen Dienst und den seiner männlichen Mitarbeiter.

Trotz der nur sporadischen Äußerungen zeigt das Neue Testament, daß die Frauen in sehr bedeutsamer und vielfältiger Weise am Missionswerk der Urkirche beteiligt waren.

VI

Zur Stellung der Frauen
in den paulinischen Gemeinden*

Von Gerhard Dautzenberg, Gießen

Es ist sicher richtig, daß manche theologischen und exegetischen Fragestellungen, obwohl sie immer möglich und selten ganz vergessen waren, gerade dann besonders hervortreten, wenn sie sich mit aktuellen Problemstellungen, Erfahrungen und Auseinandersetzungen berühren. Angesichts der gesellschaftlichen Entwicklung, die

---

* *Literatur* zum Thema „Frau" im Urchristentum, zu den Schweigegeboten und zu Gal 3, 28, auf die im Folgenden abgekürzt (mit Verfasserangabe und Titelwort) verwiesen wird: *M. Boucher*, Some Unexplored Parallels to 1 Cor 11, 11–12 and Gal 3, 28: The NT on the Role of Women, in: CBQ 31 (1969) 50–58; *M. Bouttier*, Complexio Oppositorum: sur les Formules de 1 Cor. XII.13; Gal. III.26–28; Col. III.10, 11, in: NTS 23 (1976) 1–19; *F. Crüsemann*, „... er aber soll dein Herr sein" (Genesis 3, 16). Die Frau in der patriarchalischen Welt des Alten Testamentes, in: *F. Crüsemann – H. Thyen*, Als Mann und Frau geschaffen. Exegetische Studien zur Rolle der Frau (Gelnhausen – Berlin 1978) 13–106; *G. Dautzenberg*, Urchristliche Prophetie (Stuttgart 1975); *ders.*, Tradition, Paulinische Bearbeitung und Redaktion in 1 Kor 14, 26–40, in: Tradition und Gegenwart. FS E. Schering (Bern – Frankfurt 1974) 17–29; *E. S. Gerstenberger – W. Schrage*, Frau und Mann (Stuttgart 1980); *J. Kürzinger*, Frau und Mann nach 1 Kor 11, 11 f, in: BZ NF 22 (1978) 270–275; *G. Lohfink*, Weibliche Diakone im Neuen Testament, in: Diakonia 11 (1980) 385–400 (in diesem Bd. 320–338); *D. Lührmann*, Wo man nicht mehr Sklave oder Freier ist. Überlegungen zur Struktur frühchristlicher Gemeinden, in: WuD 13 (1975) 53–83; *W. A. Meeks*, The Image of the Androgyne: Some Uses of a Symbol in Earliest Christianity, in: History of Religions 13 (1974) 165–208; *M. de Merode*, Une théologie primitive de la femme, in: Revue Théologique de Louvain 9 (1978) 176–189; *H. Paulsen*, Einheit und Freiheit der Söhne Gottes – Gal 3, 26–29, in: ZNW 71 (1980) 74–95; *E. Schüssler-Fiorenza*, Women in the Pre-Pauline and Pauline Churches, in: Union Seminary Quarterly Review 33 (1978) 153–166; *R. Scroggs*, Paul and the Eschatological Woman, in: Journal of the American Academy of Religion 40 (1972) 283–303; *D. Stein*, Le statut des femmes dans le lettres de Paul, in: Lumière et Vie 27 (1978) 63–85; *K. Stendahl*, The Bible and the Role of Women (Philadelphia 1966 – der ntl. Teil findet sich in deutscher Übersetzung in: *E. Moltmann-Wendel*, Menschenrechte für die Frau [München 1974] 147–161; die schwedische Originalfassung: Bibelsynen och kvinnan, erschienen in: Kvinnan – Samhället – Kyrkan [Stockholm 1958] 138–167); *K. Thraede*, Art. Frau, in: RAC VI 197–267; *ders.*, Ärger mit der Freiheit. Die Be-

alte das Verhältnis von Männern und Frauen betreffende Gleichheitspostulate jetzt als gesellschaftlich realisierbar erscheinen läßt, und angesichts eines sehr breiten Strebens der Frauen nach Gleichberechtigung in allen Lebensbereichen, sieht sich die Theologie genötigt, die überlieferten Optionen und Positionen zu hinterfragen. Im Bereich der neutestamentlichen Exegese muß sich dieses Fragen vor allem mit dem Corpus Paulinum beschäftigen. Denn dieses enthält quantitativ und qualitativ die wichtigsten Aussagen zur Stellung der Frauen, in ihm zeichnen sich Gemeinde- und Sozialstrukturen ab, die bis heute prägend geblieben sind. Die in ihm latent oder offenbar vorhandenen Spannungen provozieren in besonderem Maße zum Nachdenken oder auch zur Rekonstruktion einer Befreiungs- oder Unterdrückungsgeschichte.

Mein eigenes Nachdenken über die Thematik hat, wahrscheinlich nicht unbeeinflußt von der Emanzipationsdebatte, mit einer Beobachtung begonnen, die an sich leicht zu machen ist, sich mir aber bei meiner Arbeit über die urchristliche Prophetie und besonders über das Verhältnis von 1 Kor 11,2–16 zu 1 Kor 14,33–36 und zu 1 Tim 2,11–15 aufdrängte[1]. In den authentischen Paulusbriefen zeichnen sich mit Ausnahme von 1 Kor 14,33–36 Gemeindeverhältnisse bzw. eine Gemeindeordnung ab, in welchen eine Beteiligung der Frauen am Gottesdienst, an der Gemeindeleitung und an der Mission nahezu selbstverständlich ist. Die Deuteropaulinen enthalten keine Informationen in dieser Hinsicht und beschäftigen sich mit der Stellung der Frauen in den sogenannten Haustafelabschnitten, welche die Unterordnung der Frauen fordern. Die Pastoralbriefe und 1 Kor 14,33–36 setzen die Haustafeltradition fort und übertragen die Forderung nach Unterordnung der Frauen in die Gemeindeordnung. Ihr Amtsverständnis ist patriarchalisch orientiert. Die Frauen sollen im Gottesdienst schweigen. Gemeindliche Aktivitäten von Frauen sind verdächtig; sie werden nur unter dem strengen Reglement der

---

deutung von Frauen in Theorie und Praxis der alten Kirche, in: *G. Scharffenorth – K. Thraede*, „Freunde in Christus werden ...“. Die Beziehung von Mann und Frau als Frage an Theologie und Kirche (Gelnhausen – Berlin 1977) 31–182; *H. Thyen*, „... nicht mehr männlich und weiblich ...“. Eine Studie zu Galater 3,28, in: *F. Crüsemann – H. Thyen*, Als Mann und Frau geschaffen (s.o.) 107–201.
[1] Vgl. *Dautzenberg*, Prophetie 257–273; *ders.*, Tradition.

Witwenregel und nur unter Frauen geduldet. Eine Männer und Frauen gleichwertende Gemeinde- und eine patriarchalische Sozialordnung scheinen also entweder in Spannung zueinander gestanden zu haben oder in Spannung miteinander geraten zu sein, bis sich die patriarchalischen Grundsätze der Sozialordnung auch in der Gemeindeordnung durchgesetzt hatten. Diese Annahme möchte ich im Folgenden überprüfen und präzisieren.

1. Das Hervortreten von Frauen in der paulinischen Mission und in den urchristlichen Gemeinden

1.1. Frauen unter den Mitarbeitern des Paulus

Die Paulusbriefe (hier mit dem Kolosserbrief) erwähnen etwa 40 Personen, die als Mitarbeiter des Paulus anzusehen sind[2]. Unter ihnen befinden sich neun oder zehn Frauen[3]. Weitere acht Namen begegnen in der Apostelgeschichte, darunter eine Frau (Lydia, Apg 16,14.40). Die Pastoralbriefe erweitern den Kreis um zehn Namen, darunter ebenfalls eine Frau (Claudia, 2 Tim 4,21; 4,19 erscheinen die aus den Paulusbriefen und aus der Apostelgeschichte bekannten Priska und Aquila in der Grußliste). Von einigen dieser Frauen wird gesagt, daß sich in ihrem Haus eine Hausgemeinde versamml(e) (Röm 16,5; 1 Kor 1,11; 16,19; Phlm 2; Kol 4,15). Wenn schon dies außer auf den sozialen Status dieser Frauen auf ihre aktive Rolle in der Gemeinde schließen läßt, ist dies um so mehr der Fall, wo Paulus die Mitarbeit von Frauen am Missionswerk ausdrücklich hervorhebt durch die für seine Mission typische Bezeichnung als συνεργός/ Mitarbeiter[4], so für Priska Röm 16,3 und wohl auch für Euodia und Syntyche Phil 4,2f, oder durch die Erwähnung ihres κοπιᾶν/sich

---

[2] Vgl. *W.-H. Ollrog*, Paulus und seine Mitarbeiter (Neukirchen-Vluyn 1979) 1.

[3] Je nachdem, ob man den Akkusativ IOYNIAN Röm 16,7 einem weiblichen (Junia) oder männlichen (Junias) Personennamen zuordnet; die Gründe für die Annahme eines weiblichen Personennamens sind überzeugend, vgl. *Schüssler-Fiorenza*, Women 154; *Gerstenberger – Schrage*, Frau 133; *Lohfink*, Diakone 391–395 (327–331): Andronikus und Junia sind ein missionarisches Ehepaar. Der Aposteltitel geht auf die Aussendung durch den Auferstandenen zurück.

[4] Von männlichen Mitarbeitern des Paulus: Röm 16,3.9.21; 2 Kor 8,23; Phil 2,25; 4,3; Phlm 1,24; Kol 4,11; vgl. *Ollrog*, aaO. 63.72.

184

Abmühens[5], ihres Einsatzes in der Missionsarbeit (Röm 16,6.12: Maria, Tryphaina, Tryphosa, Persis).

W. Ollrog hat in seiner Untersuchung „Paulus und seine Mitarbeiter" den besonderen Charakter der paulinischen Mission als einer auf Mitarbeiter aus den neugegründeten Gemeinden gestützten Zentrumsmission herausgearbeitet[6]. Die Gemeinden werden durch die von ihnen befristet für das Missionswerk zur Verfügung gestellten Mitarbeiter zu Partnern der Mission des Paulus. So würden z. B. die Angaben über Stephanas, Fortunatus und Achaikus 1 Kor 16,15–18 verständlich: sie füllen durch ihre Anwesenheit bei Paulus ein ὑστέρημα/Mangel ihrer Gemeinden aus. Zugleich fordert Paulus die Gemeinde auf, sich ihnen und „jedem, der mitarbeitet, unterzuordnen"[7]. In ähnlicher Weise könnte man die Stellung der Phöbe als διάκονος/Dienerin ihrer Gemeinde von Kenchreä, ihre Reise nach Rom als Überbringerin des Römerbriefes und ihre Empfehlung an die römische Gemeinde verstehen (Röm 16,1 f)[8]. Wenn Röm 16, wie eben vorausgesetzt, ein ursprünglicher Bestandteil des Römerbriefes ist, würden die in 16,6.12 wegen ihrer Missionsarbeit hervorgehobenen Frauen wohl ebenfalls wie andere in der Grußliste genannte Persönlichkeiten (16,7 Andronikus und Junia[s]; 16,9 Urbanus) über den Kreis ihrer Heimatgemeinde hinaus an verschiedenen Orten in der Mission gearbeitet haben.

Die Teilnahme von Frauen ist nicht eine ausschließliche Besonderheit der paulinischen Mission. Priska und Aquila sind unabhängig von Paulus Christen geworden, sie haben zunächst unabhängig von ihm missioniert und führen ein ähnliches Wanderleben wie er[9]. Das Hervortreten von Frauen im Bereich der hellenistisch-judenchristlichen Mission ist vor dem Hintergrund der ansteigenden gesellschaftlichen Emanzipation der Frauen in der griechisch-römischen Mittelmeerwelt[10] nicht ungewöhnlich, wenn es auch ange-

---

[5] Von Paulus gebraucht für seine eigene Missionsarbeit: 1 Kor 15,10; Gal 4,11; Phil 2,26; für die Missionsarbeit von Mitarbeitern: 1 Kor 16,16; 1 Thess 5,12; vgl. *Ollrog*, aaO. 75.

[6] Vgl. besonders *Ollrog*, aaO. 160 f.   [7] Vgl. *Ollrog*, aaO. 96–100.

[8] *Lohfink*, Diakone 388–391 (324–327): Diakon ist offizielle Bezeichnung der Phöbe; der Titel erwächst aus ihrer Stellung in der Ortsgemeinde; vgl. *Gerstenberger – Schrage*, Frau 141 f.

[9] Vgl. *Ollrog* aaO. 24–27.

[10] *Thraede*, Frau 199.204.220–224; *Meeks*, Image 168–174.198.

sichts der eher patriarchalischen Ausrichtung des Diasporajudentums[11] und des palästinischen Judentums nicht allein aus der günstigen sozialgeschichtlichen Konstellation erklärbar ist. Priska, die Ehefrau des Aquila, gewinnt neben ihrem Mann ein durchaus eigenes missionarisches Profil (vgl. Röm 16,3; Apg 18,26 mit 1 Kor 16,19; Apg 18,2). Nicht nur mehr oder weniger begüterte Frauen der Ober- und Mittelschicht treten als Mitarbeiter hervor, sondern mit Persis Röm 16,12 wohl auch eine Frau, die Sklavin oder Freigelassene war[12]. Was zählt, ist der Einsatz in der Mission, der Dienst am Evangelium (vgl. Phil 4,3), den wir nach 1 Kor 12,28–30; Röm 12,6–8 im Rahmen eines charismatischen Dienstverständnisses bewerten können und der eine Unterscheidung nach Geschlechtern übergreift[13].

Mit der paulinischen Mission hören auch die Nachrichten über diesen Typ der Mitarbeitermission und über die Frauen als Missionarinnen auf. Die Angaben in 2 Tim 4,19–21 beschränken sich auf die Nennung von Personen und haben nur die Funktion, die Paulustradition zu veranschaulichen[14]. Bei Ignatius von Antiochien, Brief an die Smyrnäer 13,1–2, hat sich gegenüber den Paulusbriefen die Perspektive charakteristisch gewandelt. Ignatius grüßt zunächst „die Häuser meiner Brüder samt Frauen und Kindern und die Jungfrauen, die Witwen genannt werden", dann das „Haus der Tavia" und schließlich „Alke, die mir liebe Persönlichkeit" (so auch Ignatius an Polykarp 8,3). Hier zeigt sich die auch sonst beobachtbare Verlagerung des Interesses von der Hausgemeinde zum Haus, in welchem die Frauen ihren Platz hinter dem Manne haben, wenn sie es nicht als Witwen selber führen (IgnPol 8,2), und die Eingrenzung der fraulichen gemeindlichen Aktivitäten auf den Stand der Witwen[15].

---

[11] Siehe dazu unten 199 ff; vgl. *Meeks*, aaO. 174–179.

[12] *Thraede*, Ärger 97.

[13] Eine gewisse Auffälligkeit der Grußliste Röm 16,3–17 besteht darin, daß nur bei den unter den männlichen Mitarbeitern in 16,6.12 erwähnten Frauen das κοπιᾶν εἰς ὑμᾶς bzw. ἐν κυρίῳ hervorgehoben wird, aber nicht bei den Frauen in 16,15.

[14] *P. Trummer*, Die Paulustradition der Pastoralbriefe (Frankfurt 1978) 137.

[15] Vgl. *G. Stählin*, Art. χήρα, in: ThWNT IX, 428–454.441–454.

1.2. Das Mitwirken von Frauen im Gottesdienst

1.2.1. Der Brauch in den paulinischen und vorpaulinischen Gemeinden

Die urchristlichen, in 1 Kor 11–14 besprochenen Gemeindeversammlungen hatten gottesdienstlichen Charakter. Neben dem Herrenmahl (11,17–34) standen verschiedene Formen geistgewirkten Redens in ihrem Mittelpunkt: Offenbarungsrede, Erkenntnisrede, Psalmen – all dies entweder in verständlicher Rede oder in Sprachen und Übersetzung (14,6.13–17.27 f), ferner Prophetie und ihre Deutung und Lehre (14,6.26.29–31). Jeder (14,6), das heißt, jeder der etwas beizutragen hatte oder dem die Gabe dazu verliehen war (12,29 f), konnte und sollte sich beteiligen. Nach den eher einschränkenden Anweisungen des Paulus: „zwei oder drei" sollten in Sprachen reden und „zwei oder drei Propheten" ihre Prophezeiungen oder Offenbarungen vortragen (14,27.29), gab es eher zuviel als zuwenig Aktivität und Spontaneität (vgl. 14,30–33 a). Alles sollte dem Nutzen (14,6), der Erbauung (14,4 f.17.26), der Unterweisung, Belehrung und Ermahnung (14,14.19.31) der Gemeinde dienen. Am Beispiel des Propheten, dem, während andere sprechen, eine Offenbarung zuteil wird, die er dann auch sogleich mitteilen soll (14,30), wird als weiteres fundamentales theologisches Prinzip für die Zulassung zum Sprechen das Wirken des Geistes in der Gemeinde deutlich. Er teilt jedem mit, wie er will (12,7.11), und zwar Männern und Frauen.

Es gibt manches Befremdliche und schwer Verständliche in der Argumentation des Paulus zur Verschleierung der Frauen in 1 Kor 11,2–16 – darüber wird noch zu sprechen sein –, aber der Ausgangspunkt dieser Argumentation ist die für Paulus selbstverständliche Tatsache, daß Männer und Frauen in gleicher Weise vor der Gemeinde beten und prophetisch reden (11,4–5). In dieser Hinsicht enthält der Text keine Einschränkungen für die Frauen. Zuletzt verweist Paulus für die beizubehaltende Sitte der Verschleierung auf die „Gewohnheit", und zwar in aufschlußreicher Form: „Wir haben eine solche Gewohnheit nicht, und auch nicht die Gemeinden Gottes" (11,16). Das besagt doch wohl, daß dieser Brauch in seinen von ihm gegründeten und geleiteten Gemeinden und darüber hinaus in allen urchristlichen Gemeinden, wahrscheinlich vor allem in den als normativ angesehenen Gemeinden Judäas[16], gilt – überall dort, wo Frauen vor der Gemeinde beten oder prophetisch reden. Die Mitwirkung der Frauen im Gottesdienst ist also nicht auf das paulinische Christentum beschränkt, sondern wie die Gaben des Geistes Kennzeichen des gesamten Urchristentums, einschließlich seiner judenchristlichen Ursprungsgemeinden. Gelegentliche Hinweise auf Prophetinnen in der Apostelgeschichte (2,17; 21,9) und in der altchristlichen Überlieferung[17] bestätigen diesen Schluß. Das bedeutet aber, daß wir die Zulassung von Frauen zur gleichberechtigten Teilnahme am Gemeindegottesdienst zunächst vor dem Hintergrund der jüdischen Tradition zu bewerten haben.

1.2.2. Die jüdischen Voraussetzungen für die unterschiedslose Beteiligung von Männern und Frauen am Gottesdienst

Noch an der von Paulus in 1 Kor 14,26–33 a.39–40 entworfenen Gemeindeordnung läßt sich als traditionsgeschichtlicher Hintergrund die synagogale Praxis des zeitgenössischen Judentums aufweisen[18]. In dieser Tradition kam den Frauen eine auf Grund der patriarchalisch ausgerichteten Lebensordnungen des Judentums mehr oder weniger als selbstverständlich hingenommene passive Rolle zu. Sie nahmen zwar in aller Regel am Gottesdienst teil, was für die neutestamentliche Zeit auch aus den Angaben Lk 13,10–17; Apg 16,17; 17,4 hervorgeht[19]. Wahrscheinlich saßen sie in der Synagoge abgesondert von den Männern, wie es für das talmudische und mittelalterliche Judentum belegt ist[20]. Der archäologische Befund hat aber keine Hinweise für spezielle den Frauen vorbehaltene Räume in den alten Synagogen erbracht[21]. Kinder und Frauen können prin-

---

[16] *J. Hainz*, Ekklesia (Regensburg 1972) 235.250.252.

[17] *Dautzenberg*, Prophetie 268 f.

[18] *Dautzenberg*, Prophetie 274–288.

[19] *S. Safrai*, The Synagogue and its Worship, in: *M. Avi-Yonah – Z. Baras*, Society and Religion in the Second Temple Period (Jerusalem 1977) 65–98.76.

[20] *J. Maier*, Geschichte der jüdischen Religion (Berlin 1972) 258.

[21] *Safrai*, aaO. 94 f. Hier müßte also *A. Oepke*, Art. γυνή, in: ThWNT I, 776–790.782.787, korrigiert werden; überhaupt bietet Oepke eine zwar interessante, aber doch einseitige Zitatensammlung.

[22] TMeg 4,11; Meg 23ᵃ Bar (*Billerbeck* III 467).

zipiell zur Toralesung aufgerufen werden[22], wenn auch die Halacha[23] bestimmte: „Man läßt eine Frau nicht kommen, um öffentlich vorzulesen" (Tosefta Megilla 4, 11), – „Eine Frau soll aus der Tora nicht vorlesen wegen der Ehre der Gemeinde" (Babylonischer Talmud Megilla 23 a Baraita). Diese Spannung zwischen prinzipieller Zulassung und faktischem Ausschluß läßt darauf schließen, daß die rein männliche Prägung des Synagogengottesdienstes nicht zu allen Zeiten galt und doktrinär kaum zu begründen war.

Philos Nachrichten über die Therapeuten in De Vita Contemplativa (im Folgenden: VitCont) zeigen, daß diese einen synagogalen Gottesdienst unter Beteiligung von Frauen kannten. Die sich darauf beziehenden Angaben sind in der bisherigen Diskussion nicht genügend beachtet worden. Schon in meiner Arbeit zur urchristlichen Prophetie hatte ich viele Entsprechungen zwischen den Gottesdiensten der Therapeuten und den gottesdienstlichen Aussagen in 1 Kor 11–14 beobachtet und war dort zu dem Schluß gekommen, daß der Gottesdienst nach 1 Kor 14, 26–40 den Versammlungen der Essener und Therapeuten wahrscheinlich näher stand als dem allgemeinen Typ des jüdischen Synagogengottesdienstes[24]. Ich will den dort geführten Beweis jetzt nicht wiederholen, aber die dort nur eben gestreifte Beteiligung von Frauen schärfer in den Blick nehmen.

Für die Anlage von VitCont ist es wie für die Anlage von 1 Kor 11 bis 14 typisch, daß die Differenzierung der Gemeinschaft der Therapeuten in Männer und Frauen die allgemeine Schilderung ihres Lebens nicht beeinflußt hat. Philo erwähnt die Beteiligung von Frauen zum ersten Mal bei der Schilderung des Sabbatgottesdienstes VitCont 32 f. Er berichtet, daß der heilige Versammlungsraum/σεμνεῖον durch eine nach Art einer Brustwehr gebaute, drei bis vier Ellen hohe Mauer in zwei Einfriedungen für Männer und Frauen getrennt ist. So soll die der weiblichen Natur gemäße Zurückhaltung gewahrt werden, ohne daß die Stimme des Vortragenden dadurch unverständlich würde. Bei dem gemeinsamen Festmahl, welches entweder an jedem Sabbat oder alle sieben Wochen stattfindet, sitzen Männer und Frauen getrennt, die Männer rechts, die Frauen links (69). Jüngere Mitglieder der Gemeinschaft übernehmen den

---

[23] *Safrai*, aaO. 77; *G. F. Moore*, Judaism II (Cambridge 1962) 131.
[24] *Dautzenberg*, Prophetie 112–118.289.

Tischdienst und dienen den anderen wie Söhne ihren Vätern und
Müttern (72). Zu Beginn des Mahles hält der Vorsteher einen Vortrag über eine mit dem Verständnis der Schrift zusammenhängende
Frage (75). Nach dem Vortrag singt er einen Hymnus auf Gott, entweder einen neuen von ihm selbst verfaßten oder einen alten (80),
vielleicht auch einen biblischen Psalm. Den folgenden Teil der
Schilderung gebe ich im Wortlaut wieder: „Darnach singen auch die
anderen der Reihe nach in der gebührenden Ordnung[25], wobei alle
unter tiefem Schweigen zuhören, außer wenn sie den Schluß oder
den Refrain singen müssen[26]. Dann nämlich erheben alle[27] (Männer)
und alle (Frauen) ihre Stimme" (80). Dann endlich findet die eigentliche Mahlfeier statt. An sie schließt sich am Vorfest eine Nachtfeier
an. Zunächst bilden Männer und Frauen zwei getrennte Chöre, die
teils zusammen, teils mit Wechselgesang Hymnen singen und dazu
tanzen. Auf dem Höhepunkt der Feier vermischen sich die beiden
Chöre zu einem Chor (85). Und so singen sie „in schöner Trunken-
heit" bis zum frühen Morgen (89).

   Die Gemeinschaft der Therapeuten ist von weisheitlichen und
apokalyptischen Traditionen geprägt, sie kennt und schätzt ekstatische Erfahrungen (26) und beschäftigt sich mit den großen Themen
der jüdischen Mystik[28]. Die Zulassung von Frauen zu dieser Gemeinschaft scheint ohne prinzipielle Schwierigkeiten gewesen zu
sein. Philo, selber, wie wir noch sehen werden, eher der streng patriarchalischen Richtung des Judentums zuzuordnen, verweist für
die Zugehörigkeit von Frauen nur darauf, „daß sie von demselben
Eifer und demselben Streben beseelt seien" (32 vgl. 68). Wenn er die
Vermischung der Chöre in der Nachtfeier als Nachahmung des Sie-
gesliedes am Schilfmeer beschreibt, das von Männern und Frauen
gesungen wurde (vgl. Ex 15,1–20) und wenn er damit einen Gedanken der Therapeuten wiedergibt, könnte dahinter die Einsicht stehen, daß Männer und Frauen von Anfang an nur zusammen das
Gottesvolk bilden. Entscheidend für die Bildung der therapeuti-
schen Gemeinschaft aus Männern und Frauen werden aber neben

---

[25] Vgl. 1 Kor 14,31 (καθ᾽ ἕνα πάντες) 33 a.40; den Gegensatz dazu bildet 14,23.
[26] Vgl. 1 Kor 14,16.
[27] 1 Kor 14,26: ἕκαστος; VitCont 81: ὅταν ἕκαστος διαπεράνηται τὸν ὕμνον.
[28] *Dautzenberg*, Prophetie 110f; *I. Heinemann*, Die Sektenfrömmigkeit der Therapeuten, in: MGWJ 78 (1934) 104–117.114.

dem Beispiel bedeutender biblischer Frauengestalten wahrscheinlich noch konkrete Erfahrungen bei der Entstehung der Gemeinschaft gewesen sein. An ihrem Anfang standen auch Frauen, deren Bereitschaft, zugunsten des Strebens nach Weisheit auf das Familienleben zu verzichten (68), ebenso groß war wie die entsprechende Bereitschaft der männlichen Anfänger, und Frauen, deren charismatische Fähigkeiten sich in ihren Visionen und Hymnen eindrucksvoll äußerten.

Vielleicht knüpft die Zeichnung der drei Töchter Hiobs, die nach dem Testamentum Hiob (THiob) in den Engelssprachen Hymnen singen und die Geheimnisse der Schöpfung und des göttlichen Thrones preisen, an solche Erfahrungen an. Für das THiob ist ja schon mehrmals ein Zusammenhang mit dem Traditionskreis der Therapeuten vermutet worden[29]. Die Abfassung neuer Hymnen und Gesänge im THiob hat Entsprechungen sowohl bei den Therapeuten (VitCont 29) wie im urchristlichen Gottesdienst (1 Kor 14,26; Kol 3,16; Eph 5,19). Das Sprechen und Singen in Engelssprachen nach THiob stellt die nächste religionsgeschichtliche Analogie zur urchristlichen Glossolalie dar und legt die Vermutung nahe, daß ekstatische und pneumatische Erfahrungen im Judentum die hergebrachte Rollenverteilung der Geschlechter zugunsten einer stärkeren Selbständigkeit der Frauen aufbrechen konnten.

Diese Vermutung erhält noch mehr Gewicht durch die eschatologische Prophetie Joel 3,1 f, welche erwartet, daß der eschatologische Gottesgeist Menschen aus allen jetzt durch soziale Gegensätze getrennten Gruppen, Männer und Frauen, Alte und Junge, Freie und Sklaven, zu Propheten machen wird[30]. Zwar begegnet diese Stelle im Zusammenhang mit der urchristlichen Prophetie erst in dem späten, wenn auch sachlich bedeutsamen Zusammenhang von Apg 2 (V.17 f), aber es läßt sich doch wahrscheinlich machen, daß sie schon länger im Urchristentum benutzt wurde, um den urchristlichen Anspruch auf Leben am Ende der Zeit und auf den eschatologischen

---

[29] Zur Diskussion vgl. *A. M. Denis*, Introduction aux pseudepigraphes Grecs d'Ancien Testament (Leiden 1970) 103; *B. Schaller*, Das Testament Hiobs, in: JSHRZ III (Gütersloh 1979) 303–387.309–311. Schallers negative Stellungnahme wird jedoch den traditionsgeschichtlichen Berührungen nicht ganz gerecht; vgl. *Dautzenberg*, Prophetie 111; *ders.*, Art. Glossolalie, in: RAC XI 225–246.233 f.
[30] Vgl. *F. Crüsemann*, Frau 92–94; *Gerstenberger – Schrage*, Frau 63.

Geistbesitz zu unterstützen[31]. Auf eine breitere Auslegungsgeschichte von Joel 3,1 f im Urchristentum weist einmal die Anspielung in Tit 3,6 (Geistausgießung), zum anderen die Verwendung von
Joel 3,5 zur Rechtfertigung der universalen Völkermission in Röm
10,13; 1 Kor 1,2 (sekundär Apg 2,21.47). Es ist sehr bemerkenswert,
daß im Zitat wie auch in seinem Umkreis in Joel 3 und an seinen
neutestamentlichen Haftpunkten die drei fundamentalen Gegensätze genannt werden, von deren Aufhebung in Christus Gal 3,28
spricht. Zu „Jude – Grieche" vgl. Röm 10,12f; zu „Sklave – Freier"
vgl. Apg 2,18; zu „männlich und weiblich" vgl. „Söhne – Töchter",
„Sklaven – Sklavinnen" Apg 2,18; Joel 3,2[32]. Diesen Gegensätzen
kommt bei der Begabung mit dem Geist keine Bedeutung mehr zu,
und so auch nicht bei dem in dieser Begabung seinen Ursprung ha-
benden prophetischen Reden in der Gemeinde.

So könnte es sich erklären lassen, daß der Übergang von einer
männlich ausgerichteten Ordnung des Synagogengottesdienstes zu
der Männer und Frauen unterschiedslos je nach ihren Fähigkeiten
zu Wort kommen lassenden Ordnung des urchristlichen Gottesdienstes sich allem Anschein nach ohne größere Auseinandersetzung

---

[31] Vgl. *B. Lindars*, New Testament Apologetic (London 1961) 37f; *F. Bovon*, Luc
le théologien (Neuchâtel 1978) 243.

[32] Joel 3,2 LXX: καὶ ἐπὶ τοὺς δούλους καὶ ἐπὶ τὰς δούλας verliert in Apg 2,18 durch
die Anfügung des Possessivpronomens seinen Bezug auf die realen Abhängigkeitsverhältnisse. Diese Sinnverschiebung braucht für frühere Stadien der urchristlichen Benutzung des Zitats nicht angenommen zu werden. Sie ist vielmehr
charakteristisch für die in Apg 2 überhaupt beobachtbare Einengung des Verständnisses dieser Stelle auf das Pfingstgeschehen, vgl. *Lindars*, aaO. 38. Lindars
weist auch darauf hin, daß Apg 2 die universale Aussage von Joel 3,5 (Apg
2,21.39) faktisch, wenn auch kaum beabsichtigt auf das Verhältnis von Juden und
Proselyten einschränkt. Die von *Crüsemann*, Frau 94 („Die Sprache von Gal 3,28
ist zwar noch ein Stück radikaler, da sie anders als Joel Juden und Heiden einbezieht und sogar von der Aufhebung von männlich und weiblich redet, aber sie ist
in den bei Joel genannten Gegensatzpaaren doch bereits präformiert"), empfundene Differenz zwischen Joel und Gal 3,28 wird also zu einem guten Stück durch
die urchristliche Interpretationsgeschichte aufgefüllt. *Justin*, Dial 87,6 – 88,1,
sieht die Erfüllung von Joel 3,1 f darin, daß „man auch unter uns sowohl Frauen
wie auch Männer (καὶ θήλειας καὶ ἄρσενας; vgl. Gal 3,28 a) in Besitz von Charismen, die vom Geist herkommen, sehen kann". Die Passio Sanctarum Perpetuae
et Felicitatis will unter Berufung auf Joel 3,1 f (1,4) zeigen, daß die den Martyrin-
nen Perpetua und Felicitas geschenkten Offenbarungen und Visionen wert sind,
durch Verlesung des Berichts darüber in der Erinnerung der Kirche gehalten zu
werden (1,5; 21,11).

vollzogen hat, vielleicht in der Tat unter Berufung auf Joel 3,1 f, ohne daß man diesen Vorgang nur als „eine ganz natürliche Folge der gesellschaftlichen Emanzipation der Frau" bewerten müßte[33]. Das eigentliche Problem läge dann nicht in der Zulassung der Frauen zur aktiven Teilnahme am Gottesdienst, sondern in dem sich in 1 Kor 14,33 b–36; 1 Tim 2,11–15 dokumentierenden Ausschluß der Frauen von jeder aktiven Teilnahme. Zeigt sich an dieser Stelle, wie in der Einleitung bereits angedeutet, ein Konflikt zwischen einer offenen Gemeinde- und einer patriarchalischen Gesellschaftsordnung, der zu Ungunsten der Frauen ausging?

2. Ein Konflikt zwischen Gemeinde- und Gesellschaftsordnung?

2.1. Die Interdependenz von Gemeinde- und Gesellschaftsordnung nach den Schweigegeboten für die Frauen

2.1.1. Zur Interpretation von 1 Kor 14,33–36 und 1 Tim 2,11–15

Ich halte 1 Kor 14,33–36 mit der Fortsetzung 14,37–38 weiterhin für eine nachpaulinische Interpolation in den ersten Korintherbrief. Das schließt die aber auch nicht erwiesene Möglichkeit nicht aus, daß der Verfasser der Pastoralbriefe diesen Passus schon im ersten Korintherbrief vorfand und sich bei der Niederschrift von 1 Tim 2,11–14 an diese vermeintlich paulinische Vorlage anlehnte[34]. Der neueste Vorschlag[35] 1 Kor 14,33 b–36 zusammen mit 11,2–16 als ursprünglichen Bestandteil des ersten Korintherbriefes zu werten, unterscheidet zwischen „heiligen" Frauen, d.h. unverheirateten Frauen oder Jungfrauen, die nach 1 Kor 11,2–16 prophetisch reden dürfen, und Ehefrauen, die nach 1 Kor 14,33 b–36 schweigen sollen – aus Gründen der nach der jüdisch-hellenistischen Tradition von

[33] So *Thraede,* Frau 231, zu 1 Kor 11,5.
[34] So *Trummer,* aaO. (s. Anm. 16) 145 f. Trummers Beobachtungen reichen nicht aus, um die Interpolationshypothese zu erschüttern, die keineswegs nur auf sach-kritischen, sondern ebenso auf literar-, form-, überlieferungs- und redaktionskritischen Beobachtungen beruht. Die textkritischen Überlegungen von *G. Fitzer,* „Das Weib schweige in der Gemeinde" (München 1963) 37, führen tatsächlich auf Abwege; ihnen habe ich mich in meiner Arbeit ausdrücklich nicht ange-schlossen; s. *Dautzenberg,* Prophetie 271 mit Anm. 57.
[35] *Schüssler-Fiorenza,* Women 160 f.

den Ehefrauen geforderten „Unterordnung" und wegen eines paulinischen Vorbehalts gegen die Teilnahme verheirateter Frauen an den „Dingen des Herrn" (1 Kor 7,34; 9,5). Diese Lösung scheitert einmal schon an 1 Kor 11,2–16. Dort wird ohne Einschränkung, generisch von Frauen gesprochen (11,5: πᾶσα γυνή) und das Schleiertragen gerade mit der Funktion des Mannes als Haupt der Frau begründet (11,3 vgl. 7.9). Es hätte auf seiten der Korinther schon einiger Phantasie bedurft, wenn sie, bei denen auch verheiratete Frauen prophetisch redeten – dies will ja 14,33b–36 nach diesem Vorschlag untersagen – hier nur eine Erlaubnis für „heilige Frauen" heraushören sollten. Zum anderen übersieht der Vorschlag die Schwierigkeiten, die 14,33b–36 schon an sich, unabhängig von seiner Beziehung zu 11,2–16, im Zusammenhang der Kapitel 12–14 und im Zusammenhang 14,26–40 bereitet.

Es gehört zur Eigenart der beiden traditionsgeschichtlich gesehen in einem sehr engen Verwandtschaftsverhältnis zueinander stehenden Schweigegebote, daß die Regelung des Sprechens im Gottesdienst sehr eng mit bestimmten gesellschaftlichen Ordnungsvorstellungen verschränkt ist. Am offensten tritt diese Verschränkung in der mit Widerspruch (vgl. 1 Kor 14,36.37–38) rechnenden Regelung im ersten Korintherbrief zutage. V.34 statuiert einen Gegensatz zwischen dem Reden von Frauen im Gottesdienst und der vom Gesetz verlangten Unterordnung der Frauen. Es ist auffällig, daß weder an dieser Stelle noch in 1 Tim 2,11 gesagt wird, wem denn die Frauen sich unterzuordnen haben. Von den Haustafeln her ist an die Ehemänner zu denken (vgl. Kol 3,18; Eph 5,22; 1 Petr 3,1.5; Tit 2,5). Das Fehlen des Objektes kann aber – und das ist wahrscheinlicher – auch darauf hinweisen, daß die Forderung der Unterordnung prinzipieller gemeint ist, daß es nicht nur um die Ordnung der Familien, sondern um die Ordnung der Gesellschaft überhaupt geht. Das Schweigen der Frauen im Gottesdienst steht im Zusammenhang mit der Rolle, die Frauen in der Gesellschaft schlechthin zukommt. Würden die Frauen in der Gemeinde reden oder, wie der erste Timotheusbrief in bezug auf die gottesdienstlichen Formen der Pastoralbriefe formuliert[36], „lehren", dann würden sie „Autorität über den

---

[36] *N. Brox*, Die Pastoralbriefe (Regensburg 1969) 134: „Andere etwaige Elemente des Gottesdienstes außer solchem ‚Lehrgespräch‘ zeichnen sich hier nicht ab".

Mann ausüben"/αὐθεντεῖν ἀνδρός[37], während das in 1 Kor 14,34b zitierte Gesetz das Gegenteil, die Unterordnung fordert. Die Topoi „Unterordnung", „Schweigen" und „Haus" gehören auch in antiken Texten zusammen[38].

1 Kor 14,35 präzisiert das generelle Verbot von 14,34; zum Schweigen gehört auch das Verbot einer Beteiligung am Lehr- oder Predigtgespräch in der Gemeinde, das Stellen von Informations- oder Verständnisfragen, denn jede Art von Reden in der Gemeinde ist für eine Frau schändlich. Wenn die Frauen etwas lernen wollen, sollen sie es zu Hause tun. Dort können sie ihre „eigenen Männer" fragen. Der Rangordnung in der Gesellschaft. entspricht der Ausschluß der Frauen aus der Öffentlichkeit und die Kennzeichnung des Hauses als ihres eigentlichen Lebens- und Wirkungskreises; ferner der Verweis auf die „eigenen Männer" als die einzig zugelassenen Gesprächspartner und Vermittler zur Öffentlichkeit hin. Dies wird durch einen starken Appell an das Schicklichkeitsempfinden unterstützt und begründet: es sei schändlich/αἰσχρόν (nur noch 1 Kor 11,6!) für eine Frau in der Gemeinde zu reden. Dieser Appell fehlt in 1 Tim 2,11f, ebenso die ausdrückliche Beschränkung auf das Haus. Die Formulierungen dort sind gewissermaßen „liebespatriarchalisch" gemildert, aber nicht weniger eindeutig: die Frau soll „in Stille lernen" und überhaupt „in Stille dasein", wie es ihrem Status entspricht. Denn sie hat nach der Schöpfungsordnung nicht den gleichen Rang wie der Mann. Adam und nicht Eva wurde zuerst geschaffen (Gen 2,7.22); Eva und nicht Adam erlag der Verführung (Gen 3,13). Die Frauen stehen also nach der Ordnung der Schöpfung wie nach der Ordnung der Heilsgeschichte hinter den Männern zurück. Dennoch gibt es für sie eine Heilsmöglichkeit: „sie wird aber gerettet werden durch Kindergebären" (2,15).

Diese beiden Weisungen bzw. die von ihnen vertretenen Traditionen sind kirchenrechtlich und kirchengeschichtlich folgenreicher gewesen als alle neutestamentlichen Aussagen über das „Amt", wenigstens wenn man die letzteren nach ihrem Literalsinn bewertet. Ihr Spezifikum ist es, daß sie sich von antiken Ordnungsvorstellungen

---

[37] *Trummer*, aaO. 146: „Bevormundung des Mannes"; *Brox*, aaO. 134: „Ein unbefugtes Eingreifen auf ein Gebiet jenseits der Zuständigkeit".
[38] Siehe unten 196ff.

her mit der gottesdienstlichen Rolle der Frauen beschäftigen. Wie die oben durchgeführte Analyse zeigte, sind ja die den Gottesdienst betreffenden Weisungen aus Ordnungsvorstellungen (1 Kor 14,34 b; 1 Tim 2,11 b.12 b) abgeleitet. Es geht darum, auch im Gottesdienst ein diesen Ordnungsvorstellungen entsprechendes Verhalten durchzusetzen und diesen auf solche Weise unbeschränkte Geltung zu sichern.

2.1.2. Antike griechisch-römische Ordnungsvorstellungen und die Schweigegebote

Zu den einzelnen Elementen der Schweigegebote gibt es jeweils antike Parallelen, welche zeigen, daß die Schweigegebote an verbreitete Vorstellungen über das Verhalten von Frauen anknüpfen. Zuweilen finden sich in einem Text auch mehrere der im Folgenden einzeln aufgeführten Momente.

2.1.2.1. Zur Forderung der „Unterordnung"

a) Mit ὑποτάσσομαι Med. (wie 1 Kor 14,34)

Pseudo-Kallisthenes, Historia Alexandri Magni (spätgriechischer Alexanderroman aus dem 3. Jh. n. Chr.) I 22,4 (Rec. vetusta Kroll): πρέπον (vgl. dazu 1 Kor 11,13; 1 Tim 2,10) γάρ ἐστι τὴν γυναῖκα τῷ (Rez. B. ἰδίῳ) ἀνδρὶ ὑποτάσσεσθαι (es ist geziemend, daß sich die Frau dem Manne unterordnet).

b) Mit ὑποτάσσομαι Pass.

Plutarch, Praecepta coniugalia 33 (142D/E): τοῦτο συμβαίνει καὶ περὶ τὰς γυναῖκας. ὑποτάττουσαι μὲν γὰρ ἑαυτὰς τοῖς ἀνδράσιν ἐπαινοῦνται, κρατεῖν δὲ βουλόμεναι μᾶλλον τῶν κρατουμένων ἀσχημονοῦσι (dies trifft auch für die Frauen zu: wenn sie sich den Männern unterordnen, findet ihr Verhalten Lob; wenn sie aber herrschen wollen, handeln sie unanständiger als jene, die sich beherrschen lassen). Die Fortsetzung vom Herrschen/κρατεῖν des Mannes über seine Frau, bei welchem er sich nicht wie ein δεσπότης/ Herr, sondern wie die Seele zum Leib verhalten soll, stellt eine Parallele zu Eph 5,28 dar (5,22: die Frauen sollen sich ihren Männern unterordnen). Vorher, in 31/32 (s. unten), spricht Plutarch vom Schweigen der Frau. Er versucht durch den Verweis auf das Lob für Frauen, die sich unterordnen und nicht herrschen wollen, für die willige Annahme dieser Ordnungsvorstellungen zu werben.

Aristoteles, Politik, leitet die Unterordnung der Frauen aus ihrer Natur ab, 1254 b 13 f: ἔστι δὲ τὸ ἄρρεν πρὸς τὸ ϑῆλυ φύσει τὸ μὲν κρεῖττον, τὸ δὲ χεῖρον, τὸ μὲν ἄρχον, τὸ δὲ ἀρχόμενον (auf Grund der Natur ist das Männliche im Hinblick auf das Weibliche das Bessere, jenes das Geringere, das Beherrschende, jenes das Beherrschte); 1259b 1: Wenn es auch Ausnahmen von der natürlichen Ordnung geben mag, gilt doch τό τε γὰρ ἄρρεν φύσει τοῦ θήλεως ἡγεμονικότερον (das Männliche ist nämlich auf Grund der Natur dem Weiblichen überlegen), ebenso wie der Ältere dem Jüngeren überlegen ist (vgl. 1 Tim 2,13); ebd. 9f: zwischen Mann und Frau besteht eine dauernde Ungleichheit; 1260a 20-23 besteht gegen Sokrates (Plato, Menon 71E/73E) darauf, daß Mann und Frau unterschiedliche Tugenden haben, die Tapferkeit des Mannes zeige sich im Befehlen, die der Frau im Dienen (ἀλλ' ἡ μὲν ἀρχικὴ ἀνδρία, ἡ δ' ὑπηρετική); ebd. 28-30: darum hat jede Klasse von Menschen eigene Attribute. Wenn der Dichter (Sophokles, Aias 293) sage: „Schweigen ist die Zierde einer Frau" (γυναικὶ κόσμον ἡ σιγὴ φέρει), sei dies nicht in gleicher Weise Zierde eines Mannes. Der Text stellt eine ähnlich nahe Beziehung zwischen Unterordnung und Schweigen her wie 1 Kor 14,34. Wenn er diese außerdem aus dem Unterschied der Naturen ableitet, hat er in der heilsgeschichtlichen Begründung 1 Tim 2,13 und in anderer Weise in der Berufung auf die Natur 1 Kor 11,14 (s. unten) eine Parallele.

Seneca, De constantia sapientis 1,1, gibt also eine weit verbreitete Anschauung wieder, wenn er bei der Erörterung des Unterschieds zwischen den Stoikern und den übrigen Philosophen auf den Unterschied zwischen Männern und Frauen verweist: cum utraque turba ad vitae societatem tantundem conferat, sed altera pars ad obsequendum, altera pars imperio nata sit. Die Praecepta Delphica (Ditt. Syll III³ 395) formulieren mit dem Imperativ γυναικὸς ἄρχε (herrsche über die Frau) eine generelle Maxime.

2.1.2.2. Zum Redeverbot oder Schweigegebot

Nur selten werden Schweigen und Unterordnung in so engen Zusammenhang gebracht wie 1 Kor 14,34 und 1 Tim 2,11f, so *Aristoteles,* Politik 1260a 30 (s. oben); *Aeschylus,* Sieben gegen Theben 182-200, wendet sich allgemein gegen das Lärmen und Heulen von Frauen in der Öffentlichkeit, gegen Frauenherrschaft; die Männer sollen sich um das kümmern, was draußen ist, die Frauen sollen drinnen bleiben und keinen Schaden anrichten. *Valerius Maximus* III, 8,6 (1. Jh. n.Chr.) erinnert rhetorisch an die alten, aber durch die Bürgerkriege gelockerten Sitten: Quid feminae cum contione? Si patrius mos servetur nihil: sed ubi domestica quies seditionum agitata fluctibus est, priscae consuetudinis auctoritas convellitur, plusque valet quod violentia cogit, quam quod suadet et praecipit verecundia. Häufiger wird das Schweigen der Frauen mit Gründen der Schicklichkeit empfohlen (vgl. 1 Kor 14,35b). *Euripides,* Troerinnen 647-650: Eine Frau gehört nicht in die Öffentlichkeit; Andromache will sogar zu Hause vor ihrem Ehemann schweigen, ihn aber durch ein freundliches Gesicht für sich gewinnen.

Plutarch, Praecepta coniugalia 31, knüpft an eine Anekdote von der züchtigen Theano eine Folgerung für die kluge Frau: δεῖ δὲ μὴ μόνον τὸν πῆχυν ἀλλὰ μηδὲ τὸν λόγον δημόσιον εἶναι, καὶ τὴν φωνὴν ὡς ἀπογύμνωσιν αἰδεῖσθαι καὶ φυλάσσεσθαι πρὸς τοὺς ἐκτός. ἐνορᾶται γὰρ αὐτῇ καὶ πάθος καὶ ἦθος καὶ διάθεσις λαλούσης (Es ist also notwendig, daß nicht nur nicht der Unterarm, sondern auch nicht das Wort in die Öffentlichkeit gehört und daß man die Stimme wie eine Entblößung scheue und sie vor denen draußen hüte. An ihr erkennt man nämlich das Gefühl, den Charakter und den Gemütszustand der Redenden); ebd. 32 deutet er die Muschel, ein Wahrzeichen der Aphrodite, als Symbol der οἰκουρία/Leben im Haus (vgl. 1 Kor 14,35a ἐν οἴκῳ) und der σιωπή/Schweigen: δεῖ γὰρ ἢ πρὸς τὸν ἄνδρα λαλεῖν (vgl. 1 Kor 14,35a τοὺς ἰδίους ἄνδρας ἐπερωτάτωσαν) ἢ διὰ τοῦ ἀνδρός, μὴ δυσχεραίνουσαν εἰ δι' ἀλλοτρίας γλώσσης ὥσπερ αὐλητὴς φθέγγεται σεμνότερον (Sie soll nämlich entweder zum Manne oder durch ihn sprechen und ihren Verdruß nicht offenbaren, es sei denn durch die Zunge eines anderen, wie ja auch ein Flötenspieler einen feierlichen Ton erschallen lassen kann, als wenn er selber singen würde). Nimmt man ebd. 33 hinzu (s. oben), dann sind bei Plutarch, wenn auch locker gefügt und anders begründet, sämtliche Elemente von 1 Kor 14,34f, sofern sie sich auf das Verhalten von Frauen beziehen, vorhanden.

2.1.2.3. Das Haus als Ort der Frau (1 Kor 14,35a)

Aeschylus, Sieben gegen Theben 182–200 (s. oben); *Euripides,* Troerinnen 647–650 (s. oben); *Platon,* Menon 71 E; weiteres bei *Karl Praechter,* Hierokles der Stoiker (Leipzig 1901) 133f (Auszüge aus dem pseudoaristotelischen Liber secundus yconomicorum Aristotelis und Parallelen aus der Diatribe); *Thraede,* Bedeutung 57.64–66; *ders.,* Frau 201.206.215.

2.1.3. Zum jüdischen Hintergrund der Schweigegebote

Lassen sich so die Kernaussagen der Schweigegebote ableiten, deren faktische Geltung angesichts der steigenden Emanzipation der Frauen von der hellenistischen Zeit an bestritten wird[39] – in dieser

---

[39] *Thraede,* Frau 201.215f. Vgl. Die grundsätzlichen Überlegungen *Thraedes,* Bedeutung 35–40.86f, zur Interpretation der antiken Zeugnisse. Das Resümee ebd. 40: „Von besonderer Wichtigkeit ist die ‚Streuung‘ der Theorien in Philosophie und Vulgärethik: Von der Sophistik bis zu Plutarch gibt es Ansätze, die sich wie in der Philosophie zwischen den Extremen ‚Gleichheit‘ und ‚Minderwertigkeit‘ so in anderer Literatur zwischen ‚Achtung‘ und ‚Polemik‘, Begeisterung und Misogynie bewegen". Es genüge „vollauf, einen Teil der Belege für soziale ‚Freiheiten‘ der antiken Frau kennenzulernen und zu wissen, daß hellenistisches Denken der Praxis an Uneinheitlichkeit nicht nachstand. Die Umwelt des Neuen Testaments stellte auf beiden Ebenen verschiedene Möglichkeiten zur Wahl".

Sicht stellen sie eine konservative Option dar –, so ist ihre Genese dennoch ohne Berücksichtigung des in 1 Kor 14,34b begegnenden Hinweises auf die Vorschrift des Gesetzes und des in 1 Tim 2,13–14 versuchten Beweises für die Ordnung aus der Schöpfungsgeschichte und der die Schweigegebote mit den Haustafeln verbindenden Forderung des Sich-Unterordnens bzw. der Unterordnung noch nicht genügend erklärt.

Man hat hinter νόμος/Gesetz 1 Kor 14,34b eine Anspielung auf Gen 3,16 (LXX: καὶ αὐτός σου κυριεύσει) oder auch auf die traditionelle jüdische Sitte (Halacha) vermutet[40]. Tatsächlich begegnet in der Auslegung von Gen 3 bei *Philo,* De opificio mundi 167, die Forderung des Gehorsams der Frauen. Als Lohn für die Lust hat die Frau unter anderem den Verlust ihrer Freiheit zu beklagen: εἶτ' ἀφαίρεσιν ἐλευθερίας καὶ τὴν ἀπὸ τοῦ συνόντος ἀνδρὸς δεσποτείαν, οὗ τοῖς ἐπιτάγμασιν πειθαρχεῖν ἀναγκαῖον (dann die Wegnahme der Freiheit und die Herrschaft von seiten des ihr zugeordneten Mannes, dessen Befehlen sie unbedingt gehorchen muß). In den Hypothetika (= Hyp); einer apologetisch ausgerichteten Schrift, gibt Philo nach den erhaltenen Fragmenten in 7,1–9 einen Abriß der mosaischen Gesetzgebung. 7,3 erwähnt er als eine der verschiedenen geltenden Bestimmungen: ἄλλα δ' αὖ πάλιν ὁποῖά τινα: γυναῖκας ἀνδράσιν δουλεύειν, πρὸς ὕβρεως μὲν οὐδεμίας, πρὸς εὐπείθειαν δ' ἐν ἅπασιν (und noch anderes solcher Art: die Frauen sollen den Männern dienen, nicht um des Mutwillens, sondern um des Gehorsams willen). Man kann diesen Satz als Auslegung von Gen 3,16 auffassen. Aber wenn das der Fall sein sollte, dann handelt es sich nicht um eine von Philo selbst erarbeitete Auslegung, sondern um eine Auslegung, welche Philo in der Überlieferung vorfand[41]. Der traditionelle Charakter von Hyp 7,3 geht auch aus *Josephus,* Contra Apionem (= Ap) II 201 hervor. Dort begegnet in einer mit den Hypothetika sehr verwandt erscheinenden Apologie des Gesetzes (ab II 174)[42] unter der Überschrift τίνες δ' οἱ περὶ γάμων νόμοι (Welche Gesetze beziehen sich auf die Ehe?) (199) nach Bestimmungen über den „naturgemäßen Verkehr" und über die Eheschließung der Satz: γυνὴ χείρων, φησί, ἀνδρὸς εἰς ἅπαντα. τοιγαροῦν ὑπακουέτω μὴ πρὸς ὕβριν, ἀλλ' ἵν' ἄρχηται. θεὸς γὰρ ἀνδρὶ τὸ κράτος ἔδωκεν (Die Frau, sagt er, ist geringer als der Mann in jeder Hinsicht. Daher soll sie denn gehorchen, nicht zum Mutwillen, sondern damit sie beherrscht werde, Gott hat

---

[40] *Billerbeck* III, 468.
[41] Vgl. Hypothetika 7,6: Die Darlegungen in den Hypothetika geben Gegenstände wieder, die zu den ungeschriebenen Bräuchen und Bestimmungen gehören oder sich in den Gesetzen selbst finden. *I. Heinemann,* Philons griechische und jüdische Bildung (Darmstadt 1962) 529f: Philo hat für die Hypothetika „eine Quelle benutzt, die mit jüdischem Überlieferungsgut arbeitete".
[42] *F. H. Colson,* Philo IX (London-Cambridge 1967 = 1941) 409; *Meeks,* Image 177.

nämlich dem Manne die Macht verliehen) (201). Außer der grundsätzlichen Übereinstimmung darin, daß der Dienst bzw. der Gehorsam, den die Frauen ihren Männern schulden, von Gott gewollt ist, treffen sich beide Texte im Ausschluß der ὕβρις/der willkürlichen und mißbräuchlichen Ausnutzung der Herrschaftsstellung des Mannes. Es hat also den Anschein, daß die Forderung des Gehorsams der Frauen mit bestimmten Modifikationen für Philo und Josephus zu den charakteristischen jüdischen gesetzlichen Überlieferungen gehörte. Mit der ausdrücklichen Begründung, die „Frau sei in jeder Hinsicht geringer als der Mann"[43], könnte der Text eine bestimmte Auslegung von Gen 2–3 widerspiegeln[44], die sich unter ausdrücklicher Beziehung auf die biblische Geschichte 1 Tim 2,13–14 und in anderer Weise auch in 1 Kor 11,7ff findet (s. unten), in ihrer begrifflichen Fassung aber den Werturteilen der konservativen griechischen Ethik in ihrer Auseinandersetzung mit Gleichheitsbestrebungen sehr nahe kommt[45].

---

[43] Vgl. *Philo*, Ebr 55; 1 Petr 3,7: ὡς ἀσθενεστέρῳ σκεύει τῷ γυναικείῳ.

[44] 1 Tim 2,14: „Und nicht Adam wurde verführt, sondern die Frau ließ sich verführen und geriet in die Übertretung (παραβάσει)" steht mitsamt seiner Fortsetzung 2,15: „Sie wird aber gerettet durch Kindergebären, wenn sie in Glaube und Liebe und Heiligung verharren in Zucht" in Zusammenhang mit einer bestimmten jüdischen Tradition, welche nicht nur den Adam ent- und Eva belastete wie Apokalypse des Mose 16–21; ProtevJac 13,1, sondern in der Tat Evas die Tat der Frau schlechthin erblickte; vgl. Sir 25,24: „Von der Frau stammt der Ursprung der Sünde, und alle müssen ihretwegen sterben". Bei Philo zeichnet sich eine Affinität von Frau und Sünde und von Mann und Gehorsam ab; Quaest in Gen I 43 (zu Gen 3,8): „It was the more imperfect and ignoble element, the female, that made a beginning of transgression (παραβάσεως) und lawlessnes (παρανομίας), while the male made the beginning of reverence and modesty and all good, since he was better and more perfect"; ebd. IV 15 (zu Gen 18,11) unterscheidet männliche und weibliche Seelenregungen. Die weiblichen folgen dem weiblichen Geschlecht, welches unvernünftig und mit animalischen (?) Leidenschaften verwandt ist mit Furcht, Sorge, Wohlgefallen und Verlangen, aus denen unheilbare Schwächen und Krankheiten entstehen. Wessen Geist vom Gesetz erfüllt ist, der gleicht dem männlichen Geschlecht, er überwindet die Leidenschaften und erhebt sich über alles sinnliche Wohlgefallen und Verlangen. Damit ist die Lehre von den beiden Trieben auf die beiden Geschlechter verteilt, vgl. *E. Peterson*, Frühkirche, Judentum und Gnosis (Freiburg 1959) 215. Diese Traditionen setzen sich fort in den Pseudoklementinischen Homilien: Nicht Adam war der Übertreter (II 52,2), sondern Eva (III 22,2); der Mensch hat das σῶμα/den „Leib" und entsprechende Leidenschaften vom weiblichen Prinzip, das Pneuma mit Verstand, Einsicht und Gottesfurcht vom männlichen Prinzip, und so liegen vor ihm auch die Wege des Gesetzes und der Gesetzlosigkeit, des Himmelreiches und der irdischen Herrschaften (XX 2,3); „Der Mann ist ganz Wahrheit, die Frau ganz Irrtum" (III 27,1). Die gegenwärtige weibliche Welt hat die Aufgabe, für die künftige männliche Welt die Gerechten als ewige Söhne zu gebären (XIX 23,3), vgl. *Peterson*, aaO. 214–216. Jedoch verbinden die Pseudo-Clementinen mit der grundsätzlichen Abwertung des Weiblichen keine Folgerungen auf der Ebene der gesellschaftlichen Ordnungsvorstellungen.

[45] Vgl. oben 196f; bes. Aristot Polit 1254 b 13f: ἄρρην und θῆλυ sind φύσει κρεῖτ-

Weder Hyp 7,3 noch Ap II 201 stehen in unmittelbarem Zusammenhang mit der Ordnung des jüdischen Synagogengottesdienstes, aber beide Traktate legen es darauf ab, die auf dem sabbatlichen Gesetzesstudium in der Synagoge beruhende umfassende Kenntnis ihrer Lebensgesetze, welche die Juden von den Völkern auszeichne, ins Licht zu rücken (Hyp 7,10–13; Ap II 173–178). Der Synagogengottesdienst ist, ohne daß dies eigens gesagt wird, männlich geprägt. Er hat nach Ap II 181 eine einheitliche von Gottesfurcht geprägte jüdische Lebenspraxis zur Folge. Dies können sogar Frauen und Haussklaven bezeugen: „Übrigens kann man die Ansicht, daß Gottesfurcht das Ziel sei, auf welches alle übrigen Bestrebungen des Lebens hinarbeiten müssen, selbst aus dem Munde unserer Frauen und Haussklaven vernehmen" (ὅτι δεῖ πάντα τἄλλα τέλος ἔχειν τὴν εὐσέβειαν, καὶ γυναικῶν ἀκούσειεν ἄν τις καὶ τῶν οἰκετῶν). Hier ist wohl doch vorausgesetzt, daß die Frauen (und die Sklaven) nicht am Gesetzesstudium in der Synagoge teilnehmen und dennoch die Grundsätze des jüdischen Lebens kennen. Wie sie diese kennenlernen, sagt Philo, Hyp 7,14: Jeder (Jude) wird leicht auf alle Fragen über die väterlichen Ordnungen antworten können – καὶ ἀνὴρ γυναικὶ καὶ παισὶ πατὴρ δούλοις δεσπότης ἱκανὸς εἶναι δοκεῖ τοὺς νόμους παραδιδόναι (Und der Mann gilt als fähig, der Frau die Gesetze zu überliefern, wie der Vater den Kindern und der Herr den Sklaven).

Hier erscheint der Mann in ähnlicher Weise als Lehrer der Frau wie in 1 Kor 14,35.

Schließlich begegnet bei *Philo,* De specialibus legibus (= Specleg) III 169, unter der Überschrift „Über die Vorschrift, daß Frauen nicht schamlos (ἀναισχυντεῖν; vgl. 1 Kor 14,35 αἰσχρόν) sein sollen" eine gewisse Parallele zur Gegenüberstellung von ἐκκλησία/Gemeinde und οἶκος/Haus 1 Kor 14,35: „Marktplätze, Ratsversammlungen, Gerichtshöfe, gesellschaftliche Vereinigungen, Versammlungen großer Menschenmengen und der Lebensverkehr durch Wort und Tat unter freiem Himmel in Krieg und Frieden eignen sich nur für Männer (ἀνδράσι); das weibliche Geschlecht dagegen soll das Haus hüten und daheim bleiben (θηλείαις δὲ οἰκουρία καὶ ἡ ἔνδον μονή), und zwar sollen die Mädchen in den hinteren Gemächern sich aufhalten und die Verbindungstüre als Grenze ansehen, erwachsene Frauen aber die Haustüre".

2.1.4. Der Ort der Schweigegebote

Das Schweigegebot 1 Kor 14,34 f erweist sich als durchwegs von gemeinantiken und vor allem von jüdisch-hellenistischen Ordnungsvorstellungen bestimmt. Das Gebot stellt eine an diesen Ordnungs-

---

τον und χεῖρον. Dort auch eine entsprechende Ableitung der Herrschafts- bzw. Abhängigkeitsverhältnisse; vgl. dazu auch *Thraede,* Frau 209.

vorstellungen orientierte Reaktion auf eine freiere Praxis dar, die ein Reden von Frauen in der Gemeindeversammlung kannte und zuließ. Zwei Beobachtungen können über das bereits Gesagte hinaus zeigen, daß das Gebot zu einem anderen, späteren Stratum als zu dem der paulinischen Missionsgemeinden gehört. Nach 1 Kor 7,12–16 gehören eben nicht nur gläubige Ehepaare zur Gemeinde, sondern auch Frauen mit ungläubigen Männern (7,13) und umgekehrt. Das setzt einmal eine größere Selbständigkeit der Frauen voraus, als die angesprochenen Ordnungsvorstellungen es zulassen, es macht auch eine Regelung wie die von 1 Kor 14,35 unmöglich, nach welcher die Frauen auf Beteiligung am Lehrgespräch in der Gemeinde verzichten und sich mit der häuslichen Unterweisung durch ihre Männer begnügen sollen. Der missionarische Charakter der Gemeinde ist in 1 Kor 14,34f einer bereits ständisch orientierten, mehr nach innen gerichteten Gemeindeordnung gewichen.

Von fundamentaler theologischer Bedeutung und großer geschichtlicher Tragweite ist ferner die in 1 Kor 14,35 zutage tretende Angleichung der Gemeindeordnung an die Gesellschaftsordnung mit ihrer Unterscheidung von Öffentlichkeit und „Haus". Mit „es ist nämlich schändlich für eine Frau, in der Gemeinde zu reden", wird die Gemeindeversammlung in dieser Hinsicht auf eine Stufe mit den profanen öffentlichen Versammlungen und ἐκκλησίαι gestellt und damit die urchristliche ἐκκλησία/Gemeinde ihres sie von der Umwelt abhebenden, alle Gemeindemitglieder in gleicher Weise integrierenden Binnencharakters beraubt, da ihr der christliche οἶκος/Haus als eigener privilegierter und geschützter Binnenraum gegenübergestellt wird[46]. Vom integrierenden Charakter der ἐκκλησία bleibt, daß Frauen, wenn auch passiv, teilnehmen können, und nicht total wie z. B. bei *Philo*, SpecLeg III 169, an das Haus gebunden werden. Diese Spannungen sind in 1 Tim 2,11–14 nicht so offenkundig, aber nur weil sich das Bild der Gemeinde überhaupt gewandelt hat.

[46] *D. Lührmann*, Neutestamentliche Haustafeln und antike Ökonomie, in: NTS 27 (1980) 83–97.94, erkennt in der Ausbildung der Haustafelethik ebenfalls eine Verlagerung des Schwerpunktes im Gemeindeleben. Sind die paulinischen Missionsgemeinden entsprechend Gal 3,28 durch die Integration unterschiedlicher gesellschaftlicher Gruppen charakterisiert (s. dazu unten 216f), so ist nun „Grundlage der Gemeinde ... der *christliche* οἶκος".

2.1.5. Die Schweigegebote und die Haustafeln

Es ist auffällig, daß in den Schweigegeboten das Abhängigkeitsverhältnis der Frau vom Manne mit ὑποτάσσομαι, ὑποταγή/sich unterordnen, Unterordnung beschrieben wird wie in den neutestamentlichen Haustafeln (Kol 3,18; Eph 5,22.24; 1 Petr 3,1.5; vgl. Tit 2,5), während außerhalb des Neuen Testaments verschiedene Begriffe benutzt werden und ὑποτάσσομαι nur an zwei Stellen nachgewiesen ist[47]. Ebenso regelmäßig begegnen die ἴδιοι ἄνδρες/eigenen Männer von 1 Kor 14,35 als Objekte des ὑποτάσσεσθαι in den Haustafeln (Eph 5,22; 1 Petr 3,1.5; Tit 2,5). Auf der anderen Seite behandeln ja die Haustafeln das Verhalten der Männer zu den Frauen, der Väter zu den Kindern, der Herren zu den Sklaven und umgekehrt, während die Schweigegebote nur über das Verhältnis von Männern und Frauen reflektieren. Die Erörterung dieses Verhältnisses hat aber in der Tradition in haustafelähnlichen Überlegungen seinen Sitz, in denen die Themenkreise Vater–Kinder, Herr–Sklave ebenso vorkommen, und zwar auch in wichtigen bisher in dieser Arbeit herangezogenen Texten[48]. Das bedeutet, daß die Schweigegebote und die Haustafeln auch traditionsgeschichtlich eng miteinander verwandt sind.

Der religions- und geistesgeschichtliche Hintergrund für die Haustafeln findet sich vermutlich in der späthellenistischen Gattung der Schriften zur Ökonomik[49]. Die Tendenz dieser Schriften besteht nach Thraede[50] darin, daß sie den überkommenen „Gegensatz zwi-

---

[47] Ps Callisth I 22,4; Plut PraecConiug 33 (142 D/E); s. oben 196.
[48] Plat Menon 71 E; Aristot Polit 1259a 37 – 1260b 20; 1251a 1 – 1253a 39 (Frauen, Sklaven, Barbaren); Poetik 1449b 21 – 1456b 15 (Mann, Frau Sklave); Philo Hyp 7,3 (Frauen, Kinder, Besitz); 7,14 (der jüdische Mann unterweist seine Frau, der Vater die Kinder, der Herr die Sklaven im Gesetz). *J. E. Crouch*, The Origin and Intention of the Colossian Haustafel (Göttingen 1972) 21 f, hält Hyp 7,14 sogar für die nächste Parallele zu den Haustafeln. Weitere Beispiele bei *Lührmann*, Haustafeln 85 f.
[49] *Lührmann*, Sklave 75–80; *ders.*, Haustafeln 84–87; *Thraede*, Bedeutung 63–69.119 f.
[50] *Thraede*, Bedeutung 67. Vgl. *Lührmann*, Haustafeln 88, zum ursprünglich agrarischen Umfeld der Oikos-Vorstellung: „Ist das οἶκος-Modell am überzeugendsten unter den Bedingungen agrarischer Verhältnisse, so wird es nun übertragen auf die Verhältnisse der Stadtkultur"; ebd. 89 f zum konservativen Interesse der Gattung: „Adressat der ökonomischen Schriften sind ja die Besitzenden, die jene Werte der Freiheit und der Gleichheit für sich in Anspruch nahmen, sie aber den anderen Mitgliedern ihres Hauses mehr oder weniger vorenthielten. Die

schen (vornehmlich peripatetischem) Unterordnungsdenken und (vor allem stoischen) ‚Gleichheits'-Axiomen" einzuebnen versuchen. Die Front dieser Lehre richte sich „gegen soziale Freiheits- und Persönlichkeitsrechte der Frau, wie sie ältere Philosophie propagiert hatte". Diese Tendenz ist auf die Haustafeln und auf die Schweigegebote übergegangen. Dabei ist eigenartigerweise die jüdische bzw. judenchristliche Begründung für die Forderung der Unterordnung nur in den Schweigegeboten erhalten geblieben. Gewisse Spuren der Begründung sind aber noch in Kol 3,18 und 1 Petr 3,1.5–7 erkennbar[51]. Da aber fast alle Vergleichstexte zeigen, daß diese Forderung immer schon naturrechtlich, ontologisch oder heilsgeschichtlich begründet wurde, sind die Begründungen ebenso für die Haustafeln vorauszusetzen. Nach dem Textbefund im Kolosser-, Epheser- und ersten Petrusbrief muß aber offenbleiben, welche Folgerungen dort aus der Unterordnung für den Gottesdienst der Gemeinde gezogen wurden. Am ehesten läßt sich nach der Erwähnung der Hausgemeinde im Hause der Nympha Kol 4,15 für den Kolosserbrief noch eine Beteiligung der Frauen vermuten, während

---

Kategorie der ‚Hauswirtschaft' ist ihre Deutung und Wertung der sozialen Gegebenheiten, es fehlen uns die Deutungen und Wertungen dieser Gegebenheiten z. B. durch die Sklaven".

[51] Kol 3,18: ὡς ἀνῆκεν ἐν κυρίῳ setzt wohl eine ausgeführtere (biblische?) Begründung voraus. 1 Petr 3,1 erwartet sogar eine Bekehrung ungläubiger Ehemänner auf Grund der Unterordnung ihrer christlichen Frauen „ohne Wort", also auch auf Grund des dem Willen Gottes gemäßen, für christliche Frauen spezifischen Verhaltens; vgl. Didaskalie 3 (H. Achelis – J. Flemming, Die syrische Didaskalie [Leipzig 1901] 12, 16 ff); 1 Clem 21,6–8. Die Polemik gegen aufwendige Kleidung und Schmuck 1 Petr 3,3 (ebenso 1 Tim 2,9) und die Forderung spezifischer Frauentugenden 1 Tim 2,9 (stärker verchristlicht 1 Petr 3,4) findet sich ebenso in der späthellenistischen Ökonomik: Thraede, Bedeutung 65 f (Kallikratidas), 68 (Columella). 1 Petr 3,5 f begründet die Unterordnung im Verhalten biblischer Frauengestalten. 1 Petr 3,7 verwendet den Topos vom schwachen Geschlecht, vgl. oben 200. Die auf das Verhalten in der Gemeinde abgestellte Haustafel 1 Clem 21,6–8 befaßt sich ausführlich mit den Frauen: „… laßt uns unsere Frauen zum Guten anhalten", nämlich zu keuschem Verhalten, sanftmütiger Gesinnung, Schweigen – „sie mögen die Mäßigung ihrer Zunge durch Schweigen kundtun" – und Liebestätigkeit. Die Haustafelthemen „Ehemänner", „Unterordnung" und „Haus" sind bereits in der Einleitung des Schreibens 1,3 zur Sprache gekommen: „Den Frauen befahlet ihr, alle Obliegenheiten mit untadeligem, ehrbarem und reinem Gewissen zu verrichten und dabei ihre Männer in der gebührenden Weise zu lieben; auch lehrtet ihr sie, sich in den Schranken der Unterordnung zu halten, das Hauswesen ehrbar zu versehen".

der erste Petrusbrief nach 3,1 und 5,1–5 doch schon dem gottesdienstlichen Typus der Pastoralbriefe nahestehen dürfte[52].

Die schroffe Gegenüberstellung von „Reden" und „Sich Unterordnen" (1 Kor 14,34) und der enge Zusammenhang, welcher nach 1 Tim 2,11 zwischen dem „Lehren" und dem „über den Mann Autorität haben" besteht, zeigen, daß eine aktive Teilnahme der Frauen am Gottesdienst und die Aufrechterhaltung patriarchalischer Familien- und Gesellschaftsstrukturen auf Dauer unvereinbar waren. Frauen, die ihre Männer „fürchten" sollen (Eph 5,33), werden wohl kaum im Gottesdienst sprechen können. Die Schweigegebote stehen also wohl in einem geschichtlichen Zusammenhang mit der Durchsetzung der Haustafelethik und ähnlicher Forderungen oder Normen im Urchristentum[53]. So stellt sich die Frage, wie denn beides, die aktive Beteiligung der Frauen und die Anerkennung einer patriarchalischen Gesellschaftsstruktur in der ersten Generation, vereinbar war oder ob mit dem Hervortreten der Frauen in der Gemeinde auch eine andere Einschätzung der gesellschaftlichen Rollen- und Rangverteilung zwischen Männern und Frauen einherging.

2.2. Das Verhältnis von Gemeinde- und Gesellschaftsordnung in den Paulusbriefen

Nur wenige Abschnitte aus den Paulusbriefen sind für unsere Fragestellung unmittelbar relevant. Das mag mit dem Charakter der Paulusbriefe als Gelegenheitsschriften zusammenhängen, damit, daß sie im Unterschied zum Kolosser-, Epheser- und ersten Petrusbrief wie auch den Pastoralbriefen nicht als Lehrschriften entworfen sind. Dennoch ist es erstaunlich, daß der Konflikt zwischen Gemeinde- und Gesellschaftsordnung angesichts des starken Hervortretens der Frauen gerade in der ersten Generation der Gemeinden nicht schon dort in aller Schärfe ausgebrochen ist, sondern erst in der durch die Deuteropaulinen, 1 Kor 14,33 b–38 und durch die Pastoralbriefe belegten zweiten und dritten Generation. Oder ist dies nicht so er-

---

[52] Ebenso der 1. Klemensbrief, in welchem das Schweigegebot und die Haustafelethik in offenem Zusammenhang stehen, s. die vorige Anmerkung.
[53] Zum konservativen, Frauen und Sklaven angesichts der gesellschaftlichen Möglichkeiten benachteiligenden Zug der Haustafelethik vgl. *Lührmann*, Haustafeln 94.

staunlich? Waren die Ordnungsvorstellungen in der ersten Generation nicht so fest, sondern flexibler, so daß die Haustafelethik und
die Schweigegebote eine Art konservativer oder patriarchalischer
Reaktion darstellen? Hätte die Entwicklung von der ersten Generation aus auch in eine andere Richtung verlaufen können? Aber
warum steht an ihrem Ende eine nun auch die Gemeindeordnung
einbeziehende Verfestigung der patriarchalischen Rollen- und
Rangverteilung, weshalb konnte der Anstoß, welchen das Hervortreten der Frauen in der ersten Generation bedeutete, nicht positiver
aufgenommen werden?

2.2.1. Die nicht-patriarchalische Ausrichtung von 1 Kor 7

Die Erörterungen über Ehe und Ehelosigkeit in 1 Kor 7 sind nicht
durch das Hervortreten der Frauen in der Gemeinde ausgelöst,
sondern durch die in der korinthischen Anfrage zutage treten-
den Unsicherheiten hinsichtlich der Bewertung der Ehe.
Diese werden primär asketisch (7, 1 b.8.36) und vielleicht auch
eschatologisch (7, 29–31) begründet gewesen sein. Dennoch ist das
Kapitel für unsere Fragestellung in mehrfacher Hinsicht interessant. Die Männer und Frauen betreffenden Stellungnahmen des
Apostels sind durchgängig symmetrisch formuliert (vgl.
7, 2–4.5.8.10–11.12–16.27–28.32.34). „Beide Geschlechter werden …
in betonter Sorgfältigkeit als gleichen Rechtes und gleichen Ranges
behandelt."[54]

Entsprechend dem Ehe- und Ehescheidungsrecht wird beiden
Ehepartnern die gleiche Verpflichtung und Verantwortung zugesprochen. Der Abschnitt 7, 12–16 beschäftigt sich mit dem Zusammenleben eines christlichen und eines nichtchristlichen Partners in
der Ehe. Hier interessiert einmal die freilich auch sonst in der Antike
bekannte religiöse Selbständigkeit der Frau[55], die auch ohne ihren

---

[54] *Thyen*, Studie 177; *Stein*, Statut 71.81. *Meeks*, Image 199 f, zieht 1 Kor
11, 4–5.11–12 in diese Beobachtung ein; sein Ergebnis: „Thus Paul presupposes
and approves in the Corinthian Congregation an equivalence of role and a mutuality of relationship between the sexes in matters of marriage, divorce and charis-
matic leadership of the church to a degree that is virtually unparalleled in Jewish
or pagan society of the time".
[55] Vgl. *Thraede*, Frau 207 f; ebd. 226 f über den starken Anteil weiblicher Gottesfürchtiger am Leben der hellenistischen Synagogen.

Mann gläubig werden und so Glied der Gemeinde werden kann[56], dann die Empfehlung an den jeweils christlichen Ehepartner, die Ehe wegen der „Heiligung" des ungläubigen Partners nicht aufzugeben, aber auch sich einer Trennung nicht zu widersetzen, wenn der ungläubige Partner diese betreibt, weil er doch letztlich nicht wissen könne, ob er den ungläubigen Partner „rettet". Aus diesen Empfehlungen spricht nicht nur ein hoher Respekt des Apostels vor der persönlichen Verantwortung und Entscheidung beider Ehepartner, er legt auch den Ehepartnern nahe, einander mit einem solchen Respekt zu betrachten.

Vergleicht man damit die Weisungen der Haustafel 1 Petr 3, 1 f, so fällt sofort auf, daß in ihr nur die Frauen ungläubiger Männer angesprochen werden. Sie sollen sich ihren Männern unterordnen, damit diese durch einen gehorsamen Wandel der Frauen „ohne Wort" gewonnen werden. Weshalb ist im ersten Petrusbrief die in 1 Kor 7 sorgsam bewahrte Symmetrie aufgegeben? Literarische und gattungsgeschichtliche Erwägungen können hier vielleicht ein Stück weiterhelfen, aber sie können alleine die Frage nicht beantworten. Die Mahnungen des ersten Petrusbriefes setzen zwar mit der allgemeinen Aufforderung zur Unterordnung in 1 Petr 2, 13 ein und führen diese mit einer entsprechenden Aufforderung an die Sklaven 2, 18 und an die Frauen 3, 1 fort, und es ist erkennbar, daß die Mahnung an die Sklavenhalter, die an sich dazwischen ihren Platz gehabt hätte, weggefallen ist, weil der Brief das Motiv der „Unterordnung" betonen und theologisch ausdeuten wollte.

Aber im Anschluß an die Mahnung der Frauen folgt in 3, 7 immerhin noch eine Mahnung an die Männer. Diese ist aber nicht vom Thema der „Unterordnung" bestimmt, und bei ihr wird auch nicht an die Möglichkeit eines Zusammenlebens mit einer ungläubigen Frau gedacht, sondern an ausgeprägt christliche Ehen (3, 7 b). Wahrscheinlich spiegeln sich in 1 Petr 3 die tatsächlichen Verhältnisse. Aus der alten Kirche gibt es manche Nachrichten über Ehen von

---

[56] *Lührmann,* Haustafeln 92: Durch den Übertritt eines Ehepartners ist die Grundlage des Oikos in Frage gestellt. Aus 1 Kor 7 läßt sich aber (gegen Lührmann) nicht der Schluß ziehen, Paulus fülle dort Gal 3, 28 „erstaunlich konservativ" aus, „in dem er grundsätzlich der Erhaltung der Ehe und damit des οἶκος den Vorrang gibt". 1 Kor 7, 12 f ist an der Ehe und an der Weisung des Kyrios 7, 10 f, nicht am Oikos orientiert. Dies zeigt gerade der folgende Vergleich mit 1 Petr 3.

Christinnen mit Heiden[57]. Aber warum gibt es im Unterschied zu
1 Kor 7 keine Nachrichten über Ehen von Christen mit Heidinnen?[58] Ich kann es mir nur so erklären, daß da, wo die patriarchalische Ordnung der Ehe ausdrücklich anerkannt wird und die Unterordnung dementsprechend gefordert wird, auch die Verantwortung
der Partner für den Glauben des jeweils anderen ebenfalls asymmetrisch wird: der gläubige Mann kann seine ungläubige Frau leichter
zum Christwerden bewegen als eine gläubige Frau ihren ungläubigen Mann[59]. Ihr bleibt nur der Weg der ὑποταγή ἄνευ λόγου/Unter-
ordnung ohne Wort, wie es auch ihrer Rolle in der Gemeinde entspricht. Mit aller Vorsicht wird man also eine gewisse Parallelität
zwischen der Eheauffassung des Paulus und der Rolle der Frauen
im Gottesdienst seiner Missionsgemeinden erkennen können, wie
sie ja auch zwischen der Eheauffassung der Haustafeln und den
Schweigegeboten besteht.

Weiter ist zu beachten, daß Paulus dadurch, daß er der Ehe den
charismatischen Stand der Ehelosigkeit vorordnet (7,7), der Ehe
faktisch das Monopol bestritten hat, „den Menschen zur Erfüllung

---

[57] Vornehme Frauen, die sich dem Christentum zuwenden: *A. v. Harnack,* Die
Mission und Ausbreitung des Christentums in den ersten drei Jahrhunderten II
(Leipzig ²1906) 62 f. Dem entsprechen die romanhaften Schilderungen der Apo-
stelakten: *Thraede,* Frau 230 f; *G. Delling,* Art. Eheleben, in: RAC IV 702 f. Seit
dem Ende des zweiten Jahrhunderts wird auch von Eheschließungen zwischen
Christen und Heiden berichtet: *Harnack,* aaO. 65 f; *Delling,* Art. Ehehindernisse,
in: RAC IV 689 f; *B. Häring,* Art. Mischehe, in: LThK 7, 440 f.
[58] *Harnack,* aaO. 63 Anm. 1: „Die Fälle, daß der Mann Christ die Frau heidnisch
... war, müssen selten gewesen sein, doch siehe die Acta Marciani et Nicandri
und die Acta Irenaei". Die Kirchenordnung Hippolyts erwähnt das gemeinsame
Abend- und Mitternachtgebet der christlichen Eheleute und fügt die Weisung
hinzu: „Wenn sie aber noch nicht gläubig ward, so ziehe dich irgendwohin zurück" (41, ed. *B. Botte,* Paris ²1968, 128). Vgl. die Syrische Didaskalie (*Achelis –
Flemming* 12,16 ff): „Deinem Streite aber mit jedermann und besonders mit Deinem Manne mache ein Ende und tue ihm Einhalt, als ein gläubiges Weib, damit
nicht etwa Dein Mann, wenn er ein Heide ist, um Deinetwillen ein Ärgernis
nimmt und Gott lästert, und Du von Gott Weh hinnehmen mußt ... wenn aber
andererseits Dein Mann gläubig ist ...". Die Synoden von Elvira und Arles haben
nur die Ehe christlicher puellae mit Heiden im Blick, vgl. *Harnack,* aaO. 66; *Delling,* Ehehindernisse 690: „Nicht die Rede ist von Verbindung christlicher Männer mit Heidinnen".
[59] *Häring,* aaO. 441 deutet den in Anm. 57 und 58 genannten Befund so: „In beiden Synoden findet sich kein Verbot für Männer, heidnische Frauen heimzufüh-
ren, da dies in der Struktur der damaligen Familie wohl selten eine Gefahr bedeutete".

seiner Bestimmung zu bringen"[60]. Die von ihm vorgelebte Anerkennung des Charismas der Ehelosigkeit und zwar für beide Geschlechter (7,8) begrenzte die Gültigkeit des patriarchalischen Modells, implizierte wiederum die Achtung vor der individuellen Begabung und Entscheidung und korreliert mit der in der Mission und im Gottesdienst praktizierten Anerkennung der jeweiligen Charismen, unabhängig von der Unterscheidung nach Geschlechtern.

2.2.2. Die Spannung zwischen patriarchalischem Ordnungsdenken und theologisch begründeter Gleichrangigkeit der Geschlechter in 1 Kor 11,2–16

Die Ausführungen des Paulus zum Schleiertragen der Frauen im Gottesdienst 1 Kor 11,2–16 zeigen allerdings, daß für ihn wie für die judenchristlichen Gemeinden (11,16) die Zulassung der Frauen zum Sprechen im Gottesdienst weder den jüdischen Brauch der Verschleierung der Frauen noch die in der patriarchalischen Gesellschaftsordnung wurzelnde Anschauung von der Zweitrangigkeit der Frauen aufgehoben hatte. Der Abschnitt wirft viele exegetische Probleme auf, die bis heute nicht befriedigend gelöst sind. Für unsere Fragestellung ist es vor allem wichtig zu klären, wo der hinter dem Text stehende Konflikt anzusetzen ist. Beantwortet Paulus eine Anfrage der Korinther nach der Gültigkeit und der Begründung des im korinthischen Gottesdienst auf Grund der paulinischen παράδοσις/Überlieferung eingehaltenen Brauchs der Verschleierung der Frauen[61] oder ist 11,2 nur eine captatio benevolentiae, während die wirklichen Verhältnisse in Korinth schon von einer Aufgabe dieses Brauchs oder einer innergemeindlichen Auseinandersetzung um den Brauch gekennzeichnet sind[62]. Das Letztere ließe sich aus der Anspielung auf mögliche Streitlust 11,16a erschließen. Und hat die Anfrage oder die Auseinandersetzung ihren Anlaß in einer Modefrage[63] – in Korinth stößt die orientalische Mode der Verschleierung auf Unverständnis – oder in einer womöglich auch noch als „enthu-

---

[60] *Thyen*, Studie 177.
[61] *O. Merk*, Handeln aus Glauben (Marburg 1968) 131.
[62] *H. Conzelmann*, Der erste Brief an die Korinther (Göttingen 1969) 214f.
[63] *Thraede*, Bedeutung 104, im Anschluß an *A. Oepke*, Art. κατακαλύπτω in: ThWNT III, 564.

siastisch" zu qualifizierenden Emanzipationsbewegung[64], so daß die Frauen auf Grund der in der Gemeinde erfahrenen „Gleichberechtigung" als Charismatikerinnen nun auch den Schleier als das Symbol ihrer gesellschaftlichen Deklassierung ablehnen? Schließlich, wie stehen alltäglicher Brauch und Verhalten im Gottesdienst zueinander?

Vielleicht läßt sich die korinthische Situation mit dieser Frage am ehesten erschließen. Es ist ja eigentlich auffällig, daß Paulus in 11,6–9.10 und 11,14–15 eine Argumentation aufbaut, die auf eine Angemessenheit der Verschleierung von Frauen überhaupt hinausläuft, aber in 11,4–5 und 11,13 anscheinend nur die Verschleierung von Frauen im Gottesdienst fordert. Es ist kaum anzunehmen, daß der Brauch der Verschleierung im Gottesdienst im Gegensatz zum Verhalten im Alltag bzw. in der Öffentlichkeit geübt werden sollte. Dann besteht die korinthische Problematik darin, daß der im Alltag geltende Brauch für den Gottesdienst nicht mehr anerkannt oder praktiziert wurde – aus Gründen erfahrener charismatischer Gleichberechtigung, in diese Richtung könnte der Vergleich zwischen Mann und Frau in 11,4f weisen; aus Gründen der Praxis – wie soll eine Verschleierte ungehindert zur Gemeinde sprechen können? Und dann auch aus Gründen der erfahrenen und gelebten christlichen Bruderschaft, welche den Raum der Gemeinde von der weltlichen Öffentlichkeit abhob, so die sonst geltende Trennung von privatem und öffentlichem Bereich verwischte und das Sprechen einer nicht verschleierten Frau nicht als unschicklich oder anstößig empfinden mußte.

Paulus beruft sich erst ziemlich spät auf Schicklichkeit und „naturgemäßes Verhalten" (11,13–15). Seine Überlegungen stellen vorher zweimal einen unmittelbaren Zusammenhang zwischen der Verschleierung der Frau und ihrer dem Mann nachgeordneten Stellung in der Schöpfung her (11,3–5.7–10). Gerade diese wird durch die Verschleierung symbolisiert und durch deren Fortlassen in Frage ge-

---

[64] *J. Weiß*, Der erste Korintherbrief (Göttingen 1970 = 1910) 268; *Ph. Bachmann*. Der Erste Brief des Paulus an die Korinther (Leipzig ³1921) 348; *Gerstenberger – Schrage*. Frau 98; *Meeks*. Image 202, vermutet eine symbolische Gleichsetzung von „männlich und weiblich" als Teil der „realisierten Eschatologie" in der korinthischen Gemeinde und verweist dafür auf das Motiv „Vermännlichung" in enkratitischen Texten; dazu unten Anm. 108.

stellt (11,5: καταισχύνει τὴν κεφαλὴν αὐτῆς/macht ihrem Haupt Schande; 11,10: διὰ τοῦτο ὀφείλει κτλ./deshalb soll sie …) Die Reihe „Gott – Christus – Mann – Frau" drückt Über- und Unterordnung durch den Begriff des Hauptes (11,3) aus. Wenn die Frau in dieser Reihe die letzte Position einnimmt, zeigt sich daran, daß die Reihe in ihrer gegenwärtigen Gestalt vor allem das Verhältnis von Mann und Frau im Sinne der Überordnung des Mannes begründen und sichern soll. Ähnlich konsequent betreiben die Verse 7–9 unter Beschränkung der in Gen 1,27; 5,1 dem Menschen verliehenen Gottebenbildlichkeit auf den Mann allein und mit Berufung auf die Reihenfolge und Abzweckung der Schöpfung von Mann und Frau in Gen 2 die Sicherung und Begründung der traditionellen patriarchalischen Nachordnung der Frau[65]. Paulus bewegt sich hier im Rahmen der jüdisch-hellenistischen Ordnungsvorstellungen. Die Ausführungen in 11,7–10 sind darüber hinaus im Unterschied zu 11,3 nicht von der Christologie beeinflußt. Der Schleier scheint für Paulus beim Reden der Frauen in der Gemeinde in ähnlicher Weise deren Unterordnung zu symbolisieren wie nach 1 Kor 14,34–35 und 1 Tim 2,11 das Schweigen der Frauen.

Allerdings enthalten die Verse 11,11–12 eine gewisse Korrektur[66]. Während 11,3 u. 7–9 bemüht sind, die Frau an das Ende einer von Gott ausgehenden und den Mann überordnenden Stufenfolge zu bringen und so die Abhängigkeit der Frau vom Manne zu demonstrieren, betonen die Verse 11 und 12 die gleichmäßige und gegenseitige Abhängigkeit von Mann und Frau voneinander[67], ja die Gleichrangigkeit von Frau und Mann[68] ἐν κυρίῳ/im Herrn und führen dies

---

[65] Vgl. *Gerstenberger – Schrage*, Frau 99.
[66] πλήν hat hier nicht die Funktion, die Erörterung abzuschließen und das Wesentliche hervorzuheben (so *Bauer*, Wörterbuch 1328); es führt vielmehr einen neuen Gedanken ein, der zugleich die Bedeutung des vorhergehenden relativiert; vgl. *M. Zerwick*, Analysis philologica Novi Testamenti Graeci (Rom 1960) 379: praeter, sed; *Gerstenberger – Schrage*, Frau 99: „doch"; *J. Kürzinger*, Frau 274: „indessen, aber"; *Conzelmann*, aaO. 224: „Schon die Überleitung mit πλήν bedeutet einen gewissen Rückzug"; *M. E. Thrall*, Greek Particles in the New Testament (Leiden 1972) 20: „πλήν also develops a purely adversative function".
[67] Siehe das Spiel mit den Präpositionen ἐκ und διά in 11,12.
[68] *Gerstenberger – Schrage*, Frau 99: „Mit dieser These der Gleichursprünglichkeit und Gleichwertigkeit beider Geschlechter nimmt Paulus im Grunde das zurück, was er theologisch unzulänglich fundiert und wenig überzeugend vorher erklärt hat". *Kürzinger*, Frau 273 f, vertritt für χωρίς die Übersetzung „anders als,

mit τὰ δὲ πάντα ἐκ τοῦ ϑεοῦ/alles aber (ist) von Gott auf die Absicht des Schöpfers zurück. Wenn 1 Kor 11,11 an rabbinische Gedankengänge über die Gleichwertigkeit von Mann und Frau anklingt oder anknüpft[69], ist es um so bedeutsamer, daß Paulus an dieser Stelle im Unterschied zu 11,7–10 mit ἐν κυρίῳ ausdrücklich eine christliche Begründung einführt. Die Tragweite und das Verständnis dieser Begründung sind umstritten. Entspricht sie dem paulinischen ἐν Χριστῷ/in Christus, wie es in dem ähnlichen noch zu besprechenden Zusammenhang Gal 3,26–28 begegnet[70] oder ist an der Differenz zu ἐν Χριστῷ festzuhalten?[71] Für die Annahme einer Differenzierung spricht die auch sonst unterschiedliche Intention beider Stellen. 1 Kor 11 hält an der geschlechtlichen Differenzierung von Mann und Frau fest, betont aber ihre Gleichwertigkeit im Herrschaftsbereich des Kyrios, während Gal 3,28 die geschlechtliche Differenzierung im Horizont der eschatologischen Neuschöpfung ἐν Χριστῷ für aufgehoben erklärt[72]. Insofern ist 1 Kor 11,11 streng auf seinen Kontext bezogen, es relativiert die Überlegungen von 11,3 und 11,7–10. Das ἐν κυρίῳ besagt daher nicht, daß die Unterschiede zwar „im Herrn" aufgehoben sind, aber nicht „in uns"[73], sondern zielt auf das Verhältnis von Mann und Frau in der Gemeinde und im christlichen Zusammenleben[74]: hier gibt es keine Minderwertigkeit, aber in patriarchalischen Ordnungsvorstellungen begründete oder begründbare Gewohnheiten wie die Verschleierung der Frauen.

Das bedeutet, daß unser Abschnitt zwei unterschiedlichen Theologien oder Anthropologien Raum gibt. Die erste entspricht den traditionellen patriarchalischen Ordnungsvorstellungen, die zweite der neuen Rolle der Frauen in der Gemeinde, im Herrschaftsbereich des

---

verschieden von". Der Gedanke der Gleichrangigkeit ist jedoch nicht von dieser Übersetzung abhängig.
[69] Belege: *Billerbeck* III 440; vgl. *Merode*, Théologie 183; *Boucher*, Parallels 52.
[70] *Conzelmann*, aaO. 222.224; *Kürzinger*, Frau 275.
[71] *F. Neugebauer*, In Christus (Göttingen 1961) 136 f; *Merk*, aaO. 134.
[72] *Neugebauer*, aaO. 136.
[73] So *Conzelmann*, aaO. 224.
[74] *Neugebauer*, aaO. 137, verweist auf eine ähnliche Funktion des ἐν κυρίῳ 1 Kor 7,39. Vgl. *Thyen*, Studie 185: „Ich muß darauf bestehen, daß ‚im Herrn' nicht spiritualisiert werden darf, sondern zugleich immer, in der empirischen Realität der christlichen Gemeinde als der Repräsentantin von Gottes neuer Schöpfung inmitten einer ihrem Ende entgegengehenden Welt heißen muß".

Kyrios. Die erste wird zur Stützung der Sitte der Verschleierung herangezogen, aber dann doch durch die zweite korrigiert[75]. Die theologische Unausgeglichenheit der Argumentation läßt sich nicht harmonisieren. Im Gegenteil! Zwar fordert Paulus in 11,13-15 und 11,16 wieder die Verschleierung der Frauen, aber jetzt nicht mehr mit Argumenten, die auf der Minderwertigkeit der Frau gegenüber dem Mann aufbauen[76]. Das ist sicher kein Zufall. Nach 1 Kor 11,11 f ist eine Rückkehr zum Anfang des Abschnitts unmöglich geworden[77]. Das Nebeneinander unterschiedlicher Argumentationslinien zeigt, daß es Paulus nicht gelungen ist, eine einheitliche theologische Konzeption zum Thema der Gleichwertigkeit von Mann und Frau zu entwerfen und durchzuhalten. Vielleicht wurde er daran durch das anscheinend sehr mit allerlei Vorurteilen und Ängsten besetzte Thema der Verschleierung zusätzlich behindert. So treffen bei ihm traditionelle patriarchalische Ordnungsvorstellungen und die neue christliche Erfahrung der Gleichwertigkeit der Geschlechter aufeinander, ohne daß es zu einer echten Auseinandersetzung wie bei den Themen Gesetz und Beschneidung gekommen wäre. Daß es nicht zu einer solchen Auseinandersetzung kam, liegt wohl daran, daß der Konflikt zwischen der mehr oder weniger selbstverständlichen Praxis der Gemeinde und den patriarchalischen Ordnungsvorstellungen erst nach einem längeren geschichtlichen Zeitraum voll bewußt wurde. Als dies dann geschah, haben die Aussagen von 11,3-10 eine weitaus bessere und wirkungsvollere Resonanz gefun-

---

[75] Vgl. *J. Jervell*, Imago Dei 312; *Merk*, aaO. 134: Diese Einschränkung zum vorgenannten Beweisgang ist für Paulus unabdingbar, denn sie rückt diesen in das rechte Licht, nämlich, daß „die Aussagen keine Tragweite über das hinaus haben, was sie in der konkreten Situation beweisen wollen".

[76] Allerdings sieht auch das Verhalten gemäß der φύσις/Natur in Beziehung zur Aufrechterhaltung der durch die unterschiedliche Stellung von Mann und Frau symbolisierten Weltordnung: *Meeks*, Image 179 f mit Anm. 72 und 73. Ebd. 202: „If Paul ... in 1 Corinthians 11,2-16 is concerned to insist on the continuing validity of the symbolic distinction belonging to the humanity of the old Adam, that is in harmony with the ‚eschatological reservation' which he expresses throughout this letter".

[77] Gegen *Kürzinger*, Frau 275: „Daß mit der Aussage von V.11 über die Gleichrangigkeit von Mann und Frau ‚im Herrn' das vorher Gesagte nicht aufgehoben sein will, läßt sich schon daran erkennen, daß der Apostel die Forderung nach Verschleierung der Frauen nochmals in 11,13-16 erhebt, ohne darin einen Widerspruch zu sehen mit dem zuvor in den Zwischenversen VV.11 f Gesagten".

den (vgl. Eph 5,23)[78] als 11,11 f – vielleicht doch gegen die Intention des Paulus? – und so geriet auch das ἐν κυρίῳ unter ein von der Weitergeltung der patriarchalischen Ordnung bestimmte, es auf die Beziehung zu Christus einschränkendes Vorzeichen[79]. 1 Tim 2,15: σωθήσεται δὲ διὰ τῆς τεκνογονίας/ „sie wird aber gerettet werden durch Kindergebären" nimmt sogar diese einschränkende Interpretation noch zurück, indem den Frauen dort ein besonderer geschlechtsspezifischer Heilsweg zugewiesen wird[80].

2.2.3. Zur Interpretation von Gal 3,28

Noch grundsätzlicher als 1 Kor 11,1 f betont Gal 3,28 die Gleichstellung von Mann und Frau: „Denn ihr, die ihr auf Christus getauft wurdet, ihr habt Christus angezogen. Da ist weder Jude noch Grieche, weder Sklave noch Freier, noch Männliches und Weibliches. Denn ihr alle seid einer in Christus Jesus" (Gal 3,27 f). Freilich zeigt schon die Auslegungsgeschichte dieses Textes, daß, falls er für unsere Frage nach dem Verhältnis von Gemeinde- und Gesellschaftsordnung relevant sein sollte, diese seine Bedeutung entweder auf Grund seiner Stellung im Galaterbrief oder auf Grund anderer Verständnismöglichkeiten, nicht ohne gründliche exegetische und hermeneutische Bemühungen erkannt werden kann. Über lange Zeiten hinweg entnahm man ihm hinsichtlich des Verhältnisses von Mann und Frau nicht mehr als die für ein durchschnittliches christliches Bewußtsein nicht gerade provozierende Einsicht, daß das „Sein in Christus" die alten Unterschiede transzendiert. „Der Apostel will selbstverständlich nicht sagen, daß derartige Unterschiede äußerlich nicht mehr bestehen – Mann bleibt Mann und Frau bleibt Frau, auch nach der Taufe – *aber sie haben jegliche Heilsbedeutung vor Gott verloren.*"[81] Dieser kargen Auskunft eines neueren Galaterkom-

---

[78] *Meeks*, Image 206: „The traditional parenesis has redirected the notion of reunification to refer entirely to the relation of the whole community to Christ, while the author of Ephesians uses it only to reinforce the conventional definitions of the masculine and feminine roles in marriage".

[79] Wie *Conzelmann*, aaO. 224.

[80] Auf dieser Linie liegt auch die Paränese von 1 Petr 3,4.7.

[81] *F. Mußner*, Der Galaterbrief (Freiburg 1974) 264. Zum auffälligen Schweigen der Kommentare vgl. *Lührmann*, Sklave 54 f; ferner *Paulsen*, Einheit 74;

mentars (1974) steht allerdings seit einigen Jahren eine Vielzahl von Studien gegenüber, welche diese sich so plausibel als „selbstverständlich" ausgebende Interpretationslinie in Frage stellen[82].

Die gegenwärtige Diskussion bezieht sich zunächst auf das Verhältnis von Tradition und Interpretation und dann auf die Tragweite der in Gal 3,28 ausgesprochenen Aufhebung des diskriminierenden Unterschieds von „männlich" und „weiblich" in der vorausgesetzten Tradition und in deren paulinischer Interpretation. Verschiedenartige Beobachtungen stützen die Vermutung, daß Paulus in Gal 3,28 Tradition zitiert.

Obwohl sich Gal 3,26–29 in den gedanklichen Aufbau von Gal 3 und 4,1–7 einfügt[83], hebt der Abschnitt sich durch stilistische und inhaltliche Besonderheiten von seinem Kontext ab. Stilistische Merkmale[84]: Ringkomposition mit πάντες/alle 3,26a.28b; sie bestimmt auch den Gebrauch von ὅσοι/alle, die 3,27a. Die chiastisch verstärkte Antithetik der drei Gegensatzpaare in 3,28. Wechsel der Redeform von der 1. Person Plural in 3,25 und 4,3 zu der Anrede in der 2. Person Plural in 3,26–29. Zum Inhaltlichen: von den drei Gegensätzen in Gal 3,28a hat nur Ἰουδαῖος – Ἕλλην/Jude – Grieche eine unmittelbare Beziehung zur Thematik des Galaterbriefes[85].

Auf die Übernahme vorpaulinischer Tradition weisen ferner die weitgehenden Übereinstimmungen zwischen Gal 3,28a und 1 Kor 12,13; Kol 3,11[86], die inhaltlich vor allem hinsichtlich der „christologisch fundierten Aufhebung grundlegender anthropologischer Gegensätze" bestehen, „deren Aufzählung im Einzelnen unterschiedlich gehandhabt werden kann"[87]. Daß es sich um einen vorgegebenen Motivzusammenhang handelt, geht auch aus den paulinischen Aussagen in 1 Kor 7,19; Gal 5,6; 6,15; 2 Kor 5,17 hervor,

R. *Schnackenburg*, Neutestamentliche Ethik im Kontext heutiger Wirklichkeit, in: Anspruch der Wirklichkeit und christlicher Glaube. FS A. Auer (Düsseldorf 1977) 193–207.202; *Thyen*, Studie 188–191.

[82] Den Anstoß zur neuen Diskussion über Gal 3,28 gab *Stendahl*, Bible (1967); seine Anregungen wurden zunächst in amerikanischen Publikationen aufgegriffen: *Boucher*, Parallels; *Scroggs*, Paul; *Meeks*, Image; seit 1975 beteiligt sich auch die europäische Exegese: *Lührmann*, Sklave; *Bouttier*, Complexio; *Merode*, Théologie; *Thyen*, Studie; *Paulsen*, Einheit.

[83] *Paulsen*, Einheit 74–76; *Thyen*, Studie 126–137. [84] Vgl. *Paulsen*, Einheit 77.

[85] *Bouttier*, Complexio 9; *Thyen*, Studie 111.146.

[86] *Bouttier*, Complexio 10; *Paulsen*, Einheit 77f (Literatur).

[87] *Paulsen*, Einheit 79.

welche diesen Motivzusammenhang voraussetzen und in charakteristischer Weise abwandeln[88].

Auch Gal 3,26.27.28 b knüpfen an urchristliche Theologumena an, jedoch läßt sich kaum der sichere Nachweis erbringen, daß sie schon vor Paulus mit 3,28 a zusammengefügt wurden[89]. Immerhin zeigen sich auch im größeren Zusammenhang so viele Gemeinsamkeiten mit 1 Kor 12,13 und Kol 3,11 (neben Stilistischem vor allem der Taufzusammenhang, das Überkleidungsmotiv und der Jude-Grieche-Gedanke), daß man auch für den gesamten Zusammenhang mit der Aufnahme traditioneller Topik rechnen darf. Diese hätte ihren Ursprung in der hellenistischen Gemeinde und die Absicht, die Aufhebung der fundamentalen Gegensätze von Jude und Grieche, von Freiem und Sklaven, von Männlich und Weiblich in der Christuswirklichkeit oder im Leib des Christus zu proklamieren[90]. Paulus zieht diese Überlieferung als „unangefochtenen Grundsatz" heran, auch das spricht für die Vorgegebenheit von Gal 3,28 a[91].

Mit οὐκ ἔνι ἄρσεν καὶ ϑῆλυ/da ist nicht Männlich und Weiblich ist in dieser Tradition die Aufhebung des Gegensatzes von „Männlich" und „Weiblich" ausgesprochen. Die Formulierung dieses Gegensatzpaares hebt sich durch die Verwendung von καί/und statt οὐδέ/und nicht, wie auch durch den Gebrauch des Neutrums statt des Maskulinums von den vorausgehenden beiden Paaren ab. Beide Momente weisen darauf hin, daß an dieser Stelle bewußt an die Sprache von Gen 1,27 LXX: ἄρσεν καὶ ϑῆλυ ἐποίησεν αὐτούς erinnert wird[92]. So wird wohl bewußt von der eschatologischen Aufhebung oder Überholung des in der Schöpfung angelegten Unterschieds der Geschlechter gesprochen[93]. Wie bei den vorausgehenden Gegensatzpaaren wird hier aber nicht nur von der Aufhebung von Gegensätzen, sondern auch von der Aufhebung von Diskriminierungen gesprochen[94]. Ausgangspunkt der Reihe ist der „Jude" als

[88] *Paulsen*, Einheit 79 f; *Thyen*, Studie 110 f.

[89] *Paulsen*, Einheit 87.

[90] Vgl. *Paulsen*, Einheit 87.

[91] *Lührmann*, Sklave 57; *Thyen*, Studie 138.

[92] *Merode*, Théologie 178; *Paulsen*, Einheit 83; *Bouttier*, Complexio 7; *Meeks*, Image 181; *Gerstenberger – Schrage*, Frau 122.

[93] *Paulsen*, Einheit 83–85; *Bouttier*, Complexio 7; *Stendahl*, Bible 32; *Thyen*, Studie 111; *Gerstenberger – Schrage*, Frau 122.

der Repräsentant des Gottesvolkes, ihm entsprechen in der chiasti-
schen Anordnung der Antithesen die ebenfalls privilegierten Glieder „Freier" und „Männlich", während „Weiblich" in die Reihe der
bisher nicht Privilegierten, zu „Grieche" und „Sklave" gehört. Gen
1, 27 widerspricht an sich eher einer Diskriminierung der Frau, aber
1 Kor 11, 7 f zeigte ja schon, daß selbst diesem Text eine auf den Vorrang des Mannes abhebende Interpretation zuteil werden konnte.
Das Begriffspaar ἄρρην – ϑῆλυς/männlich – weiblich hat überdies,
häufig neben ἀνήρ – γυνή/Mann – Frau gebraucht, seinen Platz in
der Sprache der antiken Ethik, sei es daß auf die unterschiedlichen
Stände im Staat abgehoben wird (*Platon,* Leges 665 C: τὸ δεῖν πάντ'
ἄνδρα καὶ παῖδα, ἐλεύϑερον καὶ δοῦλον, ϑῆλύν τε καὶ ἄρρενα) oder
auf die Überlegenheit des Mannes über die Frau (*Aristoteles,* Politik
1254b 13 f; 1259 b 1 – neutrisch formuliert), sei es daß Mann und
Frau die gleichen menschlichen Qualitäten und Fähigkeiten zugeschrieben werden (Musonius Rufus nach Stobaeus II 31, 123 u.
126)[95]. In ethischen Zusammenhängen werden Fragen der gesellschaftlichen Rangordnung immer wieder mit der Erörterung der
Unterschiede zwischen Männern, Frauen, Sklaven und Kindern verbunden. Von daher erklärt sich, daß in Gal 3, 28 mit der Aufhebung
der alten Gegensätze zugleich die Aufwertung der bisher Unterlege-
nen proklamiert wird.

Aber in welchem Sinne wird von Aufhebung und Aufwertung gesprochen? Lassen wir die ersten beiden Gegensatzpaare zunächst
beiseite und betrachten wir nur das „da ist nicht Männlich und
Weiblich", so zeigt sich, daß sogar ein in der Schöpfungsordnung
angelegter Unterschied nun als aufgehoben erklärt wird, weil auch
dieser wie die Gegensätze von Jude und Grieche und Freiem und
Sklaven Anlaß zu diskriminierender Unterscheidung bot. Der Horizont, in welchem diese Aufhebung geschieht, kann nur als eschatologischer beschrieben werden. Es ist von der neuen Schöpfung die
Rede, welche mit der Eingliederung in Christus zur eigentlichen
Wirklichkeit wird (Gal 6, 15; 2 Kor 5, 17). Insofern handelt es sich
primär um eine theologische Aussage, die prinzipiell die gesellschaftliche und geschichtliche Wirklichkeit übersteigt[96]. Das besagt

[94] Mit *Lührmann,* Sklave 57; gegen *Paulsen,* Einheit 85.
[95] Vgl. dazu *Merode,* Théologie 184 f.
[96] *Paulsen,* Einheit 88.94.

aber nicht, daß sie nicht – wie wir gesehen haben – auf gesellschaftliche Ungleichheitserfahrungen antwortet und diese überholen will. Gerade dies ist ihre Absicht[97]. Und so wird sie auch an durchaus konkrete Erfahrungen der anfanghaften Überwindung von Ungleichheiten in den Gemeinden anknüpfen und diesen Erfahrungen einen von der Hoffnung getragenen Ausdruck verleihen.

Gerade diese Beziehung auf Erfahrung und Hoffnung der Gemeinde veranlaßte Paulus wohl dazu, sich im Galaterbrief auf diese Tradition dort zu berufen, wo er darum bemüht ist, dem Anspruch der Gegner zu begegnen, man könne nur als Glied des erwählten Volkes der Kinder Abrahams und d. h. auf dem Weg der Beschneidung Christ und des Heils teilhaftig werden[98]. Die Tradition dient ihm als wirkungsvolles „Hilfsargument zur Begründung der Abrahamskindschaft der Glaubenden"[99], weil sie „konkrete und geschichtliche Erfahrungen" benennt[100]: das Fallen scheinbar unverrückbarer Grenzen und alter Privilegien, die Begründung einer neuen Einheit in der Gemeinde, die mit dem Eintritt in die Gemeinde Christi verbundene Erfahrung eines wirklichen Bruchs „mit der Vergangenheit, der bis in die fundamentalsten Sozialbeziehungen reichte"[101].

---

[97] Vgl. *Meeks*, Image 182: „A modern philosopher might call it a ‚performative utterance' ... A factual claim is being made about an ‚objective' change in reality that fundamentally modifies social roles. New attitudes and altered behaviour would follow – but only if the group succeeds in clothing the novel declaration with an ‚aura of factuality'". *Paulsen*, Einheit 88 f, betont, daß sie „konkrete Folgerungen aus sich herausgesetzt hat", und verweist darauf, daß sich die Rolle, die Frauen „durchaus nicht nur in den häretischen Gruppen bis weit ins zweite Jahrhundert gespielt haben", nicht ohne jenes Bewußtsein erklären läßt, welches sich in Gal 3,28 artikuliert. *Gerstenberger – Schrage*, Frau 122: „Daß die üblichen Klassifizierungen vor Gott nicht gelten, ist zwar richtig, aber das hat eben auch Auswirkungen ‚in Christus', und d. h. in der Gemeinde".

[98] Vgl. *Thyen*, Studie 121.

[99] *Thyen*, Studie 146.

[100] *Thyen*, Studie 134.

[101] *Thyen*, Studie 134. *Lührmann*, Sklave 67, interpretiert Gal 3,28 zu einseitig von der „sozialen Integrationsfähigkeit" der urchristlichen Gemeinden her und achtet zu wenig auf die Begründung neuer nicht mehr durch die alten Privilegien definierter Rollen in der Gemeinde, da er Paulus unterstellt, daß für ihn „die vorgegebenen Differenzen unter den Bedingungen dieser Welt nicht grundsätzlich veränderbar sind" (69); vgl. auch *ders.*, Haustafeln (s. Anm. 46) 93. Zur Kritik an dieser statischen Sicht vgl. *Paulsen*, Einheit 88 f; *Thyen*, Studie 189. Auch *G. Theißen*, Zur forschungsgeschichtlichen Einordnung der religionssoziologischen Fra-

Dennoch müssen wir wohl zwischen der ursprünglichen Intention der Tradition und ihrer Interpretation durch Paulus unterscheiden. Wenn die Tradition „die eschatologisch begründete neue Schöpfung als endgültig" postuliert[102] und dabei unverkennbar auch ein praktisches Interesse verfolgt, so rückt sie im Galaterbrief in einen vor allem ihre theologische Aussage betonenden Kontext[103]. Im ersten Korintherbrief (12,13) greift Paulus zwar die Tradition auf, aber er beschränkt sich bei der Aufzählung der aufgehobenen Gegensätze auf die Paare „Juden–Griechen" und „Freie–Sklaven". Wahrscheinlich deshalb, weil auf der Basis dieser Tradition das Verhältnis von Männern und Frauen in der korinthischen Gemeinde problematisch geworden war[104]. Das zeigt sich an 1 Kor 11,2–16 und steht von anderen in unserem Zusammenhang nicht angesprochenen Sinngehalten der Formel „nicht mehr männlich und weiblich" her auch hinter den in 1 Kor 7 diskutierten Anfragen und Problemen[105].

Paulus spricht außer in Gal 3,28 sonst nie wie die Tradition von ἄρσεν καὶ θῆλυ/männlich und weiblich[106], wenn es um das Verhältnis der Geschlechter geht, sondern von ἄνθρωπος/Mensch 1 Kor 7,1 bzw. ἀνήρ/Mann 7,2–16; 11,3–14 und γυνή/Frau 7,1–16; 11,3–15 und vertritt in 1 Kor 11,7 eine andere Interpretation von Gen 1,27 als die in Gal 3,28 vorliegende Tradition[107]. 1 Kor 11,11: „Indes ist weder die Frau etwas ohne den Mann, noch der Mann etwas ohne die Frau im Herrn" korrigiert, wie wir gesehen haben, zwar diese diskriminierende Interpretation von Gen 1,27, aber nicht in unmittelbarer Berufung auf die Tradition von Gal 3,28, sondern eher in deren bewußter Neuformulierung. Hier wird die Unterscheidung der Geschlechter nicht negiert oder aufgehoben, sondern mit den Bezeichnungen „Frau" und „Mann" festgehalten und zugleich ihre Gleichrangigkeit „im Herrn" proklamiert. Beider Auftreten in der Gemeinde soll dem natürlichen Unterschied der Geschlechter

gestellung, in: ders., Studien zur Soziologie des Urchristentums (Tübingen 1979) 3–34.31.33, sieht die integrierende Funktion von Gal 3,28 einzig auf der Ebene symbolischer Bedeutung, ohne daß diese eine soziale Entsprechung hätte.

[102] Paulsen, Einheit 94.
[103] Paulsen, Einheit 94.
[104] Vgl. Thyen, Studie 146.
[105] Vgl. Thyen, Studie 157.174–180; Lührmann, Sklave 61 f.
[106] Röm 1,27 gehört in einen anderen Zusammenhang.
[107] Siehe oben 211 f.

entsprechen und diesen nicht durch den Verzicht auf den Schleier in Frage stellen. Die Berufung auf das πρέπον ἐστίν/es ist geziemend 1 Kor 11,13 zeigt ebenso wie die bewußte Rede von „Mann" und „Frau", wie Paulus das „nicht mehr männlich und weiblich" in seinen Gemeinden verstehen möchte, nicht in der Aufhebung der geschlechtlichen Differenz in einer Art präsentischer Eschatologie[108], für deren Vorhandensein in der korinthischen Gemeinde es ja auch sonst Anzeichen gibt, sondern in der gleichberechtigten Teilnahme von Männern und Frauen am Leben der Gemeinde unter Beachtung der den Unterschied und ursprünglich und in der Gesellschaft auch die Ungleichheit der Geschlechter betonenden Sitte.

Paulus denkt und argumentiert in 1 Kor 11,2–16 wie auch in 1 Kor 7 und 14 mehr von der Ordnung her und auf ihre Bewahrung hin, ohne doch die Ordnungen als solche, wie es dann in der zweiten und dritten Generation geschieht, festzulegen. Dennoch hat er in 11,11 eine Einsicht formuliert, die überall da auf eine Umgestaltung der Ordnung drängen sollte, wo diese der Gleichrangigkeit von Frau und Mann entgegensteht – im Bereich der Gemeinde und in dem auch nach 1 Kor 11,3.7f.11f diesem so nahe verwandten Bereich

---

[108] *Meeks*, Image 202: Das Motiv der Androgynie als der Aufhebung der geschlechtlichen Differenziertheit und der damit verbundenen Spannungen stellt ein weit verbreitetes, ursprünglich nicht im biblischen Traditionsbereich beheimatetes Ziel antiker Erlösungssehnsucht dar. Als solches begegnet es auch in der apokalyptischen Erwartung (aethHen 51,4; syrBar 51,9f; Mk 12,25) und vor allem in gnostischen Texten (z. B. EvThom 22; EvPhil 71; vgl. dazu *Thyen*, Studie 139f; *Meeks*, Image 188–194). Die geschlechtliche Differenzierung von Männern und Frauen wurde in Richtung auf die menschliche Zweitrangigkeit der Frauen interpretiert und diente so der Legitimation einer vom Vorrang der Männer bestimmten Gesellschaftsordnung, wie es sich in dem häufig zur Illustration von Gal 3,28 zitierten Dankgebet des Rabbi Jehuda äußert: „Drei Gebete muß man täglich sagen: Gepriesen, der du mich nicht als Heiden schufst. Gepriesen, der du mich nicht als Frau geschaffen. Gepriesen, der du mich nicht als Ungebildeten machtest (TBer 7,18; vgl. *Merode*, Théologie 182f; *Boucher*, Parallels 53; *Meeks*, Image 168; *Lührmann*, Sklave 57f; wahrscheinlich Übernahme eines antiken Topos: *Meeks*, Image 167; *Thyen*, Studie 143). Ein Ausweg bot sich in der Negierung des Weiblichen und im Ziel der „Vermännlichung" der Frauen (JosAs 15,1; EvThom 114; EvÄg nach Clem Al Strom III 63: Ich bin gekommen, die Werke des Weiblichen aufzulösen; Acta Pauli et Theclae 25.40; Passio Sanctarum Perpetuae et Felicitatis 10,7; vgl. *Meeks*, Image 194–197; *Thraede*, Frau 242; *Thyen*, Studie 143: „Diese Denkfigur ermöglicht Frauen nicht nur volle Mitgliedschaft und führende Positionen in den hier zu Wort kommenden Gemeinden, ... sie muß ... zugleich als Reaktion auf Rollen gelesen werden, die Frauen in solchen Gemeinden faktisch gespielt haben".

des „Hauses". Wenn der Galaterbrief nach dem ersten Korintherbrief abgefaßt wurde, was sehr wahrscheinlich ist, darf die Zurückhaltung des Paulus in 1 Kor 11,2–16; 12,13 auch nicht als ein Zurückweichen von einer einmal in Gal 3,28 erreichten Position interpretiert werden. Wir stehen vielmehr im ersten Korintherbrief wie im Galaterbrief vor einer je unterschiedlich akzentuierten Interpretation und Anwendung dieser Tradition. Die Überzeugung des Apostels von der theologischen Kompetenz seiner Gemeinden läßt ihn auch die Frage der rechten Ordnung schließlich dem Urteil eben dieser geistgeleiteten Gemeinden anheimstellen (vgl. 11,13.16). Das erklärt sein im Unterschied zu den Pastoralbriefen ausgesprochen geringes Interesse an dauerhaften Regelungen der Gemeindeordnung.

3. Zusammenfassung und Ausblick

Fassen wir die bisherigen Überlegungen und Beobachtungen zusammen. Die Paulusbriefe bezeugen ein starkes Hervortreten von Frauen im Leben der Gemeinden und in der Mission, und zwar nicht nur für den Bereich der paulinischen Gemeinden, sondern darüber hinaus zumindest für den Kreis des hellenistischen Juden- und Heidenchristentums. Dieses Hervortreten war möglicherweise durch die im griechisch-römischen Mittelmeerraum anzutreffende Tendenz auf höhere Gleichberechtigung der Frauen hin begünstigt, fand seine Begründung aber in spezifisch christlichen Erfahrungen wie der Begabung von Männern und Frauen mit dem in der Endzeit wirkenden Geist. Dies ermöglichte die Ausbildung einer Gemeindeordnung, welche patriarchalischen Vorstellungen von der Unterordnung der Frauen und von ihrem Ausschluß von der aktiven Teilnahme am Gemeindeleben widersprach oder diese zumindest für den Bereich des Gemeindelebens (1 Kor 11,2–16) und der Familie (1 Kor 7) eingrenzte. Gal 3,28 bezeugt, daß die neuen Gemeindeerfahrungen auch als ein Angriff auf patriarchalische Ordnungen verstanden wurden, und deutet diese Erfahrungen als Anbruch der neuen Schöpfung, welche die alten Diskriminierungen aufhebt.

Erste Konflikte zeichnen sich in 1 Kor 11,2–16 ab. Paulus sucht diesen Konflikten zunächst mit dem Rückgriff auf patriarchalische

Ordnungsvorstellungen zu begegnen, läßt aber nicht zu, daß diese den Kern der neuen Einheit in der Gemeinde, nämlich die Einsicht in die Gleichrangigkeit von Mann und Frau und die aktive Teilnahme der Frauen am Gemeindeleben zerstören. Zugleich ist er aber um die Einfügung der neuen Ausdrucksformen in die geltenden Anschauungen vom Schicklichen bemüht. Eine Beschäftigung mit den über die Gemeinde hinausgreifenden Fragen der Gesellschaftsordnung liegt außerhalb seines Interesses. Angesichts der verschiedenen Optionen für das Verhältnis von Mann und Frau, welche in der damaligen gesellschaftlichen Wirklichkeit vorhanden waren, stellt sich die Situation in seinen Gemeinden als eine Übergangssituation dar, welche auf Dauer in der einen oder anderen Richtung einer Festigung und Verstetigung bedurfte.

Das nachpaulinische Christentum suchte diese Festigung zunächst im familiären Bereich durch neue Orientierung an patriarchalischen Ordnungsvorstellungen zu erreichen[109]. Es nahm die Forderung der Unterordnung der Frauen wieder auf und interpretierte diese im Sinne eines christlichen Liebespatriarchalismus. Die so eingenommene patriarchalische Option wirkte mit einer gewissen Notwendigkeit auf das Gemeindeleben zurück, wie es die Schweigegebote und die Gemeindeordnung der Pastoralbriefe bezeugen. In den neuen Aussagen erscheint eine aktive Teilnahme der Frauen am Gemeindeleben als Bedrohung der vorrangigen patriarchalischen Ordnung. Die theologischen Einsichten von 1 Kor 11,11 und Gal 3,28 werden, nachdem ihnen die soziale Basis entzogen worden ist, nicht mehr wiederholt, obwohl sie ursprünglich die Funktion von Korrektiven gegenüber einer patriarchalischen Orientierung hatten. Diese Entwicklung war im Ganzen nicht notwendig, aber folgerichtig. Sie

---

[109] *Lührmann*, Haustafeln 93, betont, daß der Schritt in diese von ihm sog. „zweite Phase" des frühen Christentums nicht „ohne reflektierte Auseinandersetzung mit der ersten" geschehen ist, und sieht ihren positiven Ertrag in der Sicherung der Tradition durch den Anschluß der Gemeinde an die Oikos-Struktur. Er stellt sich aber nicht genügend der Frage, ob nicht auch die befreienden Erfahrungen der „ersten Phase" ein Recht auf „Überlieferung" gehabt hätten, bzw. welche „Kosten" die patriarchalische Option für die weitere Geschichte des Christentums gebracht hat. Darüber kann nun nur noch in einer Art „Ketzergeschichte" reflektiert werden (vgl. die Daten bei *Thraede*, Frau 237–239), es sei denn, das neuzeitliche Christentum würde wieder bewußt an die exegetisch freigelegte „erste Phase" anknüpfen (vgl. *Lührmann*, aaO. 96).

222

hat seither die Erfahrung von Kirche und Gemeinde tiefgreifend verändert und dauerhaft geprägt.

Angesichts des für unsere Gesellschaft wohl endgültigen Zerbrechens der patriarchalischen Ordnung und der breiten gesellschaftlichen Bewegung auf Gleichberechtigung der Frauen hin, gewinnt die Frage nach der sozialethischen und ekklesiologischen Relevanz der lange Zeit nur von einer Gleichheit coram Deo verstandenen Aussagen Gal 3,28; 1 Kor 11,11 und nach der Praxis der frühen Missionsgemeinden insgesamt neue Bedeutung. Die urchristliche Entwicklung zeigt eine kaum aufhebbare Interdependenz zwischen Gesellschaftsordnung bzw. gesellschaftlicher Option und Gemeindeordnung. Das sollte allen zu denken geben, welche in einer Zeit, welche die gesellschaftliche Gleichberechtigung der Frauen auf allen Ebenen anerkennt und fordert, für das Gemeindeleben an einer patriarchalischen Orientierung festhalten. Die so entstehenden schweren Konflikte können die gesellschaftliche Basis der Gemeinde bedrohen und bis ins Innerste verletzen[110], wenn es nicht gelingt, den im Neuen Testament bezeugten Erfahrungen der sich in der Gemeinde auswirkenden Gleichrangigkeit von Mann und Frau wirksames Gehör zu verschaffen[111]. Gal 3,28 entwirft zwar kein soziales Programm, aber der Text läßt sich in seinem Aussagewillen auch nicht auf den Bereich coram Deo oder auf ein bestimmtes individuali-

---

[110] Der „Preis" für die dem kirchlichen Verständnis der Schrift entsprechende Zulassung der historisch-kritischen Exegese in den Kreis der kirchlichen Wissenschaften ist noch nicht „bezahlt", wenn deren Erkenntnisse zwar auf der historischen Ebene diskutiert werden können, diesen aber kaum Auswirkungen auf das aktuelle kirchliche Leben eingeräumt werden. Aus den (polemischen) Beiträgen der amerikanischen Evangelikalen *W. H. House*, Paul, Women and Contemporary Evangelicalism, in: BS 136 (1979) 40–53, und *A. D. Litfin*, Evangelical Feminism: Why Traditionalists Reject It?, in: BS 136 (1979) 259–271, kann man lernen, was alles an exegetischen Einsichten zurückgenommen werden müßte, wenn Gal 3,28 und 1 Kor 14,33 b–36; 1 Tim 2,11–15 auf einer Linie interpretiert werden sollten, und wie sehr dann gerade die späteren Schichten des Neuen Testaments dieses Gesamtverständnis bestimmen müssen. Vgl. *Litfin*, aaO. 267: „Traditionalists believe that the Bible presents to the reader a unified world view ... Crucial to this world view, according to the Bible, are the concepts of authority and hierarchy."

[111] Vgl. die Überlegungen der Psychotherapeutin *Dominique Stein*, Statut 77: „excursus sur une certaine pratique ecclésiastique de la double verité en matière biblique" und ihre Forderungen nach einer offenen innerkirchlichen Diskussion des exegetischen Erkenntnisstandes (84 f).

stisch verengtes Heilsverständnis beschränken[112], das zeigte sich schon an der Wende der paulinischen Argumentation in 1 Kor 11 von 3–10 zu 11–16. Die Überlieferung von Gal 3,28 hat einen „Vorgabecharakter, der die Wirklichkeit nicht selbstvergessen isoliert beläßt"[113], sie darf nicht durch die Unterscheidung zweier Dimensionen „vor Gott" und „unter Menschen in der Kirche und der Gesellschaft"[114] neutralisiert werden. Sie zielt vielmehr auf eine neue Wirklichkeit gerade in der Gemeinde[115].

---

[112] Vgl. *Stendahl*, Bible 34.
[113] Vgl. *Paulsen*, Einheit 94.
[114] Vgl. *Stendahl*, Bible 35.
[115] So prononciert *Thyen*, Studie 131–137.

VII

„Es ist gut für den Menschen, eine Frau nicht anzufassen"

Paulus und die Sexualität nach 1 Kor 7

Von Helmut Merklein, Bonn

1. 1 Kor 7 und der heutige Leser

Da der folgende Beitrag sich ausschließlich mit 1 Kor 7 befaßt, sei ihm um der leichteren Lesbarkeit willen eine Übersetzung dieses relativ umfangreichen Kapitels vorangestellt. Zur Rechtfertigung der dabei vorgenommenen Gliederung bzw. drucktechnischen Gestaltung muß auf die folgenden Sachausführungen (2) verwiesen werden.

1.1. Übersetzung von 1 Kor 7

1 *Bezüglich dessen, was Ihr geschrieben habt:*
  Es ist gut für den Menschen, eine Frau nicht anzufassen!
2 Wegen der Unzucht(ssünden) aber soll jeder seine Frau haben,
  und jede soll den eigenen Mann haben.
3 Der Frau (gegenüber) soll der Mann seine Verpflichtung erfüllen,
  ebenso aber auch die Frau dem Mann (gegenüber).
4 Die Frau verfügt nicht über den eigenen Leib, sondern der Mann;
  ebenso aber verfügt auch der Mann nicht über den eigenen Leib, sondern
  die Frau.
5 Entzieht euch nicht einander,
  außer etwa aus Übereinstimmung auf Zeit,
  um euch dem Gebet zu widmen und (dann) wieder zusammenzusein,
  damit euch der Satan nicht versuche wegen eurer Unenthaltsamkeit.
6 Dies aber sage ich als Zugeständnis, nicht als Befehl.
7 Ich möchte aber (vielmehr), daß alle Menschen so seien wie auch ich;
  aber jeder hat (s)ein eigenes Charisma von Gott,
  der eine so, der andere so.

8 Ich sage aber den Unverheirateten und den Witwen:
  Es ist gut für sie, wenn sie bleiben wie auch ich.

9 Wenn sie sich aber nicht enthalten können, sollen sie heiraten;
denn es ist besser zu heiraten als (vor Begierde) zu brennen.

10 Den Verheirateten aber gebiete nicht ich, sondern der Herr:
Eine Frau soll sich vom Mann nicht trennen

11 – wenn sie sich aber doch getrennt hat,
soll sie unverheiratet bleiben oder sich mit dem Mann versöhnen –
und ein Mann soll die Frau nicht wegschicken.

12 Den übrigen aber sage ich, nicht der Herr:
Wenn ein Bruder eine ungläubige Frau hat,
und diese ist einverstanden, mit ihm zusammenzuleben,
soll er sie nicht wegschicken.

13 Und wenn eine Frau einen ungläubigen Mann hat,
und dieser ist einverstanden, mit ihr zusammenzuleben,
soll sie den Mann nicht wegschicken.

14 Denn der ungläubige Mann ist durch die Frau geheiligt,
und die ungläubige Frau ist durch den Bruder geheiligt;
denn sonst wären eure Kinder unrein, nun aber sind sie heilig.

15 Wenn aber der Ungläubige sich trennt, soll er sich trennen.
Der Bruder oder die Schwester ist in solchen Fällen nicht gebunden;
zum Frieden hat euch Gott berufen.

16 Denn was weißt du, Frau, ob du den Mann retten wirst?
Oder was weißt du, Mann, ob du die Frau retten wirst?

17 Im übrigen: Wie jedem der Herr zugeteilt hat,
wie jeden Gott berufen hat, so soll er wandeln;
und so ordne ich in allen Gemeinden an.

18 Ist einer als Beschnittener berufen worden,
soll er sich nicht (eine Vorhaut) überziehen lassen.
Ist einer mit der Vorhaut berufen worden,
soll er sich nicht beschneiden lassen.

19 Die Beschneidung ist nichts, und die Vorhaut ist nichts,
sondern die Einhaltung der Gebote Gottes.

20 Jeder in der Berufung (Stand), in der er berufen worden ist,
in dieser soll er bleiben.

21 Bist du als Sklave berufen worden, soll dich das nicht bekümmern.
Wenn du aber auch frei werden kannst, um so lieber mache Gebrauch
(vom Sklavenstand? von der Freiheit?).

22 Denn der im Herrn berufene Sklave ist Freigelassener des Herrn;
ebenso ist der berufene Freie Sklave Christi.

23 Um teuren Preis seid ihr erkauft worden;
werdet nicht Sklaven von Menschen!

24 Worin jeder berufen worden ist, Brüder,
darin soll er bleiben vor Gott.

25 *Bezüglich der Jungfrauen* aber habe ich keinen Befehl des Herrn,
   (m)eine Meinung aber lege ich dar als einer, dem vom Herrn das Erbarmen zuteil wurde, vertrauenswürdig zu sein.
26 Ich meine also, daß dies gut ist wegen der bevorstehenden Not,
   daß es gut ist für den Menschen, so zu sein.
27 Bist du an eine Frau gebunden, suche keine Trennung;
   bist du frei von einer Frau, suche keine Frau.
28 Wenn du aber doch heiratest, sündigst du nicht;
   und wenn die Jungfrau heiratet, sündigt sie nicht.
   Aber solche werden Bedrängnis für das Fleisch haben,
   ich aber will euch schonen (sie euch ersparen).

29 Dies aber sage ich, Brüder: Die Zeit ist zusammengedrängt;
   also sollen die, die Frauen haben, (so) sein, als hätten sie keine,
30 und die, die weinen, als weinten sie nicht,
   und die, die sich freuen, als freuten sie sich nicht,
   und die, die kaufen, als behielten sie (es) nicht,
31 und die, die von der Welt Gebrauch machen, als gebrauchten sie (sie)
   nicht.
   Denn die Gestalt dieser Welt vergeht.

32 Ich möchte aber, daß ihr sorglos seid.
   Der Unverheiratete sorgt sich um die Dinge des Herrn,
   wie er dem Herrn gefalle.
33 Der Verheiratete aber sorgt sich um die Dinge der Welt,
   wie er der Frau gefalle,
34 und er ist geteilt.
   Und die unverheiratete Frau und die Jungfrau sorgt sich um die Dinge
   des Herrn,
   daß sie heilig sei an Leib und Geist.
   Die Verheiratete aber sorgt sich um die Dinge der Welt,
   wie sie dem Mann gefalle.

35 Dies aber sage ich zu eurem Nutzen,
   nicht um euch eine Schlinge überzuwerfen,
   sondern zu ungehinderter Anständigkeit und Beständigkeit für den
   Herrn.

36 Wenn aber einer sich unanständig gegen s e i n e J u n g f r a u zu verhalten
   meint,
   wenn er (oder: sie) überreif ist und es so geschehen muß,
   soll er tun, was er möchte, er sündigt nicht; sie sollen heiraten.
37 Wer aber in seinem Herzen feststeht und keine Not hat,
   sondern Macht hat über seinen eigenen Willen,
   und dies im eigenen Herzen beschlossen hat, seine Jungfrau zu
   bewahren,
   tut wohl.

38 Also: wer seine Jungfrau (ver)heiratet, tut wohl,
und wer (sie) nicht (ver)heiratet, tut besser.

39 Eine Frau ist gebunden, solange ihr Mann lebt.
Wenn aber der Mann entschläft, ist sie frei, zu heiraten, wen sie will;
nur (geschehe es) im Herrn.
40 Seliger aber ist sie, wenn sie so bleibt, nach meiner Meinung;
auch ich glaube aber, den Geist Gottes zu haben.

1.2. Probleme heutiger Leser

Eine „objektive" Lektüre von 1 Kor 7 dürfte dem modernen Leser
nicht leichtfallen. Der Text nötigt zum Engagement, er reizt zum Widerspruch, ja zum Widerstand. Denn etliches von dem, was Paulus
da schreibt, scheint mit heutiger Lebensauffassung und modernen
anthropologischen und psychologischen Erkenntnissen nicht über-
einzustimmen. Daß die Ehe zur Vermeidung von Unzucht (διὰ δὲ
τὰς πορνείας, V. 2) und der eheliche Verkehr aus Gründen der Unenthaltsamkeit (διὰ τὴν ἀκρασίαν ὑμῶν V. 5) zugestanden werden,
ist aus heutiger Sicht zumindest eine unzulängliche Würdigung der
Ehe. Von Liebe, Partnerschaft und gegenseitiger menschlicher Erfüllung ist nicht die Rede. Woher rührt diese einseitige Qualifizie-
rung der Ehe? Ist die Ehe für Paulus wirklich nur remedium concupiscentiae? Hat Paulus vielleicht gar ein gebrochenes Verhältnis zur
Sexualität? Immerhin wünscht er, daß alle Menschen so seien bzw.
so bleiben wie er (vgl. V. 7 f.25 f.40), d. h. ehelos[1].

Steckt hinter all dem letztlich etwa eine Abwertung der Frau[2], wie
man sie häufig bei Männern beobachten kann, die sich skeptisch
oder kämpferisch gegen Ehe und Sexualität wenden? Ist es nicht bezeichnend, daß gleichsam als Überschrift über dem ganzen Kapitel

---

[1] Die Meinung, daß Paulus verheiratet gewesen und dann Witwer geworden sei,
die namentlich von *J. Jeremias*, War Paulus Witwer?, in: ZNW 25 (1926)
310–312; *ders.*, Nochmals: War Paulus Witwer?, in: ZNW 28 (1929) 321–323, vorgetragen wurde, wird heute nur mehr selten vertreten.
[2] Vgl. etwa *G. Delling*, Paulus Stellung zu Frau und Ehe (BWANT 4. Ser., H. 5)
(Stuttgart 1931) 154: „Paulus ist erfüllt von einer tiefen Mißachtung der natürlichen Seite der Ehe, die sich nur mit Rücksicht auf die Brüder zu einer Geringschätzung dieser Grundlage herabmindert. Das Weib ist für ihn vorzüglich Trägerin des Geschlechtlichen, wie ja auch seine erste Ursache. Deshalb ist es als solche von der gleichen Geringschätzung, ja Mißachtung betroffen."

der Satz steht: „Es ist gut für den Menschen, eine Frau nicht anzufassen" (V. 1 b)?[3] Zumindest eine Frau wird diesen Satz, wenn „man" – hier besser: „frau" – ihn objektiv und für sich betrachtet, als diskriminierend verstehen müssen. Allerdings ist V. 1 b kein für sich bestehender Satz, sondern eingebettet in einen literarischen und situativen Kontext, den es zu beachten bzw. zu erkennen gilt, zumal sich je nach Beurteilung dieses Satzes die inhaltliche Wertung mancher der nachfolgenden Aussagen nicht unerheblich verschiebt.

2. Zur Pragmatik von 1 Kor 7

2.1. Zum Verständnis von V. 1 b

Zunächst ist es semantisch nicht eindeutig, ob γυνή die Ehefrau im strikten Sinn oder die Frau im allgemeinen Sinn (als ehefähiges weibliches Wesen) meint. Im ersten Fall würde V. 1 b speziell auf Enthaltsamkeit in der Ehe abzielen, im zweiten Fall den Verzicht auf Geschlechtsverkehr überhaupt fordern. Das eigentliche Problem ist jedoch pragmatischer Art, nämlich ob V. 1 b als Äußerung des Paulus oder als Äußerung der Korinther zu verstehen ist[4]. Im ersten Fall müßte man V. 1 so paraphrasieren:

Bezüglich dessen, was ihr geschrieben habt, (dazu meine ich:) „Es ist gut für den Menschen, eine Frau nicht anzufassen!"

V. 1 b wäre dann der allgemeine *Grundsatz,* von dem her Paulus die folgenden Ausführungen in 1 Kor 7 deduziert. Allerdings käme in

---

[3] *K. Niederwimmer,* Askese und Mysterium. Über Ehe, Ehescheidung und Eheverzicht in den Anfängen des christlichen Glaubens (FRLANT 113) (Göttingen 1975) 85, bemerkt zu V. 1 b, den er für eine paulinische Äußerung hält: „Der Satz scheint bestimmt zu sein von der Ritual-Angst vor der dämonischen Mächtigkeit des Sexuellen und speziell der Frau; sie ist negativ tabuisiert."

[4] Die Übersetzungen und Kommentare entscheiden sich überwiegend für eine Äußerung des Paulus. Für eine Äußerung der Korinther sprechen sich u. a. aus die Übersetzung von *O. Karrer,* Neues Testament (München 1967), und die neue *Einheitsübersetzung* der Heiligen Schrift: Das Neue Testament (Stuttgart 1979), sowie die Kommentare von *O. Holtzmann* (Das Neue Testament nach dem Stuttgarter griechischen Text übersetzt und erklärt, Bd. 2 [Stuttgart 1926]) und *C. K. Barrett* (A Commentary on the First Epistle to the Corinthians [BNTC] [London [2]1971]); vgl. auch *A. Robertson – A. Plummer,* A Critical and Exegetical Commentary on the First Epistle of St. Paul to the Corinthians (ICC) (Edinburgh [2]1914). Weitere Autoren s. u. Anm. 7.

diesem Fall die Bedeutung γυνή = „Ehefrau" im exklusiven Sinn kaum in Frage, da der Grundsatz dann nicht für die Ausführungen über die Unverheirateten und Jungfrauen passen würde; sie stünde zudem in eklatantem Widerspruch zu den relativ ausführlichen Mahnungen an die Eheleute, sich einander nicht zu entziehen (V. 2–5).

Versteht man aber V. 1 b als Äußerung der (oder bestimmter) Korinther, so wäre folgendermaßen zu paraphrasieren:

Bezüglich dessen, was ihr geschrieben habt: „Es ist gut (oder, indirekt konstruiert, es sei gut) für den Menschen, eine Frau nicht anzufassen!", (dazu meine ich:) Wegen der Unzucht aber soll ...

In diesem Fall ist für γυνή sowohl die Bedeutung „Frau" wie auch „Ehefrau" denkbar; beides muß sich auch keineswegs ausschließen. Der Mutterboden für eine derartige korinthische Meinung oder Parole könnte der auch sonst aus 1 Kor zu erschließende Enthusiasmus gewesen sein. Dabei ist es durchaus denkbar, daß dieser Enthusiasmus sowohl zu sexuellem Libertinismus (vgl. 1 Kor 5; 6, 12–20) wie auch zum Postulat sexueller Aszese geführt hat, wenn man mit unterschiedlichen Strömungen in der Gemeinde rechnet[5]. Hinter V.1 b müßten dann Leute gestanden haben, die aus der (wohl allgemeineren korinthischen) Überzeugung, bereits an der eschatologischen Herrlichkeit Anteil zu haben, den (für ihre Gruppe) speziellen Schluß gezogen hatten, man solle mit so irdischen Dingen wie Sexualität nichts mehr zu tun haben; die Enthaltsamkeit war für sie geradezu Zeichen der bereits zuteilgewordenen Herrlichkeit[6].

Philologisch sind beide Verständnisse möglich, doch sprechen für das zweite m. E. die besseren Argumente[7]. Nimmt man nämlich V.

---

[5] Daß sich Paulus in 1 Kor 7, 1–7 gegen dieselbe Front wie in 1 Kor 6, 12–20 richtet (so: *Chr. Maurer,* Ehe und Unzucht nach 1. Korinther 6, 12 – 7, 7, in: WuD NF 6 [1959] 159–169; *O. Merk,* Handeln aus Glauben. Die Motivierungen der paulinischen Ethik [MThSt 5] [Marburg 1968] 102 f), ist unwahrscheinlich.

[6] Gegen die Existenz einer bestimmten Gruppe, welche die Parole von V. 1 b ausgegeben hat, läßt sich nicht einwenden, daß sich Paulus in 1 Kor 7 „an verschiedene ‚Stände' der *Gesamt*gemeinde" wende (*K. Niederwimmer,* Zur Analyse der asketischen Motivation in 1 Kor 7, in: ThLZ 99 [1974] 241–248, hier 243; ders., Askese [Anm. 3] 81 f). Letzteres ist gerade deswegen erforderlich, weil die Parole zu einer Verunsicherung der verschiedenen Stände und damit der Gesamtgemeinde geführt hat.

[7] Vgl. dazu: *Ph.-H. Menoud,* Mariage et Célibat selon saint Paul, in: RThPh

1 b als paulinischen Grundsatz, so wäre er zumindest recht ungeschickt formuliert, da er Paulus so fort zwingt, sich in V. 2 vor einem Mißverständnis zu schützen, d. h. zu betonen, daß dieser Grundsatz in
bezug auf die Ehe nicht gilt. Es wäre zudem Paulus ein leichtes gewesen, diesen Grundsatz seinem Anliegen entsprechender zu formulieren, etwa in Anlehnung an später tatsächlich gebrauchte Formulierungen (vgl. V. 7. 8): „Es ist gut für den Menschen, so zu sein (bleiben) wie ich." Im übrigen ist unter der Prämisse, daß V. 1 b
paulinischer Grundsatz ist, die folgende Argumentation in V. 2–5
recht merkwürdig. Um zum Ausdruck zu bringen, daß Ehe und ehelicher Verkehr als Konzession gegenüber diesem Grundsatz statthaft
sind, hätte V. 2 genügt. Die Anweisung in V. 3 mit der massiven Begründung in V. 4, die das Recht des Partners auf den Körper des anderen herausstellt, und die Aufforderung in V. 5, sich einander nicht
zu entziehen, lassen eher darauf schließen, daß V. 2–5 ein aktuelles
Problem im Auge haben, auf das Paulus Antwort geben will, und
nicht, daß die Verse eine in der Argumentation notwendige Konzession zum Grundsatz in V. 1 b darstellen. Eine passende aktuelle Problematik für V. 2–5 ergäbe sich aber, wenn man V. 1 b als Parole der
Korinther verstehen dürfte.

Damit ist eine gewisse Vorentscheidung getroffen, die sich jedoch
erst noch bewähren muß. Denn nur, wenn das vorgeschlagene Verständnis von V. 1 b gestattet, 1 Kor 7 insgesamt als semantisch und

---

(3. Ser.) 1 (1951) 21–34, hier 27 Anm. 1; *J.-J. von Allmen*, Maris et femmes d'après
saint Paul (CTh 29) (Neuchâtel–Paris 1951) 11; *J. Jeremias*, Zur Gedankenführung in den paulinischen Briefen, in: *ders., Abba. Studien zur neutestamentlichen Theologie und Zeitgeschichte (Göttingen 1966) 269–276, hier 273; *X. Léon-
Dufour*, Mariage et virginité selon saint Paul, in: Christus 11 (1964) 179–194, hier
181; *J. C. Hurd*, The Origin of 1 Corinthians (London 1965) 158–163 (vgl. dort
S. 68 auch die Tabelle über die Autoren, die V. 1 b als Zitat verstehen); *C. H. Gib-
lin*, 1 Corinthians 7 – A Negative Theology of Marriage and Celibacy?, in: Bi Tod
41 (1969) 2839–2855, hier 2841–2847 (will auch noch V. 2 zum Zitat rechnen);
H. Greeven, Ehe nach dem Neuen Testament, in: *G. Krems – R. Mumm* (Hrsg.),
Theologie der Ehe (Regensburg–Göttingen 1969) 37–79, hier 73; *R. Schnackenburg*, Die Ehe nach dem Neuen Testament, in: *ders., Schriften zum Neuen Testament (München 1971) 414–434, hier 423; *J. H. A. van Tilborg*, Exegetische Bemerkungen zu den wichtigsten Ehetexten aus dem Neuen Testament, in: *P. J. M.
Huizing* (Hrsg.), Für eine neue kirchliche Eheordnung. Ein Alternativentwurf
(Düsseldorf 1975) 9–25, hier 21. Besonders hervorzuheben ist der ausgezeichnete
Aufsatz von *W. Schrage*, Zur Frontstellung der paulinischen Ehebewertung in
1 Kor 7,1–7, in: ZNW 67 (1976) 214–234.

pragmatisch kohärenten Text zu lesen, kann es aufrechterhalten werden. Die Probe aufs Exempel würde eine eingehende Analyse des gesamten Kapitels erfordern, was hier schon aus Raumgründen nicht geschehen kann. So sei wenigstens in kursorischer Weise und vorwiegend unter pragmatischer Rücksicht erläutert, daß 1 Kor 7 unter der gemachten Voraussetzung einen verblüffend kohärenten Text darstellt[8].

2.2. Eine erste grobe Gliederung von 1 Kor 7

Zunächst läßt sich unter dieser Voraussetzung die durch das zweimalige περί ("bezüglich") signalisierte (V. 1.25) grobe Gliederung von 1 Kor 7 sehr gut erklären. V. 1 gibt das allgemeine Thema bzw. die Problematik an, wie sie sich aus der korinthischen Parole ergibt. Einige Korinther hatten aus der christlichen Berufung die Konsequenz sexueller Enthaltsamkeit gezogen. Ihre besondere Brisanz erhält diese These durch die Anwendung auf die Ehe. Auf dieses Problem geht Paulus in V. 2–16 (.17–25) ein und behandelt unter verschiedenen Aspekten das Thema „christliche Berufung und Ehe". Da die korinthische Parole in letzter Konsequenz aber jedwede geschlechtliche Betätigung verurteilte, d. h. also auch die Heirat bzw. Verheiratung der noch Unverheirateten, geht Paulus in einem zweiten Anlauf auch darauf ein. Wahrscheinlich verweist der Ausdruck „bezüglich der Jungfrauen" (V. 25) sogar auf eine direkte Anfrage der Korinther, die infolge der durch die Parole ausgelösten Tendenzen auch dieses Spezialproblem erörtert haben wollten (s. u. 2.7.).

2.3. V. 2–5

V. 2 a ist eine erste Erwiderung des Paulus auf die Parole V. 1 b. Paulus betont, daß sie im Bereich der Ehe nicht gilt. Hier soll jeder seine eigene Frau (= Ehefrau) haben! „Haben" ist nicht auf das Eingehen der Ehe (Heiraten) zu beziehen. Dies würde in eklatantem Widerspruch zu der in V. 7 a geäußerten Meinung des Paulus stehen.

---

[8] Die Feststellung *Niederwimmers*, Askese (Anm. 3) 89, daß 1 Kor 7 das Resultat widerspruchsvoller Motive sei, ist m. E. zu einem gut Teil darin begründet, daß Niederwimmer V. 1 b als asketischen Grundsatz des Paulus wertet (vgl. aaO. 83–88).

„Haben" ist antithetische Substitution von „nicht anfassen" (V. 1 b) und tendiert daher zur Bedeutung „geschlechtlichen Umgang haben" (vgl. 1 Kor 5,1 b). Dies wird durch V. 3 a bestätigt. V. 4 bringt die Begründung: In der Ehe wird das Verfügungsrecht über den eigenen Körper dem Partner übertragen. Bemerkenswert ist, daß V. 2–4 streng antithetisch (Opposition: Mann versus Frau) gebaut sind und damit Mann und Frau gleiche sexuelle Pflichten und Rechte einräumen. Aufgrund dieser Wechselseitigkeit können dann die allgemeinen Grundsätze der V. 2 f (Imp. 3. Pers.) direkt in V. 5 auf die betroffenen Eheleute angewendet werden (Imp. 2. Pers.): „Entzieht euch nicht einander!" (V. 5 a). Die Ausnahme von dieser Regel formuliert Paulus – mit einer dreifachen Bedingung – sehr vorsichtig, um dann gleich wieder zum Sachanliegen von V. 5 a zurückzukehren: Nach einer bestimmten Zeit der Enthaltung sollen die Eheleute wieder zusammensein (um geschlechtlichen Umgang zu haben). Paulus widerspricht damit direkt der korinthischen Parole in ihrer Applikation auf den ehelichen Verkehr. Daß Paulus dieses Problem gleich zu Beginn seiner Ausführungen behandelt, läßt darauf schließen, daß die Parole gerade in dieser Applikation erhebliche Unsicherheit in Korinth auslöste. Paulus ist der Parole gegenüber nüchtern: Zur Ehe gehört geschlechtlicher Umgang! Auf das mit den Begründungen V. 2.5 (wegen der Unzucht bzw. Unenthaltsamkeit) gestellte Sachproblem des paulinischen Eheverständnisses (remedium concupiscentiae?) ist später einzugehen.

2.4. V. 6 f

Durch das anaphorische *„dies* aber sage ich" geben sich die Verse als metasprachliche Äußerung, d. h. als Klarstellung zu V. 2–5, zu erkennen. „Dies" ist nicht exklusiv auf die vorangehenden Forderungen (Imperative) zu beziehen. Denn dann würde Paulus den Geschlechtsverkehr in der Ehe doch nur als Zugeständnis betrachten und damit grundsätzlich der korinthischen Applikation der Parole zustimmen, daß auch in der Ehe Enthaltsamkeit eigentlich das Beste wäre. „Dies" bezieht sich vielmehr auf die Ausführungen von V. 2–5 *insgesamt*[9]. Das relativ klare Votum des Paulus für den Geschlechts-

[9] *Schrage,* Frontstellung (Anm. 7) 232 f, bezieht „τοῦτο auf die zeitweilige Ent-

verkehr in der Ehe und der generalisierende Charakter seiner Ausführungen (besonders in V. 2: vgl. „jeder/jede") könnten zu dem
Mißverständnis führen, daß die Ehe überhaupt – und sei es wegen
der Gefahr der Unzucht – ein „Befehl" (ἐπιταγή), d. h. ein christliches Gebot sei. Demgegenüber stellt Paulus in V. 6 klar, daß sein
Plädoyer für die eheliche Geschlechtsgemeinschaft nicht zum Heiraten verpflichten will, sondern unter dieser Rücksicht als „Zugeständnis" zu betrachten ist.

Man könnte auch sagen, daß durch V. 6 insbesondere die Aussage von V. 2 –
„jeder soll seine eigene Frau *haben*" – von einer Monosemierung im Sinne
des Eingehens der *Ehe* („jeder soll heiraten und so seine eigene Frau haben") bewahrt werden soll.

Bestätigt wird diese Auslegung durch V. 7 a, wo Paulus als seinen eigentlichen Wunsch gegenüberstellt, daß alle so seien wie er, d. h.
ehelos (vgl. V. 8 b). Diese Gegenüberstellung ist nur sinnvoll, wenn
das in V. 6 auszuräumende Mißverständnis sich auf die Ehe als solche bezogen hat. Mit V. 7 a hat Paulus allerdings eine Position einge-
nommen, die man wieder leicht im prinzipiellen Sinne der korinthischen Parole mißdeuten könnte. Daraus ergibt sich die Notwendigkeit von V. 7 b: Jeder hat sein (ihm) eigenes Charisma[10].

2.5. V. 8–16

Durch den Verweis auf seine Ehelosigkeit (V. 7 a) und das alternative „der eine so, der andere so" (V. 7 c) ergibt sich für Paulus die
Möglichkeit, von der Problematik, die sich aus der Anwendung der
Parole auf das Verhalten in der Ehe ergab, überzuleiten zu der Problematik, die sich in Applikation der Parole auf die Unverheirateten
stellt. Tatsächlich spricht denn auch V. 8 von den Unverheirateten
und Witwen. Doch zeigt V. 9, daß es sich hier nur um ein Zwischen-
thema handelt, das letztlich im Hinblick auf die dennoch beste-

---

haltsamkeit vom ehelichen Geschlechtsverkehr" (233); so auch: *H. Baltensweiler*,
Die Ehe im Neuen Testament. Exegetische Untersuchung über Ehe, Ehelosigkeit
und Ehescheidung (AThANT 52) (Zürich–Stuttgart 1967) 161–163.
[10] Umstritten ist, ob V. 7 b auch die Ehe als Charisma qualifiziert ist; doch ist dies
eher unwahrscheinlich: vgl. *H. Lietzmann – W. G. Kümmel*, An die Korinther I.II
(HNT 9) (Tübingen ⁴1949) 30; *H. Conzelmann*, Der erste Brief an die Korinther
(KEK V) (Göttingen 1969) 143; *Schrage*, aaO. 233 f.

hende Möglichkeit, eine Ehe einzugehen, erörtert wird. Unter dieser Rücksicht gehören die Verse 8f mit den Versen 10f.12–16 zusammen. Während die Verse 2–5 (.6f) die Frage des Geschlechtsverkehrs in der Ehe behandelten, sprechen die Verse 8–16 von der *Ehe als Stand*. Diese Wendung der Argumentation könnte pragmatisch dadurch bedingt sein, daß radikale Vertreter der Parole von V. 1b nicht nur den Geschlechtsverkehr in der Ehe, sondern überhaupt den Stand der Ehe als christliche Möglichkeit in Frage stellten. Doch könnte es sich auch um eine Schlußfolgerung des Paulus handeln, mit der er solche zu befürchtenden Konsequenzen ausschließen wollte. In jedem Fall bekommt – setzt man V. 1b als korinthische Parole voraus – die Argumentation in V. 8–16 einen sehr sinnvollen, ja geradezu notwendigen Charakter. Was den Stand der Ehe betrifft, diskutiert nun Paulus drei Möglichkeiten:

V. 8f:
Bezüglich derer, die noch nicht oder nicht mehr im Stand der Ehe leben, teilt Paulus in bestimmter Hinsicht den Standpunkt der korinthischen Parole. Er greift sogar das „es ist gut" (καλόν) der Parole auf. Allerdings weist bereits die Tatsache, daß er das sexuell fixierte „nicht anfassen" der Parole nicht übernimmt und durch „wenn sie bleiben wie ich" ersetzt, darauf hin, daß der Standpunkt des Paulus kaum durch eine Disqualifizierung der Sexualität motiviert sein kann. Dies unterstreicht im übrigen V. 9. Paulus will seine Ausführungen in V. 8 nicht als Parole oder gar als Prinzip verstanden wissen. Ehelosigkeit erfordert das Charisma der Enthaltsamkeit (vgl. V. 7b). Wo dies nicht gegeben ist, ist der Stand der Ehe die bessere christliche Möglichkeit. So sehr also Paulus in der Bevorzugung der Ehelosigkeit mit der Parole von V. 1b übereinstimmt (V. 8), so widerspricht er jedoch in V. 9 jedem (tatsächlichen oder möglichen) Versuch, mit ihr den Stand der Ehe für die Unverheirateten als christlich unakzeptabel, d.h. als mit der christlichen Berufung nicht vereinbar, zu disqualifizieren.

V. 10f:
Dasselbe Anliegen, also Abwehr des Mißverständnisses, daß der Stand der Ehe mit christlicher Berufung nicht vereinbar sei, steht auch hinter V. 10f. Paulus betont: Im Falle, daß Christen im Stand

der Ehe leben, ist dies nicht nur mit christlicher Berufung vereinbar, sondern es ist von ihr her sogar geboten, am Stand der Ehe festzuhalten. Denn christliche Berufung bindet an das Gebot des Herrn. Daß Paulus in der Parenthese V. 11ab einen Sonderfall anführt, dürfte ebenfalls pragmatisch bedingt sein. Denn gerade in dem Fall, daß eine (christliche) Frau sich von ihrem Mann getrennt hat (wahrscheinlich vor ihrer Bekehrung)[11], könnte man möglicherweise sogar auf das christliche Verbot der Wiederheirat (vgl. Mk 10,11f) zur Stützung einer sexualitätsfeindlichen Auslegung der Parole von V. 1b verweisen. Paulus stimmt dem Verbot der Wiederheirat zu, legt es aber nicht negativ aus, sondern als Möglichkeit der Versöhnung mit dem Ehepartner[12], so daß es auch hier für den verheirateten Christen letztlich beim grundsätzlichen Gebot bleibt, den Stand der Ehe aufrechtzuerhalten.

V. 12–16:

Daß Paulus in V. 12–16 auf die Mischehen (zwischen christlichen und heidnischen Partnern) eingeht, dürfte wieder in besonderer Weise bestätigen, daß V. 1b als korinthische Parole gelesen werden muß. Denn unter dieser Voraussetzung mußte die Mischehe – noch mehr als die Ehen unter Christen – in das Kreuzfeuer der rigoros-aszetischen Kritik gelangen, zumal man hier – wie V. 14ab nahezulegen scheint – noch geltend machen konnte, daß der Christ durch solche Verbindung verunreinigt würde[13]. Paulus plädiert auch hier im Sinne des Herrenwortes für die Aufrechterhaltung der Ehe. Allerdings versteht er das Herrenwort nicht als Gesetz. Denn falls der ungläubige Partner die Ehe nicht fortführen will, „soll er sich trennen"

---

[11] *R. Pesch,* Paulinische „Kasuistik". Zum Verständnis von 1 Kor 7,10–11, in: *L. Alvarez Verdes – E. J. Alonso Hernandez* (Hrsg.), Homenaje a Juan Prado. Miscelanea de estudios biblicos et hebraicos (Madrid 1975) 433–442; *ders.,* Freie Treue. Die Christen und die Ehescheidung (Freiburg i. Br. 1971) 61–63.

[12] Vgl. *H. Merklein,* Die Gottesherrschaft als Handlungsprinzip. Untersuchung zur Ethik Jesu (fzb 34) (Würzburg ²1981) 288.

[13] Zu V. 14c siehe *J. Blinzler,* Zur Auslegung von 1 Kor 7,14, in: *ders. – u.a.* (Hrsg.), Neutestamentliche Aufsätze. FS J. Schmid (Regensburg 1963) 23–41. Vgl. auch: *G. Delling,* Nun aber sind sie heilig, in: *ders.,* Studien zum Neuen Testament und zum hellenistischen Judentum. Gesammelte Aufsätze 1950–1968 (Göttingen 1970) 257–269; *ders.,* Lexikalisches zu τέκνον. Ein Nachtrag zur Exegese von 1. Kor. 7,14, in: ebd. 270–280; *ders.,* Zur Exegese von 1. Kor. 7,14, in: ebd. 281–287.

(V. 15 a). Für diesen bestimmten Fall teilt also Paulus faktisch den Standpunkt einer möglichen oder tatsächlichen Folgerung aus der Parole. Doch ist seine Begründung eine andere. Er plädiert für Trennung, nicht weil er in der (Misch-)Ehe eine Quelle der Verunreinigung sieht, sondern weil der Christ durch das Verhalten des Ungläubigen nicht geknechtet werden darf (V. 15 b). Den Einwand, den Paulus in V. 16 sich selbst macht, lehnt er als zu hypothetisch ab[14].

2.6. V. 17–24

Die bisherige Stellungnahme des Paulus, d. h. sein Plädoyer für den ehelichen Verkehr, sein Votum für die Aufrechterhaltung bereits eingegangener Ehen, aber auch die angedeutete Favorisierung des Unverheiratet-Bleibens lassen sich in dem Grundsatz zusammenfassen, daß jeder in dem Stand bleiben soll, in dem er berufen wurde. Dieser allgemeine Grundsatz wird in den Versen 17.20.24 – jeweils leicht variiert – ausdrücklich genannt. Er bestätigt, daß die korinthische Parole als (falsche) Folgerung aus der christlichen Berufung verstanden werden muß, und stellt die eigentliche Antithese des Paulus zur Parole dar. Begründet und exemplifiziert wird der Grundsatz in den Versen 18 f. 21–23. Die konkrete Wahl der Exempel könnte zunächst als Abschweifung empfunden werden. Doch ist gerade die scheinbare Abschweifung eine weitere Bestätigung der hier vertretenen Deutung von V. 1 b. Es wurde schon öfter darauf hingewiesen, daß Paulus hier der Topik einer bestimmten urchristlichen Tradition verpflichtet ist, die das eschatologische Heil in Christus als die Überwindung ethnischer (Jude – Heide), sozialer (Sklave – Freier) und sexueller (Mann – Frau) Unterscheidungen herausstellte (Gal 3,28; vgl. 1 Kor 12,13; Kol 3,11)[15]. Es ist anzunehmen, daß auch den Korinthern diese Tradition bekannt war (vgl. neben 1 Kor 7,17–24 auch

[14] Anders: *J. Jeremias*, Die missionarische Aufgabe in der Mischehe (1. Kor. 7,16), in: Abba (Anm. 7) 292–298; er bezieht „Frieden" V. 15 c auf die missionarische Aufgabe und übersetzt V. 16: „*Vielleicht* nämlich kannst du, Ehefrau, den Mann retten..." (aaO. 296). Zur Auseinandersetzung mit Jeremias vgl. *S. Kubo*, I Corinthians VII.16: Optimistic or Pessimistic?, in: NTS 24 (1978) 539–544.
[15] Vgl. dazu: *H. Thyen*, „... nicht mehr männlich und weiblich ...". Eine Studie zu Galater 3,28, in: *F. Crüsemann – H. Thyen*, Als Mann und Frau geschaffen. Exegetische Studien zur Rolle der Frau (Gelnhausen–Berlin–Stein/Mfr. 1978) 107–197, bes. 138–145; *H. Paulsen*, Einheit und Freiheit der Söhne Gottes – Gal

12, 13). Man kann sogar vermuten, daß hinter der Parole von V. 1 b eine einseitige Auslegung dieser Tradition steht[16]. Einige hatten die Belanglosigkeit sexueller Differenzen als Programm ausgewertet: Wer in Christus ist, hat das Mann- bzw. Frau-Sein hinter sich zu lassen[17], was dann konkret auf die Forderung einer Sexualaszese im Sinne von V. 1 b hinausläuft[18]. Ob die Korinther aus der Tradition eine analoge Programmatik in bezug auf ethnische und soziale Differenzen entwickelt haben, läßt sich nicht sicher entscheiden. Im positiven Falle würde Paulus in V. 18 f. 21–23 eine weitere falsche Auslegung angreifen, im negativen Falle, der m. E. doch wahrscheinlicher ist, würde Paulus auf Punkte verweisen, in denen er mit den Korinthern übereinstimmt, um ihnen so die Unrichtigkeit ihrer Folgerung in bezug auf die Sexualität zu demonstrieren. In jedem Fall

---

3, 26–29, in: ZNW 71 (1980) 74–95 (dort S. 77 f Anm. 16 weitere Autoren); sowie den Beitrag von *G. Dautzenberg* (bes. 2.2.3.) in diesem Band. – Gegen Paulsen ist jedoch zu betonen, daß Gal 3, 28 b noch nicht den „Gedanken des σῶμα Χριστοῦ" (aaO. 86) enthält; er ergibt sich erst durch die Interpretation des Paulus, mit der er in 1 Kor 12, 12 f(.27) eine einseitige Auslegung des In-Christus-Seins von seiten bestimmter Korinther (im Sinne einer Konformität mit Christus, die ihren adäquaten Ausdruck in pneumatischer Ekstase findet und damit letztlich auf Uniformität hinausläuft) korrigiert.

[16] Schon *Thyen,* aaO. 157, stellte zu Recht fest: „das gesamte siebte Kapitel des ersten Korintherbriefes ist die paulinische *Auslegung* von Gal 3, 28 in der praktischen Absicht, das gestörte Verhältnis von Männern und Frauen in Korinth so zu ordnen, wie Paulus jene Maxime verstanden wissen will." Allerdings kann man in bezug auf 1 Kor 7, 1 b m. E. nicht einfach sagen, daß Paulus „in dem asketischen Grundsatz ... mit den Briefschreibern aus Korinth überein(stimmt)" (aaO. 174). Dies widerspricht der differenzierenden Stellungnahme des Paulus; als Grundsatz kann Paulus 1 Kor 7, 1 b gerade nicht anerkennen! Begreift man jedoch 1 Kor 7, 1 b als korinthische Parole, so wird einerseits die differenzierende Argumentation des Paulus verständlich, andererseits wird auch das konkrete korinthische Problem deutlich. „Das gestörte Verhältnis von Männern und Frauen in Korinth" (um mit Thyen zu sprechen) ist selbst in der (korinthischen) Interpretation von Gal 3, 28 begründet.

[17] Möglicherweise hat die Problematik von 1 Kor 11, 2–16 einen ähnlichen Ansatz. Man müßte dann annehmen, daß einige Frauen die eschatologische Belanglosigkeit der geschlechtlichen Differenz (Gal 3, 28) im Sinne einer überwundenen Schöpfungsordnung deuteten und dies gerade beim gottesdienstlichen Prophezeien dokumentieren wollten.

[18] Wenn diese Sicht richtig ist, ist die Annahme gnostischen Einflusses zur Erklärung der korinthischen These (so: *Schrage,* Frontstellung [Anm. 7] 220–222) nicht unbedingt nötig. Die Parole kann als enthusiastische Interpretation des christlichen Grundsatzes von Gal 3, 28 verstanden werden, was andererseits nicht ausschließen muß, daß ein bestimmtes (gnostisches?) Milieu diese Interpretation gefördert haben könnte.

erklärt sich so die scheinbare Abschweifung in V. 18 f. 21–23 als pragmatisch bedingte Logik.

Auf die exegetische Einzelproblematik der Verse 18 f. 21–23 (besonders V. 21 b) kann hier nicht eingegangen werden[19]. Inhaltlich erläutert Paulus, was christliche Freiheit ist. Der ethnische Stand (V. 18) – und das gilt analog (vgl. jedoch unten unter 3.3) auch für den sozialen bzw. sexuellen (Ehe oder Ehelosigkeit) – ist für das Heil belanglos, hier ist allein entscheidend das Halten der Gebote (V. 19; vgl. V. 10 f). Ansonsten ist der Christ frei und nicht verpflichtet, seinen bei der Berufung innegehabten Stand zu ändern. Wer z. B. seine christliche Freiheit von der Faktizität sozialer Freiheit (analog: von der sexuellen „Freiheit" im Sinne der Parole!) abhängig macht, verkennt, daß christliche Freiheit sich allein in der Freiheit schenkenden Knechtschaft Christi gründet (V. 22). Wer einer anderen Interpretation von Freiheit folgt, begibt sich in die Knechtschaft von Menschen (V. 23). Implizit fällt darunter auch die von einigen Korinthern postulierte Praxis, die das Heil von Sexualaszese abhängig machen will.

2.7. V. 25–28.39 f

Dieser Abschnitt kann relativ kurz, d. h. ausschließlich im Blick auf die durch die Parole V. 1 b bedingte Pragmatik, behandelt werden. Die eigentlich theologisch-argumentativen Passagen (bes. V. 29–31.32–35) sind ohnehin im zweiten Teil dieser Ausführungen noch zu behandeln.

---

[19] Umstritten ist vor allem, ob μᾶλλον χρῆσαι (V. 21 bβ) die Möglichkeit, doch Sklave zu bleiben (vgl. V. 21 a), oder die Möglichkeit, freizukommen (V. 21 bα), nahelegen will. Von der Semantik des Textes her sind beide Verständnisse möglich. Im ersten Fall würde Paulus durch V. 21 b den Grundsatz des Bleibens unterstreichen (so z. B.: *D. Lührmann,* Wo man nicht mehr Sklave oder Freier ist. Überlegungen zur Struktur frühchristlicher Gemeinden, in: WuD NF 13 [1975] 53–83, hier 62). Aus sprachlichen, grammatischen und sachlichen Erwägungen (ein Sklave hatte gar nicht die Möglichkeit, die Freilassung zurückzuweisen, wenn sein Herr diese beschlossen hatte! Vgl. dazu: *S. S. Bartchy,* ΜΑΛΛΟΝ ΧΡΗΣΑΙ: First-Century Slavery and the Interpretation of 1 Corinthians 7:21 [SBLDS 11] [Missoula/Montana 1973] 97 f.119) dürfte jedoch die zweite Möglichkeit zu bevorzugen sein. Vgl. *P. Stuhlmacher,* Der Brief an Philemon (EKK) (Zürich–Einsiedeln–Köln–Neukirchen 1975) 44–46; *Thyen,* nicht mehr männlich (Anm. 15) 158–160; *P. Trummer,* Die Chance der Freiheit. Zur Interpretation des μᾶλλον χρῆσαι in 1 Kor 7,21, in: Bib. 56 (1975) 344–368.

Nachdem Paulus in V. 2–16 das mit der korinthischen Parole gestellte Problem vorwiegend unter der Rücksicht „*Ehe* und christliche Berufung" erörtert und mit der grundsätzlichen Erwägung in V. 17–24 abgeschlossen hat, geht er nun die Problematik der Parole im Blick auf die Verheiratung der (noch bzw. wieder) Unverheirateten an. Mit Sicherheit sind die Ausführungen V. 25–40 pragmatisch von V. 1 b bedingt. Wahrscheinlich liegt Paulus sogar eine direkte Anfrage „bezüglich der Jungfrauen" (V. 25) vor. Dies legt nicht nur die mit περί (bezüglich) analog zu V. 1 gestaltete Einleitung in V. 25 nahe, sondern auch die Beobachtung, daß Paulus in V. 26 wiederum (wie in V. 8) „es ist gut", ja sogar „es ist gut für den Menschen" (καλὸν ἀνϑρώπῳ) aus der Parole aufgreift.

Schwer zu klären ist allerdings, worin das korinthische „Jungfrauen"-Problem konkret bestand. Umstritten ist besonders, was mit „seiner Jungfrau" in V. 36–38 gemeint ist[20]. Relativ unwahrscheinlich ist es, daß es um geistliche Verlobte im Sinne des Syneisaktentums geht, da dieses als Institut erst seit dem 3. Jahrhundert sicher belegt ist[21]. Die traditionelle Auslegung sieht in der „Jungfrau" die Tochter[22]. Dem steht jedoch als sprachliche Schwierigkeit gegenüber, daß γαμείτωσαν V. 36 (= sie sollen heiraten) doch wohl auf die Heirat zwischen dem Subjekt des Satzes (das dann nicht der Vater sein kann) und der „Jungfrau" zu beziehen ist. Am wahrscheinlichsten ist es daher, daß die Verse 36–38 die Frage behandeln, ob es einem jungen Mann gestattet ist, seine Verlobte zu heiraten[23]. Dafür spricht übrigens auch V. 26 b (sofern man ihn mit V. 36–38 in Zusammenhang bringen darf), wo auch kaum daran gedacht sein kann, daß dem Vater nahegelegt werden soll, „so zu sein", d. h. ehelos zu bleiben.

Hinter V. 25–38 dürfte also folgendes Problem der Gemeinde von Korinth stehen: Die Parole von V. 1 b hatte nicht nur die Verheirate-

---

[20] Vgl. dazu *Conzelmann*, 1 Kor (Anm. 10) 160 f; *Baltensweiler*, Ehe (Anm. 9) 175–185; vor allem: *W. G. Kümmel*, Verlobung und Heirat bei Paulus (1 Kor 7, 36–38), in: *ders.*, Heilsgeschehen und Geschichte. Gesammelte Aufsätze 1933–1964 (MThSt 3) (Marburg 1965) 310–327.

[21] Zum Material vgl. *H. Achelis*, Virgines subintroductae. Ein Beitrag zum VII. Kapitel des I. Korintherbriefs (Leipzig 1902). Ob bereits Hermas das Syneisaktentum voraussetzt (vgl. *Lietzmann*, 1 Kor [Anm. 10] 36; *Thyen*, nicht mehr männlich [Anm. 15] 179), ist zumindest unsicher: vgl. *Kümmel*, aaO. 312 Anm. 9.

[22] *J. D. M. Derrett*, The Disposal of Virgins, in: *ders.*, Studies in the New Testament I (Leiden 1977) 184–192, versucht diese Auffassung vom jüdischen Recht her zu begründen.

[23] Zu γαμίζω (V. 38) in der Bedeutung „heiraten" siehe *Lietzmann*, 1 Kor (Anm. 10) 35 f.

ten, sondern auch die jungen Männer, die eben im Begriff standen zu heiraten, verunsichert. Denn in der Konsequenz der Parole lag es auch, daß das Eingehen einer Ehe mit christlicher Berufung unvereinbar war. Auf die entsprechende Anfrage geht Paulus in V. 25–38 ein, wobei er aber nicht nur im Blick auf die jungen Männer argumentiert, sondern allgemein (und unter Bezug auf beide Geschlechter; vgl. V. 28) das Verhältnis von christlicher Berufung und Ehelosigkeit aus seiner Sicht erörtert. Die Lösungen, die er anbietet, bewegen sich ganz auf der Linie des in V. 17–24 genannten Grundsatzes und der dort dargelegten christlichen Freiheit. Zunächst stimmt Paulus mit der Aussage der Parole darin überein, daß es besser sei, ehelos zu bleiben (vgl. V. 26.27 b.32–35.37.38 b). Das entspricht auch dem Grundsatz von V. 17.20.24. Allerdings ist die Begründung des Paulus eine andere (s. u. 3.) als die der Vertreter der Parole, die die Sexualaszese zum Kriterium des Christlichen gemacht hatten. Paulus macht aus seinem Grundsatz kein Prinzip und muß insofern einer rigorosen Applikation der Parole auf die Unverheirateten widersprechen. Da der sexuelle Stand (Ehe bzw. Ehelosigkeit) wie der ethnische und soziale grundsätzlich für das Heil belanglos ist, rekurriert Paulus auf die christliche Freiheit. Da diese Freiheit aber in der Unterwerfung unter den Kyrios gründet (vgl. V. 22), realisiert sie sich im Falle bereits bestehender Ehen – gemäß dem Gebot des Kyrios (vgl. V. 10 f) – im Aufrechterhalten der ehelichen Gemeinschaft (vgl. V. 27 a). Im Falle der Unverheirateten aber, wo es keinen „Befehl" des Kyrios gibt (V. 25), muß Paulus die Möglichkeit zur Heirat als Möglichkeit christlicher Freiheit offenlassen (vgl. V. 28 ab.36.38 a), wenngleich er es aus bestimmten Gründen (vgl. V. 29–31.32–35) für besser hält, nicht zu heiraten.

V. 39 f wenden die vorausgehenden Ausführungen sinngemäß auf die „Witwen" an. Möglicherweise gab es auch zu diesem Punkt im Gefolge der Parole V. 1 b eine direkte Anfrage aus Korinth.

Zusammenfassend läßt sich sagen: Die vorwiegend pragmatisch orientierte, kursorische Analyse konnte alle in 1 Kor 7 konkret angesprochenen Fragen auf dem Hintergrund einer einheitlichen korinthischen Problemstellung erklären, so daß auch von daher die Entscheidung, V. 1 b als korinthische Parole zu verstehen (2.1.), als gesichert gelten kann.

3. Sachlich-theologische Auswertung

Unter Zugrundelegung dieser Entscheidung ist nun auf die eingangs gestellten Sachfragen zurückzukommen, wobei zugleich die tieferen theologischen Beweggründe der paulinischen Stellungnahme zu erheben bzw. – soweit sie in der Analyse schon angesprochen wurden – in mehr systematischer Weise zu durchdringen sind.

3.1. Ehe als remedium concupiscentiae?

Die Begründungen in V. 2.5 („wegen der Unzucht[ssünden], „wegen eurer Unenthaltsamkeit"), die es auf den ersten Blick nahelegen könnten, Paulus halte die Ehe nur für ein remedium concupiscentiae, sind auch im Sinn des Paulus kaum ausreichend, um das Wesen der (christlichen) Ehe zu würdigen. Hier ist daran zu erinnern, daß Paulus im Blick auf den Stand der Ehe auch positiv argumentieren kann (und muß!), nämlich mit einem Gebot des Kyrios (V.10 f). Dieses wendet er sinngemäß sogar auf die Mischehen an, die er – möglicherweise in Abwehr einer gegenteiligen korinthischen Meinung – als Mittel der Heiligung für den ungläubigen Partner herausstellt (V. 12–14). Damit zeigen sich zumindest Ansätze einer relativ positiven Wertung der Ehe. Leider ist diese Sicht in 1 Kor 7 nicht im Sinne einer Ehelehre ausgefaltet; doch ist dies im Zuge der auf Abwehr eines falschen Verständnisses bedachten Argumentation des Paulus auch gar nicht zu erwarten.

Im übrigen wird man die Begründungen für den ehelichen Verkehr in V. 2.5 keineswegs auch nur als Versuch einer christlichen Ehelehre verstehen dürfen. Die Begründungen sind vielmehr primär pragmatisch (durch die sexualaszetische Parole von V. 1 b) bedingt. Je höher der Enthusiasmus gewisser Kreise in Korinth in den Himmel zu entschweben drohte, um so nüchterner mußte Paulus argumentieren, nämlich mit der Realität, daß hochgeschraubte Aszese schnurstracks in die Unzucht führt. Christliche Berufung entführt den Christen nicht aus der irdischen Wirklichkeit und beseitigt nicht die menschliche Natur, auch nicht in sexueller Hinsicht. Daß Paulus dies mit den Stichworten der „Unzucht" bzw. der „Unenthaltsamkeit" zum Ausdruck bringt, mag aus der an einem völlig andersartigen Fragehorizont orientierten Optik der heutigen Zeit recht derb erscheinen, ist aber von der Sache her und – gemessen an der enthusiastisch-unwirklichen Konsequenz der Vertreter der korinthischen Parole – eigentlich auch höchst positiv[24].

3.2. Die paulinische Regel und ihre Handhabung

„Jeder soll in der Berufung (d. h. in dem Stand bzw. in der Relation), in der er berufen worden ist, bleiben!"[25] Dieser Satz, der in V. 17.20.24 variiert wird, stellt die eigentliche paulinische Gegenthese zur korinthischen Parole dar. Als *Regel* genommen, ist er gleichsam das Paradigma, nach dem die paulinische Argumentation in ihren Hauptzügen funktioniert, sowohl im Blick auf die Verheirateten wie auf die Unverheirateten. Doch macht Paulus – anders als die Verfechter der korinthischen Parole – aus seiner Regel kein Prinzip, d. h. keinen unter allen Umständen normativen Satz. Vielmehr wird seine Normativität je nach Stand bzw. Relation unterschiedlich ausgelegt. Entsprechend ist das paulinische Urteil gegenüber der korinthischen Parole teils von faktischer Übereinstimmung, teils von sachlicher Ablehnung gekennzeichnet.

Als unmittelbar normativ wird die Regel auf die *(christlichen) Ehen* angewendet (V. 10f). Der Grund dafür ist, daß Paulus hier an das Wort des Kyrios gebunden ist. In diesem Fall muß er daher seine Regel als direkten Widerspruch zur korinthischen Parole konkretisieren. Einer nicht-normativen Geltung der Regel in bezug auf die Ehe widersetzt sich Paulus sogar für den Fall, daß der (christliche) Ehepartner sich (vor Bekehrung?) *getrennt* hat; das Verbot der Wiederheirat hat für Paulus letztlich wohl die Funktion, die Möglichkeit der Versöhnung offenzuhalten (V. 11 ab).

In analoger Weise ist die Regel auch das normative Paradigma für die Behandlung der *Mischehen* (V. 12–14). Paulus macht zwar deutlich, daß hierfür kein Herrenwort vorliegt und „nur" er selbst spricht (V. 12a). Doch ist dies kein Grund, der getroffenen Regelung eine

---

[24] Ein Versuch, 1 Kor 7 unter Berücksichtigung der veränderten heutigen Situation zu interpretieren, findet sich bei *J.-M. Cambier,* Doctrine paulinienne du mariage chrétien. Étude critique de 1 Co 7 et d'Ep 5, 21–33 et essai de leur traduction actuelle, in: EeT(0) 10 (1979) 13–59.

[25] Daß in dem Begriff κλῆσις profaner Stand und göttlicher Ruf aufeinander bezogen sind, betont *E. Neuhäusler,* Ruf Gottes und Stand des Christen. Bemerkungen zu 1 Kor 7, in: BZ NF 3 (1959) 43–60.

mindere normative Geltung zuzusprechen, da der Apostel nur die Norm des Herrenwortes sinn- und sachgemäß anwendet. Auch hier muß Paulus seine Regel als Widerspruch zur korinthischen Parole entfalten. Allerdings besteht Paulus für den Fall, daß der heidnische Partner sich trennen will, nicht auf einer Aufrechterhaltung der Ehe. Dies ist kaum als Ausnahme zu der ansonsten normativ verstandenen Regel im Falle der Mischehen zu interpretieren, sondern zeigt eher, daß die von Paulus postulierte Normativität nicht aus einer sklavischen Bindung an den Wortlaut des Herrenwortes, sondern aus der Bindung an den lebendigen Kyrios resultiert. Davon ist noch zu sprechen.

In bezug auf den *geschlechtlichen Umgang in der Ehe* (V. 2–5) wird man kaum von einer im strikten Sinn normativen Anwendung der paulinischen Regel sprechen können. Doch hält Paulus eine ihr entsprechende Praxis (also Bleiben in der sexuellen Relation der Ehe) für das Normale, das man nur unter bestimmten Bedingungen (vgl. V. 5 bc) verlassen darf, soll nicht die Gefahr der Unzucht (V. 2) bzw. der satanischen Versuchung heraufbeschworen werden (V. 5 d). Doch legt Paulus Wert auf die Feststellung, daß aus dieser Anwendung der Regel nicht die Ehe als christliche Norm abgeleitet werden darf (V. 6).

Dies widerspräche der paulinischen Regel selbst, die im Falle der *Unverheirateten* ja die Aufrechterhaltung des ehelosen Standes postuliert (V. 8.26.27 b.37.38 b.40). Hier stimmt Paulus faktisch mit der Forderung der korinthischen Parole überein. Im Gegensatz zu dieser postuliert Paulus hier jedoch keine normative Geltung, weil er für den Fall der Unverheirateten kein Gebot des Kyrios hat (V. 25). Er versteht die Regel als Empfehlung zum Besten der Betroffenen (vgl. V. 28cd.35).

Die paulinische Regel erweist sich so als hervorragender Gegen-satz zur korinthischen Parole, der eine differenzierende Behandlung derselben gestattet. Ihre christlich nicht zu verantwortenden, gegen die Ehe gerichteten Konsequenzen können zurückgewiesen und das in ihr enthaltene Anliegen christlicher Ehelosigkeit, das auch Paulus bewegt, kann in rechter Weise betont werden. Die unterschiedliche Normativität in der Anwendung der Regel ergibt sich je nach Vorhanden- oder Nichtvorhandensein eines Gebotes des Kyrios.

Mit diesen Feststellungen ist allerdings noch nicht die Frage geklärt, was der Grund bzw. die Begründung der paulinischen Regel ist. Der Verweis auf das Herrengebot ist als Antwort unzureichend, da es die Regel wohl in bezug auf die Verheirateten begründen könnte, nicht aber in bezug auf die Unverheirateten, für die Paulus nach eigener Auskunft (V. 25) kein Herrengebot hat. Da er die Ehelosigkeit unter diesem Bezug deswegen auch nicht als normativ betrachtet, bleibt noch die weitere Frage, warum er sie – durchaus entsprechend seiner Regel – dann doch als die bessere Möglichkeit gegenüber der Ehe betrachtet (vgl. V. 7a). Die beiden Fragen nach dem Grund der paulinischen Regel und dem Grund der Bevorzugung der Ehelosigkeit hängen also zusammen.

3.3 Der Grund für die paulinische Regel

Der Grund für die paulinische Regel kann mit Sicherheit nicht darin liegen, daß Paulus die vorhandene Relation als *heilsbedeutsam* festschreiben will. Dann müßte Paulus seine Regel zum Prinzip erklären, dann könnte sie im Fall der Unverheirateten sogar im Sinne der korinthischen Parole verwendet werden. Viel eher ist sie daher darin begründet, daß Paulus die vorhandene Relation in bezug auf das Heil gerade für *belanglos* hält[26]. Ausdrücklich realisiert wird diese Auffassung allerdings nur in bezug auf Beschneidung und Unbeschnittenheit (sie sind „nichts", V. 19), nicht aber in bezug auf die Relation der Ehe bzw. der Ehelosigkeit. Dies zeigt, daß die angegebene negative Begründung der paulinischen Regel für sich genommen noch unzureichend ist und positiv ergänzt werden muß:

Die vorhandenen (irdischen, sexuellen) Relationen sind belanglos, weil die christliche Berufung eine neue, alles Heil entscheidende Relation herstellt, nämlich die Relation zum Kyrios. Indirekt kommt diese Relation zum Kyrios schon in dem Begriff des „Rufens" von seiten Gottes (V. 17) bzw. des „Berufenwerdens" (V. 20.24) zum Ausdruck, da Gottes Ruf „in die Gemeinschaft seines Sohnes Jesus

---

[26] *W. Wolbert*, Ethische Argumentation und Paränese in 1 Kor 7 (MThSt.S 8) (Düsseldorf 1981) 111: „Auf den Stand kommt es gerade *nicht* an". Aus der Belanglosigkeit darf jedoch nicht einfach gefolgert werden: „die Freiheit ist nicht revolutionär, sie ändert an den gesellschaftlichen Verhältnissen nichts" (*Niederwimmer*, Askese [Anm. 3] 105); dies ist m. E. eine unzulängliche Generalisierung, die dem Charakter der paulinischen Regel als des Gegen-Satzes zur korinthischen Parole zu wenig Rechnung trägt.

Christus, unseres Herrn," führt (1 Kor 1,9). Direkt ausgeführt ist diese neue Relation zum Kyrios am Beispiel Sklave/Freier, wo in paradoxer Antithetik „der im Herrn berufene Sklave" als „Freigelassener des Herrn" und „der berufene Freie" als „Sklave Christi" bezeichnet wird (V. 22).

Unter der Rücksicht der allein heilsentscheidenden Relation zum Kyrios scheut sich Paulus offensichtlich, die Relation der Ehe bzw. Ehelosigkeit pauschal, wie Beschneidung und Unbeschnittenheit, als heilsbelanglos zu werten. Das heißt nicht, daß Ehe bzw. Ehelosigkeit als solche nun doch heilseffizient werden. Aber unter dem Gesichtspunkt der Relation zum Kyrios ist der Verheiratete eben verpflichtet (wegen des Herrenwortes!), im Stand der Ehe zu verbleiben (die Ehe ist für ihn nicht einfach „nichts"!). Unter dem nämlichen Gesichtspunkt rät Paulus dem Unverheirateten, ehelos zu bleiben, nicht weil er der Ehelosigkeit nun doch Heilsbedeutung zuschreiben möchte, sondern weil er dem Ehelosen ein innigeres Eingehen auf die Relation zum Kyrios zutraut. Darauf ist noch zurückzukommen.

Grundsätzlich ist zu vermerken, daß die paulinische Regel, jeder möge so bleiben, wie er berufen ist, nicht in einer prinzipiell und gesetzlich verstandenen Verpflichtung auf die vorhandene Relation, der damit Heilseffizienz zukäme, begründet ist, sondern in der Bindung an den Kyrios, die allein heilseffizient ist. Die Problematik stellt sich für Paulus nicht dar als eine Frage der Bewertung irdischer (sexueller) Relationen, ob diese also heilsausschließend oder heilseffizient sind – dies ist die Problematik, die die Korinther bewegt. Für Paulus stellt sich die Problematik dar als eine Frage der Knechtschaft bzw. der Freiheit. Die Alternative ist: Knechtsein unter dem Kyrios (vgl. V. 22), d.h. alleinige Abhängigkeit des Heils von der Relation zum Kyrios, oder Knechtsein unter Menschen (vgl. V. 23), d.h. vermeintliche Abhängigkeit des Heils von einer vorhandenen oder neu einzugehenden bzw. aufzulösenden menschlichen Relation.

Angewandt auf die konkrete Auseinandersetzung mit der korinthischen Parole von V. 1 b bedeutet dies: Weil die Relation zum Kyrios einzig heilsentscheidend ist, entläßt sie den Christen in die Freiheit, so zu bleiben, wie er berufen ist, und zwingt ihn nicht, vorhandene eheliche Relationen aufzugeben und dieses Aufgeben als heilseffizient zu betrachten, wie es einige Korinther mit ihrer Forderung der ehelichen Enthaltsamkeit bzw. möglicherweise sogar mit ihrer Forderung, die Ehe aufzugeben, tun.

Auf dem Hintergrund dieser Auseinandersetzung ist daher auch das Herrenwort V. 10 f nicht als „Gesetz" zu lesen, sondern als Ausdruck christologisch bedingter Freiheit, die allerdings nicht in die Beliebigkeit entläßt, sondern als Knechtsein unter dem Kyrios zugleich zur Aufrechterhaltung der Ehe verpflichtet.

Daß auch Paulus dieses Herrenwort nicht als „Gesetz" verstanden haben dürfte, zeigt die Tatsache, daß er in Applikation eben dieses Herrenwortes auf die Mischehen V. 15 ab formulieren kann. Ein Christ, dessen ungläubiger Partner die bisherige eheliche Relation lösen will, muß diese Relation nicht krampfhaft aufrechterhalten. Er hat die Freiheit, den heidnischen Partner ziehen zu lassen, und kann dennoch in der zerbrochenen ehelichen Relation seine Bindung an den Kyrios aufrechterhalten. Die Knechtschaft unter dem Kyrios, die Freiheit ist, darf nicht zur Begründung menschlicher Knechtschaft (in diesem Falle: durch den heidnischen Partner, der durch sein eigenmächtiges Verhalten den Christen zu einer fiktiven Aufrechterhaltung der Ehe zwingen würde, während er selbst eine neue Ehe eingehen kann) führen.

Weil die allein heilsentscheidende Bindung an den Kyrios, d. h. die christologisch begründete Freiheit des Christen, das Heil nicht an irdischen (ethnischen, sozialen, sexuellen) Relationen festmachen zu müssen, der tiefste Grund der paulinischen Regel ist, muß Paulus auch die Ehe, obwohl ihre Aufrechterhaltung für ihn – entgegen der korinthischen Parole – Zeichen der Bindung an den Kyrios und damit Zeichen christlicher Freiheit ist, in bezug auf Heilsrelevanz relativieren. Das geschieht in V. 29 b–31 a, wobei die beigefügten eschatologischen Begründungen (V. 29 a.31 b) zunächst einmal beiseitegelassen werden sollen[27]. Daß diejenigen, die Frauen haben,

---

[27] Dies ist deswegen nicht illegitim, da der eschatologische Vorbehalt des ως μη unabhängig von der Situation der Naherwartung unter christologischem Aspekt für den Christen bleibende Gültigkeit besitzt. Zu Recht stellt *W. Schrage*, Die Stellung zur Welt bei Paulus, Epiktet und in der Apokalyptik. Ein Beitrag zu 1 Kor 7, 29–31, in: ZThK 61 (1964) 125–154, hier 153 f, fest, daß Paulus auch in 1 Kor 7, 29 ff (wie in Röm 13, 11 ff) „die Eschatologie von der Christologie her interpretiert". Vgl. weiter: *G. Hierzenberger*, Weltbewertung bei Paulus nach 1 Kor 7, 29–31. Eine exegetisch-kerygmatische Studie (KBANT) (Düsseldorf 1967). – Die Christologie – und nicht primär „die prophetische ‚Grundgewißheit' von der Gegenwart als endzeitlicher Entscheidungssituation" – ist m. E. auch der entscheidende Grund für die von *U. B. Müller*, Prophetie und Predigt im Neuen Te-

so sein sollen, als hätten sie keine (ὡς μὴ ἔχοντες, V. 29 b), kann nicht besagen wollen, daß die Eheleute sich der geschlechtlichen Betätigung enthalten sollen. Das würde in eklatantem Widerspruch zu V. 2–5 stehen und nur Wasser auf bestimmte korinthische Mühlen schütten. Gemeint kann nach den Ausführungen der Verse 17–24 nur sein, daß Ehe, wie im übrigen auch Lebensfreud und Lebensleid und Besitz (V. 30.31 a), nicht zur Knechtschaft führen dürfen, indem von diesen Dingen das Heil erwartet wird bzw. indem diese Dinge den Blick vom einzig heilsentscheidenden Kyrios abziehen.

Die christologisch begründete Freiheit ist schließlich auch der Grund, daß Paulus seine Regel nicht als Prinzip formulieren kann. So sehr er selbst die Ehelosigkeit für besser hält (V. 7), so kann er doch einer Sexualaszese als Programm christlicher Freiheit nicht zustimmen. Damit würde a priori das Heil von menschlichen Relationen abhängig gemacht. Der unverheiratete Christ hat daher die Freiheit zu heiraten (vgl. V. 28 ab.36.38 a.39). Erst recht muß Paulus dort, wo die vermeintliche Freiheit nur die Begierde fixieren würde, betonen, daß es besser ist zu heiraten (V. 9)[28].

3.4. Die Bevorzugung der Ehelosigkeit

Es wurde schon betont, daß die paulinische Bevorzugung der Ehelosigkeit nicht in einer ihr speziellen Heilseffizienz liegen kann. Dem würde auch die Auskunft, daß der, der dennoch heiratet, nicht sündigt (V. 28 ab.36), widersprechen. Aus diesem Grund kann auch der Satz, daß die Unverheirateten um die Sache des Herrn besorgt sind, während die Verheirateten um die Sache der Welt besorgt sind, wie sie also dem Partner gefallen (V. 32 b–34), nicht als dogmatische Aussage verstanden werden. Paulus selbst gibt dies in V. 35 zu erkennen. Die Aussage gibt vielmehr die Überzeugung des Paulus wieder,

---

stament. Formgeschichtliche Untersuchungen zur urchristlichen Prophetie (StNT 10) (Gütersloh 1975) 158–162 (Zitat: 161), im übrigen zu Recht herausgestellten Differenzen zu 6 Esr 16,36–45; vgl. auch: *Wolbert,* aaO. 121–126.
[28] πυροῦσθαι: „vom Feuer des geschlechtlichen Verlangens verzehrt werden" (*F. Lang,* Art. πῦρ κτλ., in: ThWNT VI, 927–953, hier 950). Für eschatologischen Bezug plädiert *M. L. Barré,* To Marry or to Burn: πυροῦσθαι in 1 Cor 7:9, in: CBQ 36 (1974) 193–202: „to be burned in the fires of judgement or Gehenna" (200).

die er wohl aufgrund seiner eigenen Erfahrung und aufgrund seines Wirklichkeitsverständnisses gewonnen hat. Daß es auch andere, gegenteilige Erfahrung gibt, daß nämlich das Unverheiratetsein keineswegs automatisch zum Besorgtsein um den Herrn führen muß, sondern zur knechtischen Besessenheit von der Begierde führen kann, konzediert auch Paulus (V. 9; vgl. V. 5.36 f). Allerdings ist Paulus der Ansicht, daß in der Regel die Unverheirateten der allein heilsentscheidenden Bindung an den Kyrios leichter und spannungsfreier entsprechen können. Für die Verheirateten befürchtet Paulus, daß ihre Ausrichtung auf den Ehepartner neben der (selbstverständlich auch für sie maßgeblichen) Ausrichtung auf den Kyrios zu einer ständigen existentiellen Spannung führt (μεμέρισται, V. 34 a).

Dies hängt wesentlich damit zusammmen, daß der Verheiratete unter rein menschlicher Rücksicht (d. h. wegen seiner Bindung an den Partner, für den er in dieser Welt Sorge tragen muß) der Bedrängnis der Endzeit (θλῖψις) kaum ausweichen kann (V. 28 c), während der Christ als Christ – und dies gilt auch für den verheirateten Christen und macht gerade seine Spannung aus – sich in Sorglosigkeit, die in der Sorge um den Kyrios begründet ist, über die Bedrängnis hinwegsetzen kann. Weil Paulus vor dieser Bedrängnis bewahren will (V. 28 d) bzw. weil er diese Sorglosigkeit wünscht (V. 32 a), formuliert er V. 32 b–34[29]. Die darin geäußerte Überzeugung steht also, wie vorher schon die ὡς μή-Aussagen V. 29 b–31 a, eindeutig in eschatologischer Beziehung, die in V. 29 a.31 b auch textlich realisiert ist, und zwar im Sinne der Naherwartung. Doch während die ὡς μή-Aussagen auch ohne die apokalyptische Begründung kommunikative Gültigkeit besitzen, da sie sich sachlich auch mit dem Prinzip der christologisch begründeten Freiheit begründen lassen (s. o. 3.3.), gilt dies nicht in gleichem Maße von der in V. 32 b–34 geäußerten Überzeugung, da ihr kommunikativer Wert (d. h. ihr Überzeugungsgehalt und damit auch ihr intersubjektiver Wahrheitsgehalt) nicht unerheblich von dem vorausgesetzten Wirklichkeitsverständnis abhängt. Im

---

[29] Daß V. 32 a sachlich V. 28 cd wieder aufnimmt (so zu Recht: *Baltensweiler*, Ehe [Anm. 9] 173), beachtet *Niederwimmer*, Analyse (Anm. 6) 244, zu wenig, wenn er den Eheverzicht als jene Existenzform bezeichnet, „die dem eschatologischen Charakter der christlichen Existenz im eigentlichen Sinne angemessen ist".

Klartext heißt das: Wer wie Paulus unmittelbar vor der Ankunft des Herrn lebt, wird durchaus zustimmen können, daß die Ehe und die damit verbundene Verantwortung die endzeitliche Bedrängnis besonders intensiv erfahren lassen und daß das mit der Ehe verbundene weltliche Besorgtsein um den Partner leicht in Spannung zum Besorgtsein um den Kyrios, das gerade (weltliche) Sorglosigkeit intendiert, gerät. Aus dieser Situation ist die Überzeugung des Paulus auch psychologisch verständlich.

Zu fragen bleibt aber, ob diese Auffassung in jedwede, und d. h. auch in eine nicht von der Naherwartung bestimmte, Situation übertragbar ist. Zumindest wird dort die Gefahr knechtender Frustrierung bzw. Fixierung des Unverheirateten größer sein, da ja auch er sein Leben in den Ablauf dieser Weltzeit einpassen muß und außerdem die Bedrängnis und die Nöte der Welt nicht einfach in der Sorglosigkeit des mit dem Vergehen der Welt Rechnenden übergehen kann. Er muß sich wenigstens ein Stück weit um „die Dinge der Welt" sorgen, wie sich der Verheiratete im Partner um ein Stück Welt sorgt. Das bedeutet, daß die Verantwortlichkeit der Welt gegenüber in nicht von Naherwartung bestimmter Situation weit mehr in die Verantwortlichkeit gegenüber dem Kyrios integriert werden muß, als dies in der alternativen Darstellung des Paulus erscheint, sofern nicht schon die paulinische Alternative einer gewissen rhetorischen Zuspitzung mitverpflichtet ist[30]. Dies alles soll nicht heißen, daß es außerhalb der Naherwartung keine personalen Situationen geben kann, welche die Ehelosigkeit der Ehe vorzuziehen gebieten[31]. Aber sie können nicht in Pauschalübertragung der in V. 32b–34 geäußerten Überzeugung des Paulus als gegeben vorausgesetzt werden, sondern müssen jeweils neu und personal-individuell bestimmt werden.

Im übrigen gehorcht die paulinische Bevorzugung der Ehelosigkeit nicht einem Spezialgesetz, sondern dem nämlichen Prinzip wie die Einschätzung der Ehe. Es geht in beiden Fällen um die Freiheit für den Kyrios. Von dieser Freiheit her wird jeder seine ihm eigene Entscheidung treffen müssen (vgl. V. 7bc).

---

[30] Vgl. *Conzelmann*, 1 Kor (Anm. 10) 159.
[31] Vgl. dazu: *G. Friedrich*, Sexualität und Ehe. Rückfragen an das Neue Testament (Biblisches Forum 11) (Stuttgart 1977) 69–72.

Die Bindung an den Kyrios bzw. die christologisch begründete Freiheit des Christen erweisen sich somit als der tiefste Grund der paulinischen Regel. Im Blick auf die allein heilsentscheidende Relation zum Kyrios kann Paulus mit ihr sowohl das Bleiben in der Ehe – entgegen der korinthischen Parole – wie auch das Bleiben in der Ehelosigkeit als Möglichkeit christlicher Freiheit auslegen, wobei das Erstere verpflichtende Freiheit ist, während das Zweite dem Christen durchaus noch die Freiheit läßt, sich anders zu entscheiden. Daß die Bevorzugung der Ehelosigkeit durch Paulus in einer negativen Einschätzung der Sexualität begründet ist, davon kann jedoch nicht die Rede sein.

3.5. Abwertung der Frau?

Auch die letzte der eingangs gestellten Fragen, ob hinter den Ausführungen des Paulus in 1 Kor 7 nicht doch ein Stück Frauenfeindlichkeit steckt, muß negativ beantwortet werden[32]. Die Argumentation des Paulus ist im Gegenteil für antike Verhältnisse bemerkenswert „partnerschaftlich". Die Ausführungen richten sich fast stereotyp an die Adresse von Mann *und* Frau[33]. Die Ehelosigkeit, die Paulus aus den dargelegten Gründen für die bessere Möglichkeit hält, wird nicht nur dem Mann nahegelegt (etwa weil die Frau gefährlich sein könnte für das Heil), sondern gleichermaßen auch der Frau (vgl. V. 8.34.40). Wenn Paulus in V. 27.36–38 aus der Sicht des Mannes argumentiert, so geschieht dies wohl ausschließlich aufgrund der ihm vorgegebenen Pragmatik (vgl. V. 25). Ansonsten aber ist sowohl von der Heirat des Mannes wie der Jungfrau die Rede (V. 28 ab). Das Verbot der Ehescheidung wird auf Mann und Frau bezogen (V. 10 f), ebenso wird der Fall der Mischehe sowohl aus der Sicht des Bruders wie auch der Schwester dargestellt (V. 12–15). In Fragen des ehelichen Verkehrs werden Mann und Frau die gleichen Pflich-

---

[32] Vgl. dazu auch: *A.-M. Dubarle,* Paul et l'antiféminisme, in: RSPhTh 60 (1976) 261–280.
[33] Vgl. dazu die schöne tabellarische Übersicht bei *E. Kähler,* Die Frau in den paulinischen Briefen unter besonderer Berücksichtigung des Begriffes der Unterordnung (Zürich-Frankfurt 1960) 17–21.

ten und Rechte zugebilligt (V. 2–4)[34]. Nicht die Frau wird als Werkzeug des Satans, durch das der Mann in Versuchung geführt wird, dämonisiert, sondern die mögliche Versuchung Satans betrifft gleichermaßen beide Partner; gelegentliche eheliche Enthaltsamkeit soll in gegenseitigem Einvernehmen geschehen (V. 5).

V. 1 b, der als diskriminierend für die Frau empfunden werden könnte, ist kein paulinischer Satz, sondern die Parole gewisser Korinther. Er wird auch von Paulus *so* nicht wiederholt. Wo Paulus im Folgenden direkt darauf anspielt (V. 8 b.26; vgl. V. 37 f), wird gerade die Wendung „eine Frau nicht anfassen", die man zumindest im Sinne einer Abqualifizierung der menschlichen Sexualität am Beispiel des „Sexualobjektes" Frau verstehen könnte, nicht aufgegriffen. Allerdings wird man auch den Vertretern der korinthischen Parole nicht einfach dieses negative Verständnis unterschieben dürfen. Denn wenn es richtig ist, daß die Parole aus der eschatologischen Irrelevanz der Geschlechtlichkeit (vgl. Gal 3,28) deduziert wurde, richtet sie sich nicht primär gegen die Frau, sondern gegen die Sexualität überhaupt. Doch ist die konkrete Art und Weise der Formulierung immer noch bezeichnend genug, sofern sie sich nicht einfach aus der antiken Androzentrik erklärt. Doch kann darauf nicht näher eingegangen werden.

Abschließend kann im Rückblick auf die eingangs gestellten Fragen *zusammengefaßt* werden: Die paulinische Höherbewertung der Ehelosigkeit beinhaltet keine Abwertung der Ehe bzw. der Sexualität und erst recht nicht der Frau. Die in 1 Kor 7 geäußerten Reserven gegen die Ehe (vgl. bes. V. 27 b.29–35) sind zum Teil durch die Naherwartung bedingt. Die scheinbare Bewertung der Ehe als remedium concupiscentiae (V. 2–5) erklärt sich im wesentlichen aus der Pragmatik des Textes. Worum es Paulus bei seinen Ausführungen über Ehelosigkeit und Ehe letztlich geht, ist die Freiheit für den Kyrios, die in der allein heilseffizienten Relation zu diesem begründet ist. Daß das Heil nicht in der Sexualität – sei es in ehelicher Aktualisierung, sei es in eheloser Sublimierung – gesucht werden darf, ist ein

---

[34] Vgl. *Friedrich,* Sexualität (Anm. 31) 77–82; *(E. S. Gerstenberger) – W. Schrage,* Frau und Mann (Biblische Konfrontationen) (Stuttgart–Berlin–Köln–Mainz 1980) 153 f.

christologisch gebotenes Prinzip. In bezug auf die Ehe ist dies nicht als Negativum, sondern – auch anthropologisch – als Positivum zu bewerten. Denn nur dort, wo die Ehepartner ihre Beziehung nicht mit pseudosoteriologischen Ansprüchen belasten, ist eine wahrhaft menschliche Partnerschaft möglich. In bezug auf die Ehelosigkeit bedeutet dies eine ständige kritische Bescheidenheit, da nicht die Ehelosigkeit als solche schon heilseffektiv ist, sondern die Bindung an den Kyrios, die in der Ehelosigkeit zum Ausdruck kommen soll.

VIII

Gibt es christologische Begründungen für eine Unterordnung der Frau im Neuen Testament?

Von Claus Bussmann, Duisburg

Die Vermutung dürfte nicht falsch sein, daß das Aufblühen der sogenannten feministischen Theologie zu besonderer Unsicherheit in einer kirchlichen Großgruppe führt, die – zumindest organisatorisch – von Männern geprägt ist wie die römisch-katholische Kirche; denn hier müßte, hätte die „feministische Theologie" recht, der radikalste Wandel einsetzen. Nun paßt zu der geäußerten Vermutung gut, daß in bezug auf einen Spezialfall des Themas, nämlich der Frage einer möglichen Priesterweihe für Frauen, die schärfste und grundsätzlichste Ablehnung von römisch-katholischen Theologen stammt: „Jesus ist ein Mann gewesen." Dies aber ist ein christologisches Argument. Es stammt zwar nicht aus dem Neuen Testament, regt aber zu der Frage an, ob die zweifellos in neutestamentlicher Zeit vorkommende Unterordnung der Frauen in den christlichen Gemeinden auch schon christologisch begründet worden ist.

1. Kriterien

Bei der Auswahl der Texte möchte ich zwei Kriterien anlegen:
a) das Thema „Mann–Frau" muß – zumindest latent – darin vorkommen;
b) es muß eine christologische Argumentation vorliegen.

Eine erste Durchsicht des Materials ergibt, daß ganz eindeutige Aussagen, die beide Kriterien erfüllen, kaum vorkommen. Es gibt zwar eine ganze Reihe von Indizien dafür, daß auch im frühen Christentum mehrheitlich aus männlicher Perspektive gedacht wurde (z. B. Lk 14,26; Mk 12,18–27; die Diskussion um die Rolle der Beschneidung) und die Männer den Ton angaben (fast alle „Prominenten" in der frühen Kirche sind Männer), aber beides wird nicht christologisch begründet.

Stellen, die jedoch erörtert werden müssen, sind: Gal 3,28; 1 Kor 11,2–16; Kol 3,18 f; Eph 5,21–33; 1 Petr 3,1–7.

2. Texte

2.1. Gal 3,28

Dieser Vers scheint auf den ersten Blick meine Untersuchung überflüssig zu machen; denn er behauptet die Gleichheit und Einheit von Mann und Frau, und zwar mit christologischer Begründung. Aber: Paulus beschreibt mit diesem Vers nicht die soziale Wirklichkeit der Gemeinden Galatiens, sondern stellt die grundsätzlich vom Evangelium her vorgegebene und geforderte Gleichheit von Juden und Griechen, Sklaven und Freien, Mann und Frau heraus. Schon terminologisch fällt auf, daß an dieser Stelle von ἄρσεν (Männliches) und θῆλυ (Weibliches) die Rede ist, also die geschlechtsspezifische, nicht die gesellschaftliche Unterschiedenheit im Vordergrund steht. Man könnte auch sagen, daß Paulus mit diesem Vers einen Grundsatz aufstellt, der jedwede Unterordnung der Frau in christlichen Gemeinden verbietet, aber gerade der Nachdruck, mit dem er ihn formuliert, beweist, daß er in den Gemeinden Galatiens nicht realisiert ist. Damit ist – notabene – nicht gesagt, die vermutete Unterordnung der Frau in den galatischen Gemeinden sei christologisch begründet gewesen. Das Gegenteil ist sogar wahrscheinlicher: indem Paulus für die Aufhebung der faktischen Unterschiedenheit ein neues Argument, und zwar das christologische vom gemeinsamen Getauftsein, ins Feld führt, hofft er ja auf dessen Überzeugungskraft.

Der Kontext zeigt, daß nach dem Verständnis des Paulus eine unterschiedliche Bewertung von Mann und Frau in die Zeit des Gesetzes gehört, also Menschensatzung ist, nicht jedoch der neuen Wirklichkeit des Christseins zugehört. Solange es Zwischeninstanzen zwischen Gott und den Menschen gab (das Gesetz), solange mochte eine unterschiedliche Bewertung von Juden und Griechen, Freien und Sklaven, Mann und Frau angehen; die durch Christus vermittelte unmittelbare Gotteskindschaft hebt solche auf Menschensatzung beruhenden Unterschiede auf. Aber: Diese Aufhebung ist Bestandteil der neuen, durch den Geist vermittelten christologischen Wirklichkeit, noch nicht die soziale Wirklichkeit in den Gemeinden Galatiens. Für sie ist die Aufhebung Bestandteil der Forderung, die geschenkte Freiheit nicht wieder zu verlieren (Gal 5,1) und im Geist zu wandeln (5,16).

2.2. 1 Kor 11,2–16

Wie aber sieht die soziale Wirklichkeit aus? Die erste Probe aufs Exempel der prinzipiellen Gleichstellung von Mann und Frau sieht bei Paulus nicht gut aus. Zwar geht es nur um so etwas Harmloses wie die Kleiderordnung in der Gemeindeversammlung, aber hierbei gibt Paulus den Korinthern deutlich zu verstehen, daß die Tradition hochzuhalten sei: Frauen mit Kopfbedeckung, Männer ohne Kopfbedeckung; denn: *der Kopf der Frau ist der Mann, der Kopf des Mannes Christus* (V. 3); oder: *der Mann ist Abglanz Gottes, die Frau Abglanz des Mannes* (V. 7). Ohne sofort auf den Inhalt der Aussage einzugehen, erkennt man, daß Paulus eine eindeutige Stufenleiter vorschwebt: Gott – Christus – Mann – Frau. Die uns hier vorrangig interessierende Unterordnung der Frau wird damit begründet, daß der Mann das Haupt der Frau sei; die spätere Argumentation, daß die Frau um des Mannes willen erschaffen worden sei, ist nun allerdings nicht christologisch, sondern schöpfungstheologisch. Die Linienführung im ersten Argument über das Hauptsein des Mannes bis auf Gott hin könnte vermuten lassen, daß auch dieses Argument letztlich nicht christologisch ist. Wenn die Beobachtungen, die H. Conzelmann[1] zum Thema macht, zutreffen, daß nämlich κεφαλή (Haupt) ein Alternativbegriff zu εἰκών (Abbild) ist, dann steckt hinter der gesamten Argumentation kosmologische Spekulation. Christus ist von Paulus eingefügt, die Reihe als ganze wäre dann nicht christologisch. In V. 7 liegt die Argumentation sozusagen in Reinkultur, ohne Christus, vor. Das christologische Argument hat *für unsere Frage* also nur unterstützende, nicht tragende Funktion. Im Ge-

---

[1] *H. Conzelmann,* Der erste Brief an die Korinther (KEK V) (Göttingen 1969) 213–226.

genzug dient das christologische Argument (V. 11 f) der Relativierung der vorher behaupteten Unterordnung; „im Herrn", ich möchte übersetzen: „unter Christen", sind Mann und Frau vor Gott gleichgestellt.

Man muß sich ernsthaft fragen, was Paulus bewegt, die Frage der Kopfbedeckung in der Gemeindeversammlung mit allen zu Gebote stehenden Mitteln: kosmologisches Argument mit christologischer Ausweitung (V. 3), schöpfungstheologisches Argument (V. 7–9), gesunder Menschenverstand (V. 13), Hinweis auf die Natur (V. 14) und die Praxis der anderen Gemeinden (V. 16) im traditionellen Sinne zu regeln, obwohl das christologische Argument in V. 11 eine andere Lösung geradezu anbieten würde.

– Schlägt hier das jüdische Erbe durch?
– Hat die Kleidung nichts mit dem Heil in Christus zu tun?
– Sieht Paulus in einer Aufweichung der Kopfbedeckungspraxis der Frauen für die Gemeinde gefährliche Tendenzen am Werk?

Vor allem die zweite Frage geht an den Nerv; denn was ist eine christologisch begründete Beendigung der Unterordnung der Frau wert, wenn sie sich in der sozialen Wirklichkeit der Gemeinde nicht auswirken darf? Andererseits kann man fragen, ob denn das Schleiertragen tatsächlich eine soziale Unterordnung der Frau dokumentiert? Geht es hier nicht einfach um eine Sitte, die Paulus den korinthischen Christen – vielleicht um die Gemeinsamkeit mit Christen in anderen Gemeinden zu fördern – nachdrücklich empfiehlt? Und unterliegen nicht die Männer ebenso dieser Sitte? Dann bleibt allerdings der eigenartige Eindruck, daß Paulus für eine bestimmte Sitte mit allen zu Gebote stehenden Mitteln kämpft, sogar mit Argumenten, die seiner prinzipiellen Aussage von Gal 3, 28 zuwiderlaufen.

2.3. Kol 3, 18

Diese Stelle spreche ich kurz an, obwohl hier nur ein Sonderfall der Unterordnung der Frau, nämlich die eheliche, angesprochen wird. Das Argument lautet: „Wie es sich im Herrn geziemt." Darin ist ἐν κυρίῳ (im Herrn) enthalten, das 1 Kor 11, 11 das Hauptargument für die Relativierung der Überordnung des Mannes war (ich hatte übersetzt mit „unter Christen"). Aber es liegt ein Unterschied vor zwischen „im Herrn" bzw. „unter Christen" und „wie es sich im Herrn geziemt" bzw. „wie es sich unter Christen geziemt". Das absolute ἐν κυρίῳ betont das Neue des christlichen Verhaltens, sozusagen das spezifisch Christliche, während ὡς ἀνῆκεν ἐν κυρίῳ (wie es sich im Herrn geziemt) die Anpassung des christlichen Verhaltens an die Normen der Umwelt anzeigt. Jedoch, und deshalb ist diese Stelle für unseren Zusammenhang wichtig, wird diese Anpassung christologisch begründet: ἐν κυρίῳ; und ein Teil dieser Anpassung ist die eheliche Unterordnung der Frauen. Wenn man davon ausgeht, daß der Kolosserbrief jünger ist als die Briefe an die Galater und Korinther, älter dagegen als der Epheserbrief, dann liegt Kol 3,18 der erste Beleg dafür vor, daß eine spezielle Form der Unterordnung der Frau, nämlich in der Ehe, im weiteren Sinne christologisch begründet wird. Man darf auch nicht übersehen, daß die ganze Haustafel unmittelbar an einen Abschnitt anschließt, in dem christliches Verhalten ausdrücklich christologisch begründet wird (Kol 3,1–17). V. 18 beginnt zwar ohne eine Begründungspartikel (wie V. 5 oder V. 11 οὖν), doch der Zusammenhang ist nicht ein völlig neuer. Zwar geht es Kol 3,18 nicht um ein typisch christliches Verhalten, nicht um etwas grundsätzlich Neues, wie etwa Gal 3,28, aber es bleibt bestehen, daß die Anpassung an die in der antiken Umwelt verbreitete Unterordnung der Frau in der Ehe christologisch begründet wird, wenngleich sie durch die angeschlossene Aufforderung der Ehemänner zur Liebe relativiert wird.

2.4. Eph 5,21–33

Zwei Motive aus Eph 5,21–33 sind als Einzelaussagen schon vorgekommen:
– die Unterordnung der Ehefrau (Kol 3,18)
– „der Mann ist das Haupt der Frau" (1 Kor 11,3).

Der große Zusammenhang ist derselbe wie im Kolosserbrief: Aufforderung zu christlichem Verhalten als Nachahmung Christi. Aber im einzelnen gibt es erhebliche Unterschiede.

Statt mit der Linie Gott – Christus – Mann – Frau (1 Kor 11) wird hier mit einer Parallele argumentiert: Mann – Frau so wie Christus – Kirche. Die kosmologische Spekulation ist christologisch bzw. ekklesiologisch variiert. Das hat zur Folge, daß die Unterordnung der

Ehefrau hier erstmals ausdrücklich christologisch begründet wird. Diese Unterordnung wird weder durch V. 21: „Seid einander untertan", wenn man diesen Satz als Überschrift versteht, noch durch die Forderung an die Männer V. 25: „Liebt eure Frauen, so wie auch Christus die Kirche geliebt hat", aufgehoben oder gemildert; denn gerade die zweite Aussage unterstreicht die Überordnung des Mannes[2], denn seine Verpflichtung zur Liebe ist begründet durch die Analogie zur unbezweifelten Priorität Christi gegenüber der Kirche, des Retters gegenüber der Geretteten. Vielleicht liegt in dieser Analogie zwischen der empirischen Ebene (Mann-Frau-Beziehung) und der theologischen Ebene (Beziehung Christus – Kirche) die tiefgehende Wirkung im christlichen Bereich und zugleich die Gefährlichkeit der Argumentation des Epheserbriefes begründet. Denn nicht nur für diese Analogie gilt ja, daß die Unähnlichkeit größer ist als die Ähnlichkeit, das Vertrackte der hier vorliegenden Argumentation ist, daß eine Änderung im empirischen Bereich, in den Beziehungen zwischen Mann und Frau, in Richtung auf eine „Gleichberechtigung" der Frau unmöglich erscheint, da auf der theologischen Ebene eine Änderung ausgeschlossen ist. Hier gerät die christologische Argumentation in die Gefahr, zur Ideologie zu werden.

Man kann sich allerdings fragen, ob die Unterordnung der Ehefrau nicht faktisch der christologischen Begründung vorausläuft. Wenn diese Annahme zutrifft, dann dient die christologische Argumentation der zusätzlichen Begründung eines Zustandes, den es vorher gab und der an anderer Stelle auch anders begründet worden ist. Es ist bemerkenswert, daß sich im Kolosser- und Epheserbrief nicht die prinzipielle Gleichstellung von Mann und Frau (Gal 3,28), sondern die faktisch unterschiedliche Stellung (1 Kor 11) durchsetzt. Es wäre allerdings ungerecht, wenn nun nicht hinzugefügt würde, daß die Unterordnung der Ehefrau nicht die einzige, heute schwer nachzuvollziehende, christologisch begründete Forderung des Epheserbriefes ist; die vom Mann geforderte Liebe und Hingabe, ebenfalls christologisch begründet, läßt erkennen, daß der Verfasser von einer vordergründigen „Herr im Haus bin ich"-Moral weit entfernt ist.

---

[2] Vgl. *H. Schlier*, Der Brief an die Epheser (Düsseldorf ²1958) 254.

Eine weitere Haustafel, die die Ehefrau zur Untertänigkeit ermahnt. Dieser Text ist besonders provozierend, weil er die Untertänigkeit der Frau parallel zur Untertänigkeit der Sklaven entfaltet. Insgesamt scheint für den Autor des ersten Petrusbriefes die Unterordnung vorrangige Bedeutung im christlichen Verhalten zu haben (2,13.18; 3,1), wobei nach dem Gesamtzusammenhang die Unterordnung als Konkretisierung der Enthaltung von sarkischen Begierden (2,11) gedacht ist.

Nun stellt sich die Frage nach einer christologischen Begründung der Unterordnung der Frauen nur indirekt; denn im unmittelbaren Kontext wird sie missionarisch (die Männer sollen durch das Verhalten der Frauen gewonnen werden 3,1) und mit dem Beispiel heiliger Frauen wie Sara (3,5 f) begründet. Das Problem liegt in dem anknüpfenden ὁμοίως (ebenso). Soll damit nur gesagt sein, daß sich die Frauen, ebenso wie die Sklaven, unterordnen sollen, oder steckt auch der gleiche Begründungszusammenhang in der Verbindungspartikel?[3] Das hieße nämlich, daß als Motiv für die Unterordnung der Frau auch das geduldig getragene Leiden Christi angeführt würde. Aber außer der Verbindungspartikel deutet höchstens noch der „heilige Wandel" (3,2) darauf hin, daß dem Verfasser ein innerer Zusammenhang zwischen der Unterordnung der Frau und dem leidenden Christus vorgeschwebt haben könnte. Selbst wenn es so wäre, läge aber nicht im strengen Sinne eine christologische Begründung für die Unterordnung der Frau vor, sondern ein Motiv, die faktische Unterordnung christlich zu ertragen. Nicht zu übersehen ist allerdings, daß im weiteren Sinne alle Unterordnung „wegen des Herrn" (2,13) geschehen soll. Unter die Überschrift „Haltet euch an das Vorbild Christi" werden auch antik-bürgerliche Vorstellungen wie die Unterordnung der Frau subsumiert. In jedem Falle liegt eine Verwässerung des paulinischen Prinzips von Gal 3,28 vor.

---

[3] *K.-H. Schelkle*, Die Petrusbriefe. Der Judasbrief (HThK XIII/2) (Freiburg i. Br. 1961) 99, hält die göttliche Schöpfungsordnung für die übergreifende Begründung.

3. Fragen

Wie ist zu erklären, daß ein so verheißungsvoller Auftakt wie Gal 3,28 im frühen Christentum keinen durchschlagenden Erfolg verbuchen konnte? War die grundsätzliche Einsicht des Paulus, die er Gal 3,28 formulierte, zu revolutionär, als daß sie in die alltägliche Wirklichkeit der Gemeinden Einlaß finden konnte? Oder ist vielleicht Paulus selbst die Tragweite seiner Einsicht gar nicht zu Bewußtsein gekommen? Auf das letztere könnte seine Anweisung in 1 Kor 11 hindeuten. Oder soll man sich vorstellen, daß in den Gemeinden Galatiens – und vielleicht auch in anderen – die Unterordnung der Frau tatsächlich in Richtung auf eine im privaten wie öffentlichen Raum praktizierte Gleichberechtigung hin überwunden war, und zwar aufgrund des gemeinsamen Christusglaubens, und diese „Errungenschaft" wäre von anderen Gruppen innerhalb der frühen Kirche argwöhnisch betrachtet und schließlich wieder abgeschafft worden? Und zwar wiederum unter Hinweis auf den Christusglauben, der eine klare Hierarchie kennt: Mann – Frau wie Christus – Kirche? Dann spielte die Christologie die Rolle einer Notbremse angesichts einer für gefährlich gehaltenen Entwicklung. Wieso gefährlich? Darüber kann der heutige Leser des Epheserbriefes nur spekulieren. Er kann sich fragen, welches Interesse hinter der Festschreibung der Unterordnung der Frau erkennbar wird. Dabei entpuppt sich dann die christologische Argumentation als Vorwand für die Beibehaltung einer – selbstverständlich von Männern – für richtig gehaltenen Ordnung, in der Unterordnung der Frau und Überordnung des Mannes als Abbild der allzeit gültigen Heilsordnung erscheinen. Für die heutige Situation heißt das, daß die Frage, wieso eine von Gal 3,28 ausgehende Neubestimmung der Rolle der Frau in christlichen Gemeinden als gefährlich empfunden wird, eine Frage nach der Angst der christlichen Männer ist.

Wenn im Neuen Testament sowohl das Ende der Unterordnung der Frau (Gal 3,28) als auch die Unterordnung der Frau (Eph 5,22 f) christologisch begründet werden, dann stellt sich die Frage nach dem Stellenwert der christologischen Argumentation in der Frage nach der Stellung der Frau. Dieser erscheint vergleichsweise gering; denn weder garantiert die christologische Aussage vom Einssein in Christus die tatsächliche Gleichberechtigung der Frau, noch schließt die christologische Aussage von der Überordnung des Retters Christus über die gerettete Kirche eine partnerschaftliche Beziehung zwischen den Eheleuten aus. Für die tatsächlich nicht zu leugnende Unterordnung der Frau in den Gemeinden des Neuen Testaments scheint die christologische Begründung nicht den Ausschlag gegeben zu haben.

IX

Die Haustafel des Kolosserbriefes und das antike Frauenthema

Eine kritische Rückschau auf alte Ergebnisse

Von Karlheinz Müller, Würzburg

Von den derzeit für ihre Rechte in der Gesellschaft immer heftiger rebellierenden Frauen werden mit Vorzug die sogenannten „Haustafeln" des Neuen Testaments ins Spiel gebracht[1], wenn sie ihre gewöhnlich harsche und resignierte Abrechnung mit den Überlieferungen und den Institutionen eines Christentums vortragen, das nach ihrer Auffassung nicht unerheblich die Unterdrückung der Frauen gefördert und stabilisiert hat[2]. Und das ist kein Wunder. Denn in den pragmatischen Appellen zur Unterordnung, wie sie die neutestamentlichen Haustafeln den Frauen zumuten, scheint sich der Kanon der Bevormundung und des Unrechts zu klassischer Präzision zu steigern[3], der sich von den Zeiten der alten Kirche bis in

---

[1] Vgl. *Ph. Trible,* Gegen das patriarchalische Prinzip in Bibelinterpretationen, jetzt in: *E. Moltmann-Wendel,* Frauenbefreiung. Biblische und theologische Argumente: Systematische Beiträge 12 (München ²1978) 94.

[2] Aus der neueren Literatur: *E. Moltmann-Wendel,* Freiheit, Gleichheit, Schwesterlichkeit. Zur Emanzipation der Frau in Kirche und Gesellschaft (München 1977); *A. J. Jelsma,* Heilige und Herren. Die Stellung der Frau im Christentum (Konstanz 1977); *K. Lüthi,* Gottes neue Eva. Wandlungen des Weiblichen (Stuttgart 1978); *M. Daly,* Jenseits von Gottvater, Sohn und Co. Aufbruch einer Philosophie der Frauenbefreiung (München 1980), und *C. M. Halkes,* Gott hat nicht nur starke Söhne. Grundzüge einer feministischen Theologie (GTB 371) (Gütersloh 1980).

[3] Für *S. Schulz,* Gott ist kein Sklavenhalter. Die Geschichte einer verspäteten Revolution (Zürich – Hamburg 1972) 199–200, geraten die Haustafeln geradezu zum verräterischen Emblem für ungehemmte Anpassungswilligkeit und widerstandsschwaches Sich-Treiben-Lassen des „frühkatholischen" Ethos': „Mit dieser konservativen Haustafelethik wird von den Christen, und vor allem von den christlichen Sklaven, widerspruchslose Einfügung in die bestehende Welt der sozialen Instanzen verlangt. Damit werden selbstverständlich die damaligen sozialen Verhältnisse nicht nur für zeitlos gültig erklärt, sondern auf den Willen des Schöpfergottes zurückgeführt. Eine Änderung solcher bereits statisch vorhandenen Schöpfungsordnungen ist nicht nur vom stoisch-heidnischen Hintergrund dieser Haustafeln, sondern jetzt noch mehr durch die christlich-schöpfungstheologi-

die Gegenwart[4] wie ein lebensfeindlicher Schatten auf das Geschick der Frauen in der abendländischen Gesellschaft legte[5].

Es ist also keine Frage: in einem Buch über „Die Frau im Urchristentum" müssen die „Haustafeln" ein wichtiges Thema sein. Dabei ist es allerdings nützlich, gleich eingangs die Grenzen zu markieren, an die der Neutestamentler gehalten bleiben muß, wenn er seine methodische Glaubwürdigkeit nicht verspielen will.

Er darf nämlich seine berufliche Ehre nur darin finden, jene antiken Texte eben *nicht* in das Geflecht moderner emanzipatorischer Regungen und Gewißheiten zu verspannen, sondern sie korrelational zu ihrer Entstehungszeit am Ausgang des ersten Jahrhunderts nach Christus verständlich zu machen[6]. Das aber heißt vor allem: er kann ihre objektive ethische Qualität nur aus dem Vergleich mit mehr oder weniger vagen Durchschnittsmargen für soziales Verhalten in der späthellenistischen Antike erkennen[7]. Er muß sich deshalb besonders davor hüten, das, was ihn heute stört, allzu flugs als damals zeitbedingt wegzuarbeiten[8]. Seine vordringliche Aufgabe wird es vielmehr sein, gerade die anstößige *Fremdheit* jener alten

---

sche Begründung ausgeschlossen. Das Gegenüber Gottes zur Welt wird damit kritiklos bestätigt, nicht aber kritisch herausgefordert". – Ähnlich: *ders.*, Evangelium und Welt. Hauptprobleme einer Ethik des Neuen Testaments, in: *H. D. Betz – L. Schottroff* (Hrsg.), Neues Testament und christliche Existenz. FS *H. Braun* (Tübingen 1973) 497–498.

[4] Zu K. Barth vgl. *H. Thyen*, „... nicht mehr männlich und weiblich ...". Eine Studie zu Galater 3,28, in: *F. Crüsemann – H. Thyen*, Als Mann und Frau geschaffen. Exegetische Studien zur Rolle der Frau: Kennzeichen 2 (Studien und Problemberichte aus dem Projekt „Frauen als Innovationsgruppen" des Deutschen Nationalkomitees des Lutherischen Weltbundes) (Gelnhausen – Berlin – Stein [Mfr.] 1978) 191–197.

[5] Vgl. schon *S. de Beauvoir*, Das andere Geschlecht. Sitte und Sexus der Frau (Hamburg 1951) 105 (zu Eph 5,24).

[6] Vgl. die lesenswerte „Vorbemerkung" von *H. Cancik*, Die neutestamentlichen Aussagen über Geschlecht, Ehe, Frau. Ihr religionsgeschichtlicher und soziologischer Ort, in: *H. Cancik – H. Cancik-Lindemaier – J. Scherff – C. Härlin – P. Grohmann*, Zum Thema Frau in Kirche und Gesellschaft. Zur Unmündigkeit verurteilt? (Stuttgart 1972) 24–26.

[7] Zu den damit gegebenen methodischen Problemen: *K. Thraede*, Ärger mit der Freiheit. Die Bedeutung von Frauen in Theorie und Praxis der alten Kirche, in: *G. Scharffenorth – K. Thraede*, Freunde in Christus werden. Die Beziehung von Mann und Frau als Frage an Theologie und Kirche: Kennzeichen 1 (Anm. 4) (Gelnhausen – Berlin – Stein [Mfr.] 1977) 35–40.

[8] Vgl. die Warnung von *K. Thraede*, Verkündigen oder Schweigen?, in: Zur Debatte (Themen der Katholischen Akademie in Bayern) 11 (1981) 6.

Äußerungen vor dem aufgeklärten hermeneutischen Horizont der eigenen Gegenwart zur Geltung zu bringen[9]. Zunächst aber muß an Allgemeines und Grundsätzliches erinnert werden.

1. Der Begriff „Haustafel"

Es war Martin Luther, der den Namen „Haustafel" im deutschen Idiom durchsetzte[10]. 1529 überschrieb er den zweiten Anhang seines „Kleinen Katechismus" mit den Worten: „Die Haustafel etlicher Spruche für allerlei heilige Orden und Stände dadurch dieselbigen als durch eigene Lektion ihres Ampts und Diensts zu ermahnen."[11] Und um mit einem derartigen Anliegen die „Orden und Stände" des sozialen Feldes möglichst vollzählig zu erreichen, rekrutierte der Reformator unter dieser Überschrift eine Reihe von Belegen aus dem Neuen Testament, denen man in der Tat mit geringer Mühe die Rahmenrubrik „Ermahnung" anpassen kann: Röm 13,1–2.4.9; Kol 3,19; Eph 6,1–3.4.5–8.9; 1 Petr 3,1.6; 5,5–6; 1 Tim 3,2–6; 5,5–6 und Tit 1,6–9[12].

2. Das Textfeld

Genauer besehen unterscheiden sich die hier vom Begriff der „Haustafel" (Singular)[13] okkupierten paränetischen Stücke allerdings beträchtlich. Das Ausmaß ihrer inhaltlichen Verschiedenheit ist zum Teil so erheblich, daß unter solcher Rücksicht die merkwürdige Zurückhaltung verständlich wird, welche die Lutherbibeln an den Tag legen, wie sie seit dem Ende des 16. Jahrhunderts im Druck

---

[9] Zur „hermeneutischen Bedeutung des Zeitabstandes" hat *H.-G. Gadamer*, Wahrheit und Methode. Grundzüge einer philosophischen Hermeneutik (Tübingen ⁴1975) 275–283, das Wesentliche gesagt.

[10] Zuletzt hat *L. Goppelt*, Der erste Petrusbrief/hrsg. v. F. Hahn (KEK XII/1) (Göttingen ⁸1978) 164 Anm. 1, die Herkunft des Begriffs untersucht.

[11] Die Bekenntnisschriften der evangelisch-lutherischen Kirche, herausgegeben im Gedenkjahr der Augsburgischen Konfession (Göttingen ²1955) II 523.

[12] Ebd. 523–527.

[13] *J. Gnilka*, Der Kolosserbrief (HThK X/1) (Freiburg – Basel – Wien 1980) 205(–216), gebraucht für Kol 3,18 – 4,1 den Plural: „Die Haustafeln". Das bleibt nicht nur begriffsgeschichtlich ohne Rechtfertigung (die Berufung auf „Luther",

erscheinen[14]. Nach wie vor billigen ihre Titelzeilen die Benennung „Haustafel" lediglich den neutestamentlichen Textfolgen Kol 3,18 bis 4,1 und Eph 5,22 – 6,9 zu.

Von einer ähnlichen Beschränkung ist der heute geläufige Sprachgebrauch der internationalen Forschung weit entfernt. Er orientiert sich an einer Regelung, für die ehedem Martin Dibelius eingetreten war. Sie reservierte die Rede von den „sogenannten Haustafeln" einer Serie urchristlicher und altkirchlicher „Spruchsammlungen", von denen sich sagen ließ, daß sie „die Pflichten der einzelnen Gruppen im Hause festlegten"[15]. Näherhin meinte der Heidelberger Neutestamentler damit Kol 3,18 – 4,1 sowie „Eph 5,22 – 6,9; 1 Petr 2,18 – 3,7; Tit 2,1–10; ferner noch 1 Tim 2,8–15; 6,1–2"[16]. Aber er fand ähnliche Partien auch im ersten Clemensbrief (1 Clem 21,6–9), in den Schreiben des Ignatius von Antiochien an Polykarp (IgnPol 5,1.2) und des Polykarp von Smyrna an die Philipper (PolPhil 4,2 – 6,3), im Barnabasbrief (Barn 19,5–7) und in der Didache (Did 4,9–11)[17].

Die in dieser Weise von seinem Lehrer M. Dibelius als „Haustafeln" exponierten Texte griff dann im Jahre 1928 Karl Weidinger erstmals monographisch auf[18] und legte damit endgültig den Umfang dessen fest, was die Zunft der Bibliker künftig unter dem Namen „Haustafeln" zur Kenntnis nehmen wollte.

---

ebd. 205, ist unangebracht), sondern behindert vor allem eine präzise formgeschichtliche Differenzierung. Vgl. unten: S. 267–270. Ein Beispiel einer formgeschichtlich hinderlichen, ja unbrauchbaren Definition des Begriffs der „Haustafeln" bietet: *W. Schrage*, Zur Ethik der neutestamentlichen Haustafeln, in: NTS 21 (1975) 2: „Unter Haustafeln verstehe ich wie üblich diejenigen paränetischen Stücke, die sich formal durch ihre Geschlossenheit und übersichtliche Disposition von der sonst mehr lockeren, regellosen und eklektischen Aufreihung der neutestamentlichen Mahnungen abheben und die inhaltlich vor allem das Verhalten der verschiedenen Stände (sic!) zu ordnen versuchen."

[14] Vgl. *H. Volz*, Hundert Jahre Wittenberger Bibeldruck 1522–1626 (ASUBG NF 1) (Göttingen 1954) 129–130.131–132.138.

[15] *M. Dibelius*, An die Kolosser, Epheser, an Philemon/neu bearbeitet von H. Greeven (HNT 12) (Tübingen ³1953) 48.

[16] Ebd.

[17] Vgl. zudem: *M. Dibelius*, Geschichte der urchristlichen Literatur. Neudruck der Erstausgabe von 1926 unter Berücksichtigung der Änderungen der englischen Übersetzung von 1936, hrsg. v. F. Hahn (TB 58) (München 1975) 142.

[18] *K. Weidinger*, Die Haustafeln. Ein Stück urchristlicher Paränese (UNT 14) (Leipzig 1928).

266

Wie dem auch sei[19]: Kol 3,18 – 4,1 ist in jedem Falle die älteste und kürzeste Haustafel im Neuen Testament. Und es empfiehlt sich daher, die für das sittengeschichtliche[20] Verständnis der Haustafeln im allgemeinen notwendigen Beobachtungen zuerst und vordringlich *hier* zu machen. Dabei fallen schon im Zuge einer genauen Beschreibung der Form sachlich einschlägige Entscheidungen – *auch* für das Frauenthema[21].

3. Die Form der Haustafel des Kolosserbriefes

3.1. Von der Haustafel des Kolosserbriefes werden die Frauen und Männer, Kinder und Väter, Sklaven und Herren nicht einfach nacheinander angeredet, sondern *paarweise* und *reziprok*.

Von vornherein macht derart die Gestaltung des Textes das Anlie-

---

[19] Es bleibt zu bedenken: in Kol 3,18 – 4,1 und Eph 5,22 – 6,9 werden ausschließlich(!) Ehemänner und Ehefrauen, Kinder und Väter bzw. Eltern, Sklaven und Herren angeredet. In 1 Petr 2,18 – 3,7 geht es nur noch um die erste und dritte Beziehung. In Did 4,9–11 fehlen die Frauen, in 1 Clem 21,6–8 die Sklaven. Auch in Barn 19,5–7 werden die Frauen nicht mehr erwähnt. Es ist daher ratsam, mit *L. Goppelt,* Der erste Petrusbrief (Anm. 10) 163–165, zwischen „Haustafeln" und „Ständetafeln" streng zu unterscheiden. Man sollte den Namen „Haustafel" für Kol 3,18 – 4,1 und Eph 5,22 – 6,9 reservieren. Nur hier kommt das „Haus" eindeutig und ohne Überstand in den Blick. Zu 1 Petr 2,13 – 3,7 vgl. ebd. 166. Allerdings gebraucht L. Goppelt auch den formgeschichtlich konturenschwachen Begriff der „Haustafeltradition". Vgl. *L. Goppelt,* Theologie des Neuen Testaments (UTB 850) (Göttingen ³1978) 496–497. *W. Schrage,* Zur Ethik der neutestamentlichen Haustafeln (Anm. 13) 10, redet sogar vom „Haustafelstoff" – und zählt Röm 13,1–7 dazu.

[20] Darum ging es schon *K. Thraede,* Zum historischen Hintergrund der „Haustafeln" des NT, in: Pietas. FS B. Kötting (JAC Ergänzungsband 8) (Münster 1980) 359–368.

[21] *Auch* an den einschneidenden Unterschieden der *Form* scheitert die Annahme von A. Seeberg, der „die nahe Verwandtschaft zwischen Kol 3,22 – 4,1; Eph 6,5–9; Did 4,10–11 und Barn 19,7" auf den von ihm postulierten „Katechismus der Urchristenheit" zurückführen wollte. Vgl. *A. Seeberg,* Der Katechismus der Urchristenheit. Mit einer Einführung von F. Hahn (TB 26) (München 1966) 37(–43). Hierher gehört außerdem Ph. Carrington's „code of submission": vgl. *Ph. Carrington,* The Primitive Christian Catechism (Cambridge 1940) 38 und passim. Ebenso wird man E. G. Selwyn's Rede von einem „code of subordination" bzw. von einer „Urtafel" hierher stellen müssen: vgl. *E. G. Selwyn,* The First Epistle of St. Peter (London ²1955) 437. Zusammenfassend zur Kritik dieses Erklärungsmodells: *J. E. Crouch,* The Origin and Intention of the Colossian Haustafel (FRLANT 109) (Göttingen 1972) 13–18.

VERS	ANREDE	IMPERATIV	BEGRÜNDUNG	MOTIVATION
Kol 3,18	Ihr Frauen,	seid eueren Männern untertan,	wie es sich ziemt	im Herrn.
Kol 3,19	Ihr Männer,	liebt euere Frauen und werdet nicht bitter gegen sie.		
Kol 3,20	Ihr Kinder,	gehorcht eueren Eltern in allem,	denn das ist wohlgefällig	im Herrn.
Kol 3,21	Ihr Väter,	reizt euere Kinder nicht,	damit sie nicht mutlos werden.	
Kol 3,22	Ihr Sklaven,	gehorcht in allem denen, die Kraft des Fleisches euere Herren sind, nicht in Augendienerei, um den Menschen zu gefallen, sondern in Einfalt des Herzens,		den Herrn fürchtend.
Kol 3,23		Was immer ihr tut, wirkt es von Herzen		für den Herrn und nicht für Menschen.
Kol 3,24			Wißt ihr doch, daß ihr vom Herrn als Entgelt das Erbe empfangen werdet.	Dem Herrn Christus dient.
Kol 3,25			Denn wer Unrecht tut, wird erhalten, was er an Unrecht getan hat. Und da gibt es kein Ansehen der Person.	
Kol 4,1	Ihr Herren,	gewährt eueren Sklaven, was recht und billig ist.	Wißt ihr doch, daß auch ihr einen Herrn im Himmel habt.	

gen durchschaubar, auf einer Grundordnung des Lebens bestehen zu wollen, die durch Gegenseitigkeit und Polarität geregelt werden kann. Keinesfalls wird es sich deshalb in Kol 3,18 – 4,1 um eine „Ständetafel"[22] handeln. Dagegen erhält eine solche paarweise Pointierung des paränetischen Anliegens ihre akuteste Aktualität im Lebensbereich einer antiken Familie, deren Radius im übrigen durch den angesprochenen Personenkreis nirgends überschritten wird. Aber auch die Detaillierung des sozialen Feldes wird nicht weiter vorangetrieben, als es die Kontur einer typischen Hausgemeinschaft im Altertum verlangt: der Bruder und die Schwester etwa treten ebensowenig in Erscheinung wie die Großeltern[23]. In die gleiche Richtung einer christlichen Familie weist die eingehaltene Reihenfolge. An erster Stelle kommt das engste und dichteste Verhältnis von Mann und Frau zur Sprache. Dann wird mit Rücksicht auf die direkte Abstammung der Umgang von Eltern und Kindern beredet. Erst zuletzt gerät das durch äußere Umstände manipulierte soziale Gefälle von Sklaven und Herren in den Blick. Darüber hinaus kann die Aufzählung offensichtlich nicht beliebig verlängert werden: die Haustafel des Kolosserbriefes hat ausschließlich dort Gültigkeit, wo Ehemann, Vater und Herr in einer Person zusammenfallen[24]. Das wiederum trifft nur auf die antike Hausgemeinschaft zu. Wenn man also ohne nähere Begründung davon ausgeht, „daß offenkundig *nicht* die christliche Familie, sondern die einzelnen Stände angesprochen werden"[25], so hat man wahrscheinlich bereits 1 Petr 2,13 – 3,7 oder vielleicht sogar die Pastoralbriefe (1 Tim 2,1–15; Tit 2,1–10) im Auge, welche die paarweise Belehrung tatsächlich nicht (mehr) kennen oder sie nur (noch) den Eheleuten zubilligen (vgl. 1 Petr 3,1.7). Die ziemlich grobe Voraussetzung, daß

[22] *J. Gnilka,* Der Kolosserbrief (Anm. 13) 205.
[23] Vgl. jetzt: *H.-J. Klauck,* Hausgemeinde und Hauskirche im frühen Christentum (SBS 103) (Stuttgart 1981) 18–19.
[24] Dazu: *O. Brunner,* Das „ganze Haus" und die alteuropäische „Ökonomik", in: *ders.,* Neue Wege der Sozialgeschichte. Vorträge und Aufsätze (Göttingen 1956) 44: „Alle Abhängigkeitsverhältnisse im Haus sind auf den Hausherrn bezogen, der als der leitende Kopf aus ihnen überhaupt erst ein Ganzes schafft." Und (ebd.): „Das Haus (Oikos) ist also ein Ganzes, das auf der Ungleichartigkeit seiner Glieder beruht, die durch den leitenden Geist des Herrn zu einer Einheit zusammengefügt werden".
[25] So *J. Gnilka,* Der Kolosserbrief (Anm. 13) 209.

„sich von Haustafeln (Ständetafeln) im eigentlichen Sinne nur für Kol, Eph und 1 Petr sprechen"[26] lasse, übersieht, daß die paarweise Veranlagung der Haustafel ein formal und inhaltlich unterscheidendes Kriterium des Kolosserbriefes und des von ihm literarisch abhängigen[27] Schreibens an die Epheser ist. Von hier aus führt kein direkter Weg überlieferungsgeschichtlicher Filiation zu 1 Petr 2,13 – 3,7.

3.2. Zur paarweisen und reziproken Nennung der Familienzugehörigen treten andere aufschlußreiche Formmerkmale. Den sechs Adressaten der Ermahnungen wird stets im *Nominativ Plural und mit dem bestimmten Artikel*[28] zugeredet.

Es sind nicht gewisse oder einzelne, sondern alle Frauen, Männer, Kinder, Väter, Sklaven und Herren christlicher Haushalte, die gemeint sind[29]. Auch werden die Familienmitglieder asyndetisch nebeneinander aufgereiht[30], wodurch sich der Eindruck verstärkt, daß man hier nicht den Entwurf einer differenzierenden Individualethik anraten will, sondern daß der Anspruch der Haustafel sehr viel weiter reicht. Sie hat nicht weniger im Sinn als das ethische Profil und das soziale Image des christlichen Hauses schlechthin.

3.3. Des weiteren gehen die sittlichen Appelle ausnahmslos im abrupten Pathos von *Imperativen* einher, die – ungeachtet ihrer vernei-

---

[26] Ebd. 207. Vgl. dagegen die oben (Anm. 19) namhaft gemachten Unterschiede sowie: *W. Lillie*, The Pauline House-tables: ET 86 (1975) 180: „So we limit the term ‚*house-table*' to exhortations given in the characteristic form of Colossians 3,18 – 4,1, when counsels are given in turn to wives and husbands, children and fathers, slaves and masters". Sowie (ebd.): „In any case duties to the state are not household matters. Again the exhortations in the Pastoral Epistles are rather instructions to be given by Timothy and Titus to various groups in their congregations, such as old people, young people, widows and slaves, again with a general exhortation of respect to those in authority. We might call them ‚*church-tables*'". Trotz 1 Petr 2,13–17 zählt W. Lillie jedoch – entgegen seiner eigenen Grenzziehung – 1 Petr 2,13 – 3,7 zu den „Haustafeln" (ebd.).
[27] Darüber zuletzt: *H. Merklein*, Eph 4,1 – 5,20 als Rezeption von Kol 3,1–17, in: Kontinuität und Einheit. FS F. Mußner (Freiburg – Basel – Wien 1981) 195–196.
[28] *F. Blass* – *A. Debrunner* – *F. Rehkopf*, Grammatik des neutestamentlichen Griechisch (Göttingen [14]1976) § 146,2.
[29] Vgl. ebd. § 252 unter b.
[30] *R. Kühner* – *B. Gerth*, Ausführliche Grammatik der griechischen Sprache II (Darmstadt 1963 = Hannover – Leipzig [3]1904), 340. Zur Deutung des Befundes und zum Vergleich mit dem Epheserbrief: *W. Bujard*, Stilanalytische Untersuchungen zum Kolosserbrief als Beitrag zur Methodik von Sprachvergleichen (StUNT 11) (Göttingen 1973) 44–45.

nenden Fassung in Kol 3,19b und 3,21 – ohne Umschweife zur Sache kommen.

Es stehen keine Ratschläge oder Angebote des Verhaltens zur Debatte, für oder gegen die man sich noch entscheiden könnte[31]. Vielmehr werden ethische Verpflichtungen eingeschärft, welche auf die Zweifel und die Reputation einer umständlich vernunftbegründeten Moral gar nicht angewiesen zu sein scheinen[32].

3.4. Das heißt nicht, daß diese Belehrungen völlig ohne Motivation verbleiben wollen. Im Gegenteil: eine ganze Reihe von kausalen Partikeln und Wendungen wird aufgeboten, um mit den Mahnungen auch Argumente und Erklärungen einzuprägen (Kol 3,18: ὡς; 3,20: γάρ; 3,21: ἵνα; 3,24; 4,1: εἰδότες ὅτι)[33]. Und die gleichen *Begründungen* verfolgen ihre Ziele keineswegs abseits der die Form der Haustafel tragenden Struktur, sondern sie leisten einen nicht unerheblichen Beitrag zu deren geschlossenem Erscheinungsbild[34]. Erst wenn man daran geht, sie unter inhaltlichen Aspekten miteinander zu vergleichen, ändert sich die Szene: jene begründenden Ausführungen fächern sich in eine sachliche Mehrdeutigkeit auseinander, die nach einer überlegten überlieferungsgeschichtlichen Erläuterung verlangt.

Da gibt es zunächst zwei pragmatische Hinweise auf Schickliches und Gültiges. Die Wortfolgen „wie es sich ziemt" in Kol 3,18 und „denn das ist wohlgefällig" aus Kol 3,20 appellieren offensichtlich an „fixierte gesellschaftliche Werte"[35], ohne daß man ihnen auf den ersten Blick einen Vorgang christlicher Integration abspüren könnte. Das ist auch in Kol 3,21 nicht der Fall, wo die prohibitive

---

[31] Das übersieht *E. Kähler*, Die Frau in den paulinischen Briefen (Zürich 1960) 201–202, wenn sie zu dem Schluß kommt: „Der Mensch als Mann oder Frau, Kind, Sklave oder Staatsbürger wird immer neu zu der *Entscheidung* hinsichtlich der Unterordnung aufgerufen".

[32] Schon die gewählte grammatische Gestalt der *Imperative* macht die Inanspruchnahme alttestamentlichen apodiktischen Gottesrechts als Vorgabe äußerst unwahrscheinlich: gegen *D. Schroeder*, Die Haustafeln des Neuen Testaments. Ihre Herkunft und ihr theologischer Sinn (Hamburg [Diss. theol.] 1959) 93.

[33] Nur die Mahnung an die Adresse der Ehemänner in Kol 3,19 weist keine Begründung bzw. Motivation auf, sondern nur zwei Imperative. Vgl. unten S. 314. In Eph 5,25–33 wird eine ausführliche christologische Motivation nachgebracht.

[34] Siehe den Schautext, oben S. 268.

[35] *M. Dibelius*, An die Kolosser, Epheser, an Philemon (Anm. 15) 46.

Aussage „damit sie nicht mutlos werden" die Aufforderung an die Väter motivieren soll, ihre Kinder nicht zu „reizen".

Solchen Argumenten von handlicher Opportunität tritt eine Kette theologischer Hinweise an die Seite, deren Vermittlung mit den umstehenden Markierungen ethischen Verhaltens unterschiedlich intensiv ist und daher mehrdeutig bleibt. So wird in Kol 3,18.20 lediglich die Formel „im Herrn" hinzugesetzt. In Kol 3,18 heißt es nur „den Herrn fürchtend", und in Kol 3,23 vermerkt man ohne nennenswerte Anschaulichkeit „für den Herrn und nicht für Menschen". Daß diese relativ anspruchslosen theologischen Fingerzeige nicht von vornherein und ursprünglich mit den sittlichen Appellen der Haustafel zusammengestanden haben können, ist unverkennbar. Vor allem Kol 3,20 ist dafür ein beredtes Zeugnis. Denn dort wird nicht etwa die dem Urchristentum auch sonst geläufige Regel des „dem Herrn (= Gott) Wohlgefälligen"[36] erläuternd zitiert, sondern es wird mit Hilfe der grammatisch abständigen[37] Wendung „im Herrn" der reichlich harte Versuch gemacht, eine auf dem profanen Felde arrivierte Wertung des sozial „Wohlgefälligen" herüberzunehmen und zu adaptieren. In dieselbe Richtung weist eine korrespondierende Beobachtung. Nur im Rahmen der Versreihe Kol 3,24 bis 4,1 zeigt sich die Bezugnahme auf den „Herrn" (Kol 3,24; 4,1) in ein sprachliches Netz verwoben, dessen argumentative Signale dicht genug sind, um als Ansatz einer theologischen Beweisführung ernstgenommen zu werden.

3.5. Gerade die unterschiedlich enge Begründungsstruktur der theologischen Einlassungen ist aber kaum anders verständlich zu machen, denn als verschieden weit gediehene Integrationsleistung gegenüber den ethischen Anordnungen einer *vorgegebenen* Haustafel.

Wie weit dabei deren überlieferungsgeschichtliche Vergangenheit hinter die letzte – nämlich christliche – Adaptionsunternehmung zurückreicht, wird indirekt an dem im Zusammenhang nur schwer ein-

---

[36] εὐάρεστον τῷ θεῷ bzw. τῷ κυρίῳ: Röm 12,1; 14,18; Phil 4,18 vgl. 2 Kor 5,9; Eph 5,10. Die Gewöhnung an diesen Sprachgebrauch ist so stark, daß eine Reihe von Handschriften und Clemens Alexandrinus die Lesart ἐν κυρίῳ aus Kol 3,20 in τῷ κυρίῳ verbessern.

[37] Vgl. *J. H. Moulton – N. Turner*, A Grammar of New Testament Greek III (Edinburgh 1963) 263, und *E. Lohse*, Die Briefe an die Kolosser und an Philemon (KEK IX/2) (Göttingen ²1977) 226 Anm. 7.

gängigen Imperativ „dem Herrn *Christus* dient!" aus Kol 3, 24 ables-
bar[38]. Denn obwohl sein Wortlaut im gesamten Neuen Testament
ohne Äquivalent bleibt[39], ist er die einzige Instanz, die sicheren Aufschluß darüber gibt, an wessen Autorität anläßlich der unverhältnismäßig[40] häufigen Nennung des „Herrn" in Kol 3, 18.20.22.23.24; 4, 1
erinnert werden soll. Sonst bietet die Haustafel selbst keinerlei Hil-
festellung zur Identifizierung, und man sieht sich mit der Frage, wer
der „Herr" sei, der hier so oft angerufen wird, auf den entfernteren
Kontext des Verses Kol 3, 17 verwiesen, wo zuletzt vom „Namen
Jesu, des Herrn" die Rede war.

So gesehen fördert bereits die anhand einer adverbialen Partizi-
pialkonstruktion[41] nur locker in Kol 3, 22 eingepaßte und genuin alttestamentliche[42] Phrase von der „Furcht des Herrn" den Verdacht,

---

[38] Zu lesen ist sicher der Imperativ, nicht der Indikativ, wie es die Majuskelhand-
schriften D² Ψ sowie der Mehrheitstext, alle syrischen Zeugen und Clemens
Alexandrinus nahelegen möchten, indem sie erleichternd γάρ einfügen: „*Ihr*
dient *nämlich* dem Herrn Christus". *M. Dibelius – H. Greeven,* An die Kolosser,
Epheser, an Philemon (Anm. 15) 46 übersetzen: „Der Herr, dem ihr dient, heißt
Christus". Sie lassen sich auf die nur schwach bezeugte Lesart ᾧ δουλεύετε ein.
Die Varianten machen die frühe Einsicht in einen literarischen Bruch deutlich.
Vgl. auch *C. F. D. Moule,* The Epistles of Paul the Apostle to the Colossians and
to Philemon (Cambridge 1957) 131.
[39] Vgl. *W. Kramer,* Christos–Kyrios–Gottessohn. Untersuchungen zu Gebrauch
und Bedeutung der christologischen Bezeichnungen bei Paulus und in den vorpaulinischen Gemeinden (AThANT 44) (Zürich 1963) 44 Anm. 1. Am nächsten
kommt Röm 16, 18: τῷ κυρίῳ ἡμῶν Χριστῷ.
[40] „Von 13 Verweisen auf den Kyrios im Kolosserbrief stehen 7 in der Haustafel": *E. Schweizer,* Die Weltlichkeit des Neuen Testaments: die Haustafeln, in:
Beiträge zur alttestamentlichen Theologie. FS *W. Zimmerli* (Göttingen 1977) 404
Anm. 44. Zuvor wies darauf hin: *W. Schrage,* Zur Ethik der neutestamentlichen
Haustafeln (Anm. 19) 22.
[41] Vgl. *Blass – Debrunner – Rehkopf,* § 417 Anm. 1: „zur Vermeidung zweier mit
καί verbundener Imperative". Weiterhin: *W. Bujard,* Stilanalytische Untersuchungen (Anm. 30) 63. Die Konstruktion ist griechisch. Einfluß des Hebräischen
braucht also nicht angenommen zu werden, wie *D. Daube,* Participle and Imperative in I Peter, in: *E. G. Selwyn,* The First Epistle of St. Peter (Anm. 21)
467–488, vorschlug. Damit entfällt auch die Herleitung aus einem hebräischen
Original, dessen sich das palästinische Judentum bedient haben soll.
[42] Im Neuen Testament ist die Wendung: „den Herrn = Christus fürchten"
sonst unbekannt. Dagegen reden von der „Furcht Gottes": Lk 18, 2.4; Apg
10, 2.22.35; 13, 16.26; 1 Petr 2, 17; Apk 11, 18; 14, 7; 19, 5. Merkwürdigerweise
„kennt Paulus auch diese (sc. Formel von der „Furcht Gottes") nicht": *J. Gnilka,*
Der Kolosserbrief (Anm. 13) 221 Anm. 85. Einschlägig ist, daß P⁴⁶ und der Mehrheitstext κύριον in ϑεόν verbessern und damit sekundär wieder auf den alttesta-

daß vor der urchristlichen Rezeption der Haustafel die Traditionsstufe einer jüdischen Übernahme liegt[43]. Und die Versicherung der Unparteilichkeit *Gottes*[44] beim Vollzug des Endgerichts, wie sie Kol 3,25 vorträgt, bestätigt eine solche Vermutung ganz entschieden[45].

Vor allem jedoch wird auf diesem Wege einer zweiphasigen Anverwandlung plausibel erklärbar, weswegen die Haustafel keine eindeutige Handhabe dafür zu geben scheint, wem der Satz in Kol 3,25 gelten soll, demzufolge „derjenige, der Unrecht tut, erhalten wird, was er an Unrecht getan hat". Wird an die Sklaven gedacht oder an deren „Herren"?[46] Unter der eben angesprochenen überlieferungs-

---

mentlichen Gebrauch einschwenken. Zum Ganzen vgl. *R. Bultmann*, Theologie des Neuen Testaments (UTB 630) (Tübingen ⁸1980) 561–562.
[43] So schon *E. Lohmeyer*, Die Briefe an die Philipper, an die Kolosser und an Philemon (KEK IX/2) (Göttingen ¹²1964) 158, der allerdings dann auf einer direkten Herkunft der Haustafel aus dem Judentum insistiert: „Nur im jüdischen Munde ist der Ausdruck ‚Furcht des Herrn' eindeutig. Niemals sagt das NT, daß der Herr Christus von seinen Gläubigen zu ‚fürchten' sei". Scharfsichtig hält E. Lohmeyer auch die restlichen Verweise auf den „Herrn" für jüdisch – ausgenommen Kol 3,24b (ebd. 159).
[44] Ohne Begründung legt *J. Gnilka*, Der Kolosserbrief (Anm. 13) 224, aus: „Hier wird die Unbestechlichkeit auf den Kyrios *Christus* übertragen". Vgl. *J. Gnilka*, Der Epheserbrief (HThK X/2) (Freiburg – Basel – Wien 1971) 302: „Im AT und Judentum bezieht sie sich auf Gott, ebenso noch (sic!) in Röm 2,11; 1 Petr 1,17; Did 4,10. In den Deuteropaulinen ist sie auf Christus übertragen. Diese Übertragung ist deshalb bemerkenswert, weil damit Christus als der Richter gekennzeichnet ist". Auch hier fehlen die Argumente. Zwar wird man *O. Merk*, Handeln aus Glauben. Die Motivierungen der paulinischen Ethik (MThSt 5) (Marburg 1968) 219 Anm. 138, zugestehen müssen: „Es ist nicht ganz einsichtig, ob mit κύριος Gott oder Christus gemeint ist". Und es mag auch stimmen, daß „die Parallelität mit Kol 3,24b es nahelegen" kann, „hier Christus als Gerichtsherrn zu sehen (vgl. 2 Kor 5,10 u.ö.)" (ebd.). Aber kommt ein solcher Hinweis gegen den offensichtlich stehenden Sprachgebrauch auf, der sich im Umkreis der vor Röm 2,11 nicht belegbaren Wortschöpfung προσωπολημψία niederschlägt?
Röm 2,11: οὐ γάρ ἐστιν προσωπολημψία παρὰ τῷ θεῷ
Kol 3,25: καὶ οὐκ ἔστιν προσωπολημψία
Eph 6,9 : καὶ προσωπολημψία οὐκ ἔστιν παρ' αὐτῷ (sc. κυρίῳ)
Vgl. *G. Didier*, Désintéressement du Chrétien. La rétribution dans la morale de saint Paul (Paris 1955) 186, sowie die Kommentare von *E. Lohse* (Anm. 37) 230–231; *E. Schweizer*, Der Brief an die Kolosser (EKK) (Neukirchen – Vluyn 1976) 168–169, und *H. Conzelmann*, Der Brief an die Kolosser, in: *J. Becker, H. Conzelmann, G. Friedrich*, Die Briefe an die Galater, Epheser, Philipper, Kolosser, Thessalonicher und Philemon (NTD 8) (Göttingen 1976) 201.
[45] Zur alttestamentlichen Wortverbindung πρόσωπον λαμβάνειν = parteiisch urteilen vgl. *E. Lohse*, Art. προσωπολημψία κτλ.: ThWNT VI 780–781.
[46] Klar entscheidet sich der Epheserbrief. Im Zuge seiner Auslegung von Kol 3,18 – 4,1 führt er die Warnung vor Gott, der keine προσωπολημψία kennt, in die

274

geschichtlichen Voraussetzung löst sich das alte exegetische Dilemma auf eine sehr einsichtige Weise: die älteren jüdischen Integrationselemente, welche die Sklaven ungerührt an die endgerichtliche Talio Gottes erinnerten, vertragen sich nur schlecht mit der schließlich in Kol 3,24 eingetragenen christlichen Gewißheit, daß die Sklaven ebenso wie *alle* Christen „als Entgelt das Erbe (κληρονομία)[47] empfangen werden", welches „in den Himmeln" schon für sie bereit liegt (vgl. Kol 1,5; 3,1–4). Beim Vollzug der christlichen rélecture einer längst jüdisch vereinnahmten Haustafel macht es dann auch Sinn, einen vorgegebenen Imperativ „dem Herrn dient!" durch „dem Herrn *Christus* dient!" zu komplettieren – ohne dabei das Risiko zu scheuen, aus dem geläufigen christologischen Sprachgebrauch auszubrechen. Gegenüber der jüdischen Adaptionsschicht sollte unbezweifelbar betont werden, daß der Sklave dann, wenn er seinem irdischen Gebieter zu Diensten war, schließlich dem Kyrios Gehorsam leistete, welcher ihm als der Herr über alles gelten durfte (vgl. Kol 1,15–20; 2,15; 3,1 b).

3.6. Die Spuren solcher komplexen überlieferungsgeschichtlichen Vorgänge innerhalb der begründenden und motivierenden Abschnitte beeinträchtigen sichtlich die gestalterische und logische Symmetrie der Haustafel im Kolosserbrief[48]. Sie sind jedoch ebenso unverkennbar *nicht* in der Lage, die sprachliche Form einer grundlegenderen Veränderung zu unterziehen: die entscheidenden Proportionen des stilistischen Ausdrucks bleiben erhalten[49].

Das wiederum hat mit einem inhaltlichen Gesichtspunkt zu tun, der sich von Anfang an untrennbar mit den sprachlichen Strukturen verbindet und den sowohl die christliche als auch die ältere jüdische Redaktion ohne Abstriche respektieren. Denn durch nichts wird die Gestaltung der Haustafel entschiedener und aufdringlicher gesteuert als durch ihr schlechterdings zentrales Anliegen – die Auffor-

---

Mahnung an die „Herren" ein. Eph 6,9: „Wißt ihr (sc. ihr Herren) doch, daß sowohl ihr (sc. der Sklaven) als auch euer Herr im Himmel ist und daß es bei ihm kein Ansehen der Person gibt".

[47] Vgl. *R. Hammer*, A Comparison of KLERONOMIA in Paul and Ephesians: JBL 79 (1960) 267–272, und *J. Gnilka*, Der Kolosserbrief (Anm. 13) 222 Anm. 91.

[48] Siehe oben den Schautext auf S. 268.

[49] Vgl. die Beschreibungen bei *K. Weidinger*, Die Haustafeln (Anm. 18) 50–51 und *D. Schroeder*, Die Haustafeln (Anm. 32) 79–82.

derung zu „Unterordnung" und „Gehorsam". Darauf macht nicht nur der Befund aufmerksam, daß sich hier die einschlägigen Vokabeln für „untertan sein" (ὑποτάσσεσθαι, Kol 3,17) bzw. „gehorchen" (ὑπακούειν, V. 20.22) häufen und derart ein korrespondierendes Wortfeld aufbauen, dessen Dichte die gesamte Haustafel mit einem eindeutigen semantischen Profil überzieht.

Noch weit augenfälliger ist ein anderes Indiz. Die sechs je paarweise und gegenseitig angeredeten Familienzugehörigen werden nämlich stets in der Weise genannt, daß dem Leser unmißverständlich klar wird, wie sehr es in einer Hausgemeinschaft auf die Anerkennung eines durchgängigen *Prinzips der Unterordnung* ankommt. Bei jedem der drei vorgestellten Paare ist ein Teil dem anderen untergeordnet. Ohne Ausnahme werden dabei die untergeordneten Angehörigen an erster Stelle genannt: die Frauen (V. 18), Kinder (V. 20) und Sklaven (V. 22) – *sie* sind bereits durch die formale Anordnung der auf sie hingesprochenen Appelle dermaßen exponiert, daß kein Zweifel an der Annahme erlaubt zu sein scheint, sie seien die eigentlichen Adressaten der Haustafel. Die sich dort in einer paarweisen Aufführung mit den Ehemännern, Vätern und Herren gleichfalls niederschlagende Regel der Gegenseitigkeit hat also ihre nahe Grenze an einem noch drängenderen Gefälle der Unterordnung, welches sich an einer fraglos akzeptierten patria potestas festmacht. *Nur* von den Ehemännern (V. 19), Vätern (V. 21) und Herren (Kol 4,1) wird deshalb weder „Unterordnung" noch „Gehorsam" verlangt. Und weiter: die Haustafel des Kolosserbriefes billigt und propagiert jenes auf den pater familias fixierte Ethos der Unterordnung ohne die Anstrengung ausführlicherer Beweisgänge, die ihrerseits wieder emanzipatorische Ängste oder Verlegenheiten verrieten. Eher sucht sie den Kanon familiärer Unterwerfung als naturhafte Selbstverständlichkeit zu empfehlen, der gegenüber Skrupel weder erlaubt noch möglich sind. So konfrontiert Kol 3,20 die Kinder den „Eltern", während V. 21 ausschließlich die „Väter" mit der Erziehung der Kinder befaßt zeigt, – ohne daß auch nur der Schatten einer Begründung eine solche Verengung elterlicher Gewalt plausibel machte. Dieselbe unerschütterte Sicherheit der Beharrung auf der patria potestas äußert sich in dem Befund, daß ausschließlich bei den Sklaven die Mahnung zum Gehorsam stärker ausgebaut (V. 22–23 a) und mit größerer theologischer Ausführlichkeit begründet wird (V. 23 b–25). Denn allein die Sklaven waren nicht durch den naturgegebenen Zwang des angestammten Familienbandes zur Unterwerfung unter die Regie des pater familias zu bewegen[50].

Daß die Ehemänner, Väter und Herren ohnehin nicht mit gleichem Nachdruck angeredet sind, wird man der exakt ausgewogenen Eigenart der Haustafel entnehmen müssen: lediglich die Anforderungen an die untergeordneten Teile der Familie werden nennenswert (V. 18 b.20 b), ja eingehend (V. 24–25) motiviert. Dagegen entbehren die Mahnungen an die Männer, Väter und Herren entweder überhaupt einer Begründung (V. 19) oder diese fällt unverhältnismäßig kurz und gerafft aus (Kol 3,21 b; 4,1 b).

Einmal mehr wird ersichtlich, daß eine emphatische Einschärfung der sittlichen Pflicht der Unterordnung für Frauen, Kinder und Sklaven die intentionale und eigentlich produktive Innenseite ist, welche die Form der Haustafel schließlich hervortreibt. Unter diesem wesentlichen Sachaspekt bleibt dort nichts unüberlegt oder dem Zufall überlassen. Es ist in erster Linie die Absicht, die Aufforderung zu familiärer Fügsamkeit unter die patria potestas mit Eindeutigkeit und Nachdrücklichkeit auszusprechen, welche der Haustafel des Kolosserbriefes ihren didaktischen Rang verleiht und sie nicht erst während ihres jüdischen und christlichen Aneignungsstadiums ein nahezu künstlerisches Niveau erreichen ließ.

---

[50] Anders diejenigen Exegeten, welche sich durch die überraschend umfangreichen Einlassungen an die Adresse der Sklaven in Kol 3,22–25 an eine enge Beziehung zwischen dem Kolosser- und dem Philemonbrief erinnert sehen. So vor allem *E. F. Scott*, The Epistles of Paul to Colossians, to Philemon and to the Ephesians (London 1952) 79–81; *J. Knox*, Philemon among the Letters of Paul (New York – Nashville 1959) 36–44, und *ders.*, Philemon and the Authenticity of Colossians: JR 18 (1938) 156–157; *C. L. Milton*, The Epistle to the Ephesians (Oxford 1951) 170; *E. Percy*, Die Probleme der Kolosser- und Epheserbriefe (SVSL 39) (Lund 1946) 402 Anm. 79. *O. Merk*, Handeln aus Glauben (Anm. 44) 218 Anm. 132, meint: „Daß Kol 3,25 a sich konkret auf den entlaufenen Sklaven Onesimus beziehe, ist unbeweisbare Vermutung, aber daß die ausführliche Behandlung der Sklavenfrage mit dem Anliegen des Phlm in Verbindung steht, ist durchaus denkbar". – Die entscheidenden Einwände gegen diese Annahme bei *J. E. Crouch*, The Origin and Intention of the Colossian Haustafel (Anm. 21) 11, besonders ebd. Anm. 6. Vgl. *E. Lohse*, Die Briefe an die Kolosser und an Philemon (Anm. 37) 227 Anm. 4. *E. Schweizer*, Der Brief an die Kolosser (Anm. 44) 167: „Die Paränese wird stark ausgebaut. Das könnte damit zusammenhängen, daß Onesimus Mitüberbringer ist, ist aber vor allem dadurch bedingt, daß es für Mahnungen an Sklaven kaum Parallelen gibt".

4. Die Haustafel als ältere literarische Einheit

Nicht nur die abstrahierte sprachliche Gestaltung, mehr noch die vermutlichen Spuren einer zweifachen Redaktion machen es aber außerordentlich unwahrscheinlich, daß die Mahnungen in Kol 3,18 bis 4,1 einer Front faktischen und rekonstruierbaren Fehlverhaltens in der Gemeinde von Kolossä wehren wollen[51]. Die Haustafel basiert vielmehr in *allen* ihren tragenden Bestandteilen auf einer älteren literarischen Einheit, die von ihren christlichen und jüdischen Zusätzen durchaus unterschieden werden kann.

Die Abwehr eines mit Wucht aufbrechenden urchristlichen Enthusiasmus (vgl. Gal 3,28; 1 Kor 12,13 und Kol 3,11)[52] oder die restaurativ erhobene Option für eine strengere Moral jüdischer Prävenienz in einer zu ethischer Laxheit abgeschlafften christlichen Ortskirche[53] reichen deshalb schwerlich aus, um die Existenz einer

---

[51] Es besteht keinerlei Zwang, die Paränese des Kolosserbriefes (Kol 3,1 – 4,6) gegen die „Irrlehre" in der Gemeinde (vgl. Kol 2,8–23) gerichtet zu sehen – wie immer man diese rekonstruieren mag (vgl. die bisherigen Vorschläge bei *J. Gnilka*, Der Kolosserbrief [Anm. 13] 164–167.167–170). Anders *J. E. Crouch*, The Origin and Intention of the Colossian Haustafel (Anm. 21) 150–151, der an die „existence of enthusiastic and nomistic elements in Christianity from the beginning" denkt und fortfährt: „As a result of our study we would submit that the tension between these two movements in Hellenistic Christianity is the context in which the Christian Haustafel was forged and that the Haustafel represents the nomistic tendency of Pauline Christianity. It was created to serve emerging orthodoxy as a weapon against *enthusiastic* and *heretical* threats to the stability of both the church and the social order". Die Haustafel bedarf einer solchen *antihäretischen* Rechtfertigung nicht.

[52] Vgl. *D. Schroeder*, Die Haustafeln (Anm. 32) 89–90. Im Blick auf Kol 3,22–25 spricht schon *M. Dibelius – H. Greeven*, An die Kolosser, Epheser, an Philemon (Anm. 15) 47, davon, daß „die mißverständliche Auffassung der Freiheitsbotschaft als eines Aufrufs zur sozialen Revolution" damals im Urchristentum „überall nahe gelegen habe". Vorsichtiger urteilt *E. Schweizer*, Der Brief an die Kolosser (Anm. 44) 161: „Wohl aber könnte das Mißverständnis der paulinischen Verkündigung der Freiheit für ihr Aufkommen wichtig geworden sein. ‚Alles ist erlaubt' war ja die Losung der Korinther, die sich dabei vermutlich auf paulinische Aussagen wie Gal 3,28 beriefen". Im Anschluß daran macht er selbst den entscheidenden Einwand: „Kinderemanzipation war damals gewiß nie aktuell" (ebd.). Entschiedener dagegen sprechen sich aus: *W. Lillie*, The Pauline House-tables (Anm. 26) 182, und *W. Schrage*, Zur Ethik der neutestamentlichen Haustafeln (Anm. 13) 6; außerdem: *J. E. Crouch*, The Origin and Intention of the Colossian Haustafel (Anm. 21) 157–158.

[53] *J. E. Crouch*, a. a. O. 157: „The Haustafel itself was formulated in nomistic circles to combat what was regarded as the growing danger posed by enthusiastic

Regelliste für Familienangehörige zu erklären, wie sie Kol 3, 18 – 4, 1 vorgibt. Eher liegt es nahe, damit zu rechnen, daß die Haustafel des Kolosserbriefs eine zuerst von Juden und dann von Christen aufgegriffene Parteinahme in einer gemeinantiken Debatte um das sittliche Profil der Familie und des Hauses dokumentiert[54].

4.1. Mit einer solchen Annahme kommt eine Reihe von Beobachtungen überein, die zu der Folgerung führen, daß die häuslichen Vorschriften aus Kol 3, 18 – 4, 1 nur sehr locker mit ihrem derzeitigen Kontext verklammert sind[55]. Nicht nur, daß Kol 3, 18 mit der unmittelbar zuvor ergangenen Aufforderung zum Dank (V. 15–17) ohne erkennbare Vermittlung zusammensteht[56]. Weit erheblicher ist, daß von 3, 17 und dann wieder von 4, 2 die gesamte Gemeinde undifferenziert angeredet wird, während die sechs Gruppierungen eines antiken Haushalts, an die sich Kol 3, 18 – 4, 1 wendet, im gesamten umliegenden Briefcorpus nicht mehr zur Sprache kommen[57]. Zwar

---

[54] excesses". – W. *Schrage*, a. a. O. 6, äußert sich gegenteilig: es „ist gerade gegenüber *Asketen* die Aufforderung geboten, nicht aus den Strukturen zu emigrieren, sondern alles im Namen des Herrn zu tun, der das Haupt der Mächte und Gewalten ist". Wo gibt es dafür im Kolosserbrief einen einschlägigen Text?

[54] Das setzt voraus, daß die Haustafel kein Bestandteil einer einseitig und ausschließlich innerchristlichen oder innertheologischen Auseinandersetzung ist. So K. *Thraede*, Ärger mit der Freiheit (Anm. 7) 120–125, sowie *ders.*, Zum historischen Hintergrund der „Haustafeln" (Anm. 20) 359–368, und *ders.*, Frauen im Leben frühchristlicher Gemeinden: US 32 (1977) 286–299. Vgl. aber auch D. L. *Balch*, „Let Wives be Submissive . . .". The origin, form and apologetic function of the household duty code (Haustafel) in I Peter (Yale University 1974) (Diss. Phil., Abteilung: Religion. Xerox University Microfilms, Ann Arbor, Michigan 48106) 217: „the stimulus for the adoption of this ethic in 1 Peter does not come from within the church at all; rather, it came from society, which demanded that all members of society accept Roman social-political customs, and ‚slandered' Christians who did not seem to conform. Then the church, as a ‚defense' stressed that part of the ethic which it was being accused of violating".

[55] Zwei extreme Positionen sind nur schwer mit dem Überlieferungsbefund vereinbar. Zum einen: D. *Bradley*, The Origin of the Hortatory Materials in the Letters of Paul (Yale [Diss. theol.] 1947) 181, der sich dafür ausspricht, daß die Haustafel des Kolosserbriefes „has been interpolated". Aber welche Handschrift(en) legt (legen) das nahe? Zum anderen: D. *Schroeder*, Die Haustafeln (Anm. 32) 80, der Kol 3, 18 – 4, 1 für einen „wesentlichen Bestandteil des Briefes" hält und das mit einer klassischen petitio principii begründet: „die Herausnahme der Haustafel würde eine Lücke lassen, denn dann würde Paulus sich nirgends in diesem Zusammenhang über das Leben in den Ständen äußern".

[56] Man kann nur den verbalen Anklang von Kol 3, 17 a: καὶ πᾶν ὅ τι ἐὰν ποιῆτε an Kol 3, 23 a: ὅ ἐὰν ποιῆτε namhaft machen.

[57] Vgl. E. *Schweizer*, Zur Frage der Echtheit des Kolosser- und Epheserbriefes,

sträubt sich die Haustafel nicht gegen ihren Zusammenhang, aber dieser wird keineswegs beschädigt, wenn man Kol 3, 18 – 4, 1 daraus entfernt. Im Gegenteil: 3, 17 würde in 4, 2 eine glattere und reibungslosere Fortsetzung finden, wenn die Haustafel fehlte.

4.2. Auch Sprache und Sprachhaltung verhelfen der Versfolge Kol 3, 18 – 4, 1 zum Image einer ursprünglich separaten literarischen Einheit[58]. Die Imperative der Haustafel wenden sich in kürzeren und abrupteren Formulierungen an den Leser als die paränetischen Empfehlungen ringsum[59]. Und es ist nicht ohne Signifikanz, wenn man in Kol 3, 18 – 4, 1 auf eine ungewöhnlich dichte Konzentration paulinischer und deuteropaulinischer Hapaxlegomena stößt[60].

Darf man aber alles in allem mit Gewißheit davon ausgehen, daß die Haustafel ein originär in sich geschlossener und abgerundeter Abschnitt ist, dann wird die Frage umso dringlicher, woher der Katalog ethischer Ermahnungen letztlich stammt, der sich in einer derartigen sprachlichen Konsistenz darbietet und der nach einer jüdischen Akkommodationsphase schließlich auch christlichen Gemeinden verfügbar war. Von der Antwort hängt entscheidend das Urteil darüber ab, wie sich Kol 3, 18 – 4, 1 zwischen den Koordinaten sozialethischer Anschauungen der zeitgenössischen Antike ausnimmt.

5. Die Diskussion um die Herkunft

Die hier einschlägigen Erörterungen zeigen sich bis zur Stunde von Lösungen bestimmt, die M. Dibelius in der ersten Auflage seines Kommentars zum Kolosserbrief vorschlug[61]. Er führte die neutesta-

---

in: *ders.*, Neotestamentica (Zürich 1963) 429, und vor allem *W. Bujard*, Stilanalytische Untersuchungen zum Kolosserbrief (Anm. 30) 208–210, und die Tabelle ebd. 214.

[58] Vgl. *E. Percy*, Die Probleme der Kolosser- und Epheserbriefe (Anm. 50) 19–20.36.

[59] *D. Schroeder*, Die Haustafeln (Anm. 32) 79.

[60] Kol 3, 21: ἀθυμέω; 3, 24: ἀνταπόδοσις; 3, 19: πικραίνω; 3, 22 (und davon abhängig: Eph 6, 6): ἀνθρωπάρεσκος; 3, 22 (und davon abhängig Eph 6, 6): ὀφθαλμοδουλία. Vgl. *J. E. Crouch*, The Origin and Intention of the Colossian Haustafel (Anm. 21) 11, und die Listen bei *E. Lohse*, Die Briefe an die Kolosser und an Philemon (Anm. 37) 133–135.

[61] Die 1. Auflage erschien 1913.

mentlichen Haustafeln auf „das Bedürfnis des jungen Christentums" zurück, „sich im Alltagsleben einzurichten"[62], nachdem die Naherwartung des eschatologischen Umbruchs als Irrtum erwiesen war[63]. Auf die allmählich drängenden Zwänge zu einem auch ethisch verantworteten Arrangement mit der fortschreitenden Geschichte habe das Urchristentum dadurch reagiert, daß es sich unter den paränetischen Angeboten der jüdischen Missionsbemühung umsah und dabei auf Texte stieß, welche den Präzeptensammlungen geglichen haben sollen, die sich schließlich bei Flavius Josephus (Contra Apionem 2, 198–208) und Pseudo-Phokylides (Verse 175–228)[64] niederschlugen. Daneben habe man jedoch auch „die philosophische Propaganda des Hellenismus" studiert, die sich gleichfalls „solcher Zusammenstellungen der Pflichten nach Kreisen" bediente, wofür M. Dibelius Belege aus Epiktet, Diogenes Laertios und besonders den Stoiker Hierokles zitiert[65], wie ihn Karl Praechter[66] aus Stobaios-Auszügen rekonstruiert hatte.

5.1. Es war K. Weidinger, der dann die sich bereits deutlich abzeichnende These seines Lehrers M. Dibelius von einem „in der populären Morallehre der Stoa ausgebildeten Schema"[67], das „mit

---

[62] M. Dibelius, An die Kolosser, Epheser, an Philemon (Anm. 15) 48.

[63] Ebd. 48, und M. Dibelius, Die Formgeschichte des Evangeliums (Tübingen [6]1971 = [3]1933), 241: „Die urchristlichen Gemeinden waren auf das Vergehen dieser Welt und nicht auf das Leben in ihr eingerichtet; so waren sie auf die Notwendigkeit keineswegs gerüstet, paränetische Losungen für den Alltag hervorzubringen". Aber kann man ernsthaft die ausbleibende Parusie in Anschlag bringen, um zu erklären, daß die Urchristenheit eigentlich zu schnell und nur flüchtig integrierend nach den heidnisch und/oder jüdisch vorgegebenen „Haustafeln" griff? Lebten denn die ersten Christen jemals ohne ethische Verhaltensmuster? Zeigen sie sich nicht deshalb so besonders spröde gegenüber der Entwicklung einer spezifisch christlichen Ethik, weil ihnen im wesentlichen die Ethik genügte, die sie aus dem Judentum oder aus dem Heidentum mitbrachten? Dann allerdings galten ihnen die übernommenen „Haustafeln" niemals bloß als Notbehelf angesichts der Beschwernisse einer sich verzögernden Parusie, sondern sie mußten ihnen als brauchbare und adäquate Maßgaben einer authentisch christlichen Ethik erscheinen.

[64] Vgl. jetzt die Übersetzung und den Kommentar von M. Küchler, Frühjüdische Weisheitstraditionen. Zum Fortgang weisheitlichen Denkens im Bereich des frühjüdischen Jahweglaubens (OBO 26) (Freiburg – Göttingen 1979) 261–302.

[65] M. Dibelius, An die Kolosser, Epheser, an Philemon (Anm. 15) 48–49.

[66] K. Praechter, Hierokles der Stoiker (Leipzig 1901), jetzt in: ders., Kleine Schriften, hrsg. von H. Dörrie (Hildesheim 1973) 311–467.

[67] M. Dibelius, a. a. O. 48.

oder ohne Vermittlung des Judentums"[68] in Gestalt der Haustafeln auch für urchristliche Gemeinden verpflichtend geworden sei, in der deutschsprachigen Forschung durchsetzte[69]. Er tat dies nicht ohne eine beeindruckende Ausweitung des Vergleichsmaterials (darunter Philo, De decalogo 165–167) – vor allem jedoch nicht ohne ein in sich geschlossenes und einprägsames Resümee: „So hat sich denn ergeben, daß wir ein altes Stück griechischer *Volksethik* vor uns haben. Es war davor beschützt, verloren zu gehen, da es durch die stoische Propaganda immer wieder eingeschärft wurde. Unter diesen Umständen konnte das Christentum, das sich auf hellenistischem Boden ausbreitete, kaum ohne seine Kenntnis bleiben."[70] Und es wird eingeräumt: „Allerdings besteht auch die Möglichkeit, daß das Schema erst auf einem Umweg in das Christentum gekommen ist, nämlich durch das hellenistische Judentum, von welchem das Christentum ja außerordentlich viel an Formeln, Gebeten usw. übernommen hat. Die aufgezählten Parallelen zeigen, daß das Schema hier in einer Form heimisch geworden ist, die sich von der ‚heidnischen' kaum unterscheidet. Nur die Pflichten gegen die Götter mußten wegfallen oder einer monotheistischen Formulierung weichen."[71]

5.2. Nach Zweifeln, die schon Ernst Lohmeyer[72], Karl Heinrich Rengstorf[73] und David Schroeder[74] an einer solchen Ableitung der Haustafelethik des Neuen Testaments angemeldet hatten, unterzog James E. Crouch[75] die gesamten bis 1972 namhaft gemachten Vergleichstexte heidnischer und jüdischer Herkunft einer abermaligen gründlichen Revision.

---

[68] Ebd. 49.   [69] op. cit. (Anm. 18).

[70] *K. Weidinger*, Die Haustafeln (Anm. 18) 48.

[71] Ebd. 48–49.

[72] *E. Lohmeyer*, Die Briefe an die Philipper, an die Kolosser und an Philemon (Anm. 43) 156: „Wie diese ehelichen Mahnungen, so bleiben auch die folgenden an Kinder und Eltern auf dem bekannten Boden damaliger jüdischer Sitte".

[73] *K. H. Rengstorf*, Die neutestamentlichen Mahnungen an die Frau, sich dem Manne unterzuordnen, in: Verbum Dei manet in Aeternum: FS O. Schmitz (Witten 1953) 131–145, und *ders.*, Mann und Frau im Urchristentum: Arbeitsgemeinschaft für Forschung des Landes Nordrhein-Westfalen, Geisteswissenschaften 12 (Köln – Opladen 1954). Er hält die „Haustafeln" für „Stücke spezifisch urchristlicher Prägung", in: *ders.*, Mann und Frau im Urchristentum 28.

[74] op. cit. (Anm. 32). Seine Vorstellung des überlieferungsgeschichtlichen Weges der „Haustafeln" bis hinunter zum historischen Jesus wird unten S. 312 beschrieben.

[75] op. cit. (Anm. 21).

Die ernüchternden Ergebnisse seiner Untersuchung drangen jedoch entweder nicht durch oder wurden bagatellisiert. Zu stark war die Faszination durch das Erklärungsmodell der alten „stoischen Haustafel"[76], die ihrer „Verchristlichung"[77] harrte, als daß man mit Ernst zur Kenntnis genommen hätte, was J. E. Crouch mit seiner methodisch ungewöhnlich bewußten Studie herausfand. Nicht mehr und nicht weniger nämlich, als daß die seit M. Dibelius und K. Weidinger immer wieder unbekümmert in Anspruch genommene „stoische Pflichtentafel"[78] (vgl. die „stoische Pflichtenethik")[79] keines der wesentlichen, die Form der Haustafel in Kol 3,18 – 4,1 unverzichtbar festlegenden Elemente aufweist[80].

Abgesehen von den markanten Unterschieden in der Syntax[81] gibt es dort keine Dreierstruktur der Untergebenen, da Sklaven nicht erwähnt werden. Es fehlt die reziproke Verhaltensnormierung, und auch ein analoges Insistieren auf dem Gehorsam ist unbekannt[82].

Nicht viel besser sieht der Ertrag aus, den J. E. Crouch aus der Durchsicht der „hellenistic-jewish lists of social duties"[83] gewinnt. Es gelingt ihm wieder nicht, Texte namhaft zu machen, die es wenigstens erlaubten, Dreiergruppierung und Reziprozität der sittlichen Ermahnung aus einer einheitlichen Überlieferung heraus zu erklären. Was an vergleichbarem Material letztlich bleibt, sind zwei Belege: Seneca, Epistula ad Lucilium 94, 1[84] und Philo, Hypothetica 7, 14[85], wo immerhin Frauen, Kinder und Sklaven in ihren auf den Hausherrn bezogenen sozialen Relationen genannt werden.

Daß ungeachtet dieses offen zutage liegenden Defizits die sto-

---

[76] So: *J. Gnilka*, Der Kolosserbrief (Anm. 13) 215.

[77] *K. Weidinger*, Die Haustafeln (Anm. 18) 74–79.

[78] *L. Goppelt*, Der erste Petrusbrief (Anm. 10) 170.

[79] Ebd. 171.

[80] *J. E. Crouch*, The Origin and Intention of the Colossian Haustafel (Anm. 21) 33–34. 83.

[81] Vgl. schon *D. Schroeder*, Die Haustafeln (Anm. 32) 95–97, zu den Imperativen. Die Folgerung: „der Imperativ der ntl. Haustafeln entspricht der absoluten Form des apodiktischen Rechtssatzes" (ebd. 99) ist unhaltbar. Ohne Begründung und Evidenz meint auch *J. Gnilka*, Der Kolosserbrief (Anm. 13) 214, lapidar: „Es ist die Struktur des apodiktischen Rechts".

[82] *J. E. Crouch*, a. a. O. 83.

[83] Ebd. 74–83. 84–101.

[84] Ebd. 77.

[85] Ebd. 106–107.

ischen „Pflichtenschemata"[86] nach wie vor als Bezugspunkt neutestamentlicher Sozialethik ein nahezu[87] unwidersprochenes Monopol haben[88], hat damit zu tun, daß J. E. Crouch nicht in der Lage war, die Haustafel aus Kol 3, 18 – 4, 1 anderen Texten zuzuordnen, „die von den gegenseitigen Beziehungen zwischen Mann und Frau, zwischen Eltern und Kindern, zwischen Herren und Sklaven handeln, und allein von *diesen* Beziehungen"[89].

6. Der überlieferungsgeschichtliche Kontext späthellenistischer Ökonomik

Texte solcher Art gibt es jedoch in der späthellenistischen Literatur zur Ökonomik, welche es unternahm, die gesellschaftlichen Verhältnisse im einzelnen „Haus" oder „Haushalt" – als der grundlegenden und weitgehend autarken Sozial- und Wirtschaftszelle des antiken Staates – auch unter ethischen Aspekten zu reflektieren[90]. Ihr Anliegen war es, „zu einer sinnvollen Führung der Hauswirtschaft im personalen wie im sächlichen Bereich"[91] anzuleiten[92].

Schriften „Über die Ökonomie" tauchten bis vor kurzem nur am Rande der Debatte über die Haustafeln auf[93] – meistens, ohne daß

---

[86] *O. Merk*, Handeln aus Glauben (Anm. 44) 221. Er spricht aber auch vom „Pflichtenschema" (Singular: ebd. 222).

[87] Die wichtige Ausnahme ist: *D. Lührmann*, Wo man nicht mehr Sklave oder Freier ist. Überlegungen zur Struktur frühchristlicher Gemeinden: WuD 13 (1975) 53–83, hier: 71–83.

[88] Vgl. auch *H. Schlier*, Der Brief an die Epheser (Düsseldorf ⁴1963) 250 Anm. 3; *G. Strecker*, Ziele und Ergebnisse einer neutestamentlichen Ethik: NTS 25 (1979) 11, und N. Brox, Der erste Petrusbrief (EKK 21) (Neukirchen – Vluyn 1979) 125–127.

[89] So mit Recht: *D. Lührmann*, Neutestamentliche Haustafeln und antike Ökonomie: NTS 27 (1980) 85.

[90] Vgl. *M. J. Finley*, Die antike Wirtschaft (DTV WR 4277) (München 1977) 7–19, und: *H. Klees*, Herren und Sklaven. Die Sklaverei im oikonomischen und politischen Schrifttum der Griechen in klassischer Zeit (Forschungen zur antiken Sklaverei 6) (Wiesbaden 1975) 56–141 („ökonomische Schriften").

[91] *D. Lührmann*, Neutestamentliche Haustafeln (Anm. 89) 89.

[92] Dazu genauer: *K. Thraede*, Ärger mit der Freiheit (Anm. 7) 62–69.

[93] Zuerst wohl bei *J. Hoffmann*, Die „Hausväterliteratur" und die „Predigten über den christlichen Hausstand". Lehre vom Hause und Bildung für das häusliche Leben im 16., 17. und 18. Jhdt. (Weinheim – Berlin 1959) 25: „Die Haustafeln erinnern, besonders in ihrer Gliederung, an die peripatetische Ökonomik. Wie

man sie als eigenständigen Traditionsstrom von der vielbemühten stoischen „Offizienethik" unterschied: wie etwa der von J. E. Crouch als einschlägig zurückbehaltene Vergleichstext aus Seneca, Epistula ad Lucilium 94, 1 zu jenem Schrifttum gehört[94], oder wie Hierokles, einer der Kronzeugen für M. Dibelius und K. Weidinger, nach Stobaios auch einen Traktat περὶ οἴκων bzw. περὶ οἰκονομίας hinterließ[95].

Inzwischen haben Dieter Lührmann[96] und Klaus Thraede[97] die Zahl der vergleichbaren Texte über das von Friedrich Wilhelm schon im Jahre 1915 gelegte Fundament[98] hinaus beträchtlich vermehrt, und David L. Balch[99] ist es gelungen, die zeitliche und thematische Kontinuität der Literatur „Über die Ökonomie" von Platon bis in die frühe Kaiserzeit nachzuweisen[100].

6.1. Eine traditionsgeschichtliche Zuordnung der Haustafeln des Neuen Testaments zum antiken Schrifttum „Über die Ökonomie" hat wichtige Vorteile für sich: auch hier geht es um ein Dreier- bzw.

---

bei Aristoteles werden drei häusliche Verhältnisse gesehen: das von Mann und Frau, das von Vater bzw. Eltern und Kind und das von Herr und Sklave". Dann: *A. Strobel,* Furcht, wem Furcht gebührt: ZNW 55 (1964) 60 (zu Röm 13,3f).

[94] *J. E. Crouch,* The Origin and Intention of the Colossian Haustafel (Anm. 21) 59–60 und 106, wo der Verfasser die Gattung „Über die Ökonomie" nur knapp verfehlt: „Ordinarily, slaves were not mentioned in the Stoic list of duties, and it may well be that Seneca's interest in slaves evidenced elsewhere influenced his list in Epist. XCIV. It would appear, at any rate, that the treatment of women, children and slaves as a unit stems from Judaism. It merely remains to be determined whether this grouping can be found in our Hellenistic Jewish sources".

[95] Vgl. die Hinweise bei *K. Weidinger,* Die Haustafeln (Anm. 18) 31–33.

[96] *D. Lührmann,* Wo man nicht mehr Sklave oder Freier ist (Anm. 87), und *ders.,* Neutestamentliche Haustafeln (Anm. 89).

[97] *K. Thraede,* Ärger mit der Freiheit (Anm. 7), und *ders.,* Zum historischen Hintergrund der „Haustafeln" des NT (Anm. 20).

[98] *F. Wilhelm,* Die Oeconomica der Neupythagoreer Bryson, Kallikratidas, Periktione, Phintys: RMP 70 (1915) 161–223. Ebd. 208 Anm. 1 wird unter anderem auf Eph 5,22 und 1 Petr 3,1 verwiesen. Die ökonomische Schrift des Bryson hatte eine Nachgeschichte in der islamischen Überlieferung vgl. *M. Plessner,* Der Oikonomikos des Neupythagoreers ‚Bryson' und sein Einfluß auf die islamische Wissenschaft. Edition und Übersetzung der erhaltenen Versionen, nebst einer *Geschichte der Ökonomik im Islam* mit Quellenproben in Text und Übersetzung (Antike und Orient 5) (Heidelberg 1928).

[99] *D. L. Balch,* „Let Wives be Submissive ..." (Anm. 54).

[100] Ebd. 27 die wichtige Beobachtung zur Gattungsbestimmung: „The three topoi ‚concerning the state' (περὶ πολιτείας), ‚concerning household management' (περὶ οἰκονομίας), and ‚concerning marriage' (περὶ γάμου) were so combined and interrelated that it is difficult to distinguish them clearly".

Zweierschema[101], um Gegenseitigkeit des Verhaltens, um den Versuch, aufdringliche und rücksichtslose Herrschaftsausübung versittlichend zurückzunehmen, um Leitmotive wie „Furcht" bzw. „Furcht und Liebe"[102]. Vor allem aber gibt die Erkenntnis des Zusammenhanges mit der antiken Ökonomik die Möglichkeit an die Hand, die zeitgenössische Stoßrichtung zu vermessen, in welcher sich die neutestamentlichen Haustafeln bewegen: „In ihrem nichtchristlichen Zweig bekunden sie klar genug die Absicht, das Grundmuster des Herrschens und Dienens im Bereich des Hauses auszuarbeiten, ja angesichts der Bestrebungen, Rechte des Individuums zu gewährleisten, darf man wohl sagen: sie versuchen jene Grundordnung aufrechtzuerhalten. Das geschieht zugleich so, daß sie, und zwar in erkennbar verschiedener Akzentuierung, Oben und Unten ‚humanisierend' aufeinander beziehen."[103]

6.2. Ein Exponent solcher restaurativer Bestrebungen im zeitgenössischen Heidentum ist zum Beispiel der Agrarschriftsteller Lucius Junius Moderatus Columella[104]. Er stammt aus Spanien, kennt Syrien und Kilikien aus seiner Militärzeit, besitzt schließlich Landgüter in der weiteren Umgebung Roms und wird dort mit Seneca bekannt, dessen Bruder Gallio sein Freund ist[105].

Dieser Columella verfaßt zur Zeit Neros ein umfassendes Werk „Über die Landwirtschaft", in dessen zwölftem Buch er die Umstände beklagt, welche den mittleren Landwirt von Format derzeit zwingen, eine Wirtschafterin (villica) anzustellen[106]:

„Die meisten Ehefrauen lassen sich in Üppigkeit und Trägheit so gehen, daß sie nicht einmal geruhen, sich der Wollarbeit anzunehmen, sondern hausgemachte Kleidung verabscheuen, so daß ihnen in ihrem unvernünftigen Ver-

[101] Vgl. *D. Lührmann*, Wo man nicht mehr Sklave oder Freier ist (Anm. 87) 79.
[102] *K. Thraede*, Zum historischen Hintergrund der ‚Haustafeln' des NT (Anm. 20) 363–364.
[103] Ebd. 364.
[104] Vgl. die Hinweise bei *K. Thraede*, Ärger mit der Freiheit (Anm. 7) 68–69; außerdem: *ders.*, Zum historischen Hintergrund der ‚Haustafeln' des NT (Anm. 20) 364–365.
[105] *K. Ahrens*, Columella. Über Landwirtschaft. Aus dem Lateinischen übersetzt, eingeführt und erläutert (Schriften zur Geschichte und Kultur der Antike 4) (Berlin 1972) 12–13. 21.
[106] Übersetzung: ebd. 368; Text: Rei rusticae 12, praefatio 9–10 bei *E. S. Forster – E. H. Heffner*, Lucius Iunius Moderatus Columella. On Agriculture and Trees III (The Loeb Classical Library) (London – Cambridge 1955) 178.

langen am meisten das zusagt, was man nur für viel Geld und beinahe für ein ganzes Vermögen kaufen kann; so darf man sich auch nicht wundern, daß ihnen Landwirtschaft und Umgang mit ländlichem Gerät lästig sind und daß sie es schon als eine äußerst schmutzige Arbeit ansehen, nur wenige Tage auf dem Gute zu verweilen. Aus diesem Grund hat sich, da allgemein jener alte Geist sabinischer und römischer Gutsherrinnen nicht nur aus der Mode gekommen, sondern gänzlich dahingeschwunden ist, allmählich das Amt der Wirtschafterin als notwendig erwiesen."

Was Columella hier jenseits seines konkreten Anliegens, den Beruf der Wirtschafterin sozialgeschichtlich verständlich zu machen, anprangert, ist bemerkenswert. Er redet unter der Hand von einer Lockerung alter Sitte in der Folge eines offenkundigen gesellschaftlichen Fortschritts der „meisten Frauen" seiner Umgebung. Und in der Tat scheinen die Frauen der frühen Kaiserzeit erheblich in Richtung hellenistisch vermittelter Freiheit und Gleichheit vorangekommen zu sein[107]. Unverkennbar zeichnet sich eine Liberalisierung in der Rollenzuweisung an die Frau ab, über deren Recht und Grenzen man noch keine Gewißheit hat und die man deshalb ausgiebig diskutiert – so wie Columella, der im übrigen auf eine sehr bezeichnende Weise nach einer Antwort sucht. Er bemüht nämlich die Ökonomik des Xenophon, die Cicero (De officiis 2, 87) schon im Jahre 85 v. Chr. ins Lateinische übersetzt[108] und dadurch in Rom einem breiteren Publikum zugänglich gemacht hatte[109]:

„Das hat in seinem Oeconomicus Xenophon und nach ihm Cicero, der jenes Buch ins Lateinische übertragen hat, recht gut auseinandergesetzt. Denn bei den Griechen und dann bis zur Zeit unserer Väter auch bei den Römern ist die Hausarbeit gewöhnlich Sache der Frau gewesen, während das Familienoberhaupt, ohne sich um etwas zu kümmern, nur gleichsam zum Ausruhen von den Strapazen draußen sich ins Haus zurückzog. Größte Ehrerbietung nämlich ging Hand in Hand mit einmütigem und gewissenhaftem Bemühen, und die Frau wetteiferte aufs schönste mit dem Manne, indem sie strebte, durch ihr Wirken seiner Tätigkeit zu größeren und besseren Erfolgen zu verhelfen. Man sah im Hause nichts Getrenntes, nichts, wovon entweder der

---

[107] K. Thraede, Ärger mit der Freiheit (Anm. 7) 84–85, und J. Griffin, Augustan poetry and the life of luxury: JRS 66 (1976) 87–105.
[108] Offenkundig bestand schon damals in Rom ein Bedarf an ökonomischer Ethik.
[109] Übersetzung: K. Ahrens, Columella (Anm. 105) 338; Text: Rei rusticae 12, praefatio 7–8: E. S. Forster – E. H. Heffner, Lucius Iunius Moderatus Columella (Anm. 106) 177–178.

Mann oder die Frau behauptet hätte, es gehe nur ihn oder sie allein an; vielmehr wirkten beide in der Weise miteinander gemeinsam, daß der Regsamkeit draußen der Fleiß der Hausfrau die Waage hielt."

Der belesene und gebildete Gutsbesitzer Columella zeigt sich also damit beschäftigt, die in seinem Lebensbereich spürbare Kluft zwischen der „matrum familiarum mos" (Rei rusticae 12, praefatio 10), wie sie „usque in patrum nostrorum memoriam" (ebd. 7) üblich war, und den emanzipierten Gebärden zeitgenössischer Frauen zu überbrücken.

Und er steuert in einer höchst bedachtsamen Manier gegen diese beunruhigende Erfahrung seiner Tage an. Mit Hilfe der liberalisierenden Vorstellungen einer hellenistischen Ökonomik von gemäßigter Observanz bringt er das alte römische Leitbild von der mater familias neu in Erinnerung. Dabei ist es ihm offenkundig ein Anliegen, den moralischen Abstand der Gegenwart von der idealen Vergangenheit nicht absolut zu setzen. Columella entscheidet sich vielmehr für einen pragmatischen Mittelweg. Er kann als Gutsherr die landflüchtigen Anstrengungen der „meisten Frauen" nicht gutheißen, aber er unternimmt auch keinen Versuch, die modernen Frauen seiner Tage mit der Moral eines alten „Frauenspiegels" zu disziplinieren. Statt dessen setzt er sein Vertrauen auf die Einsichtigkeit klassischer Ökonomieregeln, die ihm freiere Alternativen zu gewaltsam konservatistischen Lösungen[110] anboten. Columella beugt sich deshalb der Forderung der Ökonomik nach einer uneinschränkbaren „unanimitas" (Rei rusticae 12, praefatio 7) der Eheleute bei der Besorgung des „Hauses". Aber er stellt unter Berufung auf dieselbe Ökonomik keineswegs in Abrede, daß die Frau weiterhin ihrem Gemahl „summam reverentiam cum concordia et diligentia mixtam" (ebd.) zu erweisen habe.

Im Ganzen bot das Schrifttum „Über die Ökonomie" dem Columella somit eine Möglichkeit, die hellenistische Option für eine Humanisierung und Versittlichung der patria potestas von einem zwischen Unterdrückung und Gleichstellung vermittelnden Standpunkt aus aufzugreifen.

6.3. Wenn aber die „Form" der in etwa gleichzeitigen Haustafel

[110] Vgl. *K. Thraede*, Ärger mit der Freiheit (Anm. 7) 79–81, zu der in augusteischer Zeit einsetzenden Restauration.

des Kolosserbriefs ohnehin nur jenen Literaturresten vergleichbar ist, welche in sich häufender Anzahl aus dem späten Hellenismus überkommen sind und damals ihren Lesern noch einmal die Gesetze der Haushaltungskunst in Erinnerung zu rufen versuchten, dann liegt es nahe, aus dem Beispiel und der Bemühung des Columella einschlägige Konsequenzen zu ziehen.

Es wird diskutabel, die Textfolge Kol 3, 18 – 4, 1 als Niederschlag einer (zunächst jüdischen, schließlich) christlichen Zustimmung zu einer humanitätswilligen Mittelposition zwischen den damals allgemein in der Frauenfrage aufgebrochenen Fronten zu verstehen.

Der sozialgeschichtliche Stellenwert der auf Umwegen christlich gewordenen Haustafel wäre demzufolge keineswegs als gering zu veranschlagen. Im Blick auf konkurrierende konservative Gegenentwürfe der Antike[111] und mit Rücksicht auf zeitgenössische extreme Ableitungen aus dem stoischen Gleichheitssatz[112] bringt sich hier eine verantwortungsvoll ausbalancierte Stellungnahme für ein gemäßigt fortschrittliches und milde humanisiertes sozialethisches Verhaltensmuster zu Wort.

6.4. So gesehen spiegelt die Liste der Regeln in Kol 3, 18 – 4, 1 keine schlechthin gemeinantike Anschauung von hausbezogener Moral wider, sondern eine ganz bestimmte. Es geht um eine unter mehreren Möglichkeiten, für welche sich zuvor schon das Frühjudentum entschieden hatte, weil sie dem Strom seiner eigenen Tradition am nächsten kam – und das heißt des näheren: *weil* die überwiegend anerkannte Führungsrolle des Mannes[113] als des Hausherrn nicht wesentlich angetastet, sondern lediglich mit den „ökonomisch" einsichtigen Ansprüchen der Frau in Einklang gebracht zu werden brauchte; vor allem aber, *weil* die Reihe: Frau, Kinder, Sklaven samt den für das Schrifttum „Über die Ökonomie" typischen Motiven der Furcht und des Gehorsams längst jüdisch besetzt war[114].

---

[111] Vgl. *J. Gaudemet*, Le statut de la femme dans l'empire romain: RSJB 11 (1959) 191–222, bes. 192–193.

[112] *H. Greeven*, Das Hauptproblem der Sozialethik in der neueren Stoa und im Urchristentum (NTF 3) (Gütersloh 1935) 6–18.

[113] Zu Philo: *J. Heinemann*, Philons griechische und jüdische Bildung (Breslau 1932) 240. Vgl. *Flavius Josephus*, Contra Apionem II 201.

[114] Zu Mischna Berachot 3, 3: *J. E. Crouch*, The Origin and Intention of the Colossian Haustafel (Anm. 21) 105.

6.5. Ein solches Wissen um den überlieferungsgeschichtlichen Kontext der im Altertum seit Xenophon (etwa 365 v. Chr.) populären und dann gerade wieder am Beginn der Kaiserzeit zu größerer Beliebtheit gelangten Literaturgattung περὶ οἴκων bzw. περὶ οἰκονομίας nimmt den modernen Exegeten von Kol 3, 18 – 4, 1 alte Profilängste.

Der Neutestamentler darf sich des mühevollen Zwangs entbunden fühlen, vor einer betont finster gehaltenen Kulisse heidnischer Beharrung auf Unterwerfung und männlichem Hegemoniestreben eine strahlend helle und neuartige Bühne urchristlicher Liebe und Freiheit aufrichten zu müssen. Vielmehr demonstriert die älteste Haustafel des Neuen Testaments *an der Seite* der zeitgenössischen Textsorten zur Ökonomik – und *nur* dort – eine höchst respektable urchristliche Entscheidung für einen Mittelweg sozialer Sittlichkeit, wie er sich damals einer breiteren, gemäßigt fortschrittlichen antiken Öffentlichkeit erschloß[115].

Unter einer zeitgeschichtlich derart verankerten Meßlatte zeigt Kol 3, 18 – 4, 1 nicht nur die Flagge profilierter Kritik an allzu weit ausgreifender Liberalisierung und Emanzipation[116], sondern dieselbe Haustafel sucht mit ähnlicher Entschiedenheit eben *auch* Abstand von jener schlichten Behauptung unverblümten Herrschaftsdenkens zu gewinnen, der sich zeitgenössische Moralisten patriarchalischen Zuschnitts verschrieben hatten[117].

7. Frauen und Männer nach Kol 3, 18(–19)

Verdichtet sich aber der Eindruck, daß sich die Haustafel des Kolosserbriefs bewußt an markant unterscheidbare, zeitgenössische Rezepte für den sozialen Umgang der Zugehörigen eines Hausstandes

---

[115] Vgl. *K. Thraede*, Zum historischen Hintergrund der ‚Haustafeln‘ des NT (Anm. 20) 367–368.
[116] Vgl. die Charakteristik der Verhältnisse in der gleichzeitigen „griechisch-römischen Gesellschaft" bei *K. Thraede*, Frauen im Leben frühchristlicher Gemeinden: US 32 (1977) 286–287. Zu *dieser* Frontstellung: *ders.*, Augustin-Texte aus dem Themenkreis ‚Frau‘, ‚Gesellschaft‘ und ‚Gleichheit‘ I: JAC 22 (1979) 80 Anm. 33.
[117] Aufschlußreich für die einschlägigen Gegebenheiten in der Kaiserzeit: *K. Thraede*, Art. Frau: RAC VIII (1972) 216–217 (Nr. 3).

anlehnt und von dort aus in einer schon antiken Auseinandersetzung – nach zwei Seiten hin mäßigend – Stellung bezieht, so verliert ihr nur schwer zu leugnender „Paternalismus"[118] von vornherein seine „theologischen" Schrecken.

7.1. Zum einen entfällt nämlich endgültig jede Nötigung, Kol 3,18 bis 4,1 überhaupt und Kol 3,18–19 näherhin als Standpunkte eines inner*christlichen* Richtungsstreites in Betracht zu ziehen, mit Hilfe derer man sich gegen ein enthusiastisches und anarchisches Mißverständnis überkommener Spitzensätze wie Gal 3,28; 1 Kor 12,13 oder Kol 3,11 hätte verwahren wollen.[119]

7.2. Zum anderen büßt im Zusammenhang der skizzierten überlieferungs- und sozialgeschichtlichen Situation die Frage an hermeneutischer Brisanz ein, ob und auf welchem Wege ein Transfer der ältesten Haustafel des Neuen Testaments in die Pastoral moderner *christlicher* Kirchen noch zu verantworten sei. Denn unter anderem wird die Einsicht erschwinglich, daß *auch* die beiden Imperative in Kol 3,18–19 nicht einer „durch Sitte und Tradition festgelegten"[120], „allgemein geltenden Ordnung"[121] das Wort reden, sondern für eine spezifische ethische Ansicht sprechen. *Auch* die dort zur Kenntnis gegebenen Ermahnungen an die Ehefrauen und deren Männer schreiben keinesfalls eine auf „Unterordnung" fixierte „gemeinantike Eheauffassung"[122] fest. Sondern dabei geht es einmal mehr um das frühe christliche (und zuvor jüdische) Placet zu einer an den humanisierten Normen hellenistischer *Ökonomik* ausgerichteten *besonderen* Sittlichkeit ehelichen Zusammenlebens im „Hause", bei dessen Vollzug „Unterordnung" eben *nicht* das letzte Wort sein sollte (vgl. Kol 3,19).

7.3. Unter einer solchen Voraussetzung vermittelt aber das hintergründige Geländer ungefähr gleichzeitiger Ökonomietraditionen dem Ausleger größere Sicherheit bei der Abwehr allzu beflissener Überinterpretationen, von denen in der Vergangenheit zunächst der Wortlaut aus Kol 3,18 permanent bedroht war: „Ihr Frauen, seid eueren Männern *untertan, wie es sich ziemt im Herrn!*" Wenn man

---

[118] K. *Niederwimmer*, Askese und Mysterium, Göttingen 1975, 157.
[119] Siehe oben die Anmerkungen 52 und 53.
[120] E. *Lohse*, Die Briefe an die Kolosser und an Philemon (Anm. 37) 225.
[121] Ebd. 224.
[122] So J. *Gnilka*, Der Kolosserbrief (Anm. 13) 216.

nämlich davon ausgehen darf, daß die Haustafel des Kolosserbriefes das in der Umwelt virulent gewordene Frauenthema nach dem
Muster der moderaten und mittleren Position der Ökonomietraktate
aufgreift, dann erspart diese achtenswerte Zustimmung zu jener human gehobenen Option des späten Hellenismus für eine Zurück-
nahme willkürlicher väterlicher Hausgewalt dem Exegeten von
vornherein emanzipationswillige Unterscheidungszwänge.

8. „Unterordnung"

So wird für den Neutestamentler zunächst das beliebte Spiel mit ver-
kürzten lexikalischen Befunden ohne Reiz bleiben, dessen Unterstützung man immer wieder gesucht hat, um die semantischen Umrisse des Verbums ὑποτάσσεσθαι = „sich unterordnen"[123] einer
überlegenen christlichen Moralität zugänglich zu machen.

8.1. Dieses Spiel begann des näheren damit, daß K. H. Rengstorf
im Jahre 1953 das Argument in die Diskussion einführte, „der
Sprachgebrauch von ὑποτάσσεσθαι", wie er im Neuen Testament
unter anderem durch Kol 3,18 demonstriert werde, sei „so gut wie
spezifisch christlich"[124]. Dazu berief sich der Verfasser auf die lexi-
kographische Garantie, welche damals Walter Bauer in der vierten
Auflage seines „Griechisch-deutschen Wörterbuchs" zu leisten vermochte. Ihrzufolge standen aus der Profangräzität nur je ein Beleg
aus Plutarch und Pseudo-Kallisthenes zur Verfügung, so daß die
Folgerung von K. H. Rengstorf einigermaßen plausibel klingen
konnte: „ὑποτάσσεσθαι spielt in außerneutestamentlichen Texten
nur eine sehr bescheidene Rolle, wenn es sich um die Beschreibung
des Verhältnisses der Frau zu ihrem Ehemann handelt. Demgegenüber weist die Regelmäßigkeit, mit der das Wort in den Haustafeln
des Neuen Testaments erscheint, auf besonderes christliches Interesse an ihm hin."[125] Schien jedoch schon das numerische Defizit des
antiken Sprachaufkommens für einen urchristlichen Sonderfall zu

---

[123] *W. Bauer,* Griechisch-deutsches Wörterbuch zu den Schriften des Neuen Testaments und der übrigen urchristlichen Literatur (Berlin ⁵1963) 1677 (β), notiert:
„sich unterordnen, sich unterwerfen, gehorchen".
[124] *K. H. Rengstorf,* Die neutestamentlichen Mahnungen (Anm. 73) 132.
[125] Ebd.

sprechen, so lag es durchaus nahe, auch die Sinnlinien des Wortes ὑποτάσσεσθαι in die gleiche Richtung voranzubringen. K. H. Rengstorf unternahm das auf dem Wege eines sehr beeindruckenden Hinweises auf 1 Kor 14,34: „denn es ist ihnen (sc. den Frauen in der Gemeindeversammlung) nicht gestattet, zu reden. Vielmehr sollen sie sich unterordnen (ὑποτασσέσθωσαν), wie es auch *das Gesetz* sagt". Da er zudem das hier angesprochene „Gesetz" inhaltlich von 1 Kor 14,40 her aufzufüllen suchte, wonach „alles anständig und *ordnung*gemäß" zu „geschehen" habe[126], ergab sich dem Verfasser schließlich ein für das Urchristentum außerordentlich günstiges Urteil. K. H. Rengstorf sah „den Punkt erreicht, an dem sich die ältesten christlichen und die ältesten außerchristlichen Belege für die Mahnung an die Frauen, sich den eigenen Männern unterzuordnen bei aller äußeren Berührung scheiden. Plutarch begründet sie damit, daß es dem Ruf der Frau noch abträglicher wäre als ihrem Manne, wenn sie der herrschende Teil wäre, und Pseudo-Callisthenes verweist darauf, daß es so eben schicklich sei. Die neutestamentlichen ‚Haustafeln' verzichten demgegenüber auf jeden Versuch einer moralischen Begründung, wie sie sich vom Naturrecht ebenso wie von der Sitte her leicht geben läßt, und berufen sich allein auf Gottes *Ordnung*. Es entspricht diesem Bilde, wenn in den ‚Haustafeln' alle Glieder des oikos in ihrer Bedeutung für diesen und für seine *Ordnung* und seinen Bestand grundsätzlich gleich eingeschätzt werden. Darin aber wiederholt sich nun, nur in neuer Form, die scharfe Absage des jungen Christentums an seine gesamte Umwelt, was deren Tendenz zur prinzipiellen Unterbewertung nicht allein der Frau, sondern auch des Kindes und des Sklaven gegenüber dem Manne betrifft."[127]

Es war die Antike schlechthin, die hierbei undifferenziert auf der Strecke blieb, die man mit zwei weit auseinanderliegenden und dazu noch ihren Kontexten entfremdeten Nachweisen für ὑποτάσσεσθαι ausmanövrierte und auf das einspurige Gleis eines rüden Patriarchalismus schob. Als selbstverständliche, wenn auch nicht beabsichtigte Folge stellte sich ein, daß der tatsächliche sittengeschichtliche Rang von Kol 3,18(–19) immer mehr ins Dunkel geriet. Er entzog sich um

---

[126] *K. H. Rengstorf,* Mann und Frau im Urchristentum (Anm. 73) 23.
[127] Ebd. 29.

so vollständiger der exegetischen Erkenntnis, je mehr man nach K. H. Rengstorf daran ging, mit den gleichen und stets aufs neue kolportierten lexikalischen Mitteln ein christliches Monopol für mögliche Freiheits- und Gleichheitsbestrebungen einzurichten – so, als habe das Altertum ausschließlich für die Unterordnung der Frau plädiert und erst das Neue Testament vom Manne Rücksicht verlangt.

8.2. In dieser Spur zitiert D. Schroeder schon 1959 nur noch die Praecepta coniugalia (33,142 e) des Plutarch und fährt darauf mit deutlichen begriffsrealistischen Obertönen fort: „Hier sehen wir, daß es als empfehlenswert gehalten wird, daß die Frau dem Manne untertan sei. Rein formal wird das Wort genau so gebraucht wie im Neuen Testament. Der Sprachgebrauch ist derselbe, aber es ist nicht gleichbedeutend mit dem neutestamentlichen ὑποτάσσεσθαι; denn ὑποτάσσεσθαι wird bei Plutarch im Gegensatz zu κρατεῖν gesetzt. Es geht um die Frage, wer die Macht über den anderen haben soll. Der Mann soll die Frau regieren oder ihr befehlen, aber nicht umgekehrt. In der neutestamentlichen Haustafel ist nicht κρατεῖν, sondern ἀγαπᾶν (vgl. Kol 3,19) das Gegenstück von ὑποτάσσεσθαι. Das Wort ὑποτάσσεσθαι wird beide Male im Verhältnis der Frau ihrem Mann gegenüber benutzt, aber der Standort, von wo aus es gesprochen wird, sowohl als die Bedeutung des Wortes sind verschieden."[128] Eine Seite weiter heißt es schließlich: „damit ist klar geworden, daß die Frau im hellenistischen sowohl wie im jüdischen Raum eine untergeordnete Stelle einnahm. Es ist aber zugleich klar geworden, daß das trotzdem grundverschieden ist von dem, was in den neutestamentlichen Haustafeln mit ὑποτάσσεσθαι bezeichnet wird."[129]

Von da an scheint im Lager der christlichen Ausleger die Anschauung unausrottbar zu werden, daß die hellenistische Ethik lediglich zu einer Bejahung männlich-rigorosen „Herrschens" (κρατεῖν) fähig und willens gewesen sei.

Das konnte soweit gehen, daß Else Kähler es gänzlich unterlassen zu dürfen glaubte, sich in der zeitgenössischen Antike umzusehen und statt dessen ausgerechnet von 1 Kor 15,27–28 aus auf ein erträglicheres, geradezu christologisch fixiertes Verständnis des Verbums

---

[128] *D. Schroeder,* Die Haustafeln (Anm. 32) 122.   [129] Ebd. 123.

ὑποτάσσεσθαι stoßen wollte: wo „von Unterordnung die Rede ist, sollte der Unterordnung Jesu Christi gedacht werden, die ihm niemand befahl – auch Gott nicht –, sondern zu der er aus freiem Entschluß aufgrund seiner Einsicht in Gottes Ordnung gelangte. Wie seine Unterordnung frei von jeder Schmach, von jeder Abwertung seiner eigenen Person ist, so ist es auch die derer, die dazu aufgerufen werden: Frauen, Untertanen, Sklaven; schmachvoll wird sie erst dann, wenn Ehemänner, Obrigkeit, Herren diese Unterordnung dadurch fordern, daß sie das Wort ὑποτάσσεσθαι, das – wie wir am Beispiel Christi zeigten – Einsicht und Entscheidung verlangt, zu einem Befehls- und Gehorsamswort degradieren."[130]

Jedoch: selbst wenn man darüber hinwegsehen wollte, daß in Kol 3,18 eine freie Entscheidung ebensowenig wie ein freiwilliger Vollzug der „Unterordnung" nachweisbar mitgedacht ist, hat ὑποτάσσειν/ὑποτάσσεσθαι wenigstens in 1 Kor 15,27 (vgl. Ps 8,7) den unbestreitbar aggressiven Sinn gewaltsamer und siegreicher Unterwerfung. Und: ändert das Korrelat der Aufforderung an die Männer, ihre Ehefrauen „zu lieben" (Kol 3,19), wirklich irgend etwas an der *inhaltlichen* Eigenart der Mahnung, die Frauen sollten ihren Männern „untertan sein" – wie E. Kähler und D. Schroeder gemeinsam glauben? Offenkundig hilft es der Sache wenig, wenn man urchristlichen Schriftstellern anachronistisch zuvorkommen und sie abhalten möchte, etwas zu sagen, was modernen feministischen Grundsätzen und Strategien zuwiderläuft.

8.3. Ähnlich bedenklich stimmen die Anstrengungen solcher Exegeten, welche daran arbeiten, die alten lexikalischen Fehlanzeigen um den Profangebrauch des Verbums ὑποτάσσεσθαι für einen Beweisgang mobil zu machen, der schließlich darauf abzielt, den Anweisungen in Kol 3,18–19 geradezu gesellschaftskritische Energien zuzuführen. Was man dabei der Antike im ganzen an einschlägigen ethischen Haltungen zutraut, wird in herkömmlicher Manier sub voce ὑποτάσσεσθαι aus zwei weit entlegenen Sätzen bei Plutarch und Pseudo-Kallisthenes rekrutiert.

---

[130] *E. Kähler*, Die Frau in den paulinischen Briefen (Anm. 31) 196–197; vgl. *dies.*, Zur „Unterordnung" der Frau im Neuen Testament: ZEE 3 (1959) 6–7. Ähnlich: *E. Schweizer*, Der Brief an die Kolosser (Anm. 44) 164: „Das Verbum bezeichnet das freiwillige Sicheinordnen, wie es Christus selbst gegenüber dem Vater übt (1 Kor 15,28)".

So meint Wolfgang Schrage: „Während der Begriff (sc. ὑποτάσ-σεσθαι) in der Septuaginta und im Judentum nirgendwo auf das normale Verhältnis des Bürgers zur Obrigkeit (Ausnahme: Josephus, Bellum II 433) oder für das Verhältnis Mann–Frau und Kind–Eltern verwendet wird, gebrauchen Plutarch und Pseudo-Callisthenes ihn für die Unterordnung der Frau gegenüber dem Mann: ‚denn ziemlich ist es, daß die Frau dem Manne untertan sei‘. Unterordnung ist also (sic!) das, was sich nach damaliger Zeit und Sitte gehört.“[131] Fühlt man sich aber dazu ermuntert, ein solches Resümee zu riskieren, dann kann es nur noch als ein Akt gedanklicher Konsequenz erscheinen, wenn man endlich den Aufruf an die Männer aus Kol 3, 19 als christliches Novum propagiert und gegen den Rest einer durchgängig als autoritär vereinnahmten antiken Sozialethik hochrechnet: „Die Mahnung zur Agape gegenüber der Frau aber ist in der damaligen Zeit etwas ganz und gar nicht Selbstverständliches, sondern etwas schlechthin Unerhörtes, wie H. Greeven mit Recht betont hat[132], und nicht dadurch zu entkräften, daß ἀγαπᾶν auch außerhalb des Neuen Testaments für das Verhältnis von Mann und Frau vorkommt.“[133] Von da an wird der Schlußstrich mit großer Entschiedenheit gezogen: „Plutarch spricht an der Stelle, wo er das ὑπο-τάσσεσθαι der Frau lobt, beim Mann von κρατεῖν, Seneca sagt ‚altera pars ad obsequendum altera imperio nata est‘ (De constantia sapientis 1, 1). Auf diesem Hintergrund gewinnt die Mahnung zur Agape gegenüber der Frau erst die rechten Konturen. Und es ist zugleich evident, daß das Verhalten der Christen im οἶκος nicht einfach der Konvention entspricht.“[134]

Aber nichts stimmt hier. Vor allem ist die Balance der aufgebauten sittengeschichtlichen Relationen nicht sorgfältig genug austariert.

Geht es wirklich an, mit einem flüchtigen Halbsatz die Historia Alexandri Magni (I 22, 4)[135] aus der Feder des im 3. christlichen

---

[131] *W. Schrage*, Zur Ethik der neutestamentlichen Haustafeln (Anm. 19) 9.
[132] Vgl. *H. Greeven*, Zu den Aussagen des Neuen Testaments über die Ehe: ZEE 1 (1957) 122.
[133] *W. Schrage*, a. a. O. 12–13.
[134] Ebd. 13.
[135] Text: *G. Kroll*, Pseudo-Callisthenes: Historia Alexandri Magni I (Berlin ²1958) 22.

Jahrhundert schreibenden Pseudo-Kallisthenes in Erinnerung zu bringen und dort die gleiche Auffassung von der „Unterordnung" der Frau zu verbuchen wie bei Plutarch von Chaironeia, der schon um 125 n. Chr. starb? Und was soll man von der Haltbarkeit eines Belegnetzes denken, das neben Plutarch und Pseudo-Kallisthenes gerade noch ein vereinzeltes Wort des Seneca (4 v. bis 65 n. Chr.) erfaßt und sich sonst damit zufrieden gibt, in einer Anmerkung das Fragment einer Komödie zu zitieren, in welcher der Dichter Philemon auf einen weit verbreiteten Topos einschwenkt und wieder einmal die herrschsüchtige(!) Ehefrau karikiert?[136] Reicht das alles aus, um der gesamten Antike Konservatismus in der Frauenfrage zu bescheinigen und „auf *diesem* Hintergrund"[137] der Haustafel des Kolosserbriefs eine „kritische Komponente" zuzumuten?[138]

8.4. Wie sehr in einer solchen Rechnung der Wunsch nicht nur der Vater des Gedankens, sondern auch der Methode ist, bringt im übrigen mit der wünschenswerten Klarheit eine kritische Überprüfung jener Stelle aus den Praecepta coniugalia des Plutarch an den Tag, die seit K. H. Rengstorf alle Exegeten im Munde zu führen pflegen, wenn es ihnen darum zu tun ist, dem Altertum en bloc eine autoritäre und ungemilderte Sozialethik anzulasten. Läßt man nämlich den unermüdlich neben dem Verbum ὑποτάσσεσθαι annoncierten Text in seiner angestammten Umgebung stehen, so ergibt sich ein geradezu gegenläufiger Sinn (33, 142 e):

„Wenn reiche Leute und Fürsten Ehren auf Philosophen häufen, schmücken sie sich selbst und die Philosophen. Auf der anderen Seite jedoch steigern Philosophen weniger den Ruf der Reichen, als daß sie ihren eigenen schmälern, wenn sie den Reichen Reverenz erweisen. So steht es auch mit den Frauen. Solange sie sich ihren Ehemännern unterordnen (ὑποτάττουσαι μὲν γὰρ ἑαυτὰς τοῖς ἀνδράσιν), verdienen sie Lob. Wenn sie aber darauf ausgehen, zu herrschen (κρατεῖν δὲ βουλόμεναι), verletzen sie den Anstand mehr als die Objekte ihrer Herrschsucht. Der Mann jedoch soll über seine Frau nicht wie ein Despot über sein Eigentum herrschen, sondern wie die Seele über den Leib – voller Mitgefühl und (sc. mit der Gattin) liebevoll zusammenwachsend (συμπαθοῦντα καὶ συμπεφυκότα τῇ εὐνοίᾳ)."[139]

---

[136] *W. Schrage*, a. a. O. 9 Anm. 1.
[137] Ebd. 13.
[138] Ebd. 11.
[139] Text: *F. C. Babbit*, Plutarch's Moralia II (The Loeb Classical Library) (London 1956 [= 1928]) 320–323.

Offenkundig ist Plutarch völlig ungeeignet, um als Zeuge für eine harte und schlicht konservative Gehorsamsforderung in die Schranken geschickt zu werden[140]. Im Gegenteil: er verbürgt eine eindeutig fortgeschrittene Problemstellung – genau auf der Linie der von W. Schrage fälschlicherweise dem Urchristentum vorbehaltenen „kritischen" Gegenstimme. Daß der Hausherr dominant bleibt, stellt sich bei Plutarch *und* in Kol 3, 18–19 als ein für notwendig gehaltenes Zugeständnis an die soziale Realität der Zeit dar. Aber darum herum liegen die entscheidenden Nuancen: *auch* zur vorbildlich gemeinschaftlichen Lebensführung und liebevollen Rücksichtnahme versteht sich Plutarch ebenso wie Kol 3, 18–19.

Plutarch belegt somit die zurückhaltend versittlichende und humanisierende Richtung der antiken Auseinandersetzung um die soziale Rolle der Frau, auf welche sich schließlich auch das Urchristentum mit Kol 3, 18–19 einließ – gestützt und bestärkt durch die Regeln der damaligen Ökonomik, deren Interesse darauf ausging, die Übermacht männlicher Hegemonie im Hause auf der Basis mitmenschlicher Kooperation und Liebe im Zaum zu halten.

Nichts führt also daran vorbei, daß die Haustafel des Kolosserbriefes von den Frauen soziale „Unterordnung" unter ihre Ehemänner verlangt. Dagegen kommt auch die von Leonhard Goppelt vorgeschlagene Konstruktion eines angeblichen Sinnunterschieds zwischen der Mahnung zur „Unterordnung" an die Frau in Kol 3, 18 und der Aufforderung zum „Gehorsam" (ὑπακούειν) an Kinder (V. 20) sowie Sklaven (V. 22) nicht an[141]. Mehr als alle Kunstfertigkeit einer christlichen Semantik markiert jedoch die Nachbarschaft Plutarchs den Abstand von Kol 3, 18(–19) zu allem, was an Unterdrückung und Entmündigung der Frau etwa bei Philo[142] oder sonst im Zugriffsbereich zeitgenössischer patria potestas unterwegs war. *So* gesehen verstand sich die Option für eine durch die „Liebe" der Ehemänner (Kol 3, 19) kontrollierte „Unterordnung" der Frauen durchaus *nicht* von selbst.

---

[140] Warnungen schon bei: *K. Thraede*, Ärger mit der Freiheit (Anm. 7) 61; vgl. *ders.*, Zum historischen Hintergrund der ‚Haustafeln' des NT (Anm. 20) 360 Anm. 7.
[141] *L. Goppelt*, Der erste Petrusbrief (Anm. 10) 174–175.
[142] Vgl. *F. Geiger*, Philon von Alexandreia als sozialer Denker (Stuttgart 1932) 42–43.

9. Das „Geziemende"

Die Anleitung der Frauen zu einer solchen human limitierten „Unterordnung" erfährt in Kol 3, 18 b eine stereotyp anmutende, knappe Begründung: „wie es sich ziemt (ὡς ἀνῆκεν) im Herrn". Es ist die vordergründige und scheinbar terminologische Prägnanz des hier gebrauchten Verbums ἀνῆκεν, welche die Neutestamentler immer wieder dazu drängte, von einer genaueren Bilanzierung der inhaltlichen Aspekte des Aufrufs an die Frauen selbst abzusehen und auf einer ganz bestimmten sittengeschichtlichen Äquivalenzbeziehung zu beharren.

9.1. Seit (M. Dibelius und) K. Weidinger gilt es nämlich als weitgehend akzeptiert, daß das Prädikat ἀνῆκεν aus Kol 3, 18 b auf jene „Unterabteilung des stoischen Systems" aufmerksam mache, die nach einer Mitteilung des Diogenes Laertios „den Namen καϑῆκον trug"[143]. Konkret sei es dort um einen „Pflichtenkodex"[144] gegangen, welchen die Werbung der Stoa einer anderen und beträchtlich älteren „Zusammenfassung der wichtigsten Sittengebote" entnommen habe – den sogenannten „ungeschriebenen Gesetzen"[145]. Im einzelnen sollten diese altväterlichen νόμιμα ἄγραφα den griechischen Bürgern von ehedem eine Reihe fundamentaler Pflichten einschärfen: „die Götter fürchten, die Eltern ehren, die Toten begraben, dazu wohl noch die Freunde lieben und das Vaterland nicht verraten"[146]. Das alles aber sei „im wesentlichen dasselbe" gewesen, „was in der Stoa als καϑῆκον" begegne[147]. Die Grobmaschigkeit des derart ausgezogenen Vergleichs ließ es zu, daß K. Weidinger anfing, von einem „Schema" ethischer Unterweisung zu reden, das während der gesamten hellenistischen Epoche keine nennenswerten Veränderungen habe hinnehmen müssen: „Man kann es wagen, die ganze Zeitspanne vom dritten vorchristlichen bis zum vierten nachchristlichen Jahrhundert für Parallelen mit dem Christentum in Betracht zu ziehen; denn die Durchschnittsmoral der griechischen Gesellschaft ist in der ganzen Zeit wesentlichen Veränderungen nicht ausge-

---

[143] *K. Weidinger*, Die Haustafeln (Anm. 18) 43.
[144] Ebd. 45.
[145] Ebd. 46.
[146] Ebd. 47.
[147] Ebd. 48.

setzt."[148] War es jedoch vorstellbar, daß sich über sieben Jahrhunderte hinweg eine „Durchschnittsmoral der griechischen Gesellschaft" durchzuhalten vermochte, der „wesentliche Veränderungen" erspart geblieben seien, dann bot es sich an, noch einen Schritt weiterzugehen und die Konturen antiker Sittlichkeit noch entschlossener einzuebnen. Die Rede vom allgegenwärtigen ethischen „Schema" des hellenistischen Zeitalters nahm endgültig den Rang eines nicht mehr bewegbaren Oberbegriffs ein, der es fast erübrigte, kleinliche Differenzen im philologischen Erscheinungsbild der verglichenen Texte oder gar komplexere historische Entstehungsprobleme zu diskutieren: die neutestamentlichen Haustafeln dokumentierten ebenso wie ihre in Aussicht genommenen jüdischen Vorläufer ein geradezu widerstandsloses und ohnmächtiges Einströmen „des Schemas". Ohne größere logische Komplikationen konnte K. Weidinger versichern, „die" neutestamentlichen Haustafeln seien nichts weiter als „fortschreitend verchristlichte" Kurzformeln „für das gemeinsame ethische Empfinden im Heidentum, Judentum und Christentum"[149].

Es macht keine Umstände, einzusehen, daß es nicht leicht fallen konnte, von einer solchen Höhe theoretischer Abstraktion wieder einen Weg zu den sehr viel bunteren und beweglicheren Ausgangssituationen der konkreten antiken und christlichen Überlieferungen zu finden. Im Gefälle der sich von M. Dibelius herleitenden und durch K. Weidinger maßgebend geführten Diskussion zeigt sich die gesamte Ethik des Altertums im Korsett einer durch nichts mehr zu erschütternden Einhelligkeit und Homogenität. Und noch heute blockiert die Behauptung jenes vorgeblich universalgültigen „antiken Pflichtenschemas"[150] bzw. die Rücksicht auf ein ebenso grob vermessenes „καθῆκον-Schema stoischer und jüdisch-hellenistischer Provenienz"[151] hartnäckig die Durchschlagkraft der seit Alfred Juncker[152] verfügbaren und durch J. E. Crouch vervollständigten

[148] Ebd. 19–20.
[149] Ebd. 79.
[150] W. Schrage, Zur Ethik der neutestamentlichen Haustafeln (Anm. 19) 8.
[151] J. Gnilka, Der Kolosserbrief (Anm. 13) 214.
[152] A. Juncker, Die Ethik des Apostels Paulus II (Halle 1919) 205: „Dort (sc. in der Stoa und im Judentum) lautet sie (sc. die ‚grundlegende Fragestellung'): Wie hat sich der einzelne den verschiedenen Ständen, Kreisen, Klassen gegenüber zu betätigen? Hier (sc. in den Haustafeln) dagegen: Welche Pflichten liegen den ein-

Hinweise auf die bis in die Anstrengungen zur Formgebung hinein wirksamen *Besonderheiten* der Haustafeln in Kol 3, 18 – 4, 1 und Eph 5, 22 – 6, 9.

9.2. Im exegetischen Nachspiel zu dieser offensichtlich unverbrüchlichen Grundeinstellung geht es dann allerdings nicht zuletzt um das Verbum ἀνῆκεν aus Kol 3, 18 b: mit seiner Hilfe wird die verlangte „Unterordnung" der Frau als „sich ziemende" Tugend *gemeinantik* verrechnet.

So zum Beispiel durch Otto Merk, der deswegen noch einmal die gänzlich ungeeigneten[153] Praecepta coniugalia des Plutarch (33, 142 e) ins Feld schickt: „Ἀνῆκεν begründet und interpretiert also die Aufforderung ὑποτάσσεσθε und gibt dieser ‚Unterordnung' darum zunächst keinen anderen Sinn als den, den *die Umwelt des Neuen Testaments* ebenfalls damit verband: Es ist die Unterordnung der Frau, die im Gegensatz zum Herrschen des Mannes steht und um derentwillen sie gelobt wird (vgl. Plutarch, Praec. conjug. 142 de)."[154] Dabei gerät die Anweisung zu weiblicher „Unterordnung" nach Kol 3, 18 b unversehens in die Nähe einer beinahe naturrechtlichen Verlautbarung: „Mit dem Tag des Christwerdens war diese ‚*natürliche*' Ordnung zwischen den Eheleuten nicht aufgehoben, was schicklich und geziemend war, galt auch für christliche Eheleute weiter, die mit dem Tag ihrer Bekehrung nicht sofort in neuen Lebensgewohnheiten abseits von ihren heidnischen Nachbarn lebten, und es ist zu vermuten, daß ein geordnetes Eheleben, so wie es die Sitte vorschrieb, fern von heidnischer Lasterhaftigkeit (vgl. Kol 3, 5) nicht als ein Widerspruch zur Botschaft des Evangeliums empfunden wurde."[155] Eine derartige Einschätzung des „‚neutralen' Ausdrucks ἀνῆκεν"[156] aus Kol 3, 18 b legt dann den sozialgeschichtlichen Wert oder Unwert der Einladung zur „Unterordnung" in Kol 3, 18 a unverrückbar fest: „Dieser Ausdruck (sc. ὑποτάσσε-

---

zelnen Ständen usw. als solchen ob? Mit anderen Worten: In den heidnischen und jüdischen Schriften sind die verschiedenen Stände und Klassen als Objekt, bei Paulus als Subjekt der sittlichen Betätigung gedacht". Das Beharren auf den *Unterschieden* ist erinnernswert.

[153] Siehe oben S. 297–298.
[154] *O. Merk*, Handeln aus Glauben (Anm. 44) 214.
[155] Ebd. 215.
[156] Ebd. 214.

σϑε) bezeichnet nicht mehr und nicht weniger als den Grad des Gehorsams, der auch in der Umwelt in solchem Verhältnis üblich und schicklich war."[157]

Auf ähnliche Weise sieht sich Josef Ernst durch die Wendung καϑὼς ἀνῆκεν aus Kol 3,18b bewogen, dem Altertum ohne Abstriche sittlichen Konservatismus zu bescheinigen und „Unterordnung" der Frau als unwidersprochenes Herkommen zu deklarieren. „Die Mahnung an die Frauen, ihren Männern untertan zu sein, hält sich an die im Judentum und in der Antike geltenden gesellschaftlichen Strukturen", kommentiert der Autor ohne erkennbare Absicht der Differenzierung und fährt fort: „Das Neue Testament hat das Verhältnis der Geschlechter zunächst völlig unkritisch nach dem ‚geltenden Recht' gesehen und bewertet."[158] Ist man jedoch davon überzeugt, daß sich Kol 3,18 lediglich schlicht „auf das beruft, was üblich ist und was die Tradition vorschreibt"[159], so muß man den Zweck der ausdrücklichen Verpflichtung zur „Unterordnung" notgedrungen anderswo suchen und Christologie ins Spiel bringen, um christliche Veränderung der Sitten für die Frau wenigstens absichtsvoll anzudeuten: „Der Kyrios Jesus (sc. aus Kol 3,18bβ) garantiert nicht eine bestimmte zeitbedingte gesellschaftliche Tradition, sondern sein Anspruch gibt dem bisher Gültigen einen völlig neuen Sinn. Hier werden die Impulse für eine entscheidende Wandlung in den Ordnungen des menschlichen Zusammenlebens sichtbar."[160] Warum eigentlich? Und vor allem: wo schlägt sich das nieder?

9.3. Alles in allem suggerierte der Rückzug auf jenes „Schema der sittlichen Unterweisung"[161] der Mehrzahl der Neutestamentler eine Dispens von der Aufgabe, sich intensiver dem zeitgleichen Altertum zuzuwenden und den mannigfachen Antrieben nachzuspüren, die sich dort unter anderem mit der Behandlung des Frauenthemas verbanden. Gerade anläßlich der Frage nach einer möglichen sittengeschichtlichen Konkretion der Wortfolge καϑὼς ἀνῆκεν in Kol 3,18b gerann die Hypothese K. Weidingers allmählich zur stehenden For-

---

[157] Ebd. 215.
[158] *J. Ernst*, Die Briefe an die Philipper, an Philemon, an die Kolosser, an die Epheser (RNT) (Regensburg 1974) 235.
[159] Ebd.
[160] Ebd.
[161] *E. Lohse*, Die Briefe an die Kolosser und an Philemon (Anm. 37) 221.

mel – wie bei Eduard Lohse, der dazu bemerkt: „In der Ethik der hellenistischen Popularphilosophie, die vermutlich durch die hellenistische Synagoge den christlichen Gemeinden vermittelt wurde, fand man eine reiche Materialsammlung vor, aus der man entnehmen konnte, was allgemein als schicklich und geboten anzusehen war."[162]

Zweifellos brachte eine solche verkürzte Zusammenschau „der hellenistischen Morallehre"[163] dem Theologen Vorteile. Es bot sich ihm eine Gelegenheit, im Namen des neuzeitlichen Christentums eingängige „Sachkritik" zu demonstrieren, ohne daß die hinter den Strukturen zeitbedingter Moral vermutete kerygmatische Substanz auch nur entfernt Gefahr lief, angetastet zu werden. Und nicht nur Hans Conzelmann ergriff diese Chance: „Diese Tafeln bieten nicht eine zeitlose ‚christliche' Ethik. Sie setzen die damaligen gesellschaftlichen Ordnungen und Anschauungen voraus. Die Gültigkeit liegt vielmehr in den Voraussetzungen, aus welchen diese bürgerlichen Sätze übernommen werden. Wer diese Anweisungen mechanisch in die heutige Sozialordnung übertragen wollte, würde sie in Wirklichkeit nach Sinn und Inhalt völlig verändern und würde ihre theologische, nämlich eschatologische Voraussetzung verkennen. Das zeigt sich sogleich in der ersten Forderung, der Unterordnung der Frauen. Diese bedeutete damals einfach das Einhalten einer selbstverständlichen gesellschaftlichen Stellung, des Schicklichen."[164]

Jedoch: passen die hier vorweggenommenen zeitgeschichtlichen Daten? Wie steht es mit der Schlüssigkeit einer derartigen Sachkritik, wenn das Verbum ἀνῆκεν in Kol 3,18b nicht nur allgemein auf „die Lebensregeln" aufmerksam machen wollte, „wie sie von der hellenistischen Popularphilosophie dargelegt und eingeübt wurden"[165], sondern vom Leser verlangte, daß er sich auf die Seite einer besonderen Lebensform schlug, welche der Späthellenismus neben einer ganzen Skala anderer Vorschläge zur Frauenfrage parat hielt? Ist es auch dann theologisch noch so ohne weiteres machbar, die

---

[162] Ebd. 222.
[163] Ebd. 223.
[164] *H. Conzelmann*, Der Brief an die Kolosser (Anm. 44) 200.
[165] *E. Lohse*, a.a.O. 220.

Haustafel des Kolosserbriefes „ihrem Inhalt nach" davor in Schutz zu nehmen, wirklich „angewandtes Kerygma" zu sein?[166]

Und in der Tat spricht einiges dafür, daß Kol 3, 18–19 (bzw. 3, 18 bis 4, 1) eines von *mehreren* denkbaren ethischen Angeboten an die christliche Ehefrau als „geziemend" auswählt.

9.4. Schon das Imperfekt ἀνῆκεν vermag in diese Richtung zu zeigen. Denn es ist grammatisch gar nicht in der Lage, an „die Vergangenheit als die gebietende Autorität alles gegenwärtigen Handelns" zu erinnern, wie noch E. Lohmeyer meinte[167]. Dagegen liegt es in seiner sprachlichen Kompetenz, „eine Aussage über die Gegenwart" zu machen und somit auf etwas hinzuweisen, was „tatsächlich notwendig" ist, jedoch noch „nicht geschieht"[168]. Im Kontext von Kol 3, 18–19 wird man daher den Umstand, daß ein solches Imperfekt „eine Aufforderung enthält"[169], auch mit einer aktuellen Parteinahme für eine bestimmte Fasson des sittlichen Vollzugs vereinbaren können und nicht nur mit der erneuten Einschärfung eines ehrwürdig hergebrachten Brauchtums. Offenkundig will der Verfasser nicht umfassend auf einer „Anerkennung der bestehenden Ordnung"[170] beharren, sondern eine wohlüberlegte Entscheidung für die eine und gegen eine andere sozialethische Orientierung herbeiführen.

9.5. Zu dieser grammatischen Möglichkeit paßt die Einsicht in die Irrtümlichkeit einer Mehrzahl bisheriger Beurteilungen der antiken Szenerie. In der Folge der von K. Weidinger durchgesetzten These und aufgrund der dabei stets aufs neue zum Markte getragenen gleichen Beleggarnituren mußte sich im neutestamentlichen Geschäft der Eindruck festigen, als habe es im hellenistischen Altertum einen unüberwindbar dauerhaften, für die Frauen jener Tage gleichbleibend ungünstigen Status quo sozialethischer Denkmuster gegeben, den eben auch und gerade Kol 3, 18 – 4, 1 abbildete. Die Rede vom (stoischen) Pflichtenschema, das über synagogale Paränese vermittelt worden sei, das Beharren auf der sogenannten „Offizienethik" –

---

[166] Vgl. ebd. 220 Anm. 4.
[167] *E. Lohmeyer,* Die Briefe an die Philipper, an die Kolosser und an Philemon (Anm. 43) 156.
[168] Blass – Debrunner – Rehkopf, § 358.
[169] Ebd. § 358, 2 Anm. 3.
[170] Vgl. *J. Gnilka,* Der Kolosserbrief (Anm. 13) 226.

zuweilen ohne Nachweis auch als „Haustafeln der hellenistischen Umwelt"[171] schon im neutestamentlichen Vorfeld wehrlos vereinnahmt –, all das verstellte die Bühne der Antike wirkungsvoll und restlos. Die faktische Bandbreite der Gedanken-Modelle, welche das späthellenistische Altertum zum Frauenthema entwickelte und debattierte, blieb unvermessen und verborgen.

9.6. Daß und mit welcher Heftigkeit diese Diskussion gerade im 1. christlichen Jahrhundert geführt wurde, zeigen stellvertretend Leute wie der Philosoph Seneca, den die Exegeten gewöhnlich in sensu malo zitieren, sobald ihnen Kol 3,18–19 ins Haus steht. Aber Senecas Auffassung von der gesellschaftlichen Rolle der Frau läßt sich nicht ohne Gewalttätigkeit auf den Satz festlegen, daß „der eine Teil" der Menschheit „zum Gehorchen, der andere zum Befehlen geboren sei" (De constantia sapientis 1,1), wie das noch W. Schrage versuchte[172]. Vielmehr zeichnet sich der einschlägige Befund in der Hinterlassenschaft dieses Stoikers durch nichts mehr aus als durch Unentschiedenheit und Beweglichkeit der Einstellung – und ist deswegen besonders geeignet, eine Vorstellung von der Mannigfaltigkeit der Facetten zu vermitteln, in welchen zur frühen Kaiserzeit die soziale Reputation der Frau schillert. Die Bilanz der von Seneca erwogenen Positionen umspannt die alte Überzeugung von der weiblichen Inferiorität[173] ebenso wie das achtungsvolle Zugeständnis der Gleichwertigkeit in Bildung und Sitte[174]: die Konventionen erscheinen aufgebrochen und bieten sich in einem deutlichen Gefälle dar, auf dessen Bahn Frauenverachtung nur einer der beiden denkbaren Extremwerte ist. Durch nichts wird hingegen die den Neutestamentlern lieb gewordene Überzeugung vom ausdauernden und konservativen Einklang des Altertums in Grundfragen sozialer Sitte bestätigt. Vielmehr dokumentiert Seneca den sozialen Wandel und die Schwierigkeiten, damit fertig zu werden.

9.7. Als noch bedeutsamer wird allerdings eine andere Beobach-

---

[171] *E. Lohse,* Die Briefe an die Kolosser und an Philemon (Anm. 37) 225 Anm. 6.
[172] *W. Schrage,* Zur Ethik der neutestamentlichen Haustafeln (Anm. 19) 13.
[173] De constantia sapientis 1,1; De ira II 30,1.III 24,3; De consolatione ad Helviam 14,2; Naturales Quaestiones III 12,2. Vgl. *Ch. Favez,* Les opinions de Sénèque sur la femme: REL 16 (1938) 335–345, besonders 341–342.
[174] Vor allem: De consolatione ad Helviam 16; 17,4; 19,5. *H. Preisker,* Christentum und Ehe in den ersten drei Jahrhunderten (NSGTK 23) (Berlin 1927) 26, führt diese den Frauen günstige Einstellung auf „Entwicklung" zurück.

tung einzustufen sein. Sie läßt sich wieder an einem Seneca-Text machen, den die Exegeten bislang meist nur deswegen und nur soweit ins Spiel zu bringen pflegten, als er es ihnen erlaubte, jenes ohnehin vielbemühte und offensichtlich unverzichtbare „Schema in der allgemeinen Morallehre der Stoa"[175] an einem weiteren Exempel zu demonstrieren: an der Epistula ad Lucilium 94[176].

Im Zuge einer derartigen Beschränkung des Interesses wurde eine für Kol 3, 18–19 (4, 1) höchst aufschlußreiche Pointe übersehen. Der Anfang dieses Briefes (94, 1–4) unterrichtet nämlich den Leser über die Absicht des Seneca, eine Streitfrage wieder aufzugreifen, die um die Mitte des 3. vorchristlichen Jahrhunderts der stoische Philosoph Ariston hatte liegen lassen – das Problem näherhin, mit welchen vordringlichen Gegenständen sich die Philosophie zu befassen habe. Dabei stellt Seneca zunächst die strikte Weigerung des Ariston heraus, das Metier des Philosophen mit den auf konsequente Gegenseitigkeit angelegten Verhaltensnormen innerhalb eines Haushalts zu belasten[177]:

„Jene Sparte der Philosophie, welche sich mit den Regeln befaßt, die der Einzelperson angemessen sind und die davon absieht, den Menschen in den Rahmen des Großen und Ganzen einzuordnen, sondern statt dessen dem *Ehemann* rät, wie er sich gegen seine *Frau* verhalten, dem *Vater,* wie er seine *Kinder* erziehen und dem *Herrn,* wie er seine *Sklaven* leiten soll – dieses Stoffgebiet der Philosophie also nehmen manche als das allein bedeutsame zur Kenntnis. Die anderen Disziplinen vernachlässigen sie hingegen, als schweiften sie von unseren praktischen Bedürfnissen ab. Als ob einer für einen Lebensausschnitt als Ratgeber in Frage kommen könnte, wenn er sich nicht vorher über die Summe des ganzen Lebens Gedanken gemacht hat! Der Stoiker Ariston schätzt im Gegensatz dazu jene eben genannte Abteilung der Philosophie nur gering ein: man solle sie nicht allzu ernst nehmen, da sie nur altweiberhafte Lebensregeln anbiete. Am meisten, meint er, käme es darauf an, daß die grundlegenden Einsichten der Philosophie und die Vorstellung von der Wesensart des höchsten Gutes vorankämen; denn: ‚wer dabei gut auffaßte und lernte, kann sich dann selbst Vorschriften darüber machen, was bei dieser oder jener Gelegenheit zu tun sei'. Das ist so wie bei einem, der das Werfen lernt. Er muß ein Ziel ins Auge fassen können und seine Hand dazu ausbilden, das, was er wirft, daraufhin zu steuern. Wenn er

[175] *E. Lohse,* Die Briefe an die Kolosser und an Philemon (Anm. 37) 221.
[176] Siehe oben S. 283 f.
[177] Text: *L. D. Reynolds,* L. Annaei Senecae ad Lucilium epistulae morales II (Scriptorum classicorum bibliotheca Oxoniensis) (Oxford 1965) 363–364.

dann diese Fertigkeit durch Unterricht und Übung erworben hat, kann er – wann immer ihm danach ist – davon Gebrauch machen. (Hat er doch gelernt, nicht nur dieses oder jenes zu treffen, sondern alles, was er will.) Ebenso hat der, der sich über das Leben schlechthin unterrichtet hat, kein Bedürfnis nach stückweiser Ermahnung. Hat er doch eine umfassende Belehrung erhalten: eben nicht darüber, wie er mit seiner Frau oder mit seinem Sohne leben soll, sondern wie man überhaupt gut lebt. Darin ist ganz von selbst enthalten, wie er am besten mit seiner Frau und seinen Kindern lebt. Cleanthes wiederum beurteilt die oben genannte Sparte der Philosophie zwar als nützlich, jedoch als schwachsinnig, wenn sie nicht aus dem Großen und Ganzen herausströmt und nicht die eigentlichen Grundeinsichten der Philosophie und ihre Hauptgegenstände in ihr Erkenntnisstreben einbezieht."

Seneca gibt hier vor, darum zu wissen, daß es innerhalb der stoischen Bewegung seit Kleanthes (331–232 v. Chr.), dem Nachfolger des Schulengründers Zenon, umstritten gewesen sei, ob man das Thema der zwischenmenschlichen Beziehungen in den Schranken und mit den Akzenten der Ökonomietraktate erörtern solle oder ob sich Ökonomik überhaupt nicht als sinnvoller Gegenstand der Philosophie empfehle. Demzufolge war die Stoa unschlüssig, ob sich die Normenfelder, welche die Schriften περὶ οἴκων bzw. περὶ οἰκονομίας im Rahmen der für das Haus maßgebenden Strukturen (Mann/Frau, Vater/Kinder, Herr/Sklaven) besprachen, aus den mit Vorzug und in größerer Allgemeinheit zu lehrenden Einblicken in die „Wesensart des höchsten Gutes" ableiten ließen oder ob man sich im Schulbetrieb ihrer eigens annehmen müsse. Und Seneca gibt auch zu, daß es Leute gebe (Epistula 94, 1), die das Terrain der philosophischen Erkenntnis ganz auf die Belange zurücksteckten, auf welche die Ökonomiekonzepte ihr Augenmerk konzentrierten. Für Seneca war somit die ausdrückliche und ausschließliche Zuwendung philosophischer Einsichten an die Adresse des Ehemannes und seiner Frau, des Vaters und seiner Kinder sowie des Herren und seiner Sklaven – zu sozialen Gegebenheiten also, die in solcher Reziprozität und Begrenzung der sogenannten „Offizienethik" fehlten – ein durchaus unterscheidbarer, ja sogar alternativer Weg der Philosophie. Dieser Weg bot sich ihm keineswegs auf dem unanfechtbaren Niveau einer gemeinantiken Grundauffassung an noch war er Bestandteil eines „antiken Ethos"[178] schlechthin bzw. des „damals

---

[178] *W. Schrage*, Zur Ethik der neutestamentlichen Haustafeln (Anm. 19) 9.

Üblichen"[179] überhaupt. Seneca argumentiert nicht so, als habe er aus seinem Lebensbereich eine unbestritten gültige „sittliche Konvention der damaligen Zeit"[180] gekannt, an die er nur hätte zu appellieren brauchen. Im Gegenteil: wenn man sich der Ökonomierezepte mit ihrer Beschränkung auf das „Haus" und ihren stets im Unterschied zur politischen Öffentlichkeit[181] behandelten Elementen – Ehefrauen, Kindern und Sklaven – annehmen wollte, so verlangte das eine inhaltliche Abstimmung mit den philosophischen Prinzipien der Stoa.

9.8. In summa bietet der Fall des Seneca einigen Anlaß, dem Eindruck geschlossenen Einvernehmens gründlich zu mißtrauen, welchen die sozialethischen Anstrengungen des Altertums im Referat der Neutestamentler gewöhnlich hinterlassen. Die Äußerungen dieses Philosophen stecken voller Widersprüche und Ungereimtheiten, sobald man seine direkten und indirekten Antworten auf die Frage nach dem gesellschaftlichen Soll und Haben der Frauen seiner Tage nebeneinander aufreiht. Und man kann nicht daran zweifeln: gerade *darin* dokumentiert er die sittengeschichtliche Großwetterlage der Antike um die Mitte des 1. Jahrhunderts n. Chr. Weder in Rom noch sonstwo in seinen Provinzen gab es damals so etwas wie eine einverständliche „Ethik der hellenistischen Popularphilosophie", aus welcher das Christentum (und zuvor das Judentum) nur hätte zu „entnehmen" brauchen, „was *allgemein* als schicklich und geboten anzusehen war"[182]. Darüber hinaus verrät Seneca, wie gering das Aufkommen des zeitgenössischen Altertums an hierher gehöriger und übereinkommender Theorie gewesen sein muß – und das besonders, wenn es um die Frauen und ihr Verhältnis zu den Männern ging. Mehr als anderen konnten dabei einem Stoiker die eigenen philosophischen Voraussetzungen sogar im Wege stehen – in erster Linie die Affektenlehre, welche die Anerkennung emotional verankerter Bindungen schon im Ansatz vereitelte[183]. Um so erstaunlicher

---

[179] Ebd.   [180] Ebd.

[181] Hier urteilt *D. Lührmann,* Wo man nicht mehr Sklave oder Freier ist (Anm. 87) 80, gegenteilig: „Sieht man, daß die Ökonomie Teil der Politik war, so liegt in den Haustafeln ein latenter politischer Anspruch, setzt man die Bedingungen der hellenistischen und römischen Stadtkultur voraus". *Das* geben die Texte schwerlich her.

[182] *E. Lohse,* Die Briefe an die Kolosser und an Philemon (Anm. 37) 222.

[183] So mit Recht *K. Thraede,* Art. Frau (Anm. 117) 217 (Nr. 4).

ist es, daß Seneca ungeachtet einer so ungünstigen gedanklichen Prädisposition ein einschlägiges Sozialtheorem parat hat. In der schon am Ausgang seines Lebens abgefaßten und dem Aebutius Liberalis aus Lyon gewidmeten Schrift „Über die Wohltaten" (II 18, 1–2) kommt er darauf zu sprechen[184]:

> „Jede Verpflichtung, die zwei Menschen betrifft, fordert von beiden dasselbe. Wenn du dich darum bemüht hast, einzusehen, welche Art Mensch ein *Vater* sein muß, dann wirst du wissen, daß da noch die nicht weniger große Aufgabe ansteht, zu durchschauen, welcher Art Mensch ein Sohn sein soll. Hat der *Ehemann* gewisse Pflichten, so die Ehefrau nicht weniger. In Gegenseitigkeit erfüllen sie wieviel auch verlangt sein mag. Sie wollen eine gleichlastige Verhaltensregel. Aber eine solche Richtschnur ist eine schwierige Sache, wie Hekaton sagte."

Die Emphase, mit der sich Seneca hier für den Grundsatz der Wechselseitigkeit einsetzt, ist vor dem Hintergrund stoischer Individualethik verwunderlich[185]. Und allem Anschein nach stellt er sich bewußt in Rechnung, daß er sich damit von dem Stoiker Hekaton entfernt, der um 100 v. Chr. diesem Axiom der Sittlichkeit mit großer Skepsis begegnet war. So wie sich Hekaton im Gegensatz zu Seneca auch nicht dazu bereit finden konnte, den Aspekt der Reziprozität ethischen Verhaltens auf die Kommunikation des Herrn mit seinen Sklaven „intra domum" anzuwenden (De beneficiis III 22, 1) – auf die dritte soziale Struktur des antiken „Hauses" also. Entgegen älterer stoischer Tradition zeigt sich Seneca somit unterwegs, die Pflichten innerhalb der Familie als eine in sich geschlossene Einheit sittlicher Ansprüche und Leistungen begreiflich zu machen – als eng zusammengehöriges Feld der gesellschaftlichen Beziehungen zwischen Ehemann und Ehefrau, zwischen Vater und Kindern (De beneficiis II 18, 1–2), aber ebenso zwischen dem Hausherrn und seinen Sklaven (De beneficiis III 22, 1). Seneca setzt also dazu an, *auch* das Frauenthema im Rahmen jener Gegebenheiten eines Haushaltes zu diskutieren, welche die überkommenen Schriften „Über die Ökonomie" seit Jahr und Tag nach den ethischen Maßgaben der gutwilligen Wechselseitigkeit und freundschaftlichen Kooperation zu re-

---

[184] Text: *J. W. Basore*, Seneca. Moral Essays III (The Loeb Classical Library) (London – Cambridge 1964) 84–87.
[185] Vgl. *P. Barth*, Die Stoa (Stuttgart [3+4]1922) 101–113.

geln versuchten. Bei Seneca läßt sich demzufolge exemplarisch nachlesen, wie die Erörterung der sozialen Möglichkeiten der Frauen einen festen Kontext sittlicher Orientierung an dem durch Reziprozität gemäßigten Programm effektiver Haushaltungskunst zu gewinnen vermochte.

9.9. Man wird an das Beispiel des ungefähren Zeitgenossen Seneca denken müssen, wenn man sich daran macht, den Satzteil „wie es sich ziemt" aus Kol 3, 18 b verstehen zu lernen. Das Imperfekt innerhalb der Wendung καϑὼς ἀνῆκεν indiziert dann keinesfalls die Rücksicht auf eine in der Antike angeblich global zuhandene Durchschnittsmoral, sondern es signalisiert die Entschlossenheit, sich auf ein bestimmtes und unterscheidbares Modell des Vollzugs ethischer Verantwortung einzulassen. Dieses Modell empfahl nicht zuletzt den Frauen, den Normen späthellenistischer Ökonomik zu folgen, die zwar die Führungsrolle des Ehemannes im „Hause" fraglos anerkannten, jedoch durch ihre Appelle zu Partnerschaft und strikter Gegenseitigkeit versittlicht und humanisiert waren.

10. „Im Herrn"

Wenn sich die auffallend zahlreichen Berufungen auf den „Herrn" in Kol 3, 18.20.22.23.24; 4, 1 bereits einer vorausliegenden jüdischen Redaktion verdanken, dann ist es nicht unwahrscheinlich, daß es gerade das Wort κύριος aus Kol 3, 17 war, welches die Einbringung der älteren Haustafel in Kol 3, 18 – 4, 1 und nicht anderswo geraten sein ließ[186]. Denn streng genommen bot nur Kol 3, 17 beides: die Bedingungen für eine Stichwortassoziation und wenigstens die vage Möglichkeit einer inhaltlichen Verklammerung mit dem Aufruf zum „Gottesdienst im Alltag der Welt"[187] aus Kol 3, 17: „Und alles, was ihr in Wort und Werk tut, das alles (tut) im Namen des *Herrn* Jesus,

---

[186] Auch W. Munro's Versuch, Kol 3, 18 – 4, 1 als späte Interpolation zu verstehen, scheitert an der handschriftlichen Überlieferung: *ders.,* Col 3, 18 – 4, 1 and Eph 5, 21 – 6, 9. Evidences of a Late Literary Stratum?: NTS 18 (1972) 434–447. Vgl. oben Anm. 55.

[187] Der Ausdruck stammt von *E. Käsemann,* Gottesdienst im Alltag der Welt. Zu Röm 12, in: *ders.,* Exegetische Versuche und Besinnungen II (Göttingen ³1970) 198(–204).

indem ihr durch ihn Gott, dem Vater, Dank sagt." Offensichtlich ist die Einschaltung der Haustafel vom christlichen Verfasser des Kolosserbriefes so gemeint, daß jenes „gottesdienstliche Leben der Gemeinde seine Fortsetzung im Alltag von Ehe, Familie und Arbeitswelt"[188] haben soll.

Trifft aber diese Vermutung zu, dann wird die Frage umso dringlicher, welchen Stellenwert die Formel „im Herrn" für Kol 3,18(20) hat, nachdem festzustehen scheint, daß sich in Kol 3,18 – 4,1 eine jüdisch vermittelte Parteinahme für späthellenistische Ökonomie-Traditionen niederschlägt.

10.1. Es entsprach ihrer Vorstellung von einer relativ unbehinderten Herleitung der Haustafel aus einem allgegenwärtigen und unerschütterlich konsistenten Pflichtenformular der Stoa, wenn M. Dibelius und K. Weidinger den sachlichen Beitrag der Wendung ἐν κυρίῳ aus Kol 3,18 b(20) nur sehr gering bewerteten. „Die paränetischen Regeln, auch die aus der Umwelt übernommenen, werden (sc. von Paulus) vorgetragen als Anweisungen zum Leben ἐν Χριστῷ. Darum genügt zur *Verchristlichung* solcher Regeln mitunter ein ἐν κυρίῳ wie z. B. Kol 3,18.20. In Wirklichkeit werden solche Paränesen fremder Herkunft mit dieser Verchristlichung auf eine andere Ebene übertragen. Die Ausführung dieser Gebote gehört zum Vollzug des neuen Lebens", meinte M. Dibelius[189]. Und K. Weidinger vollstreckte die von seinem Lehrer eher angedeutete Erklärung des Befundes: „Wenn somit diese Haustafel als ein Stück christlicher Paränese anzusprechen ist, das ganz besonders deutliche Spuren seiner profanen Herkunft trägt, so ist das doch kein Einwand gegen seinen Wert innerhalb des Neuen Testaments. Denn auch die kurze Formel ἐν κυρίῳ bietet schon eine Erinnerung an die neue Lebenssphäre, die hergestellt ist durch die Erfahrung der Liebe Gottes, die er uns ‚in dem Herrn' erwiesen hat, und die im Christen eine Wendung des Sinnes hervorbringt (1 Joh 4,11) und ist selbst in dieser ganz einfachen Form ein tiefes, weil religiöses Motiv."[190]

10.2. Andere Exegeten gaben sich damit nicht zufrieden. Ihnen

---

[188] *E. Schweizer*, Der Brief an die Kolosser (Anm. 44) 164.
[189] *M. Dibelius*, Die Formgeschichte des Evangeliums (Anm. 63) 240–241 Anm. 2.
[190] *K. Weidinger*, Die Haustafeln (Anm. 18) 51–52.

war es ein Anliegen, auf den Nachweis hinzuarbeiten, daß die für genuin christlich gehaltene Formel „im Herrn" eine inhaltliche und qualitative Umwandlung der heidnischen bzw. heidnisch-jüdischen Vorlage auslöste.

So sah Hans Dietrich Wendland hinter der Wortfolge ἐν κυρίῳ eine hinzutretende Markierung des „Herrseins und der Herrschaft Christi in der Gemeinde"[191]. D. Schroeder hingegen verkehrte das bislang favorisierte Modell des Zuflusses aus der nichtchristlichen Antike und beharrte auf der Annahme, daß die Mahnungen in Kol 3, 18 – 4, 1 letztlich von Jesus selbst stammten und durch Paulus mit Hilfe der Wendung ἐν κυρίῳ christlich rezipiert worden seien, um endlich vom Apostel aufgrund stoischer Fragestellungen unter den Heidenchristen seiner Missionsgebiete zu einer griffigen Haustafel gestaltet zu werden[192]. Aber macht schon die Voraussetzung Schwierigkeiten, daß Weisungen Jesu später einer christlichen Begründung „im Herrn" bedurft hätten, so erst recht der sich vermeintlich an Paulus anlehnende Gedanke: „Der Imperativ der Haustafeln geht vom fordernden Herrn aus. So wie Jesus das Sabbatgebot aufhebt und selbst an die Stelle des Gesetzes tritt durch eine neue totale Forderung und in einer neuen Erfüllung von Gottes Willen, so wird auch hier das Gesetz nicht als überholt abgetan, denn durch den κύριος wird die totale und absolute Forderung Gottes zur Geltung gebracht. Dieses ist die Autorität unseres Imperativs: die Forderung des totalen Gehorsams, die vom κύριος selbst gefordert wird. Der κύριος tritt an die Stelle des Gesetzes."[193]

Paulus indessen erweist sich als ein schlechter Gewährsmann für solche Folgerungen. Gerade im Blick auf die Frauen und Männer aus Kol 3, 18-19 läßt sich nämlich zeigen, daß D. Schroeder gut be-

---

[191] *H. D. Wendland*, Zur sozialethischen Bedeutung der neutestamentlichen Haustafeln, in: Die Leibhaftigkeit des Wortes. FS A. Köberle (Hamburg 1958) 42–43.

[192] *D. Schroeder*, Die Haustafeln (Anm. 32) 131–132. Auf anderem Wege versucht eine überlieferungsgeschichtliche Rückführung der Haustafelethik auf den historischen Jesus: *L. Goppelt*, Jesus und die „Haustafel"-Tradition, in: Orientierung an Jesus. FS J. Schmid (Freiburg – Basel – Wien 1973) 93–106; vgl. auch *ders.*, Prinzipien neutestamentlicher Sozialethik nach dem 1. Petrusbrief, in: Neues Testament und Geschichte. FS O. Cullmann (Zürich – Tübingen 1972) 285–296.

[193] Ebd. 166.

raten gewesen wäre, zwischen einem paulinischen und einem deu-
teropaulinischen Gebrauch der Formeln ἐν κυρίῳ sowie ἐν Χριστῷ
zu unterscheiden. Der Paulus der unbezweifelbar echten Briefe bedient sich der Wendungen ἐν κυρίῳ (1 Kor 11,11) und ἐν Χριστῷ
(Gal 3,28), um die Einheit und Gleichwertigkeit der Geschlechter zu
betonen – und er reklamiert die Schöpfung, wenn es ihm auf deren
Verschiedenheit ankommt (1 Kor 11,3–10). Auch sonst scheint Paulus keine nennenswerten Versuche zu unternehmen, um Anschauungen hergebrachter sozialer Sittlichkeit (theologisch oder) christologisch zu rechtfertigen (vgl. Gal 3,28; 1 Kor 12,13 mit 1 Kor
11,3–10). An ihm läßt sich somit keine tragfähige Brücke nach Kol
3,18 (– 4,1) festmachen.

Und überhaupt: wo ist der *philologisch* wirklich verifizierbare ur-
sächliche Zusammenhang zwischen der ethischen Forderung und
ihrer Motivation durch ἐν κυρίῳ in Kol 3,18–19, der es erlaubte, mit
H. D. Wendland glaubwürdig davon zu sprechen, daß sich der Charakter der den Frauen auferlegten „Unterordnung" durch seine „Begründung" mit der Formel „im Herrn" der Sache nach geändert
hätte?

An dieser Stelle kritischer Nachfrage quälen sich die Neutestamentler spürbar. Vor allem diejenigen unter ihnen, die nicht nur den
Tatbestand einer „völlig neuen *Begründung*" für die Wendung „im
Herrn" aus Kol 3,18(20) behaupten, sondern damit „zugleich ein
kritisches Prinzip" gegeben sehen, „um darüber befinden zu können, welche ethischen Weisungen für die Gemeinde als verbindlich
anzusehen sind". Die „zwischenmenschlichen Beziehungen", sagt
E. Lohse weiter, seien „das Feld, auf dem der Christ den Gehorsam
gegenüber dem Kyrios bewährt, indem er in der ἀγάπη handelt"[194].

Wie soll aber die inhaltliche Seite jenes „kritischen Prinzips" aussehen? Was darf man sich an konkret verbleibender Ethik vorstellen, wenn in unerträglicher Abstraktion fortgefahren wird: „den aus
der Umwelt übernommenen Weisungen wurde ein grundlegend
neuer Sinn gegeben, indem ihre Befolgung als dem κύριος erwiese-
ner Gehorsam verstanden wurde"?[195] Wird hier darauf abgehoben,
„daß der Mensch, der durch die Berufung zum Glauben der Gesell-

---

[194] *E. Lohse*, Die Briefe an die Kolosser und an Philemon (Anm. 37) 223.
[195] Ebd. 222.

schaft gegenüber ‚fremd' geworden ist, sich gleichwohl in die Lebensformen der Gesellschaft, in der er steht, hineinstellt", wie L. Goppelt vorschlug?[196] Oder weist – um Joachim Gnilka zu zitieren – das ἐν κυρίῳ in Kol 3,18 darauf hin, daß „der Herr das letzte Kriterium" sei und *deshalb* „eine positive Ordnung nicht das Endgültige sein"[197] könne? Kommt die Unterstellung einer derart „eschatologisch" bedingten und ἐν κυρίῳ sozusagen subversiv bewilligten Freiheit tatsächlich gegen die Erkenntnis auf, daß die mit „Unterordnung" und „Gehorsam" befaßten Imperative die Haustafel bereits auf ihren vorchristlichen und vorjüdischen Überlieferungsstrecken fundamental prägten? Und warum soll dann das Christentum aus dem Judentum, und das Judentum aus dem Heidentum ausgerechnet einen Kanon von Aufforderungen übernommen haben, der sich mit Vorzug eben *nicht* an die Untergebenen schlechthin in der damaligen Gesellschaft wandte, sondern pointiert an die subalternen Zugehörigen eines Haushalts appellierte? Reicht es da wirklich aus, mit der matten Erklärung zu kommen: „weder erschien es ratsam, die eschatologische Ordnung in das Jetzt einzutragen, noch das Weltliche zu übergehen"?[198] Warum werden im „Hause" lediglich die „Unterordnung" der Frauen (Kol 3,18) sowie der „Gehorsam" von Kindern und Sklaven (Kol 3,22–25) christologisch begründet und ausgelegt, nicht aber das von Ehemännern, Vätern und Herren geforderte Verhalten?

10.3. Geht man indessen davon aus, daß Kol 3,18 – 4,1 eine spezifische sozialethische Position literarisch abbildet, welche von den zeitgenössischen Traktaten „Über die Ökonomie" propagiert zu werden pflegte, so wird man die Formel „im Herrn" aus Kol 3,18(20) pragmatischer und einfacher beurteilen: als Autorisierung einer urchristlichen Entscheidung zugunsten des human besonnenen Mittelweges ökonomischer Gegenseitigkeit in den konventionellen Strukturen des antiken Hauswesens. Mit Rücksicht auf die Wendung ἐν κυρίῳ bleibt für Kol 3,18 somit in Geltung, was Herbert Preisker schon 1927 nüchtern zu Protokoll gab: „Der Zusatz ‚wie es sich ziemt im Herrn' ist ebensowenig christliche Vertiefung,

---

[196] *L. Goppelt,* Der erste Petrusbrief (Anm. 10) 177.
[197] *J. Gnilka,* Der Kolosserbrief (Anm. 13) 217.
[198] Ebd. 218.

wie das ὑποτάσσεσθαι christlich bestimmte Unterordnung ist. Vielmehr wird nur betont, daß auch ἐν κυρίῳ die Naturordnung gilt."[199] Man braucht lediglich den Begriff der „Naturordnung" zu tilgen und dafür einen Hinweis auf die besonderen Anliegen der Ökonomik einzusetzen, um diese klarsichtige und christologisch zurückhaltende Würdigung noch heute akzeptieren zu können.

Dazu wird man umso mehr bereit sein, sobald man den Epheserbrief in das Kalkül einbezieht[200]. Dort nämlich widerfährt der Formel „im Herrn" aus Kol 3,18 eine ausdrückliche und weiträumige christologische Entfaltung. Eph 5,22 schärft den Lesern ein, daß die Frau sich ihrem Manne fügen solle „wie dem Herrn". Und Eph 5,23 trägt den Grund dafür nach: „der Mann ist das Haupt der Frau wie auch Christus das Haupt der Kirche ist – er selber der Retter des Leibes". Die Eindringlichkeit, mit der hier Christologie *hinzu*gebracht wird, zeigt deutlich, daß der Verfasser des Epheserbriefes im Zuge *seiner* exegetischen Behandlung des Schreibens an die Kolosser in der Wendung ἐν κυρίῳ aus Kol 3,18 *keine* umfänglicheren christologischen Implikationen vorgegeben sah.

10.4. Die gut abgesicherte Verweigerung einer zu weit getriebenen christologischen Auswertung der Formel „im Herrn" zieht allerdings eine wichtige Konsequenz nach sich. Wenn es nämlich *nicht* möglich ist, die schon auf einer jüdischen Adaptionsebene eingeschaltete Wendung ἐν κυρίῳ methodisch gesichert und überlieferungsgeschichtlich unbehindert an die großen Linien der (paulinischen) Christologie und Soteriologie anzuschließen, dann geht es auch nicht an, die Mahnungen an die Frauen und Männer in Kol 3,18-19 bzw. die Appelle der Haustafel aus Kol 3,18 – 4,1 überhaupt als damalige und ein für allemal zurückliegende sittliche Standards abzuwählen, die Formel „im Herrn" jedoch gewissermaßen unbeschädigt zurückzubehalten – wie man das zuletzt bei E. Lohse lesen konnte: „Der Inhalt der einzelnen Sätze ist durch die damaligen Verhältnisse bedingt. Sie bieten weder zeitlos gültige Gesetze noch verleihen sie einer bestimmten Gesellschaftsordnung unverlierbare Würde. Im Wandel der Zeit ändert sich auch das allge-

---

[199] *H. Preisker*, Christentum und Ehe (Anm. 174) 139 Anm. 118.
[200] Zum Vergleich im einzelnen: *F. Hahn*, Die christologische Begründung urchristlicher Paränese: ZNW 72 (1981) 96–99.

meine Urteil über das, was sich schickt und gebührt. Christliche Paränese aber hat unwandelbar die Forderung einzuprägen, dem Kyrios gehorsam zu sein. Wie dieser Gehorsam jeweils konkret zu
verwirklichen ist, wird jedoch stets neu zu prüfen und zu entscheiden sein."[201]

Eine solche Äußerung hinterläßt einen „Kyrios", dessen Zuständigkeit für „christliche Paränese" in die totale Abstraktion eines rein
formalen Prinzips ausmündet. Sie läßt außer acht, daß in Kol 3,18
bis 4,1 nicht nur die Aufforderungen an die Frauen und Männer,
Kinder und Väter, Sklaven und Herren der christlichen Haushalte
einer einschlägigen „Sachkritik" bedürfen, sondern auch der Weg
ihrer Autorisation durch eine bloße Berufung auf den „Herrn".
Beide inhaltlichen Aspekte – die sittlichen Mahnungen selbst *und*
die Weise ihrer Bevollmächtigung durch den „Herrn" sind Nieder-
schläge *derselben* unwiederbringlich *vergangenen* Denkart.

11. Ergebnisse

Daß sich sogar theologisch ambitionierte Atheisten wie Joachim
Kahl an der Diskussion um die neutestamentlichen „Haustafeln"
beteiligen und deren im großen und ganzen negatives Ansehen mit
erheblicher Energie zu einer „Realbilanz der Kirchengeschichte"[202]
ausweiten, ist ein Umstand, der Aufmerksamkeit verdient: die
„Haustafeln" werden immer wieder bevorzugt herangezogen, um
die Qualität und Redlichkeit des ethischen Anspruchs christlicher
Weltgestaltung überhaupt kritisch zu bewerten. Das macht beson-
nene Reaktionen unausweichlich.

Einen wichtigen und grundlegenden Beitrag dazu leisten alle Versuche, die sitten*geschichtliche* Reputation der „Haustafeln" des
Neuen Testaments objektiver und sorgfältiger als bisher mit dem
zeitgenössischen Altertum abzugleichen – in erster Linie das hier implizite Frauenthema, an das sich der Vorwurf der „Menschenverach-
tung"[203] meistens allzu rasch und kurzsichtig anheftete. Mit einer

---

[201] *E. Lohse,* Der Brief an die Kolosser und an Philemon (Anm. 37) 223.
[202] *J. Kahl,* Das Elend des Christentums oder Plädoyer für eine Humanität ohne
Gott (Rororo aktuell 1093) (Hamburg 1977) 17.
[203] Ebd. 19.

solchen Absicht trug sich auch der vorliegende „kritische Rückblick auf alte Ergebnisse". Sein Ertrag läßt sich wie folgt bilanzieren:

11.1. Es ist ratsam, den seit M. Dibelius einer größeren Bezugsmenge reservierten Oberbegriff der „Haustafel" auf Kol 3,18 – 4,1 und den davon abhängigen Text Eph 5,22 – 6,9 zu beschränken. Nur in Kol und Eph geht es um eine bewußte Limitierung sozialethisch einschlägiger Regeln auf die Strukturen eines antiken Haushaltes. Dort, wo das Haus erstmals verlassen wird, wie in 1 Petr 2,13 bis 3,7, liegt bereits ein Stück inhaltlich einschneidender Entwicklung vor, die schließlich über die „Ständetafeln" der Pastoralbriefe bis zu den apostolischen Vätern führt. Eduard Schweizer hat sie zuletzt zutreffend beschrieben[204].

11.2. Kol 3,18 – 4,1 ist die ältere der beiden neutestamentlichen Haustafeln. Sie gibt hinter den Merkmalen einer dazwischen liegenden jüdischen Integrationsstufe die überlieferungsgeschichtliche Zusammengehörigkeit mit den späthellenistischen Abhandlungen „Über die Ökonomie" zu erkennen. Diese Abhängigkeit ist unmißverständlich. Denn nur hier und dort kommt es zu einer sozialen Diagnose sowie zu einem ethischen Reglement, welche sich auf einer Grundlage strikter Gegenseitigkeit der zwischenmenschlichen Beziehungen von Ehefrauen und Ehemännern, Kindern und Vätern, Sklaven und Herren annehmen. In der bislang viel und nahezu ausschließlich bemühten „Offizienethik" der Stoa kommen dagegen die für Kol 3,18 – 4,1 konstitutiven Strukturen entweder gar nicht vor – wie etwa die Sklaven – oder sie sind Teil einer größeren Reihe, die gewöhnlich und ohne reziproke Verhaltensanleitung die Götter, das Vaterland, die Eltern, Brüder oder Verwandten umfaßt.

11.3. Der alten Ökonomik ging es um das Funktionieren der wirtschaftlichen und gesellschaftlichen Anstrengungen innerhalb eines „Hauses". Sie verordnete deshalb an erster Stelle den Eheleuten Harmonie nach dem Maße weitgehender Wechselseitigkeit: Mann und Frau werden zu gegenseitiger Humanität ermahnt, ohne daß es zu einer Abschaffung der nach wie vor für unverzichtbar gehaltenen patria potestas kommen konnte. Im Blick auf die soziale Rolle und Wertschätzung der Frau im Altertum markiert die Einstellung der Ökonomik nichtsdestoweniger einen sittengeschichtlichen Fort-

---

[204] *E. Schweizer*, Die Weltlichkeit des Neuen Testaments (Anm. 40) 397–413.

schritt. Denn *auch* die Belange der Frau werden mit den ökonomischen Erfordernissen eines „Hauses" abgestimmt. Und das heißt: unter solcher Rücksicht werden *auch* vom Ehemann *sittliches* Verhalten und humane Rücksichtnahme verlangt. Die Ökonomik des späten Hellenismus empfiehlt den Ehepartnern daher „Unterordnung" *und* „Liebe" wie Kol 3,18–19. Sie kennt jedoch ebenso die Motive der „Furcht" und des „Gehorsams", die in der Haustafel des Kolosserbriefes gleichfalls von Bedeutung sind.

11.4. Kol 3,18 – 4,1 läßt also keinesfalls auf eine – vorher jüdisch adaptierte – Übernahme von ethischen Richtlinien schließen, die in der Antike auf gleichem Niveau und einvernehmlich jederzeit akzeptiert gewesen wären. Vielmehr verweist die Haustafel des Kolosserbriefes auf eine Entscheidung für die *spezifische* Sittlichkeit der Ökonomik und deren sozialethisches Substrat der Gegenseitigkeit.

11.5. Unter dieser Voraussetzung läßt sich der sittengeschichtliche Rang des Umgangs mit der Ehefrau, wie ihn die Ökonomieschriften *und* Kol 3,18–19 demonstrieren, als Wahrnehmung einer *humanisierenden Mittelposition* beschreiben. Nicht nur an der Skala der von Seneca erwogenen Wertungen, auch am Beispiel des nahestehenden Plutarch und des sachlich verwandten Columella kann eine solche sozialethische Bemessung abgelesen werden. Und der Umstand, daß das Heiratsalter der Mädchen bei 13 bis 15 Jahren lag[205] und dem Manne schon deswegen ein erheblicheres Quantum an Führung und Bildung der Ehefrau zufallen mußte, erhöht ohne Frage noch die Plausibilität dieser Relationierung. Ganz abgesehen davon, daß sich das Plädoyer für den *mittleren* Weg der Haustafel des Kolosserbriefes noch durch Zeugen wie den Stoiker Antipater aus Tarsos abstützen ließe, der schon um die Mitte des 2. Jahrhunderts v. Chr. über das Verhältnis von Mann und Frau in der Ehe Dinge schrieb, hinter deren egalitärem Großmut die Ökonomik ebenso wie Kol 3,18 – 4,1 weit zurückbleiben[206].

---

[205] Zu diesem wichtigen Faktor: *K. Thraede,* Ärger mit der Freiheit (Anm. 7) 38–39.
[206] Übersetzung und Interpretation des einschlägigen Fragments 63 bei *H. Cancik-Lindemaier,* Ehe und Liebe. Entwürfe griechischer Philosophen und römischer Dichter, in: H. Cancik u. a., Zum Thema Frau (Anm. 6) 56–60. Text bei: *J. v. Arnim,* Stoicorum Veterum Fragmenta III (Leipzig – Berlin 1923) 255 (Zeile 10–25). 256 (Zeile 30–33). Zur Nachwirkung der Auffassung des Antipater bei

11.6. Die Formel „im Herrn" aus Kol 3, 18(20) deutet dann allerdings nicht eine nur mehr oder minder oberflächliche „Verchristlichung" gängiger sozialethischer Normen an, sondern sie signalisiert das positive Eintreten für eine längst vorhandene, gemäßigte Stellungnahme in der antiken Diskussion um das soziale Ansehen der Frau. Als „theologisches" Thema verbliebe so vordringlich die Frage, inwieweit christliche Voraussetzungen ethische Extremwerte vermeiden helfen und dazu anleiten, zu „mittleren" Einstellungen zu gelangen.

Musonius Rufus (25–106 n. Chr.) vgl. *A. C. van Geytenbeek,* Musonius Rufus en de Griekse Diatribe (Paris – Amsterdam 1948) 56–69.

X

Weibliche Diakone im Neuen Testament

Von Gerhard Lohfink, Tübingen

1. Vorüberlegungen

Jesus hat im Abendmahlssaal die erste Heilige Messe gefeiert. Während er sie feierte, hat er zugleich die Eucharistie als bleibendes Sakrament eingesetzt. Mehr noch: Er hat beim Abendmahl nicht nur die Eucharistie eingesetzt, sondern im Augenblick ihrer Einsetzung auch das hierarchische Amtspriestertum gestiftet, das sich schon bald aufgliederte in das Priestertum der Bischöfe und der Priester. Dieses von Jesus gestiftete Amtspriestertum ist damit in einzigartiger Weise mit der Eucharistie verbunden. Das Amt der Diakone gehört in die Nähe, sozusagen in das Umfeld des hierarchischen Amtspriestertums und steht deshalb ebenfalls in sehr enger Beziehung zur Eucharistie. Da nun Jesus mit dem Amtspriestertum nur Männer betraut hat und da er sich das gut überlegt hat – er hätte ja durchaus auch Frauen hinzunehmen können –, gibt es und kann es kein legitimes Priesteramt der Frau geben. Es gab zwar in der kirchlichen Frühzeit Frauen, die diakonische Dienste ausübten, die dann auch Diakone bzw. Diakonissen genannt wurden und die teilweise sogar durch Handauflegung in ihren Dienst eingesetzt wurden – aber diese weiblichen Diakone waren stets eindeutig vom hierarchischen Amt geschieden. Sie hatten Aufgaben zu erfüllen, für die Männer nicht in Frage kamen, vor allem bei der Spendung der Taufe. Auch heute gibt es in der Kirche wichtige Aufgaben, die der Mann nicht erfüllen kann oder bei denen er der Ergänzung durch die Dienste der Frau bedarf. Die Kirche braucht daher unbedingt die diakonischen Dienste der Frau. Aber diese *diakonischen Dienste* sind sorgfältig vom *hierarchischen Amt* in der Kirche, das sakramental vermittelt wird, zu scheiden. Deshalb: Diakonische Dienste für die Frau: Ja! – Ein Amt der Diakonin in der Kirche: Nein![1]

Der geduldige Leser hat es wohl längst bemerkt: Der vorangegangene Abschnitt skizziert ein ganz bestimmtes Vorstellungsmodell. Es ist in der katholischen Kirche nach wie vor mächtig. Es mag hier ein wenig zu grob skizziert, es mag um ein winziges überzeichnet worden sein, aber es ist Realität. So denken viele, und so stellen sich viele die historischen Zusammenhänge vor. Kompliziert wird das Ganze dadurch, daß an dem oben skizzierten Vorstellungsmodell keineswegs alles falsch ist. Manches ist falsch, manches ist auch nur sehr einseitig gesehen, und manches ist von der Sache her völlig richtig, allerdings vom historischen Ablauf her größtenteils viel zu undifferenziert vorgestellt. Sehen wir deshalb etwas genauer zu!

Zunächst einmal: Jesus hat kein Amtspriestertum gestiftet. Er hat Jünger zur Proklamation der Gottesherrschaft ausgesandt und zwölf von ihnen zu eschatologischen Zeugen für (bzw. gegen) Israel bestimmt (vgl. vor allem Mt 19, 28 par Lk 22, 29 f). Es gibt also beim irdischen Jesus Sendung und Einsetzung in ein endzeitliches Zeugenamt, aber es gibt keine Einrichtung eines Amtspriestertums. Damit soll keineswegs geleugnet sein, daß in dem späteren kirchlichen Priesteramt wichtige Elemente des ältesten eschatologischen Zeugenamtes aufgegriffen und weitergeführt sind. Aber es geht nicht an, Jesus einfach zum Stifter einer bestimmten Amtsstruktur zu erklären, die sich in Wahrheit in der Alten Kirche erst ganz allmählich herausgebildet hat und die durchaus ihre geschichtlichen Bedingtheiten in sich trägt.

Weiterhin: Das letzte Mahl Jesu mit seinen Jüngern war nicht die erste Meßfeier. Die Sakramente setzen den Tod und die Auferstehung Jesu und vor allem die Geistsendung voraus. Dasselbe gilt für das Werden der Kirche. Die Kirche ist zwar im Tun Jesu präformiert, und Jesus ist das Ursakrament allen Heils, aber das heißt

---

[1] Bei dem hier vorgelegten Beitrag handelt es sich um die nur leicht überarbeitete Fassung eines Referats, das bei einer Studientagung der Akademie der Diözese Rottenburg-Stuttgart am 18. Juni 1980 in Hohenheim gehalten wurde. Die Tagung stand unter dem Thema: „Ein Amt der Diakonin". Das Referat wurde zunächst in Diakonia 11 (1980) 385–400 veröffentlicht.

nicht, daß er in einem historischen Gründungsakt eine Kirche gestiftet und Einzelsakramente eingesetzt hat[2].

Damit hängt eng zusammen: Die Ausformung und Strukturierung von Ämtern, also dessen, was Jesus durch die Aussendung offizieller Zeugen grundgelegt hatte, blieb der sich entfaltenden Kirche überlassen – allerdings der vom Heiligen Geist belebten und geführten Kirche. Diese Kirche hat sich in einem geradezu erregenden Prozeß immer wieder neue Ämter geschaffen und alte Ämter sterben lassen[3]. Das Kollegium der sieben Männer von Apg 6,3 – es handelt sich hierbei schwerlich um Diakone, sondern um das Leitungsgremium der hellenistischen Urgemeinde in Jerusalem – wurde geschaffen, als man es brauchte. Auch das Amt der Episkopen (ἐπίσκοπος = Aufseher, Inspektor) setzte sich erst in dem Augenblick allgemein durch, als man es brauchte. Ähnlich wie das judenchristliche Amt der Presbyter (es muß immer wieder betont werden: Presbyter sind keine *Priester,* sondern *Älteste*) existierte das heidenchristliche Amt der Episkopen dabei zunächst nur in kollegialer Form. Seit Ende des 1. Jahrhunderts verschwanden dann allmählich – beginnend im Osten – die kollegialen Leitungsgremien der Ältesten bzw. der Episkopen; an die Stelle dieser Kollegien oder an ihre Spitze traten Einzelbischöfe (monarchischer Episkopat). Das war eine revolutionäre Neuerung, die durchaus notwendig war, um der drohenden Irrlehre (besonders der Gnosis) begegnen zu können. Erst recht war die allmähliche Herausarbeitung des Primats des Bischofs von Rom seit dem Ende des 2. Jahrhunderts eine revolutionäre Entwicklung gegenüber der älteren Verfassungsstruktur der Kirche.

In diesen höchst lebendigen Prozeß der Entfaltung und ständigen Umwandlung kirchlicher Ämter gehört nun auch die Entwicklung und später wieder die Rückbildung des weiblichen Diakonats[4].

---

[2] Ausführlicher hierzu: *G. Lohfink,* Hat Jesus eine Kirche gestiftet?, in: ThQ 161 (1981) 81–97.

[3] Vgl. *G. Lohfink,* Die Normativität der Amtsvorstellungen in den Pastoralbriefen, in: ThQ 157 (1977) 93–106.

[4] Einen ersten (freilich teilweise einseitigen) Überblick über die Geschichte des weiblichen Diakonats bietet *A. Kalsbach,* Art. Diakonisse, in: RAC 3, 917–928; wichtiger ist freilich: *L. Zscharnack,* Der Dienst der Frau in den ersten Jahrhunderten der christlichen Kirche (Göttingen 1902).

Seine Entwicklung, die bereits im 1. Jahrhundert begann, wurde dadurch begünstigt, daß in dieser Zeit die Eucharistiefeier zunächst noch nicht im Zentrum des Amtsdenkens und der Amtstheologie stand. Es gibt zwar im Neuen Testament schon eine sehr reiche Amtstheologie, aber es gibt keinen einzigen Text, in welchem die Eucharistiefeier mit einem Amt in Verbindung gebracht wird. Erst allmählich sah man den tiefen inneren Zusammenhang zwischen dem kirchlichen Amt und der Eucharistiefeier als dem Grundvollzug der Kirche. Zum ersten Mal ist dieser Zusammenhang bei Ignatius von Antiochien greifbar. Im Neuen Testament hingegen wird das kirchliche Amt theologisch noch ganz der Verkündigung des Evangeliums und dem Aufbau der Gemeinden zugeordnet. Gerade in dieser praktisch-missionarischen Arbeit konnte nun aber auf die Dienste der Frau nicht verzichtet werden. Hier dürften denn auch die Anfänge des weiblichen Diakonats liegen. Seine Entwicklung war eindeutig dadurch begünstigt, daß das kirchliche Amt in den ersten Jahrzehnten noch nicht von der Feier der Eucharistie her begründet wurde. Es wurde zunächst noch nicht als *sakralpriesterliches* Amt interpretiert.

Die Entwicklung eines weiblichen Diakonats wurde aber auch dadurch begünstigt, daß man im 1. Jahrhundert nicht ängstlich zwischen offiziellen kirchlichen Ämtern und nichtoffiziellen Diensten in der Kirche unterschied[5]. Diese Unterscheidung bahnt sich zwar bereits an, aber sie wird noch nicht reflektiert und ist noch überlagert durch die reiche Vielfalt an Dienstleistungen, Charismen, persönlichen Begabungen und Berufungen, die in den Dienst der Ortsgemeinde gestellt und von dieser dann anerkannt werden. Genau in diesem theologisch und institutionell noch nicht verfestigten Milieu konnte die Frau ihre Begabung in vollem Maß für den Aufbau der Gemeinden einbringen, und genau in dieser Zeit und in diesem Milieu entstand auch das weibliche Diakonat.

Aber genug der Schilderung allgemeiner Entwicklungen! Im fol-

---

[5] Charakteristisch für die Offenheit der Urkirche in dieser Hinsicht ist 1 Kor 12,27–30; dort werden in einer einzigen Aufzählung die Ämter der Apostel, Propheten und Lehrer neben freien Charismen (wie etwa Heilungsgaben) genannt, wobei ausgerechnet das Charisma der Gemeindeleitung (κυβερνήσεις) unmittelbar zwischen Diakonie (ἀντιλήμψεις) und Glossolalie (γένη γλωσσῶν) zu stehen kommt.

genden sollen zunächst drei neutestamentliche Texte vorgestellt werden, die das Gesagte veranschaulichen und bekräftigen können. Der erste Text, aus der Zeit zwischen 50–60 n. Chr., spricht von einer Frau, die bereits als *Diakon* bezeichnet wird (Röm 16,1–2). Der zweite Text gehört zwar nicht unmittelbar zum Thema Diakonat; er zeigt jedoch, daß in derselben Zeit eine bestimmte Frau *Apostel* genannt werden konnte (Röm 16,7), und das ist für die in unser Thema hineinragende Problematik „Frau und kirchliches Amt" von erheblicher Bedeutung. Ein dritter Text soll zeigen, daß es gegen Ende des 1. Jahrhunderts, in einer Zeit, in der sich die kirchlichen Ämter bereits mehr und mehr vereinheitlichen, im ehemaligen Missionsgebiet des Paulus neben männlichen auch weibliche Diakone als *feste Institution* gibt (1 Tim 3,11).

2. Diakon Phöbe (Röm 16,1–2)

Um das Jahr 55 schreibt Paulus, wahrscheinlich von Korinth aus, einen großen und theologisch umfassenden Brief an die christliche Gemeinde in Rom, der seine geplante Missionsreise nach Spanien vorbereiten soll. Gegen Ende des Briefs, unmittelbar vor einer längeren Grußliste, wird eine Frau namens Phöbe erwähnt[6]. Alles, was wir über sie wissen, wissen wir aus Röm 16,1–2. Was erfahren wir aus diesem Text?

Zunächst: Paulus empfiehlt Phöbe der römischen Gemeinde. Und zwar spricht er eine *offizielle* Empfehlung aus. Diese Empfehlung setzt voraus, daß Phöbe den Brief selbst überbracht hat oder daß sie mit den Überbringern zusammen nach Rom gereist ist. Die römische Gemeinde soll Phöbe aufnehmen, *wie es sich für Heilige ziemt,* also mit der ganzen Gastfreundschaft, die unter Christen selbstverständlich war und die besonders durchreisenden Christen gewährt wurde. Phöbe ist ja ἀδελφή (Schwester), d. h. Mitchristin der Christen in Rom. Die römische Gemeinde soll Phöbe aber nicht nur mit christli-

---

[6] Im folgenden wird – gegen alle wie immer modifizierten Epheserbriefhypothesen – vorausgesetzt, daß Röm 16 von Anfang an zum Römerbrief hinzugehört hat. Vgl. jetzt bes. *H. Gamble jr.,* The Textual History of the Letter to the Romans. A Study in Textual and Literary Criticism (Grand Rapids 1977).

cher (vgl. das ἐν κυρίῳ = im Herrn) Gastfreundschaft aufnehmen, sondern ihr darüber hinaus beistehen, wo immer sie in Rom Hilfe braucht. Paulus nennt für diese seine Bitte zwei Gründe:

Zunächst: Phöbe hat ihrerseits schon vielen Christen geholfen, auch Paulus selbst. Das „sie hat vielen geholfen, auch mir selbst" wird im griechischen Text allerdings folgendermaßen ausgedrückt: „sie ist zur προστάτις von vielen geworden, auch von mir." Über dieses προστάτις ist schon viel gerätselt worden. προστάτις ist die Beschützerin, die Helferin, der Beistand; προστάτις kann aber auch terminus technicus sein und heißt dann: die Vorsteherin, die Patronin. War Phöbe etwa die patrona oder die Leiterin einer Hausgemeinde, und hat Paulus sie in einem liebenswürdigen Kompliment als seine eigene patrona bzw. Vorsteherin bezeichnet? Gegen diese Möglichkeit spricht jedoch der unmittelbare Kontext: Phöbe ist ja nicht nur für Paulus selbst, sondern *für viele andere* zur προστάτις geworden. Man wird dieser Formulierung nur dann gerecht, wenn man προστάτις nicht als terminus technicus mit *Vorsteherin* oder *Patronin* übersetzt, sondern allgemeiner mit *Helferin*. Phöbe hat schon vielen Mitchristen geholfen, sie hat schon für viele gesorgt, auch für Paulus selbst, und deshalb sollen jetzt auch die römischen Christen für sie Sorge tragen.

Paulus kann Phöbe aber nicht nur als *Glaubensgenossin* und als *Helferin vieler* empfehlen, er empfiehlt sie auch dadurch, daß er sie den Römern als διάκονος *der Gemeinde von Kenchreä* vorstellt. Kenchreä war eine Hafenstadt, etwa 7 km südöstlich von Korinth. Phöbe ist in der dortigen christlichen Gemeinde διάκονος: Diakon oder Dienerin. Für unsere Fragestellung hängt nun alles davon ab, wie dieses Wort zu verstehen ist. Ist es bereits ein terminus technicus geworden, so daß ein bestimmtes kirchliches Amt gemeint ist, oder gebraucht Paulus hier διάκονος noch unspezifisch in dem Sinn, daß Phöbe in ihrer Gemeinde dienend und helfend tätig ist? In diesem unspezifischen Sinn kann Paulus das Wort nämlich anderswo verwenden. Er kann sich selbst als Gottes διάκονος und seinen Apostolat als διακονία bezeichnen (vgl. 2 Kor 6,3f). Selbstverständlich denkt er dabei nicht an ein Diakonenamt im engeren Sinn, so sehr sich hier auch bereits Amtstheologie anbahnt. Allerdings spricht eine ganze Reihe von Gründen dafür, daß Paulus in Röm 16,1 διάκονος bereits im Sinne einer spezifischen Amtsbezeichnung versteht.

a) Das Partizip οὖσαν – verbunden mit einem Substantiv – weist auf einen Titel hin: Phöbe *ist* Diakon.

b) Das καί vor διάκονος – man übersetzt es am besten mit „zudem" – dient der besonderen Hervorhebung des folgenden Wortes. Paulus stellt Phöbe nicht nur als Mitchristin vor, sondern zusätzlich als Diakon. Auch diese Hervorhebung ist ein Indiz für den Gebrauch von διάκονος als Amtsbezeichnung.

c) Der sich unmittelbar anschließende Genitiv τῆς ἐκκλησίας (der Gemeinde) deutet ebenfalls auf einen ständigen und anerkannten Dienst in der Gemeinde von Kenchreä hin.

d) Da auf die helfende Tätigkeit der Phöbe in V. 2 eigens und ausführlich hingewiesen wird, dürfte mit διάκονος in V. 1 mehr gesagt sein als nur eine allgemeine, nichtoffizielle Tätigkeit des Dienens und Helfens.

e) In Phil 1,1 grüßt Paulus alle Christen in Philippi mitsamt ihren Episkopen und Diakonen. Hier handelt es sich klar und eindeutig um schon verfestigte Amtsbezeichnungen. Es wäre nun aber alles andere als objektiv, angesichts der Parallele Phil 1,1 in Röm 16,1 eine Amtsbezeichnung nur deshalb abzulehnen, weil es dort um eine Frau geht.

Wir kommen also gar nicht daran vorbei: Um das Jahr 55 n.Chr. trägt in der korinthischen Hafenstadt Kenchreä eine Christin namens Phöbe, die schon vielen Glaubensgenossen geholfen hat und die von Paulus hochgeschätzt wird, die offizielle Bezeichnung *Diakon*. Dieser Titel erwächst aus der Stellung Phöbes in ihrer Ortskirche: Phöbe ist Diakon der Gemeinde von Kenchreä.

Offensichtlich gibt es zu dieser Zeit auch schon in anderen Ortskirchen Diakone: Direkt belegt ist uns das für die Gemeinde von Philippi; aber auch die römischen Christen, denen Paulus schreibt, müssen gewußt haben, was ein christlicher διάκονος ist. Wichtig scheint auch folgendes: Paulus verwendet noch nicht das Femininum διακόνισσα, welches erst für das 2. Jahrhundert belegt ist. Deshalb ist nicht einmal auszuschließen, daß schon unter den διάκονοι von Philippi (vgl. Phil 1,1) Frauen gewesen sein könnten.

Über den genaueren Aufgabenbereich der Phöbe sagt unser Text nichts. Wir dürfen aber annehmen, daß Phöbe ähnlich wie andere Mitarbeiterinnen des Paulus nicht nur karitative Aufgaben wahrnahm, sondern auch im Verkündigungsdienst tätig war. Mit Sicherheit wissen wir dies jedenfalls von Prisca, einer der wichtigsten Mitarbeiterinnen des Paulus – mit ihrem Mann Aquila eines jener Ehepaare, die für die frühchristliche Mission Außerordentliches geleistet haben. Hier soll nun allerdings nicht von Prisca und Aquila die Rede sein, sondern von einem anderen Ehepaar, das weniger bekannt ist: von Andronikos und Junia.

3. Der weibliche Apostel Junia (Röm 16, 7)

Innerhalb der schon erwähnten Grußliste in Röm 16, die für unser Wissen von der urchristlichen Missionsgeschichte äußerst wichtig ist, findet sich die folgende Grußbitte: „Grüßt Andronikos und Junia, die zu meinem Volk gehören und mit mir zusammen im Gefängnis waren. Sie ragen hervor unter den Aposteln und sie sind schon vor mir Christen geworden" (Röm 16,7).

Der hier genannten Junia ist es von seiten der Exegeten in den letzten Jahrhunderten übel ergangen. Das hängt mit tiefverwurzelten Vorurteilen zusammen, aber auch mit einer Zweideutigkeit des griechischen Urtextes. In den ältesten Handschriften steht an der entsprechenden Stelle IOYNIAN[7], ein Akkusativ. Da es in diesen Handschriften ursprünglich noch kein Akzentsystem gab, kann man IOYNIAN verschieden auflösen:

Entweder: Ἰουνίαν = Akkusativ von Ἰουνία = Junia.

Oder: Ἰουνιᾶν = Akkusativ von Ἰουνιᾶς = Junias.

Rein theoretisch ist beides möglich. Akzentuiert man auf der ersten Silbe, so hat man einen bekannten antiken Frauennamen vor sich: *Junia*. Akzentuiert man hingegen auf der letzten Silbe, so erhält man einen Namen, der nach dem Muster bestimmter antiker Männernamen gebildet ist: *Junias*. Was ist nun richtig?

Im ersten Augenblick scheint alles klar: Apostel können doch nur Männer gewesen sein. Also: Junias! Eine gewissenhafte Exegese kann so jedoch gerade nicht vorgehen. Sie wird zunächst einmal zwei Fragen stellen:

1. Wie sind die Namen Junia und Junias im Altertum überhaupt

---

[7] Von der ebenfalls sehr alten Lesart IOYLIAN kann hier abgesehen werden; sie ist mit Sicherheit sekundär.

belegt? Gab es sie beide, gab es sie gleich oft? – 2. Wie haben die Kirchenväter, deren Muttersprache noch das Griechische war und die wußten, welche „Vornamen" es zu ihrer Zeit gab, unseren Text ausgelegt? Die Antwort auf beide Fragen ist aufgrund neuester Forschungen der Amerikanerin *Bernadette Brooten*[8] überraschend eindeutig:

Zunächst einmal: Ein Männername *Junias* ist für die Antike bis heute nirgendwo nachzuweisen – weder in der Literatur, noch in Namenslisten, noch in Papyri, noch auf Inschriften. Der Frauenname *Junia* hingegen ist gut belegt und war offensichtlich ein häufiger Name.

Weiterhin: Bis ins späte Mittelalter hinein gibt es keinen einzigen Ausleger, der in Röm 16,7 IOYNIAN als Männernamen deutet. Chrysostomus, Hieronymus, Theophylakt u. a. sagen ausdrücklich, es habe sich um eine Frau gehandelt. Chrysostomus formuliert: „Wie groß muß die Weisheit dieser Frau gewesen sein, daß sie sogar für würdig gehalten wurde, den Aposteltitel zu tragen!"[9] Aegidius von Rom, der von ca. 1245–1315 lebte, ist der erste für uns erkennbare Autor, der IOYNIAN als Männernamen interpretiert. Aber erst in der Neuzeit, vor allem durch Faber Stapulensis und Martin Luther, setzt sich allmählich die männliche Deutung durch. Dies geschah nicht etwa aufgrund größeren philologischen Wissens, sondern aufgrund theologischer Denkgewohnheiten: Nur Männer können ja Apostel gewesen sein! Interessant ist, daß die Deutung der Kirchenväter nie ganz unterging; sie findet sich auch noch im 20. Jahrhundert bei denjenigen Kommentatoren, die sich in der Kirchenväterexegese auskennen, so zum Beispiel noch 1916 bei M.-J. Lagrange[10].

Erst der allerjüngsten Zeit blieb es vorbehalten, den weiblichen Apostel Junia ganz zu beseitigen: In dem großen Römerbriefkom-

---

[8] Ich danke *B. Brooten* für den Einblick in ein umfangreiches Manuskript zur Auslegungsgeschichte von Röm 16,7, das die Verfasserin demnächst veröffentlichen wird und aus dem ich viel gelernt habe. Vgl. schon jetzt: *B. Brooten,* „Junia ... hervorragend unter den Aposteln" (Röm 16,7), in: *E. Moltmann-Wendel* (Hrsg.), Frauenbefreiung. Biblische und theologische Argumente (München – Mainz ²1978) 148–151.

[9] In Epistolam ad Romanos Homilia 31,2: PG 60, 669f.

[10] *M.-J. Lagrange,* Saint Paul, Épître aux Romains (Paris ¹1916; ⁶1950) 365f.

mentar von E. Käsemann[11] wird die Auslegungstradition des 1. Jahrtausends nicht einmal mehr erwähnt, in der neuesten, 26. Auflage von Nestle-Aland[12] ist die Akzentuierung Ἰουνίαν entgegen den früheren Auflagen sogar als *Möglichkeit* aus dem textkritischen Apparat eliminiert worden, und auch die Einheitsübersetzung[13] schenkt dem Problem nicht einmal eine Anmerkung. *Junias* hat sich durchgesetzt. Die Geschlechtsumwandlung der *Junia* ist perfekt. Difficile est, satiram non scribere.

Nun wird sich das alles freilich schon bald ändern. Die Bibelwissenschaft ist zur Zeit dabei, auch unter der Rücksicht der Frauenfrage das Neue Testament genauer zu lesen als bisher[14] – und deshalb werden die philologischen Argumente und die erneute Kenntnisnahme der alten Auslegungstradition die derzeitige Exegese von Röm 16,7 bald auf den Kopf stellen. Junia war eine Frau; daran führt kein Weg vorbei.

Aber was wird nun in Röm 16,7 von dieser Frau gesagt? Zunächst einmal wird sie zusammen mit einem *Andronikos* genannt. Wir dürfen davon ausgehen, daß es sich nicht um ein Geschwister-, sondern um ein Ehepaar handelt, welches sich dem missionierenden Ehepaar Prisca und Aquila an die Seite stellen läßt. Auch Petrus und seine Frau sind hier als Parallele zu nennen. Überhaupt ist in diesem Zusammenhang die Bemerkung des Paulus in 1 Kor 9,5 wichtig: „Haben wir (Apostel) nicht das Recht, eine Glaubensgenossin als Frau (auf unseren Missionsreisen) dabeizuhaben so wie auch die übrigen Apostel und die Brüder des Herrn und Kephas?" Der unverheiratete Paulus war eine Ausnahme. Die übrigen Apostel und die Brüder Jesu nahmen ihre Frauen bei ihren Missionsreisen mit, und offensichtlich sind diese dabei selbst missionarisch tätig geworden. Wir dürfen ja nicht übersehen, daß es in der Antike Bereiche gab, die dem Mann einfachhin verschlossen waren[15].

[11] *E. Käsemann*, An die Römer (HNT 8 a) (Tübingen ³1974).
[12] *Nestle-Aland*, Novum Testamentum (Stuttgart ²⁶1979).
[13] Einheitsübersetzung der Heiligen Schrift. Das Neue Testament (Stuttgart 1979).
[14] Vgl. etwa den Beitrag von *W. Schrage*, in: E. S. Gerstenberger – W. Schrage, Frau und Mann (Biblische Konfrontationen, Kohlhammer-Taschenbücher 1013) (Stuttgart 1980).
[15] Vgl. *Clemens Alexandrinus*, Stromateis III 53,3: Durch die Frauen der Apostel „konnte die Lehre des Herrn auch in das Frauengemach kommen, ohne daß Verleumdungen entstanden".

Der Text Röm 16,7 sagt uns aber noch mehr: Paulus bezeichnet Andronikos und Junia als seine συγγενεῖς. Das bedeutet: Sie sind *Juden* wie er. Und er fügt hinzu: *Sie waren mit mir zusammen in Gefangenschaft.* Dies setzt wohl voraus, daß sie eine Zeitlang mit Paulus zusammen oder in seiner Nähe missioniert haben.

Die für uns wichtigste Aussage von Röm 16,7 ist nun freilich, daß Andronikos und Junia „hervorragend unter den Aposteln sind". Das heißt, sie sind nicht nur beide Apostel, sondern sie haben als Apostel einen guten und hervorragenden Namen; sie sind beide hochangesehen.

Gerade diese Aussage des Paulus führt uns vor Augen, wie wenig wir im Grunde über die urchristliche Mission und ihre Träger und Trägerinnen wissen. Sie zeigt uns aber auch, daß der Apostelbegriff in der ältesten Kirche viel weiter gefaßt war, als er dann später im lukanischen Doppelwerk und von dort her im landläufigen Bewußtsein erscheint. Bei Lukas deckt sich der Kreis der Apostel mit dem Kreis der Zwölf. Lukas spricht von den „zwölf Aposteln", und diese Begriffsbildung hat sich seitdem durchgesetzt. Sie ist jedoch eine sekundäre Verengung eines ursprünglich viel weiteren Apostelbegriffs. Apostel sind in der ältesten Zeit alle, die feierlich und offiziell ausgesandt werden – entweder von einer Gemeinde (vgl. 2 Kor 8,23; Phil 2,25) oder vom Auferstandenen selbst (vgl. 1 Kor 9,1; 15,7).

Für ἀπόστολος (Apostel) in Röm 16,7 kommt nur eine Aussendung durch den Auferstandenen selbst in Frage. Denn wären Andronikos und Junia nur die temporären Gesandten einer Gemeinde gewesen, so würde die Wendung „sie ragen hervor unter den Aposteln" kaum passen. Offensichtlich gehörten beide zu jener größeren Gruppe von Aposteln, die 1 Kor 15,7 zufolge eine Erscheinung des Auferstandenen hatte. Paulus hebt diese Gruppe in 1 Kor 15,7 sorgfältig vom Zwölferkreis ab. Er selbst gehörte ja auch noch zu denen, die den Auferstandenen gesehen hatten und von ihm ausgesandt worden waren. Und er leitete von dieser Erscheinung das Recht ab, sich Apostel zu nennen, obwohl er nicht dem Zwölferkreis angehört hatte. Die Wendung „sie ragen hervor unter den Aposteln" setzt voraus, daß der beschriebene Personenkreis der von Christus ausgesandten Auferstehungszeugen für die älteste Kirche eine relativ feste Größe war. Man wußte, daß es diese Urzeugen gab; man sagte, die

Kirche sei auferbaut auf dem Fundament dieser Zeugen (Eph 2,20); man kannte wohl auch viele Namen aus diesem Zeugenkreis.

Daß Andronikos und Junia zu dem beschriebenen Kreis der Apostel gehört haben, zeigt noch ein weiteres Indiz: Paulus sagt, sie seien schon *vor ihm* Christen geworden (wörtlich: „sie sind vor mir geworden in Christus"). Das heißt wohl: Andronikos und Junia hatten schon vor Paulus eine Erscheinung des Auferstandenen, die sie zu Zeugen Christi machte. Diese letzte Angabe weist in die früheste Zeit nach dem Tode Jesu, etwa in die Jahre 30–32, und sie weist nach Palästina. Wahrscheinlich gehörten Andronikos und Junia zu jenen Griechisch sprechenden Judenchristen Jerusalems, die im Zusammenhang mit der Lynchjustiz an Stephanus aus Judäa fliehen mußten, daraufhin in Samaria und Syrien missionierten und dabei zuerst die Mission unter den Heiden begannen (vgl. Apg 8,1.4; 11,19f). Wir müssen uns ja immer vor Augen halten: Paulus und seine Mitarbeiter waren nicht die einzigen urchristlichen Missionare. Da gab es Petrus, Barnabas, Apollos und viele andere – darunter eben auch Andronikos und Junia. Wie später Petrus, sind die beiden irgendwann nach Rom gekommen. Paulus weiß davon – man hat damals zwischen den einzelnen Ortskirchen vielerlei Nachrichten ausgetauscht – und übermittelt deshalb dem apostolischen Ehepaar seine Grüße.

Ist Röm 16,7 auf diese Weise richtig interpretiert, dann müssen wir uns von der Vorstellung befreien, nur die *Zwölf* seien in der Urkirche Apostel genannt worden. Es gab einen größeren und umfassenderen Apostelkreis. Wir müssen uns dann aber auch von der Vorstellung lösen, all diese Apostel seien *Männer* gewesen. Man konnte zumindest ein apostolisches Ehepaar als „Apostel" bezeichnen. Und dies braucht keineswegs so verstanden zu werden, daß bei diesem Ehepaar der *Mann* der Apostel im eigentlichen Sinn gewesen sei und die Gefährtin nur aus Höflichkeit oder aus Gründen der Einfachheit noch mit unter den Begriff „Apostel" subsumiert worden sei. Von dem Ehepaar Prisca und Aquila jedenfalls wissen wir, daß offensichtlich Prisca die für die Missionsarbeit wichtigere Persönlichkeit gewesen ist[16].

---

[16] Prisca wird – entgegen der antiken Gewohnheit – mehrfach vor ihrem Mann an erster Stelle genannt: Vgl. Röm 16,3; Apg 18,18.26; 2 Tim 4,19.

Leider läßt sich zum Thema „die Frau als Apostel" über Röm 16,7 hinaus historisch nichts ausmachen: Die Apostel gehörten alle der ersten christlichen Generation an; der Titel „Apostel" wurde nicht weiterverwendet; das apostolische Amt wurde als einmaliges „Fundament der Kirche" betrachtet und institutionell nicht verlängert. Ganz anders verhielt es sich mit dem Diakonat. Dieses endete keineswegs mit Paulus, sondern wurde weiterentwickelt. Sehen wir zu, was gegen Ende des 1. Jahrhunderts aus dem kirchlichen Dienst, den wir bei der Diakonin Phöbe beobachtet haben, geworden ist. Wir fassen dazu 1 Tim 3,11 genauer ins Auge.

4. Weibliche Diakone in einem Ämterspiegel (1 Tim 3,11)

Gegen Ende des 1. Jahrhunderts wurden von einem kirchlichen Amtsträger drei Briefe pseudonym unter dem Namen des Apostels Paulus veröffentlicht. Es handelt sich um den 1. und 2. Timotheus- und den Titusbrief. Diese Briefe sollten helfen, das paulinische Erbe zu wahren. Wir kennen sie als „Pastoralbriefe". Zur Zeit ihrer Abfassung existierten in den Gemeinden des Ostens bereits sogenannte *Ämterspiegel,* in denen Grundvoraussetzungen für die wichtigsten kirchlichen Ämter aufgezählt wurden[17]. Der Verfasser der Pastoralbriefe hat in den 1. Timotheus- und den Titusbrief Teile solcher Ämterspiegel eingebaut. So findet sich in 1 Tim 3 zunächst in den Versen 1–7 eine Zusammenstellung von Anforderungen an die *Episkopen;* dann in den Versen 8–13 eine parallele Liste von Anforderungen an die *Diakone.* Dabei wird der Abschnitt über die Diakone durch V. 11 in einer seltsamen Weise unterbrochen. Dort ist plötzlich von *Frauen* die Rede; sie sollen wie die Diakone „ehrenhaft, nicht verleumderisch, mäßig im Weingenuß und in allem zuverlässig" sein. Im Anschluß daran spricht der Text wieder von den Diakonen.

Welche Funktion hat nun der Einschub in V. 11? Redet er ganz allgemein von den *christlichen Frauen* in der Gemeinde, oder redet er

---

[17] Vgl. *H.-W. Bartsch,* Die Anfänge urchristlicher Rechtsbildungen. Studien zu den Pastoralbriefen (ThF 34) (Hamburg-Bergstedt 1965).

von den *Ehefrauen der Diakone*, oder redet er von *weiblichen Diakonen?*

Die erste Möglichkeit (christliche Frauen allgemein) ist sofort auszuscheiden, denn es handelt sich ja um einen Ämterspiegel. Die zweite Möglichkeit (Ehefrauen der Diakone) ist weniger leicht auszuschließen, denn es ist nicht ausdrücklich von διακόνισσαι oder von „Frauen, die Diakone sind", die Rede. Andererseits ist aber genausowenig von „ihren Frauen", das heißt von den Frauen der Diakone, die Rede. War es überhaupt notwendig, in einem Ämterspiegel auch an die Ehefrauen der Diakone eigene Anforderungen zu stellen? Im vorangehenden Abschnitt (V. 1–7) gibt es jedenfalls keine eigenen Anforderungen an die Frauen der Episkopen, obwohl es als selbstverständlich vorausgesetzt wird, daß ein ἐπίσκοπος verheiratet ist (vgl. 3,2.4.5). Weshalb sollten aber in einem Ämterspiegel an die Familie eines Diakons höhere Anforderungen gestellt werden als an die Familie eines Bischofs? So spricht alles dafür, daß es in V. 11 nicht um die Frauen der Diakone, sondern um weibliche Diakone, also um Amtsträger, geht. Wenn der Verfasser der Pastoralbriefe an dieser Stelle wenig exakt formuliert, so hängt dies wohl einfach damit zusammen, daß er eine bereits vorgeprägte Tradition übernommen hat.

Wir dürfen somit davon ausgehen, daß das in Röm 16,1–2 zum erstenmal bezeugte Diakonat der Frau inzwischen in den Gemeinden des Ostens längst zu einer festen kirchlichen Verfassungswirklichkeit geworden ist. Der weibliche Diakon taucht nun schon, zusammen mit den Episkopen und den männlichen Diakonen, in kirchlichen Ämterspiegeln auf.

Freilich bleibt vom Text her eine leichte Unsicherheit. Sie wird jedoch historisch dadurch ausgeglichen, daß spätere, außerbiblische Texte das Amt weiblicher Diakone in der Kirche des Ostens historisch sicher bezeugen.

So schreibt Plinius d. J. um 112 aus Bithynien, also aus Kleinasien, an den Kaiser Trajan und bittet um einen Entscheid, wie er mit den Christen in seinem Amtsgebiet verfahren soll. In diesem Zusammenhang berichtet er von zwei Frauen, die er foltern ließ, um zu erfahren, was es mit dem Leben und der Lehre der Christen auf sich habe:

„Daher hielt ich es für umso notwendiger, aus zwei Sklavinnen, die als *ministrae* bezeichnet wurden, durch Folterung zu erfahren, was daran (d. h. an dem Gerede über die Christen) Wahres sei. Ich fand nichts als verkehrten, maßlosen Aberglauben."[18]

Diese zwei *ministrae* können nur weibliche Diakone gewesen sein, denn *ministra* ist das exakte lateinische Äquivalent zu διακόνισσα. Die beiden Frauen wurden dem Plinius offensichtlich als Diakone bezeichnet (ministrae dicebantur). Dies weist auf offizielle, amtliche Titulatur im kirchlichen Sprachgebrauch hin. Daß es sich um zwei Sklavinnen handelt, wirft zudem ein interessantes Licht auf das frühkirchliche Selbstverständnis: Man wußte sich als eine Gemeinschaft von Brüdern und Schwestern, in der die Standesunterschiede aufgehoben waren[19]. Gal 3,28 („da gibt es nicht mehr Juden und Griechen, nicht mehr Sklaven und Freie, nicht mehr Mann und Frau") wurde, so gut es ging, ernstgenommen.

Zu Beginn des 2. Jahrhunderts ist uns also durch eine außerchristliche Quelle für Bithynien, den Norden Kleinasiens, die Existenz weiblicher Diakone im Sinne eines festen und offiziellen kirchlichen Amtes bezeugt. Da Pliniusbrief und Pastoralbriefe zeitlich nicht allzu weit auseinanderliegen und da auch die Pastoralbriefe auf Kleinasien verweisen, dürfte es sich bei den Frauen in 1 Tim 3,11 tatsächlich um weibliche Diakone handeln. Jedenfalls ist so am besten zu erklären, wie mitten in einem Diakonenspiegel plötzlich von Frauen die Rede sein kann.

5. Ausblick

In den vorangegangenen Ausführungen wurde versucht, die Entstehung des weiblichen Diakonats zu beleuchten. Worüber gesprochen wurde, waren freilich nur seine *Anfänge,* noch nicht seine *Blütezeit.* Für die Blütezeit kann hier lediglich auf Texte einer Kirchenordnung verwiesen werden, die sich im kirchlichen Altertum großer Beliebtheit und weiter Verbreitung erfreute, der Syrischen Didaskalie, entstanden noch vor 250 n. Chr. Hier ist nun die Entwicklung deutlich vorangeschritten. Die Tätigkeitsbereiche des weiblichen Dia-

---

[18] *Plinius,* Briefe X 96,8.
[19] Vgl. *G. Lohfink,* Wie hat Jesus Gemeinde gewollt? Zur gesellschaftlichen Dimension des christlichen Glaubens (Freiburg i. Br. 1982) III 5 u. IV 3.

kons werden zum ersten Mal klar beschrieben; sie umfassen karitative Dienste, Hausbesuche, Sorge für die Kranken, Assistenz bei der Taufe und Taufkatechese. Ausdrücklich wird gesagt: Ein vernünftiger Bischof kann ohne Diakon und ohne Diakonisse gar nicht auskommen. Er soll deshalb einen geeigneten Mann und eine geeignete Frau aus der Gemeinde *auswählen* und sie als Diakone *einsetzen*[20]. Hierbei wird terminologisch kein Unterschied zwischen der Amtseinsetzung des Diakons und der Diakonin gemacht.

Daß es sich bei dem weiblichen Diakonat um ein öffentliches, ja sogar „hierarchisches" Amt in der Gemeinde handelt, wird daran deutlich, daß in einem kühnen Bild der Bischof mit Gott Vater, der Diakon mit Christus und die Diakonin mit dem Heiligen Geist verglichen wird. Die Presbyter gleichen lediglich den Aposteln[21]. Man sieht an der Typologie, daß es in den Gemeinden, in denen die Syrische Didaskalie entstand, *je Gemeinde* nur einen Episkopen, nur einen Diakon und nur eine Diakonin, aber ein *Kollegium* von Presbytern gab. Daß der Diakon mit Christus verglichen wird, geht wohl auf das Jesuswort zurück: „Der Menschensohn ist nicht gekommen, um sich bedienen zu lassen, sondern um zu dienen" (Mk 10,45). Wenn die Diakonin als Abbild des Heiligen Geistes gesehen wird, so hängt dies damit zusammen, daß der Geist in den semitischen Sprachen Femininum ist. Für die Presbyter war in dieser trinitarischen Typologie[22] natürlich kein Platz mehr; sie konnten deshalb nur mit dem Kollegium der Apostel verglichen werden. Der Versuch der Syrischen Didaskalie, das Diakonat der Frau neben dem Episkopat und dem Diakonat des Mannes *theologisch* zu begründen und zu legitimieren, zeigt in genügender Deutlichkeit, daß es sich um ein kirchliches *Amt im strengen Sinn* handelt. Übrigens wird diese Legitimation dadurch vorangetrieben, daß über die trinitarische Typologie hinaus auch noch nach einer *biblischen* Begründung des weiblichen Diakonats gesucht wird. Der Verfasser der Syrischen Didaskalie findet sie in den Frauen, die Jesus nachgefolgt sind: „Darum sagen wir, daß (in der Gemeinde) besonders der Dienst einer dienen-

---

[20] Syrische Didaskalie 16; *H. Achelis – J. Flemming,* Die syrische Didaskalie (TU 25) (Leipzig 1904) 84 f.
[21] Syrische Didaskalie 9 (Achelis – Flemming 45).
[22] Die Typologie stammt von *Ignatius von Antiochien,* Brief an die Trallianer 3,1; dort freilich noch ohne die Diakonin.

den Frau nötig und erforderlich ist, denn auch unser Herr und Heiland ist von dienenden Frauen bedient worden, nämlich von der Maria von Magdala und von Maria, der Tochter des Jakobus, und von der Mutter des Jose und der Mutter der Söhne des Zebedäus mit noch anderen Frauen. Auch du (o Bischof) bedarfst des Dienstes der Diakonin zu vielen Dingen ..."[23]

Wie gesagt, die Blütezeit des weiblichen Diakonats wäre eigens darzustellen; hier wurden hauptsächlich seine Anfänge im ersten Jahrhundert beleuchtet. Aber nicht nur Anfang und Blütezeit, auch die allmähliche Zurückdrängung und Abschaffung des weiblichen Diakonats wären eigens zu behandeln. Dann würde sich noch einmal zeigen, was zu Beginn dieser Ausführungen behauptet wurde: Die Kirche der ersten Jahrhunderte hat sich in einem geradezu erregenden Prozeß neue Ämter geschaffen und alte Ämter sterben lassen.

Man sollte dieses „Sterben" alter Ämter nicht nur negativ sehen. Es hat zwar auch seine fragwürdigen Seiten, ist aber andererseits doch auch wieder Teil eines Lebensprozesses. Wenn in diesem Lebensprozeß bestimmte Verfassungsstrukturen untergingen, andere neu entstanden oder – was noch viel häufiger vorkam – wenn unter der Oberfläche der alten Strukturen Neues heranwuchs, das vielleicht noch lange die alten Namen trug, in Wirklichkeit aber doch Neues war, dann zeigt sich gerade hierin, daß die Kirche nicht die ein für allemal fertige Größe ist, für die sie von vielen gehalten wird, sondern daß sie das *Werk Gottes* ist, der an seinem Werk noch immer schafft bis ans Ende der Zeit. Auch für die Kirche müßte man sagen: Die Schöpfung ist noch nicht zu Ende.

Die Heilsgemeinde als das *Werk Gottes* – das ist uralte biblische Theologie, die man schon bei Deuterojesaja und dann im Neuen Testament wieder in der Apostelgeschichte finden kann. „Schaut, ihr Verächter, staunt und vergeht, ein Werk schaffe ich in euren Tagen, ein Werk, das ihr nicht glauben würdet, wenn euch jemand davon erzählte" (Apg 13,41). Das ist ja wohl nicht nur den Juden im pisidischen Antiochia gesagt, sondern auch uns. Wir müßten endlich damit ernstmachen, die Kirche nicht nur christologisch, sondern umfassend trinitarisch zu begründen.

---

[23] Syrische Didaskalie 16 (Achelis – Flemming 85).

Ohne Zweifel ist eine zu enge und zu einseitige christologische Begründung der Kirche mit schuld an der Unbeweglichkeit und Starrheit unserer gegenwärtigen Kirche. Wenn wir die Kirche nur christologisch begründen, dann kommen wir kaum daran vorbei, alle kirchlichen Entwicklungen in expliziten Stiftungsakten des historischen Jesus oder des Auferstandenen zu verankern. Dann muß Jesus im Abendmahlssaal die erste Heilige Messe gefeiert haben, dann muß er bei dieser Gelegenheit das kirchliche Amt konstituiert haben, dann ist es relevant, daß er keine Frauen zu Amtsträgern eingesetzt hat.

Aber wenn der Glaube an den *dreifaltigen* Gott das unterscheidend Christliche ist, dann kann eine rein christologische Begründung der Kirche nicht genügen. Wenn der Glaube an den dreifaltigen Gott für uns bestimmend ist, dann ist die Kirche zunächst einmal das Werk Gottes, des Vaters, der sich in unendlicher Schöpferkraft sein Volk, seine Heilsgemeinde, schafft. Und dann gilt noch heute: „Staunt und vergeht! Ein Werk schaffe ich in euren Tagen, ein Werk, das ihr nicht glauben würdet, wenn euch einer davon erzählte."[24]

Wenn der Glaube an den dreifaltigen Gott für uns bestimmend ist, dann ist Jesus Christus in diesem Werk, in welchem sich Gott sein Volk schafft, die entscheidende eschatologische Stunde und die alles entscheidende Gestalt. Jesus Christus hat Israel neu gesammelt, er hat sich für das Volk Gottes dahingegeben und so die aus Israel entstehende *ecclesia* zum Zeichen der endgültigen Hinwendung Gottes an die Welt gemacht.

Wenn der Glaube an den dreifaltigen Gott für uns bestimmend ist, dann ist die Kirche aber auch das Anwesen des Heiligen Geistes, der weht, wo er will, der als der Geist Gottes alle Grenzen sprengt und der als der Geist Jesu Christi dafür sorgt, daß das, was durch Jesus endgültig geworden ist, in immer neuen Ordnungen, in immer neuen Verfassungen, in immer neuen Ämtern und vor allem in immer neuen Charismen zum Leben kommt. Die Kirche als das Werk, das Gott durch Christus im Heiligen Geiste noch immer schafft – nur

---

[24] Die Kirche als das Werk Gottes ist ein wichtiges Thema der Apostelgeschichte. Vgl. im einzelnen G. *Lohfink*, Die Sammlung Israels. Eine Untersuchung zur lukanischen Ekklesiologie (StANT 39) (München 1975) 85-92.

eine solche ekklesiologische Sicht wäre wohl letztlich in der Lage, den Panzer des Immobilismus, der sich in den vergangenen Jahrhunderten über unsere Kirche gelegt hat, aufzusprengen. Die Kirche könnte dann begreifen, daß sie durchaus ermächtigt ist, im Geiste Jesu Christi alte Ämter sterben zu lassen und neue zu schaffen – oder einst gestorbene Ämter neu zu beleben – oder längst bestehende Funktionen und Dienstleistungen zur Würde und Verpflichtung eines Amtes zu erheben, gerade auch den gläubigen und geduldigen Dienst vieler Frauen in der Kirche!

XI

Anliegen und Ansatz
feministischer Theologie

Von Magdalene Bußmann, Essen

In dem Buch von M. Daly mit dem bezeichnenden Titel: „Jenseits von Gottvater, Sohn und Co", in dem die Autorin eine postchristliche, feministische Philosophie skizziert, steht: „Es ist z. B. nicht ungewöhnlich, daß eine Frau aufgefordert wird, zu ... männlichen Kollegen über das Thema (feministische Theologie, M. B.) zu sprechen, ohne daß andere Frauen dabei sind – oder höchstens in Gegenwart von einigen ‚angepaßten' und schüchternen Frauen. Unter solchen ‚Dialog'-Umständen gerät sie mit Sicherheit in eine Lage, in der sie ‚nicht gewinnen' kann. Wenn sie Vernunft und Überzeugungskraft beweist, wird man sie als ‚irritierend' bezeichnen. Wenn sie kluge Kompromisse macht, um ‚die Tür offenzuhalten', und dabei sich und ihre Schwestern verkauft, geht man vielleicht sanft mit ihr um, aber ihre Position, oder vielmehr ihre Nicht-Position, wird von anderen Trivialitäten, um die man sich leichter kümmern kann, geschwächt."[1]

Mit dieser Situationsbeschreibung kann ich mich in diesem Kreis nicht identifizieren, denn ich habe nicht den Eindruck, daß Sie mich – wie man so schön sagt – als Alibifrau eingeladen haben, um ihrem männlichen Wissensdrang Genüge zu tun, was das Thema „feministische Theologie" anbelangt. Ich gehe eher davon aus, daß Sie und ich daran interessiert sind, gemeinsam über dieses Problem zu sprechen und Chancen oder Perspektiven zu suchen, die diese Art, Theologie zu treiben, für Frauen und Männer bietet.

---

[1] *M. Daly*, Jenseits von Gottvater, Sohn & Co. Aufbruch zu einer Philosophie der Frauenbefreiung (München 1980) 191.

1. Entstehungsort und -situation feministischer Theologie

Feministische Theologie hat ihren Ursprungsort in den USA. Wie der Name bereits ausweist, enthält sie Kritik und Programm. Auf beides möchte ich kurz hinweisen. Feministische Theologie als Gehalt und Gestalt einer von Frauen betriebenen Theologie entstand in den sechziger Jahren aus folgender Situation:

Die Wirkungen des Zweiten Weltkrieges, die Zeit der Improvisation, in der die Geschlechterrollen und männliche/weibliche Stereotypen weniger zählten, in der man froh war, wenn das Leben überhaupt weiterging, waren weitgehend vergessen. Man kehrte zu Rollenerwartungen und starren Verhaltensmustern zurück. Den Frauen wurden Platz bzw. Rolle in der am Leistungsprinzip orientierten Gesellschaft von den Männern zudiktiert, und es wurde erwartet, daß sie sich weiterhin den Normen und Maximen der Männergesellschaft fügten. Viele Frauen, denen die Nachkriegserfahrungen noch gegenwärtig waren, durch die Männer und Frauen in gleicher Weise herausgefordert waren, konnten und wollten sich mit dieser Art von Freiheitsbeschränkung nicht mehr abfinden; sie versuchten, sich von männlichen Leitbildern und Vorstellungen zu emanzipieren, um ihren eigenen Standpunkt und ihre Rolle in Staat und Gesellschaft zu reklamieren. Verstärkt wurde die Erfahrung der Identitätsbeschränkung für die Frauen durch andere Formen der Unterdrückung: rassistischer und ethnischer Minderheiten, durch Kriege und Gewaltanwendung im Inland und Ausland. Die Frauen sahen sich in eine Reihe gestellt mit den unterdrückten, unfreien Minderheiten, die selbst keine Chance hatten, das System von Diskriminierung und Unfreiheit zu durchbrechen. Das Bewußtsein, gesellschaftlich zur Gruppe der Diskriminierten zu gehören, denen das Recht auf Selbstbestimmung verweigert wird, wurde intensiviert durch die Erfahrung, daß sich die Unterdrückung auch auf den kirchlich-religiösen Bereich bezog. Appelle an die Kirchen bzw. die Verantwortlichen in den Kirchen, sich für die entrechteten Minderheiten einzusetzen und dezidiert Stellung zu beziehen für Gewaltlosigkeit, Friede, Menschenrechte, verhallten wirkungslos.

Frauen mußten die Erfahrung machen, daß die Kirchen eher bereit waren, sich auf die Seite der Machthaber zu schlagen und damit systemstabilisierend zu wirken, als ihrem christlichen Auftrag, Gerechtigkeit, Mitmenschlichkeit und Frieden für alle nicht nur verbal zu fordern, gerecht zu werden[2].

Auf Grund dieser hier nur angedeuteten Erfahrungen wurde den Frauen deutlich, daß auch ihre Rolle in der Kirche lediglich die eines „potenzierten Laien" ist. Denn zu offiziellen Ämtern und damit zu Machtpositionen, durch die allein strukturelle Änderungen herbeigeführt werden können, sind Frauen in der katholischen Kirche ja mit (pseudo-)theologischen und kirchenrechtlichen Gründen nicht zugelassen, und im Stand der „Berufstheologen" bilden sie eine verschwindende Ausnahme ohne systemändernde Relevanz.

Die gesellschaftlich und kirchlich erfahrene Ohnmacht, für entrechtete Minderheiten wirksam eintreten zu können, verstärkte bei den Frauen das Bewußtsein und die Sensibilität für die eigene inferiore Lage in Staat, Gesellschaft und Kirche.

Diese Ohnmacht schlug nun nicht um in Resignation und ohnmächtige Wut, sondern sie schlug um in Kreativität und damit in Mut zum alternativen Engagement. In dieser Kreativität, die die Erfahrung der Ausweglosigkeit positiv übersetzt, liegt die Matrix der feministischen Theologie, die in einem Kontext gesehen werden kann mit der Theologie der Befreiung, auch mit der Theologie der Revolution.

Jedoch unterscheidet sich das Theologieverständnis der feministischen Theologie bereits vom Ansatz her von dem der universitären Disziplin gleichen Namens. Der Bezugspunkt feministischer Theologie ist die konkrete Erfahrung der Unterdrückung, der Diskriminierung, der Rechtlosigkeit, die Situation des Be- und Getroffenseins, also ein existentielles, personales Engagiertsein. Der Mensch, seine soziale, emotionale, rationale Dimension als personale Einheit ist Träger und Subjekt feministischer Theologie. Es geht also nicht darum, „über" den Menschen, „über" Gott, „über" theologische Theorien zu spekulieren und den Bezug zum Menschen darüber unter Umständen zu verlieren, sondern Ausgangspunkt feministischer Theologie ist die Situation konkreter Menschen, hier der Frauen.

Frauen bringen ihre Erfahrungen, Wünsche und Ohnmacht ein

---

[2] Vgl. *C. M. Halkes,* Über die feministische Theologie zu einem neuen Menschenbild, in: E. Moltmann-Wendel (Hrsg.), Frauenbefreiung. Biblische und theologische Argumente (München – Mainz 2. veränd. Aufl. 1978) 180.

und versuchen, aufgrund einer „neuen" Erfahrung und damit vor einem qualitativ anderen Verstehenshorizont sich und ihre gesamte Existenz theologisch zu deuten, d. h. die Frage nach Gott, der biblischen Erlösungsbotschaft, der Kirche, nach religiösen Bildern und Symbolen neu zu stellen und zu beantworten.

Frauen sind bei diesem Verständnis von Theologie nicht mehr Objekte des Theologisierens, das sie und ihre Situation weitgehend außer acht läßt. Hingegen machen Frauen sich selber zum Subjekt der Theologie und versuchen, aus dieser Einheit von Erfahrung und Reflexion den befreienden Anspruch des Christentums neu zu artikulieren und zu praktizieren. Feministische Theologie ist von daher „Theologie von unten", „praktische Theologie", die sich nur dann als glaubwürdig erweist, wenn sie das erwirkt, was sie von ihrem Anspruch her sein oder erreichen will: nämlich Subjekt-Werden aller Menschen, ob Mann oder Frau, in partnerschaftlicher Beziehung zum anderen Menschen, in der alle Formen von Unfreiheit, Rechtlosigkeit, Gewalt abgeschafft sind. Da dieses Ziel nie erreicht werden kann, kann die feministische Theologie – zumindest von ihrem Anspruch her – als Befreiungsprozeß verstanden werden, dessen endgültige Realisierung dem Eschaton vorbehalten bleibt.

Aus dem bisher Gesagten wird deutlich, daß sich in der feministischen Theologie eine erhebliche Kritik oder – etwas sanfter formuliert – eine notwendige Ergänzung zur akademisch-männlichen Theologie artikuliert. Versucht diese doch, von einem bestimmten Wissenschaftsverständnis ausgehend, mit bestimmten Methoden die Rede von Gott und der Welt in ein logisches System zu bringen. In dieser Theologie haben seit beinahe 2000 Jahren männliche Bilder und Vorstellungen, Normen, Werte und Erfahrungen z. T. lehrsatzhafte Gestalt gefunden: Haben nicht Männer Gott mit den Attributen versehen, die sie selbst als die höchsten betrachteten? Haben sie nicht eine männlich orientierte religiöse Hierarchie errichtet und den gesamten Bereich des Religiös-Theologischen von Prinzipien des Männlichen bestätigen, normieren, legitimieren und sakralisieren lassen?

Frauen hatten (und haben) keine Möglichkeit, dieses System mit ihrer berechtigten Kritik, ihren Vorstellungen und Erwartungen zu beeinflussen. In der feministischen Theologie sehen sie nun die Chance, sich, ihr Menschsein, unmittelbar theologisch zu deuten und damit eine notwendige Ergänzung zur traditionellen Theologie zu bieten, die die eine Hälfte der Menschen etwa 2000 Jahre lang nicht zu Wort kommen ließ. Jedoch ist die Phase des Sprechenkönnens und -dürfens über das Versuchsstadium kaum hinausgekommen; von daher ist es eigentlich vermessen, von „feministischer Theologie" zu sprechen, denn diese liegt nicht als fix-fertiges Konzept vor, und vom Anspruch her, Menschwerden erst für alle zu ermöglichen, kann sie nicht von einem bereits vorliegenden System ausgehen.

Ein weiterer Kritikpunkt an der Universitätstheologie ist folgender: Wissenschaftliche Theologie kann sich – jenseits von Gut und Böse, also im Bereich des A-politischen, Universitären – abspielen, ohne daß sie sich bewußt und explizit jeweils auf die menschliche Realität beziehen müßte. Der Anspruch der feministischen Theologie aber ist darauf gerichtet, unmittelbar gesellschaftsbezogen zu sein aus ursprünglichem Verlangen nach Gerechtigkeit für alle Unterdrückten; sie kann daher, will sie diesen Anspruch und damit sich selbst nicht aufgeben, nicht degenerieren zu einer apolitischen, theoretischen Universitätsdisziplin.

Soweit eine kurze Skizze über Entstehungsort und -situation feministischer Theologie, deren „Sitz im Leben" also zunächst in der gesamtgesellschaftlichen nordamerikanischen Wirklichkeit zu suchen ist. Aus diesem Grunde kann ich eigentlich auch kaum etwas Originelles zum Thema „Ansätze feministischer Theologie in Deutschland" sagen, denn diese gibt es (noch) nicht oder primär in der Rezeption und Aufarbeitung der amerikanischen Impulse. Natürlich ist die bundesdeutsche kirchliche Realität – pastorale und universitäre Situation betreffend – der amerikanischen vergleichbar, jedoch wagten Theologinnen in der Bundesrepublik Deutschland feministische Theologie als bewußte Alternative zur herkömmlichen Theologie zu betreiben erst im Kontext der Diskussion der Stellung der Frau in unserer Gesellschaft. (Ich erinnere an die Diskussion um den § 218; die Forderungen nach Chancengleichheit; gleichen Lohn; an das revidierte Scheidungsrecht ...) All das hatte zur Konsequenz, daß auch die gesellschaftliche Realität „Kirche" Anfragen und Kritik seitens der Frauen erfuhr, die sich in der Kirche nicht als gleichberechtigte Menschen repräsentiert fanden. Und – beeinflußt durch amerikanische Theologinnen – beginnen sich auch in Europa

Frauen in zunehmendem Maße mit „feministischer Theologie" zu beschäftigen. Profilierteste Vertreterin ist wohl C. Halkes, Dozentin für Feminismus und Christentum an der Universität Nijmegen. Ihren Arbeiten verdanke ich weitgehend die Impulse für dieses Referat.

2. Gott der Vater?

Ich stehe jetzt vor dem Dilemma, Ihnen Grundzüge feministischer Theologie aufzeigen zu wollen, so, als ob es „die" bzw. „eine" feministische Theologie als ausformuliertes System bereits gäbe. Daß dem nicht so ist, wird Ihnen sicherlich aus meinen Ausführungen deutlich, denn bislang werden von Theologinnen eher Anfragen, Kritik, alternative Ansätze der traditionellen Theologie gegenüber artikuliert, die sich eher unter den Stichworten: „so nicht" – „vielleicht aber könnten wir in diese Richtung gehen" formulieren lassen. Von daher sind meine Ausführungen eine Mischung von Kritik, Analyse, Vorschlägen, wie wir eventuell neu oder anders mit Altem, Vertrautem umgehen könnten.

Das eingangs zitierte Buch von M. Daly trägt den Titel „Jenseits von Gottvater". Daraus erhellt ein Anspruch der feministischen Theologie, die Rede von Gott als patriarchalisch, androzentrisch zu entlarven. Da Theologie immer von Männern betrieben wurde, ist die letzte Wirklichkeit, die wir Gott nennen, in Bildern, die Gott als Vater, als Mann, als Kriegsherr, Feldherr, Lenker der Staaten bezeichnen, ausgedrückt worden. Gehen wir auf das Alte Testament zurück, so finden wir dort zahlreiche Stellen, die Gott auch in weiblichen Bildern ausdrücken: seine Zärtlichkeit ist die einer Mutter für ihr Kind (Jes 49,14–16); er wimmert wie eine Frau, die am Gebären ist (Jes 42,13–14); Gott wird mit einer Vogelmutter verglichen (Ps 17,8; 36,7). Auch das Neue Testament enthält Bilder, die dem Erfahrungsbereich der Frau entnommen sind, in denen Jesus seine Heilsbotschaft artikuliert: das Gleichnis vom Groschen (Lk 18,8–10); das Bild von der Henne, die ihre Küken unter ihre Flügel nimmt (Mt 23,37). Aus der vergleichenden Religionsgeschichte läßt sich der Prozeß aufzeigen, wie das Gottesbild der Juden zunehmend mit männlichen Zügen ausgestattet wird und am Ende dieser Entwicklung steht Gott, der Vater, der seinen Sohn in die Welt schickt, indem er durch den Heiligen Geist Fleisch wird. Führen wir uns aber vor Augen, was es bedeutet, von Gott zu reden, dann können wir – ausgehend von der Selbstoffenbarung Gottes im Alten Testament: Ich bin der Seiende – sagen: Gott bedeutet für uns die Fülle des Seins, die Quelle des Seins aller nicht realisierten Möglichkeiten dieser Welt. Gott bedeutet als Ursprung des Seins ein Befreier auf Zukunft hin – nicht, um das Vergangene bloß zu wiederholen, sondern um es zu verwandeln. Gott ist der Gott des Exodus, der Befreiende, er ist eine dynamische Größe, von der alle Dynamik, alles Werden und Leben auf der Erde seinen Ursprung hat. Die feministische Theologie legt den Nachdruck auf Gott als eine dynamische Wirklichkeit, und es wird der Vorschlag gemacht, Gott nicht mehr mit einem Substantiv, sondern mit einem Verb zu bezeichnen: Sein, Seiendes, Seiend-Werden. Diese alles Sein bergende Kraft, die als Gotteserfahrung gedeutet wird, kann nicht mit Begriffen ausgedrückt werden, die die Transzendenz und Andersartigkeit Gottes einseitig herausstellen. Auch die Vorstellung eines Gottes, der mit und in sich selbst genug ist, widerspricht dieser Erfahrung.

M. Daly fragt provozierend: „Weshalb muß ,Gott' eigentlich ein Substantiv sein? Weshalb nicht ein Verb – die aktivste und dynamischste aller Wortformen. Ist die Benennung ,Gottes' mit einem Substantiv nicht ein Mord an diesem dynamischen Verb gewesen? … Die anthromorphen Symbole für Gott mögen der Absicht entspringen , Persönlichkeit zu vermitteln, aber sie drücken nicht aus, daß Gott lebendiges Sein ist"[3]; ich möchte sogar sagen, daß der Person-Gott die Entwicklung eines patriarchalischen Gottesbildes einseitig gefördert hat, wenn wir an den Krieger-Gott, den Richter-Gott … denken.

Frauen lehnen die patriarchalischen Gehalte des Gottesbildes ab, sie suchen nach neuen Bildern, in denen sie ihre religiöse Erfahrung, ihre Deutung der letzten Wirklichkeit ausdrücken können[4].

Sie könnten jetzt einwenden, daß ich dieses Problem zu hoch bewerte; im Grunde wüßten wir ja alle, daß Bilder die Wirklichkeit nie

---

[3] *M. Daly*, Jenseits 49.
[4] Vgl. *C. M. Halkes*, Gott hat nicht nur starke Söhne. Grundzüge einer feministischen Theologie (Gütersloh 1980) 36–38.

treffen, daß von Gott also nicht die Rede sein kann, als sei er ein Mann oder gar eine Frau. Doch wird die Frage damit bagatellisiert. Denn wenn wir bedenken, daß Bilder bzw. Symbole die Realität, die sie bezeichnen wollen, widerspiegeln – natürlich unzulänglich –, dann müssen wir feststellen, daß die Frauen keine Möglichkeit hatten, ihr Seinsverständnis, ihre Erfahrungen in die bildhaften Ausformulierungen des Geheimnisses des Seins einzubringen. Sie mußten sich bislang mit vorgegebenen männlichen Bildern und Symbolen zufrieden geben; für sie wurde festgelegt, was es heißt, von Gott zu reden, religiöse Sinnerfahrungen zu machen. Im Kontext unserer patriarchalischen Gesellschaftsordnung, in dem den Frauen jeweils eine inferiore, von den Männern bestimmte Position zukam (bzw. noch immer zukommt), bedeutet das, daß Frauen nie die Möglichkeit hatten, eigene Aussagen, eigene Bilder der letzten Wirklichkeit, Gott genannt, zu artikulieren. Frauen wurde – ohne daß ihnen diese Zusammenhänge deutlich werden konnten – ihr Sinn und ihr Sein (bzw. Seinsollen) jeweils von Männern vorgeschrieben. „Eines der Kennzeichen feministischer Theologie ist, daß sie ikonoklastisch sein will, bilderstürmend, und der Leere den Vorzug gibt"[5], weil in diesem Freiraum Erfahrungen für neue Bilder und Symbole gewonnen werden können. Denn Bilder zeigen ja die Wirklichkeit in einer neuen, überraschenden Perspektive, sie sind vielseitig interpretierbar – allerdings können sie auch sterben, d. h. nicht mehr funktionieren. Haben Bilder jedoch ihre Funktion verloren, die Wirklichkeit nicht mehr transzendieren zu können, dann müssen sie abgeschafft werden. „Die Menschen, die über ihre Daseinsfragen nachgedacht und sie formuliert haben, sind … in der Geschichte immer Männer gewesen. Die Formulierung von Glaubenssätzen und die Theologie waren immer männliche Domänen, die in einer patriarchalischen Kultur ihren Ursprung fanden … Die Männer sehen sich in der Gottesvorstellung und in der Sprache als Subjekt, die Frauen als Objekt."[6] Das hatte zur Konsequenz, daß Frauen diese Fremdbestimmung internalisierten, fromm lebten, die Kirche besuchten, die Moral hochhielten, wie die Männer es vorschrieben. Deshalb können wir die Rede von Gott als dem Vater, die männlich konzipierte

---

[5] *Dies.*, Über die feministische Theologie 183.
[6] Ebd. 185–186.

Theologie nicht mehr akzeptieren, weil die angeblich geschenkte Freiheit eine beschränkte Freiheit ist, durch die eine Gruppe von Menschen über Sein und Sinn der anderen bestimmt.

3. Feministische Bibelauslegung

Eng mit dem gerade skizzierten Komplex des Redens von Gott ist das Problem des Umgangs mit der Bibel verknüpft. In diesem Kreis möchte ich mich lediglich auf einige Stichworte beschränken, mit denen ich den Fragekreis „feministische Bibelauslegung" umreiße.

Wenn Gott für jeden Menschen die Fülle des Seins bedeutet und sich die Bibel als die Botschaft dieses Gottes und über diesen Gott versteht, dann muß auch für Frauen aus diesem Buch eine befreiende Botschaft vernehmbar sein. Beginnen wir gleich mit dem ersten Buch der Bibel, dem Bericht über die Erschaffung des Menschen. Ich beschränke mich auf den jüngeren Schöpfungsbericht (Gen 1,26–27): Und Gott sprach: „Lasset uns Menschen machen nach unserem Bilde, uns ähnlich; sie sollen herrschen über die Fische im Meer und die Vögel des Himmels, über das Vieh und alles Wild des Feldes und über alles Kriechende, das auf der Erde sich regt. Und Gott schuf den Menschen nach seinem Bilde, nach dem Bilde Gottes schuf er ihn; als Mann und Frau schuf er sie."

Diese Bibelstelle bildet den Ansatzpunkt der feministischen Theologie für eine christliche Lehre vom Menschen. Alle allzu menschlichen Bilder sind verschwunden. Der Mensch ist Mann und Frau, und beide sind Abbild Gottes; es ist keine Rede von früher oder später erschaffen, wie im älteren Schöpfungsbericht, der sich verhängnisvoll für die Stellung der Frau in Theologie und Kirche ausgewirkt hat. Dem jüngeren Schöpfungsbericht entnehmen wir, daß auch in Gott etwas von der Pluralität, die in den geschlechtlichen Unterschieden des Menschen zum Ausdruck kommt, vorhanden ist; bedeutsam finde ich, daß der Begriff „Abbild Gottes" auch beinhaltet, daß der Mensch bezogen ist und durch Beziehungen Mensch wird: einerseits trägt jeder Mensch als Geschöpf Gottes das jeweilige Seinszentrum in sich selbst, er braucht es nicht außerhalb von sich in die anderen zu verlegen. Andererseits kommt der Mensch als Abbild

Gottes erst in der Beziehung zu seinem Mitmenschen, seien es Frauen oder Männer, zu seiner vollen Entfaltung[7].

Die oben zitierte Genesisstelle stellt auch die Frau als gottebenbildlich dar, und von daher ist sie auch fähig, diese ihre Bezogenheit auf Gott auf je ihre Art auszudrücken und zu leben.

Wie gesagt, dieser Text wurde in kirchlicher Lehre und Praxis nicht wirksam, jedoch finden wir hier die anthropologische „Schlüsselstelle" der feministischen Theologie, die als kritisches Korrektiv der bisherigen Tradition gelten muß und die die Legitimation für Frauen ist, aus ihrer Perspektive die Bibel auszulegen.

Das ist ein schwieriges Unterfangen, denn wir begeben uns damit in ein Gebiet, das für Frauen tabu war (ist).

Es gibt verschiedene Möglichkeiten, mit der Bibel umzugehen, ich will sie hier nur angeben, um anschließend auf die grundsätzlichen Schwierigkeiten feministischer Bibelinterpretation zu sprechen zu kommen.

a) Frauen hören und lesen die Bibel mit neuen, offenen Ohren und entdecken plötzlich neue Dimensionen; z.B. hat das „Magnifikat" als Gesang eines jüdischen Mädchens einen ganz anderen Klang, denn Frauen gehören ja zur Gruppe der Rechtlosen, auf einer Ebene mit Kindern, Sklaven und Vieh.

b) Frauen versuchen die Bibel neu zu interpretieren und Bilder neu zu entziffern, die auch Frauen ihre eigene Gotteserfahrung anzeigen, z.B. der Name JHWH, Das/Der Seiende.

c) Frauen versuchen, die Bibel neu zu schreiben und die hin und wieder durchkommende Frauengeschichte an die Oberfläche zu holen, z.B. die Stellung der Frau in der frühchristlichen Gemeinde, oder indem sie die Frauen, die um Jesus waren, neu entdecken[8].

d) Nun zitiere ich: „Frauen können die Bibel auch bleiben lassen, was sie ist: ein patriarchalisches Buch, in dem sich Frauen, die es heute lesen, wie in einem fremden Land fühlen. Sie wollen heraus, brechen zu einem Exodus auf und ziehen weg aus dem Land der Väter, weil sie in sich selbst und ineinander eine Verheißung erkennen und hören: auf die Suche zu gehen nach dem unerfüllten Potential

[7] Dies., Gott hat nicht nur starke Söhne 39.
[8] Vgl. ebd. 57–58.

unserer Vormütter, deren nichtverwirklichte Geschichte wir jetzt in unser Heute und in unsere Zukunft bringen müssen."[9]

Um einige von den hier aufgezeigten Postulaten realisieren zu können, müssen wir jedoch im wahrsten Sinne des Wortes die Bibel und die Geschichte ihrer Auslegung „gegen den Strich bürsten", um die Frauentradition, die wie die Spitze eines Eisberges in die Bibel hineinragt, aufzuspüren.

Da die Bibel jedoch von Männern geschrieben ist, reflektiert sie weitgehend männliche Erfahrungen und stellt diese in männlichen Ausdrucksformen vor. Auch die Kanonbildung erfolgte nach Kriterien, die von Männern festgelegt wurden: für die biblischen Texte und die Auswahl derselben sind also einseitig nur Männer verantwortlich gewesen. Ist es überhaupt möglich und sinnvoll, daß Frauen dieses Buch auch für sich als verbindliche Glaubensgrundlage ansehen?

Die Auslegung der Bibel wurde von Männern betrieben, nach wissenschaftlichen Kriterien, die auf einem bestimmten Vorverständnis von als typisch männlich geltenden Eigenschaften beruhen, durch die dieses Wissenschaftsverständnis als logisch, rational, methodisch qualifiziert wurde. Haben Frauen eine Chance, die von Männern interpretierte Erfahrung von Männern so umzuformulieren, daß dieser Bibelauslegung mehr als ein müdes Lächeln („nichtwissenschaftlich") entgegengebracht wird? Die Aussagen der Bibel wollen ja kein System von Sätzen enthalten, die ewig gültig, aber unverbindlich wahr sind. Die Botschaft soll *uns heute* in unserer je eigenen Situation treffen, abhängig von kultureller, sozialer, politischer Lage. Können wir heute Dolmetscher für die Bibel sein, derart, daß sie nicht als „Steinbruch für Exegeten" dient, sondern als befreiende Botschaft für alle Menschen wirken kann?

C. Halkes formuliert die konkreten Aufgaben an der Bibel, die sich für Frauen heute stellen, so:

– „Frauen sollten die Frauenfiguren in der Bibel neu erfahren und studieren; wie sind sie aufgefaßt und wahrgenommen worden, durch wen und wozu? Sehen wir heute anders, bekommen sie mehr Farbe, mehr Konturen?

– Frauen sollten die biblische Sprache in all ihren Facetten, ihrer

---

[9] Ebd. 59.

Struktur, ihrem grammatischen Geschlecht und ihrem Wort- und Bildgebrauch untersuchen. Wird es sich dann herausstellen, daß die Bibel weniger massiv-männlich ist, als es heute den Anschein macht?

– Frauen sollten der Frage nachgehen, inwieweit die Kulturen und Religionen der Nachbarvölker ihre Spuren in den biblischen Schriften hinterlassen haben, obwohl Israel ein großer Protest dagegen war. Was haben Muttergöttinnen an Elementen eingebracht, die endlich unbefangen auf ihren Wert betrachtet werden müßten?"[10]

C. Halkes schätzt die Möglichkeiten feministischer Bibelinterpretation eher skeptisch ein, denn eine Geschichte von mehr als 2000 Jahren kann nur mit Mühe – wenn überhaupt – übersprungen werden. Und eine weitere Schwierigkeit, auf die sie hinweist: wir bleiben „doch noch mit einem nicht zu unterschätzenden Problem, mit einer belastenden Erbschaft sitzen, mit der Wirkungsgeschichte nämlich: mit der praktischen Anwendung einer äußerst einseitig maskulin und androzentrisch erlebten Bibel in den Kirchen, in der Seelsorge, in Liturgie, Predigt und Verkündigung, in der Verwaltung der Sakramente, die sich natürlich auch in der Sprache, den Bildern und der gängigen Kultur ausdrückt. Noch immer leben die Bilder der zur Sünde verleitenden Eva, der man nicht trauen kann, und der reinen niedrigen Maria, der Frau, die schweigend und ihrem Manne untertan sein muß …"[11]

Mit dem letzten Satz haben wir gleich einen weiteren Problemkreis der feministischen Theologie angesprochen, nämlich das Selbstbewußtsein der Frau als Frau in der Kirche.

4. Zwischen Eva und Maria: Auf der Suche nach Identität

Hin und wieder höre ich das Argument, die Frauen in der katholischen Kirche seien doch gut daran, sie hätten immerhin noch Maria (und andere weibliche Heilige) als Bezugs- bzw. Identifikationspersonen, wenn sie schon mit diesem „Gottvater" nicht mehr allzu viel anfangen könnten.

---

[10] Ebd. 63.   [11] Ebd.

Schauen wir näher zu, wie und ob sich diese Aussage, daß Frauen ihre religiöse und damit menschliche Identität im Symbol der jungfräulichen Gottesmutter finden können, so bedenkenlos akzeptieren läßt. Denn daß Frauen feministische Theologie betreiben, ist ja gerade ein Indikator dafür, daß eben die angebotenen Gehalte und Gestalten für sie kein Selbst-Werden im Rahmen der traditionellen Theologie und kirchlichen Praxis zulassen.

Gestatten Sie mir einen kleinen Exkurs in die Geschichte: Maria wurde jeweils kontrastiert mit Eva: durch Eva kam die Sünde in die Welt (und hier wurde der Genesisbericht strapaziert), durch Maria kam das Heil. Mit Eva wurde die Materie, das Leibhafte, das Dunkle, das Sexuelle, die Sünde identifiziert (natürlich spielen hier philosophische Einflüsse eine Rolle), mit Maria das Geistige, das Licht, das Heil, das Nichtmaterielle.

Konsequenterweise wurde im Kontext der patristischen Theologie Leiblichkeit bzw. Sexualität und Sünde in der Erbsündentheologie zusammengebunden und die Frau, die menschliches Leben gebiert, wurde als Trägerin der sündhaften Materie, als moralisch minderwertig, ja sogar verdorben angesehen.

Belegstellen in der Bibel fanden sich ausreichend, um die Inferiorität der Frau dem Manne gegenüber theologisch zu legitimieren, dem eine Frau jeweils als potentielle Verführerin zu den Sümpfen der Materie, der Sexualität nur gefährlich werden konnte. Es kam zu folgenden Parallelen, die sich nicht einmal in der himmlischen Realität schneiden, geschweige denn in der irdischen:

Mann – Christus – Erlösung – Geist/Licht – Heil
Frau – Eva – Materie/Leib – Sünde – Verderben
Jungfrau – Maria – sündlose Materie – Mittlerin des Heiles.

Für die Frau hat das folgende Konsequenzen:
Als Frau, als verheiratete Frau, hat sie keine Chance, ihren minderwertigen Status zu überwinden; das kann sie lediglich als Jungfrau, indem sie ihre Leiblichkeit und damit ihre Menschlichkeit verdrängt und ein Leben als „geistliche Frau" führt, was in früheren Zeiten in den meisten Fällen das Klosterdasein bedeutete. Den Frauen insgesamt wurde und wird Maria als Vorbild vor Augen gehalten, wie sie gottgefällig leben könnten, mit folgender Begründung: Maria war ganz offen für Gott, hat sich ihm im Gehorsam hingegeben durch ihr Jawort; Gott bestimmte sie zur Mutter seines Sohnes, deshalb blieb

sie von der Erbsünde verschont, und so konnte durch einen Menschen die Menschheit erlöst werden: durch eine Frau kam die Sünde in die Welt, durch eine Jungfrau das Heil.

Frauen sträuben sich heute dagegen, sich mit diesem Marienbild identifizieren zu sollen. Maria, die Frau auf dem Podest, ist für sie in unerreichbare Ferne gerückt, denn den Anspruch, Jungfrau und Mutter sein zu sollen, kann keine Frau akzeptieren, wollte sie nicht ihre Leiblichkeit total ignorieren und diese lediglich funktional im Sinne der Verhinderung des Aussterbens des Menschengeschlechtes zu bewerten.

Genügt aber eine Frau diesem kirchlichen Anspruch nicht, bekennt sie sich zu ihrer Leiblichkeit, ihrer Sexualität, dann kann sie die Verführerin, die Hure Eva sein, eine Gefahr für die Männer, speziell die Kirchenmänner.

Eva und Maria, beide werden von Männern gegen die Frauen ausgespielt: Frau Eva „als der Sündenbock, auf die alle Begierden des Mannes, die er zutiefst fürchtete, projiziert wurden, und die dann in die Wüste der Stille, die Stimmlosigkeit geschickt wurde; die Frau Maria, die auf einen Thron gesetzt wurde, verehrt als ,Unsere Dame' der höfischen Liebe, als die ,Madonna' ... aber auch als Symbol der Barmherzigkeit, als ,Zufluchtsort' zwischen einem strafenden Gott und dem Menschen. Daneben Maria als demütige Dienerin, von der Mädchen und Frauen ihre Dienstbarkeit in Kirche und Gesellschaft herleiten mußten."[12]

Denn Frauen hatten und haben keine Möglichkeit, das Positiv-Emanzipatorische des Marienbildes für Theologie und Kirche fruchtbar zu machen, Männer bestimmten über das Los der Frau (auch das der Frau Maria) und konnten somit – wie hier nur angedeutet werden kann – alle von ihnen als negativ empfundenen Eigenschaften auf die Frau projizieren, um so ungestört ihren männlichen Idealen von Rationalität, Herrschaft, Leistung, Leidensunfähigkeit nachstreben zu können.

Daß Frauen keine Chance haben, im kirchlichen System diesen Teufelskreis zu durchbrechen, ist klar. Als angepaßte Mitglieder der Kirche haben sie die ihnen zudiktierte Rolle, die damit verbundenen Werte und Normen, weitgehend internalisiert.

---

[12] *Dies.*, Über die feministische Theologie 188.

Denn Gott ist der Mann, repräsentiert im Mann der Kirche, die Frau selbst hat keine Möglichkeit, als Frau in diese Repräsentationskette eingegliedert zu werden. Diese Unmöglichkeit wird als Minderwertigkeit verinnerlicht, um so stärker, je mehr die Frau kirchlich sozialisiert ist und Sanktionen für ihre unverschuldete Schlechtigkeit fürchtet.

Die feministische Theologie nun bemüht sich, eben Frauen zu ermöglichen, selbst Subjekte zu werden, selbst Ich-Erfahrung zu machen. Das Marienbild kann Impulse geben, dieses Subjektwerden aller Unterdrückten zu ermöglichen. Ich möchte dazu wiederum C. Halkes zitieren, um neue Perspektiven aufzuzeigen, die durch eine Beschäftigung mit einer „anderen" Maria, als der unserer oft betulichen Frömmigkeitsgeschichte sichtbar werden:

„Wenn ich als christliche Feministin auf der Suche nach der Bedeutung von Maria bin, dann suche ich mehr als nur ein neues Leitbild für Frauen. Denn ich suche auch nach einem ganzheitlicheren Gottesbild und nach einem ganzheitlicheren, integrierteren, humaneren Bild der Kirche. Das wird sichtbar an den drei Aspekten Marias, die natürlich aufs engste miteinander zusammenhängen:
– an der prophetischen Maria als Inspiration für den christlichen Feminismus;
– an der Maria, die zum heiligen Häufchen der Armen von Jahwe gehört, Bild von Israel und das ‚weibliche Gesicht der Kirche' …
– an der Maria voll der Gnade, Braut, Tochter und Mutter Gottes, aufgenommen in den Himmel, Offenbarung der Weisheit und der Weiblichkeit, die weibliche Dimension Gottes.
Es geht um Gott und den Menschen, um den Menschen in ihrem oder seinem Aufgang zu Gott, in der Teilhabe an der Quelle des Seins, als Partner Gottes, aufgerufen durch eine Stimme in sich oder außerhalb seiner oder ihrer selbst. Wenn die Frau abgewertet und zum Anderen statt zum Partner und Gegenüber gemacht wird, dann ist die Wirklichkeit gespalten und die Bilder verkümmern, immanent wie transzendent. Neue Bilder von Maria zu entdecken, ist eine der Möglichkeiten zur Menschwerdung von Frauen, zur Ganzwerdung der Menschheit und zur Erfahrung der Dynamik Gottes."[13]

---

[13] *Dies.*, Gott hat nicht nur starke Söhne 118.

5. Die Kirche als Herrschaftsbereich der Männer

Mit all dem bereits Gesagten komme ich zu einem letzten Punkt, in dem sich alle Kritik und Neuansätze wie in einem Prisma bündeln: nämlich zur Kirche, d. h. zur hierarchisch verfaßten, durchorganisierten Institution, einem von zölibatären Männern geleiteten gesellschaftlich mehr oder weniger relevanten Machtfaktor.

Daß Feministinnen sich von diesem Apparat nicht repräsentiert, geschweige denn als Personen akzeptiert wissen, wird zunehmend deutlich, zumal wenn auch der schweigende Exodus vieler Frauen aus der Kirche, deren treueste Schafe sie ja lange Zeit waren, registriert wird. Das – gelinde gesagt – Unbehagen vieler Frauen an dieser Institution möchte ich mit einigen Strichen skizzieren: Die die Kirche von Anfang an beherrschenden Männer gingen – wie schon bei der Entwicklung der Frauentypen Eva–Maria – sehr arbeitsteilig vor: die Eigenschaften, in denen sie sich repräsentiert sahen: Macht, Stärke, Herrschenkönnen, Rationalität, kombinierten sie mit den Vorstellungen und Modellen von Aufgaben und Funktionen in der Kirche: kurz, sie waren und sind für den Bereich des Amtes und damit des Herrschens und der Öffentlichkeit zuständig.

Auf die Frauen wurden die dienenden, leidenden, emotionalen Werte projiziert, die die Männer damit loswaren und mit denen die Frauen fortan einseitig belastet waren, ohne durchschauen zu können, wieso und warum. Im Kontext der Ausprägung eines bestimmten Frauenbildes in der Kirche – jeweils orientiert an Maria, der Heiligen, und Eva, der Hure bzw. Hexe – konnten die Frauen nicht anders, als diese Rollen und Werte zu internalisieren und sich somit auch vom aufoktroyierten Selbstwertgefühl immer nur als „Gottes zweite Garnitur" bzw. als „nur Frau" in der Kirche zu verstehen. Sinn und Aufgabe wurde ihnen von Männern zugespielt, an deren Selbst- bzw. Amtsverständnis zu zweifeln den Frauen als kirchlich sozialisierte Personen als Blasphemie bzw. Sünde, die eine Strafe nach sich zog, angerechnet wurde.

Die Verbannung der Frau aus kirchlicher und damit auch gesellschaftlicher Öffentlichkeit ließ sie zuständig werden für den Bereich des Hauses, der Familie, des Privaten. Ich möchte sagen, daß im Laufe fast der gesamten Kirchengeschichte Frauen systematisch von Männern fremdbestimmt wurden, daß dieser Vorgang den Herrschenden jedoch vielfach nicht (mehr) bewußt wurde (und wird), da die Erhaltung des Systems es erforderte, daß dessen Plausibilitätsstrukturen internalisiert wurden und ein Zweifeln an denselben mit Sanktionen belegt wurde. Da die (Macht-)Strukturen in der Kirche theologisch überhöht wurden, war (ist) jede kritische Anfrage an das Amt bzw. den Amtsträger schon ein Angriff auf die gottgewollte Erscheinungsform der Kirche.

Machtpositionen in der Kirche haben Männer inne; Frauen haben keine Möglichkeit, strukturelle Reformen zu initiieren, durch die die – zwar verbal akzeptierte – Gleichwertigkeit aller Menschen auch rechtlich-institutionell garantiert werden könnte. Die Gründe, die zur Aufrechterhaltung des Männersystems von den Machtinhabern vorgebracht werden, sind wissenschaftlich längst als nicht stichhaltig ausgewiesen worden – dennoch werden sie oft in pastoral-betulichem Ton den Frauen zum Glauben dargeboten.

Wenn auch heute kirchlicherseits nicht mehr wie früher von der Unterlegenheit der Frau die Rede ist, so doch von ihrer Andersartigkeit, die sie aber genau für die Aufgaben prädestiniert, die Männer den Frauen zugestehen. Aus einer Ansprache Pauls VI. wird deutlich, wie plakativ mit dieser „Andersartigkeit" umgegangen wird, wie sich jedoch keine begründende, inhaltliche Aussage findet, um diesen Begriff einsichtig zu machen: „Uns scheint sie (die Frau) ein Geschöpf, das jegliche Bildung höchst gelehrig annimmt; daher eignet die Frau sich für alle kulturellen und gesellschaftlichen Aufgaben, insbesondere aber für diejenigen, die ihrer sittlichen und geistigen Sensibilität am meisten entsprechen."[14]

Die Bilder, in denen im Laufe der Kirchengeschichte von der „Mutter" Kirche die Rede war, entlarven männliches Denken als Herrschafts- und Machtdenken, von dem auch die „Mutter" nicht verschont bleibt, denn von ihr wird gesprochen als von „der kirchlichen Hierarchie", die wie ein geordnetes Kriegsheer ist (Konzil von Trient), von einer „perfekten Gesellschaft", die in Analogie zu einem Staatswesen mit einem bestimmten Regierungsapparat ausgestattet ist, in dem sich Herrscher und Beherrschte gegenüberstehen – mehr oder weniger ohne Verständnis füreinander. Die Kirche wird beschrieben als „Gesellschaft von Ungleichen, in der es eine von

---

[14] Zit. nach *M. Daly,* Kirche, Frau und Sexus (Olten 1970) 100.

Gott verliehende Vollmacht gibt, die den einen zum Heiligen, Lehren und Leiten gegeben ist, den anderen nicht". (I. Vatikanum). Dieses von männlich geprägten Werten geformte Kirchenbild kann für Frauen, denen in dieser Kirche die Rolle der Schweigenden, der Dienenden, der Gehorchenden zugewiesen wird, keine Bezugsgröße sein, der Begriff „Mutter" Kirche wirkt in diesem Kontext eher als Karikatur, denn diese Mutter kann keine anderen Frauen als gleichberechtigte Partnerinnen ertragen – so könnte man argwöhnen.

Doch viel heftiger als an diesen Faktor richtet sich feministische Kritik gegen die Art und Weise, wie Kirchenmänner ihre Macht über Frauen ausüben, indem sie von der angeblichen Natur, Anlage, Rolle der Frau sprechen, um in Fragen der Empfängnisverhütung, Ehescheidung ... eine bestimmte Position durchzusetzen, ohne daß die Betroffenen eine Chance haben, ihre eigenen Wünsche, Vorstellungen, Gefühle in die Debatte einbringen zu können. Ich möchte nur auf die Beratungen der römischen Kirchenmänner über Fragen der Sexualität hinweisen, wo Frauen so gut wie gar nicht repräsentiert waren, obwohl es auch um ihre persönlichsten Fragen ging.

Feministische Theologie will nun – wie viele Männer argwöhnen – die Kirche nicht kaputt machen, die Kirche nicht – aber diese Kirche muß anders werden, wenn es überhaupt möglich ist, eine beinahe 2000jährige Einrichtung mit mehr als nur einigen Schönheitspfläusterchen zu versehen. Y. Congar schreibt: „Es geht nicht bloß darum, den Frauen in einer Kirche, die weiterhin von Männern dominiert bleibt, ein bißchen mehr Platz zu machen; es geht darum, in der Kirche auf angemessene Art und Weise der menschlichen Wirklichkeit Gestalt zu geben, daß er sie als Mann und Frau schuf."[15] Feministinnen entwickeln den Begriff der „Schwesterlichkeit", um die neue Dimension aufzuzeigen, in der das Mensch-Werden von Frauen und auch von Männern – in oder jenseits der Kirche – realisiert werden kann. Schwesterlichkeit ist also nicht ein Protest gegen eine falsch verstandene Brüderlichkeit, sondern ein „neues Symbol für die Frauen, die sich in einem Bewußtwerdungsprozeß befinden, sowie für alle Frauen und Männer, die wo und wie auch immer eingeschränkt und unfrei leben. Schwesterlichkeit ist die Verbundenheit aller in einer akzeptierenden bedingungslosen Liebe und Soli-

---

[15] *Y. Congar*, Église catholique et France moderne (Paris 1965) 89.

darität. Sie wendet sich *gegen* die doppelte Moral, die Frauen verurteilt und Männer freispricht, *gegen* Übermacht, die zermalmt und zerschmettert, *gegen* eine Technik, die verunmenschlicht und entfremdet, *gegen* sexuellen Libertinismus, der die Frau erneut zum Objekt macht und sie allein als Körper sieht, *gegen* die Ausbeutung von Sklaven, Schwarzen, Machtlosen durch Supermänner und durch das Kapital, aber auch *gegen* die Vergewaltigung der Mutter Erde, der Natur und der gesamten Schöpfung, die unwirklich gemacht und ausgelaugt wird."[16]

Damit stellt sich im Grunde die feministische Theologie die gleichen Aufgaben, für die sich die Kirche einsetzt, nämlich eine Befreiung des ganzen und aller Menschen zu erreichen. Ob der Anspruch der Frauen eingelöst werden kann, hängt davon ab, wie Frauen und Männer die Worte des Paulus (Gal 3, 27 f): „Denn ihr alle, die ihr auf Christus getauft seid, habt Christus angezogen. Da ist nicht Jude noch Grieche, da ist nicht Sklave noch Freier, da ist nicht Mann noch Frau, denn ihr alle seid einer in Jesus Christus", wahr, d. h. konkret werden lassen.

6. Ausblick

Ich hoffe, daß aus diesen Ausführungen das Fragmentarische, Suchende, eher „so nicht" als „genau so" der feministischen Theologie ein wenig deutlich geworden ist. Dieser Art von Theologie geht, kann es von den Entstehungsbedingungen und vom Anspruch nur gehen um die ganzheitliche Befreiung aller Menschen, Männer und Frauen. Jedoch muß uns Frauen noch zugestanden werden, daß wir in vielen Fällen in völliges Neuland unterwegs sind, wohin wir von vornherein die Männer nicht mitnehmen können und wollen. Zu schnell könnten unbemerkt, unbeabsichtigt alte Rollen und Wertsysteme weitertransportiert werden. Es geht uns darum, unsere eigene Identität zu finden und zu benennen und diese Erfahrung der „neuen" Identität zu externalisieren und dadurch die religiöse Welt neu zu benennen. Die „Sisterhood", Schwesterlichkeit, in der diese Subjektwerdung möglich sein kann, wird durch die Dynamik des Seienden, einer neuen-alten Bezeichnung für Gott, qualifiziert.

---

[16] *C. M. Halkes,* Über die feministische Theologie 189.

Diese „Schwesternschaft" – M. Daly nennt sie kosmischen Bund – könnte kirchliche Theorie und Praxis neu inspirieren und Perspektiven in eine Zukunft aufweisen, die offen ist für Mensch-Sein. Daß feministische Theologie notwendig ikonoklastisch sein muß, habe ich bereits erwähnt. Vielleicht können wir es erreichen, neue Symbole und Bilder zu finden, in denen sich die je eigenen religiösen Erfahrungen von Frauen und Männern beschreiben und deuten lassen. Ich glaube, unsere Welt könnte humaner, wärmer, menschlicher werden, wenn es uns gelingt, die Hälfte der Menschheit aus ihrer Unterdrückung zu befreien. Ob wir es realisieren können, das hängt ab zum einen von uns Frauen selbst, ob wir aus unserer oftmals liebgewordenen – gewohnten – Rolle ausbrechen können, ob wir Kreativität und Mut genug haben, uns dieses Anliegen – sei es gelegen oder ungelegen – ganz zu eigen zu machen. Zum anderen liegt es an bestimmten Einstellungen, die sich sowohl bei Frauen als auch bei Männern finden lassen, denen eine Mitschuld am Sexismus zuzuschreiben ist:
– „das Problem nicht erkennen wollen;
– es von sich fernhalten, lächerlich machen und herabspielen;
– bei Frauen Schuldgefühle wecken;
– uns als unweiblich, Mannweib, alte Jungfer verurteilen oder Sprüche fallen lassen, wie: ‚sie hat es wohl nötig‘, ‚ihre Ehe taugt sicher nichts‘;
– das Problem abschieben: ‚in anderen Kirchen ist es auch nicht besser‘ oder: ‚schau mal, wie es in einem Land zugeht, wo eine Frau Premierminister ist‘;
– uns mit der wohlwollenden Haltung von jemandem entgegenzutreten, der Caritas übt und zu Dankbarkeit verpflichtet."[17]

Lassen Sie mich schließen mit einem Zitat von S. Truth, die 1851 sagte: „Wenn die erste Frau, die Gott geschaffen hat, stark genug war, die Welt ganz allein auf den Kopf zu stellen, sollten alle Frauen zusammen doch auch imstande sein, sie wieder in Ordnung zu bringen. Sie wollen es tun, darum sollten die Männer sie gewähren lassen"[18], und ich möchte hier noch hinzufügen, sie sollten nach besten Kräften mithelfen.

---

[17] *Dies.*, Gott hat nicht nur starke Söhne 77.
[18] Zit. nach *M. Daly*, Jenseits von Gottvater 118.

Frauen entdecken die Bibel

Herausgegeben von Karin Walter

frauenforum

Der erste Band der neuen Reihe „frauenforum"

Bücher von Frauen für Frauen geschrieben

Engagierte christliche Frauen berichten von ihren ganz persönlichen Erfahrungen und eröffnen faszinierende Perspektiven, die sie aus der befreienden Lektüre der Bibel gewonnen haben. Der Leser wird überraschende Aufbrüche spüren: der Aufbruch zu einem neuen Selbstbewußtsein der Frauen in der Kirche, aber auch der Aufbruch zu einer spezifisch weiblichen Spiritualität.

Die Autorinnen:
H.-R. Laurien, C. Halkes. G. Casel, S. Walter, E. Gössmann, H. Waach, M. Dirks, R. Ahl, L. Altwegg, H. B. Gerl, Th. Hauser, A. Lissner, H. Pissarek-Hudelist, D. Sölle

Herausgegeben von Karin Walter.
ca. 192 Seiten, Paperback. ISBN 3-451-20789-3

Verlag Herder Freiburg · Basel · Wien

Glauben Frauen anders?

Erfahrungen
Herausgegeben von Marianne Dirks

„Hier geht es um jene Erfahrungen, die für Frauen entscheidend waren, um den eigenen Glauben zu entwickeln oder zu verlieren. Zumindest wirkt ihr Glaube heute verändernd und erneuernd" (Publik-Forum).

„Eines wird in diesen ehrlichen und selbstkritischen Schilderungen fraulicher Selbstfindung in – oft schmerzlicher – Auseinandersetzung mit dem Glauben und den kirchlichen Strukturen klar: Gerade durch ihre spezifisch fraulichen Eigenschaften, die Werte des Gefühls, der Innerlichkeit, der Phantasie, vermag die Frau viel dazu beizutragen, dem Ziel eines menschlicheren Glaubens und einer menschlicheren Kirche näherzukommen" (Esther Betz in: Rheinische Post).

4. Auflage. 192 Seiten, Paperback. ISBN 3-451-19751-0

Herta Pfister

Der an uns Gefallen findet
Frauen im Alten Testament

In diesem Band läßt Herta Pfister Frauengestalten aus dem Alten Testament vor dem Leser lebendig werden, ausgehend von Eva über Sara, Rebekka, Judit und andere bis hin zu Maria, Frau der Hoffnung und Erfüllung: Mutter Jesu. Im Leben und in der Gottesbeziehung dieser Frauen wird sichtbar, was auch für den heutigen Menschen bedeutsam ist: Gott wider alle Aussichtslosigkeit vertrauen, seine Zumutungen annehmen, sich von ihm aus Ich-Bezogenheit und Angst befreien lassen.

96 Seiten, Paperback. ISBN 3-451-20715-X

Verlag Herder Freiburg · Basel · Wien